Online! The Book

"If you go online, see how much more you can gain, without the pain. Fascinating, fun, and delightfully written. The invaluable tool for everyone that makes you laugh out loud to read."

—Scott Cook, Founder and Chairman of Intuit Software

"There is only one Dvorak. He invented the idea that technology was as worth covering as news, he wrote the first gossip column on the inductry, and even has answered tech questions on call-in shows. He's the Orson Wells to Bill Gates's Kane."

—William R. Hearst III, Publisher and Venture Capitalist

"For 20 years or more, no one else has given us the same no-nonsense, in-your-face advice John C. Dvorak has. His expertise and influence among makers and consumers of software and hardware are legendary, as is the dry sardonic humor he brings to everything he writes about. If you want to know why you should go online and what to do once you get there, you can trust Dvorak's advice like you would trust your mother's—if Mom were intimately knowledgeable about computing, and if she could make you laugh while pointing out computing's foibles."

—Ron White, author How Computers Work, *10th Anniversary Edition*

"Chris Pirillo is one of those original geeks, dating back to when he first brought common sense to the Help Desk. From there he's built bridges between Silicon Valley and Hollywood, landing somewhere in a conceptual San Luis Obispo—the grey area between content and technology."

—Marc Canter, Founder Macromedia

"This is the most practical and valuable book about the Internet you can get. A perfect reference for anyone who goes online."

—Victoria Recano, "Inside Edition"

"Everything you ever wanted to know about the Internet and really ought to ask. I love this book!"

—Lance Ulanoff, Executive Editor PCMAG.COM

"Pirillo is truly the Internet guru of our times. Hundreds of thousands of his 'Gnomie' followers can't be wrong. *Online!* is a Rosetta Stone, bringing the priceless, yet nearly costless, millennial treasure of the Internet to the masses. *Online!* is the first truly practical book about the Internet, exploring the depth of its power, without the typical techno-jargon. *Online!* will leave you asking how you ever got along without it."

> —*Brett Trout author of* Internet Laws Affecting Your Company *and Chair of the Iowa State Bar Association Technology Committee*

"For hundreds of thousands of computer users, Chris Pirillo is the face of the Internet. Combining a sharp wit and the technical knowledge that comes with living computers and the Internet 24/7, Chris simplifies complex technical issues, helps computer users make informed decisions in the crowded software marketplace, and manages to entertain while still delivering the facts. By embracing technology as a way of life, this techno-geek has become the net's most trusted voice."

> —*Ken White, CEO, NextUp.com*

"Chris Pirillo is at the center of the digital universe."

> —*Robert Scoble, Technical Evangelist, Microsoft Corporation*

ONLINE!
THE BOOK

John C. Dvorak

Chris Pirillo

Wendy Taylor

PRENTICE
HALL
PTR

PRENTICE HALL
Professional Technical Reference
Upper Saddle River, NJ 07458
www.phptr.com

Library of Congress Cataloging-in-Publication Data

Dvorak, John.
   Online! : the book / John C. Dvorak, Chris Pirillo, Wendy Taylor.
   p. cm.
   Includes bibliographical references and index.
   ISBN 0-13-142363-0 (paper)
   1. Information networks. 2. World Wide Web. 3. Data transmission systems. I. Pirillo,
Chris. II. Taylor, Wendy. III. Title.

TK5105.5D895 2004
004.67'8–dc22

2003065600

Editorial/Production Supervision: Patti Guerrieri
Composition: Pine Tree Composition
Cover Design Director: Jerry Votta
Cover Design: Anthony Gemmellaro
Art Director: Gail Cocker-Bogusz
Interior Design: Wee Design Group
Manufacturing Manager: Alexis R. Heydt-Long
Executive Editor: Jeffrey Pepper
Editorial Assistant: Linda Ramagnano
Development Editors: Ralph Moore, Jim Markham, Jim Keogh
Technical Reviewer: Jim Huddleston
Marketing Manager: Curt Johnson

© 2004 Pearson Education, Inc.
Publishing as Prentice Hall Professional Technical Reference
Upper Saddle River, New Jersey 07458

Prentice Hall PTR offers excellent discounts on this book when ordered in quantity for bulk purchases or special sales. For more information, please contact: U.S. Corporate and Government Sales, 1-800-382-3419, corpsales@pearsontechgroup.com. For sales outside of the U.S., please contact: International Sales, 1-317-581-3793, international@pearsontechgroup.com.

Company and product names mentioned herein are the trademarks or registered trademarks of their respective owners.

Printed in the United States of America

First Printing

ISBN 0-13-142363-0

Pearson Education Ltd.
Pearson Education Australia Pty., Limited
Pearson Education Singapore, Pte. Ltd.
Pearson Education North Asia Ltd.
Pearson Education Canada, Ltd.
Pearson Educación de Mexico, S.A. de C.V.
Pearson Education—Japan
Pearson Education Malaysia, Pte. Ltd.

About Prentice Hall Professional Technical Reference

With origins reaching back to the industry's first computer science publishing program in the 1960s, and formally launched as its own imprint in 1986, Prentice Hall Professional Technical Reference (PH PTR) has developed into the leading provider of technical books in the world today. Our editors now publish over 200 books annually, authored by leaders in the fields of computing, engineering, and business.

Our roots are firmly planted in the soil that gave rise to the technical revolution. Our bookshelf contains many of the industry's computing and engineering classics: Kernighan and Ritchie's *C Programming Language*, Nemeth's *UNIX System Adminstration Handbook*, Horstmann's *Core Java*, and Johnson's *High-Speed Digital Design*.

PH PTR acknowledges its auspicious beginnings while it looks to the future for inspiration. We continue to evolve and break new ground in publishing by providing today's professionals with tomorrow's solutions.

PRENTICE
HALL
PTR

CONTENTS

FOREWORD

I was asked to make this personal, and that's what I've done.

When I told an associate I was writing an introduction to a book by John C. Dvorak, I was told, "Good choice. Neither one of you started with any journalism background and you're both crusty old curmudgeons who don't give a rip what anyone else thinks."

Which, if perhaps a bit extreme about me, certainly describes John to a T. Remarkable how much insight some readers have.

John and I have been writing opinion columns about computers and technology since the 1970s. We started at about the same time, and for a while we both wrote for *InfoWorld*, although our overlap was very brief back when Maggie Cannon was editor. We have very different styles. I tend to write the "Field and Stream" column—rambling accounts of what I did and what happened next, interspersed with observations on trends and how the world is going to hell (or not). John writes formal essays and short, very terse opinion columns. I hate to admit it, but what he does is harder than what I do. On the other hand, I write novels and he doesn't, although spies tell me even that's about to change.

We also used to host the best-known computer parties the world has ever known—the Pournelle-Dvorak-Hearst Party at COMDEX. It was famous because you could come to the party only if you could find it, and we got pretty clever at hiding the *real* party while steering people to a large, faked one that neither of us visited for more than 10 minutes. There are still plenty of people who think they went to the party who actually never found it.

The name of that party got shortened over time to "the Dvorak Party," and I think I know who was responsible. Dvorak openly bribed people to vote for his chili at one of the COMDEX chili cookoff contests and even paid to have pretty girls go out and rope people in to his chili booth, so my guess as to who had the colossal egomania to "shorten" the name of the party—which, incidentally, neither of us paid for (that was done by Will Hearst)—should be pretty obvious.

It wasn't as though he could have paid for it, either. I remember back at the first CD-ROM conference in Seattle. I invited John to dinner at the Pink Pig. I brought my *BYTE* technical editor. John showed up with five friends, and when it came time to pay the check, it was bigger than his expense account would handle. I never had that kind of problem at *BYTE* while McGraw-Hill owned the book, so I paid it. Then I realized this was my tech editor's first *BYTE* trip, and the bill was large enough—thanks to single-malt Scotch—to scare him. So I hustled and commissioned two technical articles about CD-ROM, and I wrote one on how CD-ROM was the wave of the future and ended up on the cover of *The New Papyrus*, saying prophetic things. It made me look pretty good, and I suppose I ought to thank John for sticking me with a check so big I had to work hard to justify spending that much money.

We started writing about computers and related technologies at the same time. We also got connected to what became the Internet very early on, back in the days when it was all a big adventure, and text adventure games such as Zork were an important part of the experience. Those were the days when electronic mail came in at 300 baud, and you could read a newspaper while waiting for the entire message to print. Even at 1,200 baud (no one called it bits/second then), you could read the text as fast as it came on screen. Even so, it worked, and because neither John nor I like working in someone else's office, we both learned to use the new capability so that we could file our stories from home or anywhere else.

At least he learned. I now have a confession.

I know John has been to Brazil and to Finland north of the Arctic Circle, because we went there together. On both of those trips, he was able to establish communications with his home base—we didn't say things like "get online" in those days because that's not quite the way it worked—and I couldn't. He also had a wealth of local information, including currency exchange rates and the best bars in Helsinki—the ones that served single-malt Scotch—which he had managed to find. This was back well before there was anything like Google or AltaVista or, for that matter, an Internet. I could usually get better technical information than he did because *BYTE*'s BIX had the most sophisticated readers in the world, but it was hopeless asking them about Helsinki cab fares or Springbank single-malt Scotch.

So. It's probably fitting that John writes a book about the Internet experience and how to use it and getting connected. He's always been pretty good at that. Sometimes better than I am. Of course, he wrote a book about OS/2 back when I knew far more than he did about it. I actually had three OS/2 systems working and interconnected and able to share a CD-ROM drive, and believe me that wasn't anything like easy in those days. I know Dvorak hadn't done it, but there he was with a book on the subject. But when I read it, I realized he'd done it again: I might know more about OS/2 than John Dvorak, but I sure didn't know more about it than his collaborators. He had the head of Team OS/2 as a co-author. And I have to admit, John has always been very good at getting people who know more than he does to write with him. And when he does that, you can rely on the result. I do.

So here's John Dvorak writing about being ONLINE. Recommended.

Jerry Pournelle
Studio City, July 2003

INTRODUCTION

This book is about everything you ever wanted to know about going online and were afraid to ask. Unlike other books of this type, we go overboard and cover everything we can think of: from getting your first modem or DSL connection to selling something using online and email marketing tricks. The book is, simply put, about everything that has anything to do with going online, presented in the most comprehensive manner we can.

The problem with past books about the Internet and the Web is that they are too focused on one or two topics. We noticed that the market lacked a book that covers everything and offers people an introduction to a topic and the ability to decide whether they want to learn more by specializing. This doesn't mean that this book is shallow because it isn't. It means that it is an in-depth primer for every topic that has to do with online, Internet, and Web activity.

The authors have worked closely with computer users and the public at large for decades, and we've all learned that there are gaps in knowledge that do not seem to be addressed by either books or magazines. There are fewer and fewer books for beginners that take a broader sweep than today's specialty book. We've further discovered that most users are neither beginners nor experts but perpetually intermediate users. There is virtually nothing out there for them, either. And finally, the expert users tend to be like the books themselves—expert in limited arenas. Out of this thinking, this book was born. It addresses common gaps in information and introduces people to new and exciting aspects of the online world they may otherwise never discover. The book is designed to be used as a reference, a guide, and an overview of all topics related to the world of online communications.

To make the book even more valuable, we've added a Web site that you can access for more in-depth information and trends that will affect the online world. The site is http://www.onlinethebook.com, and you can use it to discover additional new links and to find more features and articles on new topics of interest. Product listings and free software will be posted on the site, as well as new material written by the authors and others.

Over the next few decades, you and your friends will be spending thousands of dollars just to maintain a connection with the online world. The monthly fees add up over time, and we think it's a shame if you do not get your money's worth. We're all convinced that if you know more about the Net, you'll get more out of it. In fact, you should greatly benefit from efficient use of the Internet, enough so that the cost of being online will be offset quickly. And it's not that we think everyone should run Web sites or online businesses. It's just that the power of the Internet and the Web in particular, combined with the efficiency of email, should make your life easier. And it should also make your work life easier. After all, knowledge is power, and the online world gives you access to more knowledge than you can ever absorb.

So read this book cover to cover or browse it when you have to. But above all, keep it nearby.

ACKNOWLEDGMENTS

This book is the result of the labor of many people. The first glory goes to my wife, Mimi Dvorak, who spent months doing most of the necessary rewrite work. She has a knack for bringing things to a consumer level, whereas I would prefer more technical discussions, and Chris Pirillo would prefer discussing sales. She also is better than all of us combined when it comes to arguing with copyeditors.

Credit also to Wendy Taylor, the former editor of *PC Computing*. Wendy's job was to control the workflow and maintain contact with all the people who worked on the project. This was no easy chore because each chapter had a team of people from various companies and organizations trying to attack a specific topic with precision.

I can tell you in advance that I am going to be killed if I leave someone's name out of the thank-you list, and I promise to put it in for the second printing. Along the way, when we suddenly felt that a new topic should be covered, one of us would find someone at the last minute who has a known grasp on a topic, and we'd have them do some writing or have them give us permission to use their material, which we would then blend into the text. It's amazing how much good, specialized knowledge is out there if you know where to look for it.

The idea behind a book like this is to combine the resources of definitive experts. Jerry Pournelle chides me about this technique in his Foreword, but I have always felt that no one person can know everything about a broad topic such as telecommunications. It can't be done. When a lone individual takes on a big topic like this, you end up with too much missing information. We believe that our approach is the best approach, although it demands a lot of rewriting to keep the overall tone of the book consistent.

I know from experience that when people look over this book, they will send in notes asking why this topic or that topic wasn't included, and these will be topics that should have been included. What we want to develop here is an inclusive know-it-all bible for folks out there who find the entire online scene a little wild and wooly. It *is* wild and wooly. The more things you can do, the more comfortable you get. But as it now stands, most people get an AOL account and are afraid to try anything else.

With this in mind, I'd like to thank all the experts who contributed to the book. And a particular thanks to the companies that helped us out, namely, US Robotics, 2Wire, Netgear, Palm, Apple, Microsoft, America Online, Expert City, Zone Labs, Kaspersky Lab, Macromedia, Sun Microsystems, GlobalSCAPE, HBN Networks, Total Marketing Concepts, Interwoven, InterVoice, Texas Instruments, Toshiba, Real Networks, Expercity, Vendio (formerly Auctionwatch), and Omnipod. Writers, researchers, and friends who helped include John Markoff, Lara Chereso, Aric Mackey, Allison Wellington-Toth, Abigail Lovell, Jenny Gispen-Shultz, Penny Sanchez, Nathalie Welch, Jeff Corbett, Keith D. Little, David Kopf, Aaron Wester, Laura McCormick, Christie Cooney, Jim Semmick, Rob Rosenberger, Corey Bridges, Mendy Hill, Dennis Zenkin, Te Smith, Ben E. Brady, Dave Collins, Larry Jordan, Brian Crystal, Kevin Corson, Mike Chandler, Maureen Miller, Ben Reytblat, Noel Sweeney, Heather Hollaender, Kevin Lynch, Robyn Pollman, Todd Pollman, Mark Hale, Kathleen Means, Debbie Ryan, Michael Meadows, Brian Christal, Stephanie Leonard, Penni Sanchez, Mike Polcyn, Chip Rodgers, Deborah Shemony, Traci Renner, Ross Goldenberg, Doron Aronson, Douglas Uhlinger, Kevin Corson, Lisa Amore, Lee Kaplan, Greg Robinson, Mark Hale, Kathleen Means, Debbie Ryan, Alan Weinkrantz, David Gerrold, Jennifer Stryd, Gemma Paulo, Marlene Somsak, Ted Leonsis, John Cristofano, Brian Christal, Robert Oslin, Dave Whittle, Michelle Moody, Jim Inscore, Jonathan Schwartz, Simon Phipps, Mark Herring, Greg Bardsley, Constance Sweeny, Rodrigo Sales, David Russell, Steve Mack, Susan Morrow, Ellis Cave, William Simmelink, Jack Jia, Brian Donahoo, John Marshall, Matt Hunt, Jeff Kainz, Eric Allman, Thomas Johnson, and Tim Hillman. Coordinating all these folks took the genius of Wendy Taylor. I figure the book will be a best seller if we can sell one copy to everyone who worked on it. In addition, a special thanks goes to all the folks who let us use material from their Web sites especially Ryan Ozawa, Dr. John Suler, Daniel Lemin, Robert H'obbes' Zakon, and Greg Costikyan.

1

THE ONLINE WORLD

Today's online world has changed dramatically in the last decade. Back then, *online* to the average user meant a telephone connection directly to either another computer or to an online service, such as CompuServe or AOL. The Internet now dominates all online activity. In popular parlance, the Internet is synonymous with the World Wide Web, although it is much more, as we'll explain in this book.

The Internet can be described generally as a "network" of networks. It is a transportation vehicle for applications. In fact, the visual representations of the Net look like a road map. If lines are drawn between each connection, between larger and larger connections, and between smaller and smaller ones, the end result is a web of connections—a virtual road map.

> This book is divided into four rough sections. The first is for beginners. It is to get anyone up to speed quickly with the information needed about the Web. Each chapter has recommended Web sites (to type the address, or Uniform Resource Locator [URL] into your Web browser) to help direct you.
>
> The second section has more detailed information about downloads, email, security, and information on virus protection.
>
> The third part is about how to create a Web site, Web tools, blogging, and what you can add to your Web site (such as streaming media, RSS feeds, and XML, among other things).
>
> The fourth part is by far the densest. It is a collection of more technical information for the Web-savvy. There are chapters about how a modem works, networking, handhelds, remote access, Internet marketing, Web content management, peer to peer, the Web and the law, VoIP, and EIM.

THE NET: THERE, WHEREVER YOU ARE

The significant contribution of the Internet has been its social impact for everyday people. As the connections of the Internet encompassed a wider group of people, the social interactions increased and spread to wider interests. The three Cs of the Internet:

- Comfort: The comfort is that you can touch the far reaches of the planet, research arcane and inane subjects, talk to people, spout opinions, argue, laugh, and partake in idle chat—all from the comfort of your home. You can sit in your pajamas at 3:00 in the afternoon, and no one will know (unless you have a video camera enabled). In fact, the Internet is *open* 24/7, 365 days a year, so anytime of the day or night, you can connect, research something that you've always wanted to know about, or just idly wander around.

- Community: There are numerous communities of people on the Internet. They cover a diversity of topics from sewing to genealogy, dating, and obscure hobbies. People connect with shared interests and can interact. For millions, the Net has the same appeal as a coffee shop or pub—places where you won't be shushed and where schmoozing is encouraged. Using email and instant messages, you can readily have online conversations with friends, family, and people who share an interest.
- Chat: These are electronic conversations that take place at the keyboard, but if you have a microphone and sound card, you can have voice conversations, too.

The Internet is a source of inspiration. From one technology springs an idea to utilize a part of the Internet better or to add to it. The Internet has many connections. Not only does it connect computers, but it also connects people and Web sites. At its most simple, people connect through email, sending notes to each other without worrying whether anyone is around to "answer the phone."

The online world is exciting because it removes the factor of distance between you and the information you need, and between you and the people you want to reach. Need an Italian dictionary? It's at your fingertips. Need to get the opinion of experts in digital photography? Read a newsgroup, join a mailing list, or visit a photography community. So yes, a wired PC makes distance much less important. But suppose you can't be near your computer?

There are plenty of options to connect to the Web where *you* are, not just where *your PC* is, whether you are at work, on vacation, sitting at someone else's computer, or using a non-PC device. You can't get the entire, highly visual online experience over a wireless phone, of course, but the essentials are there, including email, messaging, shopping, Web searching, and more. When you're not at your own computer, you can access the Internet via:

- Wireless phones with Web services
- Handheld computers, such as a Palm, Handspring, or PocketPC, with a wireless connection. You can also download the Web content from the PC to your handheld before you leave.
- Pagers
- Any PC with an Internet connection at a café, on a ship, or at a friend's house
- Mobile communicators: small, two-way messaging devices with built-in keyboards, made by the makers of the popular Blackberry wireless handheld

The *Net* is shorthand for the Internet, a global network of information and communities. The World Wide Web is a part of the Net—an application—the easiest-to-use and most visual part. Other important parts of the Net include email, discussion groups, and file exchange.

Online content refers to the content available over a network. Online content is usually in the form of words and pictures, sometimes in the form of video, audio, and animation.

An *IP address* is the physical address of a computer on the Internet. For example, instead of 1234 Peach Street, the Internet uses 123.12.12.123—four sets of numbers separated by a period identifying the unique location. Each number can be 0 to 255.

A *link* is a short bit of text or a small picture that you click with your mouse to find more information. To tell whether text or a picture is a link, move your mouse arrow over it. If the mouse arrow turns into a picture of a pointing finger, you can click it. You can find links on almost every Web page.

A *clickable link* is when a Web address or URL is blue and underlined. Instead of typing the address into an Internet window, you put your mouse pointer over the blue underlined address and click your mouse button: The link will connect.

EXPLORING THE NET

What draws tens of millions of new people to the Internet every year? For many, it's the sights, sounds, and pure information of countless online destinations. The World Wide Web combines ease of use and ease of *participation*; anyone can contribute to the Web by creating his or her own Web pages easily, as we will show in this book. The Web has become the most popular way to learn about ancient civilizations or about inkjet technology, kudzu, and Cambodia. (The quickly spreading kudzu plant used to be a popular metaphor for the Net's rapid growth.) It's also the place for the information that you need to manage your life, from weather forecasts to airline schedules.

Electronic mail is the most popular and biggest single use of the Internet, but large amounts of data flow between computers on a daily basis in the form of FTP (File Transfer Protocol). FTP allows a user at one computer to enter the address of another computer virtually anywhere on the Internet and browse through the file directories until a sought-after program or document is located. FTP has opened an immense world of shareware and public domain software to the public's access. Beyond FTP is Usenet. This is a remarkable array of computer conferences that run on tens of thousands of computers around the globe. Usenet has discussion groups on every subject imaginable, from the risks of computer technology to groups about duck raising and management to child rearing theory. Some of the groups have literally become communities, linking thousands of people who share a common interest. In the Usenet world, some of the groups are an uncontrolled electronic stream of consciousness, whereas others are moderated by one of several members who serves as moderator.

Some of the most fascinating aspects of the Internet are the electronic libraries and commercial online databases. Another is the vast numbers of electronic books (eBooks) available on the Web. Users can purchase an eBook on a disk or CD, but the most popular way is to purchase and download a file from an eBook sales site on the Web. (Some books are sold, some are for a nominal fee, and some are free.) eBooks can be downloaded and read on desktop, laptop, or palm computers. You can use a specialized eBook reader, which will allow you to make notes, highlight passages, and save selected text, but special hardware and software isn't necessary to read. The book's pages are displayed in full color with graphics and photos, and they resemble the printed pages of a book. Generally, an eBook can be downloaded in less than five minutes.

The Internet isn't just about text and information. It's also about people. People meet online in a variety of ways. They meet in chat rooms on Internet Relay Chat (IRC). This is a way for people to drop in on real-time global conversations. By typing on the keyboard, they can exchange some idle chat with someone in New Zealand or Sweden. These conversations go on 24/7. And once they've found friends all over the globe, people can stay in touch with IRC and instant messaging (IM), carry on private conversations, and "see" when their friends are on their computers (see Chapter 7).

People have found a variety of ways to meet. Online dating is a big business. From the comfort and safety of your home, you can view and read about potential mates all around the world. Another way to meet people is with MOGs (massively online games) and MUDs (multiple user dungeons; the name heralds back to the board game Dungeons & Dragons) where you can interact—talk and compete against or simply play—with others online.

Music has become a highlight of the Web, so it's not all about just text or images. Of course, you can read about your favorite band or singer, but you can also download music and convert music from one file format to another. The Web has changed the face of the music industry with Napster, where users traded copyrighted music, causing lots of legal issues and challenges to arise. Plenty of alternatives to Napster abound. If you're uncomfortable with the gray area sites, there are places to find good music that's legal for downloading. Some bands have realized that offering free MP3 files can help them sell more albums. Start with Rolling Stone (www.rollingstone.com/dds/). It offers free downloads of tracks from top artists in various formats. MP3.com (www.mp3.com) is another hot spot, especially for unknown artists. (MP3. com and MP3 are not the same thing. MP3.com is a library of MP3 files, whereas MP3 is a popular music file type. For more information, Chapter 5 is all about music.)

The World Wide Web Has Much to Offer

This book is a guide to help you get on the Web and direct you to the key features. There are more things on the Web than we could cover in one book, even a thick one. This book tries to guide you to find what you really need and covers what you really need to know. There is so much more out there, though.

The world is ever changing, and the Web changes, as well. Like never before, get instant updates on world news, sports, weather, and politics. The Web is a tool. As you learn more, your tastes will change and evolve. No matter what it is you are looking for, if you know how to look (and this book will give you that knowledge), you can find what you seek.

News

The Internet is a 24-hour news source. And with an online news site— unlike your television or newspaper—you can personalize the news to your preferences. There are plenty of choices to get the news. Television networks such as CNN (www.cnn.com), BBS (http://news.bbc.co.uk), MSNBC (www. msnbc.com), and ABCNews (www.abcnews.go.com) offer something for everyone. Newspaper Web sites such as *New York Times* (www.nytimes. com), *LA Times* (www.latimes.com), and *USA Today* (www.usatoday.com) supplement their static newspapers with frequently updated, online versions. There are specialty news sites focusing on a specific topic such as TechWeb for IT news (www.techweb.com), *Sports Illustrated* for sports (http://sports illustrated.cnn.com/), United Nations (www.un.org/News/), National Geographic News for science (http://news.nationalgeographic.com/), and Zap2it for entertainment (www.zap2it.com/index).

Genealogy

Exploring genealogy is easier with the Internet. Web sites such as Family Search (www.familysearch.org/), state and country government sites, newspapers, and other significant places with archives abound. One such archive is Ellis Island (www.ellisislandrecords.org/), which can beat trying to hire some remote researcher to dig through microfiche. As people gather information and get details on locations, the next step may be to contact a government in another country or a newspaper that lists marriages and deaths. The Internet has enabled us to search our family history without the need to travel. There are specialty sites for those with a specific background, such as JewishGen (www.jewishgen.org), which helps those with a Jewish background, and Italian Genealogy Homepage for those with Italian ancestry (http://italian genealogy.tardio.com/). Cyndi's List of Genealogy Sites links to over 175,000 Web sites (www.cyndislist.com).

Travel

Book your airplane reservations and your hotel reservations online. Check competing airlines for the best price. Reserve car rentals, one-way moving trucks, and motor homes. Check the weather, (www.weather.com or www.intellicast.com). Check road conditions or highway construction projects. Check around the Web for restaurant ideas, entertainment, and historical places to visit. If it's a business trip, maybe you can look up other businesses to visit while you're there. Going to another country? No problem; many sites have currency converters and language dictionaries. If you are just exploring ideas, try Travelocity (www.travelocity.com), Lonely Planet (www.lonelyplanet.com), and Fodor's (www.fodors.com).

Finance/Investment

The Internet is a gold mine for investors in terms of up-to-date information. View the latest company press releases, news articles, and financial data on the Web. Research companies and read their financial reports—without going to the library or calling the company and asking for its report. Trade, buy, and sell stocks online. Start with Wall Street City (www.wallstreet city.com).

Food

Going nuts over what to have for dinner tonight? Dining out isn't always an option. Is your cookbook thinner than skim milk? Never fear; all the recipes you'll ever need are sitting on Allrecipes (www.allrecipes.com) and similar sites. You've probably got a cupboard full of unused ingredients; search for meals containing your favorite spice, meat, vegetable, etc. Specially formatted pages are linked so that you can print out any recipe for a 3×5 or 4×6 note card. It's finger-clicking good.

Classic Books

Name one online (and electronic) resource that has been around for decades? No, we're talking pre-Yahoo!, folks. When you want to "rent" a book, you probably go to your public library. When you want to buy a book, you might think of heading to Amazon.com. But over at Project Guttenberg (http://promo.net/pg/), you will find a group that has been making classic books available to the world in a common "text" format. There's nothing terribly recent (because of copyright laws), but here you'll find the complete works of Shakespeare, Aesop's fables, and Plato's philosophies. You can leave your library card at home this time; eBooks have already arrived, and you can start grabbing them without dropping a dime.

Interpretation

What does it mean when you dream of being chased by giant mirrors? I'm almost afraid to look! Wake up to a world of internalized subliminal processes with sites such as Dreamdoctor.com. Share your sleep-time experiences on a discussion board and look up meanings in the dream symbols dictionary. Do your dreams share a common thread with other dreamers? Love to learn about other people's dreams? I suppose that fiction is stranger than truth.

Home Improvement

Did you know that a screwdriver can double as a hammer? Did you know a butter knife can double as a screwdriver? Or that a nail file can double as a butter knife? Well, they can in *our* world. If you have a computer question, we're your guys. When it comes to home improvement, you may have to inquire elsewhere. Want some real tips for improving your home or tackling that next big project? Ask someone such as Tim Carter from Ask the Builder (http://askthebuilder.com). He knows so much, in fact, that his columns are nationally syndicated and he has own radio show in Ohio. The station, for whatever it's worth, isn't WKRP. "Baby, if you've ever wondered; wondered whatever became of my skill saw . . ." (Venus Flytrap was never much of a home builder, you know.)

Career Advice

Show me the money! No, really . . . show me the money! No, I'm serious . . . I need money. Well, who doesn't need money? Money, after all, is how we attain certain necessities: clothes, food, shelter, and digital cameras. The problem is, you have to work for money. What's up with that!? What and where are the best jobs? And more importantly, could you make more doing the same job in a different state? Before sending out those resumes, check here. Head to a site such as salary.com, and you'll see the average pay rate of an occupation, depending on its state (snow plow operators may find higher pay in Iowa than in Arizona). This destination also includes articles and advice for staying on top of the business world. Now get back to work. You need money.

Unit Conversion

There's an old story, which may or may not be true, about a dispatch taking place in the middle of the ocean: "Change your course to avoid a collision." "How?" "Turn forty degrees starboard." "Um . . . we're a lighhouse." Insane, I tell you. It's too bad that those shipmates didn't have access to this site; carrying over 8,000 units, they could have converted anything to anything. At a site such as OnlineConversion.com, specific categories have been designated for the various measurements. And thanks to the cooking section, everything's as easy as pie (with two and a half cups of flour). This URL should be etched in your memory. Whether two feet from shore or 20,000 leagues under the sea, knowing how many "Xs" are in a "Y" just might save your life.

Maps

"The entire Internet is now on a map of Antarctica." Well, I guess someone had to do it. That may sound a little strange, but oddly enough—it appears to work. Click on any one of the 17 map categories at Visual Net (http://map.net), and you can start exploring the Internet. The more you click, the narrower your search becomes. It's perfect for someone who doesn't know exactly what they're looking for and wants to see everything that's available. If map clicking isn't your cup of Java, there's always the plain ole text search. Hey, Lockergnome's there!

Consumer Protection

It seems as though everyone has either been sued or is getting sued these days, doesn't it? Well, there are plenty of frivolous lawsuits floating around, but let's not forget that there are some legitimate charges being made by consumers who just want to get what they paid for. If you think you're a little fish in a giant corporate pond, swim on over to a site such as Big Class Action (http://bigclassaction.com). Join a group of people seeking a class action or register your own complaint.

Technology

Different people tend to ask similar questions. So instead of wasting man hours and resources on answering the frequently asked questions, people put together FAQs (which, oddly enough, stands for Frequently Asked Questions). You'll find that most heavily traveled Web sites have FAQs that newcomers may read to make themselves familiar with the "rules" of that particular group. Internet FAQ Archives (www.faqs.org/faqs) is a great place to start.

Email has been around forever (as far as this e-world is concerned). For some users, it makes sense to have a Web-accessible account. For those who stay in one spot, not so much. So which service is the best one? Depends on who you are and what you need. There are all kinds of companies willing to give you a mailbox; they're now just a click away. Doesn't matter where you're from or what language you hablas. A great free guide is at Free Email Providers Guide (http://fepg.net).

Who really understands what goes on after you click on a link? Sure, with any luck, a new Web page pops up. But how does that really happen? Don't immerse yourself in technojargon—download this beautifully illustrated movie. Don't you know how data flows in a networked environment? Are packets good or bad? Who's this "Lan" guy, and why is he setting walls on fire? Young grasshopper: Sit back, watch, and learn through Warriors of the Net (www.warriorsofthe.net).

Ever notice those three little letters after the dot in a file name? For instance, the file extension for the Word document "ilovelockergnome.doc" would be "DOC." Hopefully, you're aware of the most common file extensions; sometimes a strange one will spring up. What the heck is an SCR? Or LST? Or CAB? Or . . . well, you get the idea. Filext.com is the site for you if a file extension has you flabbergasted. Just enter it into this search engine (sans dot) and extsearch.com will tell you what the extension possibly stands for (as well as its respective file type). You would have gone MAD without it, although you probably wouldn't have any idea what it meant.

You need graphics. No, I'm telling you: You need graphics. You might be designing a Web page, working on invitations, or any number of things, and this site is there to satisfy all of your graphical needs. The best part is that it's free at Flamingtext.com. Need some cool text effects? Just select the font size, the color, the style, the shadow, the bevel . . . you get the picture. There are also cool links to clip art, buttons, wallpaper, and tools—all of those things that make your fancy Web world even fancier.

You've probably seen those commercials on television featuring state-of-the-art refill systems for your inkjet. That's all fine and dandy, but different cartridges require different methods of refilling. A site such as Refill-FAQ (www.refill-faq.de) should answer any questions still lingering—if you choose to refill your cartridges (as opposed to just buying new ones when the old ones run dry). They walk you through the basics of refilling while addressing problems associated with this "money-saving" technique. Ah, I went laser four years ago and haven't looked back.

Sports

The Internet is a paradise for sports lovers. Find statistics on favorite teams and athletes. Get news and sports updates. Interact with other sports fans. Buy merchandise, and a lot more. ESPN (www.espn.com), CBS Sportsline (www.cbs.sportsline.com), and The Sports Network (www.sports network.com) offer coverage on all sports. Their updates reflect the latest seasonal sports and any hot news, such as draft picks. Sports sites categorize their pages for easy reference with the hot news on the front page. Diehard fans of specific sports can find pages dedicated to one sport. Soccer (or football to countries outside of the United States) fans can go to Federation International de Football Association (www.fifa.com) and FA (www.thefa.com) for everything soccer. All professional and amateur sports organizations have their own Web sites, such as National Hockey League (www.nhl.com), Major League Baseball (www.majorleaguebaseball.com), National Basketball Association (www.nba.com), and NCAA for college sports (www.ncaa.org). Annual or recurring events have their own Web sites, such as the Olympics (www.olympic.org), Super Bowl (www.superbowl.com), and World Cup Soccer (fifaworldcup.yahoo.com). We haven't even covered teams' or players' Web sites. Colleges, professionals, and amateur team sports and players offer sites for their teams. Do a Web search for your favorite team or player, and you should be able to get there in no time. (For information on Web searches, go to Chapter 4.)

Autos

Whether you prefer to buy a new vehicle online or locally, start your research online. Kelly Blue Book (www.kbb.com), a car buyer's guide, has a Web site where you can calculate the price and trade-in value of used vehicles. Automakers have information about every car they make and sell on their Web sites. They feature vehicle comparison charts, loan calculators, model guides, and all the information you need to know before dealing with a local dealer. Web sites such as MSN Autos (http://autos.msn.com/) and cars.com (www.cars.com) are a good place to start when you don't have anything specific in mind.

Replacement Parts

Need an updated driver? A resolution to a software problem? Information about a favorite board game? Try the Internet first before calling and waiting on hold for hours for tech support. It might be faster to search for the answer than to call tech support or every game store in town. When I upgraded to a new operating system, I needed updated drivers and got them all online. My mom had a small set of old and useful cocktail forks. I went on eBay and found more of the same brand to increase her set. When a gadget still in fine working order has a broken or missing part, go look on the Internet for replacements. It may be cheaper than replacing the gadget. Did another china plate break? Even if your china is no longer in production, try Replacements, Ltd. (www.replacements.com/), which stores sets that are no longer produced.

SUMMARY

So the Internet and today's online world is rich, indeed. Most people who begin using the Internet seldom scratch the surface, even after years of use. The only reason for this is that the Net has actually evolved over decades into this patchwork quilt of interesting and useful applications. We want to make sure you take full advantage of all the Net has to offer. It will enrich your life and contribute to your personal success. And it's fun. Use this book as your guide.

2
HARDWARE
BASICS

BEFORE HARDWARE

The first thing to consider before hardware is the *operating system* (OS). For personal computers, there are three basic versions of an OS. There is the Windows family, the UNIX family (which includes Linux), and the Macintosh OS (which runs only on Apple hardware). An OS manages the hardware and software resources—processor chip memory, disk space, where and how to store data—and it gives software application programs a consistent way to interface with the hardware so that different programs don't have to be specific to the differences in the hardware. Another thing the OS does is gives the software developers a similar format, the application program interface (API). This lets a software developer write a program that will run on many different computers, no matter what configuration it may be or what might be added. This flexibility is important. The OS manages the hardware and the resource allocation, and makes sure everything runs smoothly. As well, the OS provides a consistent graphical user interface (GUI) for the user. (All programs will have a similar pull-down menu, help command, save function, etc., so that each program doesn't have wildly different commands, as they did in the dark ages in the beginning of computing.)

All computers work in layers, for example:

Hardware—IBM-compatible PC (Personal Computer)

OS—Microsoft DOS and/or Windows

GUI—Windows was initially a GUI for DOS

Programs—Microsoft Word

Windows is by far the most popular OS, with an estimated 80% of computers running it worldwide, although under that catchall, there are a number of variations (Windows 95, Windows 98, Windows 2000, Windows XP, etc.). This is followed by the Macintosh OS, with an estimated 5–10%; then Linux, at about 4–8%.

WHAT AN OPERATING SYSTEM DOES

When you first turn on your computer, you hear the fan spinning and the disk drives start churning. The first program to run is the computer's ROM (read-only memory). This is a lot like waking up in the morning; you blink and make sure that you still have two hands, two arms, two legs, and everything is ready to go. The boot program checks the system hardware to make sure it's all connected and ready to go. The POST (power on self-test) looks for errors in the CPU, memory, and the BIOS (basic input-output systems). Once the POST is complete, the ROM will activate the drive where the boot information is stored. The OS's bootstrap loader is activated.

The bootstrap loader is a program with one function: to load the OS into active memory. Once the OS is loaded, it begins to administer the various categories of jobs it must do. These include processor, device, storage memory management, and user and application interfaces, among other mundane details. If the OS encounters an error at any point, it cannot continue. These are called *boot failures*.

If you've failed to shut your machine down correctly (such as due to a power failure), your machine will go through a special series of checks. It will try to detect and repair any damage to the file allocation tables, among other checks. If your OS is damaged or destroyed, your computer cannot work.

Other Operating Systems

There are many other OSs. Everything with a chip will have an OS to tell it what to do. These devices, grouped together as "embedded" systems, include: PDAs; cell phones; point-of-sale devices; VCRs, industrial robot controls; smart self-propelled vacuums; and the list goes on. In fact, everything that has a computer chip in it will have some programming to tell it how to operate.

There are four broad categories of OS:

- **RTOS** (real-time OS) used for machinery, scientific instruments, industrial systems, medical systems, and manufacturing devices. RTOSs have very little "user interface" and limited functionality. The system does only what it is specifically programmed to do, and the OS's main job is to manage the resources to ensure that the programmed operation executes exactly, consistently, and in precisely the same amount of time and often at a specific time. For multiple sequential moving parts, such as robotics, an error in any part of the motion would be potentially catastrophic. As an example, you wouldn't want your intelligent washing machine to spin the clothes without rinsing them.

- **Single user/single task** is an OS that allows one thing at a time by one person. A good example would be in a handheld device. You cannot switch functions without closing one and starting another.

- **Single user/multitasking** is the ability to have multiple things operating at once, such as printing and opening a new Web page or viewing a document while downloading a file. This is the classification of OS to which Windows, Mac OS, and Linux would belong.

- **Multiuser** is an OS that lets many people access a computer at the same time. This would be used on large mainframes, VMS, and UNIX systems. One such Multiuser OS is OS/390.

Windows

Windows is the number one dominant personal computer OS in the world. In fact, few people even consider that there is a choice when it comes to PCs, aside from the various versions of Windows itself. Overall, Windows is probably going to be your choice if it's your first computer. Almost every computer sold today comes loaded with one version or another of Windows. In fact, you may have a choice of OSs, such as Windows 98, Windows XP Home, or Windows 2000 Professional, depending on what machine you purchase. Low-end machines will probably come with Windows 98, whereas high-end business power machines will feature Windows XP Professional or Windows 2000.

Most people use the OS already on their machine. It's likely you'd want to use Windows if you want to stay *mainstream* to run Microsoft Office products (Word, Excel, Access, PowerPoint, etc.). Because it is the most common OS, it is easier to find assistance from your friends, co-workers, and relatives. There are other options. The big "other" is Linux for PCs. Other OSs may include OS/2 Warp and Tao OS, among other non-notables.

You are sure to hear a few of the common complaints (most often from Linux devotees) about Microsoft. These complaints include:

- **Target of virus programs**—Software virus programs target Microsoft products. Part of the reason is because Microsoft has a number of security flaws. It is a huge target.

- **Not robust**—This is geek talk with roots in Latin. In plain terms, it means reliable; in this case, it means a product able to recover from some software program error and keep running without crashing (requiring a machine reboot). *Robust*, from a programmer's point of view, is software that has been gone over, smoothed out, and refined to the point of elegance and attention to detail. Robust is one step below *bulletproof*. It's not 100% foolproof, but it's good. (According to one of Murphy's Laws, it is impossible to make anything foolproof, because fools are so ingenious.) Early versions of Windows crashed all the time, which is where this complaint originated. The truth is, some versions of Windows are more stable than other versions.

- **Unstable**—These are things such as the "blue screen of death" and "safe mode." Windows has a reputation for crashing a lot. It's gotten better with the successive versions, but the reputation persists like a high school rumor.

- **Upgrades**—A chief complaint of Linux devotees is that Microsoft makes sure its users upgrade every few years by introducing incompatibilities into new programs (such as Word 97 files not working with Word 95 files). Another complaint is that Microsoft makes sure that new computers come with Windows, which keeps the cycle going. True, but before Windows, all IBM PCs came with MS-DOS, and way back when, this was good because it standardized the market.

WINDOWS TIMELINE

Windows 1.0 was first released by Microsoft in 1985. This was a milestone product. It was the first to allow PC users to switch from the MS-DOS line command prompt way of typing commands at the C:\ prompt to using a mouse to point and click through functions. It also allowed users to switch between programs without stopping one and starting another (which was how we did it back then—two application programs couldn't run at the same time). Few people actually used Windows 1.0 or its successor 2.0.

In 1990, Windows 3.0 was released. This offered an amazing (at the time) 32-bit performance and advanced graphics, and it supported the Intel 386 processor. There were added features such as a Program Manager, File Manager, and Print Manager. The desktop was said to look more like a Macintosh, which was both ridiculed and praised.

Windows for Workgroups 3.11 was released in 1993. This was developed for businesses using local area networks (LANs) with features targeted at corporate users. Windows NT 3.1 was also released that year. This was also a business-focused OS. There were both a desktop version and a server version (Windows NT Advanced Server). Another 1993 product release was Windows NT Workstation 3.5. This supported the OpenGL graphics standard, designed to aid engineers, software developers, and scientific and high-end business users.

Windows 95, released in 1995, was the successor to Windows 3.1, Windows for Workgroups, and MS-DOS. This was the first version of Windows for home users that wasn't based on MS-DOS. There were a number of innovative changes.

In 1996, Microsoft released Windows NT Workstation 4.0. This product was strictly for business. (In 1998, it was announced that the next version of NT would be known as Windows 2000).

Windows 98 was probably the most popular version of Windows, specifically created for home users. This version performed better than past versions. It included support to read DVD disks and to connect to universal serial bus (USB) devices. (You will find computers today sold with this OS. It remains a popular but inexpensive choice. It's probably not the best choice, though.)

In 1999, Windows 98 SE (Second Edition) was released with some enhanced hardware compatibility and more Internet features. It was also the first home OS to use device drivers that also worked on the Windows NT business OS. This is by many accounts the most stable and supported Windows OS. Some ultra low-cost machines, from smaller clone builders, will use this OS. It's a better choice than plain Windows 98.

In 2000, the Windows Millennium Edition (Windows ME) was released. It would be the last OS based on the Windows 95 kernel. (Future OSs would be based on the Windows NT and Windows 2000 kernel.) One key new feature was System Restore, which would allow users to restore their PC software configuration to a date or time before a problem was encountered. Windows Media Player 7 was first in this release. When it was released, it was widely rumored that it was just a highly modified version of Windows 98 SE that was released expressly to address issues/potential rulings in the antitrust suit against Microsoft. It's not well supported by Microsoft anymore. There will be some ultra cheap machines on the market loaded with this OS. These are best to avoid.

Windows 2000 Professional was also released in 2000. This was an upgrade to Windows NT Workstation 4.0 but was also designed to replace Windows 95 and Windows 98. This OS added advanced networking, wireless products, USB devices, IEEE 1394 and infrared devices, along with improvements to Internet compatibility and mobile computing. It offers lots of support, stability, and reliable networking. It's well supported by Microsoft. Many of the early issues (such as not working with computer gaming) have been addressed with various patches and drivers. It's an inexpensive option for many computer makers. It is a good choice. A majority of business networks, as well as high-end/power users, have made this their OS choice.

Windows XP, released in 2001, was the merging of the two OS system lines (consumer and home) into one. There were, however, three versions released: Windows XP Professional, Windows XP Home Edition, and a 64-bit version called Windows XP 64-Bit Edition (for power users with workstations that had Intel Itanium 64-bit processors). The idea behind the XP products was to create a new breed of 2000 that was more user-friendly, customizable, and stable. It had more media integration and a prettier user interface. The XP Home version is a "stripped down" version of the Professional. Microsoft disabled or hamstrung a number of the features related to networking to keep corporations from buying thousands of home versions instead of paying the higher price for the Professional license.

Linux

Linux is talked about a lot. It's an *open source* design, meaning that the software source code is not proprietary. Anyone can look at it, use it, and modify it. (Most software programs purchased in shrink-wrapped packages are proprietary and come without source code.) Linux is a relatively young

OS. It's been around about a decade, whereas Windows and Macintosh can boast twice that.

The roots of Linux are UNIX, which is a very old OS used in mainframes, especially at universities across the world. UNIX and Linux come in large numbers of versions from many sources, called *distributors*. (This is unlike the single-company, proprietary Microsoft Windows.)

> **Source code** is the initial form of a computer program before it's *compiled*. Compiling is a process of translating source code into a form that can run on a computer. The compiled program is called the *object code*. There is a sequence of events to creating a computer program, just as there is a sequence of events to making a cake.
>
> The programming recipe:
>
> - Individual lines of code are written as statements in an *editor* (that simplifies the process because much of it is repetitive or has been done before).
> - This file is called the *source code* or *source statements*.
> - The programmer runs this source code through a *compiler* (another program).
> - The compiler *parses* (analyzes and translates) the lines of code and builds the *object code,* also known as the *output module*.
> - The object code is *machine code* that a computer processor can execute.
> - Some OSs (such as some mainframe computers) require an additional step, link editing, which makes sure that everything is cross-referenced. This output is called a *load module*.

> The programs you purchase in a computer store are shrink-wrapped. They have licenses. They are compiled object code, without the source code. Because compiled code is very difficult to translate back into source code accurately, vendors are assured that you won't change or enhance their programs, which insures that it stays proprietary.

Linux was created by Linus Torvalds (University of Helsinki, Finland). In 1991, he released the basic OS, which consisted of his kernel and some tools. Linus made it open source. As open source, many people have taken the source code and added to it and refined it. It's an OS that has an unlimited number of software developers at work at the same time. This is its strength (over a regular proprietary company). This is also what makes it difficult for a newcomer. Although Linux is one type of OS, it also has a vast array of variations.

There are many versions of Linux. Linux's versions are similar in that they all run the same *kernel*, which is the most basic part of the OS. Each has been adapted for a different use, so they may not look or act exactly alike, depending on how they were specialized. There are versions of Linux to create a firewall, boot the OS from a floppy diskette or CD ROM, or manage a Web server, to name a few. Linux runs on a variety of machines and chips (PC, Alpha, Sparc, Itanium, Mainframe, Sony Playstation, Sega Dreamcast, for NASA onboard spacecraft use and HP's PA-RISC, among others).

There are versions of Linux that you can purchase at a computer store like regular software, in a shrink-wrapped box containing a CD with Linux (Red Hat, SuSE, Caldera, MandrakeSoft, etc.) or you can download Linux from any of a number of various companies or individuals.

Linux uses a command line, although a GUI is available to make it look similar to a Mac or Windows machine desktop. At first, Linux was only for the very computer-savvy. It had major nerd appeal because it was alternative. Now there are a number of companies offering various versions of Linux for all experience levels. There are entry-level versions designed to be user-friendly; in fact, Linux can look very much like Windows, in every way.

 Some mainstream Linux distributors include:

Mandrake—www.mandrakelinux.com/en/

Red Hat—www.redhat.com

SuSE—www.suse.com/index_us.html

Slackware—www.slackware.com

Caldera Linux—www.caldera.com

For more information on Linux distributors, see www.linux.org/dist/index.html

A drawback of Linux is that most hardware vendors don't write *device drivers* for Linux (more about drivers later in this chapter). Without a driver, your computer won't know how to interface with the device. So before you purchase new hardware, you'll have to research whether there is a driver available. Most Linux device drivers are written, maintained, and distributed along with Linux. New hardware may not have a driver written for it yet, so you may have to wait six months or more, if a driver is even written at all. On the other hand, Linux has good support for older hardware, so you can purchase used equipment and be reasonably certain it will work.

One big complaint about Linux is the learning curve. (Although everything relating to computers has one.) In the case of a switch from Windows to Linux, there will be some things to unlearn, and there may be less help available from friends and associates. For the most part, the Linux documentation is long and technical, and it is not easy to locate specific answers.

The advantage most often cited is that Linux is stable. It's also available free or at low cost, and you can easily change from one distributor to another without any problems.

Macintosh

The Macintosh is a family of computers from Apple Computer. These are unlike PC, desktop, or IBM-based machines, which may come from many vendors. The Apple Macintosh comes only from Apple Computer. Apple Computer was an early entry into the personal computer market. The Apple I and later Apple II were popular early machines embraced by educators across the country. In 1984, the first Apple Macintosh was introduced (based on an earlier, more advanced Lisa Computer, which didn't do well for a number of reasons). The Mac was the first widely sold personal computer to feature a GUI and 32-bit processing. It came with a mouse, and the icons on the screen were the visual representations of objects (files) or actions (such as delete). Apple used a proprietary OS, Mac OS, and the Motorola 68000 series of microprocessor chips. (This is an important difference, because Intel microprocessors were the chips used by the DOS-based machines.) The current version is called Mac OS X ("OS ten") and is BSD UNIX based. From 1994 to the writing of this book, the Macintosh used a PowerPC microprocessor, a joint development of Apple, Motorola, and IBM. (Recent announcements have said that future machines will use an IBM chipset.) The Mac has a full line of personal computers with different configurations for user needs—art, business, educational, home, etc.

PC or Mac

The biggest question is the choice of a PC or a Mac. Macintoshes are completely different beasts than PCs. It's a closed system. The mouse has only one button, instead of the standard Microsoft mouse style, with two buttons. Mac software runs only on Mac hardware. The Mac interfaces and connectors are different. They will work only on Macintoshes. For the most part, the prices of software, hardware, and accessories are higher than the equivalent for a PC.

However, if something fails, such as the drive or the motherboard, you have one vendor to deal with. With a PC, it's "parts are parts." A machine from a big-name seller, such as Dell, does not use the same part from the same subcontractor manufacturer on various machines. It's about supply and demand. The subcontractor with the most plentiful and cost-effective part gets the sale. The disk drives, the CD drive, the sound card, and the motherboard all have dozens if not hundreds of manufacturers competing. A PC might have an Intel chip or an AMD processor.

The choice of PC or Mac is a highly personal one. It is based on what you need. It is based on what you want and what you do. Mac has somewhere between 5% and 10% of the total personal computer market share (depending on whose numbers you may use). These are devoted and outspoken users. Part of the appeal is that Mac has kept the same basic interface; it's excellent for editing video and sound, it's aimed at making everything easy for untrained users, and it simply *does things differently* (as one of the Apple ad campaigns noted).

> To avoid confusion and to simplify the discussion, we'll focus on PC computers. Macs have the same basic internal parts, but since it's a closed-box system, there are fewer variables. You cannot build a Mac on your dining room table from scratch, and Mac machines offer considerably fewer configuration choices than their PC counterparts.

COMPUTER INTERNALS

One look at a magazine ad for personal computers or a stroll through a computer store will both confuse and overwhelm any normal person. The sales pitch for most computer sellers seems to be to list every little performance detail, benchmark, and buzzword without offering any graspable information.

It's not that PCs are difficult. They are made up of a few different parts thrown together. The problem is that the competition is fierce. Think of it as a steady din of carnival barkers trying to get your dollar. This chapter will try to identify the key information you need and the choices you'll need to sort through.

Chip Choices

The first choice is what computer chip you want to be the brain of your computer. There are two main competing manufacturers: Intel and AMD. Each has a variety of chips designed for personal computers (and they make processors for many other kinds of devices, as well). When people talk about having a Pentium computer, what they mean is that the *motherboard/mainboard* on their machine has an Intel Pentium chip on it.

The microprocessor is the brain of your computer. It's the central processing unit (CPU). It's a toenail-sized silicon square chip with millions of switches and pathways to help your computer make decisions and carry out tasks. Older computer naming schemes were number based. The first significant IBM-PC chip was the 8088. The next was the 80286, then the 80386, then the 80486 (although the *80* was hardly ever mentioned). Each of these chip numbers represented a family of CPUs, a generation. Each was faster than the one that came before it. When the 80586 went into production, Intel decided to give it a more memorable name—Pentium. The Pentium chip was released in 1993. Things have become only more confused since. In 1998, Intel produced a new Pentium called the *Celeron*. The Celeron was an inexpensive chip for low-end home machines. The early Celerons were slow and without a cache (and Intel quickly moved to add a cache to improve performance). The Celeron chips and the Pentium chips exist in the same market. Then to make things even more confusing, Intel added the Pentium III to the marketplace, then the Pentium IV, which is currently the fastest chip. There is also the XEON, a chip designed for servers.

Likewise, AMD began to name its chips. At first, they were named K5 and K6 (which were comparable to the Pentium and Pentium II). It soon gravitated toward proprietary names, too, with Athlon and Duron.

The variation of Pentium chips (including the Pentium Celeron) began as a new Intel marketing strategy. Its "Intel Inside" chips are Pentium Celeron, Pentium II, Pentium III, and Pentium IV with speeds that range from 300 MHz to over 2 GHz. Each of these chips has different versions. There are a lot of choices on the market.

Processor Speeds

The processor speed, or clock speed, of a chip is the measure of the internal chip clock. The speeds are measured in cycles per second, Hertz (Hz). Speeds can range from 25 MHz (megahertz) to over 2 GHz (gigahertz, a billion cycles per second), with faster chips on the design board.

The clock speeds are simple: The higher the MHz, the faster the chip can process data. This means things such as drawing the screen or loading a program. However, the difference between the fastest machine and the midrange one is sometimes not noticeable. For the most part, if you will be doing a lot of Web-related things, it may never be apparent to you. (When you surf the Web, you are at the mercy of the server speeds, the Internet traffic, and other details that can cause you to wait while a page loads, no matter what chip is on your motherboard.)

The price of a new computer is directly related to the price of the chip within it. A comparison of chips (subject to extreme change):

Intel Celeron (Pentium III based)		under $50.00
CPU:	1.2 GHz	
Cache:	256 KB	
Bus:	100 MHz	

Intel Celeron (Pentium IV based)		under $100.00
CPU:	2.4 GHz	
Cache:	128 KB	
Bus:	400 MHz	

Intel Pentium IV		around $200.00
CPU:	2.6 GHz	
Cache:	512 KB	
Bus:	400 MHz	

Intel Pentium IV XEON		around $300.00
CPU:	2.66 GHz	
Cache:	512 KB	
Bus:	533 MHz	

Intel Xeon DP		almost $500.00
CPU:	2.8 GHz	
Cache:	512 KB	
Bus:	533 MHz	

Intel Pentium IV XEON		over $700.00
CPU:	3.06 GHz	
Cache:	512 KB	
Bus:	533 MHz	

Meanwhile, AMD also has a line of chips with varied prices. And even though Intel has put a lot of money into its "Intel Inside" campaign, the AMD chips are comparable in quality and function. Its pricing is competitive. (Many believe the product is better for the price.)

Motorola produces chips for Apple/Macintosh computers. The two chips that are currently in use are the G3 and the G4. The chips also come in a variety of speeds.

OVERCLOCKING

Depending on the social circle you keep, you may hear about *overclocking*. It's essentially souping up a computer, just as people optimize the performance of a hot rod engine. CPUs and video cards can be overclocked. An example of overclocking would be to alter an Intel 166 MHz to run at 200 MHz to speed up performance.

It is a way to increase the speed of the computer's CPU or other component beyond its capacity. (Many of the newer Intel chips have been redesigned so they can't be altered, they're clock-locked. Obviously, this is a way to force people to purchase newer chips instead of tinkering with the ones they already have.)

There are risks. Overclocking can do damage. It's a bad idea to just try it without a lot of research. An overclocked CPU will have more "noise" in the core, causing errors, crashes, and the dreaded *blue screen of death* (a fatal error). Making the chip run faster will cause it to run hotter. But it is an interesting subject, even from a purely theoretical standpoint or just to know what people are referring to.

For more information:

Target PC—www.targetpc.com/hardware/articles/ocguide/part1

Extreme Overclocking—www.extremeoverclocking.com

HyperperformancePC—www.hyperformance-pc.com/overclocking_faq.htm

Tom's Hardware—www6.tomshardware.com/cpu/20000711/

Cache

The cache (which is pronounced just like the word for money—cash) is a small amount of computer memory that the chip reserves for the most recently used data. A cache is short-term memory that allows the computer to locate recently used information instead of searching for it. It speeds up the access time. This speeds up computer time. There are a few different kinds of cache. In relation to the chip speed, the larger the cache, the faster the processing time is from your perspective. For Web surfing, a chip with a large cache is a good selection criterion.

Bus Speed

Another important thing is the bus speed. This speed is also measured in MHz. It's the pipeline of information to and from the CPU. The larger the pipe, the more data can be moved at a time. The newest of the Intel chips have a whopping 800 MHz, compared with archaic and outdated speeds as low as 33 MHz.

EXPANSION BUS AND SLOTS

PCI (Peripheral Component Interconnect) is an interconnection system between a microprocessor and attached devices. The expansion slots are spaced closely for high-speed operation. Using PCI, a computer can support both new PCI cards and older standard expansion cards, such as Industry Standard Architecture (ISA). PCI 2.0 is independent of microprocessor design because it synchronizes with the clock speed of the processor chip. Most PCI cards are half-sized or smaller.

ISA Industry Standard Architecture is a standard bus (computer interconnection) architecture associated with the IBM AT (1983) motherboard. It allows 16 bits at a time to flow between the motherboard circuitry and an expansion slot card and its associated device

EISA (Extended ISA) changed the standard to a 32-bit interface. It was developed in part as an open alternative to the proprietary Microchannel Architecture (MCA) that IBM introduced in its PS/2 computers. EISA data transfer can reach a peak of 33 megabytes (MB) per second.

AGP (Accelerated Graphics Port) uses your computer's random access memory (RAM) to refresh the monitor image and to support the texture mapping, z-buffering, and alpha blending required by 2D and 3D image display. AGP offers high-speed data transfer to and from RAM, optimizing the use of memory and minimizing the amount of memory necessary for high-performance graphics. The AGP main memory use is dynamic, meaning that when not being used for accelerated graphics, main memory is restored for use by the OS or by other applications. AGP runs at several times the bus speed of conventional PCI. Because of this, the data transfer rate using AGP is significantly greater than with PCI video cards. AGP employs eight sideband address lines, so multiple data transfers can take place concurrently.

MCA (Microchannel Architecture) is an interface between a computer (or multiple computers) and its expansion cards and their associated devices. MCA is distinct from previous bus architectures (such as the ISA because the pin connections are smaller. For this and other reasons, it cannot support other bus architectures. MCA is not in general use because of the proprietary and nonstandard connectors. (Other manufacturers never adopted them.) Some of the advanced design features, however, have influenced other bus designs. It is still in use in PS/2s and in some minicomputer systems.

Motherboard/Mainboard

The motherboard, or mainboard, is the foundation of the computer system. It is where the CPU resides in a special socket. It can have a number of different configurations. In other words, even though you have a Pentium III and your friend has the exact same chip with all the same speeds and features, it may be housed on a completely different style of motherboard, encased in a very different machine case.

Form Factors

Motherboards come in different shapes and sizes for different uses. Standard classes of computer housing are referred to as the *form factors*. Form factors establish standardized ground rules for manufacturers of components, cases/chassis, and other equipment. These standards make equipment and components compatible, so small motherboards fit into small machines and big motherboards fit in big machines.
Form factors include:

- Physical dimensions (board size, height restrictions, etc.)
- Mounting hole placements and locations
- Connector placement (such as power connectors, expansion slots, disk I/O, ports, and processors)
- Power specifications (voltage tolerances, power connector configurations, etc.)
- Chassis and thermal considerations (power supply placement in the case, venting, etc.)
- Power supply form factors (choices include: ATX, SFX, and TFX), which correspond to PC form factors.

PC FORM FACTORS

 Although you may not run into many of these at your local computer store, the terms occasionally come up in magazine ads.

AT/Baby AT—This has been on the market for a long time. It is a relatively cheap design. However, it has flaws (e.g., inadequate cooling of the CPU) with newer chip/motherboard designs.

ATX—This was the engineered fix for the AT form factor. Various key components were rotated and moved around to address the heat problem and increase the airflow.

MiniATX—This design has all the benefits of the ATX design and cuts cost by using a smaller footprint.

Mini-iTX—This is a proprietary, extra-small motherboard promoted by VIA Technologies and incorporates its Pentium-like chip. Very popular among hobbyists.

Micro/FlexATX—This design has fewer expansion slots (four total) and uses a smaller footprint than ATX or MiniATX. (MicroATX case/chassis requires an SFX form factor power supply.) The maximum mainboard size possible is 8.5″ × 9.5″. It is a very compact package that is showing up in the marketplace.

Extended ATX—This is identical to the ATX, just larger, 12″ × 13″. It's commonly used with dual processor motherboards.

LPX/Mini LPX—The LPX motherboard was designed to fit into the Slimline "low-profile" cases. The design goal was to reduce space usage (and cost). This was replaced by the NLX form factor.

NLX/Mini NLX—In 1997, Intel released the NLX specifications to streamline PC case assembly and for the removal of mainboards for repair. This form was designed to build low-cost, low-profile systems.

SWTX—This is for multiprocessor server motherboards, usually 4+ processors.

WTX—The WTX was a collaborative effort between Intel and other manufacturers to lay down standards for midrange workstations.

EBX—The EBX or open architecture is targeted mainly for embedded applications, such as vending machines, scientific/medical diagnostic applications, communications equipment, and kiosks. Max board size of 8″ × 5.75″.

For more information on PC form factors, see www.formfactors.org.

Memory

Memory means a lot of different things when it comes to computers. There is memory on the chip, memory cards, short-term memory, long-term memory, read-only memory, and secondary memory, among a long list of variations. It can be confusing and bewildering, much like an Englishman's encounter with the sheer number of words an Eskimo uses for snow.

Initially, the term *memory* meant strictly data storage on computer chips. *Storage* meant data archived on tapes or on diskettes.

The terms have evolved some. Now memory can also be called *physical memory*, which refers only to the ability of a chip to hold data. Now that hard disks are computer devices containing chips with physical memory, the term *storage* isn't quite correct. The storage of data on a hard disk drive is called *virtual memory*. (It is the expanse of physical memory onto a hard drive.) Memory on hard drives, floppy disks, CDs, and tapes can also be called *secondary memory* or *secondary storage*.

All computers have a certain amount of physical memory, usually called *main memory*, which is also called *RAM*.

Remember that what you need to know about what memory to buy is carefully outlined in the documentation of the computer or motherboard. Do not make substitutions. The following are basic definitions.

RAM

This is a common term meaning Random Access Memory. RAM is a network of electrically charged points where the CPU stores the data it needs to have handy and readily accessible. It is temporary, short-term memory. The "random" in RAM means that the contents of each byte can be directly accessed without regard to the bytes before or after them. RAM requires power to maintain its contents, which is why you must save your data onto disk before you turn the computer off. (This is also known as *volatile memory*.)

DRAM

DRAM (dynamic RAM) is the most common kind of random access memory on personal computer. The "dynamic" means that it must have its storage cells regularly electronically refreshed.

SRAM

SRAM (static RAM) keeps data bits in memory for as long as power is available. SRAM is used for cache memory.

EDO RAM

EDO RAM (extended data output RAM) is a type of RAM chip designed for the Intel Pentium 66 MHz chip. The purpose was to improve the speed at which the CPU could read from memory.

FPM—Fast Page Mode is the most common DRAM, so common that people simply call it DRAM, leaving off the FPM. Accessing memory is like looking up information in a book. You choose the page, then FPM gets information from that page. FPM DRAM needs to specify the row address only once for accesses within the same page addresses. Successive accesses to the same page of memory require only a column address to be selected, which saves time in accessing the memory.

EDO—An improvement over FPM design and used in nonparity configurations in Pentium machines or higher. If supported by your motherboard, EDO shortens the read cycle between the main memory and the CPU, thereby dramatically increasing throughput. EDO chips allow the CPU to access memory 10–20% faster. EDO DRAM holds the data even after the signal that "strobes" the column address goes inactive. This allows faster CPUs to manage time more efficiently (while the EDO DRAM is retrieving an instruction for the microprocessor, the CPU can perform other tasks without concern that the data will become invalid). Do not use EDO in systems that don't support it or mix EDO with FPM because serious problems will result.

SDRAM—Designed to synchronize itself with the timing of the CPU. This enables the memory controller to know the exact clock cycle when the requested data will be ready, so the CPU no longer has to wait between memory accesses. SDRAM modules come in several different speeds so as to synchronize with the clock speeds of the system they'll be used in. For example, PC66 SDRAM runs at 66 MHz; PC100 runs at 100 MHz.

DDR DRAM—This is the next generation of SDRAM technology. It allows the memory chip to perform transactions on both the rising and falling edges of the clock cycle. So with DDR SDRAM at 100 or 133 MHz, memory bus clock rate yields an effective data rate of 200 or 266 MHz.

RDRAM—Direct Rambus is a new DRAM architecture, with data transfer speeds up to 800 MHz over a narrow 16-bit bus called a *Direct Rambus Channel*. This high-speed clock rate is possible due to a feature called *double clocked*, which is functionally identical to DDR DRAM. Also, each memory device on the an RDRAM module provides up to 1.6 GB of bandwidth (twice that of PC100 SDRAM).

Other Kinds of Memory

ROM

Read Only Memory, is a memory chip that can be written to once. ROM is built into the computer memory that contains data and programming for your computer to start running (boot up). Unlike RAM, this data is not lost when the machine is turned off or otherwise loses power. The ROM's data is sustained by a small, long-life battery (that looks like a digital watch battery) in your computer. (This is also known as *nonvolatile memory.*)

PROM

Programmable ROM can be modified once. There is also EPROM, which is erasable programmable ROM or EEPROM, electrically erasable programmable ROM.

ADVANCED AND SPECIALTY MEMORY

Base Rambus or concurrent Rambus—These forms of Rambus have been used for years in specialty video applications in some workstations and video game systems, such as Nintendo 64.

ESDRAM—Essentially SDRAM plus a small amount of SRAM cache, which allows for burst operations up to 200 MHz. One advantage of on-chip SRAM is that it enables a wider bus between the SRAM and DRAM, effectively increasing the bandwidth and speed of the DRAM.

FCRAM—Fast cycle RAM was codeveloped by Toshiba and Fujitsu and is intended for specialty applications such as high-end servers, printers, and telecommunications switching systems. It includes memory array segmentation and internal pipelining (sounds cool) that speed random access and reduce power consumption.

SLDRAM—Synchronous link DRAM (like DDR) was developed by a consortium of DRAM manufacturers as an alternative to Rambus technology in the late 1990s.

VCM—Developed by NEC, virtual channel memory allows different blocks of memory to interface independently with the memory controller, each with its own buffer. This allows different system tasks to be assigned their own "virtual channels," and information related to one function does not share buffer space with other tasks occurring at the same time, which increases efficiency.

Flash memory—Flash memory is a solid-state, nonvolatile, rewritable memory. It stores data in memory cells (solid state) just like DRAM, but the data remains in memory when power is turned off (nonvolatile).

Memory Speed

When the CPU sends out a request, the memory controller passes the request to the memory and reports to the CPU when the information will be available for it to read. This entire cycle from CPU to memory controller to memory and back to the CPU can vary in length according to memory speed as well as motherboard bus speed. Memory speed is measured in MHz. Access time (the actual time required to deliver data) can also be measured in nanoseconds (ns).

Either way, memory speed indicates how quickly the memory module itself can deliver a request once it's received from the memory controller. The speed rating on memory modules is the time it takes the memory to complete a request to and from the memory controller. The time it takes between the CPU and the memory controller depends on your motherboard bus speed.

An average CPU takes about 200 ns to access RAM. When there isn't enough RAM to satisfy the CPU's needs, a virtual memory file will be created on the hard drive. This process is called *swapping*. Swapping slows a system down because it can take the CPU 12,000,000 ns to access the hard drive for the needed information. For this reason, it's important to have enough memory available to the CPU. A computer with adequate memory capacity will respond with optimal performance. Adding memory to the machine is a twisted path. It isn't "one size fits all" or even "one color and flavor fit all." Memory comes in SIMMs, DIMMs, SO-DIMMs, RIMMs, and a number of pin choices (covered later). There is some general jargon to know first.

Memory Jargon

To understand memory choices, you need to know the basic terminology and concepts that apply to all memory. Memory can have parity or be nonparity. Nonparity is the more common.

Parity

Data moves through your computer (e.g., from the CPU to the main memory), and sometimes errors occur. Parity checking is the technique to check whether data is lost or written over as it's moved from one storage location to another.

How this works is that an additional binary digit, the parity bit, is added to a group of bits as they are moved together. This bit has no use except to identify whether the bits are moved successfully. The bits are counted and sent, with the extra bit, so that the number sent is an odd number. (If the total number of bits is already an odd number, then the parity bit is set to zero; if the total number is even, the parity bit is set to 1.) At the end of the bit trip, the incoming bits are counted to make sure it's still an odd group. If the total is even, a transmission error has occurred, and either the whole trip will begin again or the system stops and an error message is sent to the user. (If there is a memory error found, the error will be reported but not fixed.)

(Parity checking is also used between modems, in addition to the description above, which is specific to intercomputer bit travels.)

Nonparity

These modules are just like parity modules without the extra chips. There are no parity chips in Apple computers, later 486 and most Pentium-class systems. The reason for this is because memory errors are rare. A single bit error will probably be harmless.

If your SIMM module has 2, 4, 8, 16, or 32 chips, it is more than likely to be nonparity. Always match new memory with what is already in your system. To determine whether your system requires parity, count the number of small, black chips on one of your modules.

Logical Parity

Logical parity is also known as *parity generators* or *fake parity*.

These are modules produced as a less expensive alternative to true parity. Fake parity modules "fool" your system into thinking parity checking is being done. This is accomplished by sending the parity signal the machine looks for, rather than using an actual parity bit. In a module using fake parity, you will *not* be notified of a memory error, because it is really not being checked. The result of these undetected errors can be corrupted files, wrong calculations, and even corruption of your hard disk. If you need parity modules, be cautious of suppliers offering bargains.

ECC

Error correction code modules are an advanced form of parity detection often used in servers and critical data applications. ECC modules use multiple parity bits per byte (usually 3) to detect double-bit errors. They also will correct single-bit errors without generating an error message.

Interleaving

The term *interleaving* refers to a process where the CPU alternates communication between two or more memory banks. This process is typically used in servers and workstations. Interleaving between memory banks produces a continuous flow of data. This cuts down the length of the memory cycle and results in faster transfer rates.

Memory Module Form Factors

Memory module form factors for manufacturers are standardized specifications of how the memory should be installed or laid out. They are like motherboard form factors, in that they allow various manufacturers to adhere to predetermined designs in an attempt to create some standardization. These form factors include: SIMM, DIMM, SO-DIMM, and RIMM. If you go to purchase more RAM memory for your machine, you will need to know what type of form factor you have and how many pins it requires.

SIMM

Single inline memory modules come in 30-pin (3-1/2″ long) and 72-pin (4-1/2″ long). These chips are installed in pairs. 72-pin SIMMs have a single notch in the middle of the module. SIMMs are installed at a slight angle in relation to the motherboard (Figure 2.1).

DIMM

Dual inline memory modules are 168-pin (5-1/4″ long). DIMMs are installed perpendicular to the motherboard. DIMMs have a notch in the middle and one just off the left side of the module (Figure 2.2).

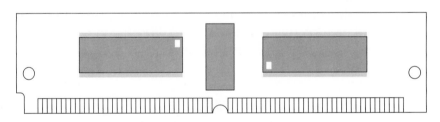

4 1/2" 72-Pin SIMM

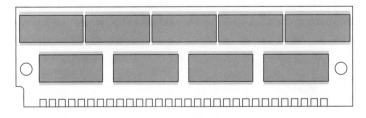

3 1/2" 30-Pin SIMM

FIGURE 2.1 **SIMMs COME IN 30-PIN AND 72-PIN VERSIONS.**

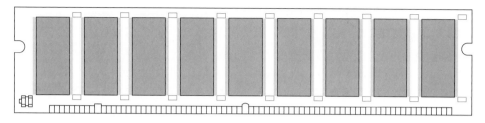

5 1/4" 168-Pin DIMM

FIGURE 2.2 **168-PIN DIMMs.**

RIMM

Rambus inline memory modules look very similar to DIMMs but have 184 pins. RIMMs transfer in 16-bit blocks. An aluminum sheath, called a *heat spreader*, covers the module to protect the chips from overheating due to the heat generated by the faster access and transfer speeds (Figure 2.3).

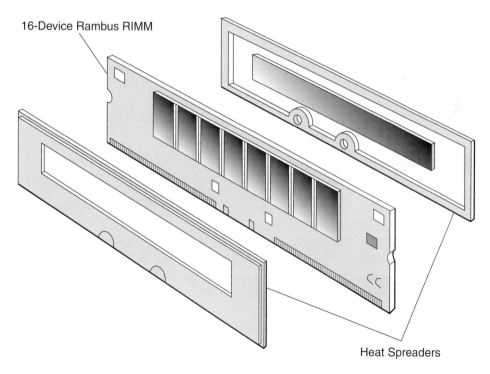

16-Device Rambus RIMM

Heat Spreaders

FIGURE 2.3 **DIAGRAM OF A RIMM WITH THE HEAT SPREADER COMPONENT.**

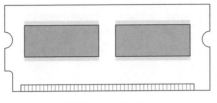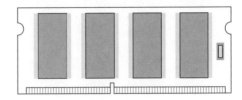

2.35" 72-Pin SO DIMM   2.66" 144-Pin SO DIMM

FIGURE 2.4   A 32-BIT 72-PIN SO-DIMM AND A 64-BIT, 144-PIN SO-DIMM.

SO-DIMM

This type of memory, called small outline DIMM, is commonly used in notebook computers. The principal difference is that the SO-DIMM is much smaller than a standard DIMM. There are two variants, a 32-bit, 72-pin and a 64-bit, 144-pin (Figure 2.4).

SO-RIMM

Similar to a SO-DIMM but uses Rambus technology and has 160 pins (Figure 2.5).

VIDEO AND GRAPHICS MEMORY

VRAM—A video version of FPM technology. VRAM typically has two ports instead of one, which allows the memory to allocate one channel to refreshing the screen while the other is focused on changing the images on the monitor. This works much more efficiently than regular DRAM in video applications, but because video memory chips are used in lower quantity than main memory, they tend to be more expensive. Some video card manufacturers will use regular DRAM instead of VRAM to save money.

WRAM—Windows RAM is another type of dual-port memory that is also used in graphics-intensive systems. It differs from VRAM because its dedicated display port is smaller and it supports EDO features.

SGRAM—Synchronous graphics RAM is a video-specific extension of SDRAM that includes graphics-specific read/write features. It also allows data to be retrieved and modified in blocks instead of individually. This feature reduces the number of reads and writes in memory, and this efficiency increases performance.

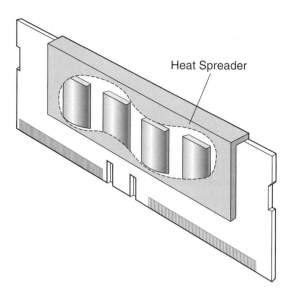

Heat Spreader

FIGURE 2.5 **FIGURE OF A SO-RIMM.**

HARD DISKS

We're going to cover hard drive basics, such as the interfaces, hard disk jargon, and RAID. We won't be covering low-voltage differential (LVD) and other very high-end technology because it's doubtful you'll want or need that kind of hardware. (However, more information about LVD is available at www.adaptec.com and www.seagate.com.)

The two most common hard drive interfaces are IDE and SCSI.

IDE

Integrated Drive Electronics is a standard electronic interface used between a computer motherboard's data paths or bus and the computer's disk storage devices. The IDE interface is based on the IBM PC Industry Standard Architecture (ISA) 16-bit bus standard, but it is also used in computers that use other bus standards. Most computers sold today use an enhanced version of IDE called *Enhanced Integrated Drive Electronics* (EIDE). In today's computers, the IDE controller is often built into the motherboard.

EIDE : Enhanced Integrated Drive Electronics

EIDE's enhancements to Integrated Drive Electronics (IDE) make it possible to address a hard disk larger than 528 MB. EIDE also provides faster access to the hard drive, support for direct memory access (DMA), and support for additional drives, including CD-ROM and tape devices. EIDE was adopted as a standard by ANSI in 1994. ANSI calls it Advanced Technology Attachment-2, also referred to as Fast ATA.

ATA/33/66/100

ATA, also known as IDE, is the most common interface for desktop and workstation computers. The numeric portion of these interfaces denotes the maximum burst transfer rate of the interface in MB per second.

As ATA disk drives have become faster internally, the need has arisen for faster interface or external "burst" transfer rates. Recent examples of this include Ultra ATA/33, Ultra ATA/66, and now Ultra ATA/100. Ultra ATA/100 is the latest generation of the ATA interface. The most significant difference between ATA/100 and the others is the increase in transfer rate. There are also some enhancements to error checking with Ultra ATA/100. In addition, these new drives include an enhanced command set to ensure compatibility with future interface additions.

SCSI

This is an acronym for Small Computer System Interface. Pronounced "scuzzy," SCSI is a parallel interface standard used by Apple Macintosh computers, PCs, and many UNIX systems for attaching peripheral devices to computers. Nearly all Apple Macintosh computers, excluding only the earliest Macs and the recent iMac, come with a SCSI port for attaching devices such as disk drives and printers. SCSI interfaces provide for data transmission rates up to 160 MB per second. In addition, you can attach many devices to a single SCSI port, so that SCSI is really an I/O bus, rather than simply an interface. Although SCSI is an ANSI standard, there are many variations and several types of connectors.

You can attach SCSI devices to a PC by inserting a SCSI board in one of the expansion slots. Many high-end new PCs come with SCSI built in. However, the lack of a single SCSI standard means that some devices may not work with some SCSI boards.

The following varieties of SCSI are currently implemented:

SCSI-1: Uses an 8-bit bus and supports data rates of 4 MB per second.

SCSI-2: Same as SCSI-1, but uses a 50-pin connector instead of a 25-pin connector and supports multiple devices. This is what most people mean when they refer to plain SCSI.

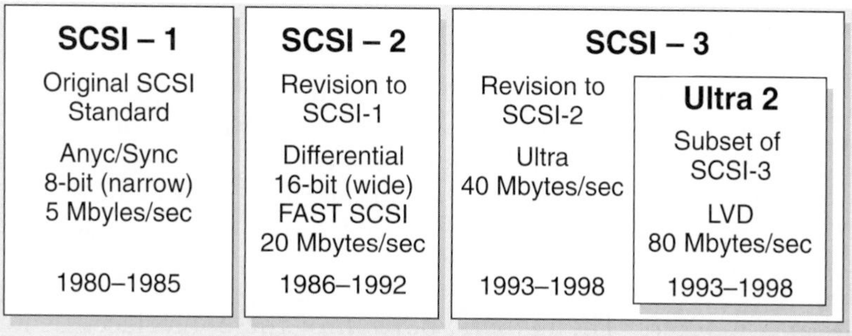

SCSI – 1	SCSI – 2	SCSI – 3	
Original SCSI Standard	Revision to SCSI-1	Revision to SCSI-2	**Ultra 2**
Anyc/Sync 8-bit (narrow) 5 Mbyles/sec	Differential 16-bit (wide) FAST SCSI 20 Mbytes/sec	Ultra 40 Mbytes/sec	Subset of SCSI-3 LVD 80 Mbytes/sec
1980–1985	1986–1992	1993–1998	1993–1998

FIGURE 2.6 THE EVOLUTION OF HARD DRIVE SCSI DEVICES.

Wide SCSI: Uses a wider cable (168 cable lines to 68 pins) to support 16-bit transfers.

Fast SCSI: Uses an 8-bit bus but doubles the clock rate to support data rates of 10 MB per second.

Fast Wide SCSI: Uses a 16-bit bus and supports data rates of 20 MB per second.

Ultra SCSI: Uses an 8-bit bus and supports data rates of 20 MB per second.

SCSI-3: Uses a 16-bit bus and supports data rates of 40 MB per second. Also called Ultra Wide SCSI.

Ultra2 SCSI: Uses an 8-bit bus and supports data rates of 40 MB per second.

Wide Ultra2 SCSI: Uses a 16-bit bus and supports data rates of 80 MB per second.

Ultra160 (LVD): Uses a 32-bit bus and supports data rates of 160 MB per second.

Hard Disk RPM and Seek Time

RPM is a measurement of how fast a hard disk's platters are spinning (in revolutions per minute). The faster the spin rate, the less time it takes for the drive to read or write a given amount of data.

Seek time is an average of how long a drive takes to move the read/write heads to a particular track on the disk. It includes controller overhead but does not include drive latency.

Hard Disk Capacity

Capacity is the amount of data that the drive can store after formatting. Most disk drive companies calculate disk capacity based on the assumption that 1 MB = 1,000 KB and 1 GB = 1,000 MB. However, a byte is made up of 8 bits and 1 MB = 1,024 KB and 1 GB = 1024 MB.

Gold is a better conductor of electricity and is more resistant to corrosion. It is also easier to apply in a thin uniform layer. Tin is much less expensive but is very difficult to apply in a thin uniform layer. When buying memory, it is recommended that you match metals. This means that if your motherboard uses gold-plated memory sockets, you purchase gold lead memory modules. The same applies if tin is used.

What's the big deal?

Dissimilar metals in contact with each other create a perfect environment for accelerated corrosion. Corrosion creates electrical current and changes the capacitance value along the circuit. Many people insist that mixing will have no effect, but the manner and quality of the gold or tin application can amplify what might have otherwise been a minute effect.

Both Compaq and Intel recommend against mixing dissimilar metals.

According to Compaq: "Contact reliability can be affected if the different metal types are mixed, for example, placing a tin-plated SIMM into a gold-plated memory socket. This metal mixing can cause accelerated corrosion, which results in bad connections and can ultimately cause system failure."

According to Intel: "Studies show that fretting (wear/corrosion) occurs when tin comes in pressure contact with gold or any other metal. Tin debris will transfer to the gold surface and oxidize. Continued transfer will build up an oxide film layer. Tin surfaces always have a natural oxide. Despite this, electrical contact is easily made between two tin surfaces. Oxides on both soft surfaces will bend and break, ensuring contact. The resistance of the oxidation layer builds up over time when one surface is hard. Increasing the contact resistance will ultimately result in memory failures. Mixing gold and tin leads doesn't always cause an immediate problem. The problem usually occurs over time and can be abated by removing the memory module and cleaning the contacts."

NETWORK CARD

The network interface card, often abbreviated NIC, is either an ISA/PCI expansion board, PCMCIA card, or USB device that you insert or plug into a computer so the computer can be connected to a network. Most NICs are designed for a particular type of network, protocol, and medium (e.g., cable), although some can serve multiple network media types. Wireless NICs are PCMCIA cards and use an adapter card for desktop machine installations.

MAC Address

Every NIC is assigned a globally unique identification number, called the MAC (media access control) address. It is a hexadecimal number that identifies the manufacturer and the network node.

Its format is: XX-XX-XX-XX-XX-XX.

The first three sets of characters indicate the manufacturer; the last three sets are to identify your network card.

Full-Duplex

Full-duplex data transmission means that data can be transmitted in both directions at the same time. For example, on a LAN with a technology that has full-duplex transmission, one workstation can be sending data on the line while another workstation is receiving data. Full-duplex transmission usually implies a bidirectional line that can move data in both directions.

Half-Duplex

Half-duplex data transmission means that data can be transmitted in both directions but not at the same time. For example, on a LAN using half-duplex transmission, one workstation can send data on the line, then immediately receive data on the line from the same direction in which data was just transmitted.

Auto-Sensing

Auto-sensing simply means that the network card will "sense" the speed of the network and automatically operate at that speed.

WOL

Wake on LAN is a feature of many network cards that allows a network professional to power on a computer remotely or to wake it up from sleep mode. By remotely triggering the computer to wake up and perform scheduled maintenance tasks, the technician does not have to visit each computer on the network physically.

Wake on LAN works by sending a wakeup frame or packet to a client machine. The Wake on LAN network adapter installed in the client receives the wakeup frame and turns on.

To use Wake on LAN technology to manage computers you need a Wake on LAN enabled network adapter, Wake on LAN enabled motherboard, and remote management software. How the card "wakes up" depends on the motherboard and the NIC. Some motherboards and NICs will "wake up" if any network traffic, such as a PING, is received. Others may require a "secret knock" or sequence of packets generated by specific software.

VIDEO CARD

Your system's video card is the component responsible for producing the visual output from your computer. Early on, the video card only had to display text—not even in color, at that. Video cards today are much more like coprocessors. They have their own intelligence and do a lot of processing that would otherwise have to be done by the system processor. This is a necessity due to the enormous increase both in how much data we send to our monitors today and the sophisticated calculations that must be done to determine what we see on the screen. This is particularly so with the rise of the graphical OS, 3D computing, and gaming.

Unaccelerated and Accelerated Video Cards

Older video cards did simple translations only. They were rather dumb in that they could only take what the processor created and send it to the monitor. The processor did all of the work of deciding what would be displayed. This was fine for older environments, such as DOS, and especially for text-based output, where the amount of information involved was small. When graphical OSs such as Windows became the norm, suddenly large amounts of data were being shuffled around on the screen. The CPU was spending a lot of time moving windows around and drawing boxes, cursors, and frames. As a result, the processor would often get bogged down, and performance would decrease dramatically.

To clear this bottleneck, companies began making cards called *accelerators*; in fact, Windows drove this effort so much that they were often called *Windows accelerators*. These were video cards that added smarts to enable them to do much of the video calculating work that had been previously done by the processor. With an accelerator, when the system needs to draw a box on the screen, it doesn't compute where all the pixels need to be and what color; it sends a request to the video card saying "draw a window at these locations," and the video card does it. The processor can then go on to do more useful work. The accelerator, for its part, can be highly customized and tailored to this specific job and, therefore, be far more efficient at it than the processor.

This offloading of video calculation work has led to a manifold increase in the power of the video subsystem in a PC. Virtually all modern video cards incorporate acceleration, some of it quite sophisticated. In essence, the video card becomes a coprocessor, working with the main CPU. Continuing the trend, new *3D* accelerators are becoming more common and offload the tremendously time-consuming work of 3D animation from the processor.

Video Memory (Frame Buffer)

The screen image that you see on your monitor can contain a fair bit of information; at the upper end, a 1600×1200 pixel screen display in true color contains almost 6 MB of data. And this is just for the displayed image, not for the data itself that the image represents.

In the early days of PCs, the amount of information displayed was much, much less. A screen of monochrome text, for example, needs only about 2 KB of space. Special parts of the upper memory area (UMA) were dedicated to holding this video data. The processor would compute what needed to be displayed and would put it into this area; then the video card would read it and display it.

As the need for video memory increased into the megabyte range, it began to make more sense to put the memory on the video card itself. The memory that holds the video image is sometimes called the *frame buffer*. A big advantage of having the memory on the video card is that VRAM is much faster than using regular system RAM.

Some motherboard designs integrate the video chipset into the motherboard itself, then use part of the system RAM for the frame buffer. This is called a *unified memory architecture*. This is mainly done for cost savings. The trade-off is much lower video performance, because in order to achieve higher resolutions and refresh rates, the video memory needs to have much higher performance than the RAM normally used for the system. A similar-sounding but different system is used by the new AGP, which lets the video processor access the system memory for doing graphics calculations but keeps a dedicated video memory for the frame buffer. This allows for more flexible memory use without sacrificing performance and is becoming a new standard in the PC world.

SOUND CARD

The modern PC sound card contains several hardware systems relating to the production and capture of audio, the two main audio subsystems being for digital audio capture and replay and music synthesis, along with some glue hardware. The replay and music synthesis subsystem produces sound waves in one of two ways:

1. through an internal FM synthesizer

2. by playing a digitized or sampled sound

The digital audio section of a sound card consists of a matched pair of 16-bit digital-to-analog (DAC) and analog-to-digital (ADC) converters and a programmable sample rate generator. The computer reads the sample data to or from the converters. The sample rate generator clocks the converters and is controlled by the PC. Although it can be any frequency above 5 KHz, it's usually a fraction of 44.1 KHz.

Most cards use one or more direct memory access (DMA) channels to read and write the digital audio data to and from the audio hardware. DMA-based cards that implement simultaneous recording and playback (or full-duplex operation) use two channels, increasing the complexity of installation and the potential for DMA clashes with other hardware. Some cards also provide a direct digital output, using an optical or coaxial S/PDIF connection.

A card's sound generator is based on a custom DSP (digital signal processor) that replays the required musical notes by multiplexing reads from different areas of the wave table memory at differing speeds to give the required pitches. The maximum number of notes available is related to the processing power available in the DSP and is referred to as the card's *polyphony*. DSPs use complex algorithms to create effects such as reverb, chorus, and delay. Reverb gives the impression that the instruments are being played in large concert halls. Chorus is used to give the impression that many instruments are playing at once, when in fact there's only one. Adding a stereo delay to a guitar part, for example, can "thicken" the texture and give it a spacious stereo presence.

Besides sound, sound cards also can double as CD-ROM interfaces. They support the three proprietary interfaces for Sony, Mitsumi, and Panasonic drives, in addition to the popular SCSI and IDE/EIDE standards. They also have an audio connector for CD audio output. The rationale for providing CD support on sound cards is that it allows a PC to be upgraded to "multimedia" capability by the addition of a single expansion card.

The hardware configuration of the AdLib sound card was the first standard of importance. But Creative Labs' SoundBlaster cards were the ones that led the way in the establishment of a much-needed standard for digital audio on PC. Creative Labs maintained its lead by following its 8-bit product with a 16-bit family. This was the user-friendly AWE32. It went far toward fulfilling users' wish lists. They were sold as an OEM kit for PC manufacturers that drop the price.

The next generation, the AWE64, launched in late 1997. It offered 64-note polyphony from a single MIDI device, 32 controlled in hardware and 32 in software. It is the current benchmark.

Most sound cards sold today should support the SoundBlaster and general MIDI standards. They should be able to record and play digital audio at 44.1 KHz stereo. This is the resolution at which CD audio is recorded. It is the reason sound cards are said to have "CD-quality" sound.

Game Audio Standards

Surround sound for the movies is prerecorded and delivered consistently to the ear, no matter what cinema or home it is replayed in. Beyond that, it's the same linear delivery, without any interaction from the listener—just like listening to music.

This is not good for games. In games, the sound needs to change interactively with the on-screen action in real time. For this reason, Creative Labs came up with its SoundBlaster mono audio standard for DOS games on PCs. As the standard matured, realism improved with stereo capabilities (SoundBlaster Pro), and quality leapt forward with CD resolution (SoundBlaster 16).

Microsoft changed the entire multimedia game standards with its DirectX in Windows 95. The idea was that DirectX offered a load of commands, also known as APIs, which did things such as "make a sound on the left" or "draw a sphere in front." Games would then make DirectX calls. The hardware manufacturers would need to ensure that their sound and graphics card drivers understood these. This is why when you start a game, there is a choice for the selection of the audio option.

The audio portion of DirectX 1 and 2 was called DirectSound. This offered basic stereo left and right panning effects to let software developers write directly to any DirectX-compatible multiple audio stream sound card for 3D audio effects. Each audio channel can be treated individually. This supports multiple sample rates and the addition of software-based effects. DirectSound becomes the sound-mixing engine. It uses system RAM to hold the different audio streams in play for the few milliseconds it must wait before being mixed and sent on to the sound card. Under ideal conditions, DirectSound can mix and output the requested sounds in as little as 20 milliseconds.

DirectX 3 introduced DirectSound3D (DS3D). This offered a range of commands to place a sound anywhere in 3D space. (It was called *positional audio*.) The downside was that it required significant CPU processing power. Microsoft was initially reluctant to allow DS3D to be accelerated by third-party hardware. So it was a while before DirectX 5 emerged, which was able to reduce the stress and demands on the main system CPU

DirectX 6 ushered in the debut of DirectMusic. This new standard enhanced versatility in composing music for games and other applications. DS3D positional audio is one of the features supported by the latest generation of PCI sound cards.

Positional Audio

Positional audio manipulates the characteristics of sounds. This can make them seem to come from a specific direction, such as from behind or from far to the left. DirectSound3D gives game developers a set of API commands to position audio elements. Furthermore, as with much of DirectX, DirectSound3D is scalable. If an application asks for positional effects and no hardware support for such effects is found, DirectSound3D provides the necessary software and uses the CPU for processing.

DS3D may have supported positional audio, but it didn't offer much support for adding reverb or individual reflections to simulate different environments. DS3D did support extensions to the API. This is significant, because it caused new sound standards to be developed. These new standards gained widespread support from game developers: Aureal's A3D technology and Creative Technology's Environmental Audio Extensions (EAX). Positional audio has given games better sound quality and added to game "feel." In some games, you can actually hear the "enemy" sneaking up behind you.

A3D

 Originally developed in 1997 in collaboration with NASA for use in flight simulators, Aureal's A3D technology has subsequently progressed through a number of versions.

ASD1 improved on DS3D by providing hardware acceleration, a more advanced distance model allowing simulation of different atmospheric environments, such as thick fog or underwater environment, and a resource manager that allows developers to take advantage of the number of 3D streams the sound card can handle and control the use of Aureal's 3D sound algorithms.

The **A3D2** version actually takes the geometry information of the room that is fed to the graphics card and uses it to render realistic sonic reflections and occlusions. Using a technology called WaveTracing, A3D2 genuinely calculates up to 60 first-order reflections, which interact in real time with the environment, then groups later-order reflections into overall reverb.

ASD3 takes the technology to the next level by adding a number of new features, such as Volumetric Sound Sources—when developers define an audio file to a sound source, the sound source must have a location so that it can be rendered in relation to the listener. This is usually done via a point source—the point where the source is. However, some sources will not "reside" in a single point; flowing water, wind, crowd cheers, etc. will actually stretch out or extend in various areas. To model these sources more accurately, ASD3 allows them to be defined as volumetric sound sources, thereby positioning them better.

MP3 playback: Previously, audio streams for 3D audio had to be WAV files. Now, MP3 files can be used, thereby both reducing their associated storage space and increasing their quality.

Reverb: The sum of all late-order reflections, Aureal's geometric reverb will work on Vortex2 (and later) cards, as well as automatically translating to EAX or I3DL2 if a sound card does not have the appropriate A3D support.

Streaming audio: Automatic support for streaming audio has been added, eliminating the complex layer of development normally required for client/server interactive entertainment applications that use existing audio solutions.

A3D2 was such a computationally complex system that Aureal developed a processor dedicated to the necessary number crunching. A3D3 requires even greater processing power, which is provided in the shape of an additional DSP (Digital Signal Processor) to accelerate the new commands.

The fact that AD3 was considered by many to be the technically superior standard proved of little consequence when, after two years of litigation with Creative Technologies, Aureal filed for bankruptcy in April 2000 and was subsequently taken over by its erstwhile rival a few months later.

EAX

First introduced with its SoundBlaster Live! soundcards in 1998, Creative Technology's EAX began as a simple way to add reverberation to DS3D. Reverb, the wash of echoes produced when sound waves bounce off walls in a room, helps us identify an environment. Gunshots in an airplane hangar sound very different than they do in a sewer pipe, for example, but DS3D ignores this fact.

EAX 1.0 was designed to provide developers with the ability to create a convincing sense of environment in entertainment titles and a realistic sense of distance between the player and audio events. The approach Creative took to achieve this was, computationally, significantly easier than the one Aureal had taken with A3D. This was simply to create predefined reverb effects for a variety of environments with different characteristics of reflections and reverberation, room types, and/or room size. EAX 1.0 provided 26 such reverb presets as an open set of extensions to Microsoft's DS3D. The API also allows for customizing late reverberation parameters (decay time, damping, level) and automatic level management according to distance.

Released in 1999, EAX 2.0 enabled the creation of more compelling and realistic environments with tools that allow the simulation of the muffling effects of partitions between environments (such as walls) and obstacles within environments (such as furniture), it being possible to apply these obstruction and occlusion features to each individual audio source. In addition, EAX 2.0 also offers global early reflections of the echoes that immediately precede real-world reverb and provide a better perception of room size and sound-source location and a tunable air absorption model. 1999 also saw the announcement of EAX 3.0, which introduced the ability to "morph" between environments, which allows developers to position and control clusters of early reflections, as well as one-shot reflections for ricochet effects, and makes full use of technologies such as HRTF for synthesizing positional audio on a single pair of speakers.

In late 2000, a number of EAX effects were incorporated into the DirectX Audio component, the functions of which were previously shared between the DirectSound and DirectMusic components of the latest release of Microsoft's suite of multimedia APIs, DirectX 8.0. A few months later, Creative unveiled an API platform for game developers wanting to incorporate Dolby Digital content into their games. Earlier sound cards had allowed Dolby Digital to be passed directly through the card and be decoded by an external decoder. However, with the 5.1 version of its successful SoundBlaster Live! sound card, Creative supported decoding directly through one of its audio products for the first time, the card being able to output straight to six discrete analog channels.

FLAVORS OF OPTICAL CD AND DVD DRIVES

Normal music CDs and CD-ROMs are made from prepressed disks and encased in plastic. The actual data is stored through pits or tiny indentations on the silver surface of the internal disk. To read the disk, the drive shines a laser onto the CD-ROM's surface, and by interpreting the way in which the laser light is reflected from the disk, it can tell whether the area under the laser is indented.

There are different formats of CDs. These are actually sorted in a rather odd way. The CD standard information is written in books. These different standards books are held bound between the colored covers of a book. A given standard is known by the color of its cover. There are Yellow Book standards and Red Book standards. (Not terribly creative, but it's how it's done.) All CD-ROM drives are Yellow Book- and Red Book-compatible. Some may boast that they have built-in digital-to-analog converters (DAC) converters. The converters allow you to listen to Red Book audio disks directly through headphone or line audio sockets.

Drive Speed Explained

CD-ROM mode 1 is the mode used for CD-ROMs that carry data and applications only. To access the thousands of data files that may be present on this type of CD, precise addressing is necessary. Data is laid out in nearly the same way as it is on audio disks: Data is stored in sectors. Each holds 2,352 bytes of data, with an additional number of bytes used for error detection and correction, as well as control structures.

In mode 1 CD-ROM data storage, the sectors are broken down further: 2,048 bytes are used for the expected data, whereas the other 304 bytes are devoted to extra error detection and correction code, because CD-ROMs are not as fault-tolerant as audio CDs. There are 75 sectors per second on the disk, which yields a disc capacity of 681,984,000 bytes (650 MB) and a single speed transfer rate of 150 KB per second. Drive speed is expressed as multiples of the single speed transfer rate, such as 2X, 4X, 6X, and so on.

ISO-9660

An ISO 9660 file system is a standard CD-ROM file system that allows you to read the same CD-ROM, whether you're on a PC, Mac, or other major computer platform. The standard, issued in 1988, was written by an industry group named High Sierra. Almost all computers with CD-ROM drives can read files from an ISO 9660 file system.

There are several specification levels. In Level 1, file names must be in the 8.3 format (no more than eight characters in the name, no more than three characters in the suffix) and in capital letters. Directory names can be no longer than eight characters. There can be no more than eight nested directory levels. Level 2 and 3 specifications allow file names up to 32 characters long. Joliet, an extension to ISO 9660 from Microsoft, allows the use of Unicode characters in file names (needed for international users) and file names up to 64 characters in length.

MONITORS/DISPLAYS

It is somewhat surprising that the technology behind monitors and televisions is over a hundred years old. The precise origin of the cathode-ray tube (CRT) is subject to controversy and can be debated. It's generally agreed that German scientist Karl Ferdinand Braun developed the first controllable CRT in 1897. He added alternating voltages to the device to enable it to send controlled streams of electrons from one end of the tube to the other. However, it wasn't until the late 1940s that CRTs were used in the first television sets. CRTs found in modern day monitors have undergone modifications to improve picture quality. But they still follow the same basic principles.

Dot Pitch

The dot pitch specification for a display monitor tells you how sharp the displayed image can be. The dot pitch is measured in millimeters (mm), and a smaller number means a sharper image. In desktop monitors, common dot pitches are .31 mm, .28 mm, .27 mm, .26 mm, and .25 mm. Personal computer users will usually want .28 mm or finer. Some large monitors for presentation use may have a larger dot pitch (.48 mm, for example). Think of the dot specified by the dot pitch as the smallest physical visual component on the display. A pixel is the smallest programmable visual element and maps to the dot if the display is set to its highest resolution. When set to lower resolutions, a pixel encompasses multiple dots.

Technically, in a CRT display with a *shadow mask*, the dot pitch is the distance between the holes in the shadow mask. The shadow mask is a metal screen filled with holes through which the three electron beams pass that focus to a single point on the tube's phosphor surface. In CRTs that use an *aperture grill* (a slotted form of mask), such as Sony's Trinitron flat screen technology, the dot pitch is the difference between adjacent slots that pass through an electron beam of the same color.

PLASMA DISPLAY PANEL

A display technology that works on the principle that passing a high voltage through a low-pressure gas creates light.

LIQUID CRYSTAL DISPLAY

This display technology relies on polarizing filters and liquid crystal cells, rather than phosphors illuminated by electron beams to produce an on-screen image.

INPUT DEVICES—KEYBOARD AND MOUSE

You can get both the mechanical and the optical mouse in both wired and wireless forms.

Mechanical

When you move a ball mouse, two rollers track the X and Y movement of a rubber ball. The rollers each connect to a shaft, and the shaft spins a disk with holes in it. When a roller rolls, its shaft and disk spin. On either side of the disk, there is an infrared light-emitting diode (LED) and an infrared sensor. The holes in the disk break the beam of light coming from the LED so that the infrared sensor sees pulses of light. The rate of the pulsing is directly related to the speed of the mouse and the distance it travels.

In this optomechanical arrangement, the disk moves mechanically, and an optical system counts pulses of light. On a typical mouse, the ball is 21 mm in diameter. The roller is 7 mm in diameter. The encoding disk has 36 holes. So if the mouse moves 25.4 mm (1 inch), the encoder chip detects 41 pulses of light.

Each disk has two infrared LEDs and two infrared sensors, one on each side of the disk (so there are four LED/sensor pairs inside a mouse). This arrangement allows the processor to detect the disk's direction of rotation. There is a piece of plastic with a small, precisely located hole that sits between the encoder disk and each infrared sensor.

Optical

The optical mouse was developed by Agilent Technologies and introduced to the world in late 1999. The optical mouse actually uses a tiny camera to take 1,500 pictures every second. Able to work on almost any surface, the mouse has a small, red LED that bounces light off that surface onto a complementary metal-oxide semiconductor (CMOS) sensor. The CMOS sensor sends each image to a DSP for analysis. The DSP, operating at 18 MIPS (million instructions per second), is able to detect patterns in the images and see how those patterns have moved since the previous image. Based on the change in patterns over a sequence of images, the DSP determines how far the mouse has moved and sends the corresponding coordinates to the computer. The computer moves the cursor on the screen, based on the coordinates received from the mouse. This happens hundreds of times each second, making the cursor appear to move very smoothly.

SUMMARY

As you can tell, the amount of gear available is phenomenal. It's wise for a person getting involved in the online world to have some understanding of what is out there. Now we can get down to business.

3

INTERNET
SERVICE
PROVIDERS

ALL ABOUT INTERNET ACCESS

The Internet is more important than the telephone to many small businesses. The average person turns to the Web to find information and products. It is a way to connect with other people. Internet services are essential, strategic business tools. Once you start to rely on them, you cannot do without them.

In fact, 70% of small businesses with broadband connections rate those Internet services as "*very important to the functioning and productivity of their businesses,*" reports a survey by a group that studies the Internet and telecommunications marketplace (The Yankee Group at www.yankeegroup. com). More surprisingly, this group notes that the majority of small businesses view fast Internet connections as more critical to their businesses than standard telephone services.

According to Helen Chan, an analyst with The Yankee Group's small and medium business technologies research and consulting:

> Small- and medium-sized businesses have learned to effectively use the Internet in a myriad of different ways, making it overall a more useful business tool than the phone. In particular, [they] have succeeded in using the Internet for customer service and building brand awareness. While voice currently beats email in adding a personal touch to exchanges that do not take place in person, broadband users are increasingly finding more based [Internet] ways to efficiently conduct and run their day-to-day business.

Now that broadband services are affordable (and readily available in most areas), the question is how to find the right ISP (Internet Service Provider). It's obvious that it isn't necessarily as easy as popping in a free trial install disk. Finding the right provider and network service can be challenging.

But do you just buy a dialup service? Do you get broadband? What type—DSL or cable access? What are DSL and cable access, anyway?

These are the kinds of questions that business owners and home users, who never thought they'd have to be their own IT department, have to answer.

Small businesses aren't alone in this predicament. Telecommuters are often in the same boat to find a service provider. Few companies have the budget to fly IT staffers to the homes of remote workers to set up their Internet connections, fiddle with routers, stretch Ethernet cable across their houses, and all that. The point is to find the right service to fit their budget.

Getting an Internet connection that the entire family can use may not be as easy as popping in an AOL installation disk. With Mom, Dad, and the kids all jockeying for a chance at the keyboard, many households have opted for broadband connections to speed things up. Parents everywhere are asking themselves: *Since when did the list of modern parenting skills include innate familiarity with all things technical?*

THE FIRST STEP

So where to start? The first question small businesses or home workers must ask is whether they need broadband services, such as DSL or cable modem service, or whether they need just dialup Internet services.

Broadband DSL

Broadband services sound more complicated than they are. DSL (digital subscriber line) users subscribe to a special telephone line. The connection offers fast access that is always on. No dialing, waiting for modems to shake hands, etc.—just pure bandwidth. Typical DSL services range from approximately $40 a month to more than $175 a month; the more money, the faster the service and the more bells and whistles. Prices can come in higher, because users must pay for the line as well as the Internet services.

DSL providers typically offer their services in tiers and with different downstream speeds (the time it takes for users to download Web pages, files, email, etc.) and upstream speeds (the time it takes to send email and other messages, share files, etc.). So an entry-level service tier may cost $45 a month and offer 768 kilobits per second (Kbps) of downstream connectivity and 128 Kbps of upstream connectivity; while a business service may cost $150 a month and offer up to 6 megabits per second (Mbps) of downstream connectivity and 384 Kbps of upstream connectivity.

However, DSL services aren't without problems. In fact, they often come with horror stories, especially when it comes to installation. To begin with, DSL services are limited by how far a user is from a telephone company's nearest central office (where all the telephone network switches and other gear reside). If a user is too far away—typically more than 18,000 feet—he or she simply cannot get the service.

If a user is within the service area, the line to his or her house must still be "qualified" by the provider. In some cases, although a user may be close enough to the central office, the copper circuit may suffer from too much interference or other issues to qualify for service. Because of these types of problems, getting DSL can sometimes be problematic, frustrating, and time-consuming. If a user is considering DSL service, the key is to ask far in advance.

Broadband Cable Modem

Cable modem service is a somewhat more straightforward but sometimes more limited service in comparison with DSL's multiple tiers. Typically, cable access is broken into residential and business service, with speed and price differences between the two. A residential service might provide 500 Kbps downstream and 128–256 Kbps upstream for $40. A business connection may deliver 1.5 Mbps or more downstream and faster upstream speeds, as well, but for more money.

It's important to note that cable providers don't serve as many location types as telephone companies. Although suburbs and other residential areas are likely to have cable TV service, small office suites and business parks might not have any cable service at all (because most businesses don't have televisions). Rural areas are not often served by cable providers.

That said, cable access has outpaced DSL installations to date. There are at least twice as many cable lines installed as DSL, according to most telecommunications industry studies.

DO I BUY OR RENT A CABLE MODEM?

Many DSL and cable services give users the option of renting units along with their monthly services, or they can buy them on their own. Typically, if the service is going to be used for any length of time, buying makes the most sense. Cable modems and DSL routers are typically priced between $150 and $500 each. Users can buy them from their service providers, online stores, or computer retailers. The key considerations in purchasing devices are ensuring that they will be compatible with the service providers' networks (most providers offer lists of compatible equipment).

What About Wireless?

In addition to wired broadband, such as DSL and cable modem services, there is an increasing number of wireless services available to small and home office users. These include Wi-Fi (wireless fidelity) and fixed wireless services. For many users in areas that are too far from central offices to get DSL or that cable providers don't serve, wireless services have heavy penetration, especially fixed wireless. Also, new wireless services are finding their way into metropolitan areas. These services cater to mobile professionals who need anywhere access.

Typical fixed wireless services resemble cable modem and DSL services. The provider attaches a terminal unit to the user's home that sends and receives the user's data, but rather than being connected to a coaxial cable or phone line, it has an antenna. Initial user reaction may be that wireless equals slow, but many fixed wireless services can offer speeds up to 3 Mbps.

But the key to all of these services' effectiveness is how well they apply to a user's specific needs. Remote workers, small businesses, etc. all have different requirements for their Internet services.

INTERNET SERVICE PROVIDERS

An ISP is a company that provides access to the Internet. There are numerous different companies that do this. The most well known national and international services are AOL, EarthLink, and Juno (although AOL is technically an online service provider because it has independent content that you cannot find on the general Internet, as well as other proprietary services). Regional ISPs include AT&T, WorldNet, IBM Global Network, MCI, Netcom, UUNet, and PSINet. There are thousands of local providers.

You can dial into an ISP or connect to one through your DSL or cable modem. The ISP will have a high-speed connection directly to the Internet, which it sublets to users. You connect to the ISP, which in turn connects to the Internet.

ISPs and the Internet

If it could be seen, the Internet would resemble a detailed road map with major highways and smaller state routes, all the way down to small alleys and country lanes. It is all about how to get a packet of data from one place to another. Routers do this job. A router consists of the computer hardware and software that sorts and sends the data packet to the right destination. The router at the ISP will send it down the line to be passed to the next router and the next router in a "fire brigade" fashion until it is passed to the destination. A router creates and maintains a table of available routes and their conditions. This information can determine the best route for a given packet. Two packets sent from the same router may take very different routes to the same destination. The router is connected between at least two networks and acts as the traffic cop. There will be a router located at a gateway (where one network meets another) and one at every Internet POP (point of presence), which makes for a lot of routers in the world.

To speed things up, there are centralized *intersections*, called *Metropolitan Area Exchanges* (MAEs). An MAE is a central location to interconnect traffic between different ISPs.

The three MAEs in the United States:

1. MAE-East in the Washington, DC area
2. MAE-West in San Jose, California
3. MAE-Central in Dallas, Texas

(In addition, there are two central MAEs that have slightly different purposes. They are explicitly for frame encapsulation [FE] and are located in Chicago and New York.)

The three major MAEs and network access points (NAPs) form what is known as the *Internet backbone* for commercial traffic. The only thing that can connect to MAE is an ISP router or a computer host that acts as a router.

> The MAEs are privately owned by MCI. For an ISP to use the MAE ports, there are certain conditions that must be met. The MCI MAE Web site outlines some of the requirements:
>
> "MCI MAE Services provide traffic exchange facilities (switching centers) that enable Internet Service Providers (ISPs) to interconnect. MCI provides as much support as possible to enable interconnection. Significant effort is needed from the ISP in the area of arranging peering or transit."

Individual ISPs work out their own peering agreements and manage routing tables. The peering agreement is an arrangement between the larger ISPs (ones with their own backbone networks) to agree to allow traffic from other large ISPs in exchange for the same privileges. (This is much like old railroad agreements to share certain sections of track.) They also exchange traffic with smaller ISPs so they can reach regional end points more directly. This is how the various "owners" of bits of the Internet put the pieces together. They worked out agreements and arrangements to share, with terms and conditions to oversee it. Peering is affected by traffic and network bottlenecks. The Border Gateway Protocol (BGP) exchanges and updates the routers regarding the Internet weather.

Bilateral peering is an agreement between two parties, and *multilateral peering* is the agreement between more than two parties. The Internet is made up of both kinds of peering arrangements. The smaller ISPs may be charged by the larger ISPs to share the resources, which may or may not include transit charges or line leases. (The MAEs also offer co-location space, where ISP equipment is located on site, which is another arrangement.)

There are also *private peering* arrangements between parties to bypass part of the public backbone network. There are exchanges through *local peering* arrangements or a combination of all. The costs of these arrangements are passed on to users as part of the ISP monthly charge. Because the service is not free to set up and run, you should be wary of any "free" ISP services.

Peering arrangements are either *priority* or *best effort*. A priority arrangement specifies reserved bandwidth for a connection. There are different rates for various amounts of service. The best effort doesn't specify a rate. Instead, a small reserved rate is set with a ceiling on the peak rate. Additional traffic up to the peak rate is possible if the bandwidth is available. (If not, the service would lag from the customer's standpoint, even to the point of timing out—meaning that a Web page might not be displayed.)

The Internet Provider

The larger ISPs have their own high-speed leased lines (long-term agreements with a telephone company to have exclusive use of the entire phone line, from point to point). Because of this, they are less dependent on the general state of a telecommunications line or the traffic that may slow things down. Larger ISPs are less affected and can offer better service to their customers. The largest national and regional ISPs are AT&T, WorldNet, IBM Global Network, MCI, Sprint, UUNet, and PSINet.

There are also smaller ISPs, sometimes known as IAPs (Internet Access Providers) to make it clear that they are independent little guys.

ISPs offer more than just Internet access. They have the equipment and the telecommunications lines to have POPs on the Web. Beyond the service type, there are the providers themselves. Finding a provider that will support business use isn't always an easy search. Service and reliability rank higher than price. What good is a cheaper service that isn't available?

Because there are so many different peering arrangements possible and because ISPs vary in their equipment, services, and abilities, there are some key points to consider and questions to ask of any potential ISP.

Stability

Stability isn't limited to the network. In today's telecom economy, plenty of small businesses and home offices often wake up to find that their service provider is front-page news and their services are history.

Insulation from Annoyances

Providers differentiate themselves on how well they insulate users from online annoyances. For instance, many providers put stringent antispam policies and technologies in place in the hope of reducing the amount of time users must otherwise spend sifting through irksome email advertisements for bad credit repair and the like. ISP EarthLink, Inc. (www.earthlink.com) has stated publicly that it has implemented "pop-up-killing" technology to block unwanted pop-up ads that can drain users' time or crash their browsers.

Not all email services are created equal, and there are providers offering more email space and throughput (some providers cap maximum message sizes) or faster email services (some providers' email systems can be slow).

Value-Added Features

Many broadband connections and often dialup services also include multiple email accounts, Web hosting space, etc. How many addresses or how much Web storage space is available may help a small business or home professional make a decision about which provider to go with.

In essence, the decisions and research related to selecting an Internet connection aren't easy, but they are necessary. Hopefully, as more and more business users, however large or small their operations might be, continue to assert that the Internet is the most critical tool for achieving their business goals, providers will respond with easier, cheaper services. But for now, it's time for users to do their homework, explore the options, and choose wisely.

DECISION SUPPORT

 Any small or home business or remote worker who depends on an Internet connection for success and survival must consider the following when selecting a service:

Do you need a broadband connection or a dialup connection?

Do you need raw connectivity or do you also need email services? Perhaps you also need Web hosting services or just simple hosting space (if you can author your own Web pages).

If you need a broadband connection, is DSL or cable modem service available in your area? If you have a choice of services, providers, or both, what are the prices? How long will installation take? If you're considering cable, what is the provider's customer service reputation? What about wireless?

Regardless of connection, what is the customer service, reliability, and responsiveness reputation for each provider that can serve you? It may turn out that a higher-priced service with a better reputation for dependability will be the better choice.

Do you have multiple computers that you need to hook up to your connection?

CHECKLIST TO CHOOSING AN ISP

There are many ISPs in the marketplace. AOL isn't the only choice. In fact, the big boys are far from the only choices. There are thousands of good, stable, inexpensive ISPs on the market. It pays to shop around.

The choice of an ISP has many factors to consider. These factors include: email considerations; a local access number (or POP); connect time; bandwidth; DNS servers; Web space; FTP space; Usenet; available technical support; billing; software installation; and the TOS (terms of service) requirements.

Email

ISPs vary on the email services offered. The minimum that an ISP should offer is one email address using a POP3 server to receive mail and SMTP to send mail. Extra features may include email aliases, extra addresses, more storage space, virus scanning, and spam filtering. A good question to ask would be, How long are both read and unread email kept before being discarded?

Email Alias

An email alias is an email address not based on the login name a user has on the system but instead containing the full name of the user and the user's mail domain. For example, on AOL, you can use only your login name as your email address. If you are John2345678 as your screen name, your email will be conducted as nothing other than John2345678@aol.com. With an email alias, it could be John.Doe@, John_Doe@, jdoe@, JohnADoe@, or anything else you want to choose. The advantage of this is that you can look more professional. For instance, email from "hotboy10" would not carry the weight that JohnAustinDoe would in business correspondence. Some ISPs offer *only* email aliases instead of email accounts.

Port 25 Blocking

Another thing to ask is whether the ISP uses *port 25 blocking*. Port 25 is the part of the server email that is sent and received. Blocking this the server can also block spam mongers who will join an ISP with the sole intent of mailing out a billion messages, up to 600 spam emails an hour. This chews up system resources for everyone and causes huge problems for the ISP, including legal ones. The downside is that there will be an extra step to send email, such as calling in through a separate number, relaying mail through another server, or having a separate email account somewhere else.

Connect Time

How much connect time comes with the basic service? The minimum should be at least 150 hours a month, 15 minutes of inactivity time, and a 4-hour session limit. A better choice would be to have unlimited access and full bandwidth for peak hours.

Key questions to ask include:

- What is the definition of "unlimited?"
- What is the penalty connection fee (over the basic service allotments)?
- Does the ISP force users to disconnect when all the modems are full?
- Are incentives used to lure people to off-peak time?

This is where doing your homework really pays off. "Unlimited" can mean a lot of things, depending on how an ISP wants to slant it.

Some "bargain" ISPs offer a great connection fee for basic service but may charge as much as $2.00 an hour in overlimit penalties. This adds up. If you routinely rack up 8 hours a day online during the week and 20 on the weekend, you could end up with a surprise bill of a few hundred dollars at the end of the month. Make sure that you check the fine print and that you are very clear on what unlimited, peak, off, daytime, nighttime, and *overlimit* hourly fees are, as well as at what point those hours start (whether one minute over is charged as a full hour or whether there is a grace period of a few minutes).

If an ISP has oversubscribed its capacity, a common practice is to "bump" off a few people when the modems are full. This is frustrating. It's different than when an ISP's terms are to bump off someone after a set inactivity period. This isn't a bad thing for the most part, because it avoids people chewing up the bandwidth when they've forgotten that they're logged on. But when an ISP routinely bounces people to manage its server capabilities, it can be very frustrating.

Bandwidth

These are simple questions. Can your account be terminated for using "excessive" bandwidth? Are you connecting straight to the ISP or are you dialing a remote terminal server that may become overloaded and create a bottleneck? Ideally, you want solid connections with minimal *bandwidth shaping*, a tool that an ISP uses to limit the amount of bandwidth used by the customers. When an ISP says it offers "unlimited access," is this unlimited bandwidth or unlimited connection time (no matter how slow it might be)?

Bandwidth is what you are buying from the ISP. It's often referred to as the "pipeline" because it is very much like being hooked to a city water supply. When everyone is using the water, you may be reduced to a trickle. When no one is using it, you'll have a gusher. Problems can restrict the flow, as can clogs. Bandwidth can also be restricted (with too small a *pipe*) or clogged (with bottlenecks or inadequate *peering*). Peering is the agreements among the companies that provide the main connections on the Internet for routing traffic among themselves. There isn't a monopoly on the Internet. No company or government owns it; instead, it's a series of arrangements, and some of these arrangements are better than others when it comes to speed and reliability.

DNS Servers

DNS (Domain Name Service) is the Internet system that translates server names to IP (Internet Protocol) addresses. (The server name is the word or words we use to identify a Web site. The IP address is a series of numbers computers use to identify the same Web site.) What DNS server an ISP has or what software is running is not apparent. DNS performance is hard to measure. It is important. It's probably more important than bandwidth but hard to measure without using it and comparing it. The minimum an ISP should be running would be two servers running BIND with lots of memory. Ideally, the server site won't be too many hops away. You'd rather have the DNS server running at your POP and not running on a central server in the middle of the country.

DNS servers may run Apache, which is an open source Web server program for many different platforms, such as UNIX and Linux, with some Windows versions. Apache is very reliable, easy to configure, secure, and inexpensive. Many ISPs use it. The other choice is typically a Microsoft product. The main downside is that a lot of security issues have surfaced, making them more prone to attack. Although these issues are being addressed, not all DNS sites will be as responsible about downloading the patches as they should be.

Web Space

This is disk space set aside on your ISP's machine. It's usually called your *home page*. You may not be interested in having a personal home page (for more information on setting up your personal Web site, see Chapter 13). We mention this only because you may find references to this on various ISP sites or you may be interested in having a personal home page. Most ISPs restrict the amount of space leased out to users. The minimum offered should be 5 MB for a personal home page, but the more space, the better. For business use, it is extremely desirable for the ISP to offer support for FrontPage, CGI scripting, and PHP/mySQL.

Some questions for the ISP are as follows:

- What happens when you hit the limit? Are your pages shut down for the month or do you incur extra charges? If so, how much?
- Will the ISP remove pages if they have *improper content*?
- How is a Web page updated? Is it a Web-based interface or full FTP access?
- Do your email inbox and home page share the same disk space and size limit?
- Are CGI scripts limited to a few provided by the ISP or can you write your own?
- Are Web logs available?
- Are Web usage reports available?

FTP Space

FTP (File Transfer Protocol) is an Internet tool used to transfer files easily. If you will be putting up a Web site on which you will want to update pages frequently, a big issue will be how to do so. The question is whether the FTP site is a small, anonymous area or whether it's larger, with password-based access control and transfer logging. Ideally, it will be the latter.

The questions you will need to ask include the following:

- Are you prohibited from making binary files available for download?
- What is the ISP's policy on copyright issues?
- Does the bandwidth count against the monthly Web page limit? (This is important in the event that your page becomes popular and there is a surge of viewers.)

An ISP has some choices as to what kind of Usenet service it will offer its clients. Usenet is an online public message exchange. One of the Usenet newsgroups is called a *binary newsgroup* with the sole purpose of distributing computer programs, pictures, sounds, and other digital files. It is important to ask whether the server contains binary newsgroups or whether it is just "read-only?" If it is read-only, you may read the newsgroups but anything you attempt to post will be quietly discarded and never appear. (It's a way of avoiding the issue of Usenet complaints, a headache to the ISP staff.) Does the ISP throttle the bandwidth to limit the usage?

If you are a Usenet junkie, look for an ISP that has another group to handle its newsgroups. Hiring people to deal specifically with these is more cost-effective and makes sense. Newsgroups are expensive to maintain when run centrally. The larger outsourcing groups include Giganews, SuperNews, and UsenetServer.com.

The minimum an ISP should offer is a one-day binary newsgroup retention and several days for text groups and posting privileges. The better services will offer longer retention and have the entire thing outsourced.

Technical Support

The minimum support you should accept from an ISP is regular 9–5 business hours, Monday through Friday. It is better for technical support to be available to you when you will most likely really need it (evenings and weekends). Keep in mind that some ISPs are staffed by people with full-time jobs, and this is a side business to them. If you are shopping only for price, you may end up with only an email or Web-based technical support. The quandary is, if you can't get online, how do you get help?

A knowledge base (ideally, the ISP will have a place where you can access information about troubleshooting or other information) and network status page (to find out about scheduled repairs or outages) are also very desirable, premium features.

Questions to ask include the following:

- Where is the technical support?
- Is technical support a long-distance call?
- How long are you on hold? (Try calling their tech support before you sign up.)
- Does this ISP support the computer and operating system you use?
- Are there online resources to help you try to figure out the problem on your own?

Billing

There are many ways to be billed/charged for your service. Email notification of an automatically billed "on file" credit card account is the most basic service. More involved billing practices include paper invoices, cash or credit card payments, money orders, and online updates of the ledger sheet of your account. The questions to ask about billing include the following:

- Are you billed for the entire first month if you sign up on the 28th or are you billed on the anniversary of your signup date?

- Does the ISP warn you and obtain updated information from you before your credit card expires (instead of letting the charge reject, then charge a fee for the declined credit card)?

- Is there a local or toll-free number to call for a billing problem?

- What is the reconnect charge if your account is closed for nonpayment?

- What are the notice requirements to cancel the service?

- If you prepay, is there any way to get a refund, and how is that refund calculated? (Prepaying is never a good idea, no matter what the price incentive might be to do so.)

SOFTWARE INSTALLATION

The ISP should at the very least have Web pages to describe how to configure Windows dialup networking (DUN). Better would be to have a downloadable installation script or a mailed-out CD-ROM with software and installation diagnostics.

TOS

Everything has terms of service (TOS) these days, or so it seems. The TOS is also known as the AUP (acceptable use policy). These are one-sided statements outlining what behavior an ISP will and won't accept from a user. They're written for a judge and jury to protect the ISP (even if the ISP doesn't enforce these rules in any way). Some outline how an ISP will punish you if you break the rules. It is a good idea to read the TOS, even if the small typeface and strange legal wording hurts your eyes and puts you to sleep. The information to glean from it includes:

- What is the refund policy?

- What must you do to cancel your account (email, fax, or registered letter)?

- What conditions may cause your ISP account to be canceled?
- Does the ISP consider your email to be private?
- Does it reserve the right to read email as it wishes?
- Under what conditions will it disclose your identity to third parties?
- What does it consider spamming or Net abuse?
- What are the charges if two people get online at the same time using the same account?
- What is the inactivity period?
- Is there a maximum length of time for a single online session?

FIND AN ISP

The Web site Find an ISP is a valuable resource for anyone looking to find an ISP. It cuts through the bull and right to the meat of the issue. It's not a flashy site. It's a sensible, information-packed one. This site is a valuable service.

It lists the top consumer problems with ISPs. (The following is the abbreviated version.)

1. Dialing a long-distance phone number by accident (to connect, the ISP says it's local, but when you get your telephone bill the next month, you find it's a toll call).
2. Paying for service in advance to "save money" (only to find the service has closed up shop a few months later, with no forwarding address).
3. Technical support that is not a free call or doesn't exist.
4. Paying with a debit card rather than a credit card. (You can dispute a credit card under the federal Fair Credit Billing Act (FCBA), but with a debit card, the FCBA doesn't apply.)
5. Busy signals and forced disconnects (oversubscribed service).
6. The noncancelable account (long holds, accidental disconnects at the customer service site).
7. Unexpected setup fees or high fees in strange places.
8. Overcharges for excessive use.
9. Submitting your personal information to a fake ISP. With the growing problem of identity theft, be wary of Web sites that seem too good and ask for too much information.

For more information, go to Find an ISP at www.findanisp.com.

BROWSERS

A browser is a client program to let your computer read hypertext documents on the Internet. Hypertext is text with hyperlinks. When an interactive browser views hypertext, certain words are highlighted with underlining and color. Clicking on the hypertext link will lead you to that Web page. A browser can be text- or graphics-based. Different browsers can have different limitations and capabilities. There are text-based browsers able to read only text files, not images or multimedia, as well as other specialized browsers.

Examples of the more common, generally used browsers include the following: Microsoft Internet Explorer (IE), Netscape, Mozilla, Opera, and iRider.

HYPERTEXT/HYPERLINK

Ted Nelson is credited with coining the terms *hypertext* and *hyperlink* in 1963 to describe a system of linked documents. Vannevar Bush is credited with the concept. He wrote a 1945 article in *The Atlantic Monthly* explaining his idea of *Memex*, a computer that linked information using "associative indexing."

For a while, there was some controversy about the ownership of hyperlinking. There was a U.S. patent no. 4873662, filed in 1976 by Desmond Sargent of the British Post Office and issued in 1989. It was construed by the owners to describe Web hyperlinks. (This patent runs out in 2006.) The BT Group (the company that is now the British Post Office and British Telecommunications) rediscovered the patent in 1997 and claimed to own anything hyperlink. It must have seen the dollar (pound?) signs. The thought of everyone everywhere paying a licensing fee to click on the blue, underlined links was more than it could resist. It pursued claims. In June 2000, it contacted Prodigy and 16 other ISPs, including America Online, asking them to buy a hyperlink license. When they all laughed, the BT group sued Prodigy as a test case in U.S. courts.

The hyperlink patent, known as the *Sargent patent*, describes a way for multiple remote users to access data stored at a central computer. The lawsuit argued that the Internet itself infringes on the patent and that Prodigy facilitates this infringement by charging and providing its users with Internet access.

The court dismissed the case. U.S. District Judge Colleen McMahon cited three problems with BT's assertions. First, the Internet had no "central computer," as outlined in the patent. Second, because the Internet itself can't infringe, Prodigy cannot be liable for contributing to infringement. Third, the Web information stored on Prodigy computers does not contain "blocks of information" or "complete addresses," as claimed by the BT filing.

Microsoft IE

This is the browser that comes with every Windows computer and will be updated throughout the life of the machine by Microsoft. It's the de facto standard browser. It's difficult to unseat as the standard browser because it is free. It has most of the features of all the other browsers but lacks some of the newer advancements. Still, there is no page it cannot read, and there are even some specialty JavaScript variations that work properly only on IE.

Netscape Navigator

This is the browser that began the browser wars and triggered the antitrust investigation against Microsoft. At one time, it was the perpetual innovative browser but because AOL bought the entire company that produced it, the browser has languished somewhat. This is slowly changing as the newest version of this browser has come under the influence of the Mozilla project, and perhaps it will reemerge as a player.

iRider

iRider is the next-generation, multipage Web browser. It can open several links at a time. You can manipulate multiple pages and download a page while you work. In fact, with a fast Internet connection, you can open pages en masse, then flip through them like a magazine. (It is much faster than opening Web pages one by one, so you save on search time.) You work with sets of pages at a time, not single pages. You can have hundreds of pages open without overtaxing memory, because the program automatically manages the memory resources.

You can query several search engines at the same time, even search engines of different categories (images, video, audio, news, shopping, etc.), then keep some pages and discard ones that don't fit your search interests.

iRider uses IE to implement basic browsing, so it's compatible with most Web pages. And pop-up ads open under your current page, so they don't get in the way. (This is better than a pop-up blocker that may block pages that you really need.)

For more information, go to www.irider.com.

Opera

Opera is called the *fastest browser on Earth*. It uses less memory and less space on the hard drive than competing browsers. It has features that other browsers don't have, such as multiple document interface (MDI), mouse gestures, keyboard shortcuts, Hotclick translation, a presentation tool, zooming, and integrated search. You can customize Opera with skins, buttons, and panels to make it look the way you'd like and easier for you to use.

For more information, go to www.opera.com.

Mozilla

Mozilla is an open source browser designed to support open Internet standards for a variety of operating systems, including Windows, Linux, and Mac OS X, among others. Fans of Mozilla cite the extra features, such as pop-up blocking, tabbed browsing, and their favorite features. Junk mail controls and blocking email viruses are other popular features. Mozilla supports popular plug-ins, such as Java, Flash, Acrobat, Windows Media Player, Quicktime, and RealPlayer.

For more information, go to www.mozilla.org.

SUMMARY

Getting a good ISP and using the right software will be the most important decision you make. Making the right decisions, meaning the decision that suits you best, will make going online a pleasure. It also means that you'll waste less time and reap the benefits of efficiency. Along the way, though, it is clear that you will have to do some experimentation. Everyone does.

4
FINDING WHAT
YOU NEED

Finding what you need is easy, once you figure out the lingo. And you need to understand a little about the structure of the Net and the schemes used to describe things. People will refer to a Web page's URL, its domain name, and its IP address often interchangeably. This can be a little confusing at first. The terms are related, although they refer to slightly different aspects of the same thing. It might be confusing for someone from another planet to understand that we are our first names, last names, social security numbers, driver's license numbers, credit card numbers, and physical addresses—all meaning *us*. In a very basic way, the URL, the domain name and its levels, and the IP address all refer to the same thing—a specific Web page located on a server someplace on the Internet.

The biggest confusion is, perhaps, the fact that the World Wide Web (WWW) and the Internet are not the same thing. The WWW is all the resources and users on the Internet that are using the Hypertext Transfer Protocol (HTTP).

In an earlier chapter, we discussed how the Internet is the massive collection of networked networks. Billions of computers are loosely connected globally to form an interchange of data across the Internet. They do so with set ways of communication, called *protocols*.

The WWW, or Web, is a regimented way to access and share information over the Internet. It is one protocol and only one. This protocol is the one used by browsers to access Web pages linked to each other (called *hyperlinks*) and documents that are text-only or that contain sounds, text, video, and graphics. HTTP is a very all-encompassing protocol.

HTTP

HTTP is what your browser automatically types in for you. All Web addresses will begin "http://." HTTP is based on the idea that all files can contain references to other files. The selection of those files will elicit related transfer requests. A Web server machine has an HTTP daemon, a program designed to wait for HTTP requests and fill them as they arrive. A Web browser is an HTTP client program that sends requests to the server machines.

When the user tells the browser to access a specific Web file by typing in the URL or clicking on hyperlink text, the browser creates an HTTP request and sends it to the IP address associated with the URL. The HTTP daemon receives the request and sends it out to the destination machine's IP address.

URL

It's common for people to say, "go to this URL." A URL is the commonly used casual term for the location of a resource on the Web. URL means Uniform Resource Locator. It is also more technically known as a URI (Uniform Resource Identifier) or URN (Uniform Resource Name). These are strings of information, usually separated by slashes, and may include long strings of other characters and numbers that identify resources in the Web: documents, images, downloadable files, services, electronic mailboxes, and other items. The URL refers to the protocol (HTTP, FTP, etc.), the domain name, and additional information, such as the path or folder where the information you are looking for is. An example URL would be: www.dvorak.org/home.htm

A URL can be much longer, and it gets confusing when a URL is dynamically generated through a content management system. For example, a URL for a *San Francisco Chronicle* online newspaper article could be:

www.sfgate.com/cgi-bin/article.cgi?file=/chronicle/archive/2003/06/16/bu15767.DTL&type=tech

The first part the www.sfgate.com is the home page. The rest of it identifies a specific article; the date of the article, 2003/06/16; and other information on where it resides on the server. So as you can see, the URL can include information about the address of a specific file page, an image file, or other files supported by the HTTP protocol.

Search engines use robot crawlers (more in a later chapter about this) to locate searchable pages on Web sites and intranets. This is some of the information they search for. (These robots are also called *crawlers, spiders, gatherers,* and *harvesters.*) Search engine robots use the same ways of looking at data as a browser (how you maneuver around the Web) to read pages, follow links, and locate every page available on a server.

So it's like following road signs to get where you want to go. The search engine crawlers wander about, mapping the attractions along the way. When you type a URL into your browser, you follow the mapped roads to access that page. When something isn't working correctly, you will get the notice that the page isn't available. The usual messages are something like these:

- Can't find Web page. The document you have requested does not exist on this server. Check for misspellings, punctuation errors, or extra spaces.

- Can't find Web page. The document you have requested is unavailable. Server is unavailable or busy. Try your request later.

A URL takes your browser to a specific file on a specific computer on the Internet. For example, the URL www.cnn.com/weather takes you to CNN's weather page. Pick a city and the URL becomes http://weather.cnn.com/weather/forecast.jsp?locCode=LFPO. www.cnn.com is the domain name that has already been identified through a domain name server. Clicking on the different links within the CNN Web site takes you to different URLs within CNN's domain name.

The problem with long, large URLs is that they are difficult to remember. If you choose to type one in, they are case-sensitive (you must use a capital letter when it is called for, lowercase when lowercase is indicated), and each individual character is important. Misspell anything or leave anything out and the page will fail to load. Worse is the fact that many of them are part of a complex content management system that designs new pages on the fly to send to users. Often, typing in the exact URL won't work because the page is created only once. Many of these URLs are so long that it is practically impossible to type them in at all. This is a recent development that is quite controversial.

The Breakdown of a Domain Name

There are different levels of domains in the domain name. The second and third levels are the most important. The third level is actually optional on some sites.

- Top Level (TLD)—.com, .net, .org, .edu, etc.
- Second Level—business, shopping, search
- Third Level—www, www1, www2, keyword (optional)

Top-Level Domain Names

The top-level domain (TLD) name is the extension, after the actual Web site name. In the 1990s, most top-level domain names were limited to .com, .net, .gov, .org, .mil, .edu, and international "country" designations.

- .com refers to a commercial organization
- .edu is for education institutions
- .net refers to networking companies
- .gov is reserved for government pages
- .org is for organizations or nonprofits

International designations are identified with two letters, such as the following examples:

- ca for Canada
- de for Germany
- uk for United Kingdom
- es for Spain

The "dot-com" craze messed things up. The demand was so high for .com that the line between .com and .net and even .org has blurred as the rules have loosened. Additional endings have been added to a growing list. Some of the new additions include:

- .biz
- .info
- .name

To confuse things more, some countries commercialized their country codes (.to is owned by Tonga, for example) and sell those as TLDs to anyone with a checkbook.

Second-Level Domain Name

Second-level domain names must be registered with one of the ICANN-accredited registrars for the name.

The middle part or the second level of the domain name is usually the part we remember best. It's the part that identifies the Web site's unique name. The full second-level name is the name plus the top level together, because you can have two names exactly the same, such as www.name.com and www.name.org, each being associated with different Web sites. It's like a first name and a last name. You may know several Bobs. But Bob one and Bob two aren't the same because one might be Bob Smith and the other Bob Wong.

The second-level domain names may contain letters, numbers, and hyphens.

The selection of a domain name is a major consideration when doing business online. Many Web sites are similar in name and intent, and this can confuse the Web surfer. Names such as *bigcar*, *big-car*, or *1bigcar* are so similar that it's confusing.

Third-Level Domain Name

Finally, the "www" part stands for World Wide Web. In giant systems, it may reference the main host server. A second server might be called *www2*. Or the www could be done without. Some Web sites don't use www, but instead start out right after the http://, and the www designation is assumed.

Each domain name is unique. When you enter www.cnn.com, you know you'll get CNN's Web site and nothing else. Putting the three parts of the domain name together means: World Wide Web: WWW; Web site: cnn; TLD: .com (for commercial).

> ICANN Internet Corporation for Assigned Names and Numbers is the nongovernmental, private, nonprofit corporation with responsibilities for IP address allocation, protocol parameter assignment and domain name system, and root server system management. (ICANN is pronounced like it looks, I-CAN, like what *the Little Engine Who Could* thought.)

IP Address

Your computer has an IP address provided by your ISP, which is your network connection. A Web site has an IP address provided by its network connection. In fact, everything hooked to the Web has an IP address. IP (Internet Protocol) is the set of rules of communication between networks. Each computer on a network must know its own address and how to send and receive information from the other networks. To be a member of the Internet, an organization needs an Internet network number. These are requested from the Network Internet Center (NIC). This number is included in any packet sent out.

There are four classes of IP addresses:

1. Class A   addresses for large networks with many devices
2. Class B   addresses for medium-sized networks
3. Class C   addresses for small networks (less than 256 devices)
4. Class D   addresses for multicast addresses

The first few bits of each IP address indicate which of the address class formats it is using.

The IP address is usually expressed as four decimal numbers, each represented by eight bits, separated by periods. Some people call it the "dot address." (And really technical purist types call it the *dotted quad notation*.)

Not all IP addresses are static, meaning they are not always the same numbers. Some IP addresses on large networks are dynamic. This means that they change and are assigned randomly from a pool. America Online does this, for example. Your IP address will change from one logon session to the next because the pool of IP addresses is shared. This can be a problem when a certain IP address has been blocked by a Web site (usually a forum) because the person who was last assigned that IP address misbehaved. The reason this system was developed was because it was determined that there were not going to be enough IP addresses to go around, and it would be easier to share them because most people weren't using them all the time.

Files hang out on a computer with a specific IP address; these files, such as HTML, JPG, GIF, PHP, and ASP, make up the Web site.

Domain Name System

The Domain Name System (DNS) is a collection of computers called *DNS servers* that keep track of what IP address is assigned to what Web site or domain name.

A *domain name* identifies one or more IP addresses used to identify a Web site. For example, www.cnn.com is a domain name, and it could have multiple IP addresses tied to that name. In other words, it's easier to remember CNN's domain name of www.cnn.com than its IP address of 64.236.16.20.

Your browser can recognize and accept an IP address if you know it.

The DNS translates domain names into IP addresses. Every time you use a domain name, the DNS translates the name into the corresponding IP address. The DNS is a separate network. If one DNS server can't figure out how to translate a certain domain name, it will turn to another to figure it out.

When you enter the URL www.cnn.com into the browser's address box, the browser connects to the nearest DNS server to request the IP address for www.cnn.com. If it doesn't know the answer, the request goes up to the next DNS server in the hierarchy. It continues to do this until a server is found containing the required information. It sends the answer back to your browser.

SEARCH ENGINES

The Web is huge. There are so many things out there that the next problem is how to find what you want if you don't know the URL. The problem is at least partially solved with search engines. The search engine is a software program used to search for the Web pages, their servers, and associated databases and links. These Internet search engines use a tool known commonly as a *spider*, although other similar tools are known as *harvesters*, *crawlers*, etc. These are automated software robots designed to creep along the Web in search of Web sites to index. (Some search engines use other tools, as well.) The program goes through all the HTML code to gather information that the search engine uses in its algorithm. They often do not go very deep into a Web site. Web pages can block the spiders in a variety of ways from sensitive information. However, if a Web site wants to get noticed by the search engines, its developers will try to make things as easy as possible for the program, to the point of voluntarily submitting its Web sites to the search engine.

> Although there are *dynamic* Web page URLs (meaning they change, or at least part of it does), most are static (stay the same). These can be dynamic by use of a programming error or dynamic because someone named the URL extension without adding a link elsewhere on the Web site.
>
> Search engine robot developers worry about dynamic URLs because they can confuse the robot and cause it to get lost in "spider traps" and "black holes" (sites with no useful information on them).
>
> For the most part, dynamic URLs are not searched or indexed, nor do they come up on search engine keyword searches. (Information contained in these types of URLs are referred to as the "invisible Web.") If a page isn't linked to the main page, neither the spider nor you will find it easily. What this means to you is that if your friends just added a page of photos onto their web page but they wanted only you to view them, there would be no way to access that page without knowing the exact URL. So if it was Bob's Web site and he added /picturesforSally.htm after his URL and you forgot whether it was pixforSally or photos or photographs, any other variation, there wouldn't be a link, nor could a search engine find it.

Algorithms

All search engines use algorithms. An algorithm describes a method of doing a task. The term is usually used in regard to software to describe program logic for a certain function. There are two types of algorithms: deterministic and heuristic (rule of thumb). Definitive ones can perform tasks that have set answers and a best method to process them. This is like searching for word on a list or finding a name in a directory. Subjective algorithms are used to process information based on an assumptive model, where there isn't one "correct" answer. These are used heavily by search engines. The various search engines use different approaches to what is "best" or a closer match to your keywords.

So algorithms are formulas of instructions and directions for the spider to gather information to rank a Web page. The search engine algorithms vary so much that a Web page could rank high on one search engine and low on others.

Optimization

There is a lot of confusion about search engine optimization (SEO) in relation to search engine spamming. Web pages are often designed to make the page as visible to search engines as possible to get a higher ranking on a specific search engine. Optimization is a way to make a page readable for a search engine, emphasize key topics, and accurately key target content. It's important to keep pages readable so the Web page doesn't become part of the invisible Web (part of the Web that search engines cannot access). So it's a cooperative effort by the Web page designer and the search engine programmer. They must work together (in the cosmic sense) to create a good end-user experience while finding ways to keep the spammers at bay.

It's important for Web designers to choose good, readable URLs. People are more comfortable with consistent and intuitive paths (names that make some sense), such as a recognized product name URL. Good names are easy to remember and minimize confusion. You'll find that names come with or without hyphens and with correct, creative, or phonetic spelling.

The basic idea behind a search engine is that you go to a search engine and type in a keyword or phrase to find out what Web pages contain them. A good search engine will return a list of Web pages to give you what you seek. Now the big battle is for search engines to return what is correct and eliminate offensive or simply wrong ones. For instance, you want to find out about *child birthday party games*, hoping to find some amusing games for a dozen six-year-olds. However, your search returns only porn sites boasting about co-eds doing drugs in their birthday suits, golf club sales sites, and web cams of "girls" emerging from cakes. These would not enhance your user experience with the search engine.

The problem is that search engines try to refine their search criteria and target data. Meanwhile, Web site promoters find ways to overcome them and spam the search engine. It is impossible for a Web page to satisfy the needs of all search engines, which is why the various search engines vary so much in their Web page returns.

Keyword Frequency/Placement/Prominence

The more often a word (or words) is cited on a specific Web page, usually the more relevant the page will be. This is the rationale behind *keyword frequency*. When a Web page repeats the same word, the search engine should see this and downgrade the rating. (Because it would be an obvious ploy to try to trigger a higher page ranking.) *Keyword placement* is a term to describe where the search engine will look for information. Places such as the title page, heading, and body text, as well as link text, can be part of the search criteria. *Keyword prominence* is how close to the start of the page a keyword appears. When the title of the Web site is an exact match, it should be more relevant than when the keyword is buried deep in the body text.

Stemming and Spelling (Fuzzy Search)

Stemming is a search engine's ability to figure out the stem words of a keyword. For instance, if you were to look up skiing, the search engine could find ski, as well as skiing.

Some search engines can correct obvious spelling mistakes. If your spelling is poor or you only guess at the spelling, the search engine would search for the exact spelling, then look for something that might be what you meant. Then it offers a corrected spelling option search, as well as any possible matching returned keywords. This is often referred to as *fuzzy search*. Google has an excellent fuzzy search. It can often figure out what you really meant, even if the word is spelled wrong, phonetically spelled, or partially spelled.

Ranking, Relevance, and Recall

The relative location of a page is how it compares with all other pages with similar information. The higher the ranking, the more likely it is that the search engine has matched the search criteria, and the more valuable it is to the user. So the higher on the list of returns a page appears, the closer it should be to your keyword criteria.

Relevance is how well the page content relates to the search criteria. It is an important part of search engine algorithms. The higher the relevance of a page, the better a search engine's algorithms reflect accurate ranking.

Recall is how well a search engine can return all matching documents. The recall would be 80% if, of 100 matching documents, the search engine found 80.

Site Popularity

The search engine will find how many other Web pages link to yours. This is a sign of popularity. A search engine may also look for the number of regular hits a site receives.

Pay for Placement

Search engines might have a fee-based engine marketing system in place. This seems sleazy, because it means a Web promoter can pay for a Web page to rank high in searches. This shortcut to ranking instead of the legitimate way—with the search engine algorithms, click counts, etc.—undermines the credibility of the search engine. It's rare that this kind of cheating works for a Web site. Users tend to ignore them. It can backfire on a search engine because users will abandon that one for one of its many competitors.

Keywords

The most common way to search is with keywords. Keywords are important. They aren't totally intuitive. For example, if you wanted to find bread recipes and put in just BREAD, (hoping to find a recipe), the returns would be lengthy. You'd get sites such as the "world hunger site" and "daily bread devotional," as well as poetry and literature with the word bread in it, along with a few recipe Web sites mixed in. Now add the word *recipe* as a second keyword. You'd type in *bread recipe*. This search would return a page of bread recipes to search through.

It's best to try the most obvious and specific words first. If you want to read about macaws, type in *macaw* instead of *parrot*.

Keyword searches are tricky at first. If you want to figure out the adhering and bondage qualities of latex paint versus oil-based paint for a cement wall, an obvious keyword search might include *latex oil bondage cement*. The results would be eye-popping, because they would be mostly about the fetish sexual domination. However, if you rethink the keyword search and instead type *painting cement latex oil*. The search return would be pages of painting discussions of the qualities of each.

The order of the words may influence the search criteria. So if a search doesn't yield what you are looking for, try flipping the words around or substituting a word for a synonym. If you want to find a description, a discussion, or a definition, try putting these following the word that represents the information you are looking for.

Most every search engine has ways other than simply the keyword way to search. So look around the search engine site to find "search preferences," "refine search," "search tools," or "advanced search tips."

Boolean Operators

In addition, almost all search engines will allow Boolean operators. Some don't use all the commands but most will use a few. The Boolean operators are AND, OR, NOT (or AND NOT), and NEAR. These tell search engines what to include or exclude in your search or whether you require that your keywords appear close to each other. Some have been replaced by more common syntax (e.g., the plus and minus signs and quotation marks).

The AND operator means the same as the plus sign (+). If you wanted to search for *old hats* you could type in: *old AND hats* or *old + hats*

That would tell the search engine to look for both those words, not either/or. So your search would come back with both those terms, although they may not be in the context you want.

You can use the AND operator as often as you need. The more you link together with AND, the more specific the search will be.

The OR operator states a preference that includes either or both results. So if you looked up *jelly OR jam* you would get listings with both or one of the words. Most search engines do not even recognize the OR Boolean operator anymore. The default in the bulk of the engines is AND, and they will substitute it if you add the OR. It's easier to look up jam, then in a subsequent search to look up jelly.

The NOT (or AND NOT) operator excludes the word after it from appearing in the search result items. The more modern way is to use the minus sign. So if you typed in *antique –looking* or *antique NOT looking* or *antique AND NOT looking*, this would all mean *+antique –looking* to a search engine. What you would get, it is hoped, would be antiques, without any of the phony antique-looking items.

You might string multiple NOTs in a sentence to make it more specific.

The NEAR operator requires the search words to appear close to each other. The modern way is with the use of quotation marks. So if you wanted to find *Bill Jones*, you would type in *"bill jones"* or *Bill NEAR Jones*. This will let the search engine know that these two words should be closely connected. You can also use the quotation marks to designate a phrase. If you looked for Alice in Wonderland you would get articles pertaining to that book or using the name of the book in some context.

You can combine Boolean operators. In the search engines supporting parentheses, you can, as an example call for a search with *cat AND (fleas OR mites)*. This would return all articles with cats and a discussion of either fleas or mites, or both.

GEORGE BOOLE (1815–1864)

Around the same time that Charles Babbage was fooling around with his Analytical Engine, George Boole, another Englishman, was making significant contributions to mathematics. His forte was in representing logical expressions in a mathematical form, now known as Boolean algebra, which extended the limits of "modern" mathematics.

In his 1847 *"The Mathematical Analysis of Logic,"* he argued that logic was a principal discipline of mathematics instead of a branch of philosophy. Other texts include *"Treatise on Differential Equasions"* (1859) and *the "Treatise on the Calculus of Finite Differences"* (1860).

He delved deeper into his ideas and refined the concept. His point was to find a way to encode logical arguments into language that could be verbally manipulated and solved mathematically.

Boole came up with some linguistic algebra, for lack of a better description. The three most basic operators were AND, OR, and NOT. These three functions are the only operators necessary to compare or perform basic mathematical functions.

Boole's system was based on a binary approach processing two objects: yes-no. They could also be expressed as *on-off*, *true-false*, or even *zero-one*.

At the time this was *not* a groundbreaking achievement. In fact, it was largely ignored until an American logician, Charles Sanders Pierce, described Boole's ideas to the American Academy of Arts and Sciences 12 years after Boole introduced the concept. Pierce then spent the next 20 years modifying and expanding on the idea. Pierce recognized the potential value for the theoretical idea of electronic circuitry and electrical logic circuits.

He introduced Boolean algebra in his university-level logic-philosophy classes.

The daily use of the Boolean operators would probably surprise George Boole. He'd be gratified at how they're in use today.

Google—www.google.com

Google is a very advanced and popular search engine. It's so popular that it's become a verb: *to google it*! Google has so many features and facets; it's deep and powerful but still easy to use.

The main page (Figure 4.1) has five search options. Each is a different way of looking for information, depending on your particular needs. The interfaces work the same in each; you type in a keyword and information is returned in a standard format:

- Web—For Web searches of more than 3 billion Web pages.

- Images—A comprehensive image search with 425 million images, indexed and available for viewing. The images may be protected by copyright. (Some of the results may contain mature content.)

- Groups—This is an archive of Usenet discussion groups dating back to 1981. These discussions range over the full human experience and provide a fascinating look at evolving viewpoints, debate, and advice on every subject imaginable. Google's search feature lets users access this information by providing relevant results from a database with more than 700 million posts.

- Directory—Whereas the regular Google Web search is the fastest way to find information, the directory is useful when you aren't sure how to narrow your search from a broad category. The directory can help you to understand how topics within a specific area are related. It can also give you an idea of the scope of any given category. The Open Directory project has 20,000 volunteer editors reviewing Web sites and classifying them by topic, which means that you'll get the benefit of both human judgment and a sophisticated ranking algorithm.

- News—This feature searches more than 4,500 news sources, worldwide. The articles are arranged to present the most relevant news first. Topics are updated continuously throughout the day. You can also search on particular keywords or trace the history of a particular issue by clicking

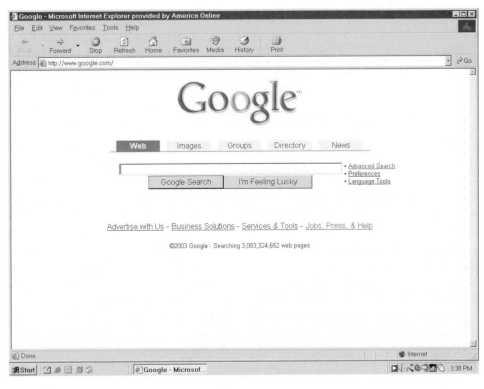

FIGURE 4.1   **GOOGLE MAIN SEARCH PAGE.**

the "sort by date" function on the page to arrange all the stories in chronological order.

Google doesn't support pop-up ads. It doesn't accept payment for placement within an actual search result. Instead, it shows advertising links to the right of the search results, clearly identified as "sponsored links." Its name is a play on the word *googol*, which is the term for the number 1 followed by 100 zeros.

Google Query/Response Features

A regular keyword search will return a lot of different variables, and Google offers some unique features that tend to blend into the results and don't stand out as features per se. These features include searches of non-HTML files, cached links, dictionary, spell check, its proprietary "I'm Feeling Lucky" option, phone book, maps, and more.

Non-HTML File Type Searches

Google searches HTML files and a number of other file types. The range of file types is ever expanding, but current ones include non-HTML file types, PDF documents, and documents with formats of Microsoft Office, PostScript, Corel Word Perfect, and Lotus 1-2-3. These will appear in Google search results when they are relevant to the query. Google also offers the user the ability to view non-HTML files as "view as HTML," which speeds the loading of the page and allows users to avoid viruses that can be carried in certain types of files.

Cached Links

Google automatically returns cached links. It takes a snapshot of each page as it crawls the Web and saves these as backup. If the original page is unavailable, Google can offer this snapshot of the page instead. It's not necessarily the most recent version of the page. The cached link will not be available for sites that have not been indexed or when the site owner has requested that his or her content not be cached.

Dictionary Definitions

Google can be used to find dictionary definitions. Enter your query into the search box. When any part of your query has a dictionary definition, this will be underlined in the center text above the search results in the dark blue tabbed area. If you search *boolean* the response would be something like this:

Example: Searched the web for **Boolean**. Results 1-10 of about 3,760,000. Search took 0.14 seconds.

Then if you click on the underlined text, the link will take you to the relevant definition from a dictionary provider, which has been selected solely on the basis of its quality.

Spellchecker

Google's spellchecking software automatically looks at your query and checks to see whether you are using the most common version of a word's spelling. If it calculates that you're going to generate more relevant search results using an alternative spelling, it will ask you *"Did you mean . . ."* with the more common spelling. If you click on the suggested spelling, it will launch a new Google search for that item. Because Google's spellcheck is based on occurrences of all words on the Internet, it is able to suggest common spellings for proper nouns (names and places) that might not appear in a standard spellcheck program or dictionary.

I'm Feeling Lucky

The *I'm Feeling Lucky* button will take you directly to the first web Page that Google would return as your keyword search. In fact, you won't see the other results at all. The "feeling lucky" option means that you spend less time in the search for the right Web page because the best one will be the one returned. So if you were looking for the state of California, you could type that in, hit the I'm Feeling Lucky button, and go directly to the main state government page without the need to wade through a dozen or more returns.

Phone Book

All Web searches now automatically include a U.S. street address and phone number lookup with the information provided through Google's search box. You'll see the publicly listed phone numbers and addresses at the top of the page results for searches with specific kinds of search criteria.

To find listings for a U.S. business, type the business name into the Google search box, along with city and state. Or type the business name and zip code. Entering the phone number with area code will also return a complete business listing.

To find listings for a U.S. residence, type any of the following combinations into the Google search box:

- First name (or first initial), last name, city (state is optional)
- First name (or first initial), last name, state
- First name (or first initial), last name, area code
- First name (or first initial), last name, zip code
- Phone number, including area code
- Last name, city, state
- Last name, zip code

If your query results in business and residential listings, both categories will be listed for your convenience. (If you want your name removed from this option, go to www.google.com/help/pbremoval.html.)

Street Maps

To use Google to find street maps, enter a U.S. street address, including zip code or city/state in the search box. When your query is recognized as a map request, the return links will be from high-quality map providers that will lead you directly to a relevant map. These maps have been selected based on their quality. (Google is not affiliated with any of the map providers used.)

Similar Pages

When you click on the "similar pages" link for a search result, Google will scout for Web pages that are related to that result. This technology is called the *GoogleScout*. The more specialized a page is, the fewer results it can find for you. However, using GoggleScout can help you to find a large number of resources without having to worry about selecting the right keywords.

Site Search

The word *site*, followed by a colon in the keyword search box, will restrict your search to a specific site. For instance, if you want to find Froogle on Google, you can type in froogle:www.google.com, and instead of searching the entire Web, Google will search only the google.com site for the answer.

Stock Quotes

To use Google to get stock and mutual fund information, enter one or more NYSE, NASDAQ, AMEX, or mutual fund ticker symbols or the name of a corporation traded on one of the stock indices. If Google recognizes your query as a stock or mutual fund, it will return a link that leads directly to stock and mutual fund information from high-quality financial information providers. (Google's financial information providers have been selected and ordered solely on the basis of their quality, based on factors including download speed, user interface, and functionality. Google is not affiliated with the financial information providers used.)

Web Page Translation

Web pages from French, German, Italian, Spanish, and Portuguese can be translated into English. Not all languages are translated, and not all pages in those languages will be translated completely. The translation software also doesn't translate text within images. The translation is often difficult to understand because the state-of-the-art technology still doesn't possess the skill of a professional translator. Automatic translation is very difficult because the meaning of the words depends on the context in which they are used. For the most part, you can at least figure out what the page is about and glean some information from it.

GOOGLE TOOLBAR

http://toolbar.google.com

The Google toolbar increases your ability to find information from anywhere on the Web and takes only seconds to install. When the toolbar is installed, it appears alongside the Internet Explorer toolbar. You can search Google without returning to the home page to begin a search. You can customize the layout of the toolbar.

It is free.

The minimum system requirements for running the Google toolbar are: Microsoft Windows 95/98/ME/NT/2000/XP/2000 Server and Microsoft Internet Explorer version 5 or later. At this time, it is not available for any other system.

Toolbar 2.0, the newest version, has a pop-up killer and an auto-fill feature. For more information, go to www. toolbar.google.com.

Google's Other Search Areas

Google also has other search areas, which are novel in their approach to searching. These include: Froogle, Google Catalogs, topic-specific searches, and Google Answers.

Froogle—www.froogle.google.com

This is a shopping search engine designed to make it easy to find information about products for sale online. By focusing entirely on product search, Froogle applies the power of Google's search technology to a very specific task: Locate the stores that sell the item you want and point you to the right place to make a purchase. Like all Google searches, Froogle ranks store sites based only on their relevance to the search items you've entered.

Google Catalogs—http://catalogs.google.com

Google has made it easy to find information published in mail-order catalogs that were not previously available online. Their exclusive Google Catalog Search includes full content of hundreds of mail-order catalogs selling everything from industrial adhesives to clothing and home furnishings. However, due to the intensely graphical nature of the pages, they are best viewed over a high-speed, broadband Internet connection. Google is not associated with the catalog vendors offered in the service.

Topic-Specific Google

Google offers topic-specific searches for Apple/Macintosh, BSD Unix operating system, Linux, and Microsoft related pages.

Google Macintosh—www.google.com/mac.html
Google BSD UNIX—www.google.com/bsd
Google Linux—www.google.com/linux
Google Microsoft—www.google.com/microsoft.html

There are also U.S. government-specific searches possible for all .gov and .mil sites at www.google.com/unclesam.

Searches for specific universities such as Stanford, Brown, and BYU, as well as hundreds more are possible. For more information, go to: www.google.com/options/universities.html.

Google Answers

Google Answers is an open forum where researchers answer your questions for a fee. When you ask a question of Google Answers, you specify how much you are willing to pay for an answer. A researcher will search for the information you want, then post it, and you will be informed via email. You are only charged for a question when an answer is found and posted. For more information, go to www.answers.google.com.

GOOGLE LABS

http://labs.google.com

This is the technology playground for Google engineers and adventurous Google users, where new ideas are displayed for you to play with and give feedback to improve them. None of these experiments are guaranteed to make it onto Google.com. It's the first phase of a development process. If you have an interest in trying out new ideas and participating by voicing your comments about what you think, this is a must-visit site.

Some of the current *play areas* include:

Google Computer, where you can donate your computer's idle time to help scientific research.

Google Viewer to view results as scrolling Web page images

Google Webquotes to view search results with quotes about them from other sites

Google Glossary for definitions of words, phrases, and acronyms

Google Sets to create sets of items from an example automatically

Keyboard Shortcuts to navigate search results without using a mouse

Voice Search to search Google with a phone call

OTHER ENGINES AND FINDERS

There are search engines and useful sites other than Google. Here are our favorites.

Yahoo!

Probably the most important service on the Web has traditionally been Yahoo! Located simply at www.Yahoo.com, Yahoo! uses Google as its underlying search engine but in itself, Yahoo! has been more of a directory than a search engine. With a directory, you are looking at what can be best described as moderated links. In other words, when you are looking for a site for collecting Corvettes, Yahoo! may have a series of important listings that have often been examined, sorted, verified, and approved for listing. In the first years of the Web boom this was easier to accomplish than it is today, and Yahoo! has to use Google as a backup. Still, Yahoo! is an amazing resource because many of the listings on the Yahoo! site cannot be found easily by using Google alone. Yahoo!, as mentioned elsewhere, also offers other services, such as email, chat rooms, want ads, and all sorts of odd features worth exploring.

KartOO—www.kartoo.com

KartOO is a metasearch engine with a visual display interface (Figure 4.2). When you click on OK, KartOO launches the query to a set of search engines, gathers the results, compiles them, and represents them in a series of interactive maps through a proprietary algorithm.

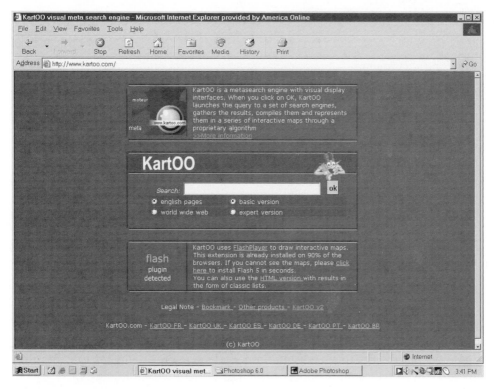

FIGURE 4.2 **KartOO main page.**

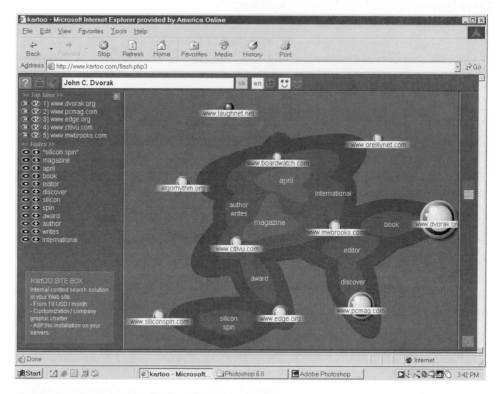

FIGURE 4.3

KARTOO SEARCH RESULT.

You enter a query and select the language of the interface. KartOO analyzes the request, questions the most relevant engines, selects the best site, and places it on a map. When you move your mouse pointer over a "ball" (map point on the screen), the description of the site is displayed. There is a show button to indicate how many Web sites are related to your request (Figure 4.3).

There is both a Flash version and a regular HTML version of KartOO. It is the most visually interesting search engine on the Web.

AltaVista—www.altavista.com

AltaVista is built on a foundation of 58 technology patents, with innovations in multilingual and translation support (Figure 4.4). AltaVista provides integrated search results to give users immediate access to relevant information, including Web pages, multimedia files, and up-to-the-minute news.

AltaVista's search technology has been a leader since debuting as the first full-text Internet search service in 1995. The company added multi-

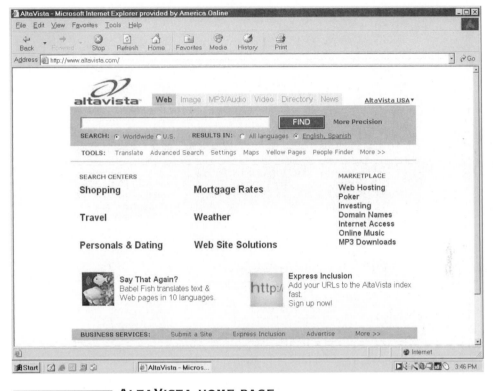

FIGURE 4.4   ALTAVISTA HOME PAGE.

lingual search with support of 25 languages in 1997. It debuted 20 local country sites between 1999 and 2001. And it launched multimedia (audio/ video/image) search support in 1999. It was the first major engine to introduce free Internet news search in 2001, and it unveiled AltaVista Prisma, a powerful assisted search tool, in 2002. Through constant innovation, AltaVista has been issued more search-related patents than any other search engine.

AltaVista is the home of Babel Fish, a text and Web page translator for 10 languages (Figure 4.5).

FAST/AlltheWeb—www.alltheweb.com

AlltheWeb is a search engine operated by Fast Search & Transfer ASA (FAST), a leading provider of real-time search and filter technology used behind the scenes of many companies as their search engine (Figure 4.6).

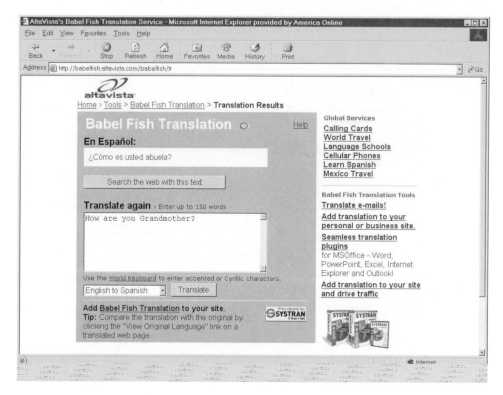

FIGURE 4.5 **BABEL FISH SEARCH RESULT.**

- AlltheWeb combines large and fast indices with powerful search features.

- AlltheWeb indexes billions of Web pages and hundreds of millions of multimedia, audio and FTP files, as well as tens of millions of PDF and Microsoft Word files.

- FAST scans the entire Web every 7–11 days to ensure that the content is fresh, without any broken links.

- AlltheWeb supports searching in 49 different languages.

- The News search feature provides up-to-the minute news from thousands of news sources all across the globe and indexes the stories every minute.

SEARCHABILITY—A GUIDE TO SPECIALIZED SEARCH ENGINES

Paula Dragutsky created the SearchAbility Web site to help people use search engines to do research on the Web. Although a general search will turn up information on a subject, it can be difficult and time-consuming to pinpoint the specific information you are looking for or find data in depth.

A specialized search engine indexes collections of materials that relate to particular fields or subjects. This material can include information at Web sites, abstracts of documents that have not been put online, data gathered by the special engine, etc. In contrast, general Web search engines index material found at Web sites about all subjects.

For most searches a general search engine will give you an overview of the information you might need. But if this only scratches the surface of what you need to know, you may need to look deeper for a specialized search engine.

Using a specialized search engine may be the only way to find what you are looking for on the Internet. The problem is that there are literally thousands of specialized search engines, with more springing up every day. This list of guides to these specialized engines can increase your chance of locating the engine that will give you access to the information you need.

This is an excellent guide to search engines. There are guides to specialized search engines listed by size, guides A–Z, giant guides, guides to search engines focusing on popular topics, guides to academic search engines, guides to search engines for children, and specialized metasearches.

For more information, go to www.searchability.com.

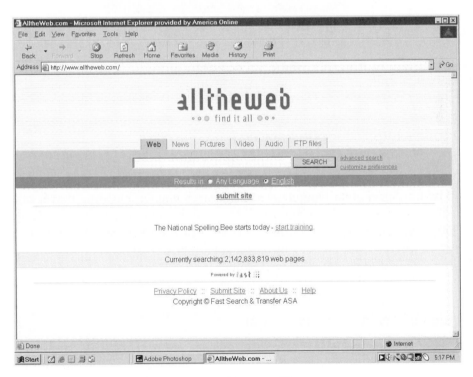

FIGURE 4.6 SCREEN SHOT OF ALLTHEWEB.

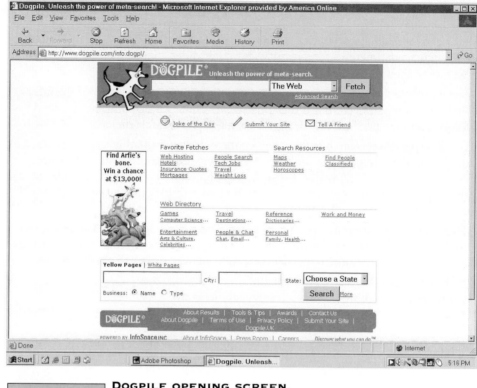

FIGURE 4.7 **DOGPILE OPENING SCREEN.**

Dogpile—http://dogpile.com

Dogpile, founded in 1996, is a popular Internet metasearch engine (Figure 4.7). The site joined the InfoSpace Network in 2000 and is owned and operated by InfoSpace, Inc. Dogpile is a metasearch engine, meaning that it takes a request, then searches the Internet's top search engines (About; Ask Jeeves; FAST: FindWhat; Google; LookSmart; Overture and many more). It combines multiple search engines into one single, powerful search engine to get more relevant and comprehensive results.

Beaucoup—www.beaucoup.com

Beaucoup is a privately held Web site owned by one person (Figure 4.8). It was started in the winter of 1995 as a small page on the back-end of a personal Web site as a list of engines used for research. There are currently over

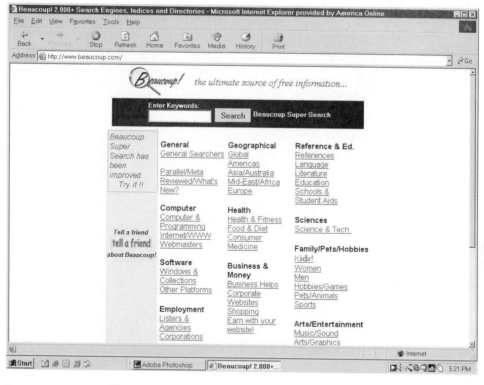

FIGURE 4.8 BEAUCOUP WEB SITE.

2,500 indices or directories on Beaucoup, unlike the typical "search engine" approach that many take. Beaucoup is different because the engines listed on the main site are all "free information" sites. They offer a lot of searchable information instead of commercial products or interests.

To use Beaucoup, click on a category, then go through the annotated listings. If you don't find what you are looking for, whatever page you are on will have the category list. Click on a new category. You are always one click away from a list of links that will take you directly to the search sites themselves.

FindArticles—www.findarticles.com

FindArticles is a vast archive of published articles that you can search for free (Figure 4.9). Constantly updated, it contains articles dating back to 1998 from more than 300 magazines and journals.

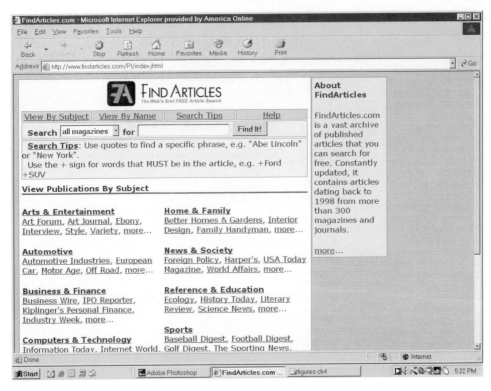

FIGURE 4.9 **FINDARTICLES SEARCH PAGE.**

You will find articles on a range of topics, including business, health, society, entertainment, sports, and more. Unlike other online collections, each of the hundreds of thousands of articles in FindArticles can be read in its entirety and printed at no cost. For detailed information on how to use FindArticles, there is an excellent online help tutorial.

FindArticles is a content-distribution partnership between LookSmart, which provides the search infrastructure, and the Gale Group, which provides the published editorial content.

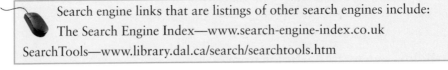

> Search engine links that are listings of other search engines include:
> The Search Engine Index—www.search-engine-index.co.uk
> SearchTools—www.library.dal.ca/search/searchtools.htm

Archive Collections—www.archive.org

The Archive is building an "Internet library" (Figure 4.10). Libraries exist to preserve society's cultural artifacts and to provide access to them. If libraries

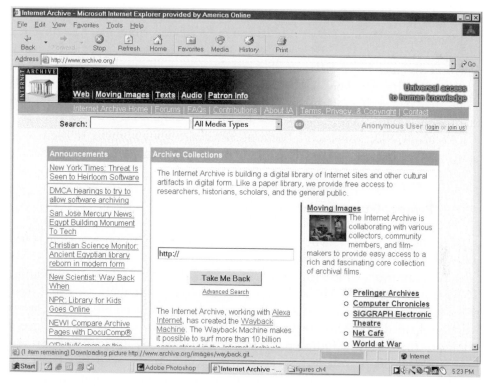

FIGURE 4.10   ARCHIVE COLLECTIONS MAIN PAGE.

continue to foster education and scholarship in this era of digital technology, it's essential for them to extend those functions into the digital world. Archive Collections is an online library and museum. There are archives of books, images, audio, software, and much more.

The Wayback Machine

The Internet Archive is working to prevent the Internet, a new medium with major historical significance, and other "born-digital" materials from disappearing into the past. Collaborating with institutions, including the Library of Congress and the Smithsonian, it is working to preserve a record for generations to come. It is the home of the Wayback Machine. This is the definitive Internet archive. You type in a URL, select a date range, then you are surfing on an archived version of the Web. Imagine surfing circa 1999 and looking at all the Y2K hype. Working with the Alexa Internet, the

Wayback Machine makes it possible to surf more than 10 billion pages stored in the Internet Archive's Web archive. The Wayback Machine was unveiled on October 24, 2001, at UC Berkeley's Bancroft Library. Visit the Wayback Machine by entering a URL or clicking on the specific collections listed on the home Web page. The Wayback Machine has old copies of Web sites from when they began. You can see what they looked like when they were infants or find out when a favorite Web site died.

Archive Collections is collaborating with numerous libraries to digitize as many texts and books as possible. Some of the projects are described next.

Project Gutenberg

This began in 1971, when Michael Hart was given an operator's account with $100,000,000 of computer time in it by the operators of the Xerox Sigma V mainframe at the Materials Research Lab at the University of Illinois. The premise on which Michael Hart based Project Gutenberg was that anything that can be entered into a computer can be reproduced indefinitely, what Michael termed *replicator technology*. The concept is a simple one: Once a book or other item (including pictures, sounds, even 3D items) can be stored in a computer, any number of copies can and will be made available. Everyone in the world or even not in this world (given satellite transmission) can have a copy of a book that has been entered into a computer.

Million Book Project

This was pioneered by Jaime Carbonell, Raj Reddy, Michael Shamos, Gloriana St. Clair, and Robert Thibadeau of Carnegie Mellon University. The goal is to digitize a million books by 2005. The task will be accomplished by scanning the books and indexing their full text with OCR (optical character recognition) technology. The undertaking will create a free-to-read, searchable digital library the approximate size of the combined libraries of the Carnegie Mellon University and one much bigger than the holdings of any high school library. The pilot, *Thousand Book Project* has already been successfully completed.

UVA

Since 1992, the Electronic Text Center at the University of Virginia Library has pursued twin missions with equal seriousness of purpose:

- To build and maintain an Internet-accessible collection of SGML texts and images.
- To build and maintain user communities adept at the creation and use of these materials.

The Center combines an online archive of tens of thousands of SGML- and XML-encoded electronic texts and images with a library service that offers hardware and software suitable for the creation and analysis of text. Through ongoing training sessions and support of teaching and research projects, the Center is building a diverse user community locally, serving thousands of users globally and providing a model for similar humanities computing enterprises at other institutions.

Liber Liber

This is a nonprofit cultural association whose aim is the promotion of any kind of artistic and intellectual expression. It supports the Manuzio project (named after the famous publisher who in the sixteenth century improved the printing techniques created by Gutenberg). The Manuzio project has the ambition to make a noble idea real: the idea of culture available to everybody. How? Making books, graduation theses, articles, or tales available all over the world at any minute for free. The Manuzio project is building a library of electronic texts freely available via modem and CD-ROM, starting with the masterpieces of Italian literature.

Arpanet

This collection consists of memoranda, interview notes, periodicals, papers, and other materials documenting the development of the Advanced Research Projects Agency Network (ARPANET) of the U.S. Department of Defense. The materials were collected by Katie Hafner in preparation for a book written with Matthew Lyon. *Where Wizards Stay Up Late: The Origins of the Internet*, which describes the system's genesis as a device to link computer resources around the world.

Open Source Books

Open source books are contributed by the community.

Internet Bookmobile

This is a mobile digital library capable of downloading public domain books from the Internet via satellite and printing them anytime, anywhere, for anyone. It will be traveling across the country from San Francisco to Washington, D.C., stopping at schools, libraries, and retirement homes—places where people understand the value of the book.

Internet Children's Digital Library

The ICDL is a five-year research project to develop innovative software and a collection of books that specifically address the needs of children as readers. Interdisciplinary researchers from computer science, library studies, education, art, and psychology are working together to design this new library. With participants from around the world, the ICDL is building an international collection that reflects both the diversity and the quality of children's literature. Currently, the collection includes materials donated from 27 cultures in 15 languages.

FTP

www.ftpsearchengine.com

FTP is the simplest way to exchange files between computers on the Internet. FTP is commonly used to transfer files back and forth for your personal home page. It is commonly used to download shareware or other files to your computer from other networks. To use FTP, you should acquire an FTP client or, to put it in simple terms, "an FTP browser." Your Web browser can also make FTP requests to download programs you find on a Web page. Using an FTP client, you can rename, add, or remove files. Doing this generally applies to your personal account FTP. Most Internet services provide free Web space. Contact your ISP to find out how to use your FTP account for a Web page.

You can also use anonymous FTP. That's what the FTP Search Engines page is for. Start by finding the files you want through your Web browser. Then search for the files on one of the supplied search engines. You can look for shareware, game demos, or missing files. Copy the link location and input this into your FTP client. You can then browse through the server directory as though it were on another hard drive. Remember that these servers have rules. Be sure to read the rules in the root directory of the server. These rules also appear when you connect with your FTP client.

THE DARK SIDE OF THE NET: PESKY MARKETING

Everything in life comes with the good and the bad. The Internet is no exception. You most likely have discovered the dark forces of the Internet in the disguises of pop-up ads, pop-unders, Flash ads blocking your reading view, spybots, and banners that make you dizzy with their animation, flashing, and bright colors. Although it doesn't happen as often, some Web pages hijack your browser and change your home page (the page you see when you load your browser each time) to an unwanted Web page.

You're ready to go surfin' on the Web and boot up your browser to begin. Whaaaatt??? This isn't your home page! Some other new home page has taken over and throws pop-up ads left and right. Thinking this is just a fluke, you close the browser and maybe even restart your PC; the same scenario happens again. Your browser has been hijacked. This is another @(#*$ advertising technique that sneaks into the PC without your knowledge. In most cases, this technique piggybacked on software you downloaded and installed or from a Web page you crossed. This has happened to us, and we've never been able to pinpoint the source.

Cookies

When you are visiting various pages on the Web, your computer will collect *cookies.* Cookies are pieces of information generated by a Web server and sent to the user's computer via the browser to be stored on the computer as small text files for future access. The purpose is to identify users and load customized pages for them.

The first time you enter a Web site using cookies, you may fill out a form with your user name, password, and interests. The next time you visit the same site, you won't have to enter your user name and password. It may even have, "Welcome, your name" instead of a generic, "Welcome." Amazon (www.amazon.com) uses cookies to recognize who you are and to serve customized pages with things that might interest you, based on the products you've reviewed in past visits. Just like their delicious taste, that's the "good side" of cookies.

Now for the bad side, as bad as high calories, except it infuriates users instead. Know that cookies can't carry a virus or anything harmful to a computer. If you look at your list of cookies, you may see cookies for sites you've never visited, especially ad.doubleclick.net. DoubleClick and other advertisers are able to track users to serve content without violating rules. Places such as DoubleClick subscribe to a media service that places ads for them, which results in sending a cookie to a user's PC. In other words, the user gets a cookie through this process without ever having visited the Web site. This is a controversial use of cookies and has led to discussions on cookies and privacy, as well as creation of features or software for blocking cookies. However, if you block all cookies, you won't be able to utilize perfectly valid Web sites.

We would like a 100% effective cure to pesky marketing. Just like the Borg of the *Star Trek* series, the players behind the marketing continue adapting to our weapons and shields. Although there are no laws outlawing such marketing, the best we can do is stay on top of the latest scum and software that destroys them.

Pop-Up Ads

Pop-up windows come in a variety of flavors. They are usually smaller browser windows, with close, minimize, and maximize (the little line, square with the heavy line at the top, and the box with the X icon in the upper right-hand corner). The pop-ups that people complain bitterly about are the ones that are unwanted advertisements that block the view of the Web page you want to view. Marketers don't seem to care that these generate a great deal of ill will. Users grumble and close the ads, often almost as quickly as they appear.

Sometimes they try and trick you by looking like a real Web dialog box, a warning or a flashing "you have won" notice. Do not be fooled. These are advertising and subversive, annoying advertising at that. It's even more infuriating when you aren't quite accurate in your rush to initiate a close window click, and the ad is activated. It opens up to full screen and overwhelms whatever you were looking at. It's frustrating. Some of the worst offending Web sites throw pop-ups on the screen so fast you cannot see what you want on the Web site.

These are not popular with most users and are an annoyance to Web surfing. Some of the smarter marketers have started doing "pop-unders," which still load, but they display under the main Web page.

GET PRACTICE CLOSING POP-UPS

There is a pop-up game called *The Realistic Internet Simulator*, where you can get practice closing simulated pop-up ads. The small simulated ads show up one after another and the clock is ticking (Figure 4.11).

At the end, the game does a tongue-in-cheek "blue screen of death" and tells you how many pop-ups you killed (Figure 4.12).

To play, go to www.2.b3ta.com/realistic-internet-simulator/.

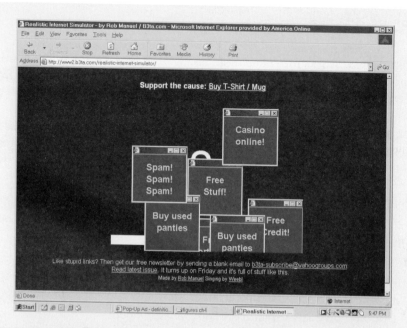

FIGURE 14.11 REALISTIC INTERNET SIMULATOR IN ACTION.

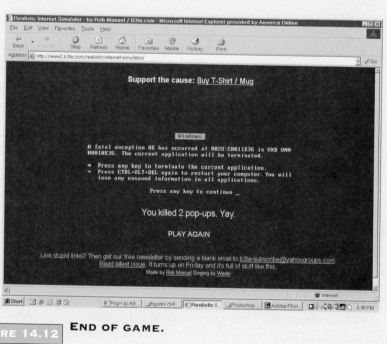

FIGURE 14.12 END OF GAME.

USENET

Usenet is a worldwide distributed discussion system. Anyone with Internet access can read and post messages. It consists of a set of *newsgroups* with names that are classified hierarchically by subject. Newsgroups exist for virtually every subject imaginable.

For a listing of Internet Usenet archives, go to www.faqs.org/faqs (Figure 4.13).

Articles or *messages* are posted to these newsgroups by people on computers with the appropriate software. These articles are then broadcast to other interconnected computer systems via a wide variety of networks. Some newsgroups are *moderated* (articles are first sent to a moderator for approval before they appear in the newsgroup). Usenet is available on a wide variety of computer systems and networks.

In the early 1980s, it was created (by Steven Bellovin, Jim Ellis, Tom Truscott, and Steven Daniel) to exchange information, mainly on university UNIX machines. It grew rapidly to become an international, decentralized information utility. By the early 1990s, it hosted more than 1,200 news-

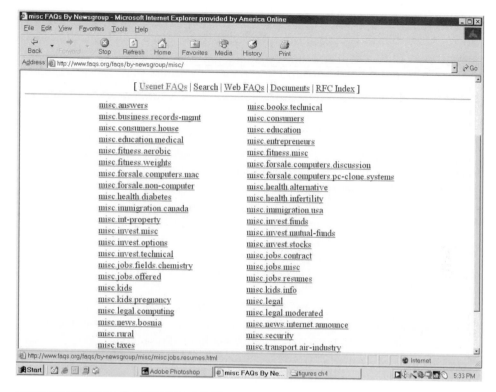

FIGURE 4.13 A LISTING OF USENET TOPICS IN THE MISC HEADING.

groups and an average of 40 MB of new technical articles, news, discussion, opinions, and ideas each day. (40 MB is the equivalent of several thousand paper pages.) By the end of the century, there were well over 37,000 groups.

There are gateways into Usenet (such as www.deja.com). Many Web browsers (Netscape and Internet Explorer) are linked, and Internet URLs that begin with "news" refer to Usenet newsgroups (such as http://news.news. announce.newusers). Google's groups section (http://groups.google.com/) is also a gateway into the newsgroups.

The correct term is *newsgroups*.

Incorrect terms include: bases, boards, bboards, conferences, round tables, SIGs, echoes, rooms, or usergroups.

People who run the news systems are called *news administrators*, not sysops.

Usenet is made up of people called *newsgroups (or groups)* who exchange articles tagged with one or more universally recognized labels. It consists of newsgroups that are listed in the periodic "List of Active Newsgroups" and/or "Alternative Newsgroup Hierarchies" postings that appear regularly in *news.lists.misc* (http://news.lists.misc).

WHAT THE USENET IS NOT

Usenet is hard to understand conceptually and is widely misunderstood. It's almost easier to say what it isn't to get an idea of what it is. According to the Usenet FAQ, this is the definitive, negative description.

Usenet is not an organization—No person or group has authority over Usenet as a whole. No one controls who gets a news feed, which articles are propagated where, who can post articles, or anything else. There is no "Usenet Incorporated," nor is there a "Usenet user's group." There are various activities organized by means of Usenet newsgroups. If they were to stop tomorrow, the Usenet would go on without them.

Usenet is not a democracy—Because there is no person or group in charge of Usenet as a whole, i.e., there is no Usenet "government," it follows that Usenet cannot be a democracy, autocracy, or any other kind of -acy.

Usenet is not fair—After all, who shall decide what's fair? For that matter, if someone is behaving unfairly, who's going to stop him or her? Neither you nor I, that's certain.

Usenet is not a right—Some people misunderstand their local right of "freedom of speech" to mean that they have a legal right to use others' computers to say what they wish in whatever way they wish and that the owners of the computers have no right to stop them.

Those people are wrong. Freedom of speech also means freedom not to speak. If I choose not to use my computer to aid your speech, that is my right. Freedom of the press belongs to those who own one.

Usenet is not a public utility—Some Usenet sites are publicly funded or subsidized. Most of them are not. There is no government monopoly on Usenet and little or no government control.

Usenet is not an academic network—It is no surprise that many Usenet sites are universities, research labs, or other academic institutions. Usenet originated with a link between two universities, and the exchange of ideas and information of ideas is what such institutions are all about. But the passage of years has changed Usenet's character. Today, most Usenet sites are commercial entities.

Usenet is not an advertising medium—It was never intended to be and shouldn't be used for that purpose.

Usenet is not the Internet—The Internet is a wide-ranging network; parts are subsidized by various governments. It carries many kinds of traffic, of which

Usenet is only one. And the Internet is only one of the various networks carrying Usenet traffic.

Usenet is not a UUCP network—UUCP is a protocol (actually a "protocol suit") for sending data over point-to-point connections, typically using dialup modems. Sites use UUCP to carry many kinds of traffic, of which Usenet is only one. UUCP is only one of the various transports carrying Usenet traffic.

Usenet is not a U.S. network—It is true that Usenet originated in the United States and the fastest growth in Usenet sites has been there. Usenet is worldwide. The heaviest concentrations of Usenet sites outside the U.S. are in Canada, Europe, Australia, and Japan.

Usenet is not a UNIX network—The systems used to read and post to Usenet are Vaxen running VMS, IBM mainframes, Amigas, Macintoshes, and MS-DOS PCs.

Usenet is not an ASCII network—The A in ASCII stands for "American." Sites in other countries often use character sets better suited to their language. Such are typically, although not always, supersets of ASCII. Even in the United States, ASCII is not universally used. IBM mainframes use EBCDIC. Non-ASCII sites exist.

Usenet is not software—There are dozens of software packages used at various sites to transport and read Usenet articles. So no one program or package can be called "the Usenet Software." Software designed to support Usenet traffic can be (and is) used for two other kinds of communication, usually without risk of mixing the two. Such private communication networks are typically kept distinct from Usenet by the invention of newsgroups named differently from the universally recognized ones.

SUMMARY

If the Internet is good for anything other than email, it has to be its incredible ability to provide users with almost any sort of information, from how to fix a car to the whereabouts of an old friend. Once you learn how to search and discover things on the Net, an amazing amount of raw information will become available for you to use in all sorts of ways. The key to success is to search a lot and use a lot of different searching tricks. Find out how other people search. Change the order of words. Use Boolean operators where appropriate. The Web and the Internet are now nothing less than a gold mine for information prospectors. Use it.

5
MUSIC

Some people think the best thing about the Internet is finding, swapping, sampling, or just reading about music. Indeed, the Web, in particular, is a gold mine in a lot of different ways for the lover of music.

When people talk about music on the Web, it's mostly about MP3 files. These are files that can be downloaded to your computer to listen to while you work. They can also be transferred to an MP3 portable player or burned onto a recordable CD disk that can be played anywhere.

CD-R OR CD-RW

 The difference between a CD-Recordable (CD-R) and a CD-Rewriteable (CD-RW) is that one can only be recorded on once, whereas the other can be reused.

The technology between the two is different.

If you have an older machine, you may have a read-only CD player installed. Or you may have a CD-recorder/player, which can write a CD-R but not a CD-RW, although it should be able to read most CD-RWs. The newer DVD writers can usually write to a CD-R disk that can then be read by a standard CD player.

CD-R	Data permanent	Disk price $0.35 to $1.00	Readable on any CD-ROM
CD-RW	Erasable	Disk price $0.50 to $2.00	Newer players only

DEFINING MP3

MP3 is short for MPEG-1 (Moving Picture Experts Group-1), layer 3, and is a name for a family of standards developed to covert audio, film, and video information to a compressed digital format. MP3 is the means both to store *and* recover information. An MP3 player can be either a computer program on your machine or software built into a dedicated device. What the player does is reconstruct music from the digitally encoded, compressed format. It decompresses the information.

MP3 was invented under the sponsorship of the Motion Picture Experts Group (MPEG) by a leading organization of applied research in Germany. The company, Fraunhofer Gesellschaft (FhG), was the company originally involved in MP3 development (and still holds key patents to the technology) in a joint cooperative arrangement with the University of Erlangen's Professor Dieter Seitzer. It was formalized by the International Organization for Standardization (ISO) and became the official standard in 1992.

MP3 is the file extension for MPEG, audio layer 3. This layer is one of three encoding methods (layer 1, layer 2, or layer 3) to compress audio data.

There is confusion about MP3—what it is and what it does—because it's a mathematically based algorithm to crunch the files into manageable packets to be shipped over the Internet's pipes without clogging or losing any pieces or sound quality. It relies on basic signal processing technology and on *psychoacoustics*—the science of hearing and communication. These are combined to determine what sounds are really unnecessary and redundant, as well as what sounds humans can really hear to compress the information into the smallest possible package.

According to Webopedia, "MP3 uses perceptual audio coding and psychoacoustic compression to remove all superfluous information. It also adds an MDCT (Modified Discrete Cosine Transform) that implements a filter bank, increasing the frequency resolutions 18 times higher than that of a layer 2."

Compression limits the sounds we can't hear or that are redundant. It removes the gaps and extra space between the sounds like a trash compactor squishes a week's worth of garbage into a cube the size of a box of diapers. The music, unlike the trash, can be restored to nearly original sound quality once it's decompressed. The MP3 can be compressed from one tenth up to one twelfth the size of the original sound file. MP3 is a so-called lossy-type of compression. MP3 does eliminate some sounds that we either can't hear or are redundant. The compression software is commonly called a *codec* by technical geeks. It is similar to the word *modem*, which is modulation/demodulation. Codec is compression/decompression.

Lossy and Lossless

Lossless and *lossy* are compression terms to describe whether compression can restore all the original data when the file is uncompressed.

Lossless

This compression technique is able to restore every single bit of data exactly like the original (uncompressed) file. This is the only choice for text or spreadsheet files (which might be seriously damaged with a loss of words or financial data). The .GIF (Graphics Interchange File) is a lossless compression.

Lossy

Lossy is a method of compression that eliminates bits of extra, useless information. This information cannot be restored when the file is decompressed. For the most part, this information isn't noticed by the user. Lossy compression is used for video and sound. With the video portion, it does cause movement to be jerky and unnatural but tolerable. For sound and still pictures, the small amount of data loss cannot be detected by most users.

The JPEG image file for photographs and images is one visual example of lossy compression. Using JPEG compression, you can decide how much loss to introduce and make a trade-off between file size, image quality, and how long you want to wait when uploading or downloading the image. The smaller the .JPEG file, the faster the download.

Perceptual Audio Coding

MP3 is able to reproduce enough of the data so that humans aren't bothered by it (the dog or cat might be, but people aren't). It's designed so the loss of data occurs in areas above and below what we humans can normally hear. This is called the *perceptual audio coding*. The idea here is that by taking advantage of the human sensory limitations, a lot of excess data can be eliminated quickly and easily.

Sound recording equipment can record information above and beyond the range of our hearing. The human auditory range is around 20 Hz (20 cycles per second) at the lowest, up to 20 KHz (20,000 cycles per second) at the highest. Although this varies from person to person, we all tend to hear better at the midrange than at either end of the spectrum. (We are more sensitive to high ranges earlier in life, before we've been exposed to high volumes for too long.) For the most part, women have a higher frequency range than men; most everyone hears between 2 KHz and 4 KHz.

PORTABLE MP3 HARDWARE

These very small players, about the size of a transistor radio, let you download music in any order you want onto them. It's like having your own music radio station, except without the commercials, deejays, and songs you don't like. The hardware is solid state, skip free, and can play for hours on one AA battery.

Initially, the record companies tried to block the sale of portable MP3 players, but then they relented. Some manufacturers compromise and incorporate digital rights management to prevent users from transferring music they have legitimately purchased from one format to another format. Hardware that uses Memory Stick and SD Flash memory may have this capability.

There are some choices when it comes to selecting the hardware. These include memory, bit rate, compatibility, and various features. Don't overlook the personal appeal. The device should have a good feel in your hand. Pick it up, push the buttons, read the display, and see whether it feels sturdy and comfortable to you. Besides features, the right human feel is important in making any decision.

The three types of MP3 units are:

MP 3 portable players that rely on flash memory.

Jukeboxes (hard disk drives or HHD) that can hold large amounts of storage.

Digital auto receivers (DARs) that incorporate your PC into conventional audio systems. (Their memory capacity is your computer's available memory.)

Memory

Typically, one minute of MP3 music requires approximately 1 MB of storage. A player that comes with a 32-MB memory card or an internal 32-MB memory board will play only about half an hour of music. It's best to have at least 64 MB of memory, which holds about an hour.

Memory Device Types

Flash memory is the smallest and lightest of the MP3 memory choices. It is *solid state*, meaning that it has no moving parts. It is rugged and a good choice because it can withstand regular human use: jogging, carrying it in a purse or backpack, or other rough use. Flash memory also has the least storage capacity. Some units have expansion slots to add extra memory cards. Although all flash memory cards do the same thing, they are not interchangeable between different devices.

There are five types of solid-state, nonvolatile memory:

1. **Memory Stick**—Developed by Sony, these are available in sizes up to 1 GB, although the GB-sized stick is seldom seen. They are smaller than comparable storage media and can be shared between the same manufacturer's devices. They also have built-in capabilities to restrict transfer of copyrighted material.
2. **SmartMedia**—The card is about as big as a matchbook and available in nonvolatile flash memory storage capacities up to 512 MB (with higher on the way). These are popular in devices such as PDAs and digital cameras.

3. **CompactFlash**—This is a small circuit board with flash memory chips and a dedicated controller chip, encased in a rugged shell that is several times thicker than a SmartMedia card. It is has storage up to 2 GB.

4. **MultiMedia Card (MMC)**—This is a tiny memory card (about the size of a postage stamp, weighing about 2 grams). It uses flash memory for portable storage between various devices. MMC was jointly created by SanDisk and Siemens AG/Infineon Technologies AG. Seldom seen.

5. **Secure Digital Card (SD)**—This is a memory card that uses nonvolatile flash memory with encryption capabilities to make storage between various devices secure and portable. It is available with storage capacities as high as 512 MB. This also has built-in capabilities to restrict transfer of copyrighted material.

DVORAK'S MUSIC TIP

If you are running Windows 98 (or newer OS), a USB connection is the best way to attach your MP3 player. (FireWire is the better choice for non-beige Macs.)

Bit Rate

The higher the bit rate, the better the sound quality, although in reality you should consider the use of the device as it pertains to the bit rate. The small flash-based portable units (for dashing around town or commuting on public transportation) don't need as high a quality of sound as an in-home, stationary device. Jukeboxes and DARs should support higher bit rate MP3s, as well as other coder/decoder formats, such as WMA, the Microsoft audio format that competes with MP3. The bit rates vary, depending on the player and the intended use. In fact, the player should automatically adjust to different bit rates. If they do not, you may have problems.

Compatibility

Not all players are compatible on all machines and OSs. Macintosh and Linux users need to make sure the product supports their requirements. Just because the unit may be USB-compatible doesn't mean the software is supported for Mac to Linux.

Features

There are lots of features, and that is the confusing part. Features vary from unit to unit and depend on the specific purpose of the MP3 player. You'll find an FM radio tuner, CD/MP3 hybrids, voice recording, memory upgrade capabilities, long play (100 songs or more), and units that have sophisticated file management systems (display and search the full song title or by artist, etc.). There are units designed for in-car use, included in PDA units or as add-on modules. (One drawback to listening to MP3s on a PDA is that music chews up memory. Until the units contain more memory, you can't simultaneously compute and listen to music.)

PORTABLE MP3 PLAYER REVIEWS

 Some Web sites with reviews and information on portable MP3 players:

Epinions.com—www.epinions.com

MP3 Shopping—www.mp3shopping.com

Portable CD MP3 Player—www.portable-cd-mp3-player.com

FTPPlanet.com—www.ftpplanet.com

MAKERS OF PORTABLE MP3 PLAYERS INCLUDE

 Samsung—www.samsung.com

Nomad—www.nomadworld.com

Archos—www.archos.com

SonicBlue—www.sonicblue.com

Apple iPod—www.apple.com/ipod/

MP3 PLAYERS IN YOUR AUTOMOBILE

 There are a few ways to get MP3 players into your car: carry one, install one, or use a wireless music adapter.

This is not a complete list. It can give you some idea of what variation there is in the marketplace.

AIWA America—CDC-MP3 is an in-dash CD player that reads CD-R and CD-RW disks encoded with MP3 files. The CDC MP3 doesn't support playlists—it has a directory structure as deep as eight levels and 32-character file names and ID3 tags—to aid in finding specific songs. The unit also includes an AM/FM receiver and an antitheft faceplate. It supports MP3, CD Auto, CD, CD-R, and CD-RW sources.

For more information, go to www.aiwa.com

PhatNoise Phatbox—is a unit that works like any traditional CD player. It is installed in the trunk of the car. It supports MP3, WMA, and WAV file formats, with various storage sizes from 5 GB to 20 GB. The unit has a separate DMS cartridge that can be removed and inserted into a USB cradle to transfer music files from a PC. The Phatbox supports up to 99 playlists, with up to 999 tracks per playlist.

For more information, go to www.phatnoise.com

Neo 35—uses a standard 3.5-inch IDE hard drive for storage so you can buy it with a 10-, 30-, or 61-GB drive or add your own. The unit supports MP2 and MP3 files. You transfer them with a PC bay installed into your computer and move the unit out of the PC to a bay installed in your car's dash. The unit supports playlists and allows music to be sorted by title, artist, album, and gender. You can also purchase an optional remote control.

For more information, go to www.ssiamerica.com.

Kima Link—is a wireless music adapter. You plug the Link-It into the headphone output of your portable music player, then set the car radio to FM 88.1, 88.3, 88.5, or 88.7. The music will transmit from your player to the car radio.

For more information, go to www.kimawireless.com.

FMP3 DIGITAL AUDIO RECEIVER/WIRELESS TRANSMITTER

A number of makers have a special wireless device to let you broadcast your MP3 music to any FM radio within range of your computer.

Akoo Kima KS-100 Wireless Audio System—connects the base unit to your computer's sound card or any other audio source, such as a TV, satellite, or stereo, and broadcasts to a receiving unit that you place near your radio. Tune the radio to either FM 88.1 or 88.3, and the base unit will send a high-fidelity stereo signal to the receiving unit up to 1,000 feet. For more information, go to www.kimawireless.com.

Netplay Radio—offers a music transmitter that connects to the audio output of any PC to broadcast your favorite Web music to any FM radio within 100 feet of your PC. For more information, go to www.netplayradio.com.

SOFTWARE

MP3 is used to encompass the programs that create and process the entire range of steps that are involved, as well as the music itself and the hardware.

There are four steps in converting a CD music selection to an MP3-encoded file so that you can listen to the selection on an MP3 player.

1. The *ripper* program moves sound sequences from a compact disk to the hard drive as a WAV file.
2. The *encoder* program converts the WAV to an MP3 file.

3. The *Player* program decodes and decompresses the compressed and encoded file to play the MP3.
4. You hear the MP3 file as normal analog sound.

Most of the MP3 players on the market come with software to rip, encode, and play selections. There are also many different programs—shareware, freeware, and commercial—on the open market.

The actual transmission of music is referred to as *peer-to-peer* (p2p). For more information on P2P, see Chapter 26.

Ripping, or Extracting Software

Ripping software is usually part of the encoding software. It is a program that can extract tracks from the audio CD and make a copy of them on a hard disk in WAV form. It is the starting point of an MP3 file. Like anything else, some programs are easy to use, and others are complicated. The ripper converts music files to WAV files for use by the MP3 encoder.

Encoder Software

An encoder is a program to convert an audio WAV file into an MP3 file. It is automatically decompressed while the MP3 is being played.

Microsoft and IBM created the WAV (short for *waveform* and pronounced *wave*) as a format to store audio files. Windows 95 was released with built-in WAV file support. This audio file format has become a standard PC audio file format for everything from system and game sounds to CD-quality audio. A .WAV file name extension is used primarily for PCs but is also a viable interchange for other computer platforms (such as the Mac).

Player, or Converting Software

Converting software, usually called a *player*, can read the files, then play them back. The player often has other features, such as equalizing the sound, playlist management (selecting the order of the songs, or shuffling), and sometimes a way to convert files into different audio formats (such as from MP3 to WAV) or other formats, such as Apple's AIF-C (Audio Interchange File Format-Compressed, which can use the extensions .aiff, .aif, .aifc), MIDI (Musical Instrument Digital Interface), UNIX files (.au or .snd), Microsoft Streaming Format (.asf, or .asx), or even less common formats, such as the open source format Ogg Vorbis.

Utility Programs

There are utility programs designed to simplify certain MP3 functions. Some utility programs in use with MP3 files include WinZip, to manage compressed archives; Syntrillium Software's Cool Edit Pro (to manage WAV files, change characteristics, or apply sound effects); and Trelliant's MP3-Wolf, which is used to locate MP3 files on the Internet, among many, many others.

MUSIC SHARING

DVORAK'S MUSIC TIP

Ogg Vorbis is a new audio compression format. It is comparable to the other compression formats—MP3, VQF, AAC, etc.—but different because it is open source and patent free.

Ogg is the name of Xiph.org's container format for audio, video, and metadata. Vorbis is the name of a specific audio compression scheme contained in Ogg.

Fans claim this program can compress files that are smaller, sound better (than MP3s), and have faster download times.

For more information, go to www.vorbis.com.

There are three main ways that people share music on the Web. The first is between friends or relatives. They send you a file; you send them a file. You each need to have a ripper/ encoder and a player to trade and listen. There are a number of shareware and commercial products that do this.

The second is going to the IRC and trading files with people you don't know. This has some drawbacks, although it's widely popular. Most often, it is actually an illegal practice that we recommend you avoid.

The third way is through music sharing sites. These sites have proprietary software you download and online manuals to guide you. You don't need a ripper or encoder because the software has it. Most people begin their journey into music sharing with music download sites.

Music Download Sites

There has been a lot in the news in the last few years about how easy it is to create an MP3 file from CD selections and make it available on the Web for downloading. The defunct Napster system was at the crux of most of the controversy as illegal trading became very popular. The mistaken idea is that only copyrighted materials are traded. This isn't so.

Many small artists not listed by the big record companies share their music to collect a wider audience. Collectors of old music, radio plays, comedies, and other audio files can trade files. Foreign music, old Broadway tunes, and specialized music and language lessons can be exchanged. Dvorak, for example, likes to collect old radio shows from the 1930s, which most often have entered the public domain.

Be aware that download sites can place pesky marketing ploys onto your machine. It's a good idea occasionally to scrape your computer clean of all the junk that can be placed to track your surfing habits, profile your shopping preferences, hijack your browser to start pages that you don't want, alter system files, etc. Be sure to read the Chapter 11 on Security for details concerning these issues. It has pointers on what to do. A good utility is Ad-Aware from Lavasoft. For more information, go to www.lavasoftusa.com.

Kazaa

Kazaa is the site that most people mention when they talk about file sharing. To get started on Kazaa, you need to install the Kazaa Media Desktop (KMD), which will allow you to download, create, and share files with other users. You open up the KMD and begin to search. The toolbar has buttons to execute the commands needed. To start to search, click the Search button and type in a keyword. If you are looking for songs by the turn of the last century's famous singing comic, the "Laird of the Music Hall," Sir Harry Lauder, type that in. When the search returns two songs you've been searching for—*A Wee Deoch an Doris* and *Roamin in the Gloamin*—you select them and download them to your machine.

There is no telling what is out there. It changes from one day to the next, depending on what other people are offering to share.

For more information, go to: www.kazaa.com.

WinMX

WinMX is a free file-sharing program to connect, download, and share files with other users through a decentralized WinMX Peer Network. You download WinMX software to begin. The requirements are Windows 98/ME/2000/XP, and a Pentium 166 w/64 MB RAM or better.

For more information, go to: www.winmx.com.

NeoNapster

NeoNapster has easy-to-use interfaces similar to the old Napster, except with no ads, banners, or pop-ups. It's connected to the Gnutella network.

The ripper/encoder program used is NeoAudio, which is an easy-to-use interface for beginners but, according to the Web site, "powerful and customizable for advanced audio users." With NeoAudio, you can extract and encode music from your CDs direct to your hard drive in a variety of formats.

For more information, go to: www.neonapster.com.

Gnutella

This is a system to exchange files over the Internet directly (meaning without going through a Web site P2P arrangement). Gnutella is similar to sites such as Kazaa in that it is a way to download or share music files with other Internet users. It is unlike them because it is not a centralized Web site. You can see the files of a small number of other Gnutella users, and they can see the files of others, in a "daisy-chain" effect. Without a centralized location, piracy has become an object of great concern for the music publishing industry.

Gnutella can handle files other than MP3 music files. (You can download any file type.)

For more information, go to http://gnutella.wego.com, www.gnutella.com, and www.gnutellanews.com.

MP3.com

MP3.com has information on how to get started and other essential MP3-related information. It covers the basics of players that rip and encode, download managers that disconnect after downloading, the best players, etc. The Web site is designed to give a new user all the information they need, including message boards and then some.

For more information, go to www.mp3.com.

ISSUES IN THE NEWS

The Recording Industry Association of America (RIAA) is the trade group that represents the U.S. recording industry. The RIAA has an enormous amount of power because the majority of record labels operate under it. Their actions have had an impact on the Internet—unfortunately, not a good one.

The RIAA made the choice when Napster was *the* place to find music on the Web to oppose it instead of embracing it as a way to distribute music on the Web. It would have been an easy sell to establish a Web presence that was bigger and better, as well as a secure pay-per-download service. The RIAA instead wanted Napster to go away, and they succeeded with that. It sued and dismantled Napster. Now it is using strange tactics to try and stop online music trading.

RIAA has requested from the courts the right to hack into people's computers. It is the big push behind preventing copyrighted material from being traded on or off the Web. The RIAA recently won a decision in court to force Verizon Communications to turn over the name of an Internet subscriber who supposedly in one day downloaded 600 song files from the file-trading network Kazaa. The head of the RIAA, Hilary Rosen, has made statements suggesting that ISPs should be held responsible for money the music industry has lost because of file trading and should pay the RIAA directly (and pass the charges along to their customers).

What is perplexing is that the RIAA has done some really dumb things. RIAA has taunted the hacker collective, which has caused the RIAA Web site to be hacked many times in many ways. It has attempted to flood the market with fake files to confuse users. The files are labeled, appear to be the correct format and file size, but are without data, or in the case of a Madonna file, scolds you. It asks what you are doing, complete with raunchy cussing.

In response, download music sites have initiated IP filtering to block the P2P downloads from known RIAA or MPAA sites, and a number of hackers have focused on both Madonna's Web site and the RIAA Web site.

In the January 3, 2003, online issue of Wired.com, Michelle Delio reported:

"The Recording Industry Association of America may not want people to share digital files, but the organization certainly seems to be in favor of open access to its Web site. On Monday the RIAA site was hacked for the sixth time in six months. This time, the defacement resulted in bogus press releases on the front door, touting the joys of cheese and interspecies romantic relationships."

The RIAA's battle cry is that artists are losing money and that CD sales are down because people are pirating them. The truth is probably closer to the fact that CDs cost pennies to make but the sticker price is close to $20 dollars. The radio station playlists are becoming narrow and uninteresting, prompting people to seek other ways to *find* the music they like. It can even be argued that the artists themselves are taking less artistic ventures. All in all, the RIAA's moves have the air of desperation.

The issue here in the eyes of many is that the RIAA wants to charge people to "loan" out CDs that they've already purchased. Unlike the pre-Internet days, people now have friends all over the world. What is the difference between sending a particularly good CD track from your favorite CD to your online friend in Austria today and in 1972 loaning your buddy Ralph your best album? The

RIAA is trying to cling to an outdated business model that didn't work 30 years ago and still doesn't. People lend their possessions to friends so they will have something to talk about, so that their friends will be swayed by the example (and admit to their good taste), and that's how it has always worked.

A recommended Web site to follow the news of RIAA is www.mp3newswire.net.

MPEG

The Moving Picture Experts Group (MPEG) develops standards for digital video and digital audio compression. It operates under the ISO. The standards for MPEG are evolving.

For information on MPEG, go to www.mpeg.org or http://mpeg.telecomitalialab.com (home page of MPEG).

SUMMARY

Few people see the disappearance of online music trading, but the recent appearance of new sites that sell lots of music at reasonable prices should stem piracy. In the long term, the industry is having to adjust and change as communication changes around the world.

6
E-Commerce: How to Buy and Sell on the Internet

It's hard to imagine now, but at one time, you really couldn't buy *anything* on the Web.

The Internet frenzy was a mad rush to build brands and acquire customers at any cost (enabled by the venture community's willingness to pay for it). It featured all the elements of a good gold rush story: fact and fiction, idealists and zealots, railroad barons and snake oil salesmen, and finally, winners and losers.

The market still is recovering from its dot-com hangover. But we're all still using the Web. It has evolved into an engine for global communication and commerce. It is a business platform that eliminates geographic barriers and provides entrepreneurs and companies access to world markets and customers once out of reach.

Thousands of online businesses serve consumers and complementary businesses at every step of the supply chain. There are online sales of everything from bulk wholesale supplies and heavy equipment to first-run consumer products, clearance overstock, and corporate capital assets.

The research group eMarketer estimates that in the United States. alone, more than half the123 million Internet users—above the age of 14—will buy goods and services online this year.

Consider these Internet statistics, released by both Forrester Research (a leading market research firm) and eMarketer (a research group often quoted for online statistics):

- Online retail sales topped $47.6 billion in 2001 (according to a June 24, 2002 Forrester Research press release available at www.forrester.com)

- EMarketer expects that business-to-business and business-to-consumer sales will grow from $75 billion in 2002, to over $100 billion in 2003 (source: eMarketer, published in an article by Michael Pastore on the CyberAtlas Web site http://cyberatlas.internet.com/markets/retailing/article/0,1323,6061_349891,00.html)

- Online retail sales will reach $195 billion by 2006. Online auctions should account for 25%, or $48 billion, according to another Forrester Research press release dated August 5, 2003.

- Annually, eBay enables $14.87 billion in gross merchandise sales, according to materials on their Web site.

SHOP.ORG

The Web site shop.org is a forum for online retailing executives to share information and insights. They have a comprehensive list of statistics and demographics available. For more information go to www.shop.org.

What is driving the growth of commerce on the Web?

Put simply, the Web is *inclusive*. It levels the business playing field, providing buyers greater opportunity and making high-volume commerce a reality for small, medium, and large businesses. The Web is scalable and flexible. You don't need a king's ransom to set up an online shop, build awareness for your products, or grow your operation. This is particularly true if you have an existing "brick-and-mortar business"; take advantage of Web-based applications from online email to commerce management systems (such as Vendio); or leverage successful online marketplaces (such as eBay); which attract a critical mass of buyers.

The Web allows businesses to expand their markets effectively without making major capital expenditures (direct mail, catalogs, print, radio and television advertising, regional and international expansion). The barriers of distance and time—even of gender and nationality—are minimized. They no longer localize a talented individual's market or, conversely, prohibit a customer from buying from the source.

The Web has consolidated into three main categories.

1. Online marketplaces: Person-to-person and business-to-consumer marketplaces that aggregate listings from multiple vendors.
2. Branded retailers and manufacturers: Traditional retailers and manufacturers that have come online.
3. Web superstores: Umbrella online retailers that sell across a number of "vertical" categories, such as Amazon.com, or vertical marketplaces that generally specialize in one category.

BUYING ON THE INTERNET

We are all a little lazier than we'd like to admit. Most of us would rather swivel our desk chairs and click the mouse a few times to buy what we need than to walk downtown or drive to the mall. The convenience of the Web frees us up to do more of what we need and love to do. (We're all looking for a bargain, too.) *Consumers*, young and old, are augmenting their buying online.

That doesn't mean that all Web buyers make the most of the opportunity. The Web can be overwhelming and frustrating, with its dizzying array of mediocre sites, direct marketing assaults, and merciless pop-ups.

A lot of us just scratch the surface, not taking full advantage of the many venues and market opportunities available to us. And that's too bad. After all, isn't shopping about getting the best product at the best price?

Getting Hooked

Most of us begin our adventure in online purchasing by buying a *new* item from a company we trust, a major retail brand or consumer manufacturer with which we have had previous experience.

It helps that the new item comes with a warranty so that we can have it repaired or replaced. There is customer support after the purchase. We are confident that the transaction will be seamless and without any headaches or hassles. We'll get a quality product. Payment will be secure. Our personal information will be protected. The item will be professionally packed and shipped. And more times than not, this is exactly what happens.

Amazon.com

More adventurous new buyers move on to something like a bookseller, such as Amazon.com. This company has spent hundreds of millions to be the retail epicenter of the Web. It's easy to trust Amazon—like a branded retailer—because it has established a solid reputation. Like other e-tailers in its league, Amazon.com has volume on its side. This allows, in theory, for it to discount items below traditional retail prices. Part of the appeal is that the $19 CD at Borders will be $13 at Amazon.com. No sales tax, either (unless you live in Washington state). Of course, you may have to pay for shipping and/or wait for your item.

eBay

eBay, too, has become one of the Web's most visible brands. It is a destination for new users. eBay continues to grow for two more basic reasons: First, it has naturally evolved into a business-to-consumer marketplace and is no longer just a person-to-person auction site for rare, "one-of-a-kind" items. It is a platform for off-the-shelf goods from legitimate businesses with bona fide standards. Second, you can get a bargain. Many dealers sell at near wholesale prices.

ONLINE MARKETPLACES

There are many different varieties of online markets. Some of the general categories include person to person, business to consumer, online store sites, discount sites, comparison shopping sites, and dealer direct sites.

Person to Person

Online marketplaces that enable individuals to auction/sell their secondary market goods. Most support multiple sales formats, from auction to fixed price. They are popular for both practical, consumer goods and rare, one-of-a-kind items. They have evolved into venues for small merchants and bigger businesses.

Business to Consumer

These online marketplaces are for the auction of discounted consumer goods consigned to the site by the manufacturer. These items are often refurbished or discontinued models.

Online Store Sites

These are marketplaces that consist of many independent online stores, operated by both small merchants and larger branded manufacturers and retailers. Site vendors usually sell in a variety of product categories, offering both new, practical goods and used, collectible items.

Discount Sites

Fixed-price outlets support a broad spectrum of vendors (manufacturers, wholesalers, liquidators, individuals), competing solely on price. Products are generally not first-run and are steeply discounted. Items for sale usually consist of discontinued products, refurbished customer returns, defectives, and used goods. Items are practical commodities, not collectibles.

Comparison-Shopping Sites

Shopping search engines that aggregate listings from multiple venues/merchants let buyers compare prices. These search sites retrieve new and used goods.

Dealer Direct

Though there are exceptions to every rule, the best prices are with smaller vendors on online marketplaces. These sell both used goods and new products. Warranties and product returns are often voided on these purchases.

These sites often cater to manufacturers by liquidating overstocks and close-outs. For the most part, independent dealer sites offer personal service, hands-on support, and premium property at a bargain.

PRODUCT SMART

So there are your options. Now what? Well, do you know exactly what you want? That's a serious question. You don't have to be an expert on the product you want to buy, but you should know enough not to fall for a deal that's *too good to be true*.

First things first: Go to the manufacturer's site and gather specific data on the item you're considering. While you are at it, here are some questions to ponder:

- Why are you buying this item? What's its purpose?
- Do you need a specialized product or will a more generic, economical one do?
- If there are multiple product lines and models to choose from, how do they differ?
- From a component standpoint, why is one model more expensive than another?
- When do you need it? If you can wait, you'll pay less.

And here's a quick to-do list:

- Record the exact model name, number, and suggested price (if available).
- Print out the specifications offered or ones you have selected.
- Record specifics on the item's product warranty. Print out the return policy.
- Shop other manufacturers to compare equivalent models in the product category.

Once you have narrowed your purchase to a few specific models, try to validate your selections. Solicit the opinions of friends, visit local merchants, and read product reviews from trusted trade magazines—print and online. Here are a few online sources of quality product reviews:

Consumer Reports (all consumer categories)—www.consumerreports.org

Good Housekeeping (home, garden, family)—
www.goodhousekeeping.com

CNET (software, computers, electronics, technology)—www.cnet.com

ZDNet (computers, electronics, technology)—www.zdnet.com

Amazon (books, music, software, electronics, tools, housewares)—www.
amazon.com

READY TO SHOP

Okay, you've done your homework and you're ready to buy. Here are eight strategies to get the best combination of price and service for your next purchase.

The less handholding you need, the less expensive your item. If you can wait a bit, many online retailers will give you a significant discount on shipping. Additionally, there's no sales tax on Internet purchases—unless you buy from a dealer, retailer, or manufacturer in your state. If price factors most in your decision, cast the widest possible net to capture the greatest diversity of Web sellers. Remember, some venues and dealers will be better than others, depending on the item you're looking for, particularly if it's rare and collectible. Some ideas include:

- Hit the manufacturer's retail site to see whether it has any discounted models.

  Upside: You'll get a new product direct with a warranty, full customer support, and more. Secure payment and shipping.

  Downside: You might have to make compromises on the product's functionality and components.

- Whether your item is a common consumer product or rare collectible, plug it into a major search engine, such as Google. Find out whether small merchants are selling your item new.

  Upside: You'll access a wide breadth of sellers and listings from small independents, online retailers, and manufacturers.

  Downside: You'll have to wade through a lot of results, some unrelated.

- Price compare at the Web superstores (Amazon.com), branded retail sites (Circuit City), and specialty online retailers. Are they reducing the manufacturer price?

Upside: Superstores offer a very wide product selection. They also usually discount MSRP (manufacturer-suggested retail price) and offer returns and rebates (shipping, multiple-item orders). All offer secure payment and shipping.

Downside: Superstore selection can be vanilla and customer support unsophisticated. Shipping and handling can negate MSRP discount.

- Do more price discovery, using a comparison-shopping engine, such as CNET Shopper, Dealtime, or MySimon, which aggregate listings from large and small resellers. You know the MSRP and retailer price. Now establish the average "street-price" or secondary market price.

Upside: These search sites are more targeted than a regular Internet search engine. They also highlight deals from small independents selling closer to wholesale prices. They find "off-price" items, which are new but discounted.

Downside: Some merchants don't offer warranties, refunds, and customer support. Sites cater most to repeatable consumer commodities, not unique material. Product can be antiquated or seasonal. Also beware of excessive shipping fees.

- Shop discount sites. Verify the average off-price, which might be a refurbished price or overstock, outlet price.

Upside: Sites host branded stores with new merchandise (warranty, refund, support), as well as small merchants that sell new "off-price" goods. Strong product diversity (apparel, business supplies, electronics, computers, housewares, and collectible material). Buyers can play it safe or fast and loose.

Downside: Some merchants don't offer warranties, refunds, and customer support. Sites cater more to "practicals" than dealer-quality collectibles. Products can be antiquated or seasonal.

- Shop the person-to-person auction sites, which also function as small merchant business-to-consumer marketplaces. Research completed auctions for your item to see current market value. Is the lowest price available at auction?

Upside: Intense seller competition means lower prices. Sites offer an incredible variety of new and used products, from rare collectibles to common practical items. They also attract communities of experts and let buyers build one-on-one relationships with quality, specialized dealers. Buyers then can buy with confidence from a dealer's own site.

Downside: Sites are *caveat emptor* (buyer beware). They are more laissez-faire and susceptible to fraud.

- Look for a deal at one of the business-to-consumer auction sites that resell refurbished or overstock products from manufacturers.

  Upside: uBid starts auctions low, and bidding is sometimes light. Can pay with credit card.

  Downside: Selection can be underwhelming because product is closeout, overstock, or refurbished. Warranties range from full to limited to none. Not a destination for rare, one-of-a-kind items.

- Don't forget to search out specialty dealers and marketplaces that cater to the product category in which you're interested, such as Guild.com, Art.net, Musician's Friend, or BookFinder.com.

  Upside: Unique, quality items, both new and secondary-market, are available. Introduces you to a community. Sites offer premium service.

  Downside: Pricing can be less attractive.

Get comfortable with all of these commerce environments and leverage the Web to its fullest potential.

RESEARCH MERCHANTS

If buying from an individual or merchant at an auction site or even one of the discount marketplaces, look at the business's feedback rating. This concept was pioneered by eBay, and all the sellers have a feedback rating. The idea has caught on for other markets. In essence, it allows buyers and sellers to make an assessment of one another before they even perform a transaction, based on a record of comments posted by previous customers.

Here's how it works: Following each transaction, the buyer and seller rate each *other's* performance, positive or negative. These ratings are combined to form an aggregate score or feedback rating. A user's overall rating is then included with each of their listings or any listing in which they participate. This enables buyers and sellers to review each other's reputation and evaluate whether they should do business together. If the seller has more than 1% or 2% negative feedback, the buyer probably shouldn't bid. Likewise, if the buyer has negative comments that indicate he or she is a deadbeat bidder (nonpaying bidder), the seller might consider refusing the bid. Feedback can also be a valuable form of advertising, strengthening a seller's overall business and brand. Best of all, feedback systems enable marketplaces to be self-regulating.

The downside is that the system can be manipulated. There's feedback padding, for example, in which a user artificially inflates his or her rating with phony transactions. To avoid getting fooled, review how long a seller has been on the site before bidding. If their high feedback rating seems to have been generated overnight and looks inconsistent with their average sales volume, it should give you some pause.

There's also feedback bombing, where a rival user might unfairly rate other users to sully their reputations deliberately. Most legitimate sites have transaction-based feedback systems to eliminate these sorts of abuses. (In general, avoid sites that don't have transaction-based feedback.)

If the feedback looks good overall (a few negatives is pretty routine), scan the seller's listing to see whether they include a business address and phone number. Many sellers include this information in their listings and "About Me" pages to increase credibility and prove they are bona fide businesses. (They also want to promote their businesses and Web sites.) If they supply phone numbers, give them a call to see how customer-friendly they are.

Professional Product Listing

The product listing also should have professional photos. (Some auction sellers employ full-time professional photographers.) Generally, avoid listings that don't have photos. In addition, beware of listings with incomplete photos that omit portions of the item. Damage might be in that area. Also, don't settle for manufacturer marketing shots. This is especially true if buying secondhand business equipment. You want to see the real thing.

Finally, watch out for listings in which the images outclass the description. The image might be stolen from another listing. Believe it or not, it happens. Take eBay seller 1gallery. The company sold a genuine Dragonfly Tiffany lamp for $50,000 on eBay, only to have another crooked seller lift the image, apply it to a phony listing, and burn an unsuspecting buyer for thousands. Fortunately, the crook was caught, but it took some real time and effort, according to 1gallery.

Things to consider:

- Does the listing include a detailed condition report?
- Does it feature technical specifications if it is a computer or consumer electronic?
- Is the product description clear, complete, and free of spelling errors?
- Does the description inform/educate?
- Are the description and title consistent? If the title says "Good," expect imperfections to be described.

AVOID FRAUD

Unfortunately, honest merchants and dealers aren't the only people who view the Web as a golden opportunity. So do the crooks. With that in mind, here are some scams to be aware of so that you don't get taken. It is better to avoid fraud than to try and take effective action after the fact.

Nondelivery

This is arguably one of the most common online frauds, particularly at person-to-person marketplaces. Because it is customary for buyers to pay for their items before they are shipped, there's always a chance the seller could take your money and disappear.

Take the strange case of a Latvian seller reported by MSNBC in 2000. This crook would list electronics for sale on eBay that he didn't have. He'd arrange to purchase the products they'd bid on by registering the eBay high bidder on an online retailer's site (usually Onsale.com) using stolen European credit cards with, obviously, the stolen cardholders name, but the winning eBay bidder's shipping information. The retailer would send the eBay winners the merchandise. The unsuspecting eBay customers would now be mixed up in credit card fraud. Meanwhile, the Latvian crook was essential transparent in the deal, and had the eBay bidders money.

SOLUTION

If available, review feedback. Buy from merchants that publish their addresses and phone numbers in their listings. Buy from businesses that offer returns and refunds. Pay with a credit card so you can perform a charge-back if necessary.

Fakes

The sports memorabilia industry has had serious problems with fakes. You buy something you think is rare and authentic, and in fact, it's just common junk. The classic example on eBay: user *golfpoorly's* phony Diebenkorn, listed in 2000. Titled "Great big wild abstract painting," it sold for $135,805 to a Dutch buyer. The crooked seller, an attorney, eventually was nailed for it.

SOLUTION

This sort of scam follows the trends. Remember Beanie Babies (ugh, who can forget)? Fakes were rampant as crooks tried to cash in on the phenomenon. If you are a serious collector, develop relationships with a group of serious dealers.

Not as Advertised

Here's another old standard. The item was described as "New" or "Mint," but it arrives with a number of imperfections and doesn't work.

SOLUTION

Don't buy poorly photographed items where pieces of the item are not shown. If the actual item isn't photographed, avoid it. If you're buying an expensive item, look for local dealers so you can pick it up. Also, always closely review seller's feedback and return policies.

Excessive Shipping and Handling

Sellers may charge you for a specific mail product, then not deliver it that way. They send it a cheaper way and pocket the cash.

SOLUTION

If at auction, give them neutral or negative feedback. Research the cost of shipping your item before buying. Closely read potential sellers' policies. If S&H is not stipulated, email them and ask. If they don't respond, skip the auction.

One qualification: Don't avoid auctions with high shipping charges out of principle. Consider the total price and whether the item is still a good value.

Dubious Discount

Here's a newer form of questionable seller behavior. A budget merchant promises a steep discount on a new, popular item. The fine print, though, requires you to buy expensive accessories to obtain the discount.

SOLUTION

Don't jump at the first good deal you see. Compare prices and service at a number of venues.

Follow the above steps and guidelines, and you'll avoid questionable deals and unscrupulous sellers. Best of all, you'll significantly reduce the costs of items you need for your family, home, and business.

SELLING ON THE INTERNET

Now it's time to talk about *your* online business and maximizing its profits.

Put simply, the Web presents an opportunity no business should pass up. It allows businesses of any size to market their products inexpensively to a global audience and sell goods and services 24 hours a day. However, this wasn't always the case. Early on, businesses used the Web to advertise their products but did not perform secure online transactions because the technology wasn't available. Fortunately, times have changed. An array of professional marketplaces, online payment services, and commerce management services have made the Web more commerce-friendly today than at any time in its short history.

With that in mind, we'll show you how to establish a business presence online in five easy steps; then we'll provide some additional ideas for the more advanced sellers. We'll explain how to:

- Determine what products to sell and where to source inventory.
- Leverage multiple online sales channels and pricing models.
- Merchandise your products and build your brand effectively.
- Manage customer communication, payment, and shipping.
- Report your auction income.

One final word of introduction: Though many of our tips may be useful for large businesses, this guide is most applicable for modestly sized operations looking to increase their customer base and profits. If you're Wal-Mart, you build Walmart.com. If you don't have millions to spend on advertising, here's the surest route to sales success on the Web.

THE BASICS: HITTING THE GROUND RUNNING

Getting started selling online is easier than you may think. All you need is some stuff to sell. You also need a place to store it and a place to sell it. It's also a good idea to have tools to manage the day-to-day details.

Selling online can be a great deal of fun and, for the right person or business, a highly profitable endeavor.

Select Your Inventory

If you currently operate an established business, you already have an idea of what products you will be selling online. However, for those merchants just starting their businesses, here are some helpful suggestions.

There are several classes of inventory you can specialize in. Depending on your background and personal experience, you may find yourself more inclined toward one type or another. Many sellers start by selling items related to a hobby or existing business.

Sell New

Selling new means offering first-run consumer products that are competitively priced and acquired from wholesalers and manufacturers.

Upside: Sellers who plan to sell in volume can profit by selling consumer products. The key with these goods is to maximize your inventory turns, because margins are typically pretty slim.

Downside: There are many alternative places to purchase consumer products on the Web, especially among well-established online brands, such as Amazon.com.

TIP

Acquire brand names as much as possible. Carry accessories or families of products useful for *up-selling* merchandise at the point of purchase.

Deal in "Off-Price" Consumer Goods

These are goods sold at a discount, enabling you to outprice other vendors and sell in volume. Generally, off-price items are overstock, acquired inexpensively from manufacturers, wholesalers, local liquidation sales, and liquidators.

Upside: You can sometimes get these goods at a deep discount when bought in bulk. For the right person, this can be a highly lucrative business if you happen to have a good sense of the market.

Downside: Off-price goods usually come in bulk, so you'll need storage space and the money to purchase these goods. Beware of buying goods that are out of season or favor—they'll be tough to sell.

TIP

If buying direct from a manufacturer or at wholesale from a middleman, you must have a business license, tax ID, upfront funds, and good credit. A shipping and receiving bay is also a must because these goods typically arrive on pallets.

Sell Used

Selling used involves the secondary market goods that are unique, rare, and collectible, acquired from dealers at shows and markets, physical auctions, estate and library sales, liquidations, and more.

Upside: You can sell fewer of these items at a higher profit margin if you know the market. Successful sellers become category experts and attract repeat buyers.

Downside: It takes time to become an expert in a particular category and to build an online reputation.

You may want to experiment and sell both new and used products. Don't be afraid to make a few mistakes in order to find the right product mix for your business.

CHOOSE YOUR SALES CHANNEL STRATEGY

The Web is unique in that it offers you multiple ways and multiple locations to sell your products. You can use this to your advantage if you understand the benefits of the different online sales formats and channels available to you.

Online Store Sites

Run an independent storefront within the context of a large marketplace, which attracts a critical mass of buyers shopping for both practical consumer goods and collectibles. Sell at a fixed price in volume.

Auction Marketplaces

Inexpensively market and sell your products to a worldwide audience in auction and/or fixed-price formats. Sell practical goods or collectible items. Enable competitive bidding on your items and achieve the truest market price. Acquire new customers and guide them to your business Web site, where the cost of business is lower.

Fixed-Price Discount Sites

Access critical masses of discount shoppers, looking for off-price merchandise. These venues are perfect for volume sellers of repeatable commodities, such as CDs, DVDs, and books.

Successful sellers tend to use a combination of all three types of sites as channels for selling goods, as well as the means to acquire customers. But don't feel as though you have to rush into all three. There is a real benefit to a more measured approach.

ESTABLISH YOURSELF ON eBAY

An easy entry is with the online market, such as eBay. This has real benefits. It's wise to gain some experience selling online prior to launching your own business site. Better to make mistakes on eBay than to damage the reputation of your own site (which will cost more money and time to build). A few sales on eBay will quickly reveal what online buyers expect and how they are different from your existing offline customers. For example:

- How detailed your online customers expect items to be described/graded
- How fast they expect to be contacted after a purchase
- How they prefer to pay for their items
- How fast they expect their merchandise to arrive
- How your product pages, sales policies, and promotions are received
- How to communicate via email effectively

Funnel Customers to Your Store

Once you are up and running on eBay and other marketplaces, start developing your own branded Web site. Remember, you want to use marketplaces, such as eBay, Half.com, Amazon Marketplace, and Yahoo! Shopping to develop awareness for your *own* Web site and drive customers there—where the cost of selling an item is less, and you can also merchandise or up-sell other products and accessories.

Your goal should be to use your site and other viable marketplaces in tandem. These secondary channels generate significant exposure for your overall business and brand, and increase your sales volume. The good news is that building a simple Web site with some basic commerce functionality is simple.

If you want something more robust, solicit Web developers and system architects in your area. These IT professionals should be versed in XML (Extensible Markup Language), which enables your Web site's back-end systems to interface with other marketplaces' databases. Using this protocol, developers can program a "crawl" that collects data related to your transactions from the site. This is particularly useful for automating fulfillment. For example, it enables you to email buyers transaction information automatically at the end of an auction.

KEYS TO PRICING PRODUCTS ONLINE

There are several different ways to price your products online. However, it does tend to be fixed price versus auction.

Fixed Price

A fixed price expedites transactions and increases overall sales volume, especially if coupled with online payments. Customers don't have to bid and wait or haggle over a price. The price they see is the price of the item.

> Upside: Fixed price is useful for common items that have an established market price, particularly product accessories and add-ons sold in volume. It also proves quite effective during the holiday season and other periods of intense buying, when shoppers do not want to wait for an auction to end.
>
> Downside: You do not know exactly when you will sell your products, as with an auction, which ends on a specific date and time.

Auction

An auction is a process where multiple buyers bid on your item, effectively establishing a market price. Successful auctions often attract multiple buyers, driving the price higher than normal market value.

> Upside: Enables competitive bidding for high-demand items. Auctions let the market determine fair-market price. Because buyers find auctions to be a fun or novel way of shopping online, prices can easily get inflated during the "chase."
>
> Downside: Not as effective for generic items that need to be sold quickly in volume. Large amounts of identical products offered at auction at the same time can result in very low realized sales prices.

There are several types of auctions.

Reserve Auction

The reserve auction allows competitive bidding with a reserve price that prevents a sale below your acceptable price. You may want to list your item for $1 to generate initial buzz and bidding but not sell the item unless the price rises above $50. It protects you from selling your product at a loss. Unfortunately, some buyers don't bid on reserve auctions because they lose the thrill of the potential bargain.

Dutch Auction

A Dutch auction is selling the same item to multiple buyers. It allows you to sell the same item—in quantity—and still benefit from competitive bidding as supply diminishes. You may list 10 identical items in a single listing. In this scenario, each winning bidder pays the price of the lowest winning bidder. Dutch auctions confuse neophyte buyers, and they may lower the overall return from listing the items separately.

Auction with Fixed-Price Option

The fixed-price option allows competitive bidding. It also allows the first bidder to have the option to purchase at a fixed price. (On eBay, this feature is called "Buy it Now.") It allows a buyer to purchase an item for an offered fixed price before bidding starts. The seller may list an item with a $1 minimum bid and a $20 buy it now price. Any potential buyer may purchase the item before any other bids have been placed for $20. Once a single bid has been placed, the buy it now offer is no longer in effect, and the item will be sold at the highest auction bid.

Successful sellers use auctions to help determine the fair market value of their goods. Once they understand the average selling price for a particular item, they can confidently list it at a fixed price in their stores. Thus, by using a combination of auctions and fixed price environments, sellers can quickly maximize their sales efforts.

MERCHANDISE YOUR PRODUCTS EFFECTIVELY

Just getting your product online isn't enough. You've also got to tell a compelling story and convince buyers that they should purchase your product. That means writing comprehensive, detailed descriptions of your products and displaying high-quality images to help your items sell. Good merchandising will help your buyers feel comfortable buying from you and not from your competition. Good merchandising includes taking quality photos and other sales enhancements.

Take Quality Photos

Invest in quality images of your products. Consider buying a good digital camera or even hiring professional commercial photographers to shoot your items. Many eBay sellers are starting to do this. The better your products look, the more they'll bring.

Use Specialized Sales Templates

A consistent, professional-looking template is best for all your listings. Avoid a lot of cute items, such as music, moving bears, and other distracting elements.

Include Merchandising Elements

Add unique elements, such as bulleted lists, fact boxes, grading charts, and photo details to your listings to distinguish them from the competition.

Also, call out your special services and incentives, particularly ones not offered by competing sellers. If you waive shipping on purchases of three or more items, create a graphic for this offer and put it in all of your listings and customer emails. If you have a toll-free help line, do this as well. These little marquees will make a real difference to buyers on the fence.

Create Professional Policies

Develop standardized *policies* that relate to each facet of your business so that your customers are well informed and regard you professionally. Your policies should cover:

- Payment (advertise what forms of payment you accept)
- Shipping (describe your carriers, mail products, and shipping schedule)
- Handling (clearly explain your combined S&H charge)
- Insurance (advertise whether you offer it; some buyers won't bid or buy if you don't)
- Refunds and returns (they increase customer confidence and bids)

Put some real thought into your policies. A well-articulated policy also will prevent needless email from customers, which can really bog down your business. Don't wait for buyers to be disappointed—*manage* their expectations before and after each purchase.

Completing the Transaction (Handling Invoicing, Payment, and Shipping)

After the sale is complete, you will need to communicate with your buyer to arrange payment and shipping. This can often take several emails to coordinate how your buyer is going to pay and what your buyer's shipping address. If buyers don't pay on time, you may to need to send several reminders.

VENDIO

Vendio is a commerce management company that provides sophisticated yet economical software to automate your Web listings, management, and fulfillment of your items, including postsale email communication between buyer and seller. Vendio will automatically send out an invoice (winning bidder notification) on your behalf to your buyer, requesting your buyer's payment preferences and shipping address. The service can notify you when your buyer has paid so you can ship the item and allows you to print a packing label and invoice automatically to be sent with your item. If your buyer doesn't respond, Vendio can also automatically send reminder notices to your buyer. They offer Web tools to automate and streamline all your online sales efforts, as well as many other services. There are many services that Vendio can offer you if you are contemplating a Web-based sales service.

For more information, go to www.vendio.com.

PAYMENTS

Have clear payment policies but offer your buyers as many payment options as possible. State clearly that you do not ship until checks clear. Require certified methods of payment for big-ticket items. Here's a review of the different payment methods available, traditional and online, with the ups and downs of each.

Personal Check

Upside: One of the most popular and easiest methods for buyers.
Downside: Checks delay shipping because the seller should wait for each check to clear before shipping.

Certified Payment

Upside: Payment is secure because it is drawn on a bank or the U.S. Postal Service (USPS). Seller can ship upon receipt of payment, expediting fulfillment.

Downside: More burdensome, expensive for buyer, who has to purchase the cashier's check/money order at a bank/post office, plus pay a fee. This also applies for "collect on delivery" from the USPS.

Online Payment

Payment processors such as PayPal that enable the routing of funds via email from a buyer's bank to the seller are becoming quite popular.

Upside: They're fast, simple to use, and reliable for both buyer and seller. Also, they enable individuals to process credit cards without obtaining a merchant account, which has restrictive requirements.

Downside: Third-party fees for sellers can add up.

Merchant Account

The seller is in control, processing credit cards via a physical terminal or a virtual one through the seller's Web site.

Upside: Individual transaction fees are lower, 2–3% as opposed to 5% and higher. Also, the seller gets paid faster, as quickly as 48 hours. Online payment processors often pay in bulk on set days of the month.

Downside: You will probably need a "fictitious business name" and business license to get a merchant account from the bank. To accept Visa and MasterCard drafts directly, you may also be subjected to a rigorous credit check because, in essence, the bank is really providing a line of credit. There are also setup and monthly fees. (A cheaper option is an online payment processor, such as PayPal.)

NONPAYMENTS

Unfortunately, buyer misconduct is a reality that all online sellers should be prepared for. Here are some strategies to address nonpayment (via bounced check or stopped payment).

Resubmit Check

Some people make honest mistakes. Before calling the cavalry, resubmit bounced checks. The check might clear. If it does, email the buyer for your extra fees.

Request Certified Payment

After three unsuccessful attempts to process the check, request payment for the original item and the bounced check fees by money order. Also send a copy of the bounced check to the buyer by certified mail so that you have proof that he or she received it.

Make Intentions Clear

If you have been defrauded on an item of significant value, send a letter by certified mail to the buyer. Explain that you intend to file a mail fraud complaint with the U.S. Postal Inspection Service if payment isn't made by a set date. In addition, tell the buyer you are going to file a complaint with your local police department, as well as hire a collection agency.

U.S. Postal Inspection Service: http://www.usps.gov/ncsc/locators/find-is.html

Prosecute

If the buyer doesn't respond, petition your local police and district attorney to prosecute under the "theft by check" statute. Also consider filing a civil lawsuit against the buyer with your local court.

FORMAL COMPLAINT

To spread the word about this crook, file complaints:

- Federal Trade Commission—www.ftc.gov/
- National Consumer Complaint Center—www.alexanderlaw.com/nccc/cb-ftc.html
- National Fraud Information Center—www.fraud.org/

These organizations investigate and prosecute debtors.

REFUNDS

If the transaction was on an auction site, request a refund of your final value fees. Also report the buyer so that he or she is warned, watched by the site, and hopefully banned. Prepare for the following buyer scams, as well.

Bid Shielding

An unscrupulous buyer places multiple bids at an auction to discourage other buyers from bidding, then cancels the bids in the waning minutes of an auction, lowering the price of the item at the last minute. An accomplice bids immediately and wins the item at a significantly reduced price. Avoid this by placing reasonable reserves on your items.

Buy and Switch

Buyers receive your item, then switch it with a fake or defective version and send it back for a refund. If successful, they receive the real item and a refund. To avoid this, keep digital photos of your items. Also put stickers and tags on your items that void returns when removed. Finally, package items carefully so unscrupulous buyers can't easily claim they were damaged during shipment.

SHIPPING YOUR PRODUCTS

Your task is to find the most convenient, secure, and economical way to package and ship your products, using a major postal/parcel service or freight company. Keep these goals in mind:

- Reduce the operational expense of shipping and handling.
- Prevent damage to your items and ensure positive customer feedback.
- Keep shipping and handling prices consistent and controlled so you can pass savings on to your customers and be more competitive in the market.

If you sell large items, consider a freight company, of which there are many. Also set up business accounts with your carriers so that you can pay on a monthly basis and negotiate more favorable rates, particularly for pickup. Here are the major carriers you'll want to research:

United States Postal Service—www.usps.com
United Parcel Service (UPS)—www.ups.com
Federal Express, overnight and ground (FedEx)—www.fedex.com

Finally, in advance of listing your items, acquire the packing supplies you'll need. They should be specific to the products you sell. Always have them on hand so you can ship the day that payment clears. Develop a standardized packing process that protects your items and impresses your customers. A sloppy, slow shipping department will kill your business.

REPORTING AUCTION INCOME

Auction income is like any other income. Although we recommend you seek the advice of a professional accountant, here are some general guidelines to consider.

Capital Gains

The IRS taxes an individual's gain on any capital asset that was sold for more than it was purchased. This can apply to any piece of property, from a share of stock to a classic car to a piece of fine art. If you are not in the trade or business but sell an item for more than it was purchased, technically the profit should be reported as a capital gain on Schedule D, Capital Gains and Losses (http://www.irs.gov/forms_pubs/index.html) with Form 1040. Realistically, most personal, nonmerchant auction transactions do not apply. Because of depreciation, personal merchandise usually sells for less than it was originally purchased. In this case, a seller has no tax liability or reporting responsibility.

File it Away

Though laborious, it's a good idea to keep file copies of all your auction transactions, as well as all receipts related to your sales, including postage, insurance, and packing materials. Finally, track all of your auction site charges, such as listing and final value fees. With this information, you will be able to itemize your expenses and make legitimate deductions.

Estimated Payments

Sole proprietors of businesses are required to file taxes quarterly (four times a year) as opposed to just once on April 15. If you claim more than $2,500 in business expenses, consider reporting as a business on Schedule C, Profit (or Loss) from Business or Profession, with your Form 1040 (http://www.irs.gov/forms_pubs/index.html). With each filing, you must include an estimated tax payment, calculated as a quarter of what you believe your total tax liability will be for the year. The filing dates are April 15, June 15, and September 15. A final return is then required on January 18 of the following year. Calculate your estimated taxable income by deducting your auction expenses from your gross sales profit.

Social Security

As a self-employed businessperson who files quarterly returns, no one withholds tax from your paycheck. This, however, does not mean you are exempt from making contributions to Social Security. Typically, this contribution is called *self-employment tax*. Applied as a fixed percentage, it must be computed at the end of the year and added to your year-end taxable income on your Form 1040.

State Sales Tax

Thanks to 1998's Internet Freedom Act, sellers are not required to collect sales tax for online transactions made with buyers *outside* their states. Sellers are required to collect sales tax on transactions made with buyers in their states of business.

DEDUCTIONS

 Ask your accountant for a checklist of standard business expenses.

ADVANCED STEPS: MAXIMIZING YOUR ONLINE PROFITS

Your Web site is up and running, and you're leveraging secondary sales channels, such as eBay. Sales are good, but you want to turn your online business up another notch. To succeed, you'll need to expand your activities and focus.

Direct Marketing

Once you capture a customer, don't let go. To encourage repeat business, collect customer data and market additional products and services to your buyers. Done correctly, you'll develop a loyal customer base.

Sales Announcements

Leverage your customer list and notify buyers when you have new goods for sale. You can easily point them to an auction listing or to your store. Remember, the more repeat buyers that transact through your store, the less in listing fees you have to pay to marketplaces.

Store Promotion

Market your online store or company Web site at the marketplaces you use. This will encourage buyers to visit your other sites and purchase items there, where your costs are lower and you have the opportunity to sell customers other items and promote your brand.

Checkout Up-Sell

Leverage merchandising services to up-sell appropriate products and accessories to customers at the point of purchase. Examples are flash cards with a digital camera or jewelry with women's clothing. Up-selling to prequalified customers can dramatically increase your revenue.

Postsale Offers

Include special offers and product rebates in your postsale emails.

Customer Management Service

Use a third-party direct-marketing service to collect customer information, build customer profiles, and email targeted promotions and rebates to your prequalified buyers.

Build Your Reputation

To generate real returns online, you'll need to develop a reputation online, one that engenders confidence in your current and prospective customers.

Online, your reputation is a function of your business's brand and your marketplace customer feedback.

Brand Loyalty

Every business, no matter how small, has to develop its own identity, or *brand*. Brand is an awareness of what sets you apart from the competition. With brand loyalty comes increased sales, higher prices, and repeat business. Here's how to develop it.

- Name Recognition

  Good branding begins with a good name. Don't be obscure, using bizarre emails as your business name. Relate your name to your expertise and category. When people think about good deals on PC parts, antique furniture, or baseball memorabilia, you want them to think of you. Also, be consistent with your name. Your third-party user names should match your company name.

- Specialize

  Establish and expand your brand in one category before moving into others. Service niches in your main category, such as swing jazz, '60s rock, and Americana in the music category. Demonstrate a broad expertise in one category, and you'll earn credibility with buyers. If you want to move into a new category, select a complementary one, such as movies and music.

- Branded Titles

  On eBay and other marketplaces crowded with competing listings, your items' titles really matter—not just what they say but also how they are formatted. Develop your own title style that brands your listings and separates them from competing listings at a glance.

TIP

 Include popular search keywords in your titles. Your listings will appear more often in buyer searches. For example, if you sell prints, include the name of the artist, work, and school.

Here's an eBay example: MARILYN MONROE ART PRINT (GREENE)

- Company Logo

  Develop a company logo and motto with the help of a graphic artist, if necessary. Include it in all of your listings and customer emails, as well as on your packing slips, boxes, and business cards.

Postsale Functionality and Automation

Many businesses underestimate the amount of time it takes to list items, process orders, and communicate with customers once the sale takes place. Managing an online business is a very time-consuming process—many sellers hit a point where there just aren't enough hours in the day.

Without some sort of automation, your revenue growth can stall. Right from the start, it is critical to automate your online operation's business activities, from listing your items to performing your postsale duties.

Automation is essential for any serious vendor intending to sell in volume at his or her online store or one of the significant online marketplaces.

SUMMARY

Because the Internet provides entrepreneurs and small businesses with unlimited access to customers and low barriers to entry, online selling has become a mainstream activity. We're entering an age where just about everyone has something to sell and now the means to sell it. For the occasional seller, eBay is a global flea market where literally one person's trash can become another person's treasure.

There is a new breed of small businesses emerging today. They exist solely because of the Internet and most likely have few physical assets—a computer, a digital camera, and perhaps some physical storage space. Yet they compete for buyer dollars with some of the biggest brands in the world—often from the comfort of a den or study. They live and die based on their online reputations. As an aggregated group, they generate billions of dollars in online sales each year.

7

MEETING PEOPLE: THE PERSONAL SIDE OF THE INTERNET

The Internet is the modern-day Tower of Babel. People from all over the world regularly communicate with people of all ages, sexes, walks of life, and from different ends of the globe. People *meet* in chatrooms. They communicate in forums. They place and answer classified ads. These are just a few of the opportunities to connect with other people.

CHATROOMS

On the Internet, you can talk to other people who are also online by using your keyboard and any number of services (with specific software). This "chatting" is through an exchange of typed messages to a central site to be read and commented on by others. Anyone, anywhere on the Internet can take part in these conversations. Most of these conversations focus on a particular topic. You can also "listen" to a lecture from an expert or interact with a famous person (such as a movie star or super model) in a cyber convention hall. Distance learning uses chat to create an online classroom experience and to allow students to interact with each other and with the instructor.

A Web site chatroom is a place for online communities of users with common interests to communicate. Forums and discussion groups, by comparison, are more like bulletin boards (as they were called some years back) where people post messages for others to read and reply by posting subsequent comments. Many chatrooms need special software. You need an account on AOL, Yahoo!, or MSN to join the main chats, and other systems, such as the IRC (Internet Relay Chat), require you download some simple software to use it.

"On the Internet, nobody knows you're a dog."

FIGURE 7.1 **THIS WAS PROBABLY THE FIRST POIGNANT CARTOON TO APPEAR IN THE *NEW YORKER* ABOUT THE INTERNET.**

With Web-based chatrooms, you simply go to a Web site, register, and choose a name (screen name, or nickname) and password. Then you go to a room of your choice. To talk to the other users (chat), you type a message into a text box. The message is posted immediately into a larger window and viewed by all in the room. Other users respond (Figures 7.2 and 7.3).

Internet chat is, for some, a very enjoyable diversion. It is a way to meet people from all over the world without leaving your house. A chatroom is part of an online service (such as America Online) or a Web site where people can communicate in a group setting. In an online simulated or virtual reality game, people use avatars (personal representation/game pieces) that can move around and interact with others.

Chatrooms usually limit the number of people for sanity's sake. Too many and it is hard to follow the conversations (unless you are a speed reader). Too few and often the conversation lags without much said, like a bad cocktail party. On IRC, there can be some mega rooms with hundreds of people. These are meeting places. People who've previously met agree to "meet" in a mega room; then they can go off into individual conversations.

In a chatroom, there can be many conversations concurrently. At first, this can seem confusing, but after a while, you learn to follow a specific message thread. A *thread* is a single conversation. It's a subject, followed by a series of replies to the original statement or question. The term originally came about from a forum or a discussion group. With those, you'd have to

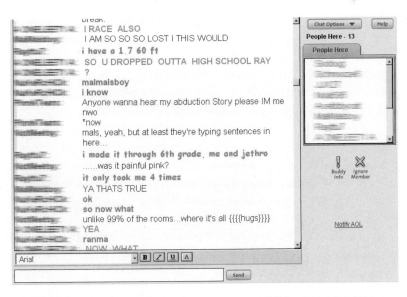

FIGURE 7.2 THIS IS AN EXAMPLE OF AN AOL CHATROOM.

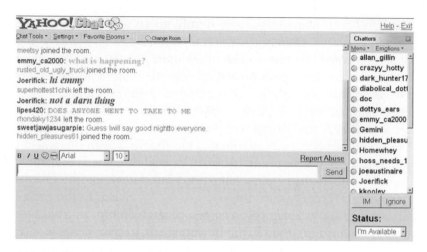

follow the "thread" of the conversation from beginning to end (or often, from the most recent back to the original post).

For that reason, most chatrooms are specific to a community of users (e.g., hobbies, interests, locations, dating, religion, politics, sports, travel, etc.). In comparison, forums and discussion groups don't have interactive messaging.

Typically, a chat has a screen with postings identified by the online handle (also known as a *screen name* or *nickname*) with automated updates of who has entered a room and left a room. To talk, users type messages into a text box, hit <Enter>, and the message is posted on the chatroom screen. The message is usually immediately visible for other users to respond. It's not a requirement to participate. When people sit and simply read the posts without commenting, they are known as *lurkers*.

TEXT TALK

Dr. John Suler is a professor of psychology at Rider University. He offers a unique perspective on what he calls *TextTalk* (see "Psychological Dynamics of Online Synchronous Conversations in Text-Driven Chat Environments," *Psychology of Cyberspace*, October 1997). He has an online book on the psychology of cyberspace at www.rider.edu/~suler/psycyber/psycyber.html. It is highly recommended if you want a fresh, entertaining perspective on the culture of the Net.

In his article, he describes his view and insight of chat:

TextTalk in online chat environments has evolved into a fascinating style of communication. In some ways, it is strikingly similar to face-to-face (ftf) dialogue. In other ways, it is quite unique. Many of its unique qualities revolve around the fact that it is an austere mode of communication. There are no changes in voice, no facial expressions, no body language, no (or very little) visual/spatial environment as a context of meaning. There's just typed words. Some people find that experience too sparse. They feel disoriented, disembodied, adrift in that screen of silently scrolling dialogue. Other people love the minimalist style of TextTalk. They love to see how people creatively express themselves despite the limitations. They love to immerse themselves in the quiet flow of words that feels like a more direct, intimate connection between one's mind and the minds of others. Almost as if the other is inside one's head. Almost as if you are talking with a part of yourself. Without the distracting sights and sounds of the ftf world, TextTalk feels like a more pure communication of ideas and experiences. For some users (like many interested in cybersex), the bare quality of typed text allows for a greater flight of imagination and fantasy.

Chat room banter can seem quite chaotic, especially when there are many people talking, or you have just entered a room and immediately dive into the ongoing flow of overlapping conversations. There are no visual cues indicating what pairs or groups of people are huddled together in conversation, so the lines of scrolling dialogue seem disjointed. You have to sit back and follow the flow of the text to decipher the themes of conversation and who is talking with whom. In almost all types of chat environments, you consciously and unconsciously set up mental filters and points of focus that help you screen out "noise" and zoom in your concentration on particular people or topics of discussion. Often, you become immersed in one or two strings of dialogue and filter out the others. With experience, you develop an eye for efficiently reading TextTalk. Some people may be better at this specific cognitive-perceptual task than others.

Dr. Suler's article can be accessed at http://www.rider.edu/~suler/psycyber/texttalk.html.

Lurking

It's not as bad as the name suggests. Unlike a cocktail party where lurkers tend to pace in the shadows, online lurkers aren't social misfits. It's just a name for people who sit back and observe the conversations going on. Lurking is a good way to assess the chatroom before you decide to join the conversation. In many cases, it's considered less rude to sit back before joining in the discussion, anyway. Not all chatrooms are the same. As strange as it might sound to someone who has never been in a chatroom, there are rules of behavior, emotional outbursts (complete with shouting), joking, light-hearted chatter, small talk, and serious discussions. Collections of people communicating do have moods. The truth is that some rooms are friendly when you enter them; others are outright hostile. Without sitting back for a moment, you'll never know if a serious debate is going on or whether it's a room full of boorish jerks.

BOTS

Short for roBOT, this is a collection of scripted commands running in a program that appears to be a regular user (it has screen name and appears to engage in conversation) but cannot respond or react outside of its prewritten script. As a very general example, the bot will say, "Hello, how are you." And you respond, "The weather is nice." It will reply, "I am well, thank you for asking." Chatrooms are full of these, usually trying to get you to go to their Web sites or to call expensive 900 numbers for dubious reasons.

Etiquette, Netiquette

The term *netiquette* is used to describe how to act in all forms of online communication: emails, forums, and chat. The rules for chatting came about through trial and error. Online groups are fundamentally a society. When people gather, in all cultures and historically, they have created rules of conduct to keep things civil.

The basic rules:

- Don't type in all CAPS (it's interpreted as yelling)
- Don't flame or bait (flaming means derogatory comments, cursing, etc.)
- No scrolling or flooding (typing the same thing, usually nonsense, over and over)
- Be polite (probably the most important thing to remember)

Follow the normal social rules and common sense in a chatroom. Few people would burst into a party—yelling, shouting, babbling inane things, and shouting obscenities—and expect to be accepted by the crowd. It's the same in a chatroom. It's best to enter, see what's going on, then add to the conversation.

Tone of Voice

Text is text. It is without body language, facial expression, or vocal tone inflection that can convey a feeling or an attitude. In the beginning, it was easy to write something and have everyone take it the wrong way and offend without intention. Humor was all but impossible. The answer to this was the *emoticon* and the acronym.

Emoticons

Emoticons (emotional icons) are ways to compensate for the missing information of text. To view the "faces" that the basic American/European emoticons represent, rotate your head 90 degrees counter-clockwise.

:)—happiness, sarcasm, or jesting

: (—unhappy

;)—winking

: o—surprise

: O—shock, surprise

: D—big grin

 There are lots of emoticons to be found online. For the most part, people use a basic few. :)

www.mueller-godschalk.com/emoticon.html

www.chatlist.com/faces.html

www.computeruser.com/resources/dictionary/emoticons.html

www.worldstart.com/guides/emoticon.htm

Acronyms

Acronyms came about because common phrases in conversation take time to type out. It's a shortcut of sorts to be able to say more with fewer keystrokes. At first, it seems like some code people are talking in, until you get the hang of it. One of the most popular is LOL, for "laughing out loud." It's so much easier than typing out "hahahahaha" or "I am laughing." Although it's used much too much and often right after someone has said something that could be taken as insulting, the LOL is to let you know that they're trying to joke or be sarcastic.

A/S/L—age/sex/location (a basic query to find out who's in the room with you)

AAMOF—as a matter of fact

BBFN—bye bye for now

BBIAF—be back in a flash
BRB—be right back
BBL—be back later
BTW—by the way
EOL—end of lecture
FAQ—frequently asked question
FITB—fill in the blank
FYI—for your information
HTH—hope this helps
IMO—in my opinion
IMHO—in my humble opinion
IMNSHO—in my not-so-humble opinion
IOW—in other words
LOL—laughing out loud
NP—no problem
OIC—oh, I see
OTOH—on the other hand
ROFL—rolling on the floor laughing
ROFLSUML—rolling on the floor laughing spitting up my lunch
RSN—real soon now
TIA—thanks in advance
TIC—tongue in cheek
TTFN—ta ta for now
TTYL—talk to you later
TY—thank you (or the Aussie version, TA)
TYVM—thank you very much
WB—welcome back
WTF—what the frick?

Chat Shorthand

Let's face it, typing to talk can get tiring. People have found ways to shorten words, especially those that are difficult to spell. The most popular of these is *prolly*, meaning *probably*. Of course, there is always the shorthand of emotions. These are usually enclosed in angle brackets.

<G>—grinning
<J>—joking
<L>—laughing
<S>—smiling
<Y>—yawning

Another common chatroom sign is actually a description of a physical action. These include: poking, hugging, kissing, tapping foot, etc. They are usually [bracketed] or {braced}, or several sets of colons may be used.

::poke:: {{{{poke}}}} [poke]
::hug::: {{{hug}}}} [hug]
::tapping foot:: {{{{tapping foot}}}} [tapping foot]

These get really old, very fast, so use them sparingly. If you use them too often, everyone will assume that you are a prepubescent girl without a very large vocabulary.

Haxor or h4x0r

Definitions of this vary, but if you are online, you will undoubtedly come across words with peculiar, almost unreadable spellings. These often include numbers and keyboard symbols, as well as letters. There may be random uppercase mixed with lowercase, creating what looks like the stereotypical ransom note. It's very popular among the younger users, and it takes a little time to adjust your eyes (brain?) to read it.

Probably the original use was as a code (like the pig Latin in WWII POW camps and grammar school) to avoid having certain words detected by someone monitoring a conversation, such as a system administrator or chatroom moderator. It's generally referred to as *Haxor*, depending on who is defining it and in what context.

Haxor is the kiddie script word for *hacker* or *to hack*. (Kiddie script, or script kiddie is a would-be hacker who doesn't have the technical skills or knowledge needed for traditional hacking methods. In other words, usually kids.) When used in a sentence (or fraction thereof) it means to win, to conquer. It is often spelled *h4x0r*. It's slang. The most common word that often accompanies haxor is the other slang word *elite*, spelled *leet, 1337*, or *31337*. The 3s are substitute Es, the 1 is an L, and the 7 is a T. It is a cry of victory, as in 133333337, to announce superiority over others.

A typical haxor sentence might look something like this:

4 7ypic41 h4x0r s3n73nc3 migh7 100k lik3 7his

The As are substituted with 4s, the Ts with 7s, the Es with 3s, and the Os with zeros.

There are variations. The same sentence might look this way:

4 7yp1c41 h4><0r 53l\l83l\lc3 /\/\1gh7 100k 11k3 7h15

In this case, the X is replaced with ><, the Ss with 5s, the Ns with l\l, and the M with /\/\.

Or even this way:

@ tYpIcAl H@X0R 53n73Nc3 MiGh7 100K 50m37HiNg lik3 7hI5.

Another thing you will often see is the use of caps, the @ sign, and numbers in sentences. In this case, all the As are replaced with @, and caps and lowercase are used interchangeably throughout the sentence.

You find Haxor used often in strange screen names on AOL or nicks on IRC. It's common to see odd combinations, such as FrE@kY N1GhTmar3 (spelling out *freaky nightmare*) or B1g f1R3 (*big fire*). It isn't necessary to learn how to type this way, but if you come across it, you'll know what it is, essentially (it's changing all the time).

There are many words used to avoid detection. Curse words, long banned by most systems, have evolved and have multiple variations on the often used "f" word, which include feck, feek, fark, foik, pha-Q, etc. Conversation might also include typed approximations of noises such as *ARGGH*, Grrrr, waaawaaa, sheesh, and boing. These are often used as a mild exclamation of upset or dissatisfaction.

JAPANESE EMOTICONS

Japanese emoticons have more variation than the Western ones. They are read vertically instead of tilting your head and getting a crick in your neck. One reason these are so different is that Western letters are one byte, while Japanese are 2 bytes, so there are more characters to chose from. Japanese sentences also contain Chinese characters called *phonograms*. These allow a greater number of characters to play with. A typical Japanese emoticon face is (^_^) instead of the Western-style :) .

The popularity of Manga, the Japanese comic books, has also influenced the emoticons, in that many of the emoticons use the same ways of expressing feelings and situations (similar to how we copy the comics, with @#%$@# !!! coming to represent cursing and ZZZzzzZzZzzz meaning sleeping). The following graphics illustrate several emoticons.

＼(◎o◎)／

"Gyaaa!" To be surprised with eyes wide open.

(·_·?)

"I don't understand."

＼(＾o＼) (／o＾)／

"Lets dance."

(-.-) ノ-=≡≡≡卍卍

Throwing Shuri-kens, a weapon that Ninjas use.

(＾人＾)

Asking for a favor (hands together in front of face).

_φ_(. .)めもめも

Writing a memo.

(＾ ₃ ＾)-☆Chu!!

Sending out a loud kiss (chu!!).

o(＾_-)O

Gentle punching as a sign of encouragement

●~*

A bomb.

∋(゜Θ゜)∈

A blowfish (fugu fish).

U・ェ・U

A dog.

(=＾·＾=)

A cat.

C:|彡

An octopus.

φ(ﾟoﾟ)/ｺﾞｯﾁ/ｺﾞｯﾁ-

"Nokotta Nokotta!" is phrase used during a sumo match. This is a sumo referee. He has a fan in his hand.

Some of the Japanese emoticons are possible with our keyset:

(;_;)/~~~~ Saying a tearful goodbye

(^.^)/~~~~~ Waving goodbye with a handkerchief

(^_-) db(-_^) Making a promise by linking little fingers with each other.

(^_-) Wink

W(`0`)W Roaring with anger

(@_@) Drunk, or giddy and dizzy

((((((^_^;) Try to leave secretly, sweating and uncomfortable.

(>_<) (>_<) Shaking head strongly in denial

(*_*) (*_*) Asking "what are you looking for?"

The Downside

Chatrooms are spontaneous, and what you type is visible to all in the room. The spontaneous and visible posts also allow the potential for problems and abuse. Because of people being people, there are terms of service (TOS) and guidelines for appropriate behavior. Many rooms also have a moderator to make sure the room's rules are adhered to. Many systems have a way to report abusive and disruptive users. There are many examples of disruptive users. Some would include dominating the conversation (really fast typists), chattering, typing nonsense, repeatedly typing the same word or phrase into the conversation (known as *scrolling* or *flooding*), flamers (posting insulting, often obscenity-laced attacks on other people).

On AOL, there are spambots, with the sole purpose of collecting screen names (which on AOL are also email accounts) to increase the amount of spam in your email box and other autogenerated messaging systems. Some of these bots will post in the chat windows links to Web sites (usually pornography, occasionally other advertising) or will directly message you (using instant messaging, IM) and try to sound very much like a real human. These are actually programs scripted to sound human. The better chat systems have found ways to block these, but they persist because they find ways around the barriers.

A Word to Parents About Chatrooms

Adolescents love chatrooms. It seems to be an extension of the age's proclivity to talk on the phone for hours, hang out together, and pass notes in class. We hear a lot from the media about kids meeting weirdos in chatrooms, then meeting in person, with horrifying results. These stories are overplayed. The media hysteria overlooks the obvious for every one horror story, there are millions of teenagers in chatrooms, playing online games, and posting to their blogs without any horrid end. Statistically, online chat is safer than hanging out in a mall or on a street corner. Still, there are things to keep in mind that must be discussed with your child (and that you should remember, too, when meeting anyone online).

First, never give out your password, personal details, home address, where you work, your school, what you do, or your name if you've just met online. Don't download files that someone offers you—for any reason—in a chatroom.

Often, online relationships take on a sort of confessional, where people divulge things that they normally would hold back when dealing with people face to face. The anonymity that allows all of us to feel more at ease in telling a total stranger things you haven't told your closest friends also obscures who it is you are telling these secrets to. This creates an aura of intimacy where you feel that you know them better than anyone else.

The problem with the obscured person on the other distant keyboard is that with the limited information we have in online chat and the fact that humans fill in the blanks as part of our nature, it's common to attribute more altruism to the other party than he or she might deserve. (This is especially true when one is new to online chat.)

Freud used the term *projection* to mean an involuntary process motivated by emotions wherein a person imposes a subjective feeling or thought on another person or situation. The tendency is to impose subjective feelings or thoughts that fill our needs. We tend to don "rosy glasses" when we talk with others online. If we have no ill will or evil intent, we assume that the other party harbors none, either. This may or may not be the reality.

Let's face it, this is no different than in ordinary life. We make mistakes about people we've known for years. Look at when the neighbors are talking about the serial murderer next door: "He seemed like such a nice man," "Real quiet, you'd never have suspected." We don't tend to assume that people are out to harm us. This extends to online, as well.

It never hurts to remember the old warning to beware of strangers. Indeed, be aware of strangers online, just as you would on the street because they may be just as strange. Talk to your kids about this aspect of online chatting. It's more important to talk about this than to try to ban it or lecture about it because it is a learning experience. With time, your kids will become naturally wary of online advances and will spot pervs and creeps. Kids talk with other kids, and they eventually put it all in perspective.

The tendency is for adolescents to become too caught up and project that what they've found is something bigger and deeper (highly romanticized). The teenage years are difficult. There is a lot of soul searching, feeling inadequate, and being lonely. Connecting with someone online is often mistaken for real love when it's only an illusion. Parents have a tendency to overreact. The worst thing to do is to declare online communications off limits. That can create a *Romeo and Juliet* romanticism about the whole thing and fan the flames. Overreacting throws the whole thing into the dark realm of secrets and lies, hidden in the shadows and obscured. You want to keep it out in the open and talk about it.

You need to reinforce the rules about not telling too much about real life or, worse, giving out an address. The point is to be aware, not reactive. You need to ask and know whether this person is planning a visit or if your child is being pushed to meet somewhere. Talk about what your children really know about this person. Find out as much as you can.

If your child has met someone online and wants to go further and meet in person, it's time to get active. Start by talking about what is safe. Ask questions; find out what they know and what they don't. Insist on calling parents, arranging logistics, being present, or inviting the person to a safe group event. If everything is truthful and honest, there won't be a problem. If the other person isn't 17 but 25 or 40, you'll hear excuses as to why that won't work. When people have nothing to hide, they don't have a million reasons and excuses.

The Reality Isn't the Same as the Illusion

Few of the amazing, incredible people online are people who look or act like the person of imagination and dreams. The guy who's perfect in every way online won't be in person. It's a simple fact of life. The people who seem so enthralling online often aren't remotely attractive to you in person. The truth of it is, attraction is more than connecting mentally. It's something ethereal that doesn't translate through the computer modem. And even if the reality and the hopes coincide and the person is perfect, distance is another obstacle. Let's face the raw truth: Most long-distance relationships don't work. They fade. Boredom sets in, and things calm down to an occasional online "hello." The point is, long-distance romances rarely work for adults and never work for adolescents. If your teen suddenly declares that they've found the greatest person in the world online, halfway around the world or across the country, nod and smile. Hey, it's fun while it lasts.

Online chat can take up huge chunks of time. If your teen is using it as a sole means of socialization to the point of ignoring schoolwork, you need to step in and limit the hours (just as you would with television or any other diversion). There are some advantages to online chat as opposed to idly watching stale sitcoms and inane cartoons on television. Online communication means one needs to type, a great skill in itself. More important is that it involves reading. The faster the chat, the faster one must read. You'll find that a reluctant reader can sit and read the screen for hours at a time. Poor spelling improves, as does coherent sentence structure. The benefits of online communication shouldn't be overlooked.

INSTANT MESSAGING

Instant messaging is like chat, except to a specific person. It's a private conversation. There are four major messaging mediums in popular use, with others on the market. Two systems dominate the market: AIM and ICQ.

ICQ (www.icq.com)

ICQ means "I seek you." It was developed independently of AOL's IM but was later purchased by AOL and is very similar to AIM. ICQ is an Internet tool to let you know who's online at any time and to let you talk directly via messaging. It's not unlike a telephone call, except that instead of you summoning people directly (by calling them), you talk to them when the program lets you know they are available. ICQ searches for them for you and alerts you when they log on.

AIM/Instant Messaging (www.aim.com)

AIM Express from AOL lets you send IMs from a Web browser, such as Netscape Navigator or Microsoft Internet Explorer, to anyone who has registered for AIM or who uses the America Online service. AIM is free to download and use. You download the software, follow the step-through directions, create a screen name, and list the people you'd like to contact online in a *buddylist*. When they are online and you are too, they'll show up on your buddylist, and you'll show up on theirs.

MSN Messenger for Windows (www.msn.com)

This service is for MSN users to connect with others on their contact list, share files, or conduct video-based IM sessions. You can chat with friends individually or up to 14 in the same conversation window.

Yahoo! Messenger (www.yahoo.com)

This is a free service, from Yahoo. All you need to do is download their messenger file, and you can connect with any other Yahoo! Messenger user.

Jabber (www.jabber.org)

Jabber is an open XML protocol for the real-time exchange of messages between any two points on the Internet. This is an IM network that offers functionality similar to AIM, ICQ, MSN, and Yahoo!. The difference is that the Jabber protocol is not associated with any large Internet company and is open source. It still hasn't caught on in a huge way.

INSTANT MESSAGE AGGREGATORS

These are actually called *multiprotocol instant messenger clients*. These allow you to connect to all the various IM networks but just have one open window on the screen (instead of a screen full). This is a relatively new type of software, and there are more on the horizon.

Odigo (www.odigo.org)

This is both an IM network and an IM aggregator. It will allow you to hook up with over 100 million users across several networks. Besides the Odigo network, you can connect with friends on AOL Instant Messenger, ICQ, or MSN Messenger.

Miranda (http://miranda-im.org)

This is an IM aggregator. It uses very little memory, requires no installation, and is flexible. The basic features are built in, but there are more than 130 plug-ins available to customize it for your needs. By using Miranda, you have one window open on your desktop but communicate with all the other IM networks.

Trillian (www.trillian.cc)

Cerulean Studios has an aggregator called *Trillian Pro*, a shareware program (the $25.00 fee entitles you to a year's worth of frequent updates and member benefits). With Trillian, you can have one desktop window to show the four major IM networks. Cerulean Studios also offers Trillian .74, which is totally free (no limits, no spyware, no ads). This program has been downloaded more than 8 million times, so it's the most well known of the aggregators.

Places to Chat Online

Online chatting has been around for a long time. Commercial services such as The Source, Portal, and CompuServe were the early people chat connections. AOL absorbed two of these operations to create the chatroom part of its service still in use today. There are two main flavors of chatrooms: AOL (and AOL-like chatrooms) and IRC-based chatrooms.

America Online

AOL was an early innovator in online chat. It offered a unique service that had it all. It was the one-stop shopping destination with online news, sports, Internet connections, email, and chat. Many people's introduction to online chat was through the AOL People Connection. This is a collection of chatrooms, each limited in size (36 maximum) and sorted roughly by interest. AOL has what it calls "features" of adding color and different fonts to your chat. These can make it very difficult to read.

AOL was once a well-controlled environment. Now, with its size (the free disks everywhere) and the budget cutbacks, the chat controls have been loosened too far. If you happen into the wrong room, the AOL chat experience will be an unpleasant one. It may be a chaotic mess with lunatics running amok, any etiquette ignored, and the TOS rules forgotten. You will witness the worst of the online experience called *chat*. To be fair, a few rooms are still rather civilized, although which ones changes hourly.

> AOL's TOS state quite clearly that it frowns on all of the following: explicit sexual language; obscene and abusive language; disruptive behavior; blatant advertising; and uncontrolled solicitations. No matter, you'll find all of those items and more with a visit to the People Connection rooms. Even flagrant violators of the TOS are not booted. You can report them, but no immediate or obvious action is taken.

The most annoying things about AOL chat are the IM bots. These are automated programs that pop up on your screen to see whether you want to IM. Most of them are from outside AOL through its AIM Instant Messenger service. They seem to gather names of who to bother by going to the chat list of who's in the room. These are (99% of the time) pornographic. You get a message: *Izzysexyhottie* wants to communicate with you. If you click OK, you end up with an automated message with a hot link to a Web site (a hot link is a link that's active, indicated with blue letters and an underline). If you click your mouse button while your cursor is anywhere near it, you'll be connected with that Web page. Some of the links are to malicious Web sites or Trojan viruses. The problem in AOL has escalated to the point that in a 5-minute period, you may get as many as 15 of these attacks by IM bots. Then there are spam bots that collect screen names and send email, mainly pornographic, to your email account on AOL.

To be called an AOLer is actually a derogatory term for someone who's not too smart or "net-savvy." AOL was the first to offer cheap and simple access and the first to release a huge number of newbies (newcomers) to the Internet. It's used as a catchall term for people who don't know much about technology.

Yahoo!

Yahoo! chat is part of the *community* section. The biggest problem with Yahoo! chat is it's graphically challenged. The screen has a tendency to jerk around because of the ads along the bottom border. The next difficulty is in finding someone's profile information. Yahoo! is slow and opens a new window over the chatroom, which obscures the ongoing chat. For the most part, the rooms are full of ex-AOL chatters. There are some spambots lurking, but Yahoo! is taking an active stance with abuse.

One of the more active features of Yahoo! is the Ignore button to block people you don't want to deal with. This is the best thing to do in the case of bots or if someone is just being rude and difficult to deal with. Use Ignore whenever someone is harassing you or saying something you'd rather not see. If the person is disruptive to the group, it's very effective to ignore the person as a group. As well, Yahoo! has a way to report abuse (http://add.yahoo.com/fast/help/chat/cgi_abuse).

Yahoo! also has two tools: Language Filter and Ignore Invitations. The language filter gives you control over what you see and don't see in the chatrooms. To strengthen or weaken your language filter, click on the Preferences button near the bottom of the screen and pick your setting. Click Save to put the new settings into effect. If you are getting too many invitations to join a room (this can become an annoyance), you can turn off the option.

For other features, go to http://help.yahoo.com/.

Yabberchat

Another, much smaller chat system is Yabberchat (www.yabberchat.com), a community chat site based in Australia. The word *yabber* is an Australian slang term for idle chat. It's a word that comes from the very foreign-sounding language of *Wuywurung*, an Aboriginal language of southeast Australia. *Yaba* means to talk. This chat system enforces its lengthy list (by American standards) of rules with room *sysops*, the chat police. In other words, the rooms are very simple, very tame, and a bit on the dull side. However, for a quick look of how a chatroom works, it's pretty simple. There are no bots, no one offers files to download, and it couldn't be much calmer.

INTERNET RELAY CHAT

Internet Relay Chat (IRC) provides a way for people from all over the world to communicate *real time* (in the moment, without delay). IRC is a collective term to mean a type of software that follows a prescribed IRC protocol.

The concepts can be confusing at first. However, we'll use the analogy of going to college. To say that you go on IRC is like saying you go to a college. But just because you go to a college doesn't mean that you know Fred's sister's kid, Jenny, who goes to Berkeley. Even if you go to Cal Berkeley, you may not know Jenny. There are many programs of study, and there are many different buildings that those subjects are sorted into, and in any one building there are many classrooms. To go to a specific classroom, you enter a building. On IRC, there are server entry points (doors to a building) and channels (rooms). The Cal campus has many buildings, but no matter how many of them you enter, you won't end up at Stanford. With IRC, if you connect with EFnet, you will not be able to be in the same channel with a friend at DALnet. The system, although similar, is made up of a totally different network of servers.

IRC is the overlying noun to describe the type of service offered on the Internet. There are many separate networks of IRC. The largest are EFnet (the original, often having more than 32,000 people online at once), Undernet, IRCnet, and DALnet. There are dozens of medium-sized and small networks.

IRC was an early improvement to the UNIX operating system "talk" program. At the time, it was limited to two users at a time. IRC allowed many people to log into the same network and chat *real time* with anyone else logged on. People started gathering in *rooms*. As rooms became too crowded, new rooms for specific interests were created. These rooms are called *channels* on IRC.

One place to find IRC help is www.irchelp.org.

To use IRC, you need the right software. This software is a client/server program (this topic is discussed throughout the book). There are various client programs for different IRC server systems and for different computers. You will need to download the right IRC client; they're available on the Internet from a variety of locations.

Some IRC Clients

- UNIX/shell—ircII
- WINDOWS—mIRC or PIRCH
- Macintosh—Ircle

Talk City (www.talkcity.com) offers an IRC client applet that it downloads for you as part of its home page, so you can start chatting immediately. (An *applet* is a small program that can be sent along with a Web page to your computer.) It is specific to Talk City's system, so you won't be able to use it to talk to other IRC systems.

Once connected to an IRC server on an IRC network, you will join one or more channels to chat. On EFnet, there are more than 12,000 channels, each devoted to a different topic. Conversations may be public (where everyone in the channel can see what you type) or private (messages between two or more people who may or may not be on the same channel).

IRC Names

IRC channel names usually begin with a pound sign (#), as in #irchelp. There are also channels with names beginning with an ampersand (&) instead of #. The same channels are shared among all IRC servers on the same net. In other words, you can be on one network server while your friend on the other side of the country can be logged onto another of the network's servers. You do not have to be on the same IRC server as your friend, just the same network.

Each user is known on IRC by a *nick*, such as *Wingding211* or *CattyPattyX99*. To avoid conflicts with other users, it's best to use a nick that is not too common (for instance, John or Betty would be poor choices).

On some nets, nicks do not belong to anyone, nor do the channels. So if you like the name Loogie, you may find that upon arriving on a server, there is already someone using Loogie. If this doesn't sit well, you may prefer networks with "services" such as Undernet, DALnet, or other smaller networks that offer nick registration and a password so that only you will have your specific nick. One thing to remember is that your nick isn't your only identifying item. Your machine's IP address will also appear, so the likelihood of confusion by seasoned users is small.

IRC NEWBIE TIP

If you have recently moved from AOL chatrooms to IRC, don't greet the channel with a "hello room" (as you would in a chatroom). If you do, you will probably be greeted with a barrage of taunts and flames, including the infamous "AOLamer!" and/or "AOLoser."

Ops and IRC Admins

Channel operators are called *ops*. They are the cops of the channel and decide who may join (or who to *ban* from joining), who must leave (*kick* them out), and who may speak (if the channel is moderated). They have complete control over their channels. In essence, they are benign dictators. In the event that you get banned from a channel, the best idea is to send a message to the ops and ask politely to be readmitted. If you are ignored, go somewhere else. These channels are a sort of club, and you don't want to be where you aren't welcome.

IRC servers are run by IRC administrators (IRC admins) and by IRC operators (IRC ops). IRC ops manage the servers themselves and on many networks do not get involved in any personal disputes, channel takeovers, restoring lost ops, etc.

IRC {SPEAK}

The best explanation of the spelling and words found in an IRC chat appears in an article on the Web site of the Institute for Journalism, Media and Communication at Stockholm University, Sweden by Sacha Ott: (www.jmk.su.se/global99/sacha/language/lang4.html)
In the article, Sacha looks at the world of IRC slang:

Most frequently found in IRC, there is a special kind of jargon developed by hackers and other online communication "addicts." In jargon the words of the language are not only truncated or spelled in an unusual

---

orthography due to the writing context but a huge amount of new vocabulary is created that does not show up in dictionaries. The writers make use of the language just like they need to fit it to their aims. If a word only exists as an adjective but is needed as a noun, a new word is composed. In that way "obvious" is a characteristic of an "obviosity" or a phenomenon that seems to be "mysterious" becomes a "mysteriosity." Other classes of nouns are composed with the endings "-iness" or "-itude" such as "lameitude."

Another way around, a verb can be created out of almost every kind of noun, or to say it in jargon: All nouns can be "verbed." Especially terms related to computer technology are often put into new contexts. The users "mouse something up" for someone, "clipboard it over" or are just "grepping for files." In addition to the grammatical changes, terms describing hardware and software face several kinds of anthromorphization. Programs or networks get confused, want something or even die. The complex behavior of the technical devices seems to give them the characteristics of a natural being.

It's not that the IRC fosters bad spelling or grammar, the misuse of words, or the bastardization of meanings—it's a human communication form. Slang is used by all cultures. It's a nonstandard vocabulary composed of coined, arbitrarily changed, and facetious words, designed to faze and befog the stranger. The ploy is to distort the language and play with it. In the process, terms are created that better express what is meant.

It's how you tell the insiders from the outsiders, or in this case, the *newbies* from the *leet*.

Dark Side of the IRC

The larger nets can be enjoyable if you are aware of the pitfalls. These "places" are just like real life. It's the big city compared with a small farm town. Each offers different experiences. A small town has comfort, community, more security, and less going on. In contrast, the city has excitement, entertainment, culture, and an abundance of everything. Crime is higher, as are things that lurk in the shadows that one must be aware of. Online mimics real life. The bigger the net, the greater the *dark side* of the IRC: illegal file trading, ad spams, pornography, Trojan/virus infections, denial of service attacks, etc. You can find just about anything you are looking for and a lot more that you may not want to see. If you are new to the IRC—be careful.

Many experienced users prefer smaller nets that still have lots of people but fewer problems or nets devoted to specific subjects, geographical areas, or languages. For beginners, it's probably best to start out on a smaller service and move up.

Illegal file trading is the exchanging of files in violation of the International Copyright Act. On the IRC, it's referred to as *warez*. For some, the only reason to be on the IRC is to exchange files. Since the demise of Napster, more people have turned to the IRC to trade music files. In addition, people trade porn, videos, and software files, among other things. Think of it as the stereotypical street corner guy whispering, "Psssst, want to buy a watch?" Don't naively ask if it's legal, or whether you get a warranty. Most likely, it's not and you won't.

Other problems on larger systems are *lags* and *splits*. A lag is when the connection is in a traffic jam and your side of the communication is delayed. If you are sitting wondering why the other person hasn't responded, lag may be the problem. They can often last more than one minute per message. Splits are when the network server suddenly has a problem. Half the room may not be able to communicate with others in the room. This is usually because connections between the servers have had a temporary glitch. Larger services with many users are more prone to these problems than are smaller ones.

 Smaller IRC networks have less than 1,000 maximum users. Because of the smaller size, these can have stricter controls over the conversation rules. This makes them more family-oriented. Some are very family-oriented.

Beyond IRC—www.beyondirc.net

Starlink—www.starlink.org

StarlinkIRC—www.starlink-irc.org

Xworld—www.xworld.org

SorceryNet—www.sorcery.net

SuperChat—www.superchat.org

Valhall.net—www.valhall.net

Warped—www.warped.net/irc/

FEFnet—www.fef.net

KnightNet—www.knightnet.net

AfterNET—www.afternet.org

Othernet—www.othernet.org

Starchat—www.starchat.net

SandNet—www.sandnet.net

Xnet—www.xnet.org

Be Wary of this IRC Slang

Pron, prOn, pr0n

Slang for pornography. They are often seen on the IRC as requests or offers for porn files. "I want prOn." "Want some kewl prOn?"

Grepping, Grep

The larger rooms have a lot of people *grepping around*. Grep is a UNIX command for searching files containing a specific pattern but has become a slang expression to search for files. On the IRC, there are people looking for files, offering to give files, and asking for files.

Warez

These are for the most part illegal and pirated copies of software. Any IRC channels that have the words *warez, appz, krackz,* and *haxkz* or variations on the theme should be avoided. They're the dark world of file trading. Unless you have a good firewall, a recently updated virus protection program, and a good lawyer (given the low tolerance climate regarding file trading), we recommend that you steer clear of these rooms.

IRC Basic Commands

Let's say you've signed on and you have chosen the handle *BettyBoo123999*. Your basic commands and text are typed in the same place. By default, commands begin with the slash character (/).

First you would begin by looking to see what channels are available on the topic you are interested in. Let's say you want to find a channel about cooking.

/list *cooking*—You find out what channels are listed that are about cooking.
/join #cookinglite—You join the channel cooking lite.
/who #cookinglite—This gives some information on other uses in the channel.
Hello Everyone—You greet everyone in the channel. They see
<BettyBoo12399> Hello Everyone.

You don't need to type in your own nick; it will appear automatically so people know who is talking in the room.

The best places to start are the channels designed for people new to IRC. These channels are on many networks: #new2irc, #newuser, #newbies, #chatback. Others that may have a little more going on include #chat and #ircbar.

Other basic commands include:

/who is (someone's nick)—to see information about them

/nick (a new nick)—to change your nick to a new one (in unregistered IRC)

/msg (someone's nick)—to send a message to someone

/ping #(channel name)—to get information on the round trip delay between you and everyone else on the same channel

/ping (someone's nick)—to get information on the delay between you and them

/dcc chat (someone's nick)—to send a specific person a request for a dcc ("direct computer to computer") chat session

/help—to get help; works on most systems

/quit—to quit

/quit Bye All—to quit and leave a parting comment

IRC Networks

There are several large IRC networks. The biggest and oldest are: Undernet, EFnet, and DALnet.

Undernet

The Undernet claims to be the largest IRC network on the Internet. It interconnects users in almost 40 countries through about 45 servers on three continents. It serves over a million people weekly in several hundred channels. Undernet is divided into regional nets, including a group of European servers and a group of American servers. Undernet offers more than 40,000 channels. It began at the end of 1992 and is seen as a rather friendly network.

The Undernet Channel Service Committee (CSC) was created in 1995 to provide channel stability and help prevent channel takeovers. This involves the use of a network bot—a computer program that appears to the system to be a person—that helps to maintain registered channels' userlists and banlists.

There are three basic steps to joining the network. The first is to locate and download an IRC chat client, configure the client, and log onto the server. Before you log on, it's best to check the most recently updated server list to connect to the closest server. That way, you'll have the fastest and best connection available.

DALnet

Founded in 1994, DALnet pioneered nickname and channel registration services, allowing users to maintain their chatroom names and identities even after logging out. In December 2000, DALnet became the first to hold over 80,000 concurrent chats, which led them to claim that they were the largest IRC network in the world. (However, most people agree that it's smaller than Undernet.) Today, the network handles over two million daily connections and supports a user base of more than 500,000 registered users. DALnet was started by a group of *Star Trek* junkies to get away from the anarchy of EFnet. DALnet strives to provide a safe, friendly place to IRC. The popularity has taken its toll; net splits and lags are common, and the network administrators aren't quite as responsive as they were in the past.

EFnet

Eris Free Network has been around since 1990. It's a large network and has well over 125,000 users and 45,000 channels. The size of it tends to make for odd politics and little cooperation between the servers. Net splits and lags are a problem. This network doesn't offer many services, so anyone can use your nickname or have your channel. It tends to be oriented toward advanced users. The general impression is that it's the wild side of the IRC. Some claim that EFnet users look down on users of other networks, and it is known as a hangout for people who fancy themselves to be *crackers* and *hackers*.

CHANNEL TAKEOVER—DEFINITION FROM VALINOR

(www.valinor.sorcery.net/glossary/channel-takeover.html)

After a net split, sometimes you will be the only person in a particular channel, and if you leave the channel and rejoin, you'll be an operator. When the net joins up again, you can try to kick and ban everyone else, and now you "own" the channel. Unfortunately for you, if the channel has been properly registered, the real channel operators will quickly end your reign of terror. On networks such as EFnet, there is no recourse if you lose a channel this way.

Forums are another way to connect with people but not directly. For that reason, forums are discussed in Chapter 4.

ONLINE DATING

In the early 1990s, it was far more likely to meet someone with similar interests and goals online, because the only people online were fellow geeks. In fact, the first online dates resembled a game of Dungeons & Dragons, the entire date taking place in cyberspace with characters created by users.

As computers began to fill more and more households and the price of Internet access went down, the likelihood of meeting someone living nearby increased. New technology made it possible to send pictures. Internet connections became quicker than ever.

Still, online dating was considered strange, especially by women, who saw it as the depths of desperation (although random interviews reveal few who would admit they've even tried). Many say they know a friend or a relative who did. This seems odd if you look at the statistics.

The Numbers

In a study released by the Online Publishers Association the online personals industry generated $53.1 million in revenue, in the first three months of 2002, alone. (Compared to the $8.2 million, for the same quarter in 2001.) The leading service, by many accounts, is Match.com, a division of Ticketmaster. An episode about online dating on Oprah quoted a figure of 3.2 million visitors to Match.com (in 2002). It is estimated that at least 15 million Americans used online personals in 2002. (The numbers for 2003 have not been released. However, the number of online dating sites has increased, so it is expected the count of current users would be significantly higher.) This is in an industry where satisfied customers cancel their accounts (who needs a matchmaker after you find someone?). There is intense competition among the sites for the Census Bureau's estimated 85 million single people in the United States.

Monthly membership for personals sites ranges from $24.95 to as low as $6.95. The average is around $19.00. Some sites require you to buy blocks of credits, the best of which offers a block of 30 credits for $30.00, each contact costing one credit. The time of the free site devoted strictly to personals may soon be over. Some free sites can be located, but the number of members is usually low.

There are, by conservative estimates, several hundred online personal ad Web sites. Sites specialize in ethnic groups, religion, region, sexual orientation, and other criteria, such as white women and black men, hefty-sized dates, sports partners, birth dates, star signs, country singles, date a doctor, advanced degrees, vegetarian, and vegan. You can even match up with a prison inmate.

Why Online Personals?

Teens and young adults have ample social situations, such as high school and college, that teem with people of the same age having similar lifestyles and interests. Once at the legal age to go to nightclubs, bars, and other adult venues, there are even more opportunities to find love. As time goes by, people get busy with career and family. Then divorces happen or spouses die. A full life of friends, career, kids, pets, laundry, and all the little time-consuming hassles of life leave a person with precious little time to fulfill the urge or dream of locating a new partner to grow old with. For this reason, the majority of personals are targeted at the 30 years and older crowd. (Young people seem to find each other, thus having no real need for matchmakers.)

What it comes down to is that you can't rely on friends and relatives to match you up anymore. Co-workers are often off limits because of corporate policies. Meeting people in the laundromat or grocery store is a quaint concept but works best in movie scripts, not in real life. Everyone is too busy, too hard-pressed for time, and living quiet, solitary lives.

But where can an *older* single go? Scattered in and among the fresh-faced twenty-somethings will be the odd character showing the ravages of early middle age, trying out tired lines and timeworn techniques. It's a kid's game. Few past their twenties care to compete or have the stamina to try. By comparison, $20 or so to meet people is a steal. And if you can do it from the comfort of your home, all the better.

The Hype

The grain of salt: Most of the information on the Web about personals sites is generated by the sites themselves. In the first quarter of 2002, consumers shelled out nearly $70.5 million for online business content for financial advice and articles (to sites such as TheStreet.com and The Wall Street Journal). These were the only Web sites to generate more revenue than pornography and personals Web sites.

Matchmaking sites have one purpose—to make money. Men are far more likely to spend money on online dating services. It should be no surprise that there are abundant articles touting online dating in men's magazines. But like an entertaining first-person experience in a men's magazine, the actual results may be a little different from the written version published. Upon closer examination of the article about online dating, it shouldn't be a shock to discover that the author also pens an advice column for a personals Web site. No doubt about it, when there is hope and desire, there is also pitch and hype.

Test Subjects

We decided to do some unbiased research. So we chose a 37-year-old single male college graduate with average looks, proportionate height and weight, and modest income. He first went to a few photo-rating Web sites where you post a picture of yourself to have it rated by visitors from all over the world, usually the opposite sex (www.hotornot.com, www.amihot.com, and www.facethejury.com). The 37-year-old was slightly above average (on a scale of 1 to 10) at 7.3 to 7.5. Not a face only a mother could love, but not GQ either. It's an effective, albeit masochistic, way to get an opinion of your external beauty, or lack thereof.

Our female subject was a 34-year old single female, also proportionate with height and weight. She holds a master's degree in business and has a respectable income and career. (She refused to post her picture to be rated.) By all accounts, she was sweet, average to slightly above average.

They each paid for a month on the top five sites. One drawback instantly noted were the incredibly detailed profiles to be filled out. Granted, the logic says that to match better, one must lay more cards on the table. No matter, it was time-consuming. They also took advantage of 20 different free trial memberships (usually lasting a week). They awaited the responses.

The Results

The first obvious problem with the big sites: The male/female ratio was not equal. (The male subject estimated 70% men to 30% women, a far cry from the hoped-for 60/40% split.) After months of trial and error, the two test subjects decided that the big money machine Web sites were not the best way to meet people.

> ## THE PROBLEM WITH FREE TRIALS
>
> The free trials were about as effective as expected in a kangaroo court. No responses were received, oddly enough, until the day after the free trial membership expired. (And they weren't local; the replies were from oddball places, such as Ethiopia and Myanmar.)

He Found

There were an abundant number of responses from the Ukraine (mail-order brides). It made filling out the profile pages seem pointless—because his criterion was strictly for women living in a 10- to 20-mile range of his zip code. In fact, most of the responses were pretty obviously spam. The give-away was that they sounded only a bit girlish: "Hi. This is going to sound strange, but I had the biggest crush on you, so I asked a friend for your e-mail address. You used to come into the store where I worked every once in awhile, and I always wanted to say something, but I never had the nerve to . . ."

Then the email would end with a link to a personal Web site. Of course, this wasn't legitimate. It was either a link to a string of pop-up porn ads or a porn site. It was disheartening.

Both subjects did get some convincing e-mails (with photos from highly attractive individuals) that had flattering details on what prompted the response and how they really wanted to meet. Of course, on closer inspection, none of these emails really referred to anything actually said in the ad; they were just some copy person's attempt at being coy and flattering. Both test subjects caught on to the ploy when they answered the email. The next correspondence directed them to a Web site with explicit instructions. To continue further contact, it was time to *upgrade to membership status*. In other words, it was a tease!

However, he did get a few genuine responses. He exchanged emails, spoke on the telephone, and had a few casual dates. What he complained about was that once it was apparent that he did not own a villa or private jet and had no stacks of cash stuffed in his mattress, the women didn't continue the connection. He felt that many of the women would delete him as soon as they found someone better looking or with more money. Another problem was that there were a number of the women who would email and speak on the phone but would not actually meet him. They would promise to but wouldn't show up or would cancel at the last minute with an implausible excuse. He considered this a considerable waste of time. He found it difficult to figure out who was honest and who was not. In email, all the women seemed sincere, including incredibly emotional outpourings and promises of romance to come. It seemed that the more demonstrative the women were online or in telephone conversations, the more likely he was never to hear from them again. It was perplexing.

She Found

First, it was odd, but she didn't get any spam. There were no listings for mail-order husbands or email from Tibet or Ghana. Sifting through the abundant emails, she saw nearly 200 emails per week, which proved to be very time-consuming.

Men lied about all sort of things. The number one lie was about income. After a few email exchanges and telephone conversations, it became clear that many of these men had barely the brains to mop up at Taco Bell, much less pull down a salary of $150K per year. Her biggest complaint was that the men tended to lie about their appearance, height, weight, age, and marital status. They often sent pictures from their college days or whenever it was that they last had hair. She found it distasteful that many of them went quickly right to the subject of sex and even sent unsolicited pictures (not always clothed, or suitable to show her mother). It was frustrating as well to find that most men in her age group sought much younger women.

Internet Dating Options

Online chatrooms are another way to meet people online. If you have a lot of time on your hands, you can join one. The problem is that people in chatrooms sometimes have their own language. It takes a while to get to know it, defeating the purpose of saving time in the matchmaking process. You can find a chatroom discussing nearly any subject you can imagine. Although it is possible to meet people for romance this way, it's probably not a good way.

WWW.CRAIGSLIST.ORG

The main site is a San Francisco-based online community. It is a good place to post personals, without charge. The San Francisco site is the oldest, and most populated. It's not uncommon to post an online personals ad and get a response within a few minutes. Sites such as these are by far a good, effective way to meet someone in your local area. It is easy to navigate and, it is free (except for help wanted postings). There are no immediate plans to charge for personals postings. There are similar craigslist sites in every major city in the country, and some have appeared in Canada and Europe.

The services that offer free online personal ads are probably the best choice. You can post an ad and see a response in as little as 10 minutes.

Dos and Don'ts of Personals

The best advice is to not to lie but not to tell too much, either. Don't post your home phone number, where you work, or where you live. The Internet is a big place. But aside from that, post as much about yourself as possible—your likes, dislikes, wants, desires—but the shorter you can say all this, the better. People don't want to read a novelette online. Poetry is never a good idea, nor is typing in verse and rhyme. Photos are important.

Scanned photos are a big selling point. Make them tasteful. Don't pose bare-chested with an assault rifle if you are a guy. If you are a woman, don't post the photo of you at the last costume party wearing a maid outfit. And for both, don't use the pictures of your wedding with the ex cropped out (leaving only the arm and part of the head). Men, for some reason, love to post photos of themselves with other women. This is also not a good idea. Photos that are blurry or shots of the scenery with a dark blob of a figure over to one side aren't very good, either.

What does work? Playing with your dogs, leaning up against your treasured car, engaged in a favorite sport, or petting your cat are all good. Professional-looking glamour shots also seem to be popular. It's not hard to find a friend with a digital camera, or you can scan in a photo with a scanner to convert shots to digital. There are also many services that will scan a photo of you for a few dollars. If you are really cheap, you can go to one of the big computer/electronics retailers and have a salesperson take a shot of you using one of the digital display models and email it to yourself.

First impressions include the email address. It's a good idea to set up a separate email account for your dating responses. (Work addresses are never a good idea.) A tame-sounding email address such as debra3242 is less scary than psychogrrrl10. Remember, you want to limit the amount of negatives.

Be lavish with the details as to why you are posting on the Internet seeking a mate. You should point out why you posted a profile, such as "very busy professional, have no time to go to bars," "I am new in town," or whatever else is the reason. Heck, even curious is better than nothing.

When writing what you are looking for in a potential mate, don't get too specific. Unless a color of hair or a very certain type of person is exactly all you want, be as general as possible. It's a bad idea for men to mention weight. It's a touchy subject with all women, because it's so subjective. (Even those who might appear extremely slender are sensitive to that issue.)

Likewise, women will do best treading lightly on both hair loss and seeking gobs of money.

Try not to brag. Tell the truth. Remember, you may actually end up meeting this person. It might be difficult to explain why you are really 260 pounds instead of the svelte 125 you claimed. People don't shrink three inches, either. Stock trader may sound more glamorous than video store clerk, and even if it's grounded in fact, 10 shares of Microsoft do not make a trader. Fashion model sounds better than part-time fitting model, but the differences are many.

The rules are different from the conventional means of meeting people.

- Return emails promptly. Nothing shows lack of interest more than infrequent communication. Online communication is not like regular, face-to-face dealings.

- Playing *hard to get* doesn't work because they can find someone who seems more motivated. A few emails are easily forgotten.

- Trying to juggle too many people is a bad idea. When there are too many emails flying about, it's easy to make a mistake and confuse one person with another.

- One week is an acceptable time period to wait before a first date.

Things to Watch Out For

You meet people faster on the Internet. Because you meet more people, you also find bad apples more frequently. Use caution and common sense. This holds true especially for women. A sincere person will not object to you taking precautions or asking questions.

Men are often targets of swindlers. Recently, the Russian police arrested an operation where two young men posed as potential Russian brides (they used photos of real women) and emailed their love and devotion, promises and intent to marry, netting more than $50,000 from American men. It's well known that many match sites are plagued with prostitutes, despite efforts to keep them out. There are also the nice-enough-sounding people who tug at heartstrings with very sad stories, asking for some help. A few dollars here or there aren't really going to go far, but some of these people make a good income off the thousands of people they convince to send small sums.

For the most part, women who are too eager to send you naked photos tend to be looking for more than love and romance. Don't go to their Web sites. Don't give them a credit card number. Don't send money. Don't buy anything. Many people have been cajoled into buying plane tickets, bus tickets, and clothing to "prove" their affection for people who are inventions of people intending to defraud. Don't believe anything unless you can verify it. Keep your wallet closed. It's best to stay in your geographic area and insist on meeting, getting to know someone's name, address, and phone number before you get too involved in the stories. The Internet is a great place for the nefarious to hide.

Be wary in giving out information about yourself too early on. Not everyone is playing with a full deck. There are lots of stories about how some ill-tempered person posted someone's home number along with a nasty ad offering sexual services for free, and the victim of the prank was inundated with calls for weeks. Be wary of hostile-sounding people and of people who move too fast and want too much too soon (such as moving in together after a few emails and perhaps a single daytime meeting). Always use your best judgment. As much as we'd like to think that it's love across a crowded Internet, take it slow. Pay attention to inconsistencies.

Women should never meet a man anywhere, except in a public place. Daytime is best for a first date. Don't give out your phone number to just anyone, especially if your phone number is listed in the telephone directory. (Reverse telephone/address directories are online, so it's not too difficult for someone to find your home address from your telephone number.) Don't send suggestive or nude photos until you've gotten to know the person. There are men (and men posing as women) who collect photos to post on the Internet.

Summary

We should always remember that the risks of meeting people in the online world are not much different than in the "real" world. Face-to-face you might have more clues (visual, verbal, dress, appearance, habits, etc.) to come to conclusions about the character of a person, but you can never really know what is in the heart or mind of another person. Online people may reveal more about themselves, their real intentions, and aspirations because of the protective screen of anonymity.

This anonymity is the real difference. People often play-act roles which they cannot play in public. Predators can hide in the shadows. Everyone is outstanding in appearance, if they do say so themselves. People will tell you their darkest secrets and aspirations with the shield in place, from the comfort of their homes and offices. (Because, online you can always disconnect and pretty much disappear without a trace.)

What it takes to make any online experience work is to understand the scene completely. Hopefully this chapter will give you the confidence to do the right thing under all circumstances.

8
GAMING

Online gaming can take many forms. There are online board and card games, role-playing games (RPGs), and multiplayer games against other humans or against a computer (some of these are "total world" gaming environments). There are sites that have a few simple games and games that involve many players. There are games that don't seem like games at all. The point isn't winning, but communicating with other people and spending time occupied while you chat. It's a huge subject.

Forrester Research estimates that online gaming will be worth $3.2 billion by 2005. They note that this growth is driven by online competitive games that have mass-market appeal, a shift away from single-person games.

MMOG (massively multiplayer online games) are extremely popular worldwide. It's reported that at least 7 million Korean users and 3 million Taiwanese users (10 million total) are paying to play the game Lineage. Sony predicted Everquest would draw in 75,000 players over the course of a few years but was surprised when the game had that many players in a few months. Current estimates have it pegged at over 800,000 playing now.

In 2002 in the United States, over $600 million was spent on MMOG titles. The most popular of these, Ultima Online, Everquest, and Asheron's Call, were all themed as medieval fantasy RPGs. War and sports games are also becoming popular. It is projected that this market could blossom into sales as high as $1.5 billion for the U.S. market alone in just a few years. (The Asian markets are expected to hit three times that number.)

Games can be played in a peer-to-peer (P2P) arrangement, with machines networked together (LANs), through wireless connections (PDAs), or through dedicated client/server arrangements with specialty Web sites. Game platforms include console games (PS2, Xbox, and Dreamcast), PC games, and Mac games, as well as handhelds (PDAs).

Gaming can also mean online gambling, a dark and murky area (we'll cover this at the end of the chapter).

COMPUTER GAME GENRES

There are a variety of computer games that you can purchase in stores to play alone on your computer. Many of the game styles have been adapted for Web games (which we will try to note, when relevant). The basic flavors of games include RPG; adventure games; combat simulations; driving simulations; sports simulators; arcade/action games; board, solitaire, and parlor games; life simulations (God games); money-making games; war and strategy simulations; children's games (often described as educational). Because we are trying to focus on Internet-related games, the categories aren't as distinct as they are in traditional commercial games. There is overlap, and many are not clear-cut definitions.

Role Playing

These once meant only Dungeons & Dragons-style games. They have evolved, and not all of them are set in barbarian-infested medieval worlds any more. A consistent element of these games is that you are your character. You create a character, name it, manipulate it, and interact with various entities, such as other people and bots (short for robots, which are generated characters that are part of the games program, so they react in predicable patterns, unlike the other human players). These are also sometimes called *NPCs* (Not Player Character).

The avatar beings, the ones created by the users, are not static. Over time, they grow smarter and stronger as the game advances. Often, the games involve you fighting one monster/critter after another until you reach the next level. Then you are challenged with a new set of critters until you hit the next level. By gamers, this is called *treadmill gaming*. It's a way to keep the carrot ahead of the player and keep things interesting and fresh.

Action/Adventure

Action games are fast paced, requiring accuracy and quick reflexes. Adventure games are animated stories where you see and control a main character (occasionally more than one) in a highly detailed story. For the most part, this is never a pure category, because it is often combined with other facets, such as RPG, combat simulation, etc. By far, these are currently the most popular in a multiuser setting.

Popular action games played in multiplayer environments include Half-Life, Quake 3, Wolfenstein; Enemy Territory; and Unreal Tournament 2k3.

Combat Simulations

These games, unlike arcade-style games, do not give you unlimited ammo and endless enemies. Instead, they attempt to be accurate simulations of planes, submarines, ships, tanks, and spacecraft, and they rely on strategy and skill. (In the case of RPG games, they include cooperation and coordination with other players.)

Popular action games played in multiplayer environments include Battlefield 1942, Medal of Honor, Allied Assault, Soldier of Fortune, Il-2 Sturmovik, Age of Empires, Blitzkrieg, and Praetorians.

Driving and Sports Simulations

These games are designed to give a quality of realism to vehicular games (cars, trains, boats, tanks, trucks, motorcycles, jet skis) and/or other sports games (skiing, fighting, baseball, golf, football, soccer, tennis, etc.). The use of this in games varies. This may be the focus of the game or it may be a side action. In either case, you either directly pilot the action or you set up the strategy and coach the action.

Popular sports games played in multiplayer environments include MotoGP, NASCAR, and Tony Hawk Pro Skater.

Arcade/Action Games

These are classic "action" games (also known as *twitch games*) where the faster your reflexes, the better you can manipulate the game controls. For the most part, these are single-player games.

Board, Solitaire, and Parlor Games

Old favorites turned into computer games include chess, checkers, Monopoly, and many others. There are a few of these that are multiplayer, but they are not as popular as the other genres. There are many solitaire games available to play as browser games or to download onto a handheld device. A number of browser game sites feature these kinds of games, often with unusual twists or with chat areas so you can connect with people while playing the games.

Reality Simulations

These are games that let you be the master of the universe (God games). Build cities; destroy them; cause famine, floods, and war. Create simulated people and make them suffer or not. Create a world from scratch; run a city, a country, a world; and unleash your wrath or benevolence.

Money-Making Strategy Games

These simulate the higher forms of gambling (stock market, commodities, securities, real estate, etc.) or let you simulate the creation and running of a corporation or climbing a corporate ladder. In the case of RPG games, this is often a facet to make the situation more realistic.

Children's Games

These are games to enhance learning (often described as educational) and to keep the kids quiet and entertained for a long time. There are ones for younger children that teach them how to use the mouse and keyboard. There are ones for older children to reinforce reading, logic, math, and spelling. Many of the Web browser "parlor" games are suitable for children. As well, there are other online resources for children's games, such as Dvorak's Personal Portal for Children.

JOHN C. DVORAK'S PERSONAL PORTAL FOR CHILDREN

This is a metasite for kids. There are kid's games, famous characters, art and coloring books, animations, girls-only pages, news-related, animals, safety, science and education, and reference Web links for kids. The links are for the most part free from excessive pop-ups or other annoying marketing ploys, and the site is reviewed frequently (by John's kids) for material that doesn't fit the strict criteria established.

For more information, go to www.dvorak.org/kidshome.htm.

Online Games

Online (Internet) games encompass a lot of territory. There are RPGs, text-based games (multiuser dungeons [MUDs] and multiuser shared hallucinations [MUSHs]), the exceedingly graphic *multiuser* and *massively multiuser* simulation environment games, simple multiplayer competition games to play in your Web browser, games to download to your laptop or handheld, and games for machines hooked together (LANs). There are free games, shareware games, commercial games, and monthly fee games.

We will sort them into three general classes of games. These are:

- Browser games
- Multiuser/massively multiplayer games
- Text-based games

NONCOMMERCIAL SHAREWARE GAME REVIEW SITES

Freeware Guide—www.freeware-guide.com
Five Star Shareware—www.5star-shareware.com

Browser Games

Browser games are also known as Java games because you must have Java enabled on your machine to play them. Usually if Java is required, you will be told so on the computer screen and taken to a download site to get the Java program. These sites are often full of parlor games or variations of old favorites. These can be either solitaire-style (one person) or multiuser. The multiuser games do not require any specialized software or any fees (generally) to play, unlike the overlapping category of multiuser games. Instead, you can play these by going to the Web site and signing in. These games are different than the "pay to play" games because they use an advertisement revenue model. (Often, the single-player games are available in a shareware version, which also funds the multiplayer game.)

There are many different browser games. We'll outline a few sites with these games, just to give some idea what is out on the Web.

Pogo—www.pogo.com

Pogo is a commercial site owned by the large game company Electronic Arts (Figure 8.1). Electronic Arts is a leading independent developer and publisher of interactive entertainment for personal computers, entertainment systems (PlayStation 2, Xbox, Nintendo Game Cube, and Gameboy). As well, they have a Web presence with EA Sports, EA Sports Big, EA Games, EA.COM, and Pogo.com.

Pogo has both games to play (free) and Pogo To Go, which are enhanced versions of the Web games that you can download to your PC and play anytime, without an Internet connection. These games give some amount of free play, then require a shareware-style fee to continue playing them off the Web.

Pogo also has a prize program. Some of the games offer prizes for playing. This makes it look like a gambling site, but it isn't. It's an incentive to keep playing. Many of the games are solitaire and classic games, such as Cribbage and Dominoes. There are also arcade-style games, puzzle games, trivia games, "freebie casino" games, word games, and more. All the games have chat (other people to talk with), even if you aren't directly interacting with them competitively.

To play, you need to sign up. They require a password, the year and month you were born, a U.S. zip code, and an email address. Then they try to entice you to sign up for a multitude of other games (which isn't required); in fact, everywhere you turn you will see advertisements.

PopCap—www.popcap.com

PopCap is a Web site game arcade that is popular on its home site and on partners such as Microsoft Gaming Zone, Yahoo!, RealOne Arcade, and Shockwave (Figure 8.2). The thing about PopCap games is that they can be found on many different platforms, from the Web to the PC to Mac to PDAs and cell phones. They're great for in-flight entertainment. The most popular game is Bejeweled (aka Diamond Mine). Other games include: TyperShark,

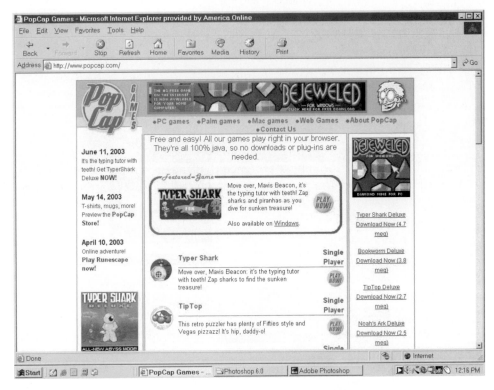

FIGURE 8.2   **POPCAP IS A FREE GAME ARCADE.**

TipTop, Dynomite, Diamond Mind, Bookworm, Candy Train, Ningpo Mahjong, Word Stalk, Insaniquarium, Big Money, Alchemy, Atomica, Mummy Maze, and Seven Seas. All are excellent games for kids or adults, with hours of entertainment value.

You can play online for free all day and all night. Most of the games are single-player puzzle games that are practically addictive. There are versions of games for the PC, Mac, and Palm to play whenever, wherever. They're shareware. So once you pay their fee, you will have an enhanced version of the game. Secret levels are unlocked, and you'll gain access to advanced help. You will also be supporting the Web site in the development of new games.

The Web site also offers some multiuser games: Atomic Poker, Lucky Penny Video Poker, and Psychobabble.

• Atomic Poker—technically not a multiplayer game because you aren't playing with anyone. It's a solitaire game, played with chat alongside. The goal of the game is to create the best poker hand possible, both vertically and horizontally. Place cards on the board by clicking an empty space.

Meanwhile, you can see what other people are winning and chat with them, although people tend not to chat much because the game takes a bit of concentration.

- Lucky Penny—also a solitaire game in that it's video poker with a PopCap twist. The ongoing chat is pretty active, and the crowd is friendly. People seem to hang around all night.

- PsychoBabble—a multiuser game in that you are playing against other people. The game is arranging a scrambled selection of "refrigerator magnets" in an attempt to make a sentence that makes some degree of sense. The other people in the room vote for what they think is the best sentence, all the while chatting with each other. The first one to 30 points wins the game.

:)Smilie Game—www.smiliegames.com

This Web site offers a number of games, including Soccer Pong, Super Bowling, Bugbuster, the Amazing Snail (which is eerily similar to the old PacMan, except with a twist), and Invaders (which is the original computer game), as well as 20 more. Their Drop4 is for two players on one browser. They plan on competitive action in the future.

This is a free site, although they do ask for donations to keep the site running.

Arcade Outpost—www.arcadegamesonline.com

This Web site is a collection of different browser games (Figure 8.3). It's simple, easy to wander around in, and has a wealth of games to occupy a bored kid on a rainy day.

 Game Spotter has links to hundreds of games you can play in your Web browser.

For more information, go to www.gamespotter.com.

Massively Multiplayer Online Games

Predating live MMPOG Internet play were online services such as Prodigy, Genie, and America Online. AOL hosted a Dungeons & Dragons game (NeverWinter Nights) and an air simulator (Warbirds). Genie ran a Massive Multiplayer feudal simulation (Hundred Years War).

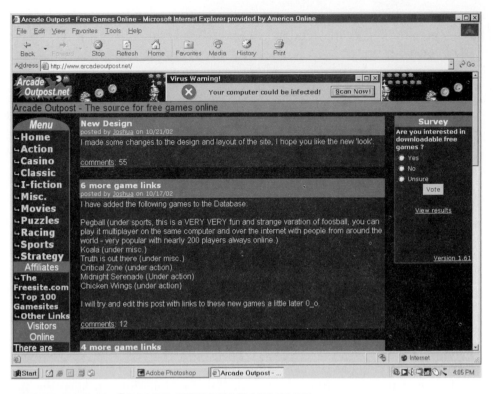

FIGURE 8.3   ARCADE OUTPOST MAIN PAGE.

Massively multiplayer games require the player to purchase the client game at a retail outlet. Then the player registers at a game site (which often requires a low monthly fee) to participate in a virtual realm and play with or against other players.

There are two types of real-time (meaning live action) multiplayer games on the Internet—P2P gaming and dedicated client/server games. (There are Web sites that offer both in one place.)

AVATAR

In 3D (virtual reality games) and in some Web chatrooms, the *avatar* is your visual representation. This word comes from the Hindu religion. An avatar is an incarnation of a deity, hence, an embodiment or manifestation of an idea or greater reality.

Peer-to-Peer Gaming Sites

P2P is a style of networking where the computers communicate directly with each other instead of going through a central server. This is often used for multiplayer online games to avoid the expense and delay of having all the traffic routed through one server.

In a P2P game, every player is on equal status with every other. During the game, all players send and receive information to every other player. There are a number of these sites to play real-time strategy games (e.g., WarCraft III, Rise of Nations). They do require that all players start at the same time. Without dedicated servers, there cannot be open games that can be started at any time. Instead, P2P games require one of the players act as the host.

P2P games have scaling problems. Every player talks to every other player. The number of communication links must work harder and faster than in client/server games. The math goes something like this: A client/server with n players must keep n links available and open. The P2P game must keep $1 + 2 + 3 + 4 + ... + (n - 1)$ links open. So a 16-player P2P game would need 100 open communications links, compared with a client/server with 16 links.

There are problems inherent in P2P gaming, because it needs very fast, reliable (broadband) connections to operate.

Client/Server Dedicated Server Games

Client/server is a computational architecture process that requires the client (user) to interact only with a server (central computer). The individual users' computers do not communicate with each other directly (as in a P2P arrangement) but instead route all communications through the central server. The client-side computer and server-side computer are two separate devices, customized with special software to carry out their specific tasks. In the case of client/server games, the individual players connect with a central host. The users purchase special client software (the retail game) to enable their computers to interact with the host.

By far, the majority of client/server games are RPG games. In these, a player's character, the avatar, interacts with the virtual world and other player's avatars. The games can be very complex, rich, and with all the social conventions and qualities of a real cultural community. An avatar might attain virtual assets—money, property, and fame—which makes the environment a more "real" one in terms of creativity and accomplishment. The avatar will own property, have specialized skills, etc.

Hybrid Gaming Arcades

Some sites support both dedicated-server and P2P gaming.

GameSpy Arcade—www.gamespyarcade.com

This is a complete gaming site (Figure 8.4). It allows players to locate and connect to multiplayer games, chat with other players, and browse the best parts of the GameSpy Network, the largest gaming network on the Internet. GameSpy Arcade matches players with similar games and interests and offers a host of features, including:

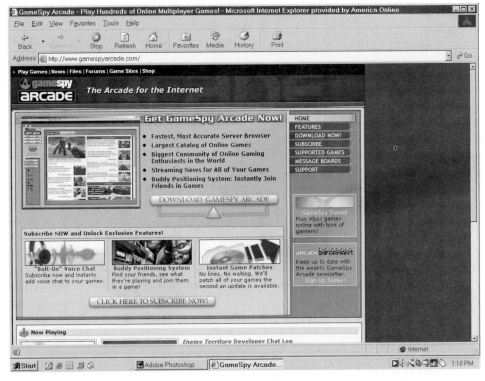

FIGURE 8.4 GAMESPY ARCADE—THE DEFINITIVE GAMING SITE.

- News and features from the GameSpy Network
- Chatrooms
- Events and tournaments
- Player Spy

It is an all-in-one tool for games. It comes bundled with a selection of free parlor games, such as backgammon, poker, spades, etc.

GameSpy Arcade supports both dedicated-server and P2P games. With both kinds of games, a wider variety of games is supported. The list of supported games is over 400 and growing. It is an excellent tool for advanced players and fans of dedicated-server games, with sophisticated filtering and rules.

This is a paid service. There is an unlimited-use trial version, but the paid version offers more and better features, including:

- Turning off of ads
- In-game voice chat
- Adding unlimited buddies to your PlayerSpy buddylist
- Unlimited file transfers
- Immediate game patching
- Priority email tech support
- Access to full versions of GameSpy 3D and Roger Wilco
- Special offers and beta tests

GAMES ONLINE

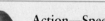

Action—Speed and Accuracy
Unreal Tournament 2003—www.unrealtournament2k3.com
Counter-Strike—www.counter-strike.net
Battlefield 1942—www.battlefield1942.ea.com
Planetside—www.planetside.com
Flight Sim
Jumpgate—www.netdevil.com/jumpgate/
FighterAce—http://fighterace.jaleco.com/
RPG—Massive
Star Wars Galaxies—www.starwarsgalaxies.com
A Tale in the Desert—www.atitd.com

Dark Age of Camelot—www.darkageofcamelot.com

Asheron's Call—www.asheronscall.com

Everquest—www.everquest.com

Strategy—Tactics

Legacy Online—www.legacyonline.net

Hyperiums—www.hyperiums.com

StarSphere—www.starsphere.net

MPOGD.com—www.mpogd.com

MPOGD.com (Figure 8.5) is a site providing information about multiplayer online games. The goal of the MPOGD is to inform the gaming community of new and existing multiplayer online games. It does not host

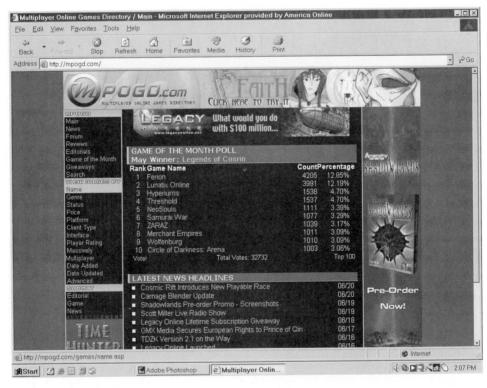

FIGURE 8.5 **MPOG GAMING DIRECTORY FOR ONLINE GAMES AND RATINGS.**

games, nor does it list games that lack online multiplayer capabilities. The site contains daily news, in-depth game reviews, editorials about current hot topics in multiplayer online gaming, a forum system where game developers and players interact, and the MPOGD Game of the Month Poll. It also features player game ratings. The most popular feature is the database of games. It lists more multiplayer online games than any other site on the Web. The games are listed in an easy-to-find format by genre, by platform, by development status, and more. (A search page is available to search by keyword.)

The game information it lists includes the following:

- Direct link to each game's official page
- Short description of each game
- Multiple screen shots
- Client program type
- Interface
- Status
- Developer
- Network
- Price
- System requirements
- Genre
- Platform
- Official MPOGD review
- Average player ratings with links to individual ratings and comments

Multiuser Dungeons

MUDs are text-based games. They are interactive, with deep story plot lines that make up for the lack of visual interest. There is not always a story, but they exhibit depth of world and lots of detail, and there are people who are very dedicated to them. (These are also known as MUDs, MUSHs, MUSEs, MUXs, and MOOs, depending on the software underlying the game. See definitions in the following sidebar.)

MUD grew out of the board game Dungeons & Dragons. MUD stands for multiuser dungeon, (or dimension, depending on who you ask). It is a structured social experience managed by a computer program and involves some minor organized context or theme, such as a rambling old castle with many rooms or a period in national history. Some are ongoing adventure games, some are educational, and some are social. MUDs existed before the Web, accessible through Telnet to a computer that hosted the MUD.

There are a number of variations on the MUD. Each is associated with a server program of that name, and the variation is mainly in the programming language used.

MOO—Multiuser Object-Oriented System

MUSE—Multiuser Simulated Environment

MUSH—Multiuser Shared Hallucination

MUX—Multiuser X-perience

VEE—Virtual Educational Environment, a MOO for educational purposes

WOO—Web-MOO, a MOO that can be accessed from the Web.

Moobie—A new person on a MOO

A MUD can have a large number of players connected to one central server. They can interact with other players (and computer-created characters) but unlike a visual based system, it's all done in text. While *mudding*, there are opportunities to solve puzzles, as well as to kill the requisite monsters (called *mobiles*—MOBs for short) to move the story along.

Although most MUDs are still entirely text-based, some new MUDs use virtual reality settings so you can see the other characters. However, the focus remains the exchange of text between all the participants logged in at a particular time.

MUD (TEXT-BASED GAMES)

For more information:

MudConnector—www.mudconnector.com

Realms—http://realms.palni.edu/muds

The MUD Resource—www.godlike.com/muds/

MUDs Online—www.mudsonline.com

For more information on MUDs, go to www.lysator.liu.se/mud/faq/faq1.html or Harley Hahn's Guide to MUDs at www.harley.com/muds.

LAN GAMING

A LAN game is a collection of online game players in the same room, playing the same game. These tend to be called *LAN parties* because

everyone shows up in the same physical location to sit at a console and play the same game shoulder-to-shoulder, both virtually and physically. Usually those who talk about "partying" in a LAN are techno-geekish in nature and not accustomed to actually holding conversations without a keyboard in front of them

LAN parties are organized by a kid with a few computers in the house or by large game companies to promote their products. There are also private LAN parties, where they rent a warehouse, wire it, and have the participants lug in their own *tricked-out* machines. These fancy eye-candy machines are called *case mods*. It means adding windows (to see inside the machine's case), lights, colors, extra fans and water cooling (for better heat control), and other artistic designs, as well as souped-up machines with overclocked chips.

For more information on LAN parties:

LAN Party— www.lanparty.com

UnReal Tournament—www.unrealtournament.com/pc/lanparties.html

For more information on case mods, go to:

Case-Mods—www.case-mod.com

Case etc—www.caseetc.com

CaseModWorld—www.casemodworld.com

Handheld Games

According to research company Datamonitor, by 2005 mobile gaming will reach more than 200 million wireless phone and PDA (handheld) units in the United States and Europe. Sprint PCS has signed up 10 content providers to supply 30 games on its wireless Web service. Verizon Wireless and AT&T Wireless also plan to offer similar services.

There are quite a few games that can be played on a PDA. PopCap offers some. There are many different freeware games available. For more information, go to one of the many directories of freeware PDA games, such as:

Palm Gaming World—www.palmgamingworld.com/arcade/arcade.shtml

Astraware—www.astraware.com/index/php

PopCap—www.popcap.com

Online Gambling

Gambling in the United States has always been a big industry. In the past, gambling could be done only at legal locations licensed by local and federal governments. First, there was only Nevada, then Atlantic City, then Indian tribal gaming and small poker rooms. Now you can gamble on your computer on the Internet.

How it works is you log onto a casino site, download the gaming programs, and use a credit card or electronic funds transfer service to cover your bets and to collect your winnings.

Internet gambling is big and growing. The General Accounting Office of the U.S. government estimates that Internet bets will total more than $4 billion in 2003 alone. The estimate is that it will reach $10 billion in 2004. There are over 2,000 online casinos by most guesses.

The problem, aside from the estimated 11 million problem gamblers, is that there is no way for an online site to tell a legal-aged gambler from an underaged one (using Mom's credit card). There is no recourse if a site uses your credit card information for nefarious purposes. In fact, there is no protection for you at all. It's no different than going to an illegal casino in the basement of some strange guy's home.

Online gambling is illegal by most definitions. There are some gray areas, but all signs point to the gut feeling that it's a bad idea.

The feds contend that Internet gambling is a tool to launder money and evade taxes. They say it's only a matter of time before organized crime will get into it in a big way. As it is, the consumer has little or no protection because it is an industry without regulatory oversight. There are no enforceable laws if the Web site sucks thousands out of an account for losses but doesn't add any money in for the winnings. It's like betting at a cockfight. If you don't get your money, don't go to the cops. The question coming up will be, "What were you doing there, anyway?"

It is unlike a traditional horse track, casino, or lottery, where there are strict laws to make sure the "house" isn't taking undue odds for its side. The Nevada Gaming Control Board has historically always been stringent in investigating and punishing casino owners who tip the odds in their favor. They want the odds for everyone walking in the door to be exactly the same. The Internet has no such controls. In fact, the people operating these sites are offshore. The moral: The individual gambler is not protected in any way when gambling in an Internet casino.

Flashy Sites

There is no doubt about it. The gambling casinos online are flashy. Chances are that they'll claim they are safe, registered, and 100% legal. However, the sad truth is that if they are so honorable, why do they throw more pop-ups, cookies, and banner ads onto your machine than even the worst of the porno Web sites? (One gambling site threw a whopping 12 pop-up ads onto my machine in less than 3 minutes.) The basic rule of thumb is that the more flashing images, slick blaring headlines, and pop-ups from a Web site, the faster you should run. (If they are "for real," why do they need to bombard you and load up your machine with junk?)

Some of these Web sites will actually hijack your machine so you cannot get the pop-ups to stop coming up; the harder you try to close the window, the faster it keeps reasserting itself. In many cases, the only thing you can do is shut down your machine to regain control. (Although, usually the command ALT F4 when clicked fast enough will stop the onslaught.)

The Big Question—Are They Legal?

This is a complicated issue. There are federal laws in place that seem to prohibit Internet gambling outright. The U.S. Justice Department has taken the stance that federal law does prohibit gambling over the Internet, including casino-style gaming. But so far, they have gone after only the people who run these casinos. There are several laws that can be cited, including:

- Interstate Transportation of Wagering Paraphernalia Act
- Professional and Amateur Sports Protection Act
- Interstate and Foreign Travel or Transportation in Aid of Racketeering Enterprises Act
- The Wire Act

The Federal Interstate Wire Act of 1961 was passed to prohibit betting operations conducted over a telephone. The Organized Crime Control Act of 1970 made it illegal to engage in a gambling business if there is a state law in place that specifically prohibits it. The Federal Travel Act prohibits all interstate communications *intent on facilitating the dispersal of gambling proceeds*. However, because the Internet is not strictly prohibited, some argue that there is some wiggle room in the law's interpretation.

The looming question is how to deal with operations located offshore, where online gambling isn't deemed illegal. Most gambling Web sites exist offshore, where gambling is legal. These are places such as Netherlands Antilles, Antigua, New Zealand, the Cook Islands, Curacao, Australia, Germany, South Africa, Sweden, Dominica, Nevis, Costa Rica, Grand Turk, Mauritius, Saint Kitts, Trinidad, and Vanuatu. They charge a fee, the online casino owner pays, and they are "registered" to operate. The site owners take the stance that they are legal.

This is where the murky area of the newborn Internet law comes in. It's not clear. (The state courts have taken the stance that Web sites are targeting the residents of their states, so they have jurisdiction. The courts' contention is that it is irrelevant that Internet gambling is legal in Mauritius or wherever.)

One State's View

U.S. federal law takes the stance that it is not illegal for individuals to operate an Internet gambling site. It is illegal to solicit bettors in the United States. In other words, it is illegal for the offshore operators to accept wagers from U.S. citizens. The government is trying to force the Web site owners to police themselves. In this way, operators who are flagrant violators are charged or threatened. The Justice Department so far hasn't gone after the U.S. citizens who place the bets (although there has been pressure on the credit card companies and the money transfer services not to do business with these kinds of services).

The states are another issue. The laws from state to state vary. Washington State is one that has gone a step further than the feds. According to the state Web site, "People in Washington State who place bets on the Internet can be charged with professional gambling in the Third Degree, which is a gross misdemeanor. You could also be charged with violating the law prohibiting the knowing transmission or receipt of gambling information. You could also be charged with Professional Gambling in the First, Second or Third Degree, depending on the amount of money and the number of people involved. Criminal penalties range from imprisonment of one to ten years and a fine of between $5,000 and $20,000." If this works, other states may follow their lead.

The Canadian government has taken the stance that running a gaming establishment over the Internet violates existing Canadian law. This will subject foreign site operators to prosecution in Canada if they solicit or accept bets from Canadian citizens.

THE BITE OF THE GOVERNMENT

Jay Cohen was a 27-year-old trader at the San Francisco Stock Exchange when he started one of the first online sports books in 1997. He went to Antigua to be legal, along with two partners, Steve Shillinger and Hayden Ware, to start the World Sports Exchange (WSE), which is a Web site that solicited people residing in the United States to place bets through the use of a toll-free 800 number and the WSE Web site. He also placed ads in various U.S. newspapers and magazines. He was charged by the U.S. under an antiquated federal anti-gambling statute. He returned to the United States to fight the charges. He lost. In February 2000, Jay Cohen was convicted of violating the Wire Wager Act. He was sentenced to 21 months in prison and fined $5,000. (Shillinger and Ware are still fugitives.) For more information www. freejaycohen.com

There have been a number of legislative attempts in the United States to further outlaw online gambling. One problem so far has been in finding a way to define gambling that won't also infringe on online gaming, such as Xbox, PlayStation, and other popular kids' enterprises. In fact, the way it's been attempted in bills such as the Leach-Oxley Bill, introduced in early 2003, the definition of gambling consistent with current federal law as "games predominantly subject to chance" would probably also outlaw chess, golf, and PacMan.

It doesn't help that the large horse racing, dog racing, and tribal gaming lobbying groups oppose most of the legislation that has been proposed to date. In fact, California bowed to the lobbying groups in 2002 by passing a law specifically making it legal to place pari-mutuel bets on off-track horse races over the Internet, as long as the bets were placed with approved locations.

Professor I. Nelson Rose, an attorney who specializes in Internet gambling (he tends to favor it) wrote about Internet gambling in an article on the Gaming Floor Web site (www.gamingfloor.com/features/Rose/Tribal_Internet_Gaming.html). Mr. Rose posed the questions, "Can Indian tribes run online lotteries, bingo and casinos? Can they license non-Indians to operate gambling sites on the Internet?"

He went on to cite several examples, including this one:

> In 1997, the Coeur d'Alene tribe in Idaho set up the first Internet Indian lottery, accepting bets for anyone located in a state with a state lottery. Non-Indian companies spent millions of dollars setting up the "U.S. Lottery," but its computers were always on tribal land. The tribe shut down the lottery, at least temporarily, after losing court cases in Missouri and Idaho.

Other tribes have followed with various ploys intended to work within loopholes. The key question is, If the tribes can license or operate Internet gambling, can they involve non-Indians in this? It all comes down to the main premise: Are the tribes sovereign? The courts will have to sort this out. For now, it is just another piece of the perplexing puzzle of Internet gambling. Right now, the key features seem to be the question of greed, the public's best interests, and the government's role in protecting us.

SUMMARY

Online gaming and even gambling is probably the fastest growing online activity and, as you can see, there are endless diversions that can be exploited online. Whether you are on a budget or have money to burn, you can find a lot of game-related entertainment online. There is something for everyone and something for every age.

9
DOWNLOADING
ONLINE
CONTENT

"I don't want a faster computer. What I need is a faster connection."

Quote from the author

This chapter covers the most repeated act in the online world—downloading. The ability to download quickly is an important part of today's online world. It's a big subject that we'll cover in stages. The first discussion is about the catchall term of *downloading*.

The terms *downloading* and *uploading* were coined to explain the acts of sending and receiving content and information between computers. An easy way to remember what these words mean is to exchange *downloading* with the word *receive* and *uploading* with the word *send*.

The Web is a content and information provider. Content and information are obtained through the process known as downloading. Downloading is repeated million of times an hour, every day, worldwide, by people who are connected via the Internet. The majority of these people are downloading information such as news and research materials. Many others download content such as movies, pictures, software, and music.

Here are some examples: When you type in a URL, you request a server to download a Web page to your machine. If you want to update your older software by downloading a new version through an FTP site (which will be covered a little later in this chapter), you are asking another computer to send you a file.

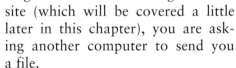

When you request your email be sent to you, a request from your computer is sent to another computer asking for the email (covered in more detail in Chapter 10). This is another example of the transaction of downloading. There would not be an Internet without the ability to download content from another location. There would be no chat lines, no newsgroups, no instant messaging—in essence, no Web and no peer-to-peer software (see Chapter 26).

TYPES OF MODEMS

Let's take a closer look at the different types of connection speeds that are currently available. Remember that your connection speeds change constantly due to the other computers you are connecting to, as well as any Internet lag that will directly affect your downloading time. Modem speeds are measured in bits per second. A bit is one unit of data. Eight bits, or a byte, constitute a word of data. This becomes all the more confusing because this word of data corresponds to 8-bit computing. Since the advent of 16-bit, 32-bit, and now 64-bit computing, word size has actually increased. But in general, we still consider 8 bits to be a byte.

When talking about modem speed, the measurement is in bits per second. So when talking about the transfer rate of so many bytes per file, you'd multiply the number of bytes by 8, then divide by the bits per second speed of the modem to get the rough download calculation.

Standard 56.6K Modem

Transfer Speed: 40–56 Kilobits per Second (Kbps)

The average time needed to download a 5-MB file is between 15 and 25 minutes, depending on the connection speed and lag time.

Modems are now standard additions to computers. The most common types of modems that are shipped with new computers today are 56-Kbps modems, also referred to as *V.90 modems*. One of the reasons that 56-Kbps modems are so popular is because there are hundreds of Internet dialup services that support thousands of 56-Kbps lines, which also happen to be regular phone lines. Another reason that they are so popular is because the connection can be made over a standard telephone line, with no special equipment other than the standard modem that came with the computer.

Mobile Wireless (Cell Phone)

Transfer Speed: 9.6–56.6 Kbps

The average time needed to download a 5-MB file using a mobile wireless connection is between 15 and 80 minutes, depending on the connection speed and lag time.

With the advent of various mobile and handheld wireless devices, such as cell phones and handheld computers, many of the same functions—downloading songs, email, and Web pages—that can be done with a more powerful home computer can be done on a handheld. However, the bandwidth of mobile wireless is still too slow to be of any practical use in downloading large files such as music and movies. It can work relatively well with email and Web pages.

Integrated Services Digital Network (ISDN)

Transfer Speeds: One Channel at 56–64 Kbps

(Two channels can be used in combination to achieve different results with speeds up to 128 Kbps.)

The major reason ISDN was created was to integrate analog voice and digital data over a single network. ISDN lines are (by comparison) complicated technology and not widely available to the home user. They involve the installation of two special phone lines, with distinct phone numbers that operate together. The phone lines are charged by the minute of use instead of a flat rate (as in the case of many other phone services). The problem for the average user is in the expense to the user because of the complexity required by the provider to insure that the correct adapters are installed at both ends of the connection (which means the service provider needs the right equipment and trained employees to support an ISDN modem). The service is still available as an alternative to DSL in some parts of the country and for special uses (such as broadcast ISDN, switched digital for Public Radio, and for some audio applications). It is an option for people who are too remote to connect with DSL and are not served by a cable modem network. Check with your local phone company to find out whether you can subscribe to this service and what the cost is in your area.

Cable or Cable Modem Termination System

Transfer Speed: 1–10 Mbps

The average time needed to download a 5-MB file with a cable modem is between 1 and 5 minutes, depending on the connection speed and lag time.

Cable modems are popular throughout the country. Cable broadcast (television) companies have expanded their business to include data transmissions along their lines. The cable modems are specialized equipment, designed to exchange the digital transmissions originating on the Internet with compatible cable modem signals in order to complete a connection. Cable modems lack the ability to allow direct connections between two or more cable modems. All transmissions must be routed through the cable modem termination system (CMTS).

Cable modems are available only through your cable company. However, just because you can get cable TV doesn't mean you can get an Internet connection. Be sure to check out the availability of this option if you are currently using ISDN or a standard modem. It offers faster downloads and connections, although the speeds vary depending on how many people are connected at a given time. The logjam may be, in part, due to the CMTS.

Digital Subscriber Line (DSL) and Asymmetric Digital Subscriber Line (ADSL)

Transfer Speed: 640 Kbps to 6 Mbps or higher

The average time needed to download a 5-MB file with a DSL or ADSL modem is between 1 and 10 minutes, depending on the connection speed and lag time.

If your home or office is close enough to your local telephone company central office that offers DSL, you can experience high-speed bandwidth over your standard telephone line. DSL installations began in 1998 and have continued to grow at an astonishing rate. DSL is replacing ISDN and will continue to compete with cable modems for small businesses and home offices.

DSL lines can carry both voice and data signals, so you can be online and chatting on the telephone at the same time. DSL's faster connection speeds are perfect for the transmission of video and audio streams, which demand the higher bandwidth it can provide.

Satellite

Transfer Speed: Typically up to 400 Kbps

The average time needed to download a 5-MB file with a satellite dish is between 2 and 10 minutes, depending on the connection speed and lag time.

Satellite modems are becoming as affordable as cable and DSL, although the availability is limited in some areas. The advantage of using a satellite modem is that you can usually deploy one just about anyplace you have good exposure to the southern sky. If you live in the country, or just can't find an Internet provider in your area, then a satellite connection is probably a good alternative. The downside is that satellite or microwave systems have a noticeable lag to them. When you are downloading, the signals come in bursts, unlike the steadier landline connections.

Using a satellite has a higher up-front cost than the other services, because the provider usually makes the user purchase the equipment. This can cost anywhere from just a couple of hundred to thousands of dollars. The nice thing is that you own it and can take it with you if you move. The lag time can be intolerable for many people. (As a service, it may be best suited for big downloads.)

Microwave

Transfer Speed: 256 Kbps to 2 Mbps

The average time needed to download a 5-MB file with a microwave dish is between 2 and 6 minutes, depending on the connection speed and lag time.

Microwave modems are almost identical to satellite modems, except that the signal does not have to travel as far; therefore, the connection lag times are less. Microwave signals are passed along with ground-based "repeaters." A drawback is that microwave modems have a higher up-front cost than the landline-based services. The equipment can cost anywhere from just a couple of hundred to thousands of dollars. It's also a very specialized technology, in that it needs the landline capable of supporting the equipment. Most of the systems require line-of-sight to the transmission tower, although newer radio versions of this technology may eliminate this requirement.

PIRILLO'S DOWNLOAD TIPS

For a download calculator, as well as a means to gauge your direct Internet connection speed, try visiting www.numion.com. For maximizing your download speeds in Windows, download CableNut for free at www.cablenut.com.

With basic information (data and access speed) you could calculate how long it would take to download a file. Most download sites offer you information to give you a rough idea of how long the information exchange will take. If you want to do a lot of downloading, the fastest transmission scheme you can afford will be the most desirable.

TRANSLATING TRANSFER RATES TO TRANSMITTED DATA

Use the following figures when determining how much data is being transmitted:

- A single bit can either be a 0 (zero) or a 1 (one).
- It takes 8 bits to make a byte.
- Kbps means kilobits per second.

- One kilobit equals 1,000 bits.
- Mbps means megabits per second.
- One megabit equals 1,000,000 bits.

For purposes of simplifying the math, it usually takes 1 byte (8 bits) of data to make up a single letter or character. In other words, the letter takes up about 8 bits (1 byte) of space.

PROTOCOLS ON THE INTERNET

The Internet has what's known as *TCP/IP protocols*, which include all of the following:

Transmission Control Protocol (TCP), which is a set of rules to exchange messages with other Internet points at the packet level

Internet Protocol (IP), which is a set of rules to send/receive messages at the Internet address level

Hypertext Transfer Protocol (HTTP) and File Transfer Protocol (FTP), which are defined sets of rules to use with other programs elsewhere on the Internet.

DOWNLOADING CONSIDERATIONS

There are many different things to consider when it comes to downloading. None of them are earthshaking, but they are worth some thought. You wouldn't want to download a huge file if you had a very slow connection speed and little time to wait. The questions of virus protection and whether the download is legal are ones that are often posed. The main considerations are:

1. What is the connection speed?
2. Should virus protection be used?
3. Is it legal content and/or information to download? Is the source reliable?
4. Do I have the right software needed to use the content or view the information?

Connection Speed

The connection speed is an important aspect of downloading content. It determines the time needed to download. No matter what type of connection you require, it all comes down to understanding speed. It's a simple rule of thumb: The slower the connection speed, the longer a download takes.

An important thing to remember about connection speeds is that you can never expect to get the maximum transfer rate every time. In fact, you will usually achieve only about 80% of the possible speed, due to what's called *net lag*. Net lag simply means that there is a slowdown somewhere that has caused your connection speeds to drop. This is similar to a traffic jam on a normally fast-moving highway. Net lag is unpredictable but does tend to pass. However, when excessive, it can be a huge annoyance.

PING AND TRACEROUTE

There are many software programs to allow you to check on your connection speed. The most commonly used program to do this is called PING. This standard network command can be used to identify whether the computer you are trying to connect to is working. This command can also be used to determine the connection speed between you and the remote computer.

The PING program works by sending a digital packet to the computer you are trying to connect to, then waits for the answer to come back. The PING command was created to allow users to find out whether another user or location is available on a network. The term *ping* was coined from World War II submarines that used to send out a sonar "pulse" from their submarines to locate (ping) enemy submarines and ships.

It is an acronym for Packet Internet Groper. When you ping, you're seeing whether a specific IP address is accessible. A packet of data is sent, and a reply is sent back. Think of it as a way of asking an IP address, "Hey are you awake or what?" That's a ping.

Traceroute

Traceroute is a command that allows you to determine the path a packet takes from a given source by returning the sequence of hops that the packet has traversed. This is a way to check for a response from a specific IP address. It's used if the "ping" isn't returned. Traceroute can help uncover why it's not answering. This is a utility that traces the route between your computer and the device you're trying to contact. It shows where problems may have occurred, and it displays the responses from each stopping point (or hop) along the way. This utility comes with your operating system. It is used to help determine a problem if PING fails.

Virus Protection

All content that is downloaded from any source, including your friends, family, and associates, should be checked with virus protection software (see Chapter 12). There are many types of viruses and worms that can be packaged and distributed along with downloaded software. In fact, almost 90% of the problems that exist with viruses, worms, and Trojan horses exist because the people who create them rely on the fact that most people do not have effective security systems in place. Kaspersky antivirus software is an example of the many programs available. By left-clicking on any file, the dialog box shown in Figure 9.1 will appear when Kaspersky has been installed.

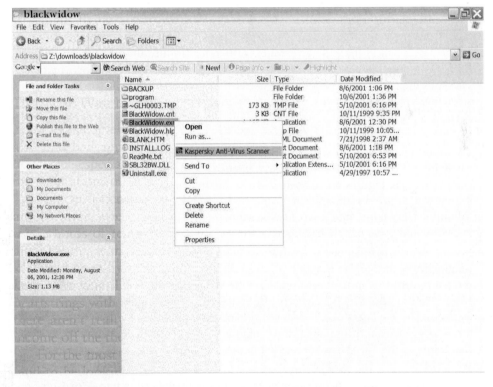

FIGURE 9-1 **BY SELECTING IT AS SHOWN, THE FILE CAN BE INDIVIDUALLY CHECKED FOR THE PRESENCE OF A VIRUS.**

Spoofing is a hot topic on the Web. It is a common problem. Spoofing occurs when a user thinks he or she is going to a certain location, only to be tricked into going to another. You can also be fooled as to the contents of the file you are downloading and find you have downloaded a completely different thing. It's the *bait and switch* of the Internet—in essence, a con job. (For more information on this, see Chapter 11.)

Content Issues

One of the hardest issues for users is whether the downloadable content and information are legal to own. The problem is that not all software available is really "free." The Internet has made it easier for people to download both legal and illegal versions of software. (Later in this chapter, we'll discuss some legal avenues to inexpensive or free software.)

WAREZ AND APPZ

Over the last few years new terms have appeared on the online landscape. *Warez* (and the lesser *appz*) generally refers to illegally obtained or bootlegged commercial software programs modified to bypass serial numbers and any encryption techniques. The software is freely distributed through various Web sites, underground networks, and chat systems, such as AOL or the IRC. The Web sites are constantly changing names, and it's a full-time job to keep track of them.

The movement is seen by some as a Robin Hood type of noble cause to allow many people to use programs that are expensive and out of reach because of the purchase price. Figures released in 2001 by the International Planning & Research Corporation estimated that online piracy cost U.S. software makers $2.6 billion in "lost sales" and a worldwide estimate of $11.8 billion. (A question arises: Would these people have purchased the software to justify those numbers?)

For a time, the people who posted warez were immune from prosecution because of a loophole in Internet law that allowed distribution as long as there was no monetary profit from it. Warez sites are free. They distribute copies of software from major vendors such as Microsoft, Symantec, Macromedia, and Adobe Systems. The NET Act of 1997 closed the loophole, making it possible for government agencies to prosecute. However, one of the problems in prosecution is that many of the Web sites are located in other countries where the law cannot reach them.

The warez community includes elements of an organized crime family or Communist cell system from the 1930s: Elaborately layered command and control and much anonymity among the members of a cell. These folks plague many commercial software vendors by making commercial programs available illegally through warez channels. Even copy-protected software is usually cracked or modified to defeat these schemes by the various warez gangs (who go by odd hacker monikers, such as Drink or Die, a defunct group believed to have come out of Russia). Anyone looking for this software can usually find it by going to Google and typing in the word *warez*, although there is no guarantee that any group is legitimate and not a government sting operation looking for you!

Although the software industry claims losses in the billions of dollars, it's hard to prove that anyone stealing software would actually buy that software in the first place. The purveyors of warez don't do it for money but claim a noble higher purpose. But this higher purpose does more harm than good, if it indeed does any good at all. If warez were not available, the alternate sources of similar software—such as quality shareware—would probably be used more. In fact, an interesting argument going around says that warez actually hurts the small shareware authors more than it does the big companies because they are the ones who really lose the sales. If this is even partially true, it is reason enough to avoid using warez.

The only category of software where the warez problem will eventually remain is computer games, especially console games. Because the warez scene is dominated by youngsters (the under-17 crowd) and few with jobs, the higher price of games ($50–$70) makes bootlegging attractive. The game companies rationalize that the high price is needed to pay for lost bootleg sales, which are indeed troublesome. So a chicken-and-egg situation has resulted. The high prices are needed to combat lost sales due to piracy. Piracy exists only because of high prices. This problem will be around for a while.

The amount of information and content that is moved across the Internet doubles every 100 days. This means that users have more things available to choose from, which could include illegal software, content, or information. The thing to keep in mind is that there have been laws enacted to counter this. So if you download music that is copyrighted, you are breaking the law. If you download warez (illegal versions of software that have been "hacked" or copied by someone), or even if you download information or pictures that are deemed illegal to own (such as the broad category of kiddie porn), it's in violation of the law. Although the possibility of being caught may be relatively low, it's still contraband. You could still be subject to some pretty heavy fines and even jail.

DVORAK'S DOWNLOAD TIP

If you want to capture a PDF (Portable Document Format) file or image to your hard disk, right-click and a dialog box will appear that will let you save the target PDF file or image. With the Mac, you just click and hold the mouse button down to get the menu.

Always check to see whether you have the legal right to download the content or information prior to downloading it. Most sites that provide downloads have license and rights of use information, which will help you understand the restrictions of use and ownership that may apply to the content and information you wish to download.

Browser Plug-ins

Downloadable information comes in a variety of formats. Many of the formats need specialized browser software to run. This browser software is called *plug-ins*. These small software programs offer extra features to decipher certain types of files or to display moving graphics, among other things. Plug-ins are usually free of charge.

PIRILLO'S DOWNLOAD TIP

If you want to clean out or manage your browser plug-ins (also known as Browser Helper Objects), try using the free BHODemon from www.definitivesolutions.com.

Plug-ins are part of a larger HTML document. These take one of three routes to get onto your computer. There are plug-ins that have the server look for the plug-in file on the destination computer. If it's not found or is an old version, a text box will pop up on the screen and ask the user to go to another Web site to download the needed program. Other plug-ins are either loaded at the time the document is displayed or the user is prompted to approve an automatic download of the plug-in. Plug-in downloads can also be hidden from the user's perspective.

In most instances when you download from the Internet onto a Windows machine, you will get the confirming dialog box shown in Figure 9.2.

SOME COMMON PLUG-INS

 Apple Quick-Time lets you experience QuickTime animation, music, MIDI, audio, video, and VR panoramas and objects directly in a Web page.

Adobe Acrobat Reader is required to view a PDF page. It allows the browser to display a document compatible with a printed format, with layout and fonts the same as those you'd see if it were a printed document. It's usually used to view a page that needs rigid formatting, such as a government form or pages of a book. It also has the ability to keep a page from being copied, or downloaded. For more information, go to www.adobe.com/support/downloads/main.html.

Macromedia Flash Player is the standard viewing for animation and other entertainment on the Web. Many Web pages have very fancy Flash graphic introduc-

---

tions that play like little movies. Although you can often skip these introductions, many are really amazing to watch. For more information, go to www.macromedia.com/downloads.

Shockwave by Macromedia is for interactive games, multimedia, graphics, and streaming audio on the Web. The download time is approximately 8 minutes on a 56K modem (3,190-K file size) at www.macromedia.com/downloads.

RealPlayer by RealNetworks lets you play streaming audio, video, animations, and multimedia presentations. To download, go to www.real.com.

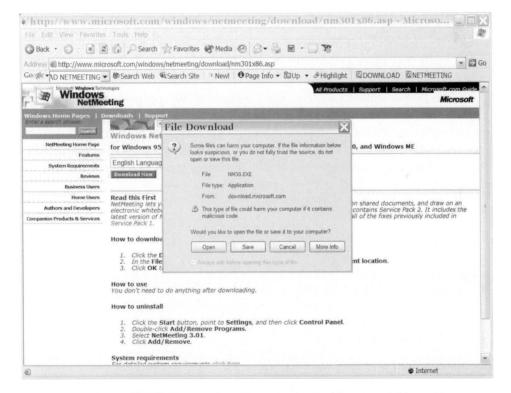

FIGURE 9.2 HERE YOU ARE GIVEN THE OPTION TO SAVE THE FILE FOR LATER USE OR TO EXECUTE IT IMMEDIATELY. IF YOU SAVE THE FILE, ANOTHER DIALOG BOX WILL APPEAR ASKING YOU WHERE YOU WANT IT SAVED. CAREFULLY CHOOSE WHERE TO PLACE THE FILE. OFTEN, A FILE IS LOST WHEN IT IS SAVED TO SOME OBSCURE LOCATION.

Shareware

There are a lot of programs that all of us would like or think we'd like, but

our pocketbook just isn't big enough to accommodate all our desires. An overwhelming consideration for most users is the cost of software. Most new PCs come preinstalled with a variety of software applications, which is an important factor, especially for a person buying his or her first system. (If you take a look at the price of even the most basic version of Office XP today, it's easy to see why.) Software prices are shockingly high. Many simply can't afford the prices of the software—enter shareware.

The idea behind shareware is simple. It's called "try-before-you-buy software." Shareware is often better than commercial software, and the great thing about it is there is no risk. If you don't like it, you go someplace else without losing money.

When you download a shareware version of an application you're interested in, you haven't committed yourself to anything. So if the software doesn't work as it should or doesn't dazzle you with its features and quality, you can uninstall it and try something else. If you're not impressed, you won't buy it. In fact, there are few commercial software programs that could not be replaced by inexpensive shareware programs.

THE HISTORY OF SHAREWARE

Shareware was an idea that appeared. It was gimmicky. The basic thought was that you give people software and let them decide whether they want to send you money for it. It wasn't so unlike the bootleg software that was everywhere, except that it would be legal. Few people really thought the idea would go anywhere, but it did.

Shareware first appeared in different places at the same time, 1982. In this case, two people, Andrew Fluegelman in Tiburon, California and Jim Knopf in Bellevue, Washington, came up with similar ideas.

Their concepts were similar: to let people try software before buying it—a sort of "play then pay" marketing concept. It was an exciting development in computers. To comprehend the climate fully, you must understand that bigger software companies had programs that were very expensive, even compared with today's prices, and of limited use. (They weren't the huge, multidimensional programs that we

---

have today.) A lot of the programs were plain junk, and there was little in the way of customer support. It was a huge gamble to spend a hundred or two for a program that might have little use. This new concept was embraced with zeal.

Andrew Fluegelman's strategy was to give out copies of his PC-TALK software freely. If people liked it, they'd pay for it. If not, no skin off his nose. Andrew claimed to coin the name *freeware*, and for a short time that looked like it was going to stick. But then he went a step further and claimed to have a copyright on the name (which he didn't) and said he'd sue anyone who used it. Everyone immediately began to look for a new moniker. (After all, who wanted a lawsuit over a silly new word?)

But in all the confusion, it's unknown who really coined the term *shareware*. There are many stories and many claims. The word crept into common usage almost overnight. However, credit should be given to journalist Jay Lucas. His article in *InfoWorld*, a computer newspaper, contained a description of software that was available for free or for a small copying charge, which he dubbed *shareware*. This reference seems to predate all others.

Jim Knopf (who was usually referred to as *Jim Button* because his software company was called *Buttonware*) had written a label program called *PC-File* (its early name was *Easy File*). He too was giving away his software. He called it *shareware*. After all, the name fit, because the intent was to use the software, make copies, and pass it around freely—to share it. If the software was useful to users and they liked it, then the request was to make a $10 donation. This donation would also include users in his mailing list for future updates and other programs.

One of Jim's first customers telephoned him to ask whether he knew that there was someone else with a very similar idea. Jim and Andrew contacted each other and decided to reference each other jointly on their distribution disks. (Which was when Buttonware renamed its Easy File program to a name that was closer to Fluegelman's PC-Talk.) It also revised its price to $25, which was the cost of PC-Talk.

Jim Knopf didn't have high hopes of becoming wealthy from this scheme. He kept his day job at IBM and considered Buttonware a hobby. After all, although personal computers were selling fairly well, they weren't commonplace things yet. They were still in the hobby category. A cute diversion was the general consensus. The hobbyist angle was furthered with the proliferation of user groups and computer clubs. These were literally clubs that met weekly or monthly to promote and encourage home computing (as it was called back then) and to help new computer owners navigate the strange and mysterious world of bits and bytes. The clubs were huge promoters of shareware and freeware. Still, not everyone belonged to computer clubs. Computer magazines had an avid following.

The turning point for shareware was when a computer writer, Doug Clapp, wrote a review of PC-File in *PC World* magazine. Jim was vacationing in Hawaii and unaware of the article. Jim returned to find that his poor neighbor (who'd agreed to watch the house while they were away) had to haul the mail into the house in grocery bags. The basement was filled with bags of mail. The avalanche was overwhelming. By the summer of 1984, he was making 10 times as much from his hobby as he was from his job.

In 1983, another shareware pioneer, Bob Wallace, entered the market. His program was called PC-Write. Bob was an early employee of a small software company called Microsoft. He was an active member in the Northwest Computer Society and the Washington Software Association. He added a new twist to shareware history. If you share your program with someone else, you could earn a commission. Wallace's idea was very popular.

The traditional software companies were outraged. They declared that it was an idea that would die out. However, as history has shown, they were wrong.

Public Domain Software

There has always been confusion with the distinction between public domain software and shareware. For clarity, public domain is free, whereas shareware is a low-cost, voluntary fee product.

Historically, public domain software was the stock in trade of BBSs (bulletin board systems), disk vendors, and users' clubs. Public domain software was available to anyone for free. (Like Linux programs are today.) Most of the early programs were freely distributed between personal computer users. (At the time, there were so few personal computer users that you had to seek others out.)

Disk dealers, people who advertised in the back pages of magazines and sent long lists of programs for a modest fee, would send shareware and public domain software on the same disk. People thought they'd paid because they paid for the disk.

The only real difference between shareware and public domain software was a message embedded on the disk asking for payment when you ran the program. The message would use words such as *voluntary*, *donation*, and *contribution*. Some added little bad mojo guilt trips, such as "your conscience will bother you" and "God will strike you dead" or "evil will follow you." They were like kid's threats. These tactics didn't add to the glamour of shareware. It made it seem silly and petty. What helped was the formation of a trade organization.

The Association of Shareware Professionals

A formative event in shareware's popularity was a conference held in 1987. All the big names at the time gathered and established a trade organization, The Association of Shareware Professionals (ASP).

The ASP began with shareware programmers. It expanded to include vendors (distributors) and BBSs. It was an answer to the disk slingers who advertised "get software free" without informing customers that there could be further fees if they wanted to use the program and register it.

The ASP convinced programmers to adhere to some standards and guidelines. Among these were money-back guarantees, software support, and an ombudsman to help in disputes between programmers and users.

PCs became popular and more mainstream. (There was a point at which the number of computers sold doubled every month.) The software industry grew at an astronomical rate. Software became more complex and so much larger that the floppy disk was at the end of its useful life. (Multiple floppies were a pain to juggle and insert in the correct order, much less keep track of. All over America, people were losing disk three from a set of five, rendering the program useless.) The CD-ROM replaced the floppy disk.

The larger companies began the evolution of the software suite—a collection of related applications (loosely or closely related tasks). Companies combined spellcheckers and word processors or spreadsheets and graphing programs. Programs that had been sold individually before were now squashed together to entice a purchase. (More for less.) Microsoft was one of the pioneers in this area.

In retrospect, the shareware concept was in danger at this point. Smaller companies couldn't compete effectively against software giants and their megasoftware packages. At the time, the Internet wasn't an effective means to send software, due to the long download times with slow dial-up modems. But with the faster modems and other innovations (ISDN, DSL, and cable modems), the shareware industry has rebounded. Now the Internet is full of interesting small shareware programs.

THE BEST ONLINE DOWNLOAD SITES

The following list of sites was compiled from a list of worldwide Internet sites that provide the best information and content on the following items. Because there are over 500 million locations on the Internet, picking the top sites is quite a challenge. Sites change, content shifts, and new sites sprout up all the time. For this reason, it is recommended that you keep up with new download sites and check on the older ones every 90 days. By following these simple steps, you will be able to maintain a quality, up-to-date list of the best downloading sites available.

 SOFTWARE

ZD Net—http://www.downloads.com
TU COWS—http://www.tucows.com

JUMBO—http://www.jumbo.com/

DigiBits Network—http://www.freewarepro.com/

Dave Central—http://www.davecentral.com/

Software Oasis—http://www.softwareoasis.com

Downloadalot—http://www.downloadalot.com/

Best Deals on the Web—http://www.bestdealsontheweb.net/

Moochers—http://www.moochers.com/

5 Star—http://www.5star-shareware.com/

WebAttack—http://www.webattack.com/

MOVIES

Movie Soundtracks—http://www.moviewavs.com/

Ultimate Movie Clips—http://www.ultimatemovieclips.com/

Bijou Flix—http://www.bijoucafe.com/

GAMES

Free Games Online—http://www.freegamesonline.com/

Happy Puppy—http://www.happypuppy.com/

The Free Games Network—http://www.free-games-net.com/

Kids Site—http://www.kidsites.com/sites-fun/online-games.htm

MUSIC

Microsoft Music—http://music.msn.com/download/

MP3.com—http://www.mp3.com

Audio Find—http://www.audiofind.com/

MP3 Grand Central—http://www.mp3grandcentral.com

Free Music online—http://www.free-music.com/

INTERNET RESEARCH SITES

NUA Internet Surveys—http://www.nua.org/surveys/

Cyber Atlas—http://www.cyberatlas.internet.com

Research Buzz—http://www.researchbuzz.com

Internet Stats—http://www.internetstats.com

PIRILLO'S FAVORITE DOWNLOAD SITES

No Nags—http://www.nonags.com

Major Geeks—http://www.majorgeeks.com

Son of Spy Freeware—http://sover.net/~whoi

Oldversion.com—http://www.oldversion.com

CFS (completely free software)—http://ww.completelyfreesoftware.com

Media Horizon Freeware—http://www.mediahorizon.net

RocketDownload.com—http://www.rocketdownload.com

Freeware Guide—http://www.freeware-guide.com

Open Source

In addition to shareware and public domain, there is another software type talked about quite a bit right now. This is open source. Open source is both a nonprofit organization and a descriptive phrase. The Open Source Initiative is a group dedicated to promote free availability to a program's source code to anyone who desires to see it and/or change it. (Source code is the set of instructions written in a programming language to direct a computer to act in a specific manner. The result is what we call software or a computer program.)

At one time, most computer software source code was available (usually for a price) to developers and to people who wanted to customize it. Programmers are all for the code to be open (available) because it allows them to fix problems and make additions. For the rest of us, it doesn't mean that much, really. However, if the code is open to all for modification, the final result may be a better program. As different versions change hands and are adapted along the way, bugs are fixed, enhancements are added, and the software itself should (in theory) be constantly improved. The idea promoted is that when other programmers can read, modify, and redistribute the code, the software evolves at a far more productive rate.

Much open source software is for very specific uses. This includes programming languages, operating systems, database programs, and the like, most of which are covered elsewhere in this book.

Examples of open source software include:

PIRILLO'S DOWNLOAD TIP

www.sourceforge.net is the world's largest repository for open source code and software. It provides a centralized place for open source developers to control and manage open source development.

- Linux: An alternative operating system based on UNIX
- Apache: Open source Web tools currently in use on around 50% of the world's Web servers (see Chapter 14)
- Perl: Probably running more scripts on Web sites than all other languages put together (see Chapter 14)
- BIND: Okay, not exactly a well-known name, but this is the baby behind the domain name system (DNS) for the whole Internet and SENDMAIL, the most widely used email transport on the Internet today (see Chapter 10)
- MySQL: A database used in Web page development (see Chapter 14)

SUMMARY

One of the primary activities of the online world is downloading. But there are security problems inherent in downloading without caution. (On one extreme, there are companies that do not allow downloading out of this fear.) In fact, one day most software and even entertainment, such as movies, will be predominantly distributed by downloading.

10
EMAIL AND SPAM

"One of these days there will only be email."

John C. Dvorak, writing in *InfoWorld*, 1982

Email is an incredible telecommunications medium to let you exchange messages with others, from one computer to another. It's the most frequently used application on the Internet. According to International Data Corporation (IDC), 5.1 billion emails were sent every day in 2000 in the United States alone. The world daily tally was over 8.2 billion. IDC projects that by 2005, the number will be around 11.5 billion messages a day in the United States and over 26.1 billion worldwide. In the United States, there are 300 million email destinations. About 90 million Americans use email at work routinely. Fifty million Americans have email at home. Of those, the average home has four different email addresses (presumably one for each member of the family).

THE ROOTS OF MODERN EMAIL

Although early networking systems and the ARPANET had email systems, the roots of the commercial email we know today were first introduced to the public as proprietary services. If you wanted to send email to a friend, you both had to subscribe to the same service and use the same software. These were "dialup" systems. None of the systems were cross-connected systems with any reliability. There were no addresses as we see today (the @ sign wasn't heard of). The proprietary systems included: MCI Mail, EasyLink, Telecom Gold, One-to-One, and CompuServe.

Most people exchanged messages and information on bulletin board systems (BBSs), in forums, and directly by modem to modem. It wasn't that difficult to call a telephone number, connect your modem, and download or upload files. (At their height, there were tens of thousands of BBS systems. Yes, people did communicate without the Internet.) Modem speeds were a big factor in connections. The earliest pre-email connections were able to transmit only about 180 words a minute (150 bits per second [bps]).

Modem speeds climbed quickly, jumping in increments of 150 bps to 14,400 bps, to a current rate of 56 Kbps.

At about the same time, companies were experimenting with Local Area Network (LAN) systems, connecting various personal computers together, sometimes with mainframes. They developed LAN-based email systems. These connected to the mainframe, or central computer, and used a terminal emulation mode, so essentially the personal computers were used as terminals had been used before. However, the email programs became more complex yet easier to use. Company networks evolved. The Internet evolved.

As the Internet became available to more people—both corporate and private—email evolved from proprietary email systems. The key innovation was an evolution in protocol from a variety of protocols to SMTP (Simple Mail Transfer Protocol), which is the main protocol in use today.

Each Internet domain has a corresponding email server. To send an email message to someone, your email client first contacts the addressee's email server, based on rules of the SMTP. First, your server asks the other server whether there is anyone there by that email address. If so, it asks to transfer the email, and the receiving server stores it until the addressee retrieves it. The most common SMTP server in use is the *sendmail* system, but there are others.

Neither Snow nor Rain nor Heat nor Gloom of Night . . .

We all have some idea how the United States Postal Service (USPS) works. You put a stamp on an envelope and drop it into a delivery box. It's then sorted, trucked or flown to the right area, then sorted again, and taken out to be delivered. Email is based on the same premise.

When you click Send to launch an email, it is directed to the hosted mail servers (typically, this is a server located at your Internet Service Provider's [ISP's] server location). The message is then sent to the recipient's mail servers. Along the way, the message will bounce off sometimes dozens of other servers. Each server will look at the domain name portion of your intended recipient's email address and will route it to the proper place. The message will finally be delivered to the intended receiver's virtual mailbox residing on the mail servers, where it will sit until the intended recipient checks for email from a local mail client application or from the Internet, if Web mail is available.

Electronic mail messages are not sent in their entirety across the network. They are broken down by the transmission protocol into smaller individual components called *data packets*. They are then packaged, relayed across the network, and finally reassembled again just short of delivery. When each message is broken down, it is given a unique identification signature. The servers used to relay the packets from point A to point B know where to send each and every one. This is the reason email messages don't collide while in transit. Each unique signature has encoded information indicating the packet size, the origin, destination, sequence data, and encryption coding that's used to construct the packets.

Timing is important when relaying information across a network. Data packets are more likely to become corrupted in transit, rather than run the risk of a collision. To help alleviate the chances of collision and minimize the risk of data corruption during packet transfers, timing sequence algorithms are used. One of the reasons files and messages are broken into smaller packages is their transfer rate of speed. Data packets can be dispersed more quickly in smaller bundles. If data corruption occurs, it's faster for the mail server to resend a single smaller packet than to resend the entire message. If data corruption does occur—usually due to static line noise—the affected packets can be resent out until the entire message is reconstructed at the receiving end.

ANATOMY OF AN EMAIL ADDRESS

Each email address is expressed as: name@domain

Each name is unique to a domain. An email address such as *bob@address.net,* although simple, has all the information needed to get it to its destination. The domain name is not the "real" name. It's an alias because we're better at remembering names than long strings of numbers. Mail servers translate this domain name into the IP (Internet Protocol) address. Every computer on the Internet has a unique numerical address used to route packets to it. Just like your postal address allows the USPS to deliver mail to your house, your computer's IP address gives the network routing protocols the information they need. The receiving server will only have one "bob"; there is only one *address.net* on the Internet, and it cannot to be confused with *address.com, address.org.*

When you send email, the email servers use the Internet's standard DNS (Domain Name System) to find the IP address. The DNS maps the domain names to IP addresses. (The job is distributed among a number of servers so that none are overloaded and there is room for growth.) You can find out your IP address on a Windows computer by opening DOS or the command prompt and typing *winipcfg* or *ipconfig.* On a Macintosh, you can check your Network control panel.

You can also find your IP address at these Web sites:

IP Info—www.lawrencegoetz.com/programs/ipinfo

The Proxy Connection—http://stealthtests.lockdowncorp.com

Privacy Net—http://privacy.net/analyze

YOUR IP ADDRESS

The IP address is broken down into 4 bytes of information (totaling 32 bits), expressed as four numbers between 0 and 255, separated by periods. There are more than 4 billion possible IP addresses. There are several databases to look up a particular IP address to see what information is available on the address:

EMAIL CLIENT APPLICATIONS

There are two main types of email in today's environment: *standalone email software* and *Web-based email.* The ability to read any electronic mail message requires an email client application.

Standalone Clients

A standalone client is a self-contained executable application. (The term *client* is used because email applications are based on the client/server architecture.) Electronic mail messages are routed from several clients to a central server. The server redirects the mail messages to an anticipated destination—another client. (A server is a machine or process dedicated to managing devices or network traffic.)

Well-known, standalone email clients are Microsoft Outlook Express and Netscape. Netscape has built-in email readers, and Outlook Express most often comes installed on your computer.

DVORAK'S EMAIL TIP

For help configuring most email clients, visit the *Grapevine Internet Services* Web site at www.thevine. net/tutorial/emailclients.htm.

There are a number of popular, alternative, and often superior standalone email clients available. These are described in the following sections.

Eudora

Eudora, from Qualcomm, may be the most popular standalone email program in use today (it's Dvorak's choice). It has two versions, Eudora Light (free) and Eudora Pro (paid). There are MAC, PC, and Palm OS versions available. Eudora has a host of features that include enhanced filtering (will match addresses against the address book), SSL (secure sockets layer) support, attachment cautions, in-line flagging of words or phrases identified as potentially offensive (its Moodwatch is a feature to warn of possible flame content for incoming or outgoing email), and email usage stats for insight into email.

For more information, go to www.eudora.com.

PocoMail

PocoMail was designed from the ground up to protect users from viruses and spam. This email client automates common email duties, including spellcheck and virus scanning. It offers a long list of features.

For more information, go to www.pocosystems.com.

Pegasus Mail

Pegasus Mail is a free, simple-to-use email program. It's recommended if you are new to email. It's been around since 1990, making it one of the oldest standalone systems. It is designed for computers running Microsoft Windows or Novell NetWare LANs. It features built-in security against viruses (including Trojan viruses), automated rule-based mail filtering, content control to trap spam and unwanted mail, support for all major Internet mail-related protocols (SMTP, POP3, IMAP4, LDAP, PH), and SSL support for secure mail access, among others. In fact, it has quite a few features, too numerous to list.

For more information, go to www.pmail.com.

EMAIL RETRIEVAL PROTOCOLS

POP3 (Post Office Protocol 3) was a protocol written in 1988 by Marshall Rose. It allows a client to retrieve email from a server (it doesn't provide for sending email; that's done with SMTP or another method). This protocol is useful for computers without a permanent network connection because it allows for the mail to be held at the "post office" (the POP server) until you are ready and able to retrieve it. POP3 will transfer your email to the hard drive of your computer when you request your mail. Your mail is sent to your computer once you request it. However, because the mail is moved to your hard disk, it is better suited to those who check their email from one location only.

IMAP4 (Internet Message Access Protocol 4) is similar to POP but newer. It supports some additional features. With IMAP4, you can read and manipulate your mail messages while keeping them on the remote mail server. You can choose which messages to download to your machine. IMAP4 is useful for accessing mail from various locations. Most newer email clients support both systems.

Web Mail

Besides the client-resident email programs, there's also Web mail. Web mail gives you the ability to send and receive email from a Web site location on the Internet or local network. Many ISPs, such as AOL, MSN, Hotmail, Yahoo!, Hushmail, and United Online, offer Web mail applications. Web mail is a terrific alternative when you need to check your mail from another computer besides your own. Some services are fee-based, and others are free.

America Online

AOL is a unique service. It offers Internet browsing access, email, chat, shopping, and news, among other features—for a monthly fee. Pick up one of the diskettes for AOL that are almost everywhere and get a chunk of time for free (there are various offers). AOL offers email with its service. You get up to seven email accounts/screen names (the same thing). AOL mail keeps the mail stored on its servers and you always read from its system, not yours. The mail is not downloaded to your machine.

For more information, go to www.aol.com.

Yahoo! Mail

Yahoo! Mail can be also accessed from anywhere. Like AOL, the mail is saved on the company servers, so that you can view your mail and save it from any computer. Yahoo! email can also be automatically forwarded to other email accounts with its External Mail feature. You can configure Yahoo! Mail to retrieve messages from most external mail accounts (as long as they have POP access). Yahoo! has both a free and a fee-based email service for domestic and international users. The free service offers 4 MB of storage and up to 100 MB if you become a "power user" for a fee. It has a fairly good spam-blocking feature, SpamGuard. It is designed to reduce the amount of spam that ends up in your mailbox by sending it to a Bulk Mail Folder that you can delete without even viewing the contents. For spam that makes it into your regular email account, you have the option of reporting (instead of just deleting) it, further refining the spam-blocking capabilities. Rocketmail, which used to be a separate service, is now part of Yahoo! Mail.

For more information, go to www.yahoo.com.

MSN Hotmail

Hotmail is one of the oldest and still the most popular of the free email services (now part of the Microsoft empire). It is easy to use, with a host of features that have become standard, along with a few features that are still unique. The downside is that it offers only 2 MB of storage space, which is exceptionally low. There are so many MSN/Hotmail users that it is difficult to get a good email address without at least four digits in your user name.

For more information, go to www.hotmail.com.

Eudora Webmail

Eudora Webmail is a free email service provided by Lycos. It offers 5 MB of storage, three-level spam protection, and an email aggregation, so you can have all your email accounts funneled into one Eudora Webmail box.

For more information, go to www.eudoramail.com.

Hushmail

Hushmail is a secure Web-based email and document storage system. Hushmail uses industry standard algorithms (specified by the OpenPGP standard) to ensure the security, privacy, and authenticity of your email. Encryption and decryption are transparent to the user. The security features work only with another Hushmail account user but between users it offers a high level of privacy and security. The site points out that the information that we all routinely send and receive can be monitored, logged, analyzed, and stored by third parties. So for sensitive transmission—legal records, personal information, or medical records—with Hushmail you can send it securely. Not even a Hushmail employee with access to the servers can read your email.

Hushmail offers a free trial membership, but then you must upgrade to a premium service. Premium fea-

DVORAK'S EMAIL TIP

Email addresses.com keeps a list of the free email services on the Web, as well as fee ones:
www.emailaddresses.com
Free Email Providers Guide has over 1,400 free email services listed in more than 85 countries, along with details and articles about free email:
www.fepg.net
Free Email Addresses is another service to find free email accounts:
www.free-email-address.com

tures include: up to 128 MB email and document storage, custom spam featuring the Human Authenticator, and the ability to send and receive large attachments, among other features.

For more information, go to www.hushmail.com.

SENDING EMAIL ATTACHMENTS

Email started out as simple text messages sent to a recipient. It didn't offer much more versatility. However, advances in the use of email created a need to deliver more than just basic content messages. Now there is the ability to send attachments. *Attachment* literally means to "attach" a file to a text message. The attached file is then transferred along with the message to the recipient, where it is automatically downloaded and placed in a designated default folder. Most email client applications give users the option to choose which desktop folder they would like to use to save the attachment.

Any file can be attached to an email message. Two of the most common file types are documents and images.

DVORAK'S EMAIL TIP

The third most common type of file attached (and the most dangerous) are malicious files containing viruses. However, your computer won't become infected with a virus unless you open or run the malicious file. For this reason, it's a good idea to have an antivirus program running in the background at all times. (For more information, see Chapter 11.)

Email File Sizes

Be aware that there are file size limitations for sending email. Each text character (such as the letter *A*) takes about 3 bytes of disk space. For roughly every 341 letters you type, it takes approximately 1 K (1 kilobyte) of file size.

Now, this may not be such a big deal when you consider that a standard hard drive is capable of storing several GB of information. But when millions of people log in to their Internet accounts, ISPs are inundated with users sending and receiving email. ISPs have set file size limits and disk space quotas on email messages and attached files, and virtual mailboxes to keep the mail servers from collapsing under the heavy traffic usage. Email will not be permitted if it's over a designated file size. These sizes can vary from 2 MB to 10 MB, depending on the system. Although a basic text message does not take up a large amount of space, file attachments and HTML emails may.

HTML Email

HTML emails usually contain the same coding as Web pages to create better-looking mail and can incorporate Macromedia Flash and graphical elements (pictures, images, etc.). File attachments in the form of photos, pictures, or images can take up a very large amount of space if not optimized. A JPEG photo saved from a digital camera and attached to email can take up several MB of space. Because every user is designated a virtual mailbox space on the mail servers, space is usually at a rare premium.

Finally, there's the issue of Internet connectivity. Most users still connect via analog modem at speeds of 33.6–56 Kbps. This means that they can transfer up to 56 kilobits of data every second. If you send an attached file that's several MB in size, you could be waiting quite a while for that message to finally be sent off to your intended receiver. What's worse is when the receiver tries to check email, only to find it choked with a large attached file. This can be most frustrating. The recipient might have another important message to check. He or she can't check for new email until the previous messages, including attached files, have been checked and downloaded first. Most email clients can limit the download size, and if your speed is slow you should consider using the option.

ARCHIVING EMAIL

After several email messages have come and gone, you'll notice that your Inbox and Outbox folders will need some cleaning. Similar to cleaning off old piled papers from your desk, archiving is a tool to clean up your electronic mailbox folders. Most email client applications have an archiving feature. When you archive messages, you are essentially moving the items from your mailbox folders to a storage folder. There are two types of archive options usually available: auto archiving and manual archiving.

Auto Archiving

Auto archiving gives you the option of setting a specific number of months before the tool archives all messages into a designated folder. You can usually choose specific settings for auto archiving. The options may include how many months should pass before cleanup occurs and which folder should contain the archived items. Auto archiving is usually already activated with a designated folder. The default duration between cleanups will vary. Microsoft Outlook, for instance, has a predetermined archive setting of two months for the Sent Items and Deleted Items folders. However, you should check your specific email program to see whether auto archiving is activated before you assume it is.

Manual Archiving

Manual archiving is not set up as an automatic function; it occurs when a user saves an email. Manual archiving is usually not the default archive setting.

Other Options

You may choose to archive messages that reside in your Outbox folder, other individual folders, groups of folders, or all folders. You may also export your folder items, although this is different than archiving them. Exporting an item will send the original item to a storage folder, but it will leave a copy in your mailbox folder, as well.

SPAM

No discussion of email would be complete without a discussion of spam. Spam's official names are *UCE* (Unsolicited Commercial Email) or *UBE* (Unsolicited Bulk Email). Spam is known to most of us as junk mail. It is flooding the Internet with millions of messages that you don't care about and don't want. If you have an email address, it's inevitable that you'll eventually end up on a spammer's list.

The problem with spam is that there are so many people on the Internet that marketers discovered it was an effective way to target their advertisements. Pop-ups, pop-unders, banners, and cookies have surrounded our every Web move, like locusts on a grain field. These were just mere annoyances until spam started to flood our email boxes. The legitimate email advertisements from real companies were one thing—you could get off their lists. The illegitimate spammers are the ones who have created the monster.

These senders lie and cheat, and you can't even respond to them. The email headers are forged, and the ISPs do not really exist. Therein lies the problem. Without controls, chaos ensues. Spam is chaos on the Internet. SMTP, the email protocol, was never designed with the idea of cheats and liars. It was designed with the assumption that people would be honest. It was never foreseen as a problem; therefore, there was never a need to verify the sender's identity or location. Always remember that many of these solicitations are cons and scams.

Is the Internet Full Yet?

The biggest problem with spam is that it clogs up the Internet. From small ISPs to large companies, the strain is felt. It makes mail servers work harder than they need to, server owners need more server space than is really necessary, and the end users spend at least 5 minutes a day (and often as long as 20 minutes) sorting and deleting unwanted spam to find their *real* email.

Just to get a basic idea of the volume, let's take the example of a high-profile company such as AOL, for instance. It has around 26 million users, and if each of those users receives an average of 35 spam email messages a day, the total is 910 million spam messages systemwide. AOL stores messages on mail servers. If each of those 910 million spam messages are a nominal 5 K each, that would be almost 5,000 GB of information that AOL must store and manipulate each day. If this number continues to escalate, you have to wonder at what point does the system break down? How much can the Internet, even with its vastness, really hold?

At the "Block All Spam" Web site, Dick Lipton, a Georgia Institute of Technology computer professor, commented on this subject. He said, "If you plot the growth of spam on any reasonable chart, clearly at some point it will exceed the capacity of the entire Internet."

In a report released to the media, Ferris Research claimed that, in 2002, spam accounted for $8.9 billion in cost to U.S. corporations. Spam is growing. It is expected that this cost will rise. It's been estimated by various sources that spam growth in the last year has been over 100%, which seems to be a conservative number.

HOW DID THE TERM *SPAM* BECOME ASSOCIATED WITH JUNK EMAIL?

 There is debate as to where the term *spam* originated. Two of the most likely places are:

An early Monty Python song, phrased as follows:

"Spam spam spam spam, spam spam spam spam, lovely spam, wonderful spam . . ."

This song is seen by many as an infinite recurrence of insignificant words.

A computer lab at USC (University of Southern California) in Los Angeles that coined the term from the meat by the same name, claiming they shared several of the same characteristics:

Nobody wants it or ever asks for it.

No one ever eats it; it is the first item to be pushed to the side when eating the entree.

Sometimes it is actually tasty, like 1% of junk mail that is really useful to some people.

Spammers' Tools

Spammers are an ingenious group. They have created a number of tools to track down email addresses. It's akin to cancer. The tools either creep along the Internet searching, bombarding email servers to try and figure out new email addresses or sending out spy messages to get some idea what you are interested in viewing and verifying your email address. New schemes will come, but the most tried and true are harvesting, dictionary attacks, and HTML mail.

Harvesting and Dictionary Attacks

There are various tools to *harvest* email addresses to use for more spam generation. The most common of the tools are Web-crawling bots (short for robot). These are also called *spiders*. They go from Web site to Web site, looking only for email addresses. They find them in Internet mailing list addresses in Web sites, on forum posts, in chat rooms, and elsewhere. Another spam tool are programs called *dictionary attacks*, which use various combinations of letters to compose and send emails to see what gets bounced back or what seems to be deliverable.

THE DIRECT MARKETING ASSOCIATIONS STANCE ON SPAM

The DMA (Direct Marketing Association), founded in 1917, is the largest business trade association interested in direct, database, and interactive global marketing. Its members include catalog companies, direct mailers, teleservices firms, Internet marketers, and other at-distance marketers.

In an April 30, 2003 press release, the DMA announced that commercial messages should not be sent when email addresses have been captured surreptitiously—a practice often called *harvesting*. In addition, the DMA announced its position against the practice of automatic algorithmic email addressing, also known as *dictionary attacks*, that spammers use in mass untargeted mailing campaigns or in order to ascertain live addresses.

According to The DMA, both practices constitute abuses to the right to send email legitimately and could ultimately undercut email as a valuable business and communications tool. The DMA's announcement was the latest move in its anti-spam campaign. In addition, the DMA is calling for bolstered law enforcement of current consumer antifraud laws, as well as federal legislation, among other things, to combat unscrupulous spam.

LEGITIMATE MARKETERS DO NOT SPAM

The spam problem is caused by hucksters. "Even other vocal antispam advocates agree that legitimate marketers are NOT the problem," said H. Robert Wientzen, President and CEO of the DMA.

The DMA requires its members' email solicitations to represent the four pillars of reputable email:

Honest subject lines
Accurate header information that has not been forged

A physical street address for consumer redress

An *opt out* that works (opt is short for *option*, meaning, to give one the option not to be included in the mass mailings)

For more information on the DMA, go to www.the-dma.org.

HTML (Spy) Mail

Advertisers and spammers have come up with better ways to track the exact receipt and time a message was "viewed" (even if you simply opened it by mistake). When you download and open one of its emails, it in turn opens an image that it grabs from its host Web page. At the same time, it sends information about your actions and your machine. In effect, that email sends out information that can be cross-referenced by the sender to track who received the message, when they read it, how many times, and from what IP address. It's used by advertisers to intrude a bit more on your privacy. The spammers verify an email address as active, so they can make money by selling their email lists, which means even more spam will be sent your way.

SPAM MAIL VERSUS OPT-IN EMAIL

A user can *broadcast* or *multicast* an email message to users. These are legitimate and convenient ways to target messages to several people at once. There is a downside, too. It can also be used to illegally send unsolicited advertising junk email to millions of users without permission from the service-provider host.

Broadcasts

Email broadcasts are when a single individual sends an email to all users on a network. It can be the best way for companies to send bulletins to all their employees. However, to simply blast out a broadcast to the entire subscriber base of a global ISP (such as AOL), it's both an amazing annoyance for everyone and explicitly forbidden by the service. It's illegal because it breached usability policies. (Unfortunately, this is rarely enforced because of the nebulous nature of spam-mongers.) Broadcasting complicates network traffic and, in some cases, has caused total network meltdowns. In the case of broadcast storms, when a broadcast message receives several responses and those, in turn, receive yet more responses, a snowball syndrome ensues, the effects of which can be catastrophic for a network mail server.

Multicasts (Narrowcasts)

Multicasts, also known as *narrowcasts*, are when users send email to a select group of recipients. Email lists are a terrific example of multicasting. An email list is a list of people who subscribe and look forward to receiving missives. Most email client applications support mailing lists and give you the ability to forward a single message to every recipient on the list. Sometimes, though, lists containing hundreds to thousands of email addresses are spammed with unauthorized advertisements that take up tons of network bandwidth.

Spam is Junk

A year ago, the estimate was that one in five spam "advertising" messages was from *legitimate* companies, but the other four fifths were pure junk or frauds. (This number has probably changed to something like one in ten.)

The legitimate companies offer a way to "opt out" of the mailing list. The spammers don't. Occasionally they have an opt out to try to look like a legitimate business. Their links either don't work or take you right to the site you are trying to avoid. As often as not, the addresses the email originated from are bogus, faked, or already closed accounts. The spam just wants you to go to a Web site. The Web site rarely has any information to contact anyone. More often than not, the Web site will, at the very least, plant a cookie on your machine and at the worst, a virus.

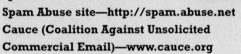

DVORAK'S EMAIL TIP

There are a Web sites dedicated to trying to find ways to combat spam:

Spam Abuse site—http://spam.abuse.net

Cauce (Coalition Against Unsolicited Commercial Email)—www.cauce.org

The Federal Trade Commission did a study that concluded that as many as two thirds of the email sent out are telling lies, and 96% of those offering ways for people to make money in business or investment are also frauds. Spam—including all those mail-order brides, miracle pills, and invitations to Web sites—totaled 6.7 million emails in the month of March 2003.

SPAM BREAKDOWN

 On any given day, the typical Spam Junk mail breakdown can be as follows:

Chain letters, pyramid schemes, get rich quick—20%

Porn sites and sex-related solicitations—20%

Real product advertising—20%

Financial offers (refinance your home)—10%

Medicines, drugs, and quack remedies—10%

Figure 10.1 shows an example of an inbox filled with spam.

```
Pamhayden            Hello there!!!
L0LA22               are you in debt?
PAMJ44               Tips and Tricks for your sex life! (Over 18)
wewpsylytd@pizz      Earn Up To $50 per Hour or More Now! xogouvmx
qc4408irete4@ex      Investigate before you invest your money.
7bx1vopoy3urs@n      gerri1188
pamna5778@vampi      f.ree online training to make big m.oney. tzo  b he
flyball45@b64v4      ADV:_Have_you_seen_the_rates
cherry6548@eudo      Refinanc.ing is easier now more than ever! qzah mn
LOSEWEIGHTubta@        Be Younger & Slimmer, FREE HGH
47na2g3kcx@yaho      NEW ! Order generic Viagra online qps zzfpu
bhinkelman@schw      Dont Let that Auto Salesman Fool You.... gufm buh kfaq
jto976@6n24w4t.      ADV:Re.f-inancing-is-easy!.....SICBW
ingalls6@i08jhw      Lower your house payment in 1 minute-----AAECANNFNR
cassi15robertau      PAIN MEDICATION...US DOCTORS..OVERNIGHT SHIPPING !! e
bib7gcdjf4c@hot      get prescription drugs without a prescription jrgbq in
Jackley810851@1      Clean Browser Cache Files!
jlvtemp@wm864ns      ADV:_How_Would_You_Like_A_5.25%_Int._On_Your_Next_Refi
legendarytimes-      [LegendaryTimes] Vol. 10 No. 17 May 24th 2003
OnlineLoveAtAOL      Precious.
legalsage@netbi      2370058no more towing costs
katievv673@aol.      Were have you been lately??  v2
SexyLilMelissa1      Hi there
```

FIGURE 10.1   SPAM.

At least 20 states have passed laws outlawing spam. But how do you bring someone to justice if they are hiding behind spoofed IP addresses and forged email headers? Clearly, something needs to be done.

THE GREAT NIGERIAN SCAM LETTER

The following is for those newcomers who have not received this infamous spam letter (or its newer variations) telling you that your name was purportedly given to someone in Nigeria and you were a "trusted person who can help." For some long-winded reason they have access to a large amount of money—usually around $20 million—that they need to get out of the country. *You* can help them. And to help them, they'll give you 10–20% of the money as a fee. Then the letter gets vague with off-the-wall and weird details. Anyway, one version of the scam works to convince you money will be transferred—by wire—into your bank account. You must get all sorts of wire transfer information, and soon your account is drained of whatever money you had. It's transferred out, not in. Duh!

What makes this interesting is that with spamming techniques, the con men do not have to spot a "mark" and target him or her anymore. Just try to scam everyone in the world and see what happens. This scam actually did begin in Nigeria and predates the Net. Apparently, real letters were sent out by hand with an elaborate package of documents. Care went into finding the right sucker. With spam broadcast mailing, this is no longer necessary. What this says to me is that quality con jobs are going to be a thing of the past, as Darwin takes over. The dumbest get ripped off instead of the richest marks.

This is urban folklore at its finest. The scam has moved from Nigeria to all over the place. (I actually doubt any Nigerians even do this scam anymore.) The last version I received was from a Mr. Nosa (no first name given). He is hiding out in the Benin Republic and has millions of dollars he needs me to help him get out of the country. Now the way this approach used to work is that you'd do a Google search of Benin and Nosa and find out there is some guy in Benin named Nosa who is famous, hiding out there, and loaded with dough. These days if you type this in, you get hit after hit regarding the Nigerian scam.

I'm impressed with the way the classic scam letter has morphed over time but still appreciate the original Nigerian scam where there is a crooked banker trying to move money out of Nigeria. I love the unique names of the supposed letter writers. My favorites include: Sandra SaviMBi and Joseph SaviMBi. SaviMBi is a popular name, apparently. Then there is Moses Mutolezi, Helen Khobi, Issa Gwazo (a personal favorite), Dan Ogaga, and Prince Tunji Abu, who apparently can type only in uppercase. Finally, I've received letters from Mahmud Daya, Prince Ahmadu A. Ahmadu (whose middle initial must stand for Ahmadu), and Dr. Francis Oputa. And a last mention goes to two identical letters from two different fakes; Dr. Thomas Okon and Dr. Raymond Okoro, both of whom were the "bank manager of Zenith Bank, Lagos, Nigeria."

Isn't the Net wonderful!

DVORAK DISCUSSES SPAM KILLER/BLOCKER SOFTWARE

The spam situation has worsened, and although people have advocated government intervention, this will just move the worst spammers offshore (where nothing can be done). This is an opportunity for some sharp operator to make money by doing real spam prevention with a good product.

Spamnix is rule-based filtering software (www.spamnix.com), and it works as a plug-in for Eudora. What makes Spamnix interesting is that it uses a set of open source governance rules to spot spam. These rules are based on a simple checklist that looks for features commonly found in the majority of spam. If you happen to get a newsletter that appears as spam because of forbidden features (e.g., ALL CAP headlines, unsubscribe comments, weird headers), you can simply put the newsletter in an exception file, and it comes through fine. From my experience, Spamnix manages to stop about 70% of incoming spam, although the company claims 95%. Still, 70% is quite good, and you can adjust the sensitivity levels of the system.

For more information, go to www.spamnix.com.

Spam Blockers, Spam Filters, Spam Killers

Filtering email is a hot topic because of spam. There are many different approaches to blocking spam. There is the strategy of filtering messages for specific content—email addresses or other types of data. There are *whitelist* or *verification* filters, where the sender of the email is checked. Another ploy is *blacklists*, which block known spam senders. *Rule-based* filtering evaluates a number of different patterns to try to "figure out" what is spam and what is not. Spam blocking is never 100% effective. Any type of strategy can also block a significant proportion of real email, as well.

DVORAK'S EMAIL TIP

The following programs are two that use a whitelist-type of Spam blocking:
Block All Spam—www.blockallspam.org
DigiPortal's Choice Mail—www.digiportal.com

MAIL BOMBS

Mail bombs are another example of email gone awry. A mail bomb is a massive amount of email sent to a specific person or system. The volumes of mail will fill up disk space on a server, or in the worst-case scenario, actually crash the server because it's too much for it to handle. Mail bombs have been used to punish Internet users who have angered someone for slights or wrongs—real or imagined. Most mail bombs are defused now with programs added to mail servers, such as Exim, an open source program.

Header and Text Analysis

Simple strings in headers, the subject line, or the body of the email text can be filtered. This is easy to do. Most email clients have at least this kind of filtering activated. The idea is good, but they often have a high false positive. (In other words, they identify real email as spam.)

Email Authentication

Email authentication is a method of blocking spam that requires senders of email to authenticate that they are the originators of the email. An email doesn't get delivered until the email server receives a confirmation from the sender. Once an email server has this information, it will deliver email from that sender as long as the sender continues to use the same email address. Should it change, the sender must reconfirm.

The problem is that this creates a barrier to communicating that some people really resent. The message, "reply to this to authenticate," that is required before your sent email will be received by the recipient has not been well accepted yet. Perhaps as the spam problem gets worse, this may become the only option.

Rule-Based Filtering

This is a type of filtering that looks at a large number of patterns and compares them with an incoming message. It ranks the email based on the number of patterns identified—so if there is too high a score, the email is deemed spam and disposed of.

Some scoring schemes are consistent—the use of forged headers and auto-executing JavaScript, for example, will instantly be deemed spam. Other rules are updated as the products change. As spam evolves, so must the rule-based filtering systems.

SpamAssassin—http://spamassin.org

Spamnix—www.spamnix.com

Spam-Smart Blocking

There are some proprietary spam-blocking techniques that have started to appear that use a combination of techniques blended together to make a dynamic smart-blocking option. This type of strategy was designed to block a polymorphic spam attack.

Polymorphic is a term that means a dynamic, rapidly changing variation. In a polymorphic spam attack, the spam can alter itself, making each version different from others that resemble it. This usually looks like a string of garbled letters. The polymorphic email will continually alter this string of letters with each email. The strategy to deal with these is to look at more information than conventional filtering—with dynamic features to change as the spam changes—combined with automatic rule updates, and other blocking filters.

Other Filtering Methods

One idea bandied about is the *Bayesian probability models* of spam. This is the idea that some words occur more often in spam, whereas other words are found in legitimate emails. (This is probably true, because none of my legitimate emails have ever arrived using the words "Russian bride" or "rock-hard all night" from any of my friends, business associates, or relatives.) A similar concept is Vipul's Razor, a collaborative spam-tracking database. It works on the theory that spam of a specific kind will come in at the same time in an avalanche. The filter will detect the duplicate messages. It will deliver the first but delete the rest.

Blacklists

This isn't very effective, given that most spammers use forged headers and email addresses, but it's a way to block known spam addresses. The idea here is to find consistent IP addresses, sites, or servers that are delivering a lot of spam and simply block all traffic.

Hand Filtering

Most people use hand filtering by reading each subject line and deleting the ones that appear rather spammish. Sometimes one may get opened in error, but for the most part, it works.

EMAIL ETIQUETTE

Email is a form of communication, and all communication is governed by certain rules. These rules are important in business because they establish a certain formality, like all business correspondence.

Addresses and Personal Names

A "personal name" is an arbitrary string that many mailers will allow you to define and is attached to your email address as a textual comment.

Always provide a personal name if your mail system allows it. A personal name attached to your address identifies you better than your address can on its own.

Use a sensible personal name: "Guess who" or other such phrases are annoying as personal names and hinder the recipient's quick identification of you and your message.

If your mail system lets you use personal names in the addresses to which you send mail, try to use them. This will often help a postmaster recognize the real recipient of the message if the address is invalid.

Example:

The address *344188@foo.chaos.com* conveys less information than if it were written as *John Devo 344188@foo.chaos.com*. Your email client may use a different protocol for adding your name.

Subject Lines

Always include a subject line in your message. Almost all mailers present you with the subject line when you browse your mailbox, and it's often the only clue the recipient has about the contents when filing and searching for messages.

Make the subject line meaningful. For example, sending a message to WordPerfect Technical Support with the subject "WordPerfect" is practically as unhelpful as having no subject at all.

If you are replying to a message but are changing the subject of the conversation, change the subject, too—or better still, start a new message altogether. The subject is usually the easiest way to follow the thread of a conversation, so changing the conversation without changing the subject can be confusing and can make filing difficult.

Message Length, Content, and Format

Try to match your message length to the tenor of the conversation: If you are only making a quick query, keep it short and to the point.

In general, keep to the subject as much as possible. If you need to branch off onto a totally new and different topic, it's often better to send a new message, which allows the recipient the option of filing it separately.

Don't type your message in all uppercase—it's extremely difficult to read. And you should note that many spam filters see such things as spam, and you may lose your message. Try to break your message into logical paragraphs and restrict your sentences to sensible lengths.

Use correct grammar and spelling. Electronic mail is all about communication. Poorly worded messages with misspelled words are hard to read and potentially confusing. Just because electronic mail is fast does not mean that it should be slipshod. The worst language-mashing I have ever seen has been done in email messages. If your words are important enough to write, they're also important enough to write properly.

Avoid public "flames"—messages sent in anger. Messages sent in the heat of the moment generally only exacerbate the situation and are usually regretted later. Settle down and think about it for awhile before starting a flame war. (Try going and making yourself a cup of coffee—it's amazing how much you can cool down even in that short a time, besides which, a cup of good coffee is a great soother. If that doesn't work, try bourbon.)

If your mail program supports fancy formatting (bold, italic, and so on) in the mail messages it generates, make sure that the recipient has a mail program that can display such messages. At the time of writing, most Internet mail programs do not support anything other than plain text in messages, although this will change over time.

Be very careful about including credit card numbers in electronic mail messages. Electronic mail can be intercepted in transit, and a valid credit card number is like money in the bank for someone unscrupulous enough to use it.

Replies

Include enough of the original message to provide a context. Remember that email is not as immediate as a telephone conversation and the recipient may not recall the contents of the original message, especially if he or she receives many messages each day. Including the relevant section from the original message helps the recipient to place your reply in context.

Include only the minimum you need from the original message. One of the most annoying things you can encounter in email is to have your original five-page message quoted back at you in its entirety with the words "Me too" added at the bottom. Quote back only the smallest amount you need to make your context clear. And it's often better to put your comments at the beginning, not at the end.

Use some kind of visual indication to distinguish between text quoted from the original message and your new text—this makes the reply much easier to follow. The greater than symbol (>) is a traditional marker for quoted text but you can use anything, provided that its purpose is clear and you use it consistently.

Pay careful attention to where your reply is going to end up: It can be embarrassing for you if a personal message ends up on a mailing list, and it's generally annoying for the other list members. There are a lot of stories in many companies about the "love letter" sent to everyone!

Ask yourself whether your reply is really warranted. A message sent to a list server that says only "I agree" is probably better sent privately to the person who originally sent the message.

Signatures

A signature is a small block of text appended to the end of your messages that usually contains your contact information. Many mailers can add a signature to your messages automatically. Signatures are a great idea but are subject to abuse; balance is the key to a good signature.

Always use a signature if you can. Make sure it identifies who you are and includes an alternative means of contacting you (phone and fax are usual). In many systems, particularly where mail passes through gateways, your signature may be the only means by which the recipient can even tell who you are.

Keep your signature short—four to seven lines is a handy guideline for maximum signature length. Unnecessarily long signatures waste bandwidth (especially when distributed to lists) and can be annoying.

Some mailers allow you to add random strings to your signature. This is well and good and can add character if done carefully. You should consider the following basic rules though:

- Keep it short. The length of your quote adds to the length of your signature. A 5,000-word excerpt from Kant's "Critique of Pure Reason" used as a signature will not win you many friends.

- Definitions of "offensive" vary widely: Avoid quotes that might offend people on the grounds of religion, race, politics, or sexuality.

- Try to avoid topical or local quotes, because they may be meaningless to recipients in other towns, countries, or cultures.

- Variable signatures are usually best if they're amusing; polemical outbursts on politics or other such topics will turn most people off, but a one-liner that brings a smile can make someone's day.

Courtesy

Electronic mail is all about communication with other people, and as such, some basic courtesy never goes amiss.

If you're asking for something, don't forget to say "please." Similarly, if someone does something for you, it never hurts to say "thank you." Although this might sound trivial or even insulting, it's astonishing how many people who are perfectly polite in everyday life seem to forget their manners in their emails.

Don't expect an immediate answer. Just because you don't get an answer from someone in 10 minutes does not mean that he or she is ignoring you and is no cause for offense. Electronic mail is all about dealing with your communications when you are able to do so.

Always remember that there is no such thing as a secure email system. It is unwise to send very personal or sensitive information by email unless you encrypt it using a reliable encryption program. Remember the recipient—you are not the only person who could be embarrassed if a delicate message falls into the wrong hands.

Include enough information. If you are sending a question to which you expect a response, make sure you include enough information to make the response possible. For example, sending the message, "My spreadsheet program doesn't work" to Lotus Technical Support really doesn't give them very much to work with; similarly, sending the message "What has happened to my order?" to a vendor is also unhelpful. When requesting technical support, include a description of the problem and the version of the program you're using; when following up on an order, include the order number, your name and organization, and any other details that might assist in tracing your order, and so on.

SUMMARY

Email is the number one use of the Internet and will continue to be for years to come. Unfortunately, the spam, the viruses, and other hazards are making email harder to use and generally risky. Expect to see new advances in email technology to emerge to fix these problems. In the meantime, always know that you can keep changing your email address if you have to.

11
SECURITY

The Internet evolved out of a project built for the U.S. Department of Defense. With such a security-minded parent, why in the world has it proven to be so full of security holes? The problem is precisely that it *was* built for security-minded scientists. Back in the late 1960s, these researchers were the only people who could access this new and very small network (known then as the ARPANET). They figured, "heck, if the only people who can log on are trusted like us government scientists, any built-in security would be redundant, right?" From that point on, we were in trouble.

The basic underlying architecture of the Internet (and personal computers, for that matter) assumes an "innocent-until-proven-guilty" stance. By default, all information on the Net is transferred in plain view for anyone to read or change, and direct computer-to-computer connections are made easily. No one thought to worry about security until it was too late. Early security precautions were usually just passwords. It wasn't until the widespread adoption of personal computers and modems in the 1980s that other measures, such as firewalls, were created.

As we'll see later in this chapter, traditional firewalls were a good start on the road to security. Essentially functioning like a moat around a castle, they were good at keeping bad guys (that is, hackers) out. Once a bad guy did happen to get in to a network, though, the old-style firewall didn't do any good. In the 1990s, we began to see the first widespread viruses that propagated via infected floppy disks, bypassing firewalls. This gave rise to antivirus products on individual computers that checked each new disk and file for viruses.

Then laptop computers became popular, and the metaphor of a moat around a static community (network) really fell to pieces. Now you've got work PCs logging in from home and home PCs logging into corporate networks. Plus, with the Internet more widely adopted than those early scientists could have dreamed, almost every computer is just one degree of separation away from every other computer. Security today has become a complex web of precautions, from the very large (national laws and policies) to the ultrapersonal (personal firewalls on individual PCs).

There are many threats one faces in this brave new Internet world. A con artist tricks you into revealing your checking account information. He goes on a spending spree, racking up tens of thousands of dollars in charges in your name. An automated computer virus infects your PC. It destroys your hard disk. It also sends out one of your most personal and confidential files to hundreds of people (including friends and co-workers). A hacker living on the other side of the planet breaks into your computer, snoops on you as you log in remotely to your company's private network. Then he gains access to the company's computer when you are logged off. A cyberterrorist plants malicious software on your computer to let him attack a government agency remotely through your PC.

THE GLOBAL VILLAGE

In the mid-1990s, there was no shortage of breathless predictions about how the Internet would usher in a new era of worldwide camaraderie. A global village, if you will, full of people eager to share knowledge and experience—people working together to bring out the best in each other. Unfortunately, what we got were the same old scammers we have in the real world.

If you're just getting online, it may only be a matter of days before you receive a virus-infected email. It might only be hours until some hacker discovers your computer and begins probing its defenses. Is it all hopeless? Should you pack up the computer, put this book on the shelf, and give up? No way!

The good news is that with a couple of tools, a few adjustments to your computing environment, and some healthy skepticism, you can secure yourself against all the menaces you're likely to encounter.

THREATS

Know your enemies. That old proverb is sound advice for the Internet. Know what the bad guys want and how they go about getting it. If you keep that in mind, you can protect yourself. Your new enemies come in many forms, both human and otherwise:

- Malware, or "malicious software," which includes viruses, snooping programs, and programs that open "back doors."
- Hackers—how they find you, how they get in, and what they do once they're there.
- Spammers—maybe they're criminals, maybe not. They're certainly an unacceptable threat to your privacy.
- Hoaxes—These run the gamut from amusing to annoying to dangerous. Best not to take chances.

WHO ARE THESE BAD GUYS AND WHY WON'T THEY LEAVE ME ALONE?

 Crackers

These are the malcontents who cause mischief and damage just for fun. Technically, this is the correct term for the bad guys usually referred to as *hackers*. Often, their sole motivation for writing viruses, creating tools, or break-

---

ing into computers is simply to show off to other crackers. If you're lucky, they will be less interested in using your stolen credit card number than in telling their friends how they procured it. At worst, these crackers are criminals; at best, they are morally stunted sociopaths who need to grow up.

Hackers

Despite its usage these days, the term *hacker* was once a compliment. A few decades ago, it simply meant someone intensely curious about the inner workings of computers and computer code. These hackers were solely interested in discovering new vulnerabilities, not exploiting them. There remain these "pure hacker" explorers today, but alas for them, the media has taken the term *hacker* and run with it as a general term for all sorts of villains. Because you don't want anyone malicious or otherwise nosing around on your computer, we'll stick with the more common (if unfair) term of *hacker* for the bad guys.

Script Kiddies

This is a contemptuous term for troublemakers who aren't especially tech literate. These kids use scripts or premade snippets of computer code that real hackers have developed. They lack imagination, but they do make up a sizable percentage of the bad-guy population. Most of the script kiddies get their kicks from simply wreaking havoc, creating a rudimentary virus, or using a hacker tool someone else created to break into your machine and delete your files.

Thieves

All sorts of real-world robbers have their online counterparts: con men, burglars, shoplifters, and more. Con men prey on your trust through sales scams or email pyramid schemes. Burglars break into computers or networks and take anything of value. Shoplifters defraud online stores, often by using credit card or bank account numbers stolen from individual computers or merchants' databases.

Corporate Spies

These are thieves and saboteurs who target rival companies. Often, they gain access to a company's confidential information by *tunneling through* the connection made by a telecommuter's computer. They can be very, very patient and rarely leave any clues of their existence.

Job Seekers

Believe it or not, some of the most pernicious viruses have been created by programmers seeking to show off how clever they are, in hopes of garnering free personal publicity. The unfortunate ones get their wish.

Hacktivists

Hacktivists are the new-millennium upgrade to the old stereotype of the bomb-throwing anarchists (or civilly disobedient protesters, depending on your point of view). These hacker activists use technology to attack political systems and symbols. Some of these attacks are aimed at causing real damage (such as shutting down an online store), and some are merely elaborate pranks that might not technically be illegal (such as collecting and posting to a Web site the travel itineraries of attendees at the World Economic Forum). The most well-known hacktivist tactic is to replace a real Web site with a parody. China, the U.S. Department of Defense, and even the White House's official Web site have all been victims of hacktivist assaults.

Spammers

The annoying "telemarketers of the Internet." Maybe they aren't technically trying to steal from you, but they're certainly out to learn all they can about you. (And their methods are legally dubious.) To top it all off, they want you to buy their junk.

MALWARE

Malware is any software that's used for malicious purposes. As if the word *malware* weren't arcane enough, hackers break it down into further mysterious subcategories such as viruses, worms, Trojan horses, and spyware. There's a lot of overlap among these categories. For example, some viruses are worms; some Trojan horses are really spyware; and some particularly nasty malware programs try and hit *every* category.

Worms

A worm is a program that propagates itself automatically across a network, from computer to computer. Each computer ends up with a fully functional (and infectious) copy of the worm. Worms are not necessarily malicious. Some worms have been built to clean up after other worms. But many allegedly harmless worms have become surprisingly dangerous when released "into the wild," as described in the following sidebar

THE GREAT INTERNET WORM OF 1988

No one was supposed to notice it. Robert Tappan Morris, a student at Cornell University, wrote a small program (only 99 lines of code) that would spread from one networked UNIX machine to another. It wasn't supposed to cause any trouble, just propagate itself quietly.

Unfortunately, Morris (by all accounts a quite sane and pleasant fellow) inadvertently found himself following in the footsteps of every mad scientist of legend. His creation was "alive," certainly, but far more destructive than he'd dreamed. Within hours, a few small bugs in Morris's worm caused the program to bring the Internet to its knees. Computers worldwide slowed to a crawl as they devoted more and more processing power to running the tiny program.

Ten percent of all computers on the Internet were infected. Even in 1988, when the Internet was mostly the domain of schools and research facilities, the cost of the lost productivity was estimated at up to $100 million. Morris himself ended up with three years' probation, 400 hours of community service, and a $10,000 fine.

It wasn't the first Internet worm, but it certainly became the most infamous. In fact, it led directly to the creation of the Computer Emergency Response Team (CERT at www.cert.org), the federally funded center for computer security expertise run in conjunction with Carnegie Mellon University.

Viruses

A virus is similar to a worm but technically unable to propagate itself without human assistance. For example, if it tricks you into mailing it, rather than automatically mailing itself, it's a virus. An older definition holds that worms merely copy themselves onto your hard disk, but viruses *overwrite* your existing files with themselves. These differentiations, though, are falling out of usage. These days, the blanket term *virus* is usually used for any malicious program that can spread itself, either automatically or with human help.

Of course, viruses often do more than simply propagate. A relatively benign one might just pop up a window with a taunting message. A nasty one could not only delete files from your hard disk, it could even override your computer's safety settings.

alt.comp.virus FAQ states:

There are no viruses which damage hardware by modifying how the mechanical parts run or their electro-magnetic characteristics. There *are* reported instances of specific hardware being damaged by the misuse of specific software. No known viruses damage hardware, and despite many suggestions to the contrary, it is unlikely that one will ever exist.

That said, there is a virus (CIH) which corrupts a system BIOS, which is not hardware damage, but is as difficult to fix. A corrupted BIOS will cause problems in the start-up of the system. The BIOS chip would need to be returned to the factory to get re-programmed. Hardware write protection of the BIOS should be used whenever possible, as should current antivirus software.

For more information, go to www.faqs.org/faqs/computer-virus/mini-faq/.

In the 1980s and 1990s, viruses were usually transmitted by the always-reliable "sneakernet," walking a floppy disk from one computer to another. Like a real virus, these programs would infect the unknowing host, then attempt to spread to everything the host came into contact with (additional floppy disks and files). Even between nonnetworked PCs, the sneakernet could spread viruses with frightening efficiency. The common viruses of the time hid in very clever places, such as Microsoft Word macros (within otherwise legit Word files) or as small hitchhikers in a disk's file structure information.

In the age of the Internet, viruses are usually spread by email, often in the form of .EXE or .VBS file attachments. You have to launch these attachments to spread the infection. Although this amounts to hiding in plain sight (attachments are easily noticed), virus infections are now more prevalent than ever. This is for two reasons: (1) some people never learn and (2) some viruses can now launch automatically from an email *without human assistance*. In fact, some viruses use the same "autolaunch" trick to download automatically and run from Web sites you browse.

The worst viruses not only autolaunch but also automatically email themselves. Usually, these viruses search your PC for email addresses, then mail themselves out to your co-workers, friends, and family. This means your closest friend could be a pod-person. Never assume a file is virus free just because you trust the sender. The sneakier viruses even alter the "From" information on the email so the recipients don't know that the email came from you. This prevents them from letting you know you're infected.

SUSPICIOUS FILE TYPES IN EMAIL ATTACHMENTS

It's impossible to come up with a complete list of all the file types that can function as virus carriers. A good rule of thumb, though, is to be suspicious of any file type that can run as a program. The standard file type for programs (and thus viruses) is .EXE, for an executable file. Another very popular file type is .VBS, which stands for Visual Basic Script, or a piece of code (a script) written in Microsoft's Visual Basic scripting language. These file types have numerous valid uses. However, because viruses are so prevalent, you should think twice before opening any email attachment. It's safest not to trust .EXE, .VBS, or any of the file types listed below unless you are expecting a specific file from someone.

Even files that don't run as programs (such as .TXT files) can be mimicked by viruses. For example, although the file BADNEWS.TXT.exe might at first appear to be a .TXT file, you can see that it's really an .EXE. Even this simple trick fools thousands of people daily into opening infected files.

The most common file types infected by viruses are:

ADE	ADP	ASX	BAS	BAT
CHM	CMD	COM	CPL	CRT

DBX	EXE	HLP	HTA	INF
INS	ISP	JS	JSE	LNK
MDA	MDB	MDE	MDZ	MSC
MSI	MSP	MST	NCH	PCD
PIF	PRF	REG	SCR	SCT
SHB	SHS	URL	VB	VBE
VBS	WMS	WSC	WSF	WSH

THE LOVEBUG

The most widespread virus of 2000 came by email with the ironic subject ILOVEYOU. Although it's called the LoveBug, *cute* is the last word you'd use to describe it. The worm caused over $8 billion in damages, and a few years after its first infection, it's still crawling around the Net, claiming new victims. The LoveBug is a dangerous combination of clever programming and "social engineering" (getting a human to unwittingly open a security hole). It arrives in your email inbox as a note from someone you know. Assuming (wrongly!) that it's safe because it comes from a friend, you open its innocent-sounding attachment, Love-letter-for-you.txt.vbs. This launches the virus. Once loose, the virus replaces files on your PC with copies of itself, then mails itself out to all the addresses in any Microsoft Outlook address book on your PC. And this time, the unsuspecting recipients think the innocuous love letter comes from you. . .

Trojan Horses

A Trojan horse is a program that hides its true nature by pretending to be something else. If a "friend" sends you a neat screen saver, be afraid. Odds are good it's a Trojan horse (or just Trojan, for short). Like any good piece of malware, the true nature of the Trojan can vary. Perhaps it's a digital "eavesdropping" program or maybe simply a virus, but the point is that it's not what it seems to be.

Many Trojans come from newsgroups or Web sites of ill repute. A favorite tactic of script kiddies is to make available a free copy of a popular software application or pornographic movie clip. Are these script kiddies doing this out of the goodness of their hearts? No, the file is actually a Trojan. By the time you figure out that the file isn't what it claims to be, you've installed the Trojan. The more clever script kiddies really do make good on their promise to deliver the game or movie in question, so you don't become suspicious as it also infects your system.

In May of 2002, the Klez virus became the most prolific virus to date. Like the LoveBug, it exploits both technological vulnerabilities and human gullibility. However, in the two years between the threats' debuts, viruses have evolved significantly.

Klez arrives in your inbox and attempts the popular "autolaunch" trick, attempting to run without your assistance. Just in case you're protected against that, though, it has one more card to play: It sometimes masquerades as a Klez removal tool! The official-sounding email advises you to run the attachment and even boldly states that some antivirus products will mistakenly identify this tool as the real Klez: "Ignore the warning, and select Continue."

Once it infects your system, Klez scours your hard disk, looking for email addresses. Next it uses its own built-in email program to mail a file (chosen at random from your PC) to all the addresses. To cover its tracks, the wily virus "spoofs" or falsifies the "From" location of the email. This keeps your computer from being implicated in the mass mailing. At least with LoveBug, everyone could tell you that you were infected. Finally, Klez overwrites files and drops a *second* virus (named ElKern) onto your PC, which also attempts to destroy your files.

Spyware

Spyware is, unsurprisingly, designed to spy on you. Most commonly, it takes the form of a "keylogger" that records to a special file everything you type. (It *logs* your *key* strokes.) This spyware usually has some method of transmitting this special file back to the hacker. This is wryly referred to as the spyware "phoning home." A keylogger can capture passwords, private correspondence, and all sorts of sensitive information. Other types of spyware include modules that monitor which Web sites you visit and which applications you run. Often, a Trojan implants spyware on its victim's PC. The hacker then sits back and waits for captured passwords and financial info to make its way back to him.

Hackers are security-minded enough to know that when spyware phones home, it points right to them. This is why the more shrewd hackers will have their spyware leave a message *somewhere else*. In these cases, the spyware drops off its payload (your information) to a newsgroup or chat channel populated only by, you guessed it, hackers. If the information isn't encrypted (encoded so that only its intended recipient can read it), suddenly hackers around the world know all about your vulnerability.

Another kind of spyware is less dangerous but no less alarming—legitimate software that secretly phones home. Although not necessarily acting as a keylogger, this sort of spyware sends market research data such as your system profile or a report of the Web sites you visit. If you're told about this back channel communication before you install the software and you give your permission, no problem. Predictably, however, some companies try to hide this from you. If they get busted, though, it always goes poorly for them. The notion that your favorite media player is sending your playlist back to Big Brother is enough to turn even the mildest grandmother into a crusading privacy activist.

One important note: Some spyware can actually eavesdrop on your Internet activity from remote locations. This type of spyware is discussed later in this chapter.

SPYWARE KILLERS

Ad-Aware

This is a popular utility from Lavasoft. It works much like a virus program except it identifies and lists programs that match its latest spyware list. There are both a freeware version and two licensed versions. The pay versions include a real-time spyware monitor to alert users if any spyware program uses RAM or tries to install itself in the system registry.

For more information, go to www.lavasoftusa.com.

BPC Spyware and Adware Remover

BulletProof Soft has a five day free trial ($29 for ongoing services) solution to spyware with its removal utility. It includes a pop-up killer and a real-time spyware monitoring tool.

For more information, go to www.bulletproofsoft.com.

Spybot Search & Destroy

This is from Patrick Kolla, a German developer. His shareware program from PepiMK Software can detect and remove spyware from your computer for the price of a donation.

For more information, go to www.spybot.safer-networking.de/.

Adware

Adware is software that is included in larger applications, such as games or file-sharing programs. These programs are free because ads are in them, and you are forced to view them. This is a fair exchange; you get a free program (that costs money and time to develop), and all you have to do is endure a few banners or pop-up ads. In fact, the free program may have told you about this in its end-user licenses that you agreed to without reading. It probably said that you agree to allow advertisers to gather statistical information about you. The point is to help advertisers target you. Most of the time, you won't even be aware that you are being reported on.

Technically, any software that displays an advertisement as part of its interface is adware. The problem with adware is that so much of it also has a habit of being spyware—not usually the keylogger kind of spyware but the gather-all-sorts-of-information-for-market-research kind of spyware. Not all adware is guilty of this, but you should be especially wary of any free ad-supported product you're thinking of downloading.

The evil part is that the spyware may search your system registry for information such as your real name, the software you have installed, or whatever information it can glean about you. This information is sent back out onto the Internet to be shared with unknown third parties.

Legitimate Spyware

Spyware is widely reviled, but cases can (possibly) be made for its legitimate uses, such as monitoring children's Internet usage or tracking criminals' computing exploits. One software company that takes great pride in the monitoring software it produces is WinWhatWhere Corporation. The product WinWhatWhere Investigator has been used in a number of high-profile law enforcement cases, most recently helping nab two Russian hackers who had stolen more than 50,000 credit card numbers. Through a complex ruse, the FBI was able to trick the suspected hackers into using a computer with the spyware secretly installed. The hackers remotely logged in to their server computer in Russia, which was loaded with the stolen credit card numbers. It was like the hackers had led the feds right to a huge storeroom of evidence and provided the keys to get in.

Remote-Access Software

Like spyware, it can be argued that remote-access software also has legitimate uses. Let's say you need to use your home PC from work, or vice versa. Remote-access software lets you connect to a PC and "drive" it from afar. Unfortunately, one person's time-saving tool is another's malware. Trojans are infamous for dropping remote-access programs onto infected PCs. This is called a *RAT* (for Remote-Access Trojan). Once installed, a RAT opens a big back door for the hacker to seize control of your system and wreak all manner of havoc: stealing your files, connecting to your employer's network, staging cyberattacks against other targets, and so on.

Malicious Web Pages

Dynamic Web pages make for a rich Web-browsing experience. Trouble is, all that "dynamic" technology can also be put to sinister purposes. Some malware authors prefer Java, JavaScript, or ActiveX, which many browsers will automatically download and run from Web pages. Java is inherently fairly secure because it's restricted to running only in its own "sandbox" where it can't access any other part of your hard disk. Still, a clever programmer can create a flawed Java applet that crashes your machine. JavaScript is less secure and can be used to cause a great deal of trouble for your browser, such as changing your settings without you realizing it. Still, its potential for mischief is limited. ActiveX is another matter entirely. Built by Microsoft, ActiveX is built to interact directly with your operating system. As such, it has the incredible potential to take control of any part of your computer *if* you give it permission.

Other Malware

These are the most common examples of malware, but there are more out there. The hackers have time on their hands and a whole world of targets to choose from. They can custom-build very specific malware that exploits even the smallest security vulnerability in a program or operating system. And bad as these automated malware attacks are, it's when a hacker uses malware such as a virus to facilitate a targeted attack that things get really nasty. We'll take a look at this in the next section.

HACKERS

In the analog world, if a burglar is going to rob your house, he follows several predictable steps:

1. He targets your house in particular.
2. He checks the locks on your doors and windows to find an open one or uses a special tool to get in.
3. He breaks in.
4. He moves quietly from room to room until he finds your valuables.
5. He leaves, just as quietly.

As we'll see, hackers have the same modus operandi.

If there's one thing a hacker loves more than breaking into your system, it's bragging to his friends about it. And it would be a mistake to think that these seemingly antisocial hackers have no friends. The hacker subculture is surprisingly complex and nuanced. In fact, the secret history of the Internet is the history of hackers. The pure hackers—the ones interested in understanding, circumventing, and ultimately *improving* complex systems—have been the very real pioneers of the Internet.

At about the same time as the ARPANET was being invented, there arose a subculture of "phone phreaks," people who could manipulate telephone systems and hardware to do all sorts of not-so-legal tricks. The most famous phreak, known as Captain Crunch, used a free whistle from a breakfast cereal (you can guess which one) that blew the precise tone needed to unlock AT&T's phone switching system. The clever (if criminal) bosun could then make free, untraceable, long-distance phone calls. As the Internet grew and personal computers became widespread, many phreaks migrated to computers, where they became known as *hackers*.

Many companies' chief technology officers today were curious hackers a decade or three back. In fact, as teenagers, the two founders of a well-known computer company (often lauded for its aesthetically appealing computers) actually met Captain Crunch. They were thus tempted into a brief life of crime selling "blue boxes" (electronic versions of the Captain's whistle) out of a Berkeley dorm; in 1969, scientists Dennis Ritchie and Ken Thompson "hacked together" a new operating system called UNIX. And where do you think the antivirus companies find engineers who are so well acquainted with viruses?

How They Find You (aka Targeting Your House)

Sometimes a hacker wants to attack a computer directly, not simply settling for an automated virus doing all the work. His first step is to find you, virtually speaking. Usually, what he needs is your IP address. This is the unique string of numbers that identifies your computer when you connect to the Internet. By default, your IP address is embedded in most types of communication that happen between your PC and any other computer. This means that a hacker can learn your IP address if you:

- visit his Web site
- visit a legitimate Web site that's been hacked
- open an email with a hidden piece of HTML called a "web bug" that secretly connects to the hacker's site

- send him an email (perhaps replying to spam, asking to be removed from the spam list)
- post to a newsgroup
- are infected with a virus that "phones home"
- share an ISP LAN with him

Importantly, even if you do none of these things, a hacker can easily find you by scanning the Net for vulnerable computers with a port scanner (see below).

Network Sniffers

One of the more ingenious ways hackers can find your IP address is with a special remote spyware program called a "network sniffer" or "packet sniffer." A network sniffer can monitor Internet traffic (the flow of packets) within an ISP's LAN or even on the Internet at large. Once the hacker begins collecting data, he can then choose to monitor the communications of just one PC. The Web sites you browse, the passwords you use at them, even the contents and recipients of your email can all be tracked, even if your PC is spyware free. The least of the information a hacker can glean is your IP address.

ISP LANs

It's a dirty little secret of many ISPs. Odds are that whenever you connect to the Internet, you're sharing a local network with other customers of that ISP. This is especially common when using a DSL connection. If you've got a hacker who can access the ISP's LAN (maybe he's actually a customer or maybe they have sloppy security), he can see and connect to your computer through standard operating system file sharing.

War Dialing

War dialing is a classic hacker technique for finding computers. A war dialer is a hacker's program that dials blocks of phone numbers, searching for some hapless PC with a modem set to auto-answer. (Remember the movie *War Games?*) If the hacker is lucky enough to find a computer on the other end of the line, he'll move on to phase two—probing your defenses.

Dialup versus Always-on Connections

Despite the benefits of always-on Internet connections via broadband, there are significant security risks. Most dialup connections use dynamic IP addressing, which means that your ISP gives you a different temporary IP address with every new Internet session. Broadband connections are usually with static IP addresses, which don't change. As you might imagine, a static IP address presents a juicier target for hackers. Once they find your address, they can just keep coming back and hammering on it.

Even if your broadband connection is with a dynamic IP address, you're saddled with that address for much longer with dialup. A dialup connection might last for only a half hour, an hour, or maybe a few hours at a time. With an always-on connection, you're connected the whole day, as long as long as your computer is turned on. That gives hackers much more time to cause trouble.

Bottom line: You need strong security, no matter what type of connection you have; both dialup and always-on have risks. But always-on keeps you a target longer.

Probing Your Defenses (aka Checking the Locks)

Once the hacker knows where your PC is, whether by IP address, telephone number, or some other method, he can *case the joint*, looking for vulnerabilities. And unfortunately, almost every aspect of your PC has security vulnerabilities: your operating system, your applications, even the hardware of your computer itself. The underground hacker community has cataloged thousands of these vulnerabilities, so all a hacker needs to do is gather some information about your unique PC. And he has many tools to help him do this.

One of the hacker's favorite investigative tools is a port scanner. Ports are used in communications between computers. Every type of communication, whether a browser's request for a Web page or an email being sent, happens through a port. They're like doors on your PC. Some are open, and some are closed. The open ones are security risks. On most computers, there are tens of thousands of ports. (These are different from the several physical ports on the back of your computer: modem port, printer port, etc. The ports we're discussing here exist only in virtual terms in software.) A port scanner, unsurprisingly, scans a specific IP address for open ports. Advanced port scanners also bypass step one, the one that targets you specifically, and just probe likely blocks of IP addresses and their ports.

Open ports are gold mines to hackers. With the right tools, they can yield a wealth of information, such as your operating system or what security programs you're running (if any). Add this to the information the hacker can gather by analyzing your other Internet communications (such as Web browsing, instant messaging, or online gaming), and he can assemble an alarmingly detailed profile of your system. Then he can just compare this with a list of known vulnerabilities and begin attacking each and every one on your system. (Often, these attacks are carried out through these same open ports that were so accommodating earlier.) These vulnerabilities or the act of attacking them are often called simply *hacks*.

HACKER COMMUNITIES AND TOOLS

How do hackers know about the latest security vulnerabilities? How do script kiddies get their hands on the latest hacker tools? Like any other hobby, they go to Web sites. They check out newsgroups. They sign up for mailing lists. No big secret. This underground society hides in plain view. Nicknames hide their real identities, but through their monikers, many are infamous the world over. Their shared arsenals include a disturbing array of specialized tools:

- virus toolkits to build new viruses
- ready-made vulnerability-exploiting scripts that can quickly be customized for an individual hacker's use in an email or Web page
- password crackers
- RATs
- war dialers
- port scanners
- network sniffers
- buffer overflow triggers
- special utilities that will break through security on different operating systems
- thousands of other vulnerability-specific tools

Some sites even have step-by-step articles showing precisely how attacks have been or should be carried out. These hacker authors take pride not from the systems they've directly hacked but by how many other hackers and script kiddies have used their tools or advice to cause trouble. Some sites publish well-organized lists of known vulnerabilities to pressure software makers to fix them. These sites are both controversial and respected, depending on who you ask. Microsoft, for instance, has criticized this practice of "full disclosure," saying that it gives hackers a heads-up for specific vulnerabilities to target. Proponents of full disclosure argue the same thing and that the software companies had better stop complaining and get to work fixing the vulnerability!

Hacking Your PC (aka Breaking and Entering)

There are tens of thousands of known hacks. Some create small holes that bring the hacker only a little bit closer to your PC. Some kick open huge doors and roll out the red carpet. Hacking into your computer is a process of trial and error. If one hack doesn't work, the hacker tries another one. And another. And another. For some hackers, the thrill of the forbidden can keep them coming back to you for months, especially if they score a few early victories.

Vulnerabilities lurk in every part of your Internet experience, from your operating system to your applications to the Web sites you visit. Some vulnerabilities are bugs (programming errors), and some are features that hackers creatively exploit.

Here are some classic ones:

- Older versions of chat program AOL Instant Messenger have a buffer overflow bug that lets a hacker remotely execute his own arbitrary commands on your PC.

- You can connect to legitimate remote-access program pcAnywhere by sending a password over the Internet, unencrypted. Hackers can snoop on this communication and discover your password. This isn't a bug but an example of an exploitable feature. (To combat this, pcAnywhere's default setting is to encrypt password communication.)

- Kazaa, often used to share MP3 music files, is easily misconfigured by users to share large areas of their hard disks, not just a limited "swap" area. Hackers routinely search the Kazaa network for email or other private files.

Password Crackers

Some hackers can even get into your PC *without* breaking your software. A legitimate remote-access program, for instance, requires a password before you gain access to your PC. Hackers attack these checkpoints with automated programs called *password crackers*. In a short amount of time, password crackers try millions of different passwords, running through the entire dictionary in what's called a "dictionary attack." (In fact, there are password crackers to target any application that requires a password, whether on your computer or on the Web.) If the password was not well chosen (see the section on choosing good passwords later in this chapter), this type of attack will eventually work. Password crackers are often used in conjunction with war dialers.

Buffer Overflows

Buffer overflows are some of the most difficult bugs for programmers to find and eliminate. They're also hacker favorites.

For their internal processing, programs often rely on buffers, which are temporary storage places for data. How a program uses temporary storage buffers, though, should be completely transparent to you, the user. You don't need to know or care. It's like a bottle of mayonnaise used by a restaurant cook. Maybe he's got a big jar of mayo in the fridge but prefers to fill up a smaller, more handy bottle for his daily tasks. This little bottle is his buffer. You as a customer don't need to know or care unless something goes wrong. (Yes, this metaphor is ultimately leading somewhere unpleasant.)

The programmer precisely defines the size of each buffer. The trouble starts when the programmer underestimates the amount of data that could be sent to the buffer. If more information is sent to the buffer than it was designed to store, the "extra" data overflows. Sometimes this extra data ends up in nearby buffers, which might be used for entirely different purposes. This can cause a program to behave very strangely, such as changing its appearance, losing some of its features, or even suddenly crashing, perhaps taking the entire operating system with it. (Have you ever had a program suddenly crash on you? Probably a buffer overflow.) Back in the restaurant, this is like the cook pouring too much mayo into his bottle. Some of it slops over into a nearby spatula drawer. Exposed to the elements, the slopped mayo soon goes bad. Someone uses a contaminated spatula on your burger, and boom. Suddenly, you've got food poisoning due to a buffer overflow.

Sometimes, buffer overflows have predictable results that open small security holes for hackers. That's bad enough, but some buffer overflows actually allow the overflow data to be processed *as though it were a direct command to the computer*. If a hacker can trigger this kind of buffer overflow, he can send any command he wants to your computer. However, even buffer overflows have limits on their size, so they don't usually allow hackers to do anything very complex. For example, it's difficult to send a buffer overflow all the commands necessary to create an entirely new back door that's invisible to you but accessible by the hacker. This is cold comfort, though. Even a small buffer overflow can accommodate a command that says, "Download and run the file at this URL." And the downloaded file can be as large and complex as needed to create a back door or cause any other sort of mischief.

Snooping on Your Hard Drive (aka Looking for Your Valuables)

If your computer is hacked, the luckiest thing that could happen is that the hacker is pleased just to have met the challenge. Challenge satisfied, he exits your computer and goes on his merry way. Maybe he leaves a single calling card to say you were hacked. Good luck waiting for that to happen.

More likely, the hacker will set up a secret back door in case something occurs to him later. The question then becomes, What *won't* he do? With access to your private files and emails, as well as possibly your financial records, he can cause all sorts of trouble for you. Identity theft is easy to perpetrate online. Additionally, he can now use your computer as the staging ground for an attack on any *other* computer. If the new target can track where the attack came from, it will lead right to you. If that happens, he'll probably have cleaned up any lingering evidence that points to him.

ATTACK OF THE UNDEAD PCs

Many hackers attack individual computers simply to assist them in taking on much larger targets. A very common version of this is a denial-of-service (DoS) attack. In a DoS, a target computer (often a server of some sort) is forced to shut down, thus denying service. Usually, a DoS is accomplished by overwhelming the target with connection requests or triggering buffer overflows.

Naturally, some servers are more robust than others and are able to resist the standard DoS. And just as naturally, hackers have stepped up to this challenge. Now the threat is the DDoS, or *distributed* denial of service attack. In a DDoS, the hacker creates a whole network of hijacked computers to attack the target. Some viruses actually turn your PC into a "zombie" or bot (robot). A zombified PC can be controlled remotely and made to attack the hacker's real target. Often, even the controlling PC is some hapless user's hacked machine, making the zombie master of all but impossible to track down. These networks of zombies (called, by straight-faced security professionals, "zombie armies") can be used again and again, as long as the real owners of the PCs never think to install security measures.

So don't just keep your PC safe for your own benefit. Do it for everyone else, lest it become . . . a zombie.

Cleaning Up (aka Leaving Quietly)

The smart hacker will take the time to erase any evidence of his presence. Especially if he wants to come back later, he won't want to leave any clues that might alert you. This includes removing any viruses that initially gave him access, fixing any software he broke to get in, or altering any logs your security software might have. If he's especially fiendish, he'll even replace your security software with a look-alike version that provides no protection.

Spammers

Civil libertarians argue that a spammer isn't quite the same level of ethical troglodyte as a hacker. That difference becomes academic, though, when you receive your twentieth "HOT XXX WEBSITES!!!" email in one day. Whether or not you lump spammers in the same category as hackers, it's a safe bet that you'd rather not be bothered by either of them. Protecting your privacy is an important part of Internet safety.

Spammers have a lot in common with hackers:

- They target you with questionable tactics.
- They snoop on you when you don't know it.
- They use all that data to build a profile of you.

Targeting

Spammers get your email address from many different sources. The most above-board method is from you explicitly giving it to someone. When you register a product, you might be asked whether you would like to receive "offers of special interest from our partners." This is a pretty good tip-off that your email will get sold to any number of third parties. Sometimes this turns out to be okay; you just get the occasional well-targeted email that actually interests you. But other times, you give your address in good faith, only to find that you've been bamboozled. Some companies promise not to give out your address but then do. Some companies sell your address not just to their "partners" but to anyone looking for a live human being on the other end. Speaking of which, don't ever reply directly to a spammed email, even if it says "Reply to this email address to be removed from this list." You'll only confirm to the spammer that you do exist. Then you'll *really* get targeted. Life is not fair.

Tragically, these are the more *reputable* spammers. The really trashy ones use programs called *email harvesters* or *spambots* to cull email addresses from newsgroup postings, bulletin boards, chatrooms, Web pages, and the like. If your email ever leaks out onto the Net in any way, a spambot will grab it. An especially sleazy tactic is from the spammers who join private email lists just to gather the names of their members.

But possibly the worst offenders are Web sites that collect your email address just by you viewing their page *even if you don't explicitly tell them*. Part of the technical specification for Web traffic includes the browser telling the Web server the client's email address. Decent sites will not take advantage of this. Pornography sites have been known to capture people's email addresses in this fashion and bombard them with all sorts of vile email. A single visit can lead to months of hardcore porn spam. A word to the wise. . .

Snooping and Profiling

The sites that grab your email address without asking can also snoop on what you're doing there. They'll track which pages you view, how long you stay there, and even what kind of Web browser you use. Often, this data is used just in aggregate form. That is, it's saved just as totals for all users. Sometimes, though, they're keeping tabs on you individually and sharing this information with other parties. In this way, sites can work together to build a comprehensive profile of you and your interests. Privacy advocates worry especially about companies matching your online profile with your real-world financial or medical profile. By the way, some companies can accomplish all of this just by getting you to use a single piece of adware, but it's worth knowing that they can track you even without that.

Keep in mind that these privacy concerns aren't reserved solely for spammers. Hackers also use many of the above techniques of targeting, snooping, or profiling.

Cookies: Good or Bad?

Cookies are small amounts of information that a server sends to your hard disk. Any client/server communication can include cookies, but usually they come from Web sites. Cookies were created to help the server deliver a more individualized experience. When a site asks you whether you want it to "remember" your ID and password for the next time you visit, it will send cookies to your PC to hold this info. The next time you visit that site, it actually checks to see whether you've got a cookie and what information is in it. Other cookies keep track of ads you've seen or pages you've visited.

Cookie usage can get quite complex, but at the heart of it, the cookie simply holds information specified by the server. As a nod to privacy, only the site that created a cookie can view it technically. In practice however, many Web sites fill their ad "slots" with HTML pointers to an ad company's server. Thus, when you browse such a page, you're also making direct contact with the ad server. The ad server can send you a cookie, which can naturally be read by this site whenever you make contact again. And by the nature of their business, ad companies serve ads on multiple sites in the thousands or tens of thousands. This means that any time you visit another site with an ad served by that ad company, you can get tracked across multiple sites. And classified, and profiled.

Hoaxes

You should always be on guard against hoaxes, whether perpetrated by a hacktivist with a cause or a con man with an angle. Even the most good-natured hoax can have unintended security repercussions. Some hoaxes are downright malicious, such as a virus that spreads itself in an email entitled "Antivirus upgrade." Some are scams, such as a site that purports (falsely) to be a billing department of AOL. Others are simply annoying, such as those that temporarily replace the InterNIC, the former domain registration service of the Internet, with a separate site to protest its monopoly.

Email Hoaxes

The most common place where you'll run into a hoax in is your inbox. Some urban legends have been forwarded from inbox to inbox for years: the dog who needs a home, the department store that stole some grandmother's cookie recipe, the software giant (Microsoft) who will pay you to forward this email. These aren't viruses, just true-sounding tales that actually convince people to forward them. Although it's possible that some incredibly wide-spread sob story is on the up and up, it's exceedingly unlikely. Do yourself and your friends a favor: Just delete it. The next generation of these hoaxes claims that certain email hoaxes are actually viruses themselves. These blare out frantic warnings such as, "If you receive an email titled PLEASE HELP POOR DOG . . . DO NOT OPEN IT! . . . It will erase everything on your hard drive . . . please share [this note] with everyone who might access the Internet." Again, try to restrain yourself from "protecting" everyone in your address book.

Other hoaxes in your inbox are more threatening. As we've seen, the Klez virus sometimes sends an infected email that actually claims to be a Klez removal tool. Social engineering attacks work only if you fall for them. Don't be the weak link in your own security.

Website Hoaxes

The worst Web hoaxes are complete scams. Be skeptical. Just because someone can cobble together a nice-looking Web site doesn't mean they're legitimate. You can probably find a Web site claiming to sell you anything. Some hoaxes are fairly complex. In 1999, a number of AOL customers got emails warning that there was a problem with their credit card bills. To resolve it, they were directed to www.aol-bills.com. This site was a scam, with no connection at all to AOL, although it looked real enough. Its goal was to trick unsuspecting users into divulging their credit card numbers.

Some site hoaxes come from very different motives. Popular with hacktivists is "hack tagging," which is defacing or replacing a Web site. For example, the Web site for the U.S. Department of Justice was hacked in 1996 and replaced with anti-DOJ propaganda and pornography. The point of hack tagging is usually to show off a blatant parody. If this happens, the security risk to you is small because you're not likely to volunteer any information at such a site. But if the vandalism is more subtle, you might be fooled. Always be on the lookout for oddities at a Web site.

AlterNIC

 Part of the fun of the Internet is getting a front-row seat to some world-class shenanigans.

In July 1997, one Eugene Kashpureff successfully replaced the Web site for the InterNIC, the sole granter of Internet domains, with his own site: AlterNIC. Technically, he redirected all traffic intended for the original site to his own by convincing the Internet's name servers that his computer's IP address was the correct one to use whenever anyone typed "internic.com" into a browser. Even before "hijacking" the InterNIC, Kashpureff's site was an outspoken critic of the InterNIC's monopoly on domain registration. He proposed opening the registration up to competing organizations, such as his.

So was the hoax an example of high-minded hacktivism or low-minded guerrilla marketing? It depends on who you ask. At the very least, Kashpureff's antics were fascinating to watch. He replaced the InterNIC (simply called "the 'NIC" by hackers in the know) twice in July, telling any reporter who would listen how he was fighting for freedom. Apparently, he was surprised when 'NIC lawyers threatened him with a lawsuit. He ultimately settled the case by showing them how he accomplished the hack and issuing a public apology. But then, to everyone's surprise, the FBI got in on the act. Not willing to settle for mere contrition, the feds wanted to send him to jail for computer fraud. They even had to extradite him from Canada over his cries that they were "overreacting." Ultimately, Kashpureff pleaded guilty to a single count of computer fraud. Faced with a maximum of five years in jail and a $250,000 fine, Kashpureff received two years' probation and a $100 fine instead.

By the way, a few years later, the InterNIC's monopoly on domain registration came to an end. You can now register a domain with a number of other accredited registrars.

MISCONCEPTIONS

It is worth keeping your distance from the popular misconceptions of even nontechnical hoaxes. If someone tells you one of these urban legends, just walk away.

The Internet is Controlled by the Government!

Not. The Internet was started by the U.S. Department of Defense, but now it's a loose collection of thousands of separate networks (a network of networks, in fact) that have all chosen to use the same communications protocols. And no, Al Gore didn't invent it.

Internet Web Sites Can View My Hard Drive!

Nope. If you visit a Web page that displays your hard drive, it's just a prank. Technically, it's an HTML trick that shows you what's on your own computer. The Web site never sees it.

One Day, the Internet Is Going to Crash!

Okay, this one might happen. It's pretty darned unlikely, though. The Internet was designed to be widespread and redundant enough to survive a nuclear war. It's conceivable, though, that some smart hacker could come up with a new Internet worm that attacks its infrastructure and takes it out of commission for a few days, tops.

PROTECTION

Now that you know what you're up against, you can defend yourself. We'll look at some proven techniques and products to help keep you secure, but the most important tool is your brain. Above and beyond the specific tactics, you've got to adopt an attitude of security. It's like driving. You've got to pay attention always. There's a lot you can take for granted, but you should be ready to react at a moment's notice if something goes wrong.

On Your Computer

The most common PC security products are antivirus, firewalls, and intrusion-detection systems. Every product has its specific uses; nothing plugs all possible security holes. This is why multilayered security is critical, just as in the real world. Every house has door locks; houses in rough neighborhoods or with a lot to protect *also* have alarm systems. As we've seen, the Internet's a pretty rough neighborhood, so don't use just a personal firewall; use an antivirus program, too. All the time.

Antivirus Programs

Let's make this simple: Get an antivirus program. Only the uninformed wade into the Internet without this basic protection. Antivirus software (often simply called *AV*) constantly scans your hard disk for viruses. If it finds any, it kills them, and sometimes even attempts to repair damaged files. A good antivirus program will scan your incoming and outgoing emails, downloaded files, and any removable media (floppy disks, CDs, etc.) that are inserted into your PC. Antivirus programs work by storing a database of known viruses' digital fingerprints (called *patterns* or *definitions*). The programs automatically download new patterns when they're available from the manufacturer. (If your antivirus software requires you to check for updates manually, do so often—at least once a week.)

Critical as an antivirus program is, though, it's not enough. By design, an antivirus program can generally look for only *known* threats, viruses that match its pattern database. A new virus can run amok for days before antivirus companies capture a sample and begin to "fingerprint" it. Even new variants of existing viruses can require a new pattern. Also, antivirus products aren't designed to protect against spyware. To plug these security holes, you need a firewall.

SOFTWARE VS. HARDWARE FIREWALL

Software firewalls intercept each network request and determine whether the request is valid. They tend to be inexpensive and easy to configure. The downsides are that they do run on your machine and take up some system resources, and you must purchase one copy for each system on your home network.

Hardware firewalls tend to be expensive unless you have multiple machines to defend (it can be cost-effective because you need only one hardware firewall instead of multiple copies of a software firewall). Because they do not run on your system, they do not take up any resources. However, they are challenging to configure.

A good Web site to read about changes in firewall technology is the Gibson Research Corporation. The site features the *Shields UP!* test to check out the security of your firewall and see whether it's configured properly, then report back any holes it may find. For more information, go to www.grc.com.

Firewalls

In addition to antivirus software, you should also have a personal firewall. Firewalls were among the first security programs on the Internet. Their initial purpose is still sound—keep the bad guys out. Today's cutting-edge firewalls, however, do much more: They also hide your PC and keep spyware from phoning home. The best ones even protect against viruses that haven't yet been fingerprinted.

Basically, firewalls work by examining the packets of information that want to come in or go out. They block intruders by rejecting attempts to probe or send in harmful commands. For instance, if a port scan asks, "Is port X open at IP address Y?" a standard firewall will send back a message that the port is closed. Now that's certainly better than replying, "The port's open; come on in!" But it gives the hacker too much information: He now confirms that there is indeed a computer there. Better still is if the firewall *doesn't respond at all*. If a hacker receives no reply to his port scan or ping (an old network tool that simply confirms whether a certain IP address is "live"), he's likely to move on to the next location. If the hacker can't find you, he can't target you. If your firewall hides the very existence of your PC, it has *stealth* capability. The port scanner is most hackers' tool of choice, so a stealth firewall is crucial. Stealthing is a relatively recent technological development, however, so only a few firewalls offer it.

Application control is another firewall feature you need. This keeps rogue applications such as Trojans or spyware from making outbound connections. A good firewall remembers which applications you allow to have outbound access. When a new one tries or an old one is altered (perhaps by a virus), the firewall alerts you.

Because firewalls already monitor inbound packets, the smarter ones check incoming email for as-yet-undefined viruses. Certain file types are common virus carriers. A quality firewall will quarantine these suspicious file types just in case. You can launch them if you want to, but your firewall protects you from accidentally infecting yourself. Naturally, some email programs (such as Microsoft Outlook) also quarantine suspicious file types. Another benefit to checking inbound packets is some firewalls' ability to stymie sites that use malicious cookies or other privacy-invading techniques. Privacy-enhanced firewalls or standalone privacy products keep servers from placing or retrieving information from your PC. Some even stop pop-up ads from cluttering your screen.

Finally, a firewall, if built correctly, is one of the few products that can actually protect itself from direct malware or hacker attacks. For example, when attacked, ZoneAlarm's defenses harden, rejecting any new Internet access attempts by programs not already connected. This last line of defense can keep malware from spreading or phoning home.

In addition to ZoneAlarm (see sidebar), other personal firewalls come from Symantec and Network Associates. However, make sure your firewall has stealth mode, application control, email filtering for suspicious attachments, and the ability to protect itself from direct attacks.

Of course, if you've already gotten a virus on your computer, installing a firewall is like shutting the gate after the horses have already escaped. That's why you should always use a personal firewall in conjunction with antivirus software.

COOL DOWNLOAD: ZONEALARM

The ZoneAlarm family of firewalls from Zone Labs is very popular with the public and has won numerous awards. The free product ZoneAlarm offers basic Internet security with stealth mode, application control, email filtering for .VBS (the file type for the LoveBug), and the ability to protect itself if attacked. ZoneAlarm Plus offers all these features plus even better network support and advanced email filtering (46 file types). ZoneAlarm Pro, the top-of-the-line product, has all the features of Plus and extra privacy and ad-blocking functionality. All three are available at www.zonelabs.com. ZoneAlarm is free for individuals and nonprofit users. ZoneAlarm Plus and Pro each cost less than $50 and are available for a one-month free trial.

Stateful Inspection Firewalls

The stateful inspection software firewall (also known as dynamic *packet filtering)* is the technology used for many firewalls on the market. The stateful firewall has two basic flavors: the packet filter and the proxy server. In the past, the methods employed were clearly defined so that comparisons could easily be made. Today for the most part, the term means a hybrid of both static packet-filtering and application-level proxy servers. When lines are blurred, confusion is created.

Pure static packet filtering will view only at the packet based at the header information level. A stateful inspection will track the connection at many levels. It may examine the header information, the contents of the packet, and the application layer. It will attempt to determine the sources and destination of the packet. Filtering decisions are based on administrator-defined rules (as in static packet filtering) and by comparing it with prior packets that have passed through the firewall.

Intrusion Detection Systems

Traditionally used on large networks, intrusion detection systems (IDSs) have recently migrated to the level of individual PCs. An IDS scans incoming (and sometimes outgoing) Internet traffic, looking for suspicious packets of data. Similar to antivirus products, an IDS compares these packets with a database of threat patterns. If it detects a match, the IDS blocks the traffic.

In theory, an IDS protects against not just viruses but also hacker attacks. However, the primary inherent weakness in an IDS is its dependence on patterns. If you are attacked by a new virus or hacker tool, your IDS might not recognize it. The most popular consumer IDS, BlackIce PC Protection, also integrates basic firewall protection. Unfortunately, it doesn't completely stealth your PC, and it doesn't scan your email. The best security for now remains a full-featured personal firewall in conjunction with antivirus protection. Keep your eye on IDS technology, though. It's a great idea that grows more useful every year.

ENCRYPTION ON YOUR HARD DRIVE

If you need to prepare for the worst possible scenario, you might want a hard disk encryption product such as DriveCrypt or the free ScramDisk. These products can make your entire hard disk or just the most important parts of it unreadable to anyone but you. If a hacker breaks into your PC or a thief actually steals the entire computer, your information remains private. These products are geared toward laptop users with ultrasensitive information, but anyone can benefit by this ultimate layer of protection.

Hardware Firewalls

Hardware firewalls were once found only in corporate networks, but they are finding their way into the home. These network appliances plug into your network and prevent access to machines except those on recognized ports. Hardware firewalls provide an additional layer of defense for one or more connected PCs.

Placed at the "gateway" through which all inbound and outbound traffic passes, a single hardware firewall can add a level of security for an entire network. However, unless you're running a network within your house, you probably don't have the need or technical acumen for a hardware firewall. Also, hardware firewalls leave certain security vulnerabilities. Because they're designed to work for entire networks, they don't monitor applications running on individual PCs. This means that a remote-access Trojan or spyware can make an outbound connection with impunity. On the other hand, software firewalls running on individual PCs can prevent this at the source. Corporations often use the multilayered security of a networkwide hardware firewall plus personal firewalls on all individual PCs.

> SofaWare offers its Safe@ product line, Safe@Home, Safe@HomePro, and Safe@Office. Its stance is that personal software firewalls are better than none; people require a more simple, secure solution. Its home hardware firewall solution is called Safe@Home. Unlike PC-based firewalls, this Internet appliance is placed between your PC and your high-speed modem (or integrates into the modem itself). With it, you are protecting your entire home network, not just a single PC. SofaWare offers additional help if you need it. For more information, go to www.sofaware.com.

OTHER APPLICATIONS

Firewalls and antivirus protection are a great start in securing your computer. Just don't think you get to stop there. You've added good defenses; now it's time to plug some holes. And they're probably more prevalent than you'd like to admit: bugs in your apps, inherently insecure products, maybe even an overly friendly operating system.

Thanks to buffer overflows and other bugs, many programs can offer a clever hacker a red carpet right onto your computer. Even your operating system itself could have bugs that a wily hacker can exploit. You should always download and run the latest patches for your programs. (Egregious security vulnerabilities are usually fixed very quickly by software companies, often before many hackers take advantage of them.) Don't let time go by without patching! The longer a security bug is known, the more tools are created to exploit it. It just gets easier and easier for hackers.

A FAVORITE VULNERABILITY

> Hackers' favorite vulnerabilities are the ones that open huge holes but don't get patched. A perennial favorite is the "MIME exploit." Normally, you have to explicitly launch or open an email attachment. If a virus exploits this bug, though, it can autolaunch just by you reading the email. The vulnerability is complicated but worth examining, so you can see how bugs can open the most surprising security holes.

Microsoft's email products, Outlook and Outlook Express, actually borrow some functionality from Internet Explorer to display HTML emails. Some versions of Explorer can be fooled by malicious HTML code into thinking that one file type is another. This can ultimately lead to Explorer opening and running a file automatically, without asking you for permission. Because Outlook and Outlook Express rely on Explorer, they can inherit this bug. This can even hit you if you simply preview a message. You should always disable the Preview feature.

By the way, vulnerable versions of Explorer can also be hit with this exploit when browsing the Web. A Web page can use the same bug to download and auto-launch malware sitting at a Web site. The Nimda virus did precisely this, and it caused over half a billion dollars in damage.

Microsoft issued an Explorer patch for this vulnerability, but many users still haven't installed it yet.

Sometimes the programs themselves are inherently insecure, even when running bug-free. Peer-to-peer communication applications, personal Web servers, and remote-access programs are especially risky. File-sharing program Kazaa, for example, lets you transport files from someone else's desktop directly to yours. If it's the file you expected it to be, great. If it's a virus masquerading as something else, you're in trouble. Security software can help you only so much if you're determined to make a dopey decision. Also, certain viruses spread through these communication tools, often bypassing firewalls and antivirus products.

Be careful if you decide to use any of the following:

- peer-to-peer apps such as KaZaA, ICQ, the Instant Messenger "chat" programs (AOL, Yahoo!, MSN), and Gnutella.
- remote-access programs or utilities such as Remote Desktop, AppleTalk Remote Access, GoToMyPC, and pcAnywhere (known lovingly by hackers as "pcEverywhere").
- personal Web servers.

They aren't necessarily unsafe, but you should know the risks before you install. If you're thinking of adding a new communications program to your PC, do some checking first. Talk to friends, check magazines, or use search engines to look up the name of the program plus words such as *virus* and *security*.

Even your operating system might be cheating on you. Unless you have a specific need for them, make sure you

DVORAK'S TIP

Always enter your own address into your address book. That way, if you get a virus that sends out emails, you'll get a copy. You'll already be infected, but at least you'll know about it.

disable all levels of file sharing, drive mapping, and (as shown above) remote access. And finally, to protect against the worst, always back up your data on a regular basis: once a month for your whole hard drive and important files daily or weekly.

Choosing Good Passwords

Spend a little time thinking up your passwords. If a hacker knows a little bit about you, he'll try the easy ones: your birthday, your spouse's name, your pet's name, and so on. Also, don't use the same word for all of your passwords: If it's cracked once, it can open up multiple vulnerabilities. Never use your email password anywhere else; if you have a POP3 email account, that password is transmitted to the mail server "in the clear" (unencrypted). Here are some guidelines for choosing passwords that are harder for password crackers to uncover:

- Make the password as long as possible.
- Don't use names or words found in the dictionary. (And don't just reverse a word. The hackers figured that one out a long time ago.)
- Use a mixture of uppercase and lowercase letters. And don't capitalize just the first letter.
- Use at least one numeral but not at the start or end.
- Use at least one "typewriter character": !@#$%^&*() but not at the start or end.

Make the password as complex as you can remember. Use the old trick of substituting numbers for sounds ("gr8" is "great"). Another favorite is to substitute numbers for letters they resemble, such as 0 (zero) for O or 3 for E. Keep in mind, though, that the hackers know all these old tricks, too, so use all the tricks at once. For example, "monkey" is an awful password; "m0N#3e" is good (assuming you were limited to six characters).

Change your most important passwords regularly at least once every two months. Don't store your important passwords in a file on your disk. If you have trouble remembering your passwords, write them down. (But leave the hard copy in a safe place—don't take it with you if you have a laptop!)

WIRELESS VULNERABILITIES

If you use a wireless network connection, you are making a hacker's job even simpler. Wireless communications are very easy for hackers to examine and even intrude on. Even if you're in your own home, a hacker could eavesdrop on your communications or trespass on your LAN, all from outside. And if you use public wireless Internet connections, for example, with American Airlines or Starbucks, you might just find yourself sitting next to a dedicated hacker just looking to monitor everything you send and receive.

Safe Surfing

The major rules here are no-brainers.

- Don't visit disreputable Web sites.
- Don't buy things from suspicious people.
- Don't assume downloads are safe.
- Don't give away your personal information.

See how they're all negatives? That's the mindset you're shooting for.

Disreputable Web Sites

The immediate danger from suspicious sites is that they're running dangerous Web content. An ActiveX hack, for example, could do all sorts of damage to your PC. Secondarily, such sites could capture your email or IP address and target you for spam or hacking. To be safe, avoid sites that obviously deal in hacker tools, pornography, and pirated software. (This is another direct parallel to the real world: If you hang out in the bad part of town, you're more likely to get mugged.)

By the hyperlinked nature of the Web, though, it's often hard to predict where the next click will take you. To be on the safe side, you should adjust your browser's security settings to at least Medium, if you use Internet Explorer. This will keep you from automatically running ActiveX. In fact, you should try surfing with High security, which should also prevent Java or JavaScript from causing trouble for you. If you don't notice any malfunctions in the Web pages you view, you should just keep your setting like that. (If you use Netscape, you can disable Java or JavaScript manually in your Preferences. Netscape doesn't support ActiveX unless you specifically install a special plug-in.)

To keep Web sites from snooping on you, try anonymous browsing. Several products and services prevent Web sites from using cookies or learning your IP address. Most accomplish this by having their own Web sites do the browsing you want, then passing that information on to you. (This idea of an intermediary fetching your content for you is at the core of proxy servers, which were once available only for large networks.) Check out www.anonymizer.com, www.idzap.com, and www.safeproxy.org.

Money and Suspicious People

If you're brave or foolish enough to visit the sorts of sites listed above, at least exercise a shred of good judgment and don't give them your bank account or credit card numbers. The same goes with online auctions—avoid folks with bad transaction history! (You'd think this wouldn't have to be said, but there's one born every minute.) If you're really going to tempt fate and buy whatever it is these spooky folks are selling, see whether they'll take a secure form of payment, such as PayPal. That way if you get burned, you lose only that one transaction and not your entire financial identity. And remember: Don't send your financial information via email. With the network sniffers out there, it's like sending it on a postcard so anyone could read it. If you get a note from your ISP asking you to resend your credit card information through email, it's probably a scam. Call your ISP to confirm.

Security and Shopping

Ironically, the one online activity that's generally pretty secure is the one that most folks worry about—shopping. If your browser has established an SSL connection with the server, the transaction itself is safe from being snooped or altered. That is, your financial info is safe *in transit* from your PC to the Web site. If you choose to buy from someone shady, you're still opening yourself up for trouble, just like in the real world. Also, hackers do target vendors' credit card databases, so even the good merchants can sometimes land you in hot water.

SSL stands for secure sockets layer. An SSL connection means that a secure layer of encrypted communication is occurring between your browser and a secure server. While this connection is maintained, any data that is transferred back and forth remains private and unalterable from hackers. (Keep in mind, though, that if you already have spyware on your machine, it will still record everything you do. If you're already compromised, a secure connection won't help you.)

By default, browsers tell you when you are entering or exiting an SSL connection. Once you've established the connection, your browser's interface should display a small lock icon (in a locked position). Check with your browser's documentation for precise information on how this looks. Also, the URL in your browser's location field starts with "https," as opposed to the usual "http."

Who Can You Trust?

Sometimes it's hard to tell who you can trust on the Internet. If thieves can build a Web site that looks as professional as AOL and that actually looks like it's *part* of AOL, how are you supposed to know the difference?

The first clue is the URL in your browser's location bar. Don't be fooled by huge URLs. Check what's toward the very left. If it starts with something such as http://www.aol.com, you're in good shape. If it's http://www.aol-bills.com, you know something might be wrong. Note that some companies do have other parties handle their online sales, so if you're buying something at one site but end up at another, it's not necessarily a bad sign. Just look for some documentation on the original site verifying that you'll be handed to another site.

What if you're confident you're at the correct site but still aren't sure whether you should trust them? Do some research! Search for articles about them at legitimate online magazines. See whether they have a phone number that actually reaches a real person. Find out how long they've been in business. See whether they have any business partners that you trust. And if you're still not convinced, consider that your better judgment is trying to tell you something, and try to find the same product somewhere else.

Free Downloads

Unsurprisingly, the Internet's denizens for its first couple of decades were largely science fiction buffs. The Net's culture (yes, it had a distinct culture) was initially shaped by them, and their effect still shows in many of the weird terms floating around the Net today. This one is appropriate for the thousands of free downloads you can find online: TANSTAAFL. It's an acronym for "There Ain't No Such Thing As A Free Lunch." Robert Heinlein popularized it in his 1963 classic *The Moon is a Harsh Mistress*. It means basically that you can't get something for nothing. If it's of high quality, it'll cost. If it's free, it'll suck eggs, no matter how much someone would have you think otherwise.

So if you think you're getting too good a deal with that free copy of Photoshop, you're downloading, you're probably right. It's a good bet that it's got a Trojan hidden in it. Of course, there are legit freebies: trial versions that work for only a month, free versions intended to impress you so much that you upgrade to a full-featured pay version, and honest-to-goodness freeware that was intended from the start to be distributed free of charge. These are all available through reputable Web sites. But at some of the more dubious Web sites and newsgroups, some hackers would have you believe that they're giving away "cracked" (fully enabled) versions of popular and expensive applications. Now does that make sense to you? That hackers, who spend their time breaking into people's PCs, are suddenly the Robin Hoods of the digital world?

Actually, some of them really *do* enjoy sharing pirated software. They call the programs *warez* (pronounced "wares," not "Juarez"). But by and large, downloading cracked software is a dangerous practice. Do the smart thing: Beware of hackers bearing software.

Personal Information

Keep your personal information personal. Does this sound obvious? If so, you'd be surprised at the amount of information people are willing to give out online. Name, social security number, yearly income, home address—it's like some people just lose their free will when confronted with a signup form.

If you're signing up for a magazine subscription through a secure server at a reputable site, then by all means give your credit card number and your mailing address. But if you're answering a comprehensive "market research" questionnaire at www.waresrule.com, you've only got yourself to blame if your credit rating takes a nosedive a few days later. If you're lucky, you'll just end up with more spam than you know what to do with.

PRIVACY POLICIES AND TRUSTE

Any site that engages in online commerce or data collection will have a privacy policy that tells you precisely what it does with any information it collects from you. The question is, does that site abide by its guidelines? Truste (pronounced "trusty") is the answer to that question. A nonprofit organization, Truste confirms for consumers that a site does indeed follow its stated policy. But note that Truste does not vouch for the *quality* of a site's privacy policy. The site's policy could be to sell your home address and yearly salary to any and every spammer with a couple of bucks. So if you're thinking of giving over personal information to a Web site, do yourself a favor and read the site's privacy policy first.

Also in the category of "what the heck were you thinking?" is giving out private information in newsgroups, forums, chatrooms, and the like. Many of these communication media are archived or otherwise available for days, weeks, or even years. The spambots will find you again and again.

Many web-interface forums allow you to pick a nickname for yourself. Go ahead. Create an alter ego. Don't be in such a hurry to use your real name. And if the forum's signup page asks your real name, just leave it blank. Maybe it will accept that. At the very least, look for a checkbox that says "Keep this information private from other forum members." If you want your new friends to contact you directly, let them know how yourself.

If you can't hide your email address (as is the case with newsgroups), consider lying. Well, maybe don't *lie*, but give the truth a tweak. If your address is person@yahoo.com, enter it as person@yahooNOSPAM.com. That will fool the spambots. Just make sure not to make it a real address that could get someone else on a spamlist. This, by the way, is known as "munging" your email address. Internet lore holds that "mung" (pronounced "munj") is an acronym for Mash Until No Good.

 Munging is when you deliberately alter your return email address so that spam bots can't decipher it. Email addresses are definable because of the unique @ sign in the address.

When munging is done, it should be done in such a way that the person reading your document (real person, not a program scanning it) can tell that it's a munged email address. Also, it shouldn't be someone else's possible email address. Five examples of a possible munged address of dvorak@aol.com would be:

DvorakNoSpam@aol.com

d-v-o-r-a-k-a-t-a-o-l-c-o-m

UsernameDvorak, domain AOL dot com

Com.AOL@Dvorak

Dvorak at aol dot com

Munged email addresses are useful in Web sites, email correspondence, chatrooms, and postings to newsgroups and special interest groups (SIGs). However, they may violate the TOS (terms of service) of some Internet providers. It should not be used when someone really needs your email address.

If you're feeling sneaky, you can also sign up with a different name or email address each time. (You can, of course, get multiple free email accounts from Yahoo!, Hotmail, and many other sites.) This way, you can track who's giving your name to the spammers, but there are so many ways spammers get away.

If You've Been Hacked

The best time to respond to a hack is before it happens. Take the time now to prepare for a worst-case scenario, and you'll be in far better shape if it ever does. Make regular backups of the important information on your PC, keep your installation disks handy, and keep a hard copy of your ISP's phone numbers, especially its "report a hacker incident" number. In fact, it's worth a call to your ISP now to confirm with it what your post-hack steps should be. They might even have extra advice for you.

If your antivirus software reports that you've been infected with a virus, it should be able to remove the infection. If you aren't running antivirus software and merely suspect an infection, purchase the software ASAP. Install it, download the latest patterns, and let the antivirus software clean (and hopefully repair) your hard disk. If the damage can't be repaired, you can always restore from those backups you've been making, right? Right?

If you're still certain you've got a virus, despite a negative result from the antivirus scan, you might have a brand-new virus that hasn't been fingerprinted yet. If this happens, you should contact your antivirus vendor. They will let you know how to get them a sample of the virus so they can make a new pattern.

If You've Been Hacked, These Are Your Priorities

Alert the authorities. Call your ISP (don't email—the hacker could be monitoring your communication to see whether he's been discovered) and ask what you should do. They will probably test your computer from afar and possibly ask you to send them your log of firewall activity. If you aren't able to reach your ISP, call your local police and see whether they have any special procedures.

Stop the attack. If you can't reach any authorities, you should disconnect your computer from the outside world.

Gather evidence against the hacker. Make a special backup of everything on your PC now, before the hacker comes back and erases any additional evidence. At the very least, save your firewall log to a floppy disk. Have backups from previous days ready for the authorities to examine.

Repair the damage. Once your ISP lets you know how the hacker got in, work with the ISP to plug any "leaks." Consider reformatting your entire hard disk and reinstalling all of your applications. If this is too daunting for you, then at least scan your PC with updated antivirus software. Set your security software to higher security settings. You've been a victim once; they might come back for you. If you have financial or other sensitive information on your PC, be ready to cope with it becoming public. (Tell the credit card companies, your bank, etc.) Consult

---

the government's Identity Theft Web site at http://www.consumer.gov/ idtheft/. If you maintain a file of various site passwords on your PC (and you shouldn't), change them all now. And keep that list on a piece of paper from now on.

Punish the hacker. At your discretion, pursue this matter further with the legal authorities.

AVOID VIGILANTISM!

A word of warning: Don't try to track a hacker down yourself. Some products, such as BlackIce and McAfee Visual Trace, let you follow a hack attack right back to the hacker. Unfortunately, the hacker will probably detect this, so you've not only ruined any stealth benefit from your firewall, you've also let the hacker know valuable information about what security software you use. This is like poking a bear with a stick. If you think you had trouble before, wait until the hacker takes it personally. If you need to know where your hacker is, use ZoneAlarm Pro or Plus, which lets you know where the hacker attacks come from. The difference is that this service is performed by the Zone Labs Web site, which hides your identity from the attacker.

STAY INFORMED

It doesn't take much to stay informed on the important security matters of the day. Regularly scan the headlines or sign up for email newsletters at technology Web sites such as PCMag.com or Lockergnome.com, and you'll see the issues that merit your attention. If you find you have a deeper interest in security and hackerdom (from the side of goodness and light, naturally), you can check out more targeted sites such as grc.com (from security guru Steve Gibson) and BroadbandReports.com (geared especially for broadband users). For information on specific viruses, go to antivirus sites such as Symantec.com.

ARE YOU A GOOD HACKER OR A BAD HACKER?

In hackerdom's fanciful language, the good guys are called "white hats" and the bad "black hats." White hats are the intellectual and spiritual heirs of the "pure hackers" of the Internet's youth. They want to know how things work, and they want to make things work better. White hats generally favor full disclosure of all bugs, trusting to the marketplace to provide the incentive to fix them. In the same spirit, they also tend to support the open source

---

movement, where companies reveal to the world the source code that makes up their applications.

Whereas black hats make hacker tools, white hats make utilities that test your system for vulnerabilities. Steve Gibson, for example, has created many such tools. The most famous is ShieldsUp, a free service. ShieldsUp runs a series of mock attacks against you from Gibson's Web site, grc.com. You can see for yourself how well your current security works. If you're coasting along without protection, it can be a sobering experience.

Other white hats dedicate themselves to spreading the gospel of security to other techies and the general public. In addition to grc.com and BroadbandReports.com, these folks hang out in discussion forums at sites such as Wilders.org, ComputerCops.biz, and of course, Whitehats.com.

One final note: There are also "gray hat" hackers who illegally break into systems, then typically let the targets know so they can plug the holes. (Often, these gray hats are consultants looking for work.) Technically law breakers, these gray hats argue that they're on the side of the angels.

SECURITY IS A PROCESS

The moral of this story is that security is not an item on a checklist. You can't just say, "Well, I'm glad my new computer comes with *Security*. Now I can relax."

Security is a process; it never ends. You must always keep your security products upgraded and software patched, and adjust to new conditions. Consider the security ramifications of everything. Want a new peer-to-peer application to share MP3s? Just be aware that you'll have to punch a hole (i.e., open a port) through your firewall to use it. Want to access your home PC from work? Make doubly sure that your remote access software is solid. Want to open the neat screensaver grandma just sent you? Call her up and make sure she's really the one who sent it (then tell her to quit sending you files that might be hiding Trojans, anyway).

On the Net, you can't afford to let your guard down. Despite its benefits, it's a rough place where everything and everyone (even dear old grandma) should be considered guilty until proven innocent. As Thomas Jefferson once said, "The price of freedom is eternal vigilance."

A GOOD SECURITY SETUP

If you're running a Windows computer, follow these steps for a good security configuration.

Turn off all file sharing.

Set your browser security settings to at least Medium.

Install ZoneAlarm Pro for a stealth firewall, application control, email filtering, and the ability to protect itself from direct attacks.

Install Norton Antivirus and keep it updated with the latest patterns to provide an additional layer of protection.

Keep all applications updated with the latest patches.

Check the tech or security sites from time to time for the latest warnings.

No computer can ever be 100% safe, but this setup puts you ahead of most other netizens.

TELECOMMUTER RESPONSIBILITIES

If you log on to your employer's network from your home computer, take care not to breach its security. If your employer's network administrator is smart, he or she has an explicit network security policy that includes a number of software products installed on each work PC. If you log on from home, though, you might not have any of these. And your home computer probably has additional vulnerabilities your work PC doesn't: your private email, the personal surfing habits of you and your family members, and insecure programs.

Even if you connect to the network through a secure connection, such as a VPN (virtual private network), your employer could still be vulnerable. If your computer is compromised, a secure connection is like a big red carpet, letting a hacker or virus enter the network with impunity. (In 2000, Microsoft itself fell prey to hackers who tunneled in through a telecommuter's hacked machine. The hackers had the run of Microsoft's internal network for *three months*.) And if you've configured your computer to autologin to your employer's network, you make it that much easier for hackers.

To be a good telecommuter, follow all the security rules in this chapter and ask your network administrator what additional safeguards you should implement.

CARNIVORE (DCS1000) AND OMNIVORE

There has been lots of misinformation about Carnivore, the original name for an email surveillance system operated by the FBI. (It's now called DCS1000, for *digital collection system*.) It is a system housed at computers at ISPs but can also collect email messages from people who are not part of a probe. It is able to intercept messages sent to or from the target of an investigation. It allows the FBI to suck one stream of data from the river of other.

The FBI calls it a *diagnostic tool,* which is a reasonable assertion. Communications networks, including the Internet, are a vehicle for criminal activists to communicate (just like the rest of us). It is a way for the justice system to obtain evidence that is unlikely to be discredited or impeached with an allegation of misunderstanding or bias. After all, it's using a defendant's own words. The gathering of information is for evidence, not intelligence . . . meaning it's not for spying but for building evidence in a case already existing.

An application for electronic surveillance will need to outline the exact details pertinent to a specific case. The offense (or offenses) committed must be specified. Where the interception is to take place (the exact telecommunications facility), a description of what sort of conversation is supposed to be monitored, and the identities of the persons are detailed.

Under Title III of the Patriot Act, applications for interception require the authorization of a high-level Department of Justice official before local United States Attorney's offices can apply for such orders. Interception orders must be filed with the federal district court judges or with other courts of competent jurisdiction. Unlike typical search warrants, federal magistrates are not authorized to approve these applications or orders. Interception of communications is limited to certain specified federal felony offenses.

The reality is, none of the people you know (unless your friends are high-level criminals) will ever be a target of an online surveillance by the Department of Justice. On the other hand, the possibility of an individual intercepting your email or gaining access to your computer files is astronomical—if you don't practice good online common sense and have security measures in place.

An earlier version, Omnivore, was an unfocused gigabyte cruncher. It did not have the *surgical* ability to intercept specific types of communication and ignored those it was not authorized to accept. Omnivore was an old technology that has since been replaced.

WORKPLACE SURVEILLANCE

You may not be aware that your employer is spying on you, but it can be. The techniques are the same as ones used by hackers. Workplace surveillance is a growing trend. Employers can use a variety of methods to track cyberslackers. Employers are not required to notify you that you are being observed, so they can do it without your consent or knowledge. It goes hand in hand with the growing number of employees using their computers for personal use and leaking sensitive information. Employers also feel compelled to watch their workers to avoid sexual harassment and discrimination lawsuits that result from offensive emails circulating within the corporate mail system. Instead of selective monitoring, it's become more prevalent to monitor everything and everyone.

There are three ways employers can easily track employees' computer usage:

Packet sniffers

Log files

Desktop monitoring programs

Packet Sniffers

If your machine is hooked to a network, one possible security breach is a *packet sniffer*. Network administrators use packet sniffers to monitor the networks and troubleshoot problems. Although this is a boon for network managers for traffic analysis, it is also a tool for hackers. The newer protocols (IPsec) are designed to prevent packet sniffing by encrypting packets, but many networks haven't implemented this encryption technology or have only a portion of the data encrypted.

The way it works is based on the way Ethernet networks send their *packets*. (The packet is part of a message that's broken into chunks for easy handling.) Any time a PC sends a packet, it is sent as a broadcast. The broadcast passes through or is seen by every PC on the network. The other PCs ignore it and pass it onto the PC that the packet is addressed to. When a packet sniffer is set up, it means some machine is peeking. There are two ways a packet sniffer can be set up: unfiltered (captures everything) or filtered (selective).

When you connect to the Internet, you are joining a network that is maintained by an ISP. The ISP's network communicates with other networks maintained by other ISPs to form the foundation for the Internet.

A packet sniffer located at one of the servers of your ISP could potentially monitor all of your online activities, such as:

Who you send email to

What's in the email you send

What you download

What Web sites you visit

What you look at on a particular site

The streaming media you use—audio, video, or Internet telephone.

Desktop Monitoring Programs

These record every keystroke, just like spyware. (In fact, it *is* spyware.) This signal can be intercepted and streamed back to the person doing the monitoring or recorded on your machine and sent as a text file. The system administrator is usually the person receiving the information, although these programs are also popular among hackers for procuring sensitive information (they're usually placed on your machine via virus programs, in the case of a hacker).

Employers can use the desktop monitoring program to read email and see what program you are using on your screen. Some capture programs written for employers have an *alert system* when an employee violates the company's policy or transmits inappropriate text.

Log Files

Your computer has log files to show what you have been doing. A system administrator can determine what you've been up to based on the contents of these logs. Web sites visited, emails sent and received, and what applications have been used can all be tracked.

Deleting the history or an email or even a file doesn't erase the trail. A log file can be stored in the operating system, Web browsers (the cache), application file backups, and email. If the machine is part of a company network or machines connected, the network administrator can view the log files remotely. If suspicious activity is suspected, an employer can check the computer when the employee isn't present.

Employers, Employees, and the Truth

Employers can track employees with cameras, tap phone conversations or voice mail, or monitor computer usage.

The U.S. Constitution does not grant any express right to privacy. The Supreme Court has historically upheld an implied right, but this right does not extend to employees when it comes to employers. The courts seem to be siding with the employers in that because the company owns the space and equipment and is footing the bill and compensating for time, it has the right to monitor employees.

SUMMARY

The future of the Internet threats isn't pretty. The hacker communities thrive, sharing new hacks and simpler hacker tools with more people than ever before. The new viruses are increasingly insidious and complex. We've already seen new, disturbing trends, such as viruses that can actually reengineer their own code; as they spread, they evolve (!) so that antivirus software can't recognize them. And we'll only see more "blended threats," such as Klez viruses that target multiple vulnerabilities at once.

On the other hand, the future of Internet *security* is bright. It's an exciting and lucrative industry, so some of the smartest people in the world are working very hard to keep you safe. Products such as ZoneAlarm Pro successfully defend against "unknown" threats, even protecting against malware that has not been identified yet. And unlike in the Internet's infancy, every new technology or product these days is analyzed for security almost from the get-go, if not by its own makers then by the hacker communities themselves. Vulnerabilities don't stay that way for long.

Besides, the most important component of security isn't really *firewall X* or *antivirus product Y*. It's you. You're the final arbiter of what software goes on your machine and what Web sites you visit. You can learn what's out there and adjust your defenses appropriately. It's all in your attitude.

RECOMMENDED READING

U.S. government site about identity theft—www.consumer.gov/sentinel

"Free technology newsletters for the world's most curious users"—www.lockergnome.com

Gibson Research Corporation. Useful forums and security utilities—www.grc.com

News and forums for broadband Internet users—www.broadbandreports.com

---

12

VIRUSES AND THE DAMAGE THEY CAN DO

The destructive arsenal of computer viruses is truly frightening. Erase a file? Yes. Modify a document's content? No problem! Steal confidential data? Simple! The point is that computer viruses are like full-scale computer programs, just like Windows or Word. They can do tremendous damage to your computer.

GLOSSARY OF TERMS

VIRUS: A malicious program. It can illegally and clandestinely embed its copies into other programs.

NETWORK WORM: A malicious *program* type. It spreads by itself using various computer resources: email, Web sites, IRC channels, local networks, etc.

TROJAN: A malicious program. When started, it performs destructive or undesired actions on the computer.

POLYMORPHIC VIRUS: This virus type modifies its appearance by using encryption methods. Consequently, these viruses contain no constant code blocks at all, which makes it harder for an antivirus program to recognize and remove them.

STEALTH VIRUS: This virus presents a veneer of temporary recovery to conceal its presence in a system. For example, these viruses temporarily restore the infected file when an antivirus program requests this file. Once the file is checked, the virus infects it again.

IN THE WILD: This means that a computer virus has made it from the inventors' computer and out to infect computers by itself.

MALWARE: *mal* in French means "bad." Malware is bad stuff. It's a term for viruses and their kin.

There are several categories of viruses that produce varying degrees of damage to a computer:

- *Harmless* viruses do not affect computer operation in any way except by consuming a portion of the hard drive's free space.
- *Paper-tigers* also consume hard drive space but may also produce graphics, sound, and/or other kinds of generally harmless effects.
- *Harmful* viruses may seriously interfere with the computer's performance.
- *Hot* viruses may corrupt programs, cause data loss, damage files and system areas principal to the computer performance, and even decrease the life of computer hardware.

How a Virus Works and Operates

Despite the fact that there are a great number of known viruses, rarely are two identical. Practically all viruses are unique in the ways they infect computer systems and operate within them. However, most harmful and hot viruses manifest themselves as parasitic, overwriting, or companion viruses.

Some companion viruses rename the target file, memorize its new name (for subsequent execution of the master file), and write their own code to disk under the name of the infected file. For example, the XCOPY.EXE file is renamed to XCOPY.EXD, and the virus saves itself as XCOPY.EXE. Upon execution of XCOPY, the virus code gets control first and later starts the original XCOPY in XCOPY.EXD.

PIRILLO'S VIRUS TIP

The easiest way to be infected by a digital nasty is to open an email attachment. Even if you know the person who sent it, don't trust the file. Have your antivirus program running when you open the attachment.

DVORAK'S VIRUS TIP

Cheap trick—when I travel and use dialup lines I hate waiting for large photos and other files to download at slow speeds. So I now limit my email downloads to the first 5–10 K of the file. This also has the advantage of keeping any virus attachment in email from downloading. I discovered the most common email viruses tend to be over 80 K in size. So now, even at home, I limit any email to 80 K and grab the rest of the file if I determine it to be safe. This simple trick prevents almost all bad attachments from getting through.

History of Computer Viruses

There are a lot of opinions as to when the first computer virus was born. What we know for sure is that Charles Babbage, the father of computing, would not have had one on his machine. On the other hand, the Univax 1108 and IBM 360/370 computers in the middle 1970s already carried viruses.

Charles Babbage (1791–1871)

Babbage is often called the father of computing, although he never actually built a computer. He never was able to secure funding to build a working model.

The device he envisioned, the Analytical Engine, encompassed concepts that later came to be an integral part of the modern computer. It was designed to manipulate symbols, sequential control, branching, and looping. It was intended to use loops of Jacquard's punched cards (an 1800s invention of a French silk weaver, Joseph-Marie Jacquard, to control the warp and weft threads of a loom by recording patterns of holes in a string of cards. This invention was later used in player pianos, music boxes, and data entry for early computers). The Analytical Engine would make decisions based on the results of previous computations. In keeping with the modern technology of the time, it would be steam driven. This was the second computational device Babbage dreamed up. The first was the Difference Engine, a mechanical device to compile mathematical tables.

A contemporary of Babbage was Augusta Ada Lovelace, the daughter of the poet Lord Byron. She fully understood the concepts and vision of Babbage. She was a gifted mathematician and designed a program to compute a mathematical sequence known as the *Bernoulli numbers*. Because of this work she is credited with being the first computer programmer, and long after her death in 1979, the programming language Ada was named after her.

Babbage held a chair at Cambridge. He was a mathematician (primarily in the calculus of functions) and an inventor. His inventions include: the cowcatcher, dynamometer, standard railroad gauge, uniform postal rates, occulting lights for lighthouses, Greenwich time signals, and the heliograph ophthalmoscope (a device to study the retina of the eye). He found beauty in diverse things: in stamped buttons, ciphers, lock picking, stomach pumps, railways, and tunnels. He was a promoter of man's mastery over nature.

He was fascinated by fire. He once was baked in an oven at 265 degrees for five or six minutes, and on another occasion he was lowered into Mt. Vesuvius to view molten lava. He was offbeat, especially for Victorian times. He argued that miracles were not violations of laws of nature but could exist in a mechanistic world. He was not good at speaking in public. He admitted he was too impatient, too severe with criticism, too crotchety. He wasn't much of a diplomat.

He didn't like music, and he despised street musicians. (He calculated that 25% of his work power was destroyed by street disturbances.) He wrote letters to the *London Times* complaining about this outrage. He was able to get "Babbage's Act" enacted, which outlawed street nuisances. However, it wasn't enforceable and was unpopular. It made him the target of ridicule. A steady parade of street performers wandered and lingered outside his home. One brass band played for five hours.

Perhaps because of these and other eccentricities, he was denied funding by the British government. History has said that even if he were able to create this machine, it wouldn't work because it was too advanced for the technology of the times. However, five years after Babbage's death, an obscure American inventor, George Barnard Grant, presented a full-scale difference engine of his own design at the Philadelphia Centennial Fair. This machine was 8 feet wide and 5 feet high, with over 15,000 moving parts, less graceful or inventive than Babbage's visions, but it worked. Evidently, the technology could tolerate the demands. It's a shame that the father of computing never saw his "child."

The idea of a computer virus was probably developed much earlier than that of the Internet, but the concept wasn't documented until the twentieth century in books by John von Neumann. He was forthright and outspoken about his discoveries and concepts of the early computers. He studied self-reproducing mathematical models that came into being in the 1940s. In 1951, he suggested a method that demonstrated the possibility of implementing of such models. Later on, in 1959, the *Scientific American* magazine published an article by L. S. Penrose devoted to self-reproducing mechanical frameworks. The main peculiarity of this article described a simple, two-dimensional model of such frameworks capable of activation, propagation, mutation, and capture. On the basis of this article, another scientist, F. G. Stahl, using the machine code on an IBM 650, put the model into practice.

JOHN VON NEUMANN (1903–1957)

von Neumann was a Hungarian-born mathematics wiz who became one of the original six professors of mathematics at the Institute for Advanced Studies (IAS), founded in 1933 at Princeton University. (He remained in this position for the rest of his life.) He is known as a visionary and a pioneer in fields such as game theory, nuclear deterrence, and modern computing.

He is most famous for a paper written in the late 1930s (with F. J. Murray) on a mathematical theory of the "rings of operators" (now called *Neumann algebras*). These are powerful tools in quantum physics. His vision was in describing the character of a dimensional structure by the space the structure would take up as it rotates. These groups of rotations associated with the rings of operators make it possible to describe a space with continuously varying dimensions.

von Neumann was in the thick of things when the ENIAC came on the scene and could see how applied mathematics was involved—mechanical computation or what we now call computers. He could see the concept of computers to be applied to mathematics for specific problems instead of the way his peers saw things (for computers to be used for the development of tables). These contributions are widespread and enduring. The *Von Neumann Architecture for Computers* organized the computer into four main parts: the *arithmetic unit*, the *control*, the *memory*, and the *input-output system*. He is credited for the concept that data and programs can be stored in the same space. The machine can alter either the program or the data within it. The question is, did this create the opening for viruses to develop?

It must be noted that the creation of the theoretical basis for the future development of computer viruses was not the purpose of any of these researchers. Quite the contrary—all these scientists were seeking to improve the world, to make it more fit for human needs. After all, this research created a basis for later progress in robotics and artificial intelligence. We cannot blame these researchers simply because new generations abused their ideas.

Eventually, all the theoretical studies of scientists and harmless praxes of engineers sank into oblivion, and the world learned that the theory of self-reproducing frameworks could be applied for other purposes.

Here They Come . . .

In the early 1970s, a virus called *Creeper* was detected on the military computer network ARPANET (the predecessor of the modern Internet). This program was written for the once popular Tenex operating system and could enter networks by modem absolutely on its own and transmit a copy of itself to a remote system. On infected systems, the virus declared itself by the following screen message: I'M THE CREEPER . . . CATCH ME IF YOU CAN.

Later on, the *Reaper* program was created for the purpose of deletion of the irritating but generally harmless virus. In fact, it was a virus that performed some functions of an antivirus program: It propagated across the computer network, detected copies of *Creeper*, and deleted them. It is difficult to know whether it was the first case of confrontation between two virus writers, or whether the virus writers were actually the same person or a group of people.

In 1974, a program called *Rabbit* appeared on mainframes, doing nothing but replicating and propagating copies of itself via data media. But the speed of its replication justified its name. This program cloned itself, occupied system resources, and in this way, decreased system productivity. When a copy of *Rabbit* reached some predetermined threshold of replication, it caused malfunctions in the operation of the infected system.

In the beginning of the 1980s, computers became more and more popular in offices, as well as in homes. An increasing number of programs were being written not by software companies but by individuals. With telecommunications technologies, it became possible to distribute these programs through common access servers or Bulletin Board Systems (BBSs) and the like. Computer enthusiasts shared software. Later on, BBSs at popular universities transformed into global databases covering all the industrially developed countries. They provided the quickest possible data exchange between even the most distant points on the planet. As a result, a lot of miscellaneous

Trojans appeared. These were not capable of replication but when started, they detrimentally affected computer systems.

Blame It on the Masses

Current computer viruses were ushered into being in 1981. At the time, the first personal computer for the masses, the Apple II, was rapidly gaining popularity. The wide popularity of Apple II, the availability of its documentation, its exposure to external interventions, and its feature allowing creation of user programs focused the interest of virus writers on this platform. It's no wonder the first mass computer epidemic occurred on these computers, initiated by the *Elk Cloner* virus. Elk Cloner is credited as the first computer virus to be "in the wild" (outside of a single computer or lab). It attached itself to the Apple DOS 3.3 operating system and spread by embedding itself to the boot sector of floppy diskettes. It seemed impossible and caused ordinary users to associate viruses with extraterrestrial civilizations attempting to conquer our world. The impression produced by this virus was enhanced by its manifestations: *Elk Cloner* turned over the display, made text displays blink, and screened various messages:

```
ELK CLONER:
THE PROGRAM WITH A PERSONALITY
IT WILL GET ON ALL YOUR DISKS
IT WILL INFILTRATE YOUR CHIPS
YES, IT'S CLONER
IT WILL STICK TO YOU LIKE GLUE
IT WILL MODIFY RAM, TOO
SEND IN THE CLONER!
```

The Infections Spread

Finally, in 1983, viruses captured the attention of the scientific community. Len Adleman used the term *computer virus* to describe self-reproducing computer programs at a computer security seminar. Fred Cohen (father of contemporary computer virology) used a VAX 11/750 system to demonstrate a viruslike program capable of rooting itself into other objects and defined the term *computer virus*.

However, the term *virus* had been used previously in novels of the 1970s. The earliest was in a 1972 science fiction novel by David Gerrold, *When HARLIE was One*. In it was a description of a fictional computer program called a *virus* and a counteragent called an *antibody*. In John Brunner's 1975 novel, *The Shockwave Rider*, programs called *tapeworms* crept through a machine with the ultimate goal of deleting data it found.

Best-selling science fiction author David Gerrold first used the term *computer virus* in one of his stories, although John Brunner is credited with popularizing the term. We asked him to explain the real history. Here is his recollection.

The film *2001* came out in May 1968 and by the end of the summer, a lot of folks in the science fiction community were talking about HAL and various forms of artificial intelligence. That year, the World Science Fiction Convention, called Baycon, was held in the Berkeley area. One of the panels was about the progress toward silicon entities and was called "The Road to HAL Is Paved With Good Inventions."

During the panel, several programmers gave the short course in computers to an audience that (at the time) knew nothing of computers except there were lots of blinking lights and thick bundles of punch cards involved. (Remember this was a decade before the appearance of the first desktop computer.)

One of the fellows on the panel talked about how computers would call each other up on the phone and exchange data. In fact, he said, it was possible for one computer to send a program to another computer, even taking over its functions. He then mentioned an apocryphal story of a programmer who wrote a program to do just that. The program was called VIRUS. The story had it that the programmer then wrote a second program to sell to companies that own computers, called VACCINE.

At the time, I was already working on a short story about an artificial intelligence called HARLIE. Almost immediately after finishing the first story, I realized HARLIE was too interesting for one story and the questions he'd asked demanded further exploration. I wrote a second story, then a third and then a fourth. At some point in the narrative, the funding company threatens to terminate the HARLIE project. The hero, a fellow named David Auberson, then discovers HARLIE had been phoning other computers, reprogramming them undetectably and stealing unused processor cycles. He also begins to suspect HARLIE is offloading parts of his identity elsewhere. I had the hero repeat the story I'd heard at the convention about the VIRUS and VACCINE programs and used that as the springboard for the extrapolation of HARLIE's own adventures as a hacker/cracker.

Eventually, HARLIE saves himself by blackmailing his would-be executioners with material he has downloaded from other computers he has cracked into. All of the HARLIE stories were published in Galaxy Science Fiction and then compiled into a novel called WHEN HARLIE WAS ONE. Ballantine Books bought the novel and published it in late 1972. It was nominated for both the Hugo and the Nebula awards, coming in second to Isaac Asimov's THE GODS THEMSELVES for both.

> In 1975, John Brunner published THE SHOCKWAVE RIDER, which is arguably the first real novel about cyberspace. John and I often chatted at conventions and occasionally exchanged letters and I admired him enormously. In the novel, his hero Nickie Haflinger is a phone phreak, someone who can tap into the global data network, Brunner postulated a software agent, a program that would spawn copies of itself to prowl through the global network looking for information. He called it a tapeworm. Later, in the mid-eighties, researchers at Xerox PARC dubbed the first actual self-propagating computer program a "worm" after the tapeworm Nickie Haflinger used in the novel.
>
> Over the years, there's been some confusion over who wrote what. The copyright pages of our respective novels should set the matter to rest. I'm the guy who first used the term "virus" and "vaccine" in a novel and John Brunner is the fellow who named the "worm."
>
> –David Gerrold

The first epidemic of a virus for IBM-compatible computers came in 1986. Within several months, the *Brain* virus infected boot sectors of diskettes, spreading almost all over the world. The reason for this success was the complete lack of preparedness of the computer industry to deal with a computer virus. On one hand, antivirus programs were not so popular as they are now; on the other hand, users didn't follow basic rules of antivirus security. Heck, who knew about them? It seemed improbable that a virus would find its way to an isolated machine. The effect of this epidemic was compounded by the lack of knowledge about computer viruses. Right after the Brain virus was detected, science fiction writers began to publish books devoted to computer viruses that may have made it even harder for a computer user to take the threat seriously.

Big and Little Brother Are Watching

The *Brain* virus was written in early 1986 by Basit Farooq Alvi (a 19-year-old programmer from Pakistan) and his brother Amjad.

There are a number of versions of the story, but the most common was they sold proprietary software that was being widely pirated (as was the fashion of the times). But, presumably to make ends meet, they also began to supplement their business by selling pirated popular American programs such as WordStar, Lotus 1-2-3, and dBase. The brothers, in a peculiar moral logic, decided their unscrupulous customers (the people buying the pirated software) should be punished. College students were credited with passing around copies of expensive commercial software programs. These programs were often recopied and passed around and backed up on school computers. This is the accepted story of how the Brain was said to have spread. (In other versions of the story, it was an experiment intended to study the extent of computer piracy in their country. The problem was it didn't stay in their country.)

By today's standards, the Brain was harmless. It wasn't devious. In fact, they placed a message containing their names, address, and the phone number of their store into the virus. It was probably the first and only known example of a traceable virus. And, except for infecting boot sectors and replacing diskette labels with the phrase "(c) Brain," the virus did not produce any harm: It did not produce any side effects and didn't corrupt any data. There was no intentional damage, although diskette access was slowed down and an occasional diskette drive became too bogged down to run right. This, however, was the first known IBM PC computer virus.

The hubbub that surrounded Brain wasn't because of the damage but because it did travel. It traveled before the Internet was in popular use. This was amazing. It traveled quickly, one machine at a time. In 1987, it was found in computers at the University of Delaware and George Washington University. By 1988, 100 machines at the *Providence Journal Bulletin* were infected. *Time Magazine* did a feature story about it and the threat of viruses. No matter what the real story about Brain was, the subsequent history of computers was inseparably linked with computer viruses.

After that, the scene heated up. In 1987, viruses such as Alameda, Jerusalem, Lehigh, Miami, Cascade (a partially encrypted virus), and Stoned were discovered. Stoned was another harmless virus. Occasionally, it would suddenly display the message "your PC is now stoned! Legalize Marijuana" when the computer was booted up.

The media got involved, and antiviral software companies began to spring up. Viruses became a real part of computing. They occupied

PIRILLO'S VIRUS TIP

It's completely safe to have more than one antivirus software package installed on the same computer. Just don't run more than one solution at the same time.

new platforms and applications, found new ways to infect computers, and replicated themselves practically every day. New virus types appeared, using sophisticated methods of hiding in the system and making them much more difficult to search for and neutralize. Categories were devised to sort them, such as stealth viruses, polymorphic viruses, multiplatform viruses, companion viruses, and others. A virtual explosion of computer viruses marked the end of the twentieth century and the beginning of the twenty-first.

DVORAK'S VIRUS TIP

Try different scanners. Each antivirus program has different characteristics. Try a few before you decide which one to keep. They all uninstall quite easily.

The Top Historic Viruses

Computer viruses are complicated, multicomponent monsters. The term *computer virus* is a catchall phrase that includes viruses, network worms, and Trojan features. These days, virus writing is a fashionable occupation among students, many of them attempting to prove they are pros in this business. As a result, the contemporary Internet, instead of being a means of communication and data exchange, has turned into a virus distribution tool. It is difficult to predict what will happen with viruses on the World Wide Web in the next four to five years. We can, however, outline the main tendencies in a historical retrospective. The following sections do just that.

Vienna

The first computer virus infecting COM files was called *Vienna*. Its appearance and expansion (practically all over the world) caused a great response and a lot of disputes about its real author. Franz Swoboda was the first person to raise a stink about it in 1987. The virus was spread in a program called *Charlie*. Of course, the computer community wanted to know the source of this pandemic. Franz Swoboda claimed he received this virus from a person, Ralf Burger, who in turn accused Swoboda of sending it to him. Whatever the case, Burger gave it to Berdt Fix, who disassembled it (the first time anyone was able to do it). He changed some of the code to make it less infectious. The result was a virus that only caused the computer to hang, a dubious improvement.

Michelangelo

This was *the* media darling of a virus. The virus was, at best, an obscure or unknown threat until a computer manufacturer, Leading Edge, announced that 500 computers had been shipped with a virus in them. The same day, a second computer maker issued a press release touting its decision to include antiviral software with its computers. The next day, United Press International reporter Jack Lesar filed a newswire quoting John McAfee (the owner of an antiviral software company McAfee and Associates) as saying that the virus could erase data from hard disks of hundreds of thousands of computers around the world. The hype continued, reaching a frenzy with stories in every major newspaper, in television news reports, and on such shows as *Nightline, Good Morning America,* and the *MacNeil-Lehrer News Hour.* The media blitz continued until March 6 but then fizzled out when nothing of consequence occurred.

As a result of the fuss, the profits of different antivirus companies skyrocketed, and the media took a more conservative approach of reporting about any computer viruses.

Macro.Word95.Concept

This was the first known macrovirus infecting MS Word documents. It was detected in August 1995. Within one month, this virus filled up the computers of MS Word users around the world and took a leading position in statistical researches conducted by various computer-related mass media. That year, at the beginning of September, Digital Equipment Corporation (DEC) distributed diskettes containing *Concept* among delegates of the DECUS conference in Dublin. Fortunately, this was quickly discovered, and the virus was isolated. Today, about 100 variations of this virus circulate.

Win.Tentacle

Windows was not immune from viruses. The first virus for Windows caused a global pandemic (March 1996). Previously, viruses for Windows were the stuff of rumors and in collections of people who were interested in such things. The Win.Tentacle virus was important because previous viruses had been found in the wild (meaning floating around in the public domain, as opposed to in the laboratory) on boot, DOS, and macro roots of infection.

Win95.CIH

This virus (also known as Chernobyl) was discovered 1998. This was the first known virus capable of destroying computer BIOS. The virus accessed the Flash BIOS chip and overwrote it with odd symbols. As a result, the computer could not be booted and required replacement of this chip in order to solve the problem. It's credited with doing multimillions of dollars in damages to the world economy. The epidemic was made worse because it found its way to some popular Web servers that then distributed the virus through downloaded games.

I-Worm.Happy

Also known as SKA, this virus was the ideological pioneer of the contemporary Internet worms distributing their copies via email. "Happy" attached itself to messages with New Year's congratulations. When started, the virus, indeed, displayed festive fireworks on the user screen, then attached its copy to every outgoing message.

I-Worm.Loveletter

Also known as ILOVEYOU and The Love Bug, this notorious script Internet worm was famous for its brilliant manipulation of a user's feelings. To force the recipient (of sound mind) to execute the worm file the *Loveletter*, the author fabricated a touching love letter. And the attachment supposedly included the love proof. What inventive souls these virus writers have!

Macro.Word97.Melissa

This was the first known Internet worm to infect MS Word documents and send copies to email addresses found in the MS Outlook address book.

Win95.Babylonia

This is an extremely complicated and dangerous virus created by the virus writer known by the nickname Vecna. Vecna, whomever it may be, began the new stage in evolution of the virus industry. *Babylonia* was the first worm with remote self-updating. The system registry is modified to monitor Internet connections. If an Internet connection is made, the virus will attempt to connect to a Web site in Japan and download updates or replace missing parts of its file. When all the parts of the virus are downloaded, the virus will then use them to spread. It's a parasitic Windows virus with worm and back-door abilities. It's a memory-resident, multipartite stealth virus. In short, it has characteristics of many other viruses. As the virus code writers became more advanced, these schemes were used in other viruses. For example, this technology was applied in Sonic, Hybris, and many other worms.

I-Worm. Bubbleboy

The first known Internet worm to cause mass pandemic used a "hole" in the Internet Explorer security system, penetrating into computers. It's embedded within an email message of HTML format without an attachment. In MS Outlook, one must open the email, but that is not the case with MS Outlook Express. It can be activated with the preview page. Due to this, infection actually occurs at the moment the message is read, and the recipient doesn't even need to execute the worm file. When released, it executes its script and at the next Windows startup will do one or more of the following:

- Change the registered owner in the registry to "bubbleboy"
- Change the registered owner to "vandelay industries"
- Send itself to every contact in the address book of Microsoft Outlook
- Set the registry keys so it won't send out a second set of emails

These by no means are the extent of the viruses out in the wild. But they are the significant developments to the beast, so far.

ANTIVIRUS PROGRAMS

In the short period of time computer viruses have existed, the antivirus industry has produced an amazing array of antivirus tools. Some are now out of date, replaced by new, more effective techniques. Certainly, new strategies will develop. It's an endless arms race. The appearance of a new virus finding a new vulnerability in the operating system's security will cause a protective response from the companies in the business of antiviral software. The tools will always keep changing. Some are more effective than others, and often an antivirus program will use a combination of techniques.

There are five types of antivirus programs: scanners, monitors, CRC scanners, immunizers, and behavior blockers, all of which are discussed in the following sections.

Scanners

Antivirus scanners are the pioneers among antivirus types. They were invented as a response to the first computer viruses. The ploy of antivirus scanners is to search for virus masks (i.e., their unique program code) in files, sectors, and system memory. Virus masks for known viruses are described in the antivirus database. If the scanner finds a known program code sequence, it notifies the user.

However, a problem with scanners is that even a slight modification of viral code can make it invisible to the scanner. In fact, the program code of two copies of the same virus may differ. For example, there are many versions of the notorious Chernobyl virus. The antivirus companies had to update their virus-definition for each variation. Not all viruses have a signature code. Polymorphic viruses contain no constant code blocks. They are devious in the way that they infect a file. This type of virus modifies itself using enciphering methods while still able to preserve its functionality.

The indissoluble bond of a scanner to its database results in another problem. When a new virus is detected, there is some lag time for an antivirus company to release the appropriate database update. During the time gap, the end-users are unprotected. The companies are getting better at improving the delivery time of appropriate antidotes; in some cases it takes minutes, but it's not always as fast as the virus can replicate. They may distribute across the world in a few seconds through email!

Due to this potential lag time, in the 1990s, antivirus experts developed and implemented a tool to detect unknown viruses—the *heuristic analyzer*. This tool checks objects by analyzing the instruction sequence in their contents, accumulating the statistics and making a decision on whether the object is infected with an unknown computer virus. However, the tool can produce false alarms. It's not foolproof. And it doesn't guarantee virus removal. In the struggle against polymorphic viruses, another approach was invented: algorithmic languages describing all possible versions of the code and code decryption systems (emulators).

Finally, the antivirus scanner checks files on the user's request after the user starts it. It requires the user constantly to stay attentive and concentrated. Sometimes the user may forget to check some suspicious file (for example, one from the Internet) for viruses that may result in his or her computer being infected. The scanner is able to detect a virus when the virus is already in your system.

A disadvantage of a scanner is size (the antivirus database is cumbersome and due to its size, results are in slow, virus-checking speeds). However, scanners are able to suppress distribution of Internet worms, effectively delete viruses from infected files and boot sectors, and restore them. (Full recovery is possible if the virus has not deleted the original contents of the infected object.)

Monitors

With the development of computer hardware and improvements in operating systems, it became possible to develop a more advanced antivirus program. These are the antivirus monitors. There are now three main types: file monitors, monitors for mail programs, and monitors for specific applications.

It's a variation on the antivirus scanner because it permanently resides in computer memory and checks all used files in real time (meaning when it's actually happening). Up-to-date monitors check programs twice: when started and closed. The goal is to eliminate a resident virus.

To enable your antivirus protection, you need to load the monitor at the operating system or application start. The following are usually done automatically by your antivirus package during installation:

- Add the monitor-start instruction to the list of programs to be started automatically or to the appropriate system registry field.

- Register the monitor as a system service to be started under any account.

- Integrate the monitor with the mail program or some other application.

The beauty of this type of anti-virus monitor is that it operates in the background. This allows the user to forget about scanning every new file. It's all done automatically. If a malicious program is detected, the monitor, depending on its settings, will cure the file, block it from being executed, or isolate it by moving it to a special quarantine directory for further study.

File monitors are used on workstations, as well as on file and application servers. Server-based monitors must support multithreading (they must be able to process more than one file at once). Otherwise, they may affect the operating speed of both the server and the entire network.

Monitors for mail programs are antivirus modules integrated with server- or client-based mail processing programs. In fact, they become part of the mail program and automatically check for viruses in all messages processed by this program. Mail monitors consume less system resources than file monitors and are more stable because a system conflict at the application level is less likely than at the operating system level.

Mail monitors are able to check all incoming/outgoing messages at the delivery/send level. These monitors are not able to detect a virus per se but block all the components of an infected message: attached files, messages at any nesting level, embedded OLE objects, and the message body. This is a comprehensive approach.

Monitors for specific applications check objects in the background; however, this is done within the framework of the applications they are intended for. Antivirus monitors for MS Office 2000 are an example of this group of monitors. Similar to their mail cousins, these monitors integrate into the program and reside in computer memory when the program runs. These monitors also check all the used files in real time and report all detected viruses.

Antivirus monitors are fully automated, and that makes them easier to use than antivirus scanners. Another advantage is that they detect, contain, and block a virus at the earliest replication stage. However, monitors use huge antivirus databases. They can be less stable in performance. This is why some system

administrators choose to check their server resources regularly with an antivirus scanner.

Integrity Checkers

This technology of protection is based on an assumption that viruses are ordinary computer programs. The key indicator of a virus program as opposed to a regular program is that the virus is able to illegally create new objects and/or to embed its copies into existing objects (files, boot sectors). In other words, viruses leave "footprints" in a file system and can be traced and detected. These tools look for the traces.

Integrity checkers calculate mathematical values known as *checksums* or *CRC values* (Cyclic Redundancy Code) for disk sectors, files, and the system registry and store these in a database along with information such as file sizes, the latest modification date and time, and other details. Once this database has been created, whenever the integrity checker is started up, it recalculates these values and checks them against the database. If the values differ, the program informs the user that files have been modified or infected by a virus.

In 1990, the first stealth viruses, Frodo and Whale, destroyed the reputation of this type of antivirus. The stealth feature allowed the viruses to substitute infected files and/or sectors with the virus-free original ones, once the antivirus program attempted to read from there. These viruses intercept system calls to the disk in order to substitute the infected file or sector with the virus-free copy whenever it is accessed. In response to that flaw, newer integrity checkers "learned" a new trick: They accessed disks directly via the IOS (input/output subsystem) driver without using the appropriate interrupts. This feature allowed the program to detect and kill even the most dangerous stealth viruses.

The current advanced integrity checkers offer some advantages over other antiviral programs. They have an extremely high speed of operation and low hardware requirements. They are able to restore files and boot sectors damaged by viruses, including the unknown ones. Their performance approach is based on knowledge of the file characteristics of the specific infective virus. Modification of a protected object is what attracts the program's attention. When changes occur, the integrity checker will restore this object to its original state. It focuses on the infection methods used by viruses.

With this strategy, the integrity checkers do not need huge antivirus databases. In fact, depending on the particular software product, they have a very small demand—typically 300–500 KB.

Alas, they do have some weak points. These checkers cannot detect a virus as soon as it appears in the system. In fact, the virus may be able to function undetected for some time. The integrity checkers cannot detect a virus in new files (email, files on diskettes, files restored from backups, files extracted from archives) because there is no informa-

tion about these files in their databases. Unfortunately, some viruses use this feature and infect newly developed files, thereby staying "invisible" to integrity checkers.

Immunizers

There are two types of immunizers: those that inform a user that an infection exists and those that block infection by a particular type of virus.

Immunizers that inform usually add code to the end of a file (employing techniques similar to those that viruses use) and check the file for changes each time it is accessed. A weak point of such immunizers (in fact, a lethal one) is that they will fail to inform a user if a file has been infected by a stealth virus. They cannot detect a stealth virus. (Their presence will be masked.)

The second type of immunizer protects a system from a particular virus. (Viruses will not reinfect files already infected by versions of itself, because the files will be modified so that they are recognizable.) The concept of this type of immunizer is to make the file appear that it is already infected. For example, to protect a COM file from the Jerusalem virus, you just have to add the corresponding MS-DOS string to this file. To provide protection from a resident virus, the program imitating the virus copy should be placed into the computer memory. When you start up the system, the virus detects this program and recognizes this system as already infected.

Infection-blocking immunizers can't offer universal protection. It's impossible to immunize files against all the known viruses by employing different methods of the infection assessment. But as a half-measure, these programs can be used to provide a reliable antivirus protection from new and unknown viruses until scanners have been updated so they are able to detect them. However, not many companies use these techniques anymore.

A typical email reads as follows:

Subject: Virus Alert

I have just been notified that my address book has been infected with a virus and, as a result, yours has also because your name is in my address list. The virus is called jdbgmgr.exe. Norton or McAfee anti-virus programs cannot detect it. It sits quietly for 14 days in your hard drive. It is sent automatically into your address book and distributes itself to your contacts via their email address and infects their hard drives.

To get rid of it:

1. Go to Start, then Find or Search.
2. In files/Folders, write the name jdbgmgr.exe
3. Be sure to check your "c" drive.
4. Click Find or Search.
5. The virus has a teddy bear logo with the name jdbgmgr.exe. DO NOT OPEN!!!!
6. Right click on it and delete it.
7. Go to the Recycle bin and delete it there also.

IF YOU FIND THE VIRUS, YOU MUST CONTACT EVERYONE ON YOUR MAILING LIST. SORRY FOR ANY INCONVENIENCE.

Some gullible friend (who bought into this nonsense) usually signs the note. The trick to avoiding being suckered by any such thing is to go to Google and type in the key information (such as the file name) followed by the word "hoax." If there's a hoax involved, it will send you to a site (or multiple sites) explaining the hoax. In the case of jdbgmgr.exe, it's a utility file used by the OS to make certain Java applets run correctly. The reason this hoax was so popular seems to be because the utility uses a crazy teddy bear icon, which just seemed suspicious. (The programmer of the utility file may have liked teddy bears?) Don't be fooled by hoaxes foisted upon you by well-meaning friends. For more information on virus hoaxes, go to the following Web sites:

http://www.symantec.com/avcenter/hoax.html (Symantec)

http://www.stiller.com/hoaxes.htm (Stiller Research)

http://vil.mcafee.com/hoax.asp (McAfee)

Behavior Blockers

The biggest problem with all antivirus programs is that they don't protect the user from new and unknown viruses. The computer is unprotected until antivirus manufacturers develop an "antidote." This may take several weeks. This has been a vexing problem.

How do you protect your computer from unknown viruses? There is no simple answer to this question. It's hoped that an answer maybe found in the future. There are some promising trends in antivirus software development. These trends will include behavior blockers.

A behavior blocker is a memory-resident program intercepting various events. It doesn't search for virus signatures (known virus code) but monitors activity and looks for virus-suspected action. When something dubious is detected, the blocker prohibits the actions or asks the user for instructions.

The idea is not a new one. Antivirus programs have tried to employ this tactic, but it was difficult to customize and demanded that the user have an in-depth knowledge of computer technologies. The technology has been successfully used in some data security fields. For example, the Java applets have a strictly limited action scope (defined permitted actions). This suppresses attempts to perform any prohibited action (for example, file deletion), which, from the user viewpoint, could be suspicious or threaten data integrity.

The file behavior blocker cannot independently define the performer of a virus-suspected action (virus, operating system, or some utility). It is obliged to ask a user for instructions. It's often the user who makes a decision for the blocker to work, which means the user needs adequate knowledge and experience. This is the main reason blocker techniques have not been widely used. This situation may be improved with the invention of an artificial intelligence to determine independently the purpose of any virus-suspected action.

It's expected that with the development of computer technologies, especially in the field of artificial intelligence, efficiency and simplicity of blockers will increase. In the foreseeable future, this type of antivirus program has the best chance of mastering the difficult task of preventing unknown viruses from spreading. This technique will become the main tool of antivirus protection.

Our recommendation is simple: The best protection is a combined approach. Use a variety of antivirus methods. Each type of antivirus program has its advantages and disadvantages. In combination, they can successfully compensate for each other and increase the security level.

One of the ploys used by people trying to propagate viruses and Trojan horses around the Net is to trick the user into clicking on something they should not be clicking on. Usually, it's some warning about a particular virus with the recommendation that you click someplace on the document to fix the problem. This is almost always a bad idea, even when it comes from a trusted source, such as your antivirus provider. Even links back to the antivirus company should not be clicked on. If you think you need something from the antivirus company, go to the Web site yourself by opening a browser and typing in the Web site by hand if you do not already have it bookmarked as a "favorite."

How to Avoid Viruses

Computer safety is a matter of computer competence. With a few simple rules, anyone can be a computer safety expert.

Rule 1: Update Your Antivirus Program Regularly

Antivirus scanners are able to detect and delete a computer virus that is found in its antivirus databases. There is antivirus software available that is capable of searching and deleting unknown viruses, such as those described in the current edition of the antivirus database. An excellent example is one of the best antivirus tools, the heuristic engine developed by Kaspersky Lab, which provides a 92% average detection rate of unknown processed viruses. However, this is not enough if you want absolute protection from computer viruses.

It is very important to update your antivirus database regularly. The more often you update the database, the more protected your workplace is. The best solution is to update daily; however, if you have a virus, you may need to update several times during the day with updates sent over by your antivirus software supplier. Therefore, it is advisable to set your event scheduler (usually supplied with the most contemporary antivirus programs) to download updates two to three times per day: in the morning, in the afternoon, and in the evening.

Rule 2: Be Careful with Email Attachments

Don't start or execute any attachment that has arrived in your mailbox if you don't know who sent it. It's a good practice to not execute any attachment until after it has been processed by an antivirus scanner.

Software sent by your friends may be infected. You never know whose computer is infected with a virus that could send an email without human help to your mailbox. The well-known viruses, such as Loveletter, Melissa, etc., use this method. The virus can make one's computer act pretty sneaky sometimes. To make matters worse, the messages contain text to encourage the reader to execute the attachment. (If the encouraging message is a sexual innuendo, this may not go over well with your boss, mother-in-law, or kids' teachers, especially if it also adds a virus to their systems.)

No less important is the fact that files with "absolutely safe" formats may also contain viruses. You are mistaken if you think that files with extensions such as PIF or DOC are unable to carry malware. Even these formats can hide a virus. Other extensions, such as JPG or TXT, can have hidden second extensions.

Rule 3: Limit the Number of People Authorized to Use Your Computer

The ideal situation is when you are the sole user of your computer. But if this is not possible, you should assign limited access rights to others using your computer and clearly define the operations they are allowed to perform. First of all, we are talking about the use of mobile media, the Internet, and your email. It is very important to control all possible sources of viruses and forbid other people from working with them.

Rule 4: Install Patches for the Software You Use in a Timely Manner

Some viruses use "holes" in the operating system and in applications. Antivirus programs are able to protect against this kind of malware, even if you have not installed the corresponding patch. But it's still a good habit to go to the antivirus's Web site regularly to download and install new patches. As well, go to the Microsoft site for updates to Windows and other Microsoft products.

Rule 5: Always Check for Viruses on Mobile Media before Use

Approximately 85% of all registered cases of computer infection are delivered by email and via the Internet. However, given that fact, it's important not to ignore other routes of infection. Do not ignore the traditional transport for malware: mobile media (diskettes, compact disks, etc.). Check for viruses before you use the programs on your computer. (An obvious exception would be for diskettes you intend to format.)

Rule 6: Be Careful with Software from a Credible Source

You may believe that a site you visit is virus proof; after all, it is a famous company. But it may not be. Sometimes these sites offer infected software to their visitors, unbeknownst to the site administrators. For several weeks, a Microsoft site offered a Word document infected with the macrovirus Concept.

Sometimes even licensed software CDs contain viruses. Or a computer taken in for maintenance is returned with the hard drive infected with a virus. (As a rule, repair shop technicians use the same diskettes to install software and test the hardware, transferring a virus from one computer to another.) So if your computer has been serviced, remember to check it for viruses.

In short, cover your back. Don't be afraid; just be aware. Even software from credible sources could contain unintentional viruses.

Rule 7: Combine Various Antivirus Technologies

Do not limit your antivirus protection to an antivirus scanner started manually or automatically by the built-in task scheduler. Other technologies, if applied in combination with an antivirus scanner, can ensure the antivirus protection of your data. These include:

- **antivirus monitor**—a memory-resident program to check all your files in real time before they are opened, executed, or installed
- **integrity checker**—to check files, folders, and disk sectors for any indication of a virus infection, such as file modification
- **behavioral guard**—to search for viruses, not according to their unique code, but according to a sequence of their actions

A combination of antivirus technologies will successfully protect your computer.

Rule 8: Create a Virus-Free Startup Disk for Your Computer and Keep It in a Safe Place

Sometimes an infected computer cannot be started. This does not mean a virus has deleted data from your hard drive. What it means is that your operating system can no longer be loaded. To solve this problem, you should use a virus-free startup diskette containing an antivirus program. This will help you to recover. A boot disk will enable you to start your computer and delete viruses in your operating system.

Do you use several operating systems and, therefore, several file systems on one computer?

Standard startup diskettes developed by an antivirus program support the operating system they have been created in. In this case, it is advisable to use the Rescue Kit function integrated into the Kaspersky Antivirus Platinum and Gold packages. This function creates a set of startup diskettes based on the Linux operating system and contain a preinstalled copy of the antivirus program for Linux. Linux supports all the popular file systems: FAT (DOS), FAT32 (Windows 95/98), NTFS (Windows NT/2000), HPFS (OS/2), EXT (Linux). This function will enable you to restore your computer even if you use several operating systems.

Rule 9: Back Up Your Files Regularly

Protect your valuable data with regular backups in case your computer becomes infected or you have a problem with hardware. It is advisable to back up your most valuable data using external media: diskettes, disks, magnetic tapes, CDs, etc.

Rule 10: Do Not Panic!

Computer viruses aren't unavoidable disasters. They aren't mysterious. They aren't magical. Viruses are computer programs, except they aren't designed for productive work. They're made to replicate themselves and penetrate files, computer systems, and network resources. A virus can cause your computer to perform strange tasks, as dictated by the virus (without your knowledge or permission).

Ordinary, albeit mischievous, people create viruses. These people are not as dangerous as the potential reaction to a virus. The worst thing to do is panic. Avoid hasty decisions or cures worse than the illness to try to disinfect your computer.

First, if you are a corporate network user, contact your network administrator. If you are working at home, contact the antivirus company if you are unsure how to use the program. Once you've identified what the virus is, go to the Web to find patches or strategies to eliminate the virus from your system.

> **DVORAK'S VIRUS TIP**
>
> **An interesting and entertaining Web newsletter concerning viruses, security issues, and wry insights is the Crypt Newsletter at http://sun.soci.niu.edu/~crypt/.**

ANTIVIRUS SOFTWARE COMPANIES

Aladdin Knowledge Systems

An Israeli company that develops a wide range of software and hardware products related to computer security. This company is famous for its antivirus software product called *eSafe*, which has for a while used the antivirus kernel developed by Kaspersky Lab. For more information, go to www.ealaddin.com.

Computer Associates

This American company develops a wide range of computer software, including antiviruses. It has been most notable in its acquisition of competitors. In 1996, Computer Associates (CA) merged with Cheyenne Software, the manufacturer of InocuLAN antivirus, and in 1999 bought Cybec, the author of Vet Antivirus. However, overall, its antivirus products are only average. This is probably due to the dissipation of resources from the mergers; therefore, both the CA antivirus projects are far behind the leaders. For more information, go to www.cai.com.

F-Secure

A Finnish company (previously known as Data Fellows) that has the product called *F-Secure Antivirus*. It is notable in that it uses three antivirus engines at once (including the Kaspersky Antivirus engine). This product suffers from slow speeds and compatibility problems but is an excellent medicine for those suffering from viral paranoia. For more information, go to www.f-secure.com.

Kaspersky Labs

Kaspersky Labs is a Russian developer of antivirus software packages. Its products combine traditional technologies (antivirus scanner and antivirus monitor) and up-to-date inventions (behavior blocker and integrity checkers) and include round-the-clock technical support and twice-a-day updating of the antivirus databases. (Dvorak uses this product.) For more information, go to www.kaspersky.com.

Network Associates

This is one of the larger, U.S.-based companies. The company has developed quite a wide range of antivirus tools for all customers, from home users to huge corporations. Its products have received mixed reviews. It is an aggressive marketer and advertiser. For more information, go to www.mcafee.com.

Norman Data Defense Systems

Norman Virus Control is a high-quality, top notch antivirus program that is very good. In addition to antivirus protection products, the company also offers personal firewalls and cryptographic and access-control systems. (By the way, it's of interest to note the company's flagship product is Norman Virus Control—not Norman Antivirus—because in Norway, the Norman Data Defense Systems (NDDS) homeland, the word for Antivirus means virus program.) For more information, go to www.norman.com.

Sophos

This British company concentrates on antivirus technologies for the corporate market. It's really not available for the home user. For more information, go to www.sophos.com.

Sophos is also the founder of well-known British magazine *Virus Bulletin*. In April 1989 in a small English pub in Oxford, the company top managers—Jan Hruska, Peter Lammer, and Ed Wilding—came up with the idea of an independent periodical to publish reliable information about computer viruses. Several months later, another British antivirus company (Dr. Solomon's) launched its own publishing project called *Virus Fax International*. In 1990, the periodical was renamed *Virus News International* and later, *Secure Computing* or *SC Magazine*. Of course, the magazines, *Virus Bulletin* and *SC Magazine*, are excellent sources of independent and constructive information.

Symantec

Symantec has been around awhile. It has merged with and purchased a lot of its competition. (If we published the entire list of competitors absorbed by the company, it would occupy several pages.) The most famous are Central Point Antivirus; the antivirus product of the Fifth Generation Systems company called Untouchable; the Novi antivirus from Certus International; LANDesk Virus Protect from Intel; ViruSweep from Quarterdeck; and a recent purchase, SecurityFocus.com, the Internet portal related to IT security issues. They have a wide range of products and are very active in press releases and marketing. The reaction to their products is mixed, depending on your source of information. For more information, go to www.symantec.com.

Symantec's company history is full of surprises and funny things. For example, in 1988, one of its best known programmers, Peter Norton, declared in *Insight Magazine* that computer viruses were an "urban myth." He claimed they were a myth of the same kind as alligators in New York sewers. "Everyone knows about them but no one's ever seen them." Nevertheless, this delusion did not prevent Symantec from starting its own antivirus product, Norton Antivirus, in December 1990. In 1996, a Symantec marketing PR release declared that users needed Norton Antivirus for a new threat, "to fight more sophisticated polymorphic viruses." In 1996, the joke was that these weren't new viruses; they'd been identified and were old news in 1992. And on a humorous note, Symantec declared the period between February 15 and March 15 to be "Virus Awareness Month," even though it's not a month. Hmmm, sounds peculiar.

Trend Micro

This is a Chinese developer of antivirus software. It is famous for its variety of products. The company offers software products for various mail and Internet gateways at the corporate level. It also develops the software product called PC-Cillin for home users. For more information, go to www.antivirus.com.

TOMORROW AND BEYOND

Recently, the problem of antivirus protection for computerized home appliances, mobile phones, and handheld computing devices has become a topic in the computer press, at IT conferences, and among IT specialists throughout the world. The reason is clear: The world is moving toward the integration of information technology into nearly all fields of human activities.

It's predicted that in a few years, people will be able to schedule and regulate the operating mode of washing machines, VCRs, lights, and other home appliances with a computer. Just imagine, your computer will control the start time and operating mode of your microwave, oven, or toaster. Create a control program once, and you can be sure that every morning you will have your breakfast ready before you enter the kitchen. Another vision is that home appliances will be connected to the Internet, and the repairman will show up at the door to fix a pending disaster of the washing machine because the machine sent out a "help me" message.

It's not a dream scenario that home appliances will be computerized and connected to the Internet. Currently, various home appliance manufacturers compete with each other by offering new features and services. They're looking for new ways to market products and get the edge on the competition. To offer new upgrades to existing appliances (for a fee) and to get information about your habits and usage of a machine would give new marketing inroads for the manufacturers. It's an interesting view of the future.

However, apart from these possible advantages (depending on your viewpoint), the concept of attaching an appliance to the Internet or other network would also present an opportunity for computer viruses to enter with malicious commands. Appliances running amuck—sounds like a made-for-TV horror movie.

Mobile Phones

On August 19, 2002, Sun Microsystems and some partners announced the distribution of the Mobile Information Device (MID) standard based on the Java programming language (Java 2 Platform Micro Edition [J2ME]) for use on mobile phones. At the same time, Motorola, one of the biggest companies in the development of wireless technologies, released an application programming interface (API) allowing the development of additional programs for its wireless devices.

To most people, this may seem to be just a collection of abstract technical terms; however, the significance is that it is an important milestone in the evolution of mobile phone functionality. The further integration of the Java programming language will enable third-party applications to be used on mobile phones and allow end users to write their own programs and to share them.

It is certainly a huge step forward on the way to evolving mobile phones from just a connection medium to a multipurpose communication portal. Java language resources allow wireless devices to be powered by nearly any additional application. It's limited only by the equipment functional capability. Java technology dramatically enhances the overall consumer experience by augmenting static text with interactive, graphic, easy-to-use services.

Nevertheless, the new functioning capability will provide an opportunity for writing useful programs, as well as malicious ones. Currently, there are computer viruses that attack mobile phones by sending obtrusive SMS messages. In the future, however, viruses will almost certainly do more damage and actually work more like a computer virus, except they will be directly in mobile phones.

Three conditions will need to exist for the presence of a resident virus. First, there must be widespread popularity of a particular platform or equipment; the second requirement is the availability of development tools; the third condition is insufficient protection.

The variable is the third point, insufficient protection. As it turns out, Java technology has already proven to be reliable and secure in practice.

During the years it has existed, a few Java viruses have been detected but are more conceptual rather than posing a real danger. The Java operating principal, based on providing a secured virtual space for every application, almost fully suppresses any possibility of viruses appearing in the wild on this platform. So far, there isn't any reason to believe that J2ME is less secure than any other version of Java. However, before reaching a definitive conclusion, we need time for a number of tests. Even if J2ME proves to be an absolutely secure platform, one of the most vulnerable areas in any security system still exists—the human factor. This problem can be solved through user education.

Linux

In the near term, the Linux operating system will see more attacks. Antiviral software experts believe that there will be a pandemic of Linux viruses. The debate continues about how strong the Linux immune system is (from a virus protection viewpoint). However, recently it has turned to a full-scale fight, with the gauntlet being thrown down by the Linux camp. They claim that the operating system is a virus-proof architecture.

Linux cannot be absolutely immune from viruses. Even if Linux's nonsusceptibility seems to be absolute, there are no guarantees that tomorrow or next week someone won't find a tiny hole to push an "elephant" through. Linux virus resistance cannot be described as absolute, even with great reservations. In its day, Windows NT was proclaimed a virus-free platform. It was a fairy tale.

The first obvious shortcoming is the Linux source code is readily available. Unlike closed platforms, where virus creation takes many months of hard work in order to disassemble the program code, the Linux source code is readily available. A virus could be written easily in a couple of minutes.

Thus, the traditional diversity of computer fauna native to, for example, DOS or Windows, could be increased to become a real nightmare. A new category of viruses integrating into the kernel of an operating system could happen.

It is worth mentioning that in all the years in which Windows viruses have been created, a Windows kernel virus has never been discovered. A kernel virus is different from the common viruses that target a program or feature of the operating system. A kernel virus would target the core (aka kernel) of an operating system. A virus that attacks and infects a file can *infect* the kernel program files. But, it cannot be a kernel virus unless it has been written to specifically target features of kernel files (their physical location on disk, a special loading, calling or other convention).

The benefits of Linux for the user (the open source code) could also be an open book to malware creators. Once created and released, it would spread.

The procedure of infection is quite simple. Once a virus has been started from an active process under the root account (most inexperienced Linux users use this account), it patches the kernel or creates new modules. The problem is that none of the Linux distributions require digital signatures of modules to prevent them from being illegally changed. (It will just upload them into memory.) As a result, the virus is activated each time the infected computer is rebooted. The most threatening element that a virus can add to the system is new functionality designed only to create devastating incidents. The simplest example is unauthorized management of a computer, allowing for accessing any data storage and reloading of additional malicious modules. Besides, open source code significantly simplifies the process of searching and exploiting the breaches within the Linux security structure, which requires just a simple analysis of the system code. The corresponding exploits under Windows are accomplished accidentally or by a long-term, well-directed disassembling of the Windows kernel, but this is a rare occurrence. Applying patches for Windows (which are usually released quickly) is very simple and requires a minimum of effort from the end user. Under Linux, it can become much more complicated because a patch requires a user to recompile the source code itself (which is not always successful), and to add to the difficulty, not all Linux distributions are completely compatible with each other.

Despite the conventional wisdom, Linux is not immune to memory-resident viruses. The first background Linux virus, Siilov, acts in a similar fashion to ordinary Windows viruses by modifying the table of entry points and intercepting the main function for executing files. Another well-known way of pushing background Linux viruses into the system is by changing the list of system services (daemons). Just like system services in Windows NT; they are automatically uploaded into memory, where the viruses are able to infect the system.

Detection and disinfection of any Linux viruses would require considerable improvements, including a complete redesign of antivirus engines of the existing antiviral products. It doesn't help that the Linux community has little demand for antiviral products. When a virus hits, help will be slow to come from unprepared antivirus vendors.

Another security flaw with Linux is the script language, which enables script viruses such as the Loveletter to exist. The most advanced of these languages (for instance, Perl) has even greater functionality than Visual Basic Scripting edition (VBScript), which is used for the creation of the majority of script viruses. Perl scripts can perform all file operations (creation, modification, deletion), collect and send off sensitive information, gain access to email, etc. The Perl scripts require no compilation to execute and are available in the source code. This feature of all script languages, including VBScript, is why there are now more than 40 variations of the Loveletter virus. To create a new virus variant, one needs to find a virus sample (available for free on the numerous virus-related Web sites on the Internet), modify a couple of strings, and bingo! (A new virus is ready.)

Then take into account that Perl and many other script languages for Linux are platform-independent. This means that Perl scripts originally developed for Windows generally will work on Linux, as well. Obviously, they are not fully portable and compliant with all platforms because the methods of file infection are different between Windows and Linux, due to the fact that the file formats are different. However, this turns out to be more of a disadvantage than an advantage for Linux. Linux Perl viruses can be successfully cleaned and the infected files restored. If a Windows Perl-based virus corrupts a Linux file, the file restoration may be less successful.

There are no fundamental obstacles in Linux to the existence of mass mailing viruses such as Melissa or LoveBug. First, in the same way that a Windows virus exploits Outlook, a Linux virus can gain access to the Sendmail gateway and send out infected messages to all the addresses found on the computer. (It's also doubtful that the mentality of an average Windows user is different from the mentality of an average Linux user.) If Linux becomes popular, we will see "love letters," "CVs," "million dollar checks," etc. attachments opened. This will lead to global epidemics comparable to contemporary Windows outbreaks.

The biggest reason a Linux-based widespread viral epidemic hasn't happened is because Linux is still not a widespread platform. It is not a desktop standard used on millions of PCs all around the world in all industries. Linux is far behind the popularity of Windows and hasn't become a target for that reason. This is true, notwithstanding that almost every week a new Linux virus is discovered. Even though many of them are squalid and botched, these attempts are becoming more and more aggressive, and what is frightening is that many are successful. It is obvious that with increased Linux popularity, a global epidemic looms on the horizon.

SUMMARY

Viruses are a permanent part of computing and have become even more important with the emergence of the online world. It's easy to fight. Be careful. Follow some of the tips we've mentioned, but more importantly, get some antivirus software and keep it updated. That's the best insurance.

13
Get Your Web Site

For your first site, create a personal Web site with typical information that people like to share: resumes, photos, and other information. A simple personal site will give you all the tools you need to get started building more complicated sites. There are numerous way to do this. Here are some of the basics. And note that today's blogging services (covered in Chapter 15) can also accomplish much of what we outline here.

HTML

Conventional Web pages are created using Hypertext Markup Language (HTML). This language tells the Web browser how to display information to people who visit your Web page. If you go to any Web page, you can select View in your Web browser, then Source from the pull-down menu. Then you will see the HTML code (as well as other languages embedded within the HTML code) that make the page display properly, show images, and link to other Web pages.

Early in Web page designing, people used HTML with text editors. Then visual authoring tools emerged to enable users to create Web pages with the type of interface they were used to (such as the interface they use with Microsoft Word to create documents). Instead of using HTML around a word to make it appear bold, the tools would allow you to highlight text and click a button. It became more visual, less programming-like.

DO'S AND DON'TS OF WEB DESIGN

After you visited enough Web sites, you get a sense that there are two categories: sites that are easy to use and the rest of the Web sites. Some of the most popular sites online, such as Yahoo! and Amazon, have put a lot of emphasis on keeping a clean, simple design that is easy to navigate. This is a daunting task, given the rate at which the Web grows. These companies try to emphasize simplicity and ease of use. They try to avoid an overload of information, so users don't become overwhelmed. Google, a top online search engine, is very simple. There is one image, a search form, and some text links to keep the experience fast and easy. It's a good example to follow.

There are a few rules you can follow that will put you ahead of the pack:

Leave Breadcrumbs

Like Hansel and Gretel, it's a good idea to make sure your visitors can find their way back through your site. If you are building a site for a small business, make sure that if they have to click on a support page to get to a page with phone numbers, somewhere on the phone page there are links back to both the support

---

page and the home page. Yahoo! does this perfectly; you can always navigate its site architecture at the top of every search listing.

Stay Consistent

Use the same style on every page. Some people want clouds on their contact page and a river for their bio page; although that might be a beautiful nature calendar, it doesn't make for a cohesive Web site.

Understandable Links

People want to know where a link will take them before they click it. So, "Click here to see my pictures," or a graphic marked "Pictures" will tell them what they will see when they click through.

Build the Site as You Go

A lot of people become very ambitious when starting their first site and end up with 20 separate areas, 18 of which are marked "under construction." But if you build it as you go, everything you do becomes a "new" area, rather than an old section you finally got around to updating.

Readable Colors

A lot of people try to differentiate their site by using purple text on a pink background. There is only one thing that differentiates Web sites—content. People go to a site to find information they aren't finding anywhere else. Most people aren't looking for a site because they want to read pink text on a purple background.

Professional Voice

Although emoticons, abbreviated words, and misspellings might be acceptable in email, it doesn't take too long after seeing them on a site *B4 I leave cuz it gets old fast.* :-)

WEB SITE HOSTING

Research your hosting options first. Learning about your hosting provider's capabilities can help you plan for future growth. If you are creating a Web site for your business, the cost of hosting should be a consideration in your monthly budget.

On the other hand, if the Web site will be for fun or for the purpose of learning, a free hosting option may be what you're looking for. If your project is "The John C. Dvorak Fan Site" (somebody please!), and you're operating without a budget, a service such as Yahoo! GeoCities may be the best solution.

Regardless of your budget, the pop-up ads and banners that free hosting providers add to your Web site may be less than desirable. To that end, you'll need to know what options exist and what to look for when researching commercial hosts.

Do Your Research

Over time, the cost of bandwidth has significantly decreased, resulting in an almost saturated hosting market. It seems that almost anyone who can afford a T1 line and a server has decided to break into the hosting business. For the moment, keep your eyes off the price and shop.

Find out the size of the hosting company's backbone. Is it hosting on a T1 or a T3? A full T1 can transfer 1.5 Mbps (megabits per second). This is adequate for a small hosting company with a handful of clients, but doesn't leave much room for growth. A full T3 can transfer 45 Mbps, meaning it can accommodate 30 times the traffic of a T1. If you can find a host with a T3 pipe or greater, it would be ideal. Even if your Web site doesn't grow to enormous levels, it's good to know that other busy sites on the same network won't slow you down.

Find out how long a hosting company has been in business. Are they seasoned professionals or are they still wet behind the ears? New hosting companies can certainly have potential, but companies in the business for a few years already have a good protocol in place. A hosting company with a solid network, regular backup schedule, and experienced customer and technical support is worth every penny. Surprisingly, these key elements are sometimes missing from hosting providers. Above all, you don't want to set up a site with a host and find that overnight it is out-of-business and you are down.

Before you settle on your choice, be sure to read and understand the company's TOS (terms of service). Familiarize yourself with any contract terms or bandwidth consumption restrictions. Educate yourself on its billing policy and find out what is required to upgrade your hosting package if you ever need to expand.

Domain Names

A domain name is an easy-to-remember host name that translates to your Web site's unique numeric address (IP address). Rather than typing an IP address into your browser, you would normally submit a domain name, such as amazon.com. You may want to acquire your own domain name.

Before you rush out to grab the first name you can think of (if it's available), you should know whether the hosting provider will support that level of service. Most commercial hosting providers do, but free hosting services typically do not. Many of the larger free hosting (nonvirtual) providers (such as Yahoo! Geocities and Lycos Angelfire) offer paid hosting upgrades with support for domain names. And some will even help you go through the process of getting the domain name.

Hosting Options

There are two hosting options: virtual and nonvirtual.

Virtual

The most common level of hosting provided by commercial hosting companies is virtual hosting. Virtual hosting lets you have your site hosted with your own custom domain name, such as http://www.myname.com. When you signup for virtual hosting, your hosting "space" is set up on a server with several other virtual hosting clients. You should ask your hosting company how many virtual clients exist per server and whether the server's hardware can accommodate their volume.

Most companies offer many bells and whistles to entice you into signing up for virtual hosting. Make sure you know what your minimum feature set is before being sold on other features.

- Maximum hard drive space
- Maximum data transfer per month
- Number of email aliases (names@mydomain.com)
- FTP access (for transferring files to and from your Web site)

Growth potential is important, and your hosting company should offer upgrades to your virtual hosting account. Here are a few things to look for.

- Server-side scripting—Perl, ASP, PHP, ColdFusion, or JSP support
- Database support—Microsoft Access, Microsoft SQL Server, or MySQL
- SSL (secure sockets layer)—Security for e-commerce applications
- Web site traffic statistics
- Additional email aliases

Have a good understanding of your needs before you sign a contract. A company may offer you 450 MB of storage for only $10 more a month, but that may be a lot more space than you need. It's good to take your hosting provider's advice, but don't be pressured. If you're negotiating with a company that applies forceful sales tactics, it may be time to move on.

Nonvirtual

Nonvirtual hosting is really budget hosting. You aren't able to use your own URL, so you'll end up with a Web address such as www.theirhostname.com/myname. It is simply a page on the host's Web site. The downside is that it's more difficult for people to remember. The costs may outweigh the negatives, depending on your budget and needs.

"ADULT" WEB HOSTING

Most host sites will not allow adult erotica content on their servers, just as they will not allow information that is counter to what the general population regards as "good taste" (i.e., Nazism, racism, hate groups, etc.). In addition, there may be more restrictions on your Web content than simply the host site. There is a fine distinction between what is legal or illegal in explicit sexual material, and this varies by jurisdiction. (Countries, states, counties, cities, and communities prohibit certain kinds of content on a Web site.)

Sites that contain questionable material should always have a warning page at the entrance. In fact, it's a good idea to use a warning page if anything at all might be considered even remotely offensive to the general population. (This would include things that you might find to be interesting and fascinating, such as a collection of horrid car accident pictures, graphic open-heart operation images, any of your displayed body parts, no matter how photogenic, or your vast collection of exposed cellulite-at-the-beach photos.) The rule of thumb would be to err on the side of caution.

It's best to explain in detail to the host provider what you intend to put on the Web. Even if its service implies that it will accept that kind of material, be sure to make certain it does.

Be aware that adult erotica can generate gigabytes of traffic, which can be very expensive and may crash smaller servers or interfere with other Web site traffic. This is a key reason why most hosting providers do not want "that kind of Web page" on their servers. The ones that do allow it will charge a hefty price for additional traffic above and beyond the minimum you contract for.

Obviously illegal, sexually explicit material has no place on the Web.

Windows vs. UNIX/Linux

It's not apparent whether a site is hosted on a Windows server network or a UNIX or Linux network. Both are solid. Each can offer an assortment of enhancements. Most open-source server-side scripting applications, such as PHP and Perl, are supported on both platforms. Typically, due to the differences in overhead, UNIX or Linux hosting will be less expensive than Windows server hosting. You may want to ask what platform your Web site is hosted on. But your focus should be on the security of the network.

Alternatives

If your Web site explodes into success, you can expect the Web site's traffic to increase. If you outgrow your bandwidth restrictions as a result, you may outgrow your hosting provider, as well.

There are two alternatives to virtual hosting: dedicated and co-located hosting. These *enterprise-level* solutions are expensive. Expect to pay anywhere between several hundred dollars to as much as $1,000 or more monthly for this level of service.

Dedicated Hosting

Your Web hosting company provides you with your own server. Due to the cost of acquiring the hardware, most companies that offer dedicated hosting will require a minimum hosting term to recover costs.

Co-Located Hosting

You purchase your own server and software, and have it installed at your hosting provider's facility.

Price Sensitivity

In a market as competitive as Web hosting, some companies undersell their bandwidth and services. It's good to look for bargains, but if it seems too good to be true, it usually is. It's not unheard of for a struggling hosting company to go out of business overnight. It means inevitable downtime for you while you struggle to find a new host and move your Web site. The price may indicate its health. If it's way lower than competitors, this may be a warning to beware.

You should expect to pay between $20 and $50 monthly for a basic, virtual hosting Web site account. You will find better deals, but you may be sacrificing customer service or quality. Take your time, and make sure all your questions are answered before you seal the deal.

Hit charges—Charges by how many times, over a minimum, that your Web site is viewed.

Predefined CGI scripts—These make your site interactive. Some may be provided.

User-written CGI scripts—Can you install scripts you write?

Automail responders—These are used to send back automatic notes to email received.

Commercial use—Not all hosts want commercial traffic.

Discount for nonprofit corporations—Some give a break to charities.

Shell account—This is a way to edit your HTML files on the server instead of transferring them.

Email account or email forwarding—This is a POP mail account or a way to forward mail.

Access reports—These provide information about the number of users and who they are.

Database available/use—Is there a database available on the server?

JAVA available—Can you use Java on your Web site?

Secure server—This will accept credit cards securely.

RealAudio—Is there a server stream for audio?

Mailing lists—Will the host allow mailing list use from the account?

Microsoft FrontPage—Not all Web sites are set up for this program.

Space can/can't be resold—Can you sell space on your Web site, essentially subletting?

Payment accepted by credit cards—Can you pay your monthly fee with a credit card?

ColdFusion—Again, not all Web sites are set up for this program.

Telephone help support—This may or may not be provided.

ABOUT DOMAIN NAME REGISTRATION

There are benefits to registering a domain name for your Web site. If your Web site is for business purposes or for reasons beyond a vanity Web site, a domain name is an affordable way to add "branding" to your online services. Additionally, it's usually much simpler to remember than the URL provided by your ISP (compare home.earthlink.net/~joesgarage to www.joesgarage.com). Portability is another added benefit. If you decide in the future to switch to a new ISP, your domain name and any email addresses associated with your domain name can come with you.

Registering a Domain Name

To purchase a domain name, you must find an accredited registrar. There is a variety of domain name registrars to choose from. A simple search for "domain name registrars" in your favorite search engine will reveal more sources than you can count. For a list of accredited registrars by the ICANN Organization (Internet Corporation for Accredited Names and Numbers), go to http://www.icann.org.

Be sure to browse the TOS of each registrar you research. There are a few things to look for in a registrar that will help you decide which one is right for you.

- **Cost**—See what the registrar charges to register a domain name and look for registrars that offer discounts for extended registration periods (two years or more).

- **Ownership**—You may find registrars who offer free domain registration if you agree to pay for other services they provide, such as Web site hosting. In those cases, it's possible that the registrar or reseller owns the domain and not you.

- **Ease of Use**—Find out how easy it is to manage your registration. Determine whether the registrar provides a method for you to login securely and change your contact information or ISP name servers.

 The following offer domain name registrations with a variety of different service levels. Read their TOS, pricing, and customer service policies to make a comparison.

Verisign / Network Solutions—www.netsol.com

DNS Central—www.dnscentral.com

InterNIC—www.interNic.net

Go Daddy—www.godaddy.com

DNS Registration

You'll want to have everything in order when you've settled on your domain name registrar. Be prepared to submit the following information to your registrar.

Contact Information

When you register, you'll be asked for some key contacts: administrative, technical, and billing. These can be different individuals or the same. In fact, they can all be you. The administrative contact is a name for general correspondence. The technical contact is for technical questions. Often, you will use the name of the hosting provider's technical person. The billing contact is who to send the bills to when payment is due.

DNS/Name Servers

To attach a domain name to a Web site numeric IP address, the registrar will ask you for two name server addresses. You can get this information from your hosting provider. If you haven't yet selected a provider, most registrars will give you the option of "parking" your domain on their name servers until you do.

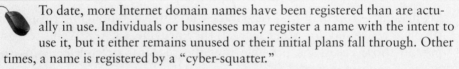 To date, more Internet domain names have been registered than are actually in use. Individuals or businesses may register a name with the intent to use it, but it either remains unused or their initial plans fall through. Other times, a name is registered by a "cyber-squatter."

A squatter is a person or entity who registers a domain name for the purpose of reselling it at an inflated price. There are people actually making businesses out of purchasing hundreds upon thousands of names with the intent to resell them. If you find that the name you want is owned by a squatter or a reseller, you're better off not playing their game. It's not unusual for a reseller to charge thousands of dollars for a domain name that would have cost you around $20, had you found it first. Your best bet is to choose another. Create a list of names that you feel are acceptable. Prepare to scratch some of them off the list because they may already be taken.

HTML EDITORS

In searching for the right HTML editor, you'll discover that there are many different offerings to choose from. In addition to commercial editors that you can purchase, there is a variety of freeware and shareware editors available. Your skill level or personal comfort zone will be what determines whether you choose a WYSIWYG editor or a text markup editor.

WYSIWYG is an acronym meaning "What You See Is What You Get." The editing environment of a WYSIWYG editor can be compared with using a word processor. As you type your document in the word processor, you're seeing a representative example of how it will appear on the printed page. Various buttons or options on the toolbar allow you to manipulate your text and align specific sections as you desire. The concept of WYSIWYG editing is similar to that of a word processor. You start with a blank canvas and type and format your content directly on the screen as you want it to appear on the Web. Using the tools the editor provides, you can add graphics or photos and position them as desired. The editor builds the HTML for you while showing you a representative example of your Web site as it will appear online.

If you're not too experienced in HTML, a WYSIWYG editor may be the best place to start. These editors give you the power of Web publishing while minimizing the learning curve. Some of the commonly used editors include Dreamweaver, GoLive, FrontPage, and WebExpress.

Macromedia Dreamweaver

Dreamweaver is a powerful alternative and arguably one of the best WYSIWYG editors on the market. Its unique user interface makes many of its tools readily available but is different enough to stump a user who is making the transition from another WYSIWYG editor, such as FrontPage. The dockable panels and tabbed windows are welcome features to users with experience in desktop publishing, and its integrated file explorer provides quick and easy access to files.

Surprisingly, Dreamweaver provides fantastic support for dynamic development, a rare occurrence in a WYSIWYG editor. In addition, to support and code libraries for ColdFusion, Macromedia's server scripting environment, Dreamweaver provides support for ASP, ASP.NET, JSP, and PHP. Additionally, strong XML and CSS support make Dreamweaver an excellent choice.

For more information, go to www.macromedia.com.

Adobe GoLive

GoLive is another easy-to-use editor with tools similar to the others. The unique interface provides a drag-and-drop approach to Web page building. Users can choose items from "Object" panels, such as Web forms or frame elements, and drag them into place. The editor provides support for PHP and JSP server scripting, and a JavaScript library contains a code base similar to that of other editors.

GoLive provides a JavaScript text editor that may be difficult for the novice Web page author to understand. The editor doesn't provide debugging options, so if you use this method to include JavaScript, you may run into some problems.

For more information, go to www.adobe.com.

Microsoft FrontPage

FrontPage may be the simplest editor to learn if you are a frequent user of the Microsoft Office suite of desktop applications. Its user interface is similar to that of other Microsoft products. It has familiarity for Microsoft Word and other Microsoft Office programs. Its feature set gives users tools to create modern Web sites, including a CSS (Cascading Style Sheet) editor and built-in JavaScripting

Despite the editor's popularity, it does have its shortcomings. FrontPage's easy Web site publishing tools work seamlessly, but only if your Web site is hosted on a server with Microsoft's FrontPage extensions installed. Extra work is required if your site is hosted without such a configuration. If your Web site contains Microsoft's ASP server-side scripting code, FrontPage will preserve it and keep it intact. If your pages contain PHP, Macromedia ColdFusion, or another server-side scripting type, you run the risk of mangling the code in FrontPage, rendering it useless.

For more information, go to www.microsoft.com/frontpage/.

MicroVision Development's WebExpress

An often overlooked alternative, WebExpress is an equally powerful WYSI-WYG editor. WebExpress contains all the tools you would expect from a professional WYSIWYG editor, plus a few surprises. The editor's Image Text Editor allows you to add text to any graphic or image, providing a clean and easy way to create navigation buttons. Combine its library of Web-ready artwork and page templates with its remarkably low cost, and you've got a product that's worth anybody's time.

Despite the meaning of the label *WYSIWYG*, none of these editors can guarantee that what you're seeing while you design your Web site is exactly what others will see in their own browsers. However, as these products have evolved, more care has been taken to ensure that they produce HTML that conforms to cross-browser compatibility standards.

For more information, go to www.mvd.com.

HTML Text Editors

For those who are familiar with HTML or would like to be, an HTML text editor may be a more suitable choice. An HTML editor gives the author the freedom to compose HTML code manually while providing tools or short-cuts to make the process faster. Unlike a WYSIWYG editor, an HTML editor's canvas is not visual, but rather raw lines of HTML code. The development environment is usually enhanced with color-coding of HTML tags and preview panes to view the results of your work as you progress.

Like WYSIWYG editors, there's no shortage of product offerings for HTML editors. Here are a few to consider.

AceHTML by Visicom Media, Inc.

An overlooked but powerful editor is AceHTML, an outstanding choice at an affordable price. It provides a large assortment of tools that make the creation process a lot easier and faster. The file explorer is convenient and speeds things along nicely. AceHTML makes fantastic use of its JavaScript tools and provides an awesome interface for creating button rollover effects. The editor provides support for all server-side scripting languages, as well.

For more information, go to www.visicommedia.com.

CoffeeCup HTML Editor by CoffeeCup Software

CoffeeCup is an excellent editor with a solid history. If you're looking for experience, look no further. It comes with a variety of tools that are easy to use and that make the development process much simpler. CoffeeCup does ship with a JavaScript library, but prepare to do some cutting and pasting. The work-in-progress preview pane is nice, and the Web publishing tools are easy to set up and use.

For more information, go to www.coffeecup.com.

Hot Dog Professional by Sausage Software

Easily one of the best editors on the market due to its ease of use, Hot Dog Pro provides all the tools you would expect from a professional HTML editor. Its file explorer allows you to open your documents for editing quickly and easily. The toolbars make most features easily available. Hot Dog provides support for all server-side scripting languages except Macromedia's ColdFusion.

For more information, go to www.domain.com.

HTML vs. WYSIWYG Editor

Clearly, choosing the right type of editor is a personal choice. It depends on your level of comfort with HTML. WYSIWYG editors minimize the learning curve but can inhibit or prevent a user from learning HTML. Additionally, implementing custom server-side scripts can be a cumbersome task in the WYSIWYG environment. HTML text editors are the best choice for users who want more hands-on control of their Web site structure, but some HTML knowledge is expected.

Alternatives

If you consider yourself an HTML guru or don't care to shop for an editor, you can use tools that you already have. Any plain text editor, such as Notepad, Pico, or vi, can be used to write and save HTML files. For the inexperienced, Microsoft Word has some primitive yet functional HTML authoring capabilities.

WEB GRAPHICS

Web graphics are a crucial ingredient in every Web page. Although the most obvious examples of Web graphics are pictures and company logos, a lot of sites use them for everything from their site navigation to background images.

Macromedia Fireworks was specifically created to address the creation of Web graphics. It automates the work behind creating site navigations, rollover graphics, pop-up menus, and buttons. You may have already worked with a graphics program such as Adobe Photoshop—Fireworks works great with Photoshop files, and it has additional features that help make your graphics files ready for the Web.

A good way to see how Fireworks is special is to look at "rollover" graphics. This term is used to describe images that change when someone moves the mouse over them. Before Fireworks, developers had to create three separate graphics to do a rollover. A rollover graphic is used a lot in site navigation, where a button will change color when your mouse is over it, then will change yet again if you click on the button.

Developers initially had to write code to load the images in the background (so there wouldn't be a delay when you mouse over the button), change the graphic when the mouse is over the graphic, then change it to a third graphic when the user selected that graphic. In Fireworks, this task is fast because it is one automatic process. Fireworks provides a step-by-step wizard for creating these graphics.

One of the main concerns of Web graphics is their size, because the larger you make an image or the higher its resolution, the longer it takes for end users to

---

download. Although you do need high-resolution pictures to make prints, you need to use small, more compact images on your site to make the end-user experience faster. Fireworks has a wizard to make Web graphics as small as possible without losing quality. This is just as important for site navigation as it is for the photos you want to add to your site from your digital camera.

ADDING GRAPHICS

Adding graphics to your Web site can mean the difference between a flat, two-dimensional Web site and an enhanced, appealing-looking layout. If you have a logo, adding it to your site can identify your brand. It's important not to go overboard with your graphics, however. Internet connection speeds vary, and a site with heavy graphics can mean a long wait while your site downloads to the user's browser.

Compatibility

When including images in your HTML, you must be sure to use image types that are compatible with all browsers. If your company logo is a high-resolution, four-color (CMYK: cyan, magenta, yellow, black) graphic, it will not appear in all browsers. A low-resolution, three-color (RGB: red, green, blue) graphic would be the best choice.

A small assortment of graphic types can be used on the Web. These are the most commonly used.

GIF

A GIF (Graphics Interchange Format) can display in both grayscale and color but is limited to a palette of 256 colors or fewer. This is the best choice for simple graphics of solid colors. A GIF file can be identified by its *.gif* file extension.

JPEG

A JPEG (Joint Photographic Experts Group) can display images with over 16 million colors, making them the best choice for photographs or complex images. You can identify a JPEG file by either a *.jpg* or *.jpeg* file extension.

Make Your Own Graphics

Custom graphics are easier talked about than done. First, there is a learning curve to figure out how to use the tools. Next is the difficult part—having creative or artistic skills to design your own creation. If you are inclined, there are powerful applications on the market to create Web designs.

Adobe Photoshop

Photoshop is one of the best products on the market for designing Web graphics. However, its many uses make it one of the most expensive products on the market.

For more information, go to www.adobe.com.

Macromedia Fireworks

Fireworks is as powerful as Photoshop, though not as widely used. It is a more reasonably priced, excellent alternative.

For more information, go to www.macromedia.com.

Paint Shop Pro

Paint Shop Pro is priced for the everyday consumer, but it's no slouch in the feature set department. If money is an object, Paint Shop Pro is a good budget choice.

For more information, go to www.jasc.com.

AceDesign

This product is still up and coming, but it has a lot of potential. AceDesign has many desirable features of the more expensive packages at a remarkably low price.

For more information, go to www.visicommedia.com.

All of these programs provide tools for optimizing your graphics for Web sites. Keep these optimization points in mind.

Low Resolution—Saving your images with a resolution of 72 dpi (dots per inch) will comply with Web standards.

Compression—To compress your images without degrading their quality, you can reduce download time and produce a faster-loading Web site.

Choose Wisely—If you create a single or two-color image, you can save it as a GIF to produce a smaller file than you would get as a JPEG.

Graphic Libraries

A quick stop at your local software retailer is all you need to find huge assortments of clipart software packages that are suitable for Web sites. These packages range in price between $20 to several hundred dollars, depending on quantity and quality.

You can also find several sources online for downloading clipart or stock images. Both free and pay services are available, with comprehensive catalogs and search functions to help you find precisely what you need.

Getty Images

Getty Images is an online source for Web-ready photographs and illustrations. Users can browse the searchable catalog and download images for use on the Web. A variety of both paid and free images are available.

For more information, go to www.gettyimages.com.

Nova Development

Nova Development offers a wide selection of Web-ready artwork for purchase. Nova's Art Explosion series provides a large assortment of clipart and images that are suitable for use on the Web.

For more information, go to www.novadevelopment.com.

Don't go overboard when adding graphics to your Web site. Adding too much will make your site cluttered and visually unappealing. Web sites with heavy image content take longer to download to the user's browser.

WEB TOOLS TO ENHANCE YOUR WEB SITE

There are tools available to enhance your Web site further. This is a brief description of the major tools. A more detailed description is available in Chapter 14.

JavaScript

JavaScript is a scripting language that can be used to add some interactive elements to a Web site, such as a button rollover effect, for example. JavaScript source code can be placed directly into the HTML of a Web page and is now widely supported by virtually all Web browsers.

JavaScript's ability to interact with an HTML source makes it a powerful language, and because of its open architecture, anyone is free to use it without license.

Java Applets

A Java applet is a program developed in the Java language that is designed to be executed by a Web browser. Java applets can be invoked from HTML source code to provide effects that go beyond the static, client/server environment of Web browsing.

Some examples of Java applets that you may have seen before are scrolling news headlines or browser-embedded games.

Server-Side Scripts

Unlike JavaScript, which is executed by the user's Web browser, a server-side script is a program that is executed on the Web server. When a browser requests a server-side script, such as PHP or ASP, the script is executed on the Web server. The results are translated into HTML, then sent to the user's browser.

Some examples of server-side script applications are Microsoft ASP, Macromedia ColdFusion, PHP, JSP, and Perl. Before deciding which server-side script to use, be sure to check with your hosting provider to find out which ones they support.

Script Sources

In addition to the script libraries that may exist in your HTML editor of choice, a variety of online resources also exist. To download and try a variety of different scripts, check out some of these valuable resources.

Fresh Meat

A searchable database of various JavaScripts and Java applets plus several PHP, Perl, ASP, and ColdFusion server-side scripts.

For more information, go to www.freshmeat.net.

The JavaScript Source

One of the largest JavaScript libraries on the Internet.

For more information, go to http://javascript.internet.com.

Resource Index

A large library of Perl and PHP scripts.
For more information, go to www.resourceindex.com.

Cascading Style Sheets

CSS is an easy method of adding font, border, and color styles to your Web pages. For example, rather than hard-coding a <font> tag in your HTML to define the typeface and color, you can define a CSS style once and apply to all or part of the text on a given page.

The most convenient use of CSS is to define your styles in an external file and reference it using the <link> tag in your HTML header. For example, if you were to compose your site's CSS in a file called *styles.css*, you could include it in your HTML with the following syntax.

```
<link rel="stylesheet" href="styles.css" type="text/css" />
```

This method of using CSS is especially convenient when making global changes to fonts or styles that carry across your entire Web site.

Most recent HTML editors ship with built-in support for editing CSS. If you're using an editor without CSS support, consider trying TopStyle Pro by Bradbury Software. You can find more information on TopStyle at http://www.bradsoft.com.

For more detailed information on CSS and a few links to tutorials, visit the World Wide Web Consortium at www.w3.org.

XML

Some people will tell you that XML is a flat-file data source. Others say that it is God's gift to planet Earth. The middle-ground definition would be that it is a convenient and flexible way of sharing data.

XML stands for Extensible Markup Language and uses a tag-based syntax similar to HTML to display data. Many different flavors of XML exist, with compatible applications that can parse XML files and interpret them in a useful way.

XML can be useful to you if you want to provide other Web sites with the ability to publish or syndicate content that originates from your site. For example, a corporate Web site may want to allow people to syndicate its company press releases and can do so by way of XML.

One of the simplest uses of XML is the RSS (Rich Site Summary) format. RSS can be easily implemented to share news or press releases and can almost always be found on Web blogs. Because of its lightweight, simple syntax, RSS has been widely adopted as the method for sharing headlines. News services such as CNET, CNN, Salon.com, and Slashdot use the RSS XML format.

For an in-depth tutorial on how to begin using RSS-XML on your Web site, point your browser to www.mnot.net/rss/tutorial/.

FLASH

Flash is an outstanding product by Macromedia to allow you to integrate rich content that breaks out beyond the boundaries of your Web browser, much like Java applets. The difference is speed and outstanding audio and visual capabilities. Flash can be used to create multimedia elements with motion and sound or an entire user interface.

The Macromedia Flash Player is required on the user's end to view any Flash elements that you incorporate into your Web site, but many of the latest browsers ship with Flash plug-in support already built in. Flash elements on your Web site must be downloaded first before the user can view them, which is something to consider before going "all Flash."

Designing or building multimedia Flash content is no simple task and will require a bit of studying before you can really take off. Fortunately, a few smaller software packages allow you to take advantage of some of the simpler features of Flash without the learning curve.

Swish

This inexpensive product allows you to create Flash effects on text or logos without having to be an expert in Flash technology. A free trial download is available.

For more information, go to www.swishzone.com.

Firestarter

Another inexpensive product, Firestarter, is an affordable alternative that allows you to create Flash elements quickly and easily without the heavy learning curve. Produced by CoffeeCup Software, this product also has a free trial version.

For more information, go to www.coffeecup.com.

Swift 3D

Slightly more expensive than the previously mentioned products, Swift 3D provides more bang for the buck. It's a bit more complicated than the others, but it allows you to create three-dimensional Flash elements with ease.

For more information, go to www.swift3d.com.

Usability

Usability is a huge issue on the Web. Although larger sites have really risen to the task of making their sites as intuitive and usable as possible, there are millions of sites online that haven't. The issue is that every time you visit a site, you have to learn how to use it, whereas every time you get a Windows application, it will probably look and behave very similarly to other Windows applications. The simple explanation is that HTML and Web authoring tools have really leveled the playing field as to who can participate. Anyone with an account on America Online can host up to six different Web sites created with AOL's own tool, Dreamweaver, or some HTML saved with Word.

Although putting the power to publish in everyone's hands is great in a utopian sense, it does mean that there is no way to ensure that everyone creates Web sites that are useful and easy to navigate. In fact, many sites seem to intentionally go out of their way to be difficult to navigate.

Usability gurus such as Jakob Nielsen (http://www.useit.com/) have pushed for a simple set of guidelines and rules to make Web sites easier for everyone to use. Unless there is a business reason to make a site more usable, a lot of people will continue to think bad navigation and hard-to-comprehend site architectures are part of their sites' "uniqueness" and not something that needs to be fixed.

Macromedia Flash has been branded as a thorn in the side of Web usability in the past, but that's similar to blaming Microsoft Word for a bad novel. It is just as possible to make beauty as it is an atrocity with any authoring tool. Macromedia has tried to get out in front of the issue and put "best practices" online to help people avoid common mistakes in Macromedia Flash authoring. Web sites dedicated to the specific issue of Macromedia Flash usability have even formed, such as www.flazoom.com. Chris MacGregor and a host of developers cover basics such as navigation all the way up to advanced topics, such as user retention and building accessible content for users with disabilities.

People looking for good usability to emulate online don't have to look far. Everyone has sites they prefer that have a clean, understandable navigation where they seem to accomplish more faster than on other sites. The best thing to do is go to sites like Amazon.com, which spend a lot of money on usability every year, and see how it manages information and organization on its site.

Accessibility

Accessibility is building your Web site so that it can be easily accessed by all people, including those who use special software or hardware to browse the Web. For example, some people need to be able to enlarge their text to read it better, whereas many blind users use special software that reads Web sites to them.

Depending on your audience, accessibility is not only good practice, but it can also be required by law. The federal government has mandated that any content on its Web sites must be accessible to all users. Known as the Section 508 guidelines, these rules for accessibility have placed a renewed emphasis on making sure the Web remains a platform available to everyone.

Before you begin the process, you should have a clear idea of your Web site's objective. Take the time to plan or outline your site's content. Based on your outline, plan the layout of your site, including any navigational links. Drafting the content of your pages first before coding any HTML can also expedite the development process.

SUMMARY

Though this chapter is not the definitive resource for creating Web sites, we hope you're ready to give it a shot. Using the many free or low-cost resources available on the Internet, you should have plenty of opportunities to practice and refine your skills.

14

WEB
PROGRAMMING
LANGUAGES

There are Web page programs for the novice, and there are Web development tools for the more advanced. *Web design tools* is the term you'll hear the most often. It is a catchall for various scripting programs and programming languages. These differ from the more common programs, such as Photoshop, GoLive, Dreamweaver, FrontPage, and others that are WYSIWYG tools that do most of the programming for you. They vary in difficulty but can generally be used by anyone. Most of the powerful Web sites, though, are programmed with more complicated languages.

These languages have more advanced abilities, including the integration of other development tools to add other code to a Web page. HTML (Hypertext Markup Language) is the basis for the World Wide Web. It supplies the code behind every Web page with a standard structure and format content for display in Web browsers. Many people write in HTML with tools such as Notepad on Windows or SimpleText on the Mac. Editors are also available.

W3SCHOOLS

Excellent Web design tutorials are on the Web. One such site is W3Schools. This is a free e-learning portal supported by sponsors. It is a frequently updated Web site. Its focus is on IE5 (Internet Explorer version 5.0) because, according to the Web site, "it's the only practical way to demonstrate XML (Extensible Markup Language) on the Web in your browser."

Tutorials include: HTML, CSS, XHTML, WAP/WML, XML, XSL, DTD, DOM, SOAP, XSchema, Xforms, JavaScript, DHTML, VBScript, WMLScript, Flash, SQL, and ADO.

There is also information on Web browsers and Web-building software.

For more information, go to www.w3schools.com.

CLIENT-SIDE VS. SERVER-SIDE LANGUAGES

Advanced languages can reside on the user's computer (client) or might often be sitting on the server. Some are programmed on the client and reside on the server. Some are completely on the server. Let's examine a few of these. (Note this is an overview. Any one of these topics could take up an entire book.)

Client Side

Client-side languages include HTML, WML, XML, JavaScript, and VBScript. The client (Web browser) executes these scripting languages. Java can be either client-side or server-side, depending on the purpose and design. Java that is for the client side is called an *applet*; if for the server side, it is called a *servlet*.

By having the browser do the work, your server gets a performance boost. The downside to doing the major processing on the client side can be security risks, as well as allowing your code to be viewable to anyone in the world. Many larger corporate sites are using Java to decrease the load on their servers.

Beyond programming, other client-side operations may include Flash and ActiveX controls.

HTML

HTML defines the presentation of a Web document. A variety of tags and attributes are used. Although there is a standard, not all browsers wandering the Net react the same to a given set of HTML instructions. That's one of the tricky things about the Web—there are so many variables.

The World Wide Web Consortium (W3C) is the group that oversees changes to HTML. Its Web site offers information on the latest version of HTML, as well as standards, tutorials, tips, software utilities, and other guidelines. For more information, go to: www.w3.org/Markup.

WML

Wireless Markup Language (WML) is an XML-based language used to specify content and user interface for Wireless Application Protocol (WAP) devices; the WAP forum provides a Document Type Definition (DTD; see sidebar) for WML. WML is supported by almost every mobile phone browser around the world.

As mobile devices become more Internet enabled, WML will be there to deliver content. It is still in the early stages of life but is limited only by the mobile devices on the market.

DTD

A DTD states what tags and attributes are used to describe content in an SGML (Standard Generalized Markup Language), XML, or HTML document, where each tag is allowed, and which tags can appear within other tags.

For example, in a DTD, one could say that LIST tags can contain ITEM tags, but ITEM tags cannot contain LIST tags. In some editors, when authors are inputting information, they can place tags only where the DTD allows. This ensures that the entire document is formatted the same way. Applications will use a document's DTD to read and display a document's contents properly.

HDML

Handheld Device Markup Language (HDML) is used to format content for Web-enabled mobile phones. HDML is Openwave's (formerly known as *phone.com*) proprietary language, which can be viewed only on mobile phones that use Openwave browsers.

HDML came before the WAP standard was created. It uses Openwave's Handheld Device Transport Protocol (HDTP) instead of WAP. HDML and the Openwave gateway are most popular throughout North America. In Europe, WML and the Nokia WAP gateway and browser are the emerging standard. However, some versions of Openwave browsers do interpret basic WML.

XML

XML is a markup metalanguage developed by the W3C and is a pared-down version of SGML, designed especially for Web documents. It allows designers to create their own customized tags, to enable the definition, transmission, validation, and interpretation of data between applications and between organizations.

VBScript

VBScript is based on the Visual Basic programming language but is much simpler. In many ways, it is similar to JavaScript. It is a language developed by Microsoft and supported by Microsoft's Internet Explorer Web browser. Although it is based on Visual Basic, it is considered to be more similar to JavaScript. It allows Web authors to include interactive controls, such as buttons and scrollbars, in Web pages.

JScript and JavaScript

JavaScript is used to add dynamic functions to a Web page, such as blinking buttons and movement. JScript is Microsoft's extended implementation of ECMAScript (ECM-262), an international standard based on Netscape's

JavaScript and Microsoft's JScript languages. JScript is implemented as a Windows script engine. This means that it can be "plugged in" to any application that supports Windows Script, such as Internet Explorer, Active Server Pages, and Windows Script Host.

JScript is one choice to use for simple tasks (mouseovers on Web pages) or advanced tasks (updating a database with Active Server Pages [ASP] or running logon scripts for Windows 2000). JScript relies on external "object models" to carry out much of its work. For example, Internet Explorer's DOM (document object model) provides objects such as "document" and methods such as "write" to enable the scripting of Web pages.

ActiveX

A loosely defined set of technologies developed by Microsoft, ActiveX is a hybrid of two other Microsoft technologies called *OLE* (Object Linking and Embedding) and *COM* (Component Object Model). ActiveX can be very confusing because it applies to a whole set of COM-based technologies. However, most people think only of ActiveX controls, which represent a specific way of implementing ActiveX technologies.

An ActiveX control can be automatically downloaded and executed by a Web browser on a Microsoft platform. ActiveX is not a programming language but rather a set of rules for how applications should share information. Programmers can develop ActiveX controls in a variety of languages, including C, C++, Visual Basic, and Java. An ActiveX control is similar to a Java applet. Unlike Java applets, however, ActiveX controls have full access to the Windows operating system. This gives them much more power than Java applets, but with this power comes a certain risk that the applet may damage software or data on your machine.

To control this risk, Microsoft developed a registration system so that browsers can identify and authenticate an ActiveX control before downloading it. Another difference between Java applets and ActiveX controls is that Java applets can be written to run on all platforms, whereas ActiveX controls are currently limited to Windows environments.

POPULAR INTERNET BROWSERS
MS Internet Explorer
Mozilla
Opera
Netscape

Safari
Konqueror
Galeon
Phoenix
Chimera
Multizilla
OmniWeb
K-Meleon
Lynx
WebTV
ANT Fresco
Netscape
ICab
AmigaVoyager

Server Side

These tools help you add content to Web pages with Server-Side Includes (SSI). These are a means of creating "template" Web pages, which places some text in a set of Web pages or applies a consistent appearance across a set of Web pages. SSIs are often called simply *Includes*.

The HTML text for a template is put in one file, then each individual page contains special instructions to include this file. If you need to change the overall appearance of the whole site, only the template needs to be changed.

When your Web page is requested by a browser, your server software will first retrieve your Web page. Then it will see instructions to parse the SSI (directives you've added to your HTML page) and will dynamically create the final page sent to the requesting browser. This final page includes whatever is in the template. This all resides on the server side of the Web.

SSI is a feature of Web server software. Apache and Microsoft IIS (Internet Information Services) both support them. The syntax will differ, depending on the Web server software used. Not all Web servers allow the use of SSI.

Server-side languages include Hypertext Processor (PHP), Perl (Practical Extraction and Report Language), Python, Tool Command Language (TCL), and VB. Server-side languages are more secure and, in many cases, more powerful. These languages are compiled on the server. They perform their job, then send the results to the browser. There is a penalty for the increased control, security, and functionality. It is performance. It is minimal, but the performance delay is higher than with client-side languages, because the server may have to compile your code on every single request for each visitor.

CGI

Common Gateway Interface (CGI) is a specification for transferring information between a WWW server and a CGI program. A CGI program is any program designed to accept and return data that conforms to the CGI specification. The program could be written in any programming language, including C, Perl, Java, or Visual Basic.

CGI programs were originally the most common way for Web servers to interact dynamically with users. Many HTML pages that contain forms, for example, use a CGI program to process the form's data once it's submitted. Another increasingly common way to provide dynamic feedback for Web users is to include scripts or programs that run on the user's machine, rather than the Web server. These programs can be Java applets, JavaScript programs, or ActiveX controls. These technologies are known collectively as client-side solutions, whereas the use of CGI is a server-side solution because the processing occurs on the Web server.

One problem with CGI was that when a CGI script is executed, a new process is started. For busy Web sites, this may slow the server noticeably. A more efficient solution—more difficult to implement—is to use the server's API, such as ISAPI or NSAPI. Another increasingly popular solution is to use *Java servlets*.

PROGRAMMING TUTORIALS

There are many different Web tutorials to aid in learning the tricks and tips of programming languages. ProgrammingTutorials.com is a portal for online programming tutorial sites. Its goal is to become an invaluable resource to the programming community and especially novice programmers or those who want further exposure to a language or technology. Tutorials it has available include: Ada, ASM/Assembly, ASP, C, C++, C#, CGI, Cobol, Delphi, HTML, Java, JavaScript, Perl, Python, Qbasic, SQL, Tcl/Tk, Visual Basic, VRML, XML, and others (such as Lisp, GNU, Eiffel, etc.).

For more information, go to www.programmingtutorials.com.

PHP

PHP was created in 1994 by Rasmus Lerdorf. In 1997, PHP development entered the hands of other contributors. Two of them, Zeev Suraski and Andi Gutmans, rewrote the parser from scratch to create PHP version 3 (PHP3), now at version 4 (PHP4). PHP is an open-source, server-side scripting language used to create dynamic Web pages. PHP can be embedded in HTML, or the entire page can be generated using PHP. In an HTML document, PHP script (similar syntax to that of Perl or C) is enclosed within special PHP tags. Example: <?PHP ?>

PHP is embedded within tags, so you can jump between HTML and PHP instead of writing heavy amounts of code to output HTML. PHP is executed on the server; the client cannot view the PHP code. PHP can perform any task that any CGI program can do, but its strength lies in its compatibility with many types of databases.

Perl

Perl is a programming language developed by Larry Wall, especially designed for processing text. Because of its strong text-processing capabilities, Perl has become one of the most popular languages for writing CGI scripts.

Python

An interpreted, object-oriented programming language that was developed by Guido van Rossum. The name is rumored to have come from one of van Rossum's favorite television shows, *Monty Python's Flying Circus*. Python is very portable because Python interpreters are available for most operating system platforms. Although Python is copyrighted, the source code is open source, and unlike GNU software, it can be commercially resold.

TCL

Pronounced T-C-L, this is a powerful interpreted programming language developed by John Ousterhout. One of the main strengths of TCL is that it can be easily extended through the addition of custom TCL libraries. It is used for prototyping applications, as well as for developing CGI scripts, though it is not as popular as Perl for the latter.

VB

Visual Basic is a programming language and environment developed by Microsoft. Based on the BASIC language, Visual Basic was one of the first products to provide a graphical programming environment for developing user interfaces. Instead of worrying about syntax details, the Visual Basic programmer can add a substantial amount of code simply by dragging and dropping controls, such as buttons and dialog boxes, then defining their appearance and behavior. Although not a true object-oriented programming language in the strictest sense, Visual Basic nevertheless has an object-oriented feel. It is sometimes called an event-driven language because each object can react to different events, such as a mouse click.

ASP

ASP is a specification for a dynamically created Web page with an *.asp* extension that utilizes ActiveX scripting, usually VBScript or JScript code. When a browser requests an ASP page, the Web server generates a page with HTML code and sends it back to the browser.

ColdFusion

ColdFusion is a product created by Allaire Corporation of Cambridge, Massachusetts (in 2001, Allaire merged with Macromedia) that includes a server and a development toolset designed to integrate databases and Web pages. With ColdFusion, a user could enter a zip code on a Web page, and the server would query a database for information on the nearest movie theaters, then present the results in HTML form. ColdFusion Web pages include tags written in ColdFusion Markup Language (CFML) that simplify integration with databases and avoid the use of more complex languages, such as C++, to create translating programs.

CFML is a tag-based Web scripting language supporting dynamic Web page creation and database access in a Web server environment. In the language, ColdFusion tags are embedded in HTML files. The HTML tags determine the page's layout while the CFML tags import content based on user input or the results of a database query. Files created with CFML have the file extension *.cfm*.

SUMMARY

There are a lot of ways to do advanced programming on a Web site, and most practitioners choose one or two and perfect those methods. The question you have to ask yourself is which route to take. The best way to determine this is to examine Web sites you like and find out from the webmasters exactly what tools are being used to create the sites. Then begin to study those tools and languages. And always remember that there is no one best way.

15
THE BLOG PHENOMENON

One of the most interesting trends on the Internet is the proliferation of personal Web-published commentary generically referred to as *blogs*. A blog can be defined as a chronologically ordered series of short, frequently updated essays, series of commentaries, or "posts." But there is more to it than that.

The term originated from "Web log," or "weblog" and was further promoted by pyra.com simply as a "blog" at its www.blogger.com site (although www.pita.com is considered the original source of easy-to-use Web logging). People who blog are called *bloggers*, and right now there are thousands of blogs on the Net.

Blogging goes beyond software posting and uses an entire system that allows for easy creation. With a blog, there is no coding to do. The blog is usually more attractive than sloppy HTML done by an amateur, and by nature it demands updating so that the material is kept current. People can't resist updating the diary and apologize if they don't do it—as though anyone really cares.

You have to be dedicated to a Web site to keep it current. Not so the blog; it's more addictive. Hobbyist blogs have emerged. For example, some people like to watch a lot of movies and review them. They see movies and immediately post their comments. Some of these homebrew reviewers are better than the pros.

JOHN C. DVORAK ASKS, "WHY?"

Why, exactly, do people want to have other people read these ramblings? Many are incriminating! Ask a weblog addict why he or she does it, and you'll get a range of answers that tend toward the "because it's easy" or "because it's fun!" bromides. Here are a few obvious possibilities:

Ego Gratification

Some people need to be the center of attention. It makes them feel good about themselves to tell the world what important things they've been doing and what profound thoughts they've been having. Curiously, although this looks like the most obvious reason for a blog, I think it's probably the least likely reason, because it's too trite and shallow.

Antidepersonalization

When people begin to think they are nothing more than a cog in the wheel of society, they look for ways to differentiate themselves. The blog proves they are different. Just read it. You'll see.

Elimination of Frustration and the Need to Share

Day-to-day life, especially in the city, is wrought with frustration, and the blog gives people the ability to complain to the world. You get to read a lot of complaining in these logs. But it seems some people genuinely like to "share," and this is one way.

Wanna-Be Writers

A lot of people want to be published writers. Blogs make it happen without the hassle of getting someone else to do it or having to write well—although there is good writing to be found. Some is shockingly good. Most of it is miserable. I expect to see those Open Learning classes around the country offering courses in blog writing.

Whatever the reason for the blog phenomenon, it's not going to go away anytime soon. The main positive change—far fewer cat pictures (Figure 15.1)!

FIGURE 15.1 AFTER JOHN RAN A COLUMN CRITICAL OF BLOGS, THIS PICTURE OF HIM WITH A GRUMPY CAT HEAD SOON APPEARED ON VARIOUS BLOGS.

There are some various views published on the Web about when and what was the first blog on the Web. Rebecca Blood's history notes that Jorn Barger created the term in late 1997, and in 1999 only 23 blogs were in existence. (Although she doesn't cite an individual pioneer or first blog.) The citations are two blog-tracking Web sites (www.jjig.net/portal/tpoowl.html and the Eatonweb Portal http://portal.eatonweb.com). But for such a small amount of history, there appears to be much confusion over its real beginnings.

Dave Winer claims that the first blog was the first Web site on the Web (http://info.cern.ch/). The site was built and maintained by Tim Berners-Lee at CERN (an acronym for the French name of the European Laboratory for Particle Physics). The Web page pointed to other sites on the Web as they came online. The National Computer Security Association (NCSA) *What's New* page began to log the same sorts of things, then Netscape took the baton. Dave Winer's history makes the claim that he did his first blog in February 1996 as part of the *24 Hours of Democracy* Web site. (This was a project dreamed up and promoted by Mr. Winer to let people post essays about what democracy meant to them.) There is no doubt that a genre appeared and was defined and embraced.

If these histories seem a little thin, it's because they are narrow in their scope. The history may have deeper roots. The fact that people are spouting opinions for the world to read isn't peculiar to computers. In the dialup BBS world (which came before the Web gained popularity), there was an abundance of *personal diaries, online journals,* and *narratives*. It wasn't unusual for a BBS sysop to have a page of updates and tidbits of information about what was going on around the homestead. In fact, what we would define as blogs or public diaries are called BBSs in Japan. The history of the contemporary Japanese BBS is directly linked to the dialup BBS public diaries.

As the Web began to gain momentum, so did the proliferation of *home pages, vanity pages, portals, links and commentaries,* and *newspages*. The differences appear to be in the semantics.

Diary or Blog?

There are many different views about this. The confusion is within the group calling themselves *bloggers*. Hundreds of online diary authors keep blogs (Figure 15.2, for example). Thousands of people use blog sites and software to keep journals. So what is the difference?

A traditional blog is focused outside the author and his or her site. A Web journal, conversely, looks inward—the author's thoughts, experiences, and

FIGURE 15.2 AN EXAMPLE OF A DIARIST-TYPE OF BLOG. THIS ONE BELONGS TO GRETCHEN PIRILLO.

opinions. Some sites, of course, do both. So to see the "perfect blurred" line better, you have to step back a bit.

Online diaries and journals have been around almost as long as the World Wide Web. What we call blogs today didn't really pop up until 1998 (although some say NCSA link pages dating back to 1993 counted as the first).

The Nebulous Blog

The basic definition of a weblog by Jorn Barger: (Weblog Guru) "A weblog (sometimes called a blog or a newspage or a filter) is a Web page where a weblogger (sometimes called a blogger or a pre-surfer) logs all the other Web pages she or he finds interesting."

The alternate definitions—notably *pre-surfer*—helps clear things up a bit. Originally, weblogs were basically richer (and often automated) link lists, as in "Click here to see an article on human cloning, here's what I think about cloning, click here to post what you think about cloning."

Instead of forwarding "check this out!" URLs to your friends, you could post them on the Web for anyone to see. A weblog's popularity would grow depending on the uniqueness and novelty of the sites you linked and the commentary you'd provide about them. And the appeal for the readers was simple: Why waste hours trying to be entertained, educated, or disgusted on the Web when someone else is happy to do all the surfing for you?

Evolution

Automation is a central reason why weblogs exploded. People created a variety of ways to start and maintain weblogs. Scripts such as Noah Grey's Greymatter made linking, reviewing, and commenting a point-and-click affair. And Web-based services such as Blogger minimized the need for extensive HTML tweaking (and partner site Blogspot provided free, weblog-friendly hosting). Five minutes and a few forms later, and anyone could be a blogger.

It should be no surprise, then, that people enjoyed simply speaking their minds and started dropping the "link" root of weblogs, instead taking advantage of *weblog tools* as an easy path to online publishing or, more specifically, to simple and irresistible expression. "Here's what I think about cloning and here's what I had for lunch."

Today it's quite possible that more people are using blogger and weblog tools to keep online journals than to comment on the Web. (The only difference to visitors, really, are generally shorter entries and the "newest-on-the-top" convention. This is when the newest entry appears first, and previous entries are lower on the page.) And that's probably why newcomers figure that's what weblogs are all about.

But it's not. Longtime bloggers at great link-and-commentary sites such as Slashdot would be the first to say so. (I mean, who wants to be associated with online diarists?) And that's why online journalers started weblogs without a hint of redundancy—their journals are about them, and their weblogs are about where they go on the Web.

TYPES OF BLOGS

There are many categories of blogs on the Web. These are general outlines of what is out there.

FIGURE 15.3 *DIGITAL WEB.* THIS IS A MAGAZINE THAT USES BLOGGER SOFTWARE TO PRODUCE ITS LOOK AND FEEL AND TO GENERATE FORUM CONTENT. TYPICAL OF THIS GENRE, IT IS VERY SPECIALIZED.

Topical

Topical blogs (Figure 15.3, for example) are usually about the events of the day or major trends. They're more like newsgroups, because they may focus on a particular subject or slant. They tend to have links and commentary where they regularly update and comment about the links.

Political Blogs

This is a specific type of topical blog where the author(s) usually hold forth with strongly held political opinions. These are forums for strong debate.
Jane Galt—www.janegalt.net
Andrew Sullivan—andrewsullivan.com (Figure 15.4)

Fan Blogs

This type of site is a natural extension of the desire for fans to write and talk about their favorite celebrities.
U2 FanCams—www.u2fancams.com/index2.html
WeezerIsland—www.weezerisland.com

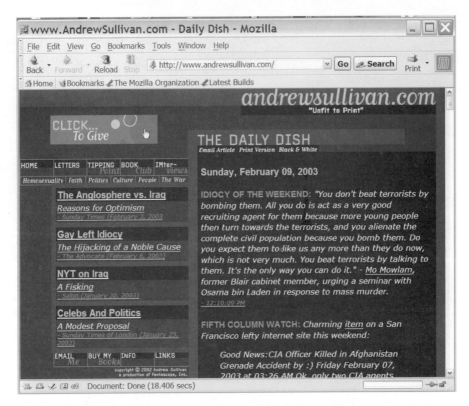

FIGURE 15.4
ONE OF THE MOST POPULAR BLOGS. ALTHOUGH THIS SITE USES BLOGGING SOFTWARE, IT IS CLOSER TO A PERSONAL AND PROFESSIONALLY PRODUCED MAGAZINE SPECIALIZING IN POLITICAL COMMENTARY.

Real-life celebrities are online, too. Hollywood stars provide in-depth analysis, commentary, and more often than not, shameless self-promotion in their blogs. Regardless, it is still a way for their fans and detractors to keep regular tabs on their daily lives.

Jeff Bridges—www.jeffbridges.com
Mariah Carey—www.mariahcarey.com
Melanie Griffith—www.melaniegriffith.com
William Shatner—www.williamshatner.com
Gene Simmons—www.genesimmons.com
Wil Wheaton—www.wilwheaton.net

Technical Blogs

This is a catchall term for any kind of blog that presents news, information, or discussion of technical topics in a blog format. If you have a particular technical expertise, this is a category where you might find a blog to match it. The list of sites is extensive. Here are a few examples.

Slashdot.org—slashdot.org
Meryl's Notes—www.meryl.net/blog/index.html
Zeldman—www.zeldman.com/
Scripting News—www.scripting.com/

LOOKING FOR LIKE MINDS? TRY HERE!

The Pepys Project—pepys.akacooties.com
Globe of Blogs—www.globeofblogs.com
Blogchalking—www.blogchalking.tk
BlogTree—www.blogtree.com
Wander-Lust—wander-lust.com

Parenting

In these blogs, parents talk about their children and the trials and triumphs of raising kids, adopting, or special problems, such as congenital birth defects. They are very good sources of information for other parents.

Raising Hell—www.rhzine.com
The Mommies—mommies.northern-town.com/

Rant Blogs

A rant blog is simply one person raging against the world. They can be very humorous.

Snarky Bitch—www.snarkybitch.com
Pick Up Your Own Damn Socks—pickupyourowndamnsocks.com

Business Blogs

This is a relatively broad and new category. These sites allow professionals, such as journalists, lawyers, and educators, to keep in touch with their clients as a replacement for email.

Diary

Although technically not a blog (but a diary or a journal), this group encompasses the vast, ever-growing segment of people who feel a real need to post information about themselves. These blogs are often very personal in nature. The line between information and exposé is a thin one. People post their thoughts for a curious and voyeuristic public. Blogs can be exceptionally revealing, occasionally telling too much. The dramas of life can unfold, although many offer mostly mundane tidbits.

WWW.DIARIST.NET

Diarist.net was the first site (June 1998) dedicated entirely to online diaries and journals. This site, run by fans of the genre, has become a central resource for this unique form of expression, exhibitionism, examination, and voyeurism.

Picture This

Photologs are updated online photo albums. They are great for a far-flung family to keep up with a new member. They are also an art outlet for many. There are group photo collections.

The Mirror Project—www.mirrorproject.com
Picture Yourself—www.pictureyourself.org
Cityscape Project—cityscape.inkdeep.com
The eye project—www.waferbaby.com/photos/eye/
Photojunkie—www.photojunkie.org
Noah Grey—www.noahgrey.com
A Life Uncommon—www.lifeuncommon.org
pixelog—www.pixelwannabe.com/pixelog/
Snap!—www.love-productions.com/snap/
Shutterblog—www.shutterblog.com
Picture Fish—www.picturefish.com

If you think you'd like to set up your own photolog, here are great tutorials to check out:

Photolog Tutorial—blogstyles.com/photo/tutorial.php
Five Step Photolog—www.moonpost.com/jeremy/photolog5steps.html

HOW TO BLOG

There are many established and emerging blog tools available to the novice. These are sometimes called *content management systems*. Their purpose is to help you to put together your blog without special programs or much technical knowledge. Some of the novice, entry-level programs are listed below, with a brief outline of their basic services.

Blogger

Pyra Labs was one of the first to offer an easy-to-use, automated Web-based tool to allow literally anyone to publish on the Web instantly. It is blog publishing without writing any code or installing any server software or scripts. You have control over the look and location of your blog, although it also has several predesigned templates available. There are two sites and many choices of services.

For basic entry level, go to www.blogspot.com. Four options are available to the newcomer. The first is free. It's the Blog*Spot, which offers text only, no FTP access, and a 250-MB transfer limit. The Blog*Spot Add free has no ads; it's $15.00 per year. It also offers a turnkey Web hosting service. The Blog*Spot Plus25 has 25 MB for images and text, with FTP access, multiple blogs, no ads, and 1-GB transfer rates. The cost is $5.00 a month (or $50.00 annually). The Blog*Spot Plus 100 offers 100 MB of space, FTP access, multiple blogs, no ads, and a 3-GB transfer rate. The cost is $10.00 a month (or $100 annually), with various plans as low as $5.00 a month.

The more advanced site is www.blogger.com. It offers Blogger Pro, an advanced Web-publishing tool. It offers: spellchecking; title fields (to give your posts headlines); image posting; posting to the future or past (so you can move items around in your blog); draft posts; archiving; BlogSend (to broadcast your blog via email); and RSS generation (to syndicate your blog). Other features are planned in the near future.

You don't have to use its hosting, but it's offered, as is a domain registry (you can also move a previously purchased domain to the site). It has 24/7 customer support and free email forwarding. Most of its services require FTP access. It's designed for ease of use for the newcomer and flexibility for the more technically savvy. (Your template can include script, such as ASP or ColdFusion pages.)

LiveJournal

LiveJournal.com is a service to allow you to create and customize your own "live journal," a journal that you keep online. You can update with short entries many times a day or with long entries a few times a week, however you'd like to use it. It's free, it's fun, and it's easy to use!

To create a journal, you need to create a new account. To keep the riff-raff out (control growth, prevent abuse, and keep the community tight), LiveJournal requires an account registration code. Most people get a code from an existing LiveJournal user. If you don't know a LiveJournal user, you can gain access by paying $5.00 for two months ($15.00 for six months, or $25.00 for 12 months). After your paid account expires, your account remains active indefinitely, except without the paid user features.

Paid user features include all of the following:

- a LiveJournal.com email address
- personalized domain name
- faster server access
- journal customization
- text messaging
- up to 10 pictures of yourself (choose one to use on each entry)
- automatic poll survey/booths to make voting poles and full surveys inside your journal entries embedded in your text

The steps are simple. You create an account, then you create your journal by filling out an online form where you will select a user ID and password and enter your email address and your name. Then you'll receive a *Welcome to LiveJournal* email, which will allow you to complete your journal creation by validating your email address. Then you can set up your personal information. You can either update your journal on the Web or download and use a client program for your platform. The Web journal update is much like filling out an email form and hitting a button to "update journal." If you run into any problems, there are online support and community information (one is called the *Newbie Lounge*) where you can explore how LiveJournal works.

Perhaps more interesting for programmers, LiveJournal is an open source project, run by the people who use it and care about it. The source code to the server and all the clients is available under various open source licenses, mainly the GPL (GNU General Public License). They welcome any and all contributors to the project in the lj dev (LiveJournal development) community.

Blog-City

The basic Blog-City service (www.blog-city.com) is free. You can have your own blog, complete with the ability to publish text-based information as you wish. Included with the basic package is the ability to allow your guests to contribute their comments to your site. There aren't many restrictions on the service, except that they ask you keep your comments nonoffensive and to use common decency when using the service. The premium service ($2.00 a month) has more features to allow greater flexibility of customization.

Blog-City makes it easy to create stunning entries without having to use HTML tags. Using the HTML editor, you can format your entry the way you want it to look. You can also link images or photos by copying and pasting from another browser window. In addition, you can edit previously published or unpublished blogs and add links. It also has a feature that will give up-to-the-minute statistics to show you which pages are the most popular and which one's aren't.

BLOG TOOLS

If you have a server or access to one or are looking for something a little more challenging than the cookie-cutter novice systems, there are many tools on the Web to create and customize a blog. There are going to be features you'll want to have in your blog that may or may not be available, depending on the tool you are using to publish your blog. A quick list of features you might want to consider:

Commenting

The ability to comment or post on a blog comes with most of the content management systems listed above. For tools without the ability to record comments, there are several add-on commenting systems that can be added to your blog to provide that functionality.

Searching

If you have a lot of posts, eventually you may want to have the ability to search them.

Web Hosting

Many blog tools require you to have your own Web hosting. In fact, many Web hosts now feature blog-specific hosting plans tailored to the smaller file sizes of blogs.

Affordability

Many blog tools are free for you to use under their licenses, although they often do ask you to make a donation to support the authors' hard work, which is usually done in addition to their regular daytime jobs. Often there will be a free version and an upgraded, fee version. This "upsizing" model, where you can pay to get extra features, is becoming more prevalent.

Customizable

An important feature to many bloggers is the ability to make a blog their own by putting a stamp on it where the appearance is unique to them. This is often done with HTML templates or some kind of Web programming. PHP (discussed a little later) is another way to customize the blog.

Archiving

Many blog tools have the ability to store older posts or entries in an archive so you or your readers can refer back to them. Once you have readers, they are likely to link to specific posts in your blog. As time moves on, your archived entries will still provide valid links for others to access. Most major blogging tools have the ability to store archived posts.

Commenting

Commenting on blogs has taken off and isn't looking back. The number of commenting systems available to install and use on a blog is growing daily. There is increasing demand for the ability to "talk" to a blogger via his or her blog and share opinions.

Guestbooks

Guestbooks are for visitors to leave a quick note to the site owner about his or her work. Given such a description, guestbooks could be considered a form of commenting. However, they don't have the ability to leave a comment for a specific post, just for the site as a whole.

Multiple Authors

Dual and group blogs have begun to emerge. These allow two authors to post in a back-and-forth conversation style.

SAY WHAT?

Ever wonder what all of the blog-related terminology floating around really means? Samizdata.net has put together a Blog Glossary. Here you can find definitions of common words and phrases such as *blogorrhea*, *blogosphere*, *Google bomb*, *permalink*, *warblog* and more.

For more information, go to www.samizdata.net/blog/glossary.html.

SOME POPULAR BLOGGING TOOLS

There are many different blogging tools. Some are geared toward the novice, and others are designed for the serious blogster.

Movable Type

Movable Type is a little more demanding. It is not a hosting service, nor is it a menu-driven, novice program. The core requirements are: an account on a Web server that allows you to run CGI (Common Gateway Interface) scripts;

Perl (version 5.004_04 or greater on the Web server); an FTP program to upload the necessary files to your server; JavaScript and cookies enabled on your browser; and support for the DB-File Perl module or MySQL and DBD::mysql.

It's a CGI program that must be installed on your system. If you have never installed a CGI program, the process may be intimidating only because you may not be familiar with some of the techniques involved. But the Web site offers installation instructions. You should be able to install the program using an FTP program and a text editor.

Movable Type is described as a decentralized, Web-based, personal publishing system designed to ease maintenance of regularly updated content. This content can consist of (but is not limited to) entries in a weblog or online journal, photographs in an online photo gallery, news headlines on a newspaper site, or articles in an online magazine. See Figure 15.5 for an example.

Since it's release in October 2001, Movable Type has grown to be a full-featured and robust system that is constantly updated and integrated with the day's latest advances in personal publishing. Movable Type's greatest strength lies in its flexibility, due to these components:

- Flexible data storage—The system supports both MySQL and Berkeley DB for your data storage, with plans to support PostgreSQL and Oracle in the future. Berkeley DB is available on almost all systems with Perl installed.

- XML-RCP API—implements the Blogger and MetaWeblog XML-RCP APIs, allowing you to use existing client tools (BlogBuddy, Bloggar, BlogApp, etc.) to manage your blog.

- Extensible, library-driven code—if you have experience programming in Perl, you can write custom dynamic applications using the Movable Type libraries.

- TrackBack—Movable Type's TrackBack system allows peer-to-peer communication and conversations between weblogs.

- XHTML/CSS Compliance—Movable Type's default templates produce accessible, standards-compliant pages for your weblog.

Movable Type has a donation (honor) system. For a $20 donation you get listed on its "Recently Updated" list in the movasletupe.org, which is sent out to all the donors. For a $45 donation, you'll be listed on the board and be entitled to receive extra personal support via instant messaging or email. Additionally, if you donate, you'll be able to subtract that amount from any future pay version (with extra features) of the software.

FIGURE 15.5 THE LOCKERGNOME NEWS SITE IS PRODUCED USING MOVABLE TYPE BLOGGING SOFTWARE.

> **TIP**
>
> A small disclaimer—we make no recommendation of one blogging tool over another. This is just a small sample of some of the more popular ones to be found. It is not a complete list of weblog creation tools but just a sampling of a select few.

Greymatter

Greymatter (www.noahgrey.com/greysoft) is a program for use in creating and maintaining a weblog, journal, news/updates page, or similar type of site. Unlike other services, Greymatter is a downloadable program.

Greymatter is primarily meant for "power users"—those who consider themselves fairly experienced with the Web and the creation/maintenance of the types of sites listed above. Greymatter's main focus is on customization and control. It is the original open source weblogging and journal software for your server. It has: fully integrated comments; searching; file uploading and image handling; customizable output through dozens of templates and variables; multiple author support; and many other features. It may have the simplest installation process and interface of all the blogging tools offering this level of functionality.

Requirements to run Greymatter include an FTP client, a Web account that offers full support for Perl 5 software, and a modest comfort level with HTML.

pMachine

pMachine enables you to publish virtually any kind of Web content—from a basic weblog to a full-blown interactive magazine. PMachine gives you complete control over the presentation, behavior, and interactivity of your site. It will allow weblogs to be collective (one in which your visitors can submit entries and other visitors can add comments to those entries). The collaborative nature of a collective weblog adds a higher level of dialog and interactivity to your site.

PMachine has a unique feature called *pBlocks* that allows contact to automatically change each time someone visits. With pBlocks, you can do simple things such as showing a different image each time a page is loaded or complex things such as changing the entire look of the site for each visit. PBlocks can also be used to store static information, such as a list of your favorite links. You can update this information whenever you have access to a browser and the Internet. You can have an unlimited number of pBlocks at your disposal so you can use them in many different capacities. With the RSS Headline Syndication feature, you can publish your weblog to an XML page. These are a few of the features the program has to offer. pMachine Version 2.2 has over 50 new features and enhancements. These range from subtle interface requirements and usability improvements to full-on new features, templates, and tags. There are two versions of the program: pMachine Free (a scaled-down version) and pMachine Pro. The current price for the pMachine Pro noncommercial license is $45. The commercial license version is $125.

pMachine was written in PHP and runs on any server that has PHP version 4 or higher and mySQL 3.23.x or higher.

PHP is a free scripting language that runs on Web sites. It's an open-source, cross-platform alternative to Microsoft's Active Server Pages (ASP) technology and Allaire's ColdFusion.

PHP is a server-side scripting language for Web programmers. PHP commands can be inserted alongside and embedded in the page's HTML. The commands are executed on the Web server to generate dynamic HTML pages. Much of it is a combination of Perl, Java, and C concepts. The syntax structure borrows heavily from C, making it an easy language to learn for novice programmers. PHP performs sophisticated mathematical calculations, provides network information, and offers mail and regular expression capabilities. PHP's strongest feature is its easy database interface. It supports the most popular database servers, including mySQL, Oracle, Sybase, mSQL, Generic ODBC, and PostgreSQL, among others.

PHP's Origins

PHP was created in 1995 by Rasmus Lerdorf to find out who was reading his resume. At the time, he was working as an independent contractor and sending potential employers the URL. He created a Perl CGI script that inserted a tag into the HTML code of his page and collected information on the visitors.

He was hired by the University of Toronto to help build a dialup system for the school. It needed a Web-managed system to tie together a student database, Cisco terminal servers, and a number of other components. He couldn't find a tool he liked to do this, so he created a simple set of tools. One tool logged into an mSQL database, and the other was a data interpreter. He kept finding new needs and wrote new tools, ending up with about 30 different small CGI programs written in C, then combined them all into a single C library. He wrote a simple parser to pick tags out of HTML files and replace them with the corresponding function in his C library. The parser grew to include conditional tags, then loop tags and functions. He never really set out to create a scripting language. He was just adding functionality to the macro replacement parser. The real strength was that PHP tried to find the shortest path to solve a Web problem. However, he made the wise decision to give up control, open up the project, and give anyone who asked full access to the PHP sources. It gained popularity, was almost completely rewritten by a group of six developers, and in turn was reborn as PHP.

SKINNING A BLOG

The appearance of a blog is a result of a person's style, just like the color and cut of a person's hair or the way they wear a hat. Not everyone has the ability (or time) to create their own designs. Some choose to have weblogs professionally designed. Others opt to use free "template services." There are other options, as well. For instance, when you sign up for its services, Blogger provides a limited number of templates to choose from. Blogplates.net and Blogskins.com offer more options. Their free template services include installation instructions written for the content management system used. It is easy to find one to fit your personality.

The upside is that even if you don't understand how to create graphics and write HTML, your blog can give a professional look to your site. The downside is that the look will not necessarily be unique. The chances are, with 10,000+ registered users at Blogskins.com, that there will be several other blogs that will bear a strong resemblance to yours.

Web page design is mostly realized in HTML. There are scripting languages to make the job easier. If you understand the basic PHP code, domesticat.net has created an excellent tutorial on *skinning a weblog*. Several different designs are available. The server you use will need to have a server-side scripting language, as well as, other considerations. For more information visit the tutorial at: www.domesticat.net/skins/howto.php.

OTHER FREE BLOG TEMPLATE SITES

Blog Designs—www.blogdesigns.com

Greymatter Templates—www.foshdawg.net/gm/templates

Miz Graphics—www.mizjenna.com/~mizgraphics

AT A LOSS FOR WORDS?

Memes are devices for a blogger to generate conversation in their blogs by answering a set of defined questions or topics (Figure 15.6). They are an aid for when the words just don't seem to flow from brain to keyboard.

A "meme" is the transmission of information by words, however; that's where the root concept and the use of it in the blogging world end. Memes, in the blogging sense, are a crutch for people who can't think of what to write about. They are benign questions, like one would use to hold up a sagging conversation on a blind date or at a dull cocktail party. It's for when the conversation just doesn't flow. Where were you born (city or state or just country), what is your favorite number or color, what about that weather, how about those 49ers? The stuff chitchat is made of that also gives people some basis from which to get to know each other.

If bloggers are still at a loss for what to say (even with the helpful suggestions of the memes) there is the Topics Blog (http://topics.blogspot.com). It is updated on an almost-daily basis.

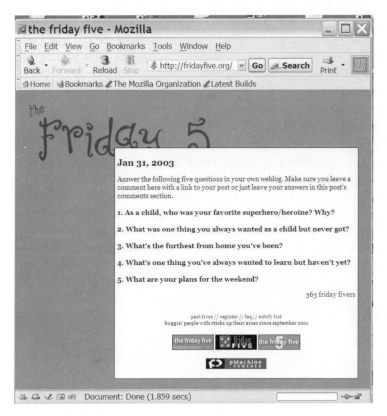

The friday five - Mozilla

File Edit View Go Bookmarks Tools Window Help

Back Forward Reload Stop   http://fridayfive.org/   Go   Search   Print

Home   Bookmarks   The Mozilla Organization   Latest Builds

the friday 5

Jan 31, 2003

Answer the following five questions in your own weblog. Make sure you leave a comment here with a link to your post or just leave your answers in this post's comments section.

1. As a child, who was your favorite superhero/heroine? Why?

2. What was one thing you always wanted as a child but never got?

3. What's the furthest from home you've been?

4. What's one thing you've always wanted to learn but haven't yet?

5. What are your plans for the weekend?

363 friday fivers

past fives // register // faq // notify list
buggin' people with sticks up their arses since september 2001

the friday five   friday FIVE   the friday 5

pMachine POWERED

Document: Done (1.859 secs)

FIGURE 15.6   EXAMPLE OF A MEME SITE.

THE SCIENTIFIC VERSION OF MEME

Life, looked at in a very scientific way, is a giant chemical process. It began about 4 billion years ago with the origin of the first self-replicating cells. From there, cells grouped together and interacted with hormones, pheromones, and other chemical means. Once life had eyes and ears and brains, new ways were found to communicate. Although chemical communication continued (smell), some rapid, nonchemical means evolved (sound and sight). This meant that living creatures could communicate with greater distance. With sounds, the beings could warn, react, comfort, and locate each other. Linguists and anthropologists spend great amounts of time in pondering the concepts of how humans came to use language.

Somehow, some way, humans did develop the ability to associate long strings of sounds with distinct meaning.

Language consists of several cognitive abilities:

- Mental semantics (the ability to make virtual mental images that represent objects, feelings, and situations)

- Syntax (the relations and interactions of the semantics)
- Vocal flexibility (the ability to make the sounds needed)
- Linguistic syntax (the brain must process the word order to comprehend and communicate to others)

Memes are broad bits of transmissible information. Using the word *earth*, for example, will convey meaning for both the dirt we stand on and the planet we cannot see from where we stand but the imagined globe that has come to symbolize our collective home. So a meme is defined as an information pattern held in an individual's memory that can be copied to another's memory through communication. Some have even compared this with a virus. It describes when a thought can take hold and spread. Thoughts can spread by hearing another person speak or by reading a book or newspaper.

Glenn Grant, a memeticist, identifies a *meme* as "a contagious information pattern that replicates by parasitically infecting human minds and altering their behavior, causing them to propagate the pattern. Individual slogans, catch phrases, melodies, icons, inventions and fashions are typical memes. An idea or information pattern is not a meme until it causes someone to replicate it, to repeat it to someone else."

The Internet has provided a new media to spread a meme.

PUBLICITY AND POPULARITY

Publicizing your blog can happen in several different ways, but it all boils down to reaching an audience. One very popular way is by linking your page to other personal blogs (A-list blogs or celebrity blogs) with comments. It is a way to spread the word about your existence. Get your site linked on a page such as popdex or blogdex.

The A-List

On many blogs, there are many common links that are just the same people, over and over. The term for this is the *A-lister*. These are the people everyone quotes from. They are the sites that other bloggers want to emulate.

CHRIS PIRILLO'S TIP

These are some of the memes on the Web. They include the Monday Mission, This or That Tuesday, The Friday Five, Saturday Scruples, and Participation Positives.
Monday Mission—www.promoguy.net
This or That Tuesday—www.ailurophile.com
Friday Five—fridayfive.org
Saturday Scruples—www.villasantiago.com
Participation Positives—
blog.orangeclouds.org/positives.html

Popdex

This is a self-styled "current-events/weblog/news-search engine." (The Popdex home page calls itself the *website popularity index*.) It crawls the Web and indexes 7,500+ Web sites and weblogs each day. By submitting your site to this service, it's possible to be linked on its top-40 page—a listing of the top 40 scored topics of the day. The URL is www.popdex.com.

Blogdex

If you have a topic you've written and it begins to be linked around the Web, perhaps on multiple and big name sites, you may find yourself on MIT's Blogdex page. This site features the top 25 most recent links in the blogging community. The URL is blogdex.media.mit.edu.

Google

Search Engines such as Google are just one way to have your blog put "out there." These can be a little more unreliable than being listed in a superdirectory such as Yahoo! or DMOZ because a search hit is usually random, and the reader may not be interested in what you have to say, regardless of the scintillating content. Even megadirectories have their flaws because a reader must often drill down by several topical levels to get to a page listing your blog.

Measurement Devices

Additionally, there are blog measurement tools, which can indicate the position your blog may occupy in the *blogosphere*. Sites such as Weblogs.com and Blogrolling.com have the ability to list how many times your peers have linked to your site and rank them accordingly. The URLs are www.weblogs.com and www.blogrolling.com.

Webrings

These are a method of linking related sites and have been around before there were even weblogs. Webrings allow you click forward or backward within a so-called ring of sites until eventually you can arrive back at your own site. This is a clever way to allow sites with related interests, such as cooking blogs or Civil War blogs, to link to one another easily.

EXTRA, EXTRA!

Want to read more about blogs in the news? Visit Blognews, Blogroll, and NetHistory for links to the most recent articles and media coverage online.

Popularity Contest

Blogging can also be viewed as one big exclusionary popularity contest with steel doors that can be very hard to break down. Faced with the sheer numbers of popular blogs, it might be easier to "complain about 'em" rather than "join 'em." Again, this goes back to the high school mentality most of us never truly grow out of, no matter how hard we might try. "If the popular kids are doing it, then I don't want any part of it." Not only is this attitude seen in the mainstream, directed at blogging in general, it can also be found in the blogging community, directed toward certain so-called A-list bloggers. Parody blogs often creep up in the blogworld. Blog comments are full of inside jokes and slams of the popular crowd. One thing to remember, however, is that if they are talking about you, they are *talking* about you. Vanity and blogging do go hand in hand.

> The word *blog* is under consideration for inclusion in the *Oxford English Dictionary. New York Times* language watcher William Safire has written about them. UC Berkeley's Graduate School of Journalism offered a course in weblogging for the Fall 2002 semester. Several media agencies promote reporters' blogs in their standard news portals.

Comments

Browsing any number of blogs, you'll find a commenting system in place. And where there's smoke, there's fire. Or in this case, where there is the ability to comment, there will be comments. Bloggers, by nature, offer their opinions on topics they believe to be important.

Why do we want comments? If the blogger is prepared to offer their opinion to the world, often they are willing to see opinions offered up in turn. The Internet has often been referred to as the ultimate democracy: Any person with the means to get on the World Wide Web has the ability to have a voice, and it can be as loud as the effort they put into expressing it. Comments are a natural extension of this online democracy. For every voice and opinion and blog out there, hundreds and thousands more will find a way to agree or disagree.

Awards and Rewards

Although comments provide bloggers with oft-desired recognition, attention, and adoration, several blog-related awards have also emerged to give credit where it is due. Most notable are the Bloggies (bloggies.com). In 30 categories, the Bloggies have handed out awards voted on by peers. There is also a parody-based Anti-Bloggies (antibloggies.com) with categories such as most updated blog, most caffeinated blogger, worst abuse of the third person, and most banal content. In June of 2002, yet other awards, "the Bloggys" (bloggys.kevins-blog.com) emerged. These are awarded on a monthly basis in five categories.

Blognews Blogroll—blognewswire.net/blognews.html
NetHistory—nethistory.urldir.com/media/

Blog Parties

People who blog tend to make close, lasting friendships with others in the blog world. Blog authors share things in their daily journals that even those closest to them might never know. Because the communication can be so deeply personal, the relationships that grow from reading journals tend to develop that way from the very start. It isn't as though you are talking to a complete stranger after knowing so many intimate details about the author. And even with blogs that aren't so personal in nature, like-minded interests tend to create bonds and spark conversations between author and reader. Several regional blog meetings and gatherings, as well as technology conventions, have developed to bring bloggers together in real life. Some of these are official gatherings, and others are impromptu "let's all meet at…" occasions.

By visiting Blog MEETUP, users are able to register and find other bloggers in their own cities. Local meetings are held for each group a few times a year, and email notices are sent to the participants to remind them when and where a few weeks in advance. Several larger metropolitan areas have their own Web sites and/or blogs to keep the locals in touch and plan events. Every March in Austin, Texas, people gather for South by Southwest (SXSW), a conference and festival of events for entertainment and related media industry professionals, including the film industry and interactive media. Several members of the blogging community attend SXSW and provide live commentary throughout the event and social schedule. Gnomedex, a technology-based conference sponsored by Lockergnome, is also a popular meeting spot. And in August 2002, several bloggers in and outside of the United States gathered in Las Vegas for Blog-Con. In its own words, "Blog-Con is not really a Conference, it's not really a Convention. Blog-Con is a Convergence, a gathering, a meet and greet fest for bloggers."

Blog MEETUP—blog.meetup.com
SXSW (South by Southwest)—www.sxsw.com
Gnomedex—www.gnomedex.com
NYC Bloggers—www.nycbloggers.com
H-Town Blogs—h-townblogs.blogspot.com
DFW Blogs—www.dfwblogs.com
Blog-Con—www.blogcon.com
D.C. Bloggers—groups.yahoo.com/group/weblogs-social-dc/

The Blogging Glass House

In this information age, it is easy for your friends, family, employers, and detractors to find out more about you than you want them to know. More than one blogger has been fired for talking about their bosses or companies in a negative light. Parents have discovered their children's secrets. The wives of married men have discovered more about the husband's lover than the person behind the blog counted on. A blogger never knows who is reading his or her site. It is unwise to divulge too many personal details. What may seem to be mundane details about daily routine and physical location could attract unwanted attention. There are several ways around this.

Password the Blog

With a password, only the people who you want in can get in. Strict control over access can offer a sense of security. However, this also limits your involvement in the blogging community. It will be difficult for others to discover your blog and get to know you if they are greeted by a password prompt instead of welcoming words.

Nom de Plume

A pen name will help insure that no one can surf to Google.com, type in your name, and instantly tie you to your blog. In fact, after being "discovered," quite a few bloggers have closed up shop and reemerged anonymously at a different URL with a different site name. The author at bloganon.com recently closed her original blog after her mother happened across it. "Jessica" describes herself as newly bisexual and did not want her mother subjected to public discussion about her private, daily life. Now she has the freedom to talk about whatever she wishes to without the threat of it being brought up over Sunday dinner or risk parental disapproval over how she chooses to live her life.

KEEPING UP WITH THINGS

Want to be notified when your favorite blog updates? Register at bloglet.com and receive a daily digest of recent content from your favorite blogs via email! (Please note, a blog must be registered in order to subscribe to it. You will need only an email address to subscribe.) Don't have a favorite blog yet? Then just sign up for updates from the Top Sites at bloglet.com instead.

Blogging by nature has no set rules. Blog content emerged as an alternative to the traditional media sources online. The tone of most blogs is "personal conversation," rather than official commentary. So how does one go about imposing etiquette guidelines on a community that has thumbed its nose at tradition from the start?

In *The Weblog Handbook: Practical Advice on Creating and Maintaining Your Blog* (Perseus Publishing, 2002), author Rebecca Blood states, "In general, etiquette in the weblog world is based on the same principals as it is in the physical world. Common sense and courtesy rule the day."

Just as in the early newsgroups on the Internet, the more popular the blog, the more likely the voice of dissent will rear its ugly head. It is common for blog authors to experience "trolls" and "flames" in their comments. These are negative messages by visitors who only wish to insult, provoke, and/or personally attack the site owner. It is quite common to read the advice "don't feed the trolls" when online. If ignored, generally the person, or troll, will go away. If acknowledged, the author (and visitors to the site) can invite permanent bickering and upheaval. It is always best to take the high road in such instances—and never to attack another blogger publicly yourself.

Popular blog authors might also encounter readers who are starstruck. These individuals usually have nothing to add to the general conversation other than "look at me" and "be my friend." It is best to keep blog comments focused on the subject at hand, rather than constant praise of the individual behind the curtain. Although notes of appreciation are always welcome and encouraged, constant praise can cross the line and cause the opposite reaction from its recipient.

Responsibility

When does commentary become plagiarism? The best advice is "cite your source." If the thoughts are not your own, do not claim them as such. If you are basing your blog entries on another blog entry, say so. Link to the original author in your entry. You would want to know whether someone else was talking about you, so it's only polite to offer the same courtesy in return. When citing a news article or online publication, state it as such. Information travels quickly on the Internet, and someone who is reading is likely to know it is not your own work. Your credibility depends on your honesty.

Linking

Another major source of bickering is whether to notify a site author when you are linking to their site on your own. (Opinion on this is split 50-50.) If you have content on your site that may be objectionable to the linked party, the question arises: Will they want their name tied to yours? The act of linking is generally thought of as a compliment. However, the common courtesy would be to email and ask.

With the invention of services of blog link list management systems (blog rolling.com and freshblogs.com), combined with the ease of link additions and the sheer volume of links, it is less likely that the practice of emailing for link permission will continue. It is a common courtesy but not a required one.

BLOG, TO GO!

Meryl.net has written a wonderful tutorial on making your blog available to PDA users. It includes instructions for creating a PDA-friendly template and registration with AvantGo.com, making your blog truly readable from anywhere!

For instructions, go to http://www.meryl.net/articles/archives/000857.php.

ANTIBLOG SENTIMENT

People who have never owned a blog of their own are more likely to roll their eyes at a friend who stops to record a life moment than to dig deeper beyond the surface and examine the phenomenon and what drives it for themselves. And with so many blogs already out there, a beginner doesn't even know where to turn first. Suddenly feeling overwhelmed, it might be easier to complain about the unknown and to load a news outlet in their browser instead.

Complaints generally center on the vanity issue. What could be so important about *your* life that *I* will want to read about it on a daily basis? The phrase "old spam every day versus steak twice a week" is often heard.

Media outlets are the worst critics. It's true that some bloggers' writing skills leave something to be desired. But is there more behind the complaints? There is a common belief among the bloggers that blogs are a threat to the mainstream media. Suddenly, anyone can be "published." The degree on the wall or years spent in the journalism trenches are no longer factors. Blog authors are not competing for market share or advertising dollars. If you can type it, you can publish it and have a daily audience of hundreds, even thousands.

Web logging, or blogging, looks to be the fastest-growing hobby on the Internet, and I've been studying the phenomenon to death. I intend to do my own blog, but I wanted to have a better understanding of what constitutes a really great blog.

The way I see it, there are two kinds of blogs. Authors promoting books or newsletters can set up faux blogs or periodicals posing as blogs to get attention from other bloggers. To me, the true blog is a legitimate journal of day-to-day life. I've deconstructed over 100 such blogs. This analysis led me to produce some formulas for a successful blog. Here are my Eight Rules for the Perfect Blog.

1. **The Right Attitude.** Make it clear that you spend the day, week, or month sitting on your rump reading other blogs instead of looking for work. Or if you actually work, make it clear that you are writing the blog at work because you hate your job.

2. **Community.** Prove that you're a dedicated blogger by citing at least five other blogs that you just read. Praise them ad nauseum. Then comment on links that their authors discovered and cut and paste these links to your blog. If you're trying to jazz up your blog, italicize the text that you cut from the other blog. Add a sentence or two as to why each link is so cool. Teasers work well too. "Can you believe this?" or "What is he thinking?" or "How can anyone be so wrong?"

3. **Humility.** Blog daily. If you miss a day, use the next day's entire blog entry to apologize profusely. Explain in detail the fascinating adventure you had that caused you to miss a day of blogging. Make sure to rave about how great blogging is and why everyone should blog and how blogging will change the world.

4. **Rich Language.** Show that you're an independent, free spirit by adding a lot of profanity to your text. Profane headlines and general cursing show people that you are an autonomous thinker not bound by the silly conventions of society—those lousy rules that make you have to work for a living when you should be getting a check from the government just for being alive!

5. **Jargon.** Pepper your text with words such as *screed, grok, gonzo, meme,* and other bloggerisms to show that you are a hip and with-it blogger. Women bloggers should use the word *sister* a lot.

6. **Controversy.** Make sure your blog page has a list of your favorite bloggers and hound them to put your blog on their lists. If you get removed from someone's list, make a public outcry and demand to be returned to the place of honor or threaten to take the other blogger's name off your list. Go through this routine weekly with someone.

7. **Humor.** Give your blog a cute name, perhaps even using a pun. "Blog on the Run." "Blogday Afternoon." "Bloggin' Fool." "Hot Blog and Relish." Or

name the blog after a title of a great novel: "The Sound and the Fury," "The Naked and the Dead." In a pinch, use "My Blog."

8. **Specialize.** If you want to trumpet the fact that you're a rockin' techie, constantly harp on Linux and link to the cool scripts you've written. Link to a lot of anti-Microsoft diatribes. Use 6-point type and no page breaks, so the blog looks like source code when it's displayed on the screen. Add color to make it even more unreadable. Use the word *warez* now and again.

To promote the idea that you're an artiste, use dark gray sans serif type on a black background. Put the links in red. Put a lot of poetry in the blog. In fact, write the whole blog in poetry. Tell others to contribute. Run everything you get.

If you're a woman who hates men, make sure to use a lot of odd misspellings, such as *womyn* and *grrls*, to let men know that you hate them. Make lame comments about how all men are pigs in case they still don't get it. Moan about your life and blame it on men. Reference your miserable high-school years. Name names.

If you are a lunatic fan who has fallen in love with a rock singer, actress, or actor without ever meeting him or her, your blog should contain a lot of pictures of the target of your affection—possibly nothing but pictures. Go on and on about how hot the person is. Do yourself a favor and avoid showing pictures of the secret hidden-in-the-closet shrine you made.

Finally, for all bloggers, consider using a cat name—Snowball, perhaps—as your own.

SUMMARY

No matter what you might think of the blogging concept it's now obvious that it is here to stay in the many forms it has taken. And while blogs about cats might trivialize its importance, the specific blogging software that has been developed is now a mainstream product. It can be used for many purposes, classic blogging only being one of them. In fact, blogging tools are part of the evolution of software and the Internet. While there is a social aspect to blogging its real contribution are the new tools that can easily be used by everyone for all sorts of things. Try them out yourself.

16
STREAMING MEDIA

Streaming media is a catchall term. It includes the software to distribute media files, as well as the files themselves. Audio and video files created specifically for the Internet are streaming media. So are the presentations that include them. Streaming media can be traditional, such as Internet radio stations, or completely new. An example would be distance learning courses with audio, video, and slide presentations.

Virtually every computer sold today includes multimedia components for high-quality video and audio playback. With your computer (and streaming media), you can listen to radio stations from around the world, watch movie previews, and even earn a degree from a distant university.

Streaming media has progressed by leaps and bounds in the last few years. RealNetworks pioneered the concept in 1994. What began as distorted, low-quality audio streams has now progressed to CD quality audio and full-screen DVD video. This has come about rapidly. In contrast, it took radio and television a generation to establish themselves as communications mediums.

Of course, none of this could have happened without the amazing foresight of the original architects of the Internet and some incredible work from a handful of companies. A chain of events was set in motion that has led to the media-rich Internet we enjoy today.

BACKGROUND

Originally, the Internet was conceived of as a way for people to share research data. Not just any people, but research types, government agencies and universities. These researchers, being clever people, decided to try to share much more than just text. It wasn't long before people devised methods for sharing other types of digital information, such as graphics, photos, and audio files. As the Internet became a "common man's" tool and access was shared with the masses, these methods of sharing images had some drawbacks. The fundamental problem was in the size of the files. The images people wanted to share were many times larger than text files. These large files took a long time to upload and download. In some cases, the files were so large that sharing them on the Internet was impractical.

Even if the file size wasn't a problem because people were willing to wait, the situation was far from optimal. It didn't make sense to download a complete audio file before you could listen to it. For example, if you wanted to listen to the first five minutes of an hour-long lecture, you had to download the *entire hour* before listening to any of it. It became clear that a new method of distributing media files was necessary.

WHAT IS STREAMING?

Streaming offers a new approach to the tedious wait for an entire file to download: the file is played back as it arrives. This approach eliminated the time spent waiting for files to download. If you didn't like what you heard, you could stop the download. Pretty simple. It was a lot like Costco's food samples: Try it; see whether you like it. Why invest the time in an audio file that you don't like? The idea was brilliant.

Streaming is different from downloading. Downloaded files are stored on the hard drive before they are played. Streaming media players store a small amount of data known as a *buffer* on the hard drive. The buffer ensures smooth playback. Streaming media files are discarded as they are played. This provides the people who own the content with a level of security, because the entire file is never stored on the computer. Downloaded files can easily be duplicated and shared.

Streaming also enables users to control their viewing experience. If users want to rewind or fast-forward through a presentation, they can do so with traditional VCR-like controls. Streaming media can also be broadcast so that many people can "tune-in" to the same event.

Streaming can be combined with other Internet technologies to create interactive entertainment or educational presentations. The global reach of the Internet means that broadcasts can be worldwide without the prohibitive cost of satellite technology. And with most streaming media platforms offering free versions of their software, anyone can become a broadcaster.

STREAMING MEDIA TODAY

The combination of a worldwide distribution mechanism and high-quality media files make streaming media an extremely powerful new medium.

- Consumers use streaming media to share media files, such as videos of family events.

- Businesses use streaming media to communicate with their customers and as an internal communications tool.

- Educational institutions use streaming media both on campuses and for distance learning applications.

- Government agencies use streaming media much as businesses do, for internal and external communications.

Streaming media is everywhere on the Internet, and streaming media usage continues to trend upward. These days, it's hard to find a commercial Web site that doesn't include some form of streaming media.

Internet Radio

Thousands and thousands of Internet radio stations are available to the discerning listener. Some of these are Internet rebroadcasts of terrestrial signals (regular AM and FM radio stations), and others are Internet-only stations. Terrestrial stations can extend their audiences beyond the limits of their transmitters by streaming their signals. Internet-only stations also do not need a costly and often unavailable FCC license to broadcast. Internet-only stations can also offer personalized programming to their listeners, reaching more people via the Internet than they would with a terrestrial station.

Entertainment Sites

Entertainment sites, like the radio sites, may have programming rebroadcast from an existing source (television shows or movie previews) or with programs created specifically for the Internet. Entertainment sites often offer supplemental content to existing broadcast content. For example, the reality shows (the rage at the moment) may be broadcast for an hour a week on television but can offer additional coverage (sometimes up to 24 hours a day) on Web sites for the fans that can't get enough.

Internet-only entertainment sites create their own content, often combining the interactive capabilities of Internet technologies with traditional storytelling. Others offer a platform for independent artists who might not have a chance to break into traditional media outlets.

News Sites

News sites have been particularly successful. In fact, many of the largest news events have been huge catalysts for streaming media. The live broadcast of President Clinton's testimony and the news surrounding the World Trade Center attacks in 2001 were huge streaming media events.

Wednesday, September 12, 2001, was the single biggest day in traffic to the Real Broadcast Network (RBN), which peaked with over 113,000 concurrent users and 11.4 million accesses to content. RBN is the content delivery network of RealNetworks and streams content from ABC, NPR, and other news outlets. Channels that offer programmed content to RealPlayer users hit all-time highs as well, with the average usage for the news channels on September 11 and 12 (including ABC, CNN, FOX, and NPR) up more than 1000% above normal usage levels.

News and streaming media are a perfect match. Using streaming media allows news outlets to provide additional information that may not make the live broadcast, or in the case of live events, to offer video not seen on regular television due to time constraints.

Subscription Services

Subscription services are now offered on many streaming media sites. Pioneered by the adult content industry, they continue to be hugely profitable. Until recently, however, subscription services have been the exception to the rule.

People have been reluctant to pay for online content for a number of reasons. The biggest complaints are the inferior quality and the programming. However, stream quality has improved in the last few years, and many consumers are now connecting to the Internet at broadband speed. More important, programming executives are also improving the online experience by providing better content.

Virtually all the major U.S. sports organizations have exclusive subscription programming available on the Internet. A number of the major television networks are offering Internet exclusives. The major movie distributors are said to be making plans, as well.

The attitude is similar to that of the cable television industry in the early 1980s. It's difficult to say at this point where it all will lead. Streaming media subscription services are still at an early stage. It's expected that people will eventually get more media from the Internet and perhaps pay for it.

HOW STREAMING MEDIA WORKS

Streaming media works like a Web page from a user's perspective. Click on a link, and the video or audio begins to play a few moments later. This may appear in the browser window or in a separate streaming media player. Though the functionality appears similar, there are fundamental differences.

When a browser requests a Web page, it requests the code to display the page, then downloads all the graphics, photos, and animations needed to display the page. If some files take longer to download, the browser may wait for the files to be completely downloaded before displaying the page. No doubt you've seen this. (It's most noticeable when traffic on the Internet is heavy.)

Streaming media does not have the luxury to wait. The whole point of streaming media is to provide a continuous audio or video experience. Delays, stutters, or gaps in the playback are unacceptable. Streaming media files are sent in *real time* (meaning as it happens). The amount of data sent in real time is determined by the user's connection to the Internet, called *bandwidth*.

Bandwidth

When it comes to streaming media, bandwidth is everything. For a successful streaming media experience, the *bit rate* of the file being streamed must not exceed the client's bandwidth. In fact, streaming media files should have a bit rate significantly lower than the maximum connection rate. (Imagine trying to suck too thick a milkshake through a very small straw.)

Internet bandwidth is never constant. Often, the bandwidth available is less than the maximum advertised. For that reason, it's best to be conservative in the creation of streaming media files. Table 16.1 lists some common connection speeds and their theoretical maximum bandwidths, along with recommended streaming media bit rates.

In addition to the user's bandwidth, the streaming media provider must be concerned with total bandwidth usage. For example, an Internet radio stream may be as slim as 20 Kbps. If 100 clients want to listen to the same stream simultaneously, the server needs 2,000 Kbps, or just under 2 Mbps of bandwidth. This is well over a T1's total connectivity to accommodate all of them.

Now imagine a full-screen, DVD-quality movie being streamed at 750 Kbps. If 10 people try to watch this on an office network (intranet), the network would grind to a halt. Those same 10 people would clog up an entire 10-Mbps connection to the Internet. These are things to be considered in

TABLE 16.1   **INTERNET CONNECTION METHODS AND DATA RATES**

Connection Type	Theoretical Bandwidth in kilobits per second (kbps)	Recommended Streaming Media Bit Rate
28.8 Modem Dial-up	28.8Kbps	20Kbps
56K Modem Dial-up	37Kbps**	34Kbps
ISDN Line	64Kbps	50Kbps
xDSL Line (including ADSL, RDSL, etc.)	Typically 256Kbps	225Kbps
Cable Modem	Typically 384Kbps	300Kbps
T1 Line	1.54Mbps	300-500Kbps
Intranet	10Mbps	500-750Kbps or above

** 56K modems only achieve maximum data rates by compressing the data being transmitted. Since streaming media is already heavily compressed, the maximum data rate is substantially lower than 56Kbps.

offering this sort of programming on the Internet. Streaming media systems can be simple or very complex, but they are all built from the same building blocks.

STREAMING MEDIA SYSTEM COMPONENTS

There are different streaming media systems, but they all share common underlying architecture. Media files are created and converted to a streaming format with a streaming media *encoder*, streamed to users by a streaming media *server* and played back on the user's computer using a streaming media *player*.

Encoders

Raw audio and video files are too large to be streamed across the Internet. Encoding software converts raw media files to a format that can be streamed by reducing the file size while attempting to maintain as much of the original quality as possible. To give you an idea of the task an encoder faces, consider the bit rate of CD audio. When audio is digitized, it is *sampled* 44,100 times a second, each sample being 16 bits long, one sample each for the left and right sides of a stereo signal.

$$44,100 \times 16 \times 2 = 1,411,200 \text{ bits per second, or } 1,378 \text{ Kbps}$$

So to stream a CD audio file to a dialup modem user, the bit rate has to be reduced from 1,378 Kbps to 34 Kbps, a ratio of 40:1. This is no simple task. Along the way, some tough compromises have to be made. The encoder attempts to maintain the highest possible quality level while satisfying the bit rate requirements. Additionally, the encoder packages the streaming media files to make them more loss resistant. After files have been encoded, they must be placed on a streaming server to be made available to the public.

Servers

Streaming media servers are the software applications to stream files to streaming media players. They are similar to Web servers. They service requests from multiple clients. They differ because the streaming media server maintains a connection to each client until its individual streaming media presentations are finished. This persistent connection enables interactive control over the presentation.

Streaming media servers distribute both live files and archived files. (These archived files are also called *on-demand* files.) During live broadcasts, the server maintains a connection to the encoder providing the live stream. Just as streaming media servers can stream to multiple players, they can also receive streams from multiple encoders. Some streaming media servers also offer advanced features, such as advertisement insertion, digital rights management (DRM), playlist generation and management, and a host of other management features.

Streaming media servers can handle thousands of simultaneous connections. The CPU of the service determines the maximum number of simultaneous requests that can be handled, along with the amount of RAM the server has, the bit rates of the files being streamed, and the total bandwidth available to the streaming media server.

Players

A streaming media player is software. This is what communicates with the streaming media server and displays the streaming media files on the user's machine. A streaming media player can function as a standalone application or be embedded in a Web page. Streaming media players generally offer control. They let the user pause or rewind the stream. Some players have additional features to allow the user to record or bookmark favorite streams and adjust the parameters of audio and video playback.

Most Internet users have at least one streaming media player installed on their systems. Some have more. All the streaming media players are free. Users can download and install a free player in the event they encounter a stream they can't play. Until recently, most streaming media systems required a proprietary player. Viewing QuickTime movies required a QuickTime player. Windows Media files required a Windows Media player. RealAudio and RealVideo files required RealPlayer. This all changed with the release of the universal RealOne Player v.2.0, which is able to play all major streaming media formats. In addition, the Helix Universal Server from RealNetworks streams all the major formats, as well as other data types (see The Helix Community sidebar later in this chapter).

PROTOCOLS AND CODECS

Streaming media encoders, servers, and players must have a way to communicate with each other. They are able to convert files to and from the streaming media format. This is where *protocols* and *codecs* come in.

Protocols are a set of rules to determine how communication takes place between software applications. There are a number of different streaming media protocols in use, such as RTSP (Real Time Streaming Protocol), RTP (Real Time Protocol), and MMS (Microsoft Media Server). They are similar to HTTP, the protocol used to deliver Web pages, but optimized for streaming media delivery.

Codecs are the software the encoder and player use to encode and decode the streams (the word *codec* is a contraction of *coder-decoder* or *compressor-decompressor*). Codecs use all sorts of tricks to reduce the file size of raw media files. These range from simple (reducing the screen size of a video file or reducing the frequency response of an audio file) to advanced mathematical manipulations designed to model the way we perceive audio and video.

Audio codecs use loudness to determine what is most important in a file. Loud sounds are encoded, and quiet sounds are deemed less important. Video codecs use motion as a determinant. Things that don't move are not re-encoded from frame to frame; only things with movement are. When there is a lot of motion in the frame, the codec must attempt to encode the whole frame. This is not always possible at lower bit rates.

Sometimes the file size compression is so drastic that the quality is compromised. Codecs are by no means perfect. Streaming media codecs are known as *lossy codecs* because a certain amount of the data must be discarded to keep the minimum file size. However, codec technology is improving all the time. And in conjunction with increased bandwidth, the quality of streaming media will continue to improve.

STREAMING MEDIA PLATFORMS

The earliest streaming media experiments were done using the MBONE (multicast backbone), a network of highly specialized servers on the Internet. Participating in these broadcasts required a fairly high level of expertise and a high-powered computer. Another early technology was CU-SeeMe, developed at Cornell University, which allowed point-to-point video conferencing. However, it wasn't until RealNetworks released the first version of Real-Player that streaming media really caught on.

In the ensuing years, many streaming media companies came and went, some were bought and absorbed by other companies, and some just fell by the wayside. Although there are still a number of fringe streaming media players, the vast majority of the streaming media market is dominated by three platforms: RealNetworks, Microsoft's Windows Media Group, and Apple's QuickTime.

RealNetworks

RealNetworks (originally Progressive Networks) has the distinction as the first commercial entry into the world of streaming media. Its first release of RealAudio player was in 1995. Initially an audio-only application, RealPlayer quickly grew to include video, animation, and other data types.

The current version of RealPlayer is now RealOne Player. It has a fully featured Web browser and a *context pane* to the right of the video playback window that streaming media authors can use to provide contextual information about their streams. Included is TurboPlay for near-instant playback of audio and video content for broadband PC users, full-screen Theater Mode, DVD playback support, complete MP3 support, full-speed CD ripping and burning support, music library management, and access to more than 1,700 radio stations.

Windows Media

Microsoft originally licensed early RealNetworks streaming technology. They gave it a facelift and called it *NetShow*. As the competition between the two companies heated up, Microsoft released a completely new streaming platform and formed a department dedicated to streaming media. This is the Windows Media Technologies group.

The Windows Media Player is deeply integrated into the Windows operating system. Because of this, the Windows Media Player rarely needs to be downloaded. In addition to running on standard PC computers, a version of the Windows Media Player also runs on Windows CE, its handheld device operating system.

Microsoft does not sell the Windows Media Player. It is available as a free download. The new player sports a new look and extensive feature set that includes CD ripping and burning; music library management, including dynamic playlists; and DVD and high-definition video playback capabilities, as well as 5.1-channel surround audio.

QuickTime

Apple has offered multimedia capabilities in its computers longer than anyone else but was a late entry into streaming media. QuickTime movies used to be delivered with a *progressive download* technology.

In progressive download technology, the entire file is downloaded to the user's hard drive. The playback begins when enough of the movie has been downloaded so that playback can be uninterrupted. Progressive download technology is suitable for short-form entertainment (songs or movie trailers) but is not a true streaming technology. There is no user control and live broadcasts are impossible.

QuickTime released a streaming server because of these shortcomings. It also made its server software open source, so anyone could download the source code and modify it. The QuickTime player can be downloaded for free, but to encode or edit files, you must purchase QuickTime Pro.

THE STREAMING MEDIA PROCESS

Installing the various components of a streaming media system is only half of the equation. "Streaming media" also refers to the files that are streamed. These files have to be created.

Streaming media files can be created from scratch or from preexisting content, such as a CD or videotape. They can be broadcast live or encoded for later broadcast or *on-demand* streaming. No matter what sort of streaming media you create, the process breaks down into four basic steps: creation, encoding, authoring, and serving.

Creation

This is where the original audio and video files are created. It can be as simple as a microphone and a tape recorder or as lavish as a multicamera shoot on a sound stage. Creating raw material for streaming media presentations is the same as any other broadcast medium. The higher the production values, the better the end product is going to look.

In addition to audio and video animation and still images, other unique data types, such as codecs, can be included. Support for these unique data types varies between different platforms.

You can record your audio and video either directly into your computer or to an intermediate format, such as videotape. It's usually a good idea to record to both so you have a backup, should either method fail. Recording audio or video into your computer is called *capturing* or *digitizing*. The quality of the capture is dictated by the quality of the raw media and the sound card (or video capture card). The better the capture, the higher the quality of the file will be.

Audio

Audio content is straightforward to produce. There's no reason your streaming audio files shouldn't sound professional, for a number of reasons:

- Good audio equipment is cheap.
- Audio is malleable.
- Audio codecs do a great job at low bit rates.

If you're producing your own audio content from scratch, there are tools you should invest in. A good microphone is essential, and a small mixing desk is also very helpful. You can use the sound card that comes with your multimedia computer. (Although investing in a professional-quality sound card is a good idea, if you can afford the cost.)

The most important aspect to audio production is the level at which you record your audio files. All audio recording hardware and software comes with meters to set the recording levels. Make sure you record your audio as loud as possible but without distortion.

There are a number of audio tools to optimize this. They are available in both hardware and software versions. (A full discussion of all the tools at your disposal is beyond the scope of this chapter. If you're serious about audio production, consider purchasing a book dedicated to the subject. Several are listed at the end of the chapter.)

Video

Video content is tougher to produce than audio content. The reasons are the opposite of why audio is easy:

- Video equipment is expensive.
- Video is difficult to manipulate.
- Video codecs have to be extra savage to achieve the desired bit rates.

The bad news is that video equipment is expensive. The good news is the prices have dropped drastically in the last few years, with quality improving. A good quality DV (digital video) camera can be purchased for under $2,000. A professional-quality tripod is crucial. You should also invest in a small, portable lighting kit and some reflectors. Video quality is completely determined by the amount of light available. If you control the light, you control the quality of your streaming video files.

Try not to move the camera when shooting video for the Internet. Video codecs use motion in the frame to determine what is important and what to encode. If you move the camera, everything in the frame moves, which makes it difficult for the codec to determine how to encode the frame. Pans, zooms, and tilts should be avoided if at all possible. Whatever you do, don't try to shoot without a tripod. Even the steadiest camera operator can't hold a camera absolutely still, and the smallest amount of motion makes it more difficult for the video codec.

Once you've shot and digitized your video, you'll have the opportunity to edit and/or process it in a video-editing program. You can cut out sections of the video you don't want and adjust the overall quality of the video. However, video processing is somewhat limited. You won't be able, for instance, to make the narrator in your video brighter without making everything in the frame brighter. This is why it is so important to light your subjects correctly when initially shooting the video.

Video editing programs also offer lots of fancy editing options, such as wipes, dissolves, and hundreds more. If possible, avoid using fancy edits. Keep the cuts between scenes clean and simple, because they encode better.

After you've edited and processed your file, you may need to *render* a new version. Rendering is simply writing the video out to a new file with all the edits and processing included. Some video editing programs allow you to render directly to a streaming media format. If your video editing program does not offer this functionality, you must render a master version before you can move to the next step, which is encoding your file.

Encoding

After you've created the raw media, you have to convert it to a format to be streamed. This is known as *encoding*. Encoding is done using the tools provided by the streaming media platform you're using. Some video and audio editing tools have streaming media encoding built in. The result should be the same either way.

RealMedia files are encoded using the RealSystem Producer and the Helix Universal Producer. Windows Media files are encoded with the Windows Media Encoder. QuickTime encoding is done using QuickTime Pro. The encoding software for all three major streaming media platforms is straightforward and easy to use. Essentially all encoding boils down to a few simple choices: choosing a bit rate, a screen resolution for video files, and the codecs to use.

 RealNetworks' Helix Universal Producer allows encoding in all three formats, making it easy to use RealAudio, RealVideo, as well as QuickTime, Windows Media, etc.

Choose a Bit Rate

Encoding streaming media files involves decisions based on your *target audience*. These decisions are based primarily on the bandwidth your target audience has. The idea is to create files that stream at bit rates low enough to reach your target audience without rebuffering. If you're trying to cater to people with differing bandwidths, you may choose to encode streaming media files at different bit rates to offer your audience a choice.

For example, you may broadcast video to dialup users at home and to people working at their offices with broadband connections. In this case, you might choose to encode a 20-Kbps file for the dialup users and a 100-Kbps version for broadband users. That way, you reach the largest possible audience and offer a higher quality experience to your broadband audience.

Choose a Screen Resolution and Codecs

After you settle on bit rates, the next choice is based on the content. For streaming video, the biggest decision is the screen size or resolution you want to offer. For a 20-Kbps stream, you'll want to encode at a much-reduced screen size, such as 160x120. At 100 Kbps, you can choose to offer a 240x180 or 320x240 screen size, depending on what type of content you're encoding.

All the encoding software tools enable you to choose a video codec. In general, you want to use the latest and greatest codec, but this might force your audience to upgrade their player software. For this reason, some people stick to legacy codecs until they feel most people have upgraded their streaming media players.

Another codec choice you must make is between a speech and a music codec for your audio. Speech content and music content are sufficiently different that codecs can be optimized for one or the other. Choosing the proper codec can make a world of difference to the audio quality.

Multiple Bit Rate and SureStream Files

With these, it is possible to fine-tune your streaming media files for each target audience. The problem you end up with is lots of files and too many links on your Web site. This may confuse the end-user and make file management a headache.

To alleviate this, both RealNetworks and Windows Media provide a mechanism to include multiple streams in a single file. These files are known as multiple bit rate (MBR) files in Windows Media parlance and SureStream files in the RealNetworks world.

Both MBR and SureStream files allow you to specify different audio and video codecs for each stream in the file. When a player connects to the server, it reports how much bandwidth it has available. The server then chooses the appropriate file to stream, based on this information. Only a single link is needed on the Web site, and only a single file has to be managed on the streaming server.

Another benefit of having multiple streams in a single file is so the server can "shift down" to a lower quality stream if bandwidth becomes constricted. For example, if you're watching a 300-Kbps MBR video stream and suddenly your bandwidth falls below that, the server can "switch" to a lower bit rate stream (say a 100-Kbps file). Although the quality would be lower, the player rebuffers, and the experience continues instead of dropping dead in its tracks.

Advanced Encoding Choices

In addition to the basic encoding choices you must make, there are also advanced encoding options that you can take advantage of to create better streaming media files. Some have to do with how the media is encoded, and others address how the media is preprocessed before it is encoded. Following are some advanced encoding options with a brief description of each.

- **De-interlace Filter:** Removes artifacts from video that result from interlaced (e.g., broadcast television) video being displayed on a noninterlaced (e.g., computer) monitor.

- **Inverse Telecine Filter:** Removes extra frames that are inserted into video content when film content is transferred to video.

- **2-Pass Encoding:** An encoding mode where the encoder makes two passes through the media file to determine how to encode the file. Results in a higher quality streaming media file but takes twice as long.

- **Variable Bit Rate (VBR) Encoding:** An encoding mode that is unsuitable for streaming video but results in higher quality encoded files.

There are other advanced encoding options available, but they are far beyond the scope of this chapter to discuss. For the most part, the presets available in the encoder will produce acceptable results, but if you really want to delve into the esoteric world of audio and video compression, there are a number of excellent books available, listed at the end of this chapter.

Authoring

Authoring your presentation means deciding how to present your streaming media files. The simplest method is to place a link on a Web page for the user to click on. This can launch a standalone *pop-up* player application or launch a Web page with a player embedded in it. If you decide to embed your player in a Web page, there is the option of using the controls with the player or creating your own and linking them to the player with JavaScript.

These methods work equally well. It's really a matter of how you want the presentation to look and function, and how much work you want to put into it. However, one concept common to all of them that is a bit tricky is the *metafile*.

Metafiles

The word *metafile* is a recent addition to our language. A metafile is a file that contains information about another file. In this case, the metafile contains the address of the streaming media file. Computer programmers refer to them as *pointers* because metafiles "point" to other files. They are necessary because of the way that browsers, servers, and streaming media players operate.

When you click on a Web page link, your browser sends a request to a server with HTTP, the protocol that Web servers use. Because streaming media files should be served from a streaming media server, we need a way to hand off control from the browser to the streaming media player, so that the streaming media player can communicate directly with the streaming media server. This is done with the metafile.

When a browser receives a metafile, it knows to hand it off to the appropriate streaming media player (or browser plug-in). The streaming media player opens the file and starts a separate connection to the streaming media server. In this way, the Web server and browser are kept completely separate from the streaming media, which is why you can still surf the Web while watching streaming media files.

Creating Metafiles

At their simplest, metafiles merely contain the location of the streaming media file. Each of the three streaming media platforms uses a slightly different syntax in their metafiles. Table 16.2 lists some sample metafile contents for each streaming media platform.

The samples are the simplest versions possible. Metafiles can also contain additional information and tags that control how the file is played back. For

| TABLE 16.2 | SAMPLE METAFILE CONTENTS |

Platform	Metafile Contents
RealNetworks	rtsp://www.myrealserver.com/myStream.rm
Windows Media	`<asx version="3.0">`
	`    <entry>`
	`        <ref href="mms://www.mywmserver.com/`
	`        myStream.wmv" />`
	`    </entry>`
	`</asx>`
QuickTime	rtsptext
	rtsp://www.yourqtserver.com/yourMovie.mov

instance, you can specify title and copyright information, how many times a stream should be played, or streams for different bandwidths.

Embedded Players

Sometimes it is preferable to embed the streaming media presentation in a Web page instead of launching the presentation in a separate player. This is often done because the streaming media provider wants to have control over the appearance of the player. Web page designers can design the space around the embedded player and keep the look and feel consistent with the rest of the Web site.

Embedded players can be placed in HTML tables or frames. The rest of the HTML page can be designed just as any other Web page is, using the same tools that designers are familiar with. Most Web page design tools now come with functionality built in that easily enables you to embed a streaming media player. Special code is used to embed a streaming media player in a Web page. This code communicates with either a *plug-in* or an *ActiveX control*, which is the embedded version of the streaming media player. Plug-ins and ActiveX controls are essentially the same thing but used for different browsers. Plug-ins are used for Netscape-based browsers, and ActiveX controls are used on Internet Explorer. Both enable you to embed all or part of a streaming media player inside a Web page.

The embedded player code is slightly different for the Netscape plug-in and the Internet Explorer ActiveX control. Luckily, you can combine the code for both the plug-in and the ActiveX control and end up with a Web page that works on most browsers. The following is an example of an embedded QuickTime player:

```
<object classid="clsid:02BF25D5-8C17-4B23-BC80-D3488ABDDC6B"
        width="160" height="136" >
  <param name="src" value="media/MyMovie_ref.mov">
  <embed src="media/MyMovie_ref.mov"
width="160" height="136" >
  </embed>
        </object>
```

The first line, the `<object>` tag, tells Internet Explorer that the code specifies an embedded object, and the `classid` attribute identifies the embedded object as a QuickTime player. The `width` and `height` attributes specify that the player is 160 pixels wide and 136 pixels tall. The `<param>` tag immediately following specifies the streaming media file location to the ActiveX control. The final `</object>` tag signifies the end of the embedded object code.

The `<embed>` tag contains the Netscape plug-in information, specifying the width and height of the player, as well as the location of the streaming media file. Internet Explorer ignores `<embed>` tags, and Netscape, in turn, ignores ActiveX tags. The embedded player code is similar for RealPlayer and Windows Media player, the most important difference being the appropriate `classid` attribute for the ActiveX control.

There are a number of optional tags that can be used when embedding media players. These vary slightly between the different players, but in general offer ways to control the appearance and functionality of the embedded player. Most if not all the functionality of the standalone players can be specified using these tags.

As with metafiles, each streaming media player offers slightly different functionality and uses different syntax for its embedded players.

Controlling Embedded Players Using JavaScript

Sometimes it is desirable to have a way for other objects on a Web page to interact with an embedded streaming media player. For example, imagine a Web page that displays pictures of different musical artists. It might be nice to have a song play automatically when an artist's picture is clicked. To do this, the browser needs to connect the images with the embedded streaming media player. This can be done using JavaScript.

JavaScript is a standardized programming language that enables the manipulation of objects inside a browser. JavaScript provides dynamic control without having to send requests back to the Web server. You can manipulate images, check entries in a form, and control embedded objects.

The amount of control you have varies between the different streaming media players. Each has a different set of *methods* that are used to control or extract information from the player. You can control playback by issuing *play*, *stop*, and *pause* commands. You can specify new files to be played or find out information about the current file, such as the title or author of a stream.

JavaScript isn't rocket science but does require a basic understanding of programming techniques. Simple JavaScript routines can be copied and pasted from one Web page to the next, but advanced JavaScript implementations require someone who is comfortable working with code. There are a number of excellent JavaScript references available if you'd like to find out more. You should also check the documentation for the platform you're working with.

Serving

Serving is the last step in the streaming media process. Your audience has no way of seeing your files until you place them on a server. Serving is, therefore, very important, because it is the last link between your content and your audience.

Serving streaming media files is basically a four-part process. First you *design* a network infrastructure, then *implement* it. Once in place, you must *maintain* your servers. Servers generate *log files* that list in detail every interaction with the server. This data can be used to *analyze* the infrastructure and traffic patterns. At some point, you may want to revisit your server architecture and implement a new design.

Designing your server architecture can be as simple as installing software and placing files on the server. If your serving needs are modest, there is no reason why a single server will not suffice. In fact, streaming media servers can coexist on the same computer as a Web server. Provided that you have enough bandwidth, a single server is able to serve thousands of streams simultaneously.

As your needs expand, you may want to add additional servers to handle higher traffic loads or to provide more reliability in case one server fails. If you're catering to a geographically dispersed audience, you may want to place servers at different locations or use different ISPs.

The demands of a streaming media system are similar to the demands of a large Web server architecture. If you plan on implementing a large streaming media system, chances are that you already have a sizeable Web server infrastructure that was designed and implemented by your network administrator. Chances are that this infrastructure can be used for your streaming needs. The main difference is that streaming media files are much larger and require more bandwidth than Web pages.

Once the streaming server architecture is up and running, all you have to do is place your encoded streaming media files on the server and link to them using a metafile. Each time a streaming media player requests a file, an entry is made into the server log file, detailing which file was requested, who requested it, and how long they listened to it. Streaming servers also maintain error log files. Each time an error occurs, an entry is made detailing what went wrong and when it occurred.

Streaming server log files are very important because they provide a window into your server performance, as well as a road map to where your programming efforts are best concentrated. By analyzing the data in the log files, you can determine which files are the most popular. With your error files, you can determine whether you need to add more servers or bandwidth or revisit your server architecture.

There are a number of streaming server log file analysis packages available. Additionally, because log file formats are relatively standardized, Web server analysis packages can also be used, although they won't do analysis specific to streaming media, such as the amount of time a user listened to a particular stream.

ADVERTISING

Given the expense of running a streaming media system, most commercial streaming media providers would like to realize some revenue from their streams. One way of doing this is via advertising. Streaming advertisements can be inserted before streams play, during stream playback, or after the requested stream has played. Banner ads can also be embedded in a Web page or streaming media presentation. For an effective advertising system, the ads must be rotated according to a set of rules. They must also be tracked so advertisers can be given a record of how many people actually saw their ads.

Digital Rights Management

Digital Rights Management (DRM) systems protect and manage the copyright of files. DRM systems provide this functionality by encrypting files and allowing playback only if the user has a valid license to do so. The terms of this license can be very flexible, offering free access, timed access, pay-per-view access, or any combinations thereof.

For example, you may offer a music track for people to download for playback on their computers, but you may not want them to burn it to a CD-ROM. Or you may allow a track to be downloaded for free but cease to play or "time out" after a given amount of time.

Streaming media files can be protected using DRM. The way it works is as follows:

1. The streaming media file is encrypted by the DRM application and placed on the streaming server.
2. The licensing information is placed on a DRM server.
3. If a DRM-protected file is requested from a streaming server, the user is directed to the DRM license server to acquire a license.
4. After the user acquires the license, the streaming media server serves the encrypted file, and the player plays the file according to the license terms.

For more information about DRM solutions, please refer to the respective manufacturer's Web sites.

THE STREAMING MEDIA BIBLE BY STEVE MACK

For more information on streaming media, *The Streaming Media Bible* (John Wiley & Sons, April 2002) is a good choice. It contains over 800 pages of need-to-know information, covering all aspects of streaming media. The book has separate sections dedicated to creation, encoding, authoring, and serving streaming media. It also has a complete section dedicated to live broadcasting on the Internet, as well as real-life case studies. Each section has an introductory chapter introducing the concepts covered in the section, followed by chapters packed full of valuable information.

LIVE BROADCASTING ON THE INTERNET

One of the great advantages of streaming media is the ability to do live broadcasts. Streaming live broadcasts is the same as creating on-demand streaming media files, with the important exception that you get only one shot at it. If something breaks, the broadcast stops. You don't get a second chance.

When broadcasting live streams, it is crucial to have backup systems in place. You should have two of everything, from the microphones and cameras all the way to the streaming servers. The one piece of equipment you don't have a backup for is sure to be the one that fails.

Live broadcasting places unusual demands on streaming media systems. Each stage in the streaming media process is affected. The most important thing to do is plan ahead. If you put a little extra thought into a live broadcast, you'll be prepared for the worst scenarios.

In the creation phase, you won't have the luxury of assembling your presentation one step at a time. Everything happens at once, so all your equipment has to be tested and ready to go. If you're broadcasting from a remote location, you have to make sure that adequate power, space, and connectivity are available.

Encoding live broadcasts should be the same as encoding on-demand files, although you may want to be extra conservative with your bit rates. Live events tend to attract larger audiences, which puts a strain on bandwidth conditions. Choosing a lower bit rate may prevent your streams from rebuffering.

Authoring live presentations should also be the same as on-demand presentations, but again you may want to simplify your presentation. There's a huge difference between 100 people looking at your Web page over the course of a day and 10,000 trying to load the same Web page all at once.

The same applies to your streaming media servers. The servers will be under greater strain than they are at any other time, because the entire audience will be connecting *simultaneously*. Besides the obvious bandwidth concerns, you also must ensure that your streaming servers are up to the task. You'll need to use load balancing to make sure the streaming loads are evenly distributed among your servers.

The most important thing to remember in a live broadcast situation is to test everything well in advance. You should test the on-site connectivity; test your encoders, your audio and video equipment, your servers, and your Web servers. Then test them all again, trying to simulate a heavy load if at all possible. The more you test, the better chance you have of identifying and solving problems before the actual event.

THE HELIX COMMUNITY

The Helix Community was started by RealNetworks to develop a comprehensive, standardized platform for digital media delivery. As part of the Helix Community, RealNetworks allows access to its source code under a variety of licensing options to allow individuals flexibility. For instance, new player releases on alternative platforms, such as Linux, had been delayed in the past because the employees at RealNetworks simply did not have the time or resources to do the work. With open source, people interested in providing for alternative platforms now have a means to do so.

As the number of devices that support streaming media increases, the programming resources necessary to support them all become burdensome. By allowing other companies and developers access to the code, RealNetworks is hoping the Helix platform will be widely adopted. Additionally, by opening the Helix platform to talented developers around the world, RealNetworks stands to benefit from their programming ideas and skills.

MPEG-4

MPEG-4 is an open standard developed by the Motion Picture Experts Group (MPEG) that combines digital television, interactive graphics, and interactive multimedia. It provides a framework for creating multimedia applications and presentations. The MPEG-4 standard covers a vast range of applications, one of which is streaming media. MPEG-4 includes audio and video codecs for use in streaming media applications, as well as specifications for delivering streaming media across a wide variety of networks. MPEG-4 includes methods for creating interactive presentations and DRM capabilities for protecting copyright.

As a standard, MPEG-4 is something of a double-edged sword. Standards take time to develop and, therefore, are rarely the best technology available. RealNetworks and Windows Media codecs already surpass those available in MPEG-4. On the other hand, the interoperability that comes with being a standard cannot be overlooked, particularly by manufacturing companies who don't want their hardware becoming obsolete.

MPEG-4 includes intellectual property from many major companies. So even though MPEG-4 is an open standard, those wishing to implement it are subject to licensing fees payable to the MPEG-4 licensing group. One notable example from a streaming perspective is the file format, which is based on the QuickTime file format.

MPEG-4 has yet to truly make a mark on the streaming media space, but the promise of true interoperability will probably win out in the end. Imagine authoring a single presentation that automatically scales from a full-screen presentation on a multimedia computer to a slide show on a cell phone, and you begin to realize the potential of MPEG-4. Both QuickTime and Real-Networks have pledged to support MPEG-4. (The Windows Media Group currently has no plans to support MPEG-4, even though some of their codec technology is included in the MPEG-4 standard.)

Non-PC Devices

The last few years have seen a number of non-PC devices appear on the market with streaming media capabilities. These include multimedia-enabled cell phones, set-top boxes that add Internet capabilities to televisions, and gaming consoles. The lines between these new gadgets continue to blur as more functionality is added with every new release.

This points to a bright future for streaming media, but not one without its challenges. It's wonderful that streaming media presentations can now be authored for a wide range of devices, but not all these devices will have the same capabilities. Some will be capable of rendering full-screen video; others will be capable of only slide shows or audio-only presentations.

SUMMARY

Regardless of the challenges ahead, streaming media usage continues to increase daily. More and more Web sites are adding streaming media, and the number of streaming media players installed is on the rise. As more and more devices become media-enabled, the role of streaming in today's media landscape will continue to expand.

REFERENCES

 There are a number of good books available if you'd like to learn more about streaming media.

Compression for Great Digital Video: Power Tips, Techniques and Common Sense. Ben Waggoner, CNP Books, August 2002. The "World's Greatest Compressionist" tells all in this essential encoding reference.

Digital Video and Audio Compression. Steven J. Solari, McGraw-Hill, March 1997. An in-depth reference for folks who really want to know how codecs work, although maybe a little difficult to locate new.

JavaScript Bible. Danny Goodman, John Wiley & Sons, 4th edition published April 2001. A must if you are serious about JavaScript.

Matters of Light and Depth. Ross Lowell. Lowell-Light Manufacturing, April 1999. A ten-year labor of love by one of the best in the business. This is a must-have for people who want to learn about lighting design.

Modern Recording Techniques. David Huber and Robert E. Runstein, Focal Press, 5th Edition, June 2001. A good, thorough book about audio production.

The MPEG-4 Book. Edited by Fernando Pereira and Touradj Ebrahimi. Prentice Hall PTR, July 2002. The place to start with the MPEG-4 standard.

Principles of Digital Audio. Ken Pohlman. McGraw Hill Professional, 4th Edition February 2000. The "bible" of digital audio.

QuickTime for the Web. Steven Gulie. Morgan Kaufmann, 3rd Edition June 2003. A great place to start for folks who want to learn about QuickTime. Entertainingly written.

SMIL: Adding Multimedia to the Web. Mary Slowinsky and Tim Kennedy. Sams, December 2001. The first seriously comprehensive book about SMIL.

Video Compression Demystified. Peter Symes. McGraw Hill Professional, December 2002. For those who really want to learn about compression technologies.

17
HOW A MODEM (REALLY) WORKS

Modems have become an integral part of everyday life. They are taken for granted. We use them daily perhaps without even thinking about it. We use them to connect to the Internet to surf the Web, read an email message, or send a fax. Modems are everywhere: in the malls and gas stations where we use our credit cards; ATMs for instant cash; vending machines even have modems to monitor product inventory; and in many other devices we come into contact with every day. Few of us are probably aware how big a role modems play in our modern lives.

A hint as to what a modem does can be found in the word itself. *Modem* is actually a contraction of two words: *modulate* and *demodulate*. In its simplest form, the modem modulates (or converts) your computer's digital signal because computers "speak" in binary 0s and 1s, represented by different voltage levels into an analog (tonal) signal that can be carried by standard copper twisted-pair telephone line to another modem. The analog signal is then demodulated back into its original digital form (Figure 17.1) for the benefit of the receiving computer. Your modem also handles the dialing/answering functions and controls data transmission.

The term *modem* has become a confusing one because marketing, DSL, and cable providers decided to call their digital network adapters (often called a *terminal adapter* or TA) and *cable modem termination system* (CMTS) by the same name as the traditional modulator/demodulator. In reality, these are three separate technologies. Their offspring and closely related cousins are united by the same term, which has muddled the terminology. It's not a good fit. In fact, it becomes downright confusing to try and explain without adding exceptions and confusing "well, except in the case of...". This chapter will attempt to cover the basics of a very large subject. For most of us, if a modem is working, that is enough. (Personally, I don't care what it's called, as long as it works.)

A basic, traditional "dial-up" modem is one that you purchase, plug into your machine (internally or externally), and connect to a plain, voice-grade

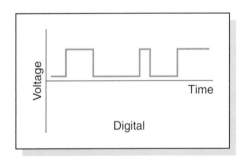
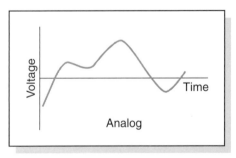

FIGURE 17.1 MODULATION—DIGITAL AND ANALOG.

(pick up the handset, dial, and speak) telephone line. This type of modem modulates your computer's outbound digital signal to an analog signal (from electrical impulses to beeps and burps) and then demodulates incoming signals from the analog signal to a digital one your computer can use. Modems are needed because the telephone line is looking for an analog signal while the computer generates a digital one.

Confusion came about when terminal adapters and cable modem termination systems were also referred to as modems without any distinction made between the various technologies or what they do and how they do it. This is further confused by the fact that your ISP will also use a device that is also called a modem. The reality is that some marketing guy decided that the public had enough trouble understanding what modems did in the first place, so why confuse them with more new (more technically accurate) terminology?

The *cable modem* and *DSL modem* are very different from a telephone line modem. It can be argued that they do not modulate/demodulate because they do not change the signal to/from an analog signal. Others have argued that, although the technologies differ, they both alter the original signal and then convert it back again.

Most discussions of modems that you may run across in the magazines and elsewhere usually describe the technology of a plain "telephone" modem. It's the traditional, basic flavor, describing a specific technology that everything evolved from. Unfortunately, even the generalities aren't always perfectly accurate for the full spectrum of all that is called modem. (It is like talking about ice cream without naming a flavor.)

Cable, DSL, and ISP Modems

The cable modem is a device that hooks a PC to a digital cable line. It is really an adapter because the digital data rate of your computer is not compatible with the cable system's digital system. A cable modem does not actually do any modulation or demodulation. It changes a digital signal from one format to another. A cable modem attaches through a standard Ethernet card in the computer. The cable modem attaches to the round coaxial cable (one that you typically attach to your television set). The cable modem will change the digital signal to a digital signal that the cable company's hardware can manipulate. At the cable company there will be other hardware to further refine and change the signal to interface with other services (i.e., telephone lines).

The digital network adapter for DSL has a variety of different technologies that also fall under the same nouveau moniker of modem. A DSL modem can be a *discrete multitone technology* (DMT), a *carrierless amplitude modulation* (CAP), or a *multiple virtual line* (MUL). The distinctions are minor, unless you're intensely interested in the subject. For the most part, all terminal adapters work the same, as they are all called DSL modems. A DSL modem is a device to convert a computer's digital signal into the type of digital signal used by the telephone company's equipment. They do not create an audible audio signal, but instead generate another digital signal.

The DSL technology uses the same existing twisted pair wires that your telephone uses. (Your telephone wires are always spoken of in pairs. All telephone technology today takes place over one pair of wires, unlike in the past where two pair were common.) The DSL modem is hooked to the phone line, just as a regular telephone modem is. Besides not making the switch from digital to analog, the major difference is what happens outside your home.

The ISP modem is a device that would more accurately be called a multiplexor or concentrator. Its function is to convert signals from great numbers of modems all receiving incoming digital signals into one large compressed signal for transmission over a telephone cable (these are called T1, T3, E1, ISDN, PRI, etc.) and, on the receiving end, split the signals into individual ones.

A Little Modem History

Modems can be traced back to the 1950s. They were developed to transmit data to North American Air Defense via telephone lines. The first commercial modems didn't appear until 1962, with the Bell 103 protocol developed by AT&T. The Bell System 103 Series was the first modem with full-duplex transmission and Frequency Shift Keying (FSK) modulation. It was capable of transmission rates up to 300 bits per second (bps). The follow-up product, the Bell 212 Series, boosted data rates to 1200 bps (that's four times faster than the previous product) and employed improved Phase Shift Keying (PSK) modulation.

1965 brought the development of the automatic adaptive equalizer. This invention compensated for differences in signal attenuation rates and smearing data symbols, and was necessary for creating the V.22bis standard at 2400 bps. This, along with the adaptive echo canceller, paved the way for higher data rates: 9.6 kilobits per second (Kbps) (1984), 14.4 Kbps (1991), 28.8 Kbps (1994), and 33.6 Kbps (1996).

Early modems were controlled entirely by dipswitches and buttons. The early command sets were chaotic. Each modem manufacturer had its own command set for its own modems, and these command sets were mostly incompatible with modems from other manufacturers. Hayes Microcomputer Products changed all of that when it started amassing much of the market share for personal computer modems. Hayes's early dominance influenced the rest of the industry to include command sets similar to the Hayes version.

Because Hayes modem commands begin by getting the modem's attention with the mnemonic "AT," it is not uncommon to hear the phrase "Hayes AT-compatible" or "AT-compatible" when referring to the standard AT command set.

Eventually, intelligent (or "smart") modems began to appear that were capable of being controlled via commands entered over the serial interface. Most newer modems are loaded with all sorts of features and functionality. This is because you have an intelligent modem. And how did your modem become so smart? Command sets. A modem's command set is a palette of instructions that allow the modem to activate its various features on demand, like dialing a particular phone number, activating data compression, selecting an error correction protocol, or preparing to transmit a fax. These commands can also be entered manually through your computer keyboard. Modems often store configuration settings and/or status information in S registers. Some modems have dozens of S registers. For example, if a modem is set to autoanswer on an incoming ring, the number of times the phone will be allowed to ring before answering is usually stored in the S0 register.

Other modem command examples include:

- ATD5555555555—dial telephone number 555-555-5555
- ATM0—turn off modem speaker
- ATL3—set maximum volume
- ATS0=3—respond after three rings to incoming calls (S register 0 is set to 3)

All of this may seem complicated, but it turns out to be less complex than it might at first appear. Recent standards have made modem command sets similar for basic commands like the ones shown. Moreover, your computer is able to identify your particular modem (brand and model) via the communication software being used. In the case of Windows operating systems, Windows knows what command to send your modem to perform a specific function because that modem has already been identified by the operating system during the modem's installation. This is why you can configure a connection in Windows mostly by clicking checkboxes and entering a phone number.

An exception to this is the "Extra Settings" field found in Modem Properties. This is where you could enter an advanced command. For instance, if you experience connection problems, your modem manufacturer might recommend that the modem be sent a special configuration command prior to any connection, perhaps to force a particular connection speed.

In 1997, there was a standards "war" between two competing versions of 56-Kbps technology. On one side was U.S. Robotics with x2; on the other side was Lucent Technologies, Motorola, and Rockwell with K56flex. Because there wasn't a unified standard, x2 modems and K56flex modems were not capable of connecting to the same servers at the increased data rate. In 1998, the V.90 56-Kbps standard was ratified, ending the 56-Kbps technology conflict, ensuring compatibility between various modems, and reaching the theoretical maximum for a modem given the capacity of the Public Switched Telephone Network (PSTN). The 56-Kbps modem standard was later tweaked and given additional functionality and greater upload speeds with the advent of the V.92 standard in 2001.

MODEM MILESTONES

 1962—AT&T manufactures the first commercial modem, the Bell System 103 Series.

1965—AT&T developed the automatic adaptive equalizer, which allows for data transmission at higher rates and cuts signal attenuation interference.

1976—U.S. Robotics founded the world's #1 selling modem brand (as of this book's writing).

1977—Dennis C. Hayes invented the PC modem and founds D.C. Hayes Associates, Inc.

1984—Modems capable of transmitting up to 9.6 Kbps (V.32); early V.32 modems cost more than the high-end PCs they were designed to work with.

1984—Initial guidelines for ISDN implementation appeared in CCITT, now known as ITU, recommendation I.120.

1989—DSL first developed, initially for purposes of transmitting video.

1991—Modems capable of transmitting up to 14.4 Kbps (V.32bis).

1994—Modems capable of transmitting up to 28.8 Kbps (V.34).

1996—Modems capable of transmitting up to 33.6 Kbps (V.34bis).

1997—U.S. Robotics (x2) and Lucent Technologies/Motorola/Rockwell (K56flex) introduced rival 56-Kbps standards, precursors to the V.90 standard.

1998—V.90 standard approved, replaces the two previously competing 56-Kbps technologies.

2001—U.S. Robotics Corporation shipped first V.92 modems fully tested for interoperability with major equipment providers.

Modern Technology Today

So why was the conversion from digital to analog and back again necessary? The raw digital data that one dial-up modem needs to send to the other modem consists of frequencies from zero to several hundred kilohertz (kHz), depending on the serial port speed. The PSTN was designed to carry analog voice signals from about 300 to 3400 hertz, so the raw data cannot be sent over the phone network. Back a few years, this would be the extent of the data conversions. But with today's ultra-fast modems the typical user's digital data undergoes more refinement. The analog signal then passes through the copper wires from the home to a central office (CO) where it undergoes an analog-to-digital conversion (meaning it is converted to a digital representation of the analog signal). So there are actually two different digital signals in the typical V.90 connection: the raw data and the phone company's digitized analog signal. This digitized signal is sent from your CO to another CO. It is then reconverted by your Internet Service Provider's (ISP's) digital server modem back into the original raw data sent by your modem.

In the reverse path, the server directs your ISP's raw digital data into the phone company's digitized representation of an analog signal. This data is passed from CO to CO and converted from digital to analog to be sent to your home. The server is digitally connected to the phone network, and there is only one digital-to-analog conversion in the path from the server to your modem's receiver. A V.90 modem is able to exceed V.34 speeds and it is why two analog modems cannot talk to each other at V.90 speeds (the faster modem would have to "drop down" to a slower speed to become compatible). V.90 and V.34 modem signals are illustrated in Figure 17.2.

Following is a simplified overview of what happens when you dial up to the Internet (Figure 17.3).

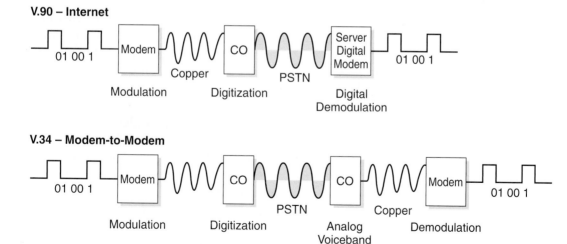

V.90 – Internet

V.34 – Modem-to-Modem

FIGURE 17.2   **V.90 AND V.34 MODEMS.**

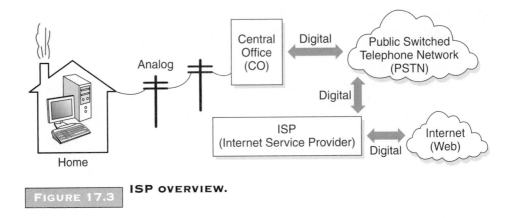

FIGURE 17.3

ISP OVERVIEW.

1. Your modem dials your ISP's access number (phone number) and establishes a connection.
2. Your modem modulates your computer's data into an analog-modulated signal.
3. The modulated signal is sent over the PSTN (and through various COs) to your ISP's server/modem.
4. The ISP's modem demodulates the analog signal back into its original form.
5. The ISP's server processes the data and forwards that information on to the specified Internet destination. That destination is embedded in the data using networking protocols. (More on these protocols later.)

How Modems Communicate

There are three basic methods that modems use to communicate with one another: full-duplex, half-duplex, and simplex. When two modems communicate with each other simultaneously (information is transmitted in both directions at the same time), the modems are operating in full-duplex mode (or sometimes called just *duplex*). When you surf the Web, your modem sends commands to the host server while simultaneously receiving Web page data based on those commands. (All current modems are full duplex.)

If two modems communicate one at a time but not simultaneously, the modems are operating in half-duplex mode; walkie-talkies operate in half-duplex mode. The primary application for half-duplex mode is faxing. Faxing relies mainly on one-way transmissions and was invented at a time when full-duplex modems of equivalent speed were very expensive.

When modems can transmit information in one direction only (like a one-way street), the modems are operating in simplex mode. Simplex mode is capable of sending files in a single direction and does so without employing any sort of error correction.

STANDARDS AND PROTOCOLS

Today, there are a number of industry standards that allow equipment from one manufacturer to communicate with equipment from another manufacturer. Telecommunications standards include Bell and ITU-T. The Bell standards (for example, Bell 103 and Bell 212A) have been followed primarily in the United States and are, relatively speaking, obsolete. The ITU-T (International Telecommunications Union Telecommunication Standardization Sector), formerly known as CCITT, covers international standards followed worldwide. All the standards prefixed with "V" are ITU-T standards. For example, the latest modulation scheme is V.92.

STANDARD DEFINITION

V.8–Covers the initial handshaking process.

V.17 fax—For making facsimile connections at 14,400 bps, 12,000 bps, 9,600 bps, and 7,200 bps.

V.21—For modems operating in asynchronous mode at speeds up to 300 bps, full duplex, on PSTNs.

V.22—For modem communications at 1,200 bps, compatible with the Bell 212A standard observed in the United States and Canada.

V.22bis—For modem communications at 2,400 bps. Includes an automatic link negotiation fallback to 1,200 bps and compatibility with Bell 212A/V.22 modems.

V.27ter—For facsimile operations, specifies modulation at 4,800 bps with fallback to 2,400 bps.

V.29—For facsimile operations, specifies modulation at 9,600 bps with fallback to 7,200 bps.

V.32—For modem communications at 9,600 bps and 4,800 bps. V.32 modems fall back to 4,800 bps when line quality is impaired.

V.32bis—Extends the V.32 connection range: 4,800, 7,200, 9,600, 12,000, and 14,400 bps. V.32bis modems fall back to the next lower speed when line quality is impaired, fall back further as necessary, and also fall forward (switch backup) when line conditions improve.

V.34—Allows data rates as high as 28,800 bps.

V.34+—An enhancement to V.34 that enables data transfer rates as high as 33,600 bps.

V.42—Defines a two-stage process of detection and negotiation for LAP-M error control.

V.42bis—An extension of ITU-T V.42 that defines specific data compression scheme for use during V.42 connections.

V.44—For modem data compression. It provides for a 6:1 compression ratio.

V.90—For 56-Kbps modem communications. It uses the digital telephone network to increase the bit rate of the receive channel by eliminating the analog-to-digital conversion commonly found in modem connections. V.90 connections require a modem with V.90 technology calling a digitally connected ISP or corporate host site compatible with V.90.

V.92—For advanced 56-Kbps modem communications. This technology offers three new features to enhance the V.90 standard: Modem on Hold, Quick Connect, and V.PCM Upstream. The V.92 technology can be utilized only if a V.92 modem is dialing into an ISP that supports and provides a digital V.92 signal.

Modulation

Modulation is a method for adding information to a carrier signal by altering that signal's strength, phase, or frequency. The modem converts digital 0s and 1s into an analog audio signal. Some of the more common types of modulation include:

- Amplitude Modulation (AM), which blends data onto the carrier by modulating the height of the carrier wave.

- Frequency Shift Keying (FSK), which modulates the frequency of the wave.

- Phase Shift Keying (PSK), which modulates the phase angle of the wave.

As modem speeds have increased, so has the complexity of the modulation. V.22 modems, capable of 1200 bps transmission, used Quadrature Phase Shift Keying (QPSK). V.22bis added adaptive equalization and Quadrature Amplitude Modulation (QAM). V.32 and V.32bis modems added trellis coding and echo cancellation, allowing the full frequency band to be used in both directions at the same time. V.34 and V.34+ modems added line probing, precoding, and shell mapping.

Pulse Code Modulation (PCM) is used in V.90 and V.92. V.90 uses PCM for transmitting downstream data only (from the sender to your modem), whereas V.92 uses it in both directions: upstream and downstream. PCM lets the electrical voltage of the line follow the value of the bytes sent. This method is complex and requires a great deal of precision but is actually simpler than advanced QAM schemes. PCM requires less computing than other forms of modulation and is capable of theoretical speeds up to 56 Kbps without requiring the use of carriers or phase shifts.

You might wonder why PCM wasn't implemented earlier instead of some of the more elaborate methods that yielded only 33.6 Kbps. The catch with

PCM is that it doesn't work between two analog modems. A PCM signal can travel from your modem to the CO, where it is digitized and sent digitally through the PSTN. This signal can travel halfway around the globe, if need be, but will be irreversibly damaged by the eventual reconversion back into an analog signal by the remote CO when being delivered to the target analog modem. The good news is that a new species of "target modem" became very popular for Internet usage: digital modems. Digital modems are used by ISPs and do not connect to analog lines but instead connect directly to the digital trunks of the PSTN. Therefore, V.90 became the standard of choice for Internet connections and as most connections today are done with the Internet, analog modems have become synonymous with 56K.

In V.90, the upstream channel (from your modem to the receiver) is still V.34. In the V.92 standard, PCM is also implemented on the upstream channel but at a lower speed than the downstream connection. The theoretical limit is 48 Kbps.

Baud and bps

You'll sometimes see references to baud. Baud rate refers to the number of symbols per second.

Each symbol may encode one or more bits. Baud rate is actually the signaling rate of the line; i.e., the number of voltage or frequency transitions per second. The term *baud* has often been incorrectly used to refer to bits per second (bps). For technical reasons, baud rate is limited on a telephone line. This is why older modulation schemes, such as FSK, are not capable of high throughput rates. The aim of modern modulation techniques is to pack as much information into one voltage or frequency transition as possible (from 1 bit per symbol in FSK to 7 bits per symbol in V.90). Hence, the accurate term to express data rate is bps. Larger bps rates are often expressed in Kbps. For example: 56,000 BPS = 56 Kbps, or 56K.

Transmitting Data: Synchronous and Asynchronous Transmissions

Much like a vinyl record that will deliver understandable music only if played at the right speed, two computers need to agree on a clock in order to communicate properly. Modems transmit data in one of two modes: synchronous or asynchronous.

Synchronous

Synchronous transmissions send data as a continuous stream of characters. Before any data is sent, the modems involved (both the sender and the receiver) are synchronized according to a timing clock or signal so that the modems can correctly identify the characters being received. This synchronization is kept in check by the inclusion of a uniquely coded series of 0 and 1 bits in the bit stream: These are the synchronization characters (sometimes referred to as *sync characters*). The receiving modem reviews the incoming synchronization characters and synchronizes itself to the incoming bit stream. Once the two modems are in synchronization, data transmission can take place.

This streaming data is broken up into bundles of characters referred to as *frames*. The data transmission itself is continuous and without gaps, with synchronization characters between the bundles of characters.

Asynchronous

Asynchronous transmissions allow for "uneven" timing intervals between characters, unlike the continuous streaming nature of synchronous transmissions. Individual characters are processed one by one as they arrive at the receiver. Asynchronous transmission of a character begins with a start bit (0), continues with the bits representing the character, and completes the character with a stop bit (1). When idle, the line remains in the "stop" state (1); thus, the next character to follow will announce itself to the receiver with its start bit (0). Each character is a self-contained unit wrapped with a start and stop bit.

Communication between your computer and your modem via a serial port is asynchronous because the serial port is asynchronous. The modem converts this to a synchronous data flow before modulating the data, saving the burden of transmitting start and stop bits with each character.

Flow Control Protocols

Modems have the capability to store data when the rate the modem receives data from the computer (DTE rate) is greater than the rate at which it can process and transmit data to the remote modem (DCE rate, or "link rate"). It can also do so when noise on the phone line requires data to be retransmitted. A data buffer in the modem holds the data until it can be transmitted. Flow control provides a means to suspend and resume data flowing into the modem. Without flow control, the modem's data buffer could run out of room, causing an overflow and loss of data.

Example: A public parking garage can be equipped with a traffic light at its entrance that displays green only when there is available space. When the parking garage is full, the light changes to red. If a parked car leaves the full garage, the light will turn green again, indicating an open parking spot. Once another car takes that empty parking spot, the light changes back to red.

There are two types of flow control: software and hardware.

- Software flow control, also known as "Xon/Xoff," reserves two characters of the computing alphabet (Xon or Ctrl-Q code 17 and Xoff or Ctrl-S code 19) to use as flow control characters. The transmitting device can send data to the receiving device (in this case, the modem) until the data buffer in the receiving device reaches its high-water mark. At that point, the receiving device sends an Xoff control character to the transmitting device. Once the receiving device has cleared out enough of the buffer to get below the low-water mark, the modem sends an Xon control character to the transmitting device. One limitation of Xon/Xoff is that these characters must not appear in the file that is being transmitted. If they do, the transfer could be halted without the possibility of restarting. This is why Xon/Xoff is very rarely used nowadays.

- Hardware flow control, also sometimes referred to as "RTS/CTS," takes place on the physical connection between the computer and the modem. On a serial link, extra signals exist beyond the transmit and receive signals. Clear-to-Send (CTS), when on, indicates that the receiving device (the modem, in this case) is ready to receive. Whenever the receiving device's data buffer reaches its high-water mark, the receiving device simply turns off CTS until the buffer clears out to the low-water mark again, and the receiving device is ready to accept more data. RTS (originally, Request-to-Send), driven by the computer, is used similarly in the other direction. Because RTS and CTS are physical hardware signals, there is no way for either end to misinterpret the contents of the file as a flow control signal. This is why hardware flow control is preferred over software flow control.

Flow control appears throughout the telecommunications data path: between your computer and your modem; between the remote modem and its computers; and between two modems. Flow control between modems is done by sending Receiver Not Ready (RNR) and Receiver Ready (RR) frames to stop and restart data flow.

Fax Standards

Many people aren't aware that their modems are also capable of sending faxes. There are standards to ensure compatibility between different fax/modems (or faxmodems). The two main standards for fax transmissions are Fax Group 3 (or G3) and Fax Group 4 (or G4). Fax Group 3 is by far the more commonly used of the two. It uses the ITU-T T.30 and T.4 protocols to organize the transmission of ID information, fax pages, retransmission of bad pages, coding (compression) of the page data, as well as the negotiation of page size, resolution, and coding method. Fax Group 4 is more robust than G3 and can handle greater compression ratios with higher resolutions and even two-dimensional image compression. G4 can also use ISDN (Integrated Services Digital Network) lines for sending faxes.

In the computer domain, faxmodem "classes" have been designed to standardize the commands used by your software to control faxing operations. This ensures that software designed for a specific faxmodem will also work with any modem in that same class. The two relevant classes are:

- Class 1: Application software on your computer performs most of the processing work.
- Class 2.0: The modem itself performs most of the processing, rather than the central processing unit (CPU). Class 2.0 fax is a standard and not the same as Class 2 fax.

File Transfer Protocols

Protocols were developed to simplify file transfers between computers. Xmodem is a file transfer protocol that was developed in 1978 and is the de facto standard. Xmodem sends 128-byte blocks of data with a checksum attached to each block. The checksum is the total value of all bytes in the block. The sending modem waits for an acknowledgment after sending each block. The receiving modem recalculates the checksum and sends back either a positive acknowledgment or a negative acknowledgment. If the received checksum doesn't match the recalculated one, a negative acknowledgment is sent, and the block is resent.

At 128-byte blocks, Xmodem is relatively slow. Zmodem, an enhanced file transfer protocol, adjusts the packet size depending on phone line conditions and ends each data block with CRC-32 (cyclic redundancy check) error checking. This method of transfer assumes that the sent data is mostly uncorrupted. Negative acknowledgments are sent only when necessary so the sending modem doesn't stop between each block. This lets data "stream" at higher rates. Zmodem has a crash recovery ability to resume botched data transfers at the error point instead of needing to retransfer the entire file from the beginning.

Error Correction and Data Compression Protocols

When Modem A sends data to Modem B, that data may pick up errors or become corrupted along the way. There are two ways to solve this problem: either Computers A and B both use a data transfer program, with an error-correcting file transfer protocol (like Xmodem or Zmodem) or Modem A and Modem B handle error correction between themselves. The latter solution is preferred. If the modems guarantee the quality of the data link, all programs using them will benefit from it, not only file transfer programs, but also your Web browser and others.

To perform error correction, Modem A will break down the data stream into small blocks and attach a "signature" to each. (This signature is an algorithm that reflects the contents of the data block.) These are either checksums or CRCs. CRCs are the more powerful of the two.

Upon receipt of the block, Modem B recomputes the code. If the code matches, the data is assumed to be uncorrupted. (Modem B may send an acknowledgment message back to Modem A.) However, if the two codes do not match, a negative acknowledgment or "reject" block is sent by B to A. There are two main error correction protocols used in the modem world: MNP4 and V.42.

- Microcom Networking Protocol 4 (MNP4) was created by Microcom and was the first widely used industry standard error correction protocol. Since 1988, MNP4 has been largely replaced by Link Access Protocol-Modem (LAP-M), another error detection and correction method under the ITU standard: V.42.

- V.42 typically creates blocks of 128 or 256 characters and uses a 2-byte CRC for error control. It allows anticipation; Modem A can send up to 16 blocks in advance to Modem B before requiring a positive acknowledgment from Modem B, instead of stopping at each block and waiting for an acknowledgement. These acknowledgements are numbered, so that if Modem A is currently sending block #134 and it receives a reject for block #130, it will then go back and resend blocks 130, 131, 132, etc. One advanced feature of V.42 worth noting is "selective reject," which allows the receiving modem (Modem B, in this example) to request that only the single erroneous block be resent (block #130), then continuing with the current blocks: 135, 136, etc. For fast modems that operate on poor lines where block retransmissions are expected to be frequent, selective reject can be a major performance enhancement.

Data Compression Protocols

Data compression allows you to cram more information onto a storage device (hard drive, floppy disk, etc.) and also helps to speed up data transmissions. Data compression techniques typically use a "dictionary" to translate original chunks of data into smaller "words." The sending compressor will:

- Identify sequences of bits or characters that are often repeated.
- Assign these sequences a shorter "name" in its dictionary.
- Send the short dictionary names instead of the original data to the receiver.

The receiver then has all of the necessary information to reconstruct the original data. The compressor performs these tasks as the data is sent "on the fly," and the dictionary is regularly updated. One of the performance characteristics of a compression scheme is its dictionary size. Data compression ratios vary depending on the type of data:

- Text: 1.5–32 times compression.
- Executable files (programs): 1.5 times.
- ZIP or compressed images: 1 time or possibly more. The modem compressor generates two outputs: compressed data and transparent data. The V.42bis controller compares the two outputs and essentially sends the better optimized of the two.

In general, you can expect compression ratios comparable or slightly lower than what is achievable by commonly available file compression utilities, because again, the modem is trying to perform these compression tasks "on the fly" and, therefore, does not have a full overview of the entire file being transmitted.

Here is a listing of some of the more common compression standards:

- Microcom Networking Protocol 5 (MNP5)—created by Microcom in 1987
- V.42bis—standardized in 1989
- V.44—an enhancement of V.42, improving efficiency for data streams that alternate highly compressible with less compressible data

It is important to note that data compression works only on error-corrected links. Modems typically use MNP5 in conjunction with MNP4 and V.42bis or V.44 in conjunction with V.42.

Internet Protocols: TCP/IP

A commonly understood language is needed for two people to communicate in any kind of meaningful way. For several computers to communicate successfully in a network, there needs to be a commonly understood protocol. This protocol defines how the computers should package data, indicating the data's purpose and destination. Protocols make it possible for any computer to join a network, transfer data among the different computers, and allow each computer to easily retrieve the data intended specifically for it.

TCP/IP

TCP/IP is the communication protocol of the Internet, which allows all types of computers to transmit data to one another via a common set of rules.

TCP/IP was originally developed by the Department of Defense to allow data communication between different networks and is actually a multilayer protocol made up of a higher layer (Transmission Control Protocol, TCP) and a lower layer (Internet Protocol, IP). TCP provides the transport functions to ensure that the total amount of data sent is received correctly at the destination point. IP handles the addressing tasks for all of those "packets" of data. (Think of TCP as the certified mail process. The IP is the letter carrier.) The network device that receives the packets reviews the addressing (IP address) of each packet and forwards the packet to its intended destination. Once all of the packets are received at the destination point, regardless of the paths they took to get there, the packets are reassembled back into the original message in its entirety.

IP Address

An IP address is a 32-bit number that identifies the sender/receiver of packets being transmitted through the Internet. Each IP address contains two pieces of information: a network number and a device number (for a specific computer, server, etc., on a specific network). There are two types of IP addresses: static and dynamic.

Static IP addresses are permanent Internet addresses assigned to computers; dynamic IP addresses are temporary. This is because of the vast number of devices that connect to the Internet and the limited number of static IP addresses available. Dynamic IP addresses are assigned to devices for the duration of the Internet session and reassigned many times over to other devices for the duration of their sessions.

Client/Server

TCP/IP communication is often point-to-point, traveling from the origination point directly to its destination. The client/server relationship used by TCP/IP means that for every communication, there are both a client and a server. The client sends a request for action that is then fulfilled by the server.

When you connect to the Internet, your computer (the client) sends a request for a Web resource to a remote program (the server) that provides the resource.

Accessing the Internet from your computer through your ISP requires yet another protocol, which allows for authentication of the user, determines when you log on and log off, pre-formats the data you send so it is IP-compatible, and is also capable of multiplexing several other protocols over the same link, if needed. The protocol most widely used today is Point-to-Point Protocol (PPP).

PPP includes error detection and operates in full-duplex mode, making it faster and more efficient than older protocols. PPP is also capable of supporting multiple, simultaneous users over a single line.

Modem Architectures

Different types of modem hardware are distinguished by their architecture, i.e., where the processing takes place in the modem or in the computer. There are three general types of modem hardware: controller-based, controller-less (or Winmodems) and softmodems.

Controller-based modems do all of the processing work, freeing up your computer's processor to handle other tasks and provide the best overall performance. Internal models plug into one of the expansion slots inside your computer, and external models plug in through a serial or USB port. External RS-232 modems are always controller-based modems.

Controller-less modems rely on the resources of the host computer for some processing power. Modulation functions are handled by a specialized microprocessor in the modem (often referred to as a DSP, or Digital Signal Processor), whose primary function is to perform intensive signal-related computation. Data compression, AT command functions, and general supervisory functions are handled by a driver (a program that comes with the modem) and executed by the host computer. Controller-less modems are commonly referred to as Winmodems because they are most often found in Windows-based computers.

Softmodems are software-based and rely totally on the host computer to handle all of the supervisory and data pump/modulation functions. This can potentially slow down a computer's overall performance. The modem itself is little more than an interface for the phone jack. Most new name-brand computers come equipped with a softmodem because it saves the computer manufacturer considerable cost. It's a good idea to upgrade/replace the included modem for better performance.

The types of modem architectures and their functions discussed in this section are detailed in Figure 17.4.

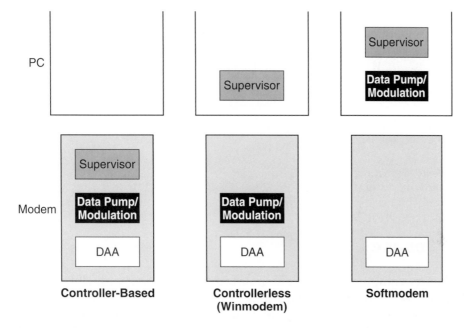

PC

Modem

| Controller-Based | Controllerless (Winmodem) | Softmodem |

FIGURE 17.4   MODEM ARCHITECTURES AND FUNCTIONS PERFORMED.

Modem Types

Your modem can be further classified as either external, internal, or PC card, depending on how it interfaces to your computer.

External Modems

These are just as you would imagine, i.e., a piece of hardware separate from your computer that is plugged into the phone jack and into the computer itself, with the modem in the middle. The two types of external modems are serial modems and universal serial bus (USB) modems.

Serial Modems

Serial modems plug into a computer's RS-232C standard serial interface using an RS-232C cable. The physical connectors at the ends of the RS-232C cable can have either a 9-pin or a 25-pin configuration. (These two connector configurations are also known as DB-9 and DB-25 connectors, respectively.) Older Macintoshes will have a rounded port known as an ADB port, which is

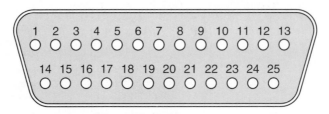

FIGURE 17.5 **RS-232C CONNECTOR.**

functionally similar to the RS-232C. All serial modems are controller-based modems. Figure 17.5 is an example.

DB-25 Connector

Newer computers, both PCs and Macintoshes, come with USB ports. The USB port is a versatile standard that supports data rates up to 12 Mbps and allows for a number of different devices to be plugged into a single, commonly configured port. Modems, joysticks, scanners, CD drives, and wireless networking adapters are just some of the more common devices plugged into USB ports. The USB port conveniently supplies power to these devices, often saving the need for an external power supply. These devices can be plugged in, out, or even interchanged with other devices while the computer is still on. This saves the trouble of having to reboot the computer (as would be necessary with most RS-232C devices). Unplugging a device and replacing it with another device without having to reboot is called "hot swapping."

Be sure to check which kind of ports your computer has before running out and buying an external modem. A USB cable is not compatible with a serial port, and a serial cable is not compatible with a USB port.

Internal modems plug directly into a desktop computer's motherboard via an open expansion slot. There are three expansion slot standards: ISA, EISA, and PCI.

- ISA (Industry Standard Architecture) is an outdated bus architecture standard that runs at 8 MHz and supports only 16-bit data transfer between the motherboard and the expansion slot's associated device.

- EISA (Extended ISA) is also an outdated bus architecture standard and a more advanced version of ISA that runs at 8 MHz and supports 32-bit data transfer.

- PCI (Peripheral Component Interconnect) runs at 33 MHz or 66 MHz and supports 32- and 64-bit data transfers. PCI is a local bus system that allows for faster throughput between the CPU and peripheral devices. PCI is the standard found on most new computers.

PC card (or PCMCIA card, for the long name) modems are designed for plugging into notebook computers. The PCMCIA comes from Personal Computer Memory Card International Association, the organization that specifies the standard. PC card modems are available in both controller-based and controller-less versions. There are currently three different types of PC cards. Each type of card is about the size of a credit card but with varying thickness (Figure 17.6).

- Type I cards (3.3 mm) are used for general memory expansion.
- Type II cards (5 mm) are used for modems, SCSI, etc. A PC card modem is a Type II card and is capable of fitting in both Type II and Type III card slots.
- Type III cards (10.5 mm) are used mainly for data storage, e.g., hard drives.

Interrupt Requests

Interrupt requests (IRQs) help modems, along with other peripheral devices, communicate with a computer's processor. An IRQ is the location inside the computer where an assigned device is expected to send status messages to the computer. These messages are called *interrupts* and commonly inform your computer of the completion of a service request, that incoming data needs interpreting, or of the detection of an error. Your computer processes the interrupt signal and decides what action to take.

Problems can occur when more than one peripheral device is assigned to the same IRQ and both attempt to send an interrupt simultaneously. On an ISA bus, this can cause a short in the bus, resulting in no effect at all, damage to the peripherals involved, or possibly even damage to your computer's motherboard. Each communication port of your computer has an IRQ

FIGURE 17.6 U.S. ROBOTICS 56K MODEM PC CARD (MODEL 3056).

assigned to it, and most modems will support any one of several different IRQs to keep multiple devices from sharing the same one, reducing the chance for possible conflicts. The PCI bus allows IRQs to be shared, and PCI modems are designed to be able to share an IRQ with other PCI peripherals.

Conflicts can occur when two devices are assigned to the same physical port, e.g., when a device is physically removed from its port without "uninstalling" the appropriate drivers and replaced with another device. In such cases, your computer still looks for the old device that was assigned to that location and does not recognize the new one. This can be avoided by simply following the uninstall instructions that came with your computer gear.

BANDWIDTH: VOICEBAND AND BROADBAND

Voiceband

This refers to the transmission of (voice) information over a relatively narrow band of frequencies, called the *voice spectrum* (about 0–3,500 Hz), for which telephone networks have been designed. Your dialup 56-Kbps modem is an example of a voiceband modem. For the sake of the scope of this chapter, voiceband technologies discussed include dialup 56-Kbps analog modems, modem doubling, and ISDN; broadband technologies will include cable, DSL, and satellite Internet access.

Broadband

This is the buzzword you've been hearing a lot about. You might not know what it is, but you've probably heard of it. Broadband covers a "wider" band of frequencies than voiceband by:

- Utilizing frequencies above those for which the PSTN lines were originally designed
- Using different transmission media, such as coaxial cable, optical fiber, or radio transmission

NOTE
Broadband provides data rates much faster than voiceband.

56K

When you go out to your favorite computer store to buy an analog dialup modem, unless you go out of your way to do otherwise, you'll be purchasing a 56-Kbps modem. 56K (as it is colloquially known) has been commonplace since about 1998 as part of the V.90 standard.

And About that 56K Claim...

So you've gotten yourself a 56K modem but aren't achieving speeds of 56 Kbps? Actually, the modems are indeed capable of 56-Kbps speeds, but the Federal Communications Commission (FCC) limits your ISP's downstream rate to 53.3 Kbps. (This isn't the case in all countries, for example, in the United Kingdom, speeds go up to a full 56 Kbps.) To maximize that 53.3 Kbps, keep the following in mind:

- Your ISP's server must be able to support a V.90 or V.92 56-Kbps signal. Contact your ISP for a listing of dialup connections and the modulations supported.

- The telephone line between your modem and ISP must be able to support a 56K connection with no more than one analog-to-digital conversion. If more than one analog-to-digital conversion occurs in your telephone operator's network between you and your ISP, your modem will likely drop down to 33.6 Kbps (V.34); modem-to-modem connections are V.34 connections.

> **NOTE**
>
> To utilize the added functionality of V.92 (Modem on Hold, Quick Connect, and V.PCM Upstream), your ISP's server must be able to support the V.92 standard. Ask your ISP whether it indeed does this.

V.92

In 2000, further enhancements were made by the ITU in what is now known as V.92. V.92 offers three major enhancements over V.90 56K: Modem on Hold, Quick Connect, and V.PCM Upstream.

- Modem on Hold works with your phone company's Call Waiting and Caller ID features to let you take incoming voice calls while you're still online. Not only is the caller identified to you, but also you have the option to "suspend" your Internet connection while you take the incoming call. This saves on the cost of maintaining multiple phone lines and keeps you from being cut off completely from your phone while you surf the Web.

- Quick Connect can shorten up your dialup time when making familiar connections. Your modem compares the connection you're currently trying to make with previous connections you've made on the same phone line, and if line conditions are similar, your modem bypasses portions of the training sequence, getting you connected faster.

- V.PCM Upstream facilitates faster upstream rates of up to 48 Kbps—quite an improvement over the 31.2 Kbps of V.90. You can adjust upstream and downstream rates to favor faster downstream communication or provide a more "balanced" communication flow, which increases upstream data rates while slightly reducing downstream rates. This kind of flexibility comes in handy for those situations when you need to send large email messages, spreadsheets, presentations, or photos or for uploading files onto a corporate local area network (LAN).

New computers will likely include dialup 56K modems as standard equipment. They are reliable and easy to use but limited in bandwidth and, therefore, in their practical applications. For increased bandwidth for business applications and for those who spend a good deal of time on the Internet (for online gaming, research, streaming audio/video, etc.), broadband is better.

Modem Doubling

Combine the bandwidth of two modems together, and you've got modem doubling, or two-channel bonding. Though not widely supported by ISPs, modem doubling is capable of connection speeds up to 112 Kbps (56K × 2) over an analog phone line. So how is it that you get twice the connection rate of 56K dialup modems? Basically, you're using two modems at the same time.

Modem bonding is one such method of modem doubling that inverse-multiplexes data packets between the two modems, essentially giving half of the data to each modem, then recombining the data upon receiving. This is possible due to Multilink Protocol Plus (MP+). An advantage of modem bonding is that the two modems work together to form a redundant connection. If one of the modems should go down or lose its connection, the other modem keeps the connection up and running—no dropped connections.

As originally conceived, Integrated Services Digital Network (ISDN) was the replacement technology for the analog network. It provides a total bandwidth of 144 Kbps, parceled into three channels—two 64-Kbps "bearer" channels (or B-channels) for transmitting digital information (voice, data, or video) and one 16-Kbps "signaling" channel (or D-channel) for transmitting call setup information and packet-switched data. ISDN is a dialup technology that uses your existing twisted-pair copper telephone lines to transmit and receive data while allowing for simultaneous use of your telephone for voice calls. The two B-channels are independent from one another and can be used to transmit voice or data to two independent destinations. ISDN comes in two variants: BRI and PRI. The version described previously is ISDN BRI (Base Rate Interface).

The other version is ISDN PRI (Primary Rate Interface) and is installed over a high-speed circuit T1 (T1s run at 1.544 Mbps). ISDN PRI provides the user with 23 B-channels and one 64-Kbps signaling channel, or if multiple PRI circuits are installed, they can share the signaling channel and use all 24 B-channels on the additional circuits. ISDN PRI is typically used by ISPs (you most likely dial into them with your analog modem or ISDN Terminal Adapter) and large corporations for voice and data communication needs.

Because ISDN uses existing telephone network infrastructures, it can be fairly inexpensive and convenient to implement in residential homes and small businesses looking for high-speed connectivity for a variety of applications, including videoconferencing, telecommuting, Internet browsing, transferring files, and running large-scale applications.

Terminal Adapter

A *Terminal Adapter* (TA) is the interface between your computer and the ISDN line; i.e., it lets non-ISDN equipment such as your home computer work on an ISDN line. TAs are often mislabeled as ISDN "modems." An ISDN TA neither modulates nor demodulates; transmitted data ISDN is 100% digital. The TA actually converts PSTN (bipolar) signaling to a more computer-friendly (unipolar) signaling. TAs come in two types: passive and active.

- Passive TAs are to ISDN TAs what controller-less modems are to modems, i.e., they are primarily internal devices that are light on processing capabilities and rely on the host computer for their functionality (D-channels and B-channels), transceiver, and bus interface (PCMCIA, ISA, PCI).

- Active TAs are the controller-based modems of the TA world. Active TAs include additional hardware, are functionally more robust than passive

TAs, and typically include a protocol processor, user interface logic, and a voice coder/decoder. An ADPCM interface is often included to allow for making standard analog voice calls via one of the ISDN B-channels. RS-232, Ethernet, and USB are the most commonly available interfaces.

The TA may or may not have an integrated network terminator (or NT1). An NT1 unit performs digital loop-back functions and signal conversion for the TA so that the signal can be delivered to the ISDN terminal.

ISDN helps provide extra bandwidth when dialup 56K isn't enough and broadband is either overkill or just not available in a given geographical area. It's practical for telecommuters, streaming audio/video, and running a small home office. Remote office employees, small businesses, and heavy Internet users (online gaming, research, streaming audio/video, and the like) should consider going with one of the broadband technologies—cable or DSL.

CABLE

Almost everyone is familiar with cable TV. Just as that all-too-familiar coaxial cable can bring us more television channels than we know what to do with, that same cable is capable of bringing broadband Internet access into our home or place of business.

How Does a Cable Modem Work?

If you thought about buying a cable modem from your favorite computer store to plug into your existing cable line in the hopes of getting free Internet access, don't. Cable Internet services will require you to pay a fee for the services received. The signal coming down your cable TV line is actually made up of many separate signals, with each television channel receiving a 6-MHz portion of the available bandwidth. "Available" becomes a keyword here. Cable is a shared resource, meaning that there is a finite amount of bandwidth available that is split up among applications and users.

> **EXAMPLE**
>
> Cable bandwidth is like the water pressure in your home; i.e., the more people that run the water at the same time for cleaning dishes, taking a shower, doing a load of laundry, or whatever, the less water pressure each person gets for his or her task. It's the same way with cable Internet access. The more users you get online at the same time, the slower your access will be.

Cable modems are not true modems in the classic analog-to-digital sense but more like ISDN terminal adapters. They are capable of speeds as high as 43 Mbps or more, but you won't be seeing anything of that magnitude reaching your home computer. Because bandwidth is shared among all users, you're more likely to see practical speeds of around 1.5 Mbps for downstreaming and 256 Kbps for upstreaming.

Just as each channel grabs a 6-MHz portion of available bandwidth, cable Internet service does the same thing. Instead of a television signal on this particular channel, you're getting Internet access. Because of the way the Internet is used, more for downstreaming (receiving) than upstreaming (sending), a smaller portion of that 6-MHz bandwidth is allocated for upstreaming—typically about 2 MHz.

Basic Components

Cable modems can be either internal or external devices. Some of the newer digital cable set-top boxes have an integrated modem for Internet access. (Though that doesn't mean you'll have Internet service.) The basic components of a cable modem are the tuner, demodulator, modulator, media access control (MAC) device, and microprocessor.

- The tuner locks onto the downstreaming Internet signal, one that would normally be an unused cable TV channel, and sends the modulated Internet signal to the demodulator.

- The demodulator converts the downstreaming data into simple signals more easily processed by the analog-to-digital (A/D) converter. At this point, the signal is converted into binary 0s and 1s. An error correction module then finds and fixes any transmission problems.

- The modulator converts upstreaming data into a signal friendlier to transmission across the cable network.

- The MAC device is the hardware/software interface for the DOCSIS (Data Over Cable Service Interface Specification) protocols.

- The microprocessor handles all of the computing functions related to modem operations.

Most cable modems are external devices. Internal versions are also available, but these are the exception to the rule because external models are easier for service providers to deploy and install in the field. The coaxial cable used for data transmission was developed in 1929 and is essentially a copper wire sheathed in a layer of insulation, copper mesh, and another layer of insulation on the outside (Figure 17.7).

Back at the cable company (or cable head-end), upstreaming data traffic from individual cable modem users is combined by a cable modem termination system (CMTS) onto a single signal, converted into IP packets, and forwarded to an ISP router for Internet transmission. All data downstreamed to and upstreamed from individual cable modems goes through the CMTS; there is no direct communication between individual modems. This methodology can allow simultaneous Internet access for up to 1,000 cable modem users and all on the same 6-MHz channel!

CableLabs Certified Cable Modems, originally known as DOCSIS, is the de facto standard for cable modems in the United States (Euro-DOCSIS covers international standards). It specifies the protocols, modulation techniques, and hardware used in cable data transfer.

Cable Internet access provides true broadband speeds and always-on connectivity that is ideal for business applications, streaming audio/video, remote office networking, online gaming, students who spend a lot of time researching their subjects, and anyone who simply wants the convenience and supe-

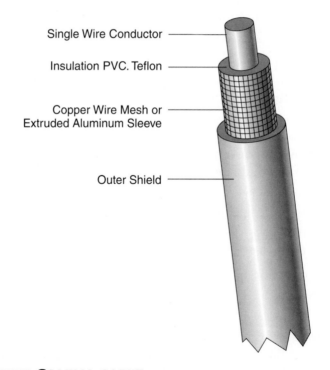

Single Wire Conductor

Insulation PVC. Teflon

Copper Wire Mesh or
Extruded Aluminum Sleeve

Outer Shield

FIGURE 17.7 **COAXIAL CABLE.**

rior performance of broadband. Here is a recap of some of the advantages of cable Internet access:

- Downstream data rates up to 1.5 Mbps.
- Upstream data rates up to 256 Kbps.
- Always-on connectivity (no need to "dial up" for each Internet session).
- Operates on existing coaxial cable.
- Allows for simultaneous Internet access and cable TV use.

If cable Internet access interests you, contact your cable company for additional information and availability in your area.

DIGITAL SUBSCRIBER LINE

Digital Subscriber Line (DSL) is another broadband technology that, like cable, uses your existing infrastructure to pipe high-speed Internet access into your home or office in a continuous, always-on connection—no dialing up. However, instead of using your cable service's coaxial cable, DSL uses traditional twisted-pair copper telephone lines. This saves a lot of time, trouble, and money by eliminating the need for costly infrastructure upgrades common with other technologies. This makes DSL a practical alternative to cable Internet access for small businesses and residential homes.

How Does DSL Work?

Just like a coaxial cable can simultaneously carry television signals and provide Internet connectivity, DSL performs a similar feat via phone lines. DSL utilizes the available bandwidth of common twisted-pair analog lines to connect digitally on both the downstream and upstream connections at speeds greater than 8 Mbps and 640 Kbps, respectively (as much as 2.3 Mbps in both directions). This kind of bandwidth is far greater than standard 56K or ISDN dialup modems and is in direct competition with cable Internet access providers in many areas.

With DSL, your phone line does double duty, i.e., not only can you download huge files off your favorite Web site, but you can also make and receive telephone calls simultaneously without any degradation in sound quality.

How is this possible? It's all in the way we speak. Typical conversational tones have a frequency range between 0 and 3,400 cycles per second (Hertz, or Hz). Twisted-pair copper lines have the capability to handle millions of

Hz, as long as the line is not too long (0–18,000 feet is the typical range). So your DSL modem uses these high frequencies above the voiceband to exchange data. At the central office (CO), additional DSL equipment installed by the service provider (or operator) processes the high frequencies (data) while letting the original PSTN equipment in the CO handle the low frequencies (voice calls) via CO splitters. This means that DSL is available only in those areas covered by a CO that is not too far away and is equipped with the required equipment. Filters are put on telephony devices or a splitter is installed at your phone box to "separate" voice from data to ensure perfect sound quality. DSL is typically installed in small businesses and residential homes. The modem itself connects to your computer via an Ethernet network interface card (NIC) or USB connection.

Bus-related technologies, like cable, have to share available resources among multiple users. DSL isn't a bus-related technology, because it operates on the user's private phone line, so the available bandwidth is more consistent to the end-user.

Just as there is more than one type of ISDN, there are also numerous variations on the DSL theme. So-called xDSL is a family of different DSL technologies. Although there are many types of DSL (Asymmetric DSL, ISDN DSL, Symmetric DSL, Very high data rate DSL, etc.), Asymmetric DSL (ADSL) is the most widely deployed form in residential homes and offices.

ASYMMETRIC DIGITAL SUBSCRIBER LINE

ADSL technology makes the most of its bandwidth by catering to the asymmetric nature of Internet data transmission, i.e., most of the channel bandwidth is allocated for downstreaming data with a relatively small portion reserved for upstreaming. For the sake of comparison, the U.S. Robotics USB ADSL Modem (Figure 17.8) is capable of producing downstream rates of up

FIGURE 17.8 U.S. ROBOTICS SURECONNECT ADSL ETHERNET MODEM (MODEL 9001).

to 8 Mbps and upstream rates of up to 1 MB. That's quite a difference in rates, but it also makes sense when you consider how we use that bandwidth, e.g., telecommuting, virtual office networking, streaming audio/video, etc.

How Does ADSL Work?

Like other forms of DSL, ADSL modems are able to cram a lot of bandwidth over twisted-pair copper telephone lines due to signal processing techniques that utilize those frequencies not used for standard voice service. Multiple channels are created using Frequency Division Multiplexing (FDM) and echo cancellation to carry voice and data traffic.

FDM creates two broad frequency bands for data transfer, i.e., one for upstream data (30–138 kHz) and the other for downstream data (138 kHz–1.1 MHz), leaving a 0–4 kHz sliver for "plain old telephone service" (POTS). Each band is further multiplexed to allow the two data bands to overlap one another, with echo cancellation employed to separate the two. Back at the customer site, a splitter is used to separate the digital data from the voice signal.

G.Lite, or ADSL Lite (officially known as G.992.2) was developed by the Universal ADSL Working Group, a global consortium of telecommunication and other interested companies, as a standard installation method for ADSL lines. G.Lite voice and data operate in a manner similar to ADSL, but slower. This eliminates the need for a splitter or a service call from your DSL provider. Data rates, though somewhat slower than full-rate G.DMT ADSL, still yield up to 1.5 Mbps downstream and up to 512 Kbps upstream. Unfortunately, certain technical difficulties kept G.Lite from becoming a standard.

G.DMT is full-rate ADSL (officially known as G.992.1). Its specifications call for downstream rates of 8 Mbps and upstream rates of 800 Kbps over standard telephone lines at a distance up to 18,000 feet. G.DMT uses discrete multitone (DMT) modulation, effectively dividing the upstream and down-stream channels into subchannels of approximately 4 kHz each. These sub-channels each occupy a narrowly defined frequency range, optimizing data throughput.

DSL, like cable Internet access, is an always-on broadband technology. It provides a convenient, high-speed solution for streaming audio/video, telecommuting/remote office networking, online gaming, conducting research, and any number of business applications. Here is a recap of some of the advantages of DSL Internet access:

- Downstream data rates up to 8 Mbps.
- Upstream data rates up to 800 Kbps.

- Always-on connectivity (no need to "dial up" for each Internet session).

- Operates on existing twisted-pair telephone line.

- Allows for simultaneous Internet access and telephone use.

If DSL interests you, contact your telephone company for additional information and availability in your area.

SATELLITE INTERNET ACCESS

The latest option for those seeking high-speed Internet access is another new variation on an old theme. Just as satellite dishes competed with cable decades ago for premium movie channel services, dishes are now back, offering satellite Internet access to compete with cable and DSL. In a practical sense, satellite Internet access isn't so much of a competing technology as much as it is an alternative in areas where cable or DSL services are not available. Satellite Internet access is a somewhat pricey option at this time, though with downstream rates from 150–1,200 Kbps and upstream rates around 50–150 Kbps, available bandwidth is far greater than dialup connectivity.

SPUTNIK

The first artificial satellite, Sputnik (Russian for "Satellite"), was launched by the Soviet Union on October 4, 1957. It was about the size of a basketball and weighed 183 pounds.

How Does Satellite Internet Access Work?

Satellite Internet access operates via geostationary (fixed-position) satellites that beam microwaves from about 22,300 miles above the Earth's equator to your dish antenna and transceiver (transmitter/receiver). Satellite Internet access is available in two forms: two-way and one-way.

A typical two-way satellite Internet connection allows for upstream and downstream transmissions via satellite (Figure 17.9). Here is an example of a typical two-way satellite data transmission:

1. Your transceiver (connected to your computer) passes the digital signal to your dish antenna, which beams the information to the satellite (transponder).
2. The transponder forwards/beams the digital signal to a network operations center (NOC) back on the ground.

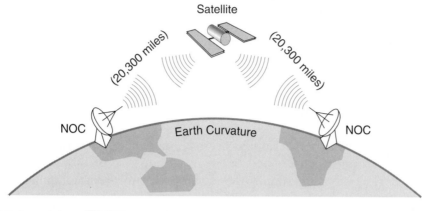

Satellite

(20,300 miles)   (20,300 miles)

NOC   Earth Curvature   NOC

FIGURE 17.9 SATELLITE ILLUSTRATION.

3. The NOC forwards the data request on to the Internet via land-based infrastructure.
4. Data returning from the Internet follows the same process (in reverse) back to your computer.

In theory, this entire process takes only about half of a second, but in practice it takes longer, so this isn't the method of choice for online gamers. (The time delays inherent in satellite communication can be somewhat distracting to online gamers.) A two-way setup provides always-on Internet connectivity that makes access convenient.

A one-way satellite Internet access transmission downstreams data from the transponder to your dish antenna but does not allow for transmitting data upstream in the same manner. One-way satellite Internet access requires that you transmit upstream data through a dialup connection but only downstream data travels via satellite.

It is worth noting that because satellite Internet access operates off "line-of-sight" communication, transmissions are susceptible to heavy precipitation signal degradation (rain fade) and occasional solar interference. A variation of this technology called *fixed wireless* uses cell towers and has less latency but even more line-of-sight problems.

SECURITY PRECAUTIONS

Whether you choose dialup 56K, ISDN, cable, DSL, or even satellite Internet access, a concern for any computer user is security. Any computer that accesses the Internet does so at potential risk. Every year, news headlines report on the latest and most destructive network hacker attacks.

Maybe you think there isn't anything particularly interesting on your computer, or at least not interesting enough to a total stranger that would warrant your taking any special security precautions. Do you ever do your yearly tax return on your computer, send important work-related documents to co-workers in the office, or order merchandise over the Internet? If so, you could be at risk.

Now don't panic. Such attacks are rare, and there are some simple precautions that you can take on your own to boost security and limit your exposure. Here are a few simple options for protecting your computer.

- Personal firewalls are software programs that work to detect and prevent hacker attacks on your computer. There are many kinds of personal firewall software programs available, and most are relatively inexpensive.

- Network firewalls are hardware-based devices that create a barrier between your network and the Internet. Network firewalls are available as separate devices and are often an included feature of routers and other networking devices, allowing you to protect multiple devices at a time. Network firewalls are a must for broadband technologies that offer always-on Internet access because such a connection offers more opportunity for those looking to gain access to your network.

- Some modems have built-in dial and dialback security that work by having the host system (the network that you are dialing in to) disconnect the caller (your computer, for instance). Then, they dial the authorized phone number for that caller (your computer), establishing a network connection between the network and your computer. The U.S. Robotics Courier V.Everything 56K Analog Corporate modem is just such a modem that features dialback security (Figure 17.10).

FIGURE 17.10 U.S. ROBOTICS COURIER V.EVERYTHING 56K ANALOG CORPORATE MODEM (MODEL 3453).

You have many more security options available to you than the few mentioned here. (For more information on security, refer to Chapter 11). Visit your local computer store for advice on the kind of security measures that would work best for your particular networking needs.

You'll notice that when it comes to broadband Internet access, you might not have a choice between cable and DSL services. More often than not, you'll find that either one or the other is available in your area, but not both. It is also common practice for broadband ISPs to provide the modem to their subscribers. Call your local cable service or phone company to find out what broadband options are available in your area.

If you're used to dialup Internet access, you might be surprised how much broadband Internet access can change your Web-surfing habits. The high data rates allow for streaming music and movies, sending graphic-intensive presentations, Web-based broadcasting, and plenty of other uses that just aren't practical through a dialup connection. Also, the "always-on" nature of both DSL and cable make using the Internet more like a utility (like your TV or phone), so checking the weather forecast, monitoring your checking account balance, sending instant messages, and many other applications become more practical and better integrated into your daily life. Once you get used to the increased capabilities of broadband, you might wonder how you ever got along without it.

SUMMARY

Don't be intimidated by the vast selection of modem choices available to you. With what you now know about modems and with some assistance from your local computer store, finding the right modem to fit your particular needs just got a lot easier.

RECOMMENDED READING

The Irwin Handbook of Telecommunications, 4th Edition, by James Henry Green, McGraw-Hill Trade, February 2000.

Computer Networks and Internets, with Internet Applications, 3rd Edition, by Douglas E. Comer and Ralph E. Droms, Prentice Hall, February 2001.

Newton's Telecom Dictionary, 19th Edition, covering Telecommuniations, Networking, Information Technology, Computing and the Internet by Harry Newton, CMP Books, March 2003.

Understanding Data Communications from Fundamentals to Networking, 3rd Edition, by Gilbert Held, John Wiley & Sons, December 2000.

18
NETWORKING

A home network can be many things to many people. To most, it is a means by which to share an Internet connection between multiple computers simultaneously. Beyond PCs, it enables an entirely new range of devices to share the Internet connection. Whether it be networked PCs, televisions, or telephones, more and more devices will start featuring the ability to connect to a home network for Internet connectivity. For example, personal video recorder (PVR) technology is becoming more and more popular and soon will allow us to download content not only from television, cable, and satellite services, but from the Internet as well.

Although the greatest benefit of a home network is clearly its shared, simultaneous access to the Internet, other benefits exist as well. A home network lets you share files and/or printers between computers in the home. Giving family members access to files on one PC from another can be powerful. The same goes for printers. A child can look at the family calendar on Dad's PC or print her science report using the color printer connected to Mom's PC. Additionally, many kids these days are hosting "LAN parties," where they play computer games against one another from different PCs in the same house. Many computer games are designed with this kind of functionality, and this can be safer than having children interact with strangers on the Internet.

A home network is all of these things and more. It primarily provides a means by which to connect devices together. In this chapter, you will learn a little about what makes a network tick and what makes most sense for your particular needs.

WHEN DOES IT MAKE SENSE FOR ME TO NETWORK MY HOME?

If you decide to subscribe to broadband Internet service, you will quickly discover its benefits, as discussed previously in this book—higher speed (bandwidth) and an "always-on" connection that renders dialing up with your modem each time you want to connect unnecessary. With that higher bandwidth, you will realize there's enough speed to share that connection with others in your home and not see a noticeable drop in performance. If you secure a broadband connection, you will likely see performance ranging from 384 kilobits per second (Kbps) all the way up to 2 megabits per second (Mbps). Comparing that with your 56-Kbps dialup modem today, that's a 6x to 35x improvement.

Another reason to think about getting networked when you move to broadband is security. The benefit of an always-on connection carries a caveat. To ensure that your connection doesn't become an available means for shady characters to hack into your system, you need to institute security measures, which are built in to many home networking solutions today. While you could purchase firewall software to load on each PC in the home, this type of software requires quite a bit of time and repeated effort to manage. Given that every Internet-accessing device is connected through the home network, built-in security provides complete security for the whole home, not just for your computers. The key is to find a home networking solution that offers truly robust security, which we'll cover in a few pages.

Finally, if you have multiple computers in your household being used by different family members, all of whom want to be on the Internet at the same time, this too becomes a potential trigger for home networking. In this context, family members can also share printers or other peripheral devices without having to move the resources around and/or purchase additional equipment.

NETWORK COMPONENTS

A network runs on hardware—specifically, a modem for Internet connectivity, a hub/switch or router for multiple device connectivity to that modem's Internet connection, and network adapters for each device you want to connect. Each one of these devices has what is referred to as a Media Access Control (MAC) address. This helps identify each point on the network where traffic may or may not be directed.

The Internet is a network. On it, data typically travels in "packets." Without diving into a muddled mess of terminology, let us first outline how these packets travel back and forth.

Adapters

An adapter (or network interface card, NIC) is either an internal computer card or an external device that is installed in/on a computer so that it can connect to a network. There are four forms that adapters will traditionally take: USB adapters, PCI cards, PC cards, and those already built into the motherboard. USB adapters are external adapters that plug into a USB port on the outside of the PC, then connect to the network using wires or wireless means. PCI cards are internal cards that plug into a PCI slot on the PC's motherboard, then connect from the back panel of the PC to the network using wires or wireless means. A PC card is most often used for notebook computers and is plugged into a PC card slot on the side of the computer to provide either wired or wireless connectivity to the network. Leading adapter manufacturers include D-Link, Netgear, and Linksys. Figure 18.1 provides an example of each of these types of adapters.

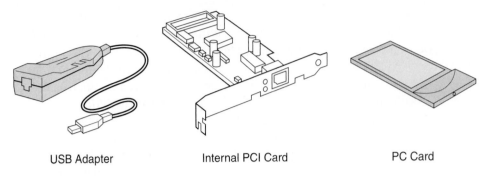

USB Adapter   Internal PCI Card   PC Card

FIGURE 18.1 **USB ADAPTER, A PCI INTERNAL CARD, AND PC CARD.**

Hub

In general, a hub is the central part of the home network that terminates connections from each of the computers in the home. The term evokes an image of the center of a wheel, where the hub is the center that holds all of the spokes in place, connecting all of the PCs that sit at a distant location at the end of each spoke. The hub is a place of convergence where data arrives from one or more PCs and is forwarded out to all other endpoints (down the spokes), regardless of whether the traffic was intended for that endpoint. In other words, a hub aggregates data and broadcasts it back out to all devices on the network, consuming bandwidth needlessly.

Switch

A switch performs the same function as a hub but with more intelligence. (It is also more expensive). A switch is capable of directing traffic to specified devices so that bandwidth on the home network isn't needlessly consumed. For home networks connecting to the Internet through a modem and hub/switch. There is no inherent security provided. (See Chapter 11 for information on security.) A switch is a device that forwards packets between LAN segments. Switches operate at the Data Link Layer (Layer 2) and sometimes the Network Layer (Layer 3) of the OSI Reference Model. (See the sidebar on OSI, later in this chapter.)

A switch will build a list of MAC addresses and update it automatically as necessary. It is a device that separates a network into segments. A switch is similar to a hub in both appearance and function. But, unlike a hub, each port is a network segment onto itself. A switch repeats data only to the recipient/port specified by the MAC address, whereas a hub repeats to all ports.

Switches can improve performance of a network because the switch is capable of delivering full bandwidth to each port. There are three switching modes: store-and-forward, cut-through, and fragment-free.

TECHNICALLY SPEAKING: THREE FLAVORS OF SWITCHES

Store-and-forward

This has a higher latency than other switching methods. With this method, the entire contents of the packet are copied into the onboard buffers of the switch, and CRC (Cyclical Redundancy Check) calculations are performed. The switch then determines whether the packet is free of corruption. If so, the switch looks up the destination address in its routing table and forwards the packet to the next node. If the packet is corrupted, it will drop the packet, causing the sending station/device to resend the packet.

Cut-through

The cut-through method (aka real-time method of switching) has a much smaller latency time because the entire packet is not copied to the switch buffers. As soon as the destination address is captured by the switch, the route to the destination node is determined, and the packet is dispatched out the corresponding port. This method is much faster than the previous one and allows the destination to do the CRC computation and determine the integrity of the packet.

Fragment-free

This is a small compromise between the other two methods. Usually, the first 64 bytes of the frame are sufficient to determine whether the frame is corrupted, because this is often where the corruption starts. This method checks these first 64 bytes; if intact and uncorrupted, the frame is forwarded. The frame is still subject to the same CRC calculation at the destination that all frames are, so any corrupt packets not dropped here will be caught and dropped at the destination.

Router

A router is an intelligent device. It routes packets to the proper destination on the basis of the destination network address in the packet. A router is configured with the gateway address information of the upstream router that it connects to on the network.

A router establishes its identity in one of two ways (depending on the type of router). The first, is DHCP, which takes the IP address assigned by the service provider. The other way is with a static IP address that is assigned manually during router configuration.

Some routers also provide DHCP services for the internal network. These routers will assign IP addresses from the private network address range

(192.168.0.0–192.168.255.255). These IP addresses would be assigned to computers on the network, but all traffic to and from the Internet would have the IP address of the router. This feature provides limited security since threats on the network cannot directly attack a specific computer on the internal network. Hackers for instance would be unable to connect to an internal network computer since the IP address (i.e., 192.168.1.1) is not publicly routable. Meaning packets from the "hacker" or other threat would not have a valid network route since millions of other computers may also have this private network IP address.

BRIDGE

A bridge is a device with two or more ports to forward frames from one LAN segment to another. It performs many of the same functions as a switch but is mainly used to connect two or more dissimilar networks, such as Ethernet and token ring, or Ethernet or Fiber optic.

Brouter

A brouter (bridging router) is a device that, as a bridge, is protocol independent and can filter LAN traffic; as a router, it can forward network packets based on the network destination. Brouters can both bridge multiple protocols and provide routing for those protocols (if they are routable). Most networks today employ switches instead of brouters.

Wireless Access Point

A wireless access point is a hub and switch rolled into one, without the wires.

Wireless Bridge

Wireless bridges are for point-to-point communications (e.g., building to building). A wireless bridge's range can be up to 15 miles or more when properly equipped. But they need to be installed in pairs for long-range capabilities.

Residential Gateway

A residential gateway is a multifunction router. It does everything that a router does. It also includes a built-in modem and a higher-performance processor for managing data, video, and voice tasks. It provides options to connect PCs that are both in the same room as the router (using Ethernet and/or USB) and PCs in other rooms from the router (using Home Phone line Networking Alliance—HomePNA). Residential gateways have built in firewalls that can properly protect the entire home from hacker attacks as well as (or better than) a software firewall. Such high-performance products are what have been of strongest interest to broadband service providers because they minimize customer problems and provide the most positive Internet experience for most users. The leader, 2Wire Inc., provides additional information on such products at its Web site at www.2wire.com.

Leading residential gateway manufacturers to consider include 2Wire, Cayman, and Motorola. Their products are offered predominantly by broadband service providers.

HISTORICALLY SPEAKING: HISTORY OF THE OSI MODEL

Much of the work on the design of Open Systems Interconnection (OSI) was actually done by a group at Honeywell Information Systems, headed by Mike Canepa, with Charlie Bachman as the principal technical member. This group was chartered, within Honeywell, with advanced product planning and with the design and development of prototype systems.

In the early and middle 1970s, the interest of Canepa's group was primarily on database design, then on distributed database design. By the mid-1970s, it became clear that to support database machines, distributed access, and the like, a structured distributed communications architecture would be required. The group studied some of the existing solutions, including IBM's system network architecture (SNA), the work on protocols being done for ARPANET, and some of the concepts of presentation services being developed for standardized database systems. The result of this effort was the development by 1977 of a seven-layer architecture known internally as the distributed systems architecture (DSA).

Meanwhile, in 1977, the British Standards Institute proposed to the International Organization for Standardization (ISO) that a standard architecture was needed to define the communications infrastructure for distributed processing. As a result of this proposal, ISO formed a subcommittee on Open Systems Interconnection (Technical Committee 97, Subcommittee 16). The American National Standards Institute (ANSI) was charged to develop proposals in advance of the first formal meeting of the subcommittee.

Bachman and Canepa participated in these early ANSI meetings and presented their seven-layer model. This model was chosen as the only proposal to be submitted to the ISO subcommittee. When the ISO group met in Washington, DC in March of 1978, the Honeywell team presented its solution. A consensus was reached at that meeting that this layered architecture would satisfy most requirements of OSI and had the capacity of being expanded later to meet new requirements. A provisional version of the model was published in March of 1978. The next version, with some minor refinements, was published in June of 1979 and eventually standardized. The resulting OSI model is essentially the same as the DSA model developed in 1977.

Although of considerable conceptual influence, the OSI model was never adopted completely as the basis for real-world systems. TCP/IP, the means of Internet interconnection, though it logically supports ISO/OSI functionality, has only four layers in its architecture.

WIRED OPTIONS

White meat or dark, manual or automatic, good or evil, and now wired or wireless. This is the biggest decision to make when it comes to installing a home network. Consider your current and future network requirements, skills and abilities, and budget.

Of your wired options you'll most likely hear a lot about Ethernet, fiber optic, and telephone wire. We'll survey the top ones, then cover the options existing and upcoming in the wireless department.

TWISTED PAIR (CATEGORY 1–7)

This utilizes a thin-diameter wire (22–26 gauge) commonly used for telephone and network cabling. The wires are twisted around each other to minimize interference from other twisted pair in the cable. (Alexander Graham Bell invented this and was awarded a patent for it in 1881.) Twisted pair have less bandwidth than coaxial cable or optical fiber.

Twisted-pair cables are available unshielded (UTP) or shielded (STP). UTP is the most common. STP is used in noisy environments where the shield protects against excessive electromagnetic interference (EMI). Both UTP and STP come in stranded- and solid-wire varieties. The stranded wire is the most common and is also very flexible for bending around corners. Solid-wire cable has less attenuation and can span longer distances but is less flexible than stranded wire and cannot be repeatedly bent.

Ethernet

Ethernet is recommended. It is your first choice to connect a PC when it is located in the same room as your hub/switch, router, or gateway. It is ideal for home networking, given the dependability of the technology and the speed at which it operates. It can be less ideal for PCs located outside of the same room as the router or gateway because it depends on special CAT5 wiring (meaning *category 5*, there are 5 twists in the wire per inch). You'd need to run this throughout your house, which can be a hazard if it's exposed. To run it on or in walls is a significant project.

ETHERNET

Ethernet networking is the tried-and-true, low-cost networking option. It's the workhorse of hundreds of thousands of commercial and private computers worldwide. This networking technology uses twisted-pair copper wires, with dependable transfer rates up to one gigabit.

Pros

Low cost

Relatively easy installation

Stable, high transfer rates—up to 1 gigabit

Established, well-supported technology

Cons

Susceptible to EMI—Electric heaters, fluorescent lighting, electric motors can interfere.

Difficult to retrofit—If you're not remodeling, it means drilling and cutting walls, as well as crawling around attics and crawl spaces.

Maximum segment length of 100 meters (328 feet)—A network wire is limited to 100 meters in length.

Ethernet is the most widely installed networking technology and is by far the least expensive and most reliable. This technology is here to stay. Ethernet is an established standard (802.3) coming from the Institute of Electrical and Electronics Engineers (IEEE), a standards-making body responsible for many computing standards. What this means is that anyone manufacturing products uses, in essence, the same blueprint to ensure that it works with other manufacturers' products. An Ethernet network typically uses special wires, called CAT5, to connect all the PCs together through a hub/switch/router/gateway. Most Ethernet networks operate at 10 megabits per second (Mbps) and can autosense what the rest of the network can achieve and perform at both 10 and 100 Mbps.

Another advantage of Ethernet is that most PCs ship with Ethernet (or, as it's sometimes identified, a network interface card [NIC]) already built in these days. If you aren't sure whether your PC has Ethernet already, you can find out by looking for an extra-wide phone jack, called an RJ-45 connector (see Figure 18.2), on your PC. It is very likely that it is included.

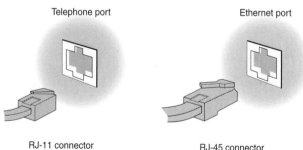

Telephone port   Ethernet port

RJ-11 connector   RJ-45 connector

FIGURE 18.2 **THE RJ-11 AND RJ-45 CONNECTORS.**

USB is a great alternative for connecting your PC to a router or gateway; however, not all routers and gateways include a USB port for direct PC connectivity. If you purchase one that does, it provides the lowest-cost means by which to connect your computer, given that almost every PC these days has a USB port. Although slightly less expensive than Ethernet, it also provides slightly lower speed for connectivity, at around 4 Mbps versus Ethernet's 10 Mbps.

USB ports, which are small and rectangular, are located on the back of the computer. Desktop computers typically have two USB ports (Figure 18.3) and notebook computers commonly have one. USB connection is recommended for additional PCs that might be located in the same room as your router or gateway, assuming you have used up your Ethernet ports for other PCs in the same room and/or for Ethernet-connected devices.

Home Telephone Line Networking

Because many people have used their phone lines for years to dial up the Internet from their PC using a V.90 modem, it becomes a natural move to envision connecting multiple PCs together and to connect to the Internet using phone lines in the walls. Using simple adapter products, this becomes easily achievable. Home phone line networking should likely be your top choice for connecting desktop PCs into your home network. It prevents the need for you to run new wires (CAT5) through your walls for Ethernet net-

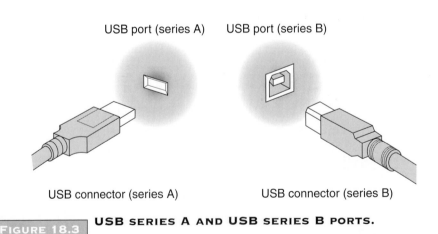

USB port (series A)   USB port (series B)

USB connector (series A)   USB connector (series B)

FIGURE 18.3 **USB SERIES A AND USB SERIES B PORTS.**

working, while keeping the cost of your home network low. Of course, this requires that your router or residential gateway also support home phone line networking; however, this is becoming more and more common because most service providers today offer phone line networking products to support this option.

Phone line networking technology provides a mechanism for connecting computers together using existing telephone wires throughout the home. Phone line networking is standardized by HomePNA, which has supported its development since 1998.

The current specification, HomePNA 2.0, supports data rates of 10 Mbps over standard telephone lines. It is similar to Ethernet in managing data transmission. The first specification, HomePNA 1.0, represented the introduction of the technology and was somewhat less than reliable. HomePNA 2.0 represents a huge leap forward over 1.0 in reliability and performance.

One of the best features of the technology is that it enables data communications between computers without interfering with regular voice communications, dialup modems, and/or DSL. In other words, you can have two computers networked over your phone line to a residential gateway that is connected to DSL on the same line while you simultaneously call your mother in Florida, using the same line. This is achieved by having each signal operate at a different frequency on the phone wire, avoiding conflict.

One unique aspect of HomePNA technology is that it has the capability of prioritizing different types of data traffic. This prioritization mechanism is called *quality of service*. This allows certain types of multimedia services to perform better than other networking technologies. Specifically, voice, video, and other multimedia streaming services benefit greatly from quality of service. For this reason, HomePNA is a likely candidate as the technology of choice for next-generation entertainment and multimedia appliances around the home, such as digitally networked telephones.

To create a home phone line network, you need either a PCI HomePNA card (see Figure 18.4) installed in your computer or an external HomePNA adapter (such as the 2Wire PC Port adapter shown in Figure 18.5). These devices make it possible to connect each additional computer through the phone line. In addition, your modem, router, or residential gateway should support HomePNA. Look for the HomePNA 2.0 certification mark for your best shot at reliable performance.

Again, home phone line networking (HomePNA) is a good choice if you are connecting secondary computers to your residential gateway. The secondary computer can be located either in the same room as the HomePortal or in a different room.

Fiber Optics

What happens when you take long strands of hollow, flexible glass or plastic and shoot light through them? You get fiber optics! There are two main designs for communications-type optical fiber: multimode fiber and

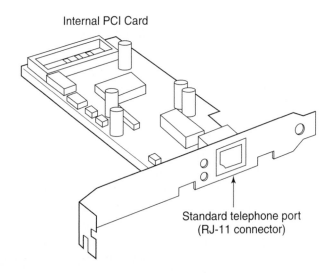

Internal PCI Card

Standard telephone port
(RJ-11 connector)

FIGURE 18.4 INTERNAL PCI HomePNA NETWORK CARD.

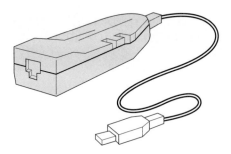

FIGURE 18.5 **2WIRE PC PORT IS A HIGH-SPEED USB TO HOMEPNA ADAPTER.**

single-mode fiber. Each is the size of a human hair, with identical outer diameters of 125 μm (micrometers, 1 millionth of a meter). The important difference is in the size of each fiber's core. The core of a single-mode fiber is 7–10 μm in diameter, and the core diameter of a multi-mode fiber is much larger, generally 50 μm or 62.5 μm. Core size is critical to how a fiber transmits data. Light propagates down the fiber core in a stable path known as a *mode*. Just as electrons transmit information down a copper wire, photons do the same thing in a fiber-optic system. The difference is that photons carry more information than electrons, and they do it faster.

DVORAK'S TIP

For more information on HomePNA technology and to find HomePNA products, consider the following Web sites:

www.homepna.org

www.2wire.com

www.dlink.com

www.netgear.com

www.linksys.com

Multimode fiber (Figure 18.6) is optical fiber that is designed to carry multiple light rays or modes concurrently, each at a slightly different reflection angle within the optical fiber core. Multimode fiber transmission is used for relatively short distances because the modes tend to disperse over longer lengths (called *modal dispersion*).

Single-mode fiber (Figure 18.7) is optical fiber that is designed for the transmission of a single ray or mode of light as a carrier and is used for long-distance signal transmission. It is sometimes called *monomode*.

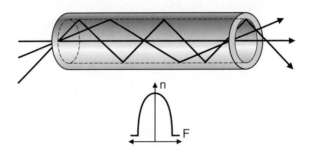

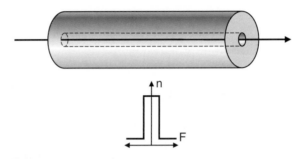

FIGURE 18.6 MODAL DISPERSION.

FIGURE 18.7 MONOMODE.

FIBER OPTICS

Fiber optics or optical fiber, however you want to refer to it, uses beams of light to transmit data through a small glass or plastic strand. It is capable of high transfer rates in the gigabits. Although fiber optics isn't really something you'd want to install for a home network, it is still worth mentioning for new construction (if you are willing to shell out the additional money as well as if you like a challenge or are slightly masochistic).

Pros

Extremely high transfer rates—*Gigabits*, enough said

Immune to EMI

Distance—Able to carry a signal long distances (miles) without assistance

Cons

Higher cost

Difficult to install and repair—Can't bend it very much, and patching is *very* difficult

Extremely difficult to retrofit into an existing home—Same issues as Ethernet wiring

Wireless

Wireless networking, also referred to by the IEEE as 802.11, is an outstanding option for connecting to the home network, especially for PCs located in rooms far from the router or gateway, or for mobile PCs that you want to tote from room to room. Two caveats: First, the cost of wireless networking may be higher than other connectivity options discussed; prices are coming down fast. Second, certain wireless networks may be difficult to set up; installation procedures are becoming easier for the lay person. The technology is so new that the setup process varies dramatically from manufacturer to manufacturer, so getting a network set up may test even the most patient person. That said, 802.11 wireless comes in different flavors, recognizable by the letter that follows.

802.11b

This was the first of the 802.11 technologies really to get traction in the marketplace and established itself as the wireless technology of choice. It is a 2.4-GHz technology touted at 11 Mbps. However, it performs at speeds below that, depending on distance and what sits between the wireless PC and the wireless router or gateway node that the PC is connecting to (called an *access point*). Walls of differing material can have a significant impact on wireless performance. Also of significance is that many cordless handsets operate at the same frequency, 2.4 GHz, and can cause interference with your network. However, it's great for simple surfing, email, and other data applications. And there's nothing like sitting in your living room, wire free, surfing the Net.

Wireless connectivity is most popular for notebook computers. It offers easy portability. The popular adapter type is a PC card based on the PCMCIA (Personal Computer Memory Card Internal Association) wireless adapter (Figure 18.8), which looks like a flat, metal credit card with a piece of black plastic (the antenna) attached at one end.

But, for desktop computers, research has shown that wireless is a popular connectivity option. It works well for households that want to connect a

FIGURE 18.8 AN 802.11B WIRELESS ADAPTER.

computer to the network in a room without a phone jack for HomePNA or Ethernet wiring (Figure 18.9).

802.11A, 802.11B, 802.11G

Pros
No wires to install
Availability of "turnkey" networking kits
Flexible—Access the network from anywhere in and around your home
Easy expansion—Additional systems can be added to the network with little effort
Cons
Varied network bandwidth—Network speed varies widely with conditions
Interference with other devices on the 2.4-GHz spectrum (microwaves, cordless phones, etc.)

802.11a and 802.11g

Although the 802.11 standard is here to stay, there remains some question about what comes next. The 802.11a specification operates at radio frequencies between 5 GHz and 6 GHz, achieving data speeds as high as 54 Mbps, but most commonly, communication takes place at around 24 Mbps. The trouble with 802.11a is that, given its operation at a higher frequency, it is impacted

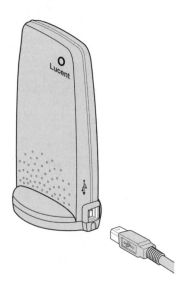

FIGURE 18.9 THE USB WIRELESS ADAPTER PROVIDES HIGH-SPEED WIRELESS INTERNET ACCESS AND NETWORKING.

even more adversely by walls and obstacles than is 802.11b. Accordingly, 802.11a has come to be regarded as more suitable for the business environment, where there are fewer walls between wireless PCs and access points.

That said, the next big advance for wireless networking in the home and small office will be 802.11g. It is the most recently approved standard. It offers wireless transmission at 2.4 GHz at up to 54 Mbps, but most commonly (like 802.11a) will operate at around 24 Mbps. Compared with the 11 Mbps of the 802.11b standard, 802.11g represents a leap forward. It is likely to become a standard offering, much like 10/100 autosensing cards have become for Ethernet.

> WiFi (wireless fidelity) is the certification mark that indicates that the manufacturer has built to the industry specification, ensuring interoperability with other 802.11 products. For more information on WiFi technology and products, consider visiting the WiFi Alliance Web site at www.weca.net. Another site of interest is 802.11-Planet (www.80211-planet.com).
>
> When considering the purchase of 802.11 products, it is important to look for WiFi-certified products.

Emerging Technologies

Many of you will have likely heard of other products and technologies that could serve to connect devices across your home network. We'll do our best to outline several technologies that fit into this category.

Bluetooth

Bluetooth is a wireless technology designed initially to enable devices to communicate over short distances. (Also see Chapter 19.) At one time, it was thought of as a mechanism to let PCs connect wirelessly and share a high-speed connection to the Internet. However, because Bluetooth operates in the 2.4-GHz frequency band, it conflicts with the more popular WiFi products (802.11b wireless technology, which has come to be the standard for wireless PC networking). Due to the conflict between technologies, Bluetooth has shifted its focus to serve as a personal area networking (PAN) technology, where WiFi serves as a local area networking (LAN) technology. In other words, Bluetooth is optimal for connecting devices that you carry or use in your immediate vicinity—mobile phones to computers to personal digital assistants (PDAs) to home and business phones to pagers. It is not optimal to provide shared access to the Internet. The maximum range of Bluetooth is approximately 10 meters, with a data exchange rate of 1. Recent efforts within the Bluetooth development community have suggested the possibility of allowing both Bluetooth and WiFi devices to operate simultaneously in the vicinity of one another.

To learn more about Bluetooth, visit its Web site at www.bluetooth.org.

IEEE 1394 (or FireWire)

Much like Bluetooth, FireWire is a distance-constrained, high-speed technology for connecting devices in the immediate vicinity of one another. FireWire technology provides transfer speeds up to 400 Mbps, faster than any other LAN technology available on the market, and can support up to 63 devices connected to one another. At such data rates, FireWire has become regarded as an ideal technology for multimedia applications, such as transferring video from a digital video camera into one's PC for creating and editing digital home movies. It is an established standard (1394) coming from the IEEE, again meaning that anyone manufacturing products uses the same blueprint to ensure that it works with other manufacturers' products.

FIREWIRE (IEEE 1394)

Networking with FireWire means you can transfer data at 100–400 Mbps with little latency but this is limited to 15 feet between computers (without the use of repeaters). Repeaters can be placed between 15-foot cables for a maximum distance of 237 feet. You are limited to a maximum of 63 devices on the network.

Another option to increase the distance between your FireWire network-enabled computers is to use a FireWire-to-fiber transceiver. These are starting to appear on the market and allow a FireWire signal to travel up to 40 km, or 24.856 miles. Right now, they are in the $500 range but should come down. An Ethernet to fiber transceiver is currently only about $120.

1394 is an established IEEE standard, but equipment is expensive, making it a not-so-economical choice for home networking, when compared with other technologies. FireWire is ideally suited for connecting PC peripherals that require high-speed connectivity. And, although there are efforts to migrate IEEE 1394 in the direction of a networking technology, don't expect to see progress here any time soon.

Pros

High transfer rates with little latency

Cons

Limited to 63 devices

Distance—Maximum of 15 feet between devices without using repeaters

Higher cost

Although many technology companies would consider FireWire a candidate for home networking, it has several things going against it. First, 1394 requires new wires around the home or office. If one wanted to locate a PC in another room, it would require stringing new wiring from one room to another. Second, the equipment is expensive, making it a not-so-economical choice for home networking, vis-à-vis other technologies. Although it is ideally suited for connecting PC peripherals that require high-speed connectivity. There

DVORAK'S TIP

To learn more about 1394/ FireWire, visit the following Web sites:

**www.1394ta.org
www.apple.com/firewire/**

are efforts to migrate FireWire in the direction of a networking technology, but don't expect to see progress here any time soon.

Powerline Networking (HomePlug Powerline Alliance)

The newest player in the world of connectivity technology is Powerline networking. The concept here is that just about every room in the home or office has a power outlet through which devices can be connected to one another in the same room or from room to room. Accordingly, Powerline technology leverages the existing wires to keep the cost and complexity of connectivity down. Further, the technology does not interfere with electrical service, allowing you to plug lamps and appliances into the same outlet without interference.

POWERLINE NETWORKING

Powerline communication-style technology has been attempted for years but never worked very well. An electrical power line is a noisy and unstable medium in which to manage data communications, which results in varying throughput rates and reliability. These challenges associated with powerline networking have become less problematic, due to recent advancements.

Pros

Easy install—Wired network without installing wires

Low cost

Cons

New technology bugs

Questionable reliability and security

Peak 14 Mbps throughput

Powerline networking was recently established as a standard by the HomePlug Powerline Alliance, meaning that anyone manufacturing products uses the same blueprint to ensure that it works with other manufacturers' products. In this particular instance, 13 industry-leading companies formed the alliance in March of 2000 and agreed on the HomePlug 1.0 specification in June of 2001. First products shipped in early 2002, so this is still an early technology that may need to shake out a little, but it has at least been recognized as a standard. Important is that the historical challenges associated with Powerline networking have become less problematic. Traditionally, the power line is a "noisy" medium in which to manage data communications. In other words, homes maintain many sources of electrical noise that can interfere with data signals. Accordingly, throughput rates can be impacted. However, recent strides have diminished the impact.

Compared with Powerline technology, tried-and-true Ethernet provides a low-cost, high-reliability in-room solution for connectivity. Phone line technology provides a low-cost, high-performance solution for connectivity with quality of service and wireline guarantees. Wireless is simply cool and allows nearly ubiquitous access to the Internet from anywhere in the home. The question to be resolved is whether powerline networking products will be able to carve out a niche for themselves amidst alternatives.

PIRILLO'S TIP

To learn more about Powerline networking or Powerline technology, visit any of the following Web sites:

www.homeplug.org
www.intellon.com
www.enikia.com

HOME NETWORKS FOR DIALUP

If you have dialup Internet service, you are limited to connection speeds of 28–56 Kbps. With such limited bandwidth, your options for sharing your Internet connection across your home are limited both by bandwidth and available technology. On the bandwidth side, sharing a 28-Kbps connection would, in essence, provide two users on a home network with only 14 Kbps, which is a step in the wrong direction for most. Accordingly, in a dialup context, most people will want to think of a home network as a means by which files and printers can be shared between computers. In this model, each PC has its own adapter and, depending on the adapter types, connects to the other computers through a hub or switch.

Should you become determined to find a solution for Internet connection sharing (ICS), there are a limited number of options available. The most affordable of these requires using Windows. It is possible to configure your computer for ICS where a single PC in the home manages the dialup connection to the Internet, then shares that connection with other PCs that are connected to it through a hub and/or switch.

PIRILLO'S TIP

Valuable Web sites for information on ICS configuration include:

Microsoft Windows XP configuration:
www.microsoft.com/windowsxp/pro/using/howto/networking/ics.asp
Microsoft Windows 98 Second Edition configuration:
www.microsoft.com/insider/articles/ics.asp
Microsoft Windows 2000:
http://support.microsoft.com/?kbid=237254
Apple users go to www.apple.com, click support, then search for "Internet connection sharing."

LAN Modems

Although not the most affordable solution, a LAN modem can eliminate some of the complexities associated with Windows. These include:

3Com OfficeConnect 56K LAN Modem and 3Com OfficeConnect Dual 56K LAN Modem each provide connectivity for PCs with Ethernet adapters to plug into Ethernet ports of this device to share a 56-Kpbs modem connection (around $250).

Netgear's RM356 provides connectivity for PCs with Ethernet adapters to plug into Ethernet ports of this device to share a 56-Kpbs modem connection (around $300).

HP 802.11b Wireless LAN Small Business Access Point from Hewlett Packard provides connectivity for PCs with wireless 802.11 adapters to plug into Ethernet ports of this device to share a 56-Kpbs modem connection (around $400).

The one benefit of home networking through dialup is that very few service providers maintain and/or enforce terms and conditions that limit multi-PC access through a broadband connection. In other words, only some service providers limit their support of home networking, especially in a broadband context.

Home Networks for Broadband

If you have broadband Internet service, your bandwidth is enough to accommodate multiple simultaneous connections throughout your home. Unfortunately, the solutions for sharing access are not so clear anymore and depend greatly on your service provider and associated service.

SERVICE PROVIDERS: FACT AND FICTION

A couple of questions always arise in one's mind when considering equipment and support plans from service providers. I'll do my best to separate the facts from the fiction.

Service providers don't usually offer the best technology available on the market—FICTION

The first question often asked is if it makes sense to find your own equipment, perhaps at a better price or with more features, than what is offered by the service provider. In most cases, the service provider has screened the products on the market to ensure that the product it offers to you (a) works on the network, (b) is familiar to its support technicians for easy troubleshooting, and (c) is best of breed with regard to security, installation ease, and features offered. In addition, most providers today offer products at a price competitive with what you would find at retail. Further, many subsidize said equipment so as to retain you as a broadband customer. The thinking here is that the more devices you connect to their broadband services, the more addicted you will become to their offerings, and the less likely you will be to turn to another provider. This works out to your benefit in terms of initial cash outlay.

If I buy home networking products in retail, the provider won't troubleshoot any of my broadband problems until I disconnect my home network—FACT (in most cases)

Most service providers are not prepared to answer questions regarding the various networking products on the market that they don't offer themselves. This is the reason that they typically ship a specific modem, adapter cards, and/or related products. This ensures that they have a baseline from which to provide customer care and assess the root cause of any problem. That said, if you install a home network and call for support when experiencing a service outage (they do happen in the broadband world), it is likely that the service agent will troubleshoot the problem starting from the desktop, working backward toward the modem, then to the network. Without fail, if you try to answer their questions while you have a home network installed, it will prove impossible. They consistently discover that you have a home network and will ask that you call back at a later time after you have set up your home according to the directions provided with your installation package in a non-networked configuration. The only way around this is to purchase a support plan.

The key here is whether the benefits of such packages are pertinent to you. In most instances, you pay the service provider approximately $10 per month for a home networking support plan. What do you get for your money? First, you get access to that provider's service and support lines for the setup of your home network. For those out there who are technical, this doesn't seem like a very good return on your investment. However, for those of you starting out with networking, having an expert available 24 hours a day, 7 days a week is of high value, especially at the beginning, when you are setting up.

Once you have your home network up and running, the support plan provides an ongoing resource for you to turn to as you (a) add more computers and devices to your network, (b) change technologies you use on any given computer (say, for example, that you want to enable your notebook computer to use a wireless connection and it's Ethernet-connected today), and (c) add more software to your PC, which may or may not have an impact on your network's performance. This can prove to be a great resource for the beginner and intermediate user.

In addition, most service providers are now realizing that to sustain the value proposition to the established user, they must also offer incremental value-added services for home networking customers for the $10 per month. Accordingly, a new range of services called *broadband applications* are being introduced by providers in conjunction with the monthly fee to further reward and retain home networking customers. Examples of these services include enhanced firewall service, parental control service, and remote access services. These packages offer significant enhancements over the traditional software-based offerings available on the market today and are network based, so they can provide support for all devices in the home without the need for loading software on the PC.

Assuming that I don't have any problems with my broadband service and/or don't need to call customer care, the service provider won't know if I've bought my own home network or not—FACT.

Service providers are set up to hand out a single IP address to each household that subscribes to their services. When you set up a router or residential gateway to receive and manage that IP address for the house, that provider does not have visibility into how many computers you are supporting in your home. Accordingly, should you choose to buy a router at retail and set it up at home, it may very well work, and you'll get along just fine. Just make sure that you have a neighbor or cousin who can assist you if you run into trouble. And be aware that you may miss out on some other great offerings from your service provider.

DSL Service Providers

If you have or intend to subscribe to DSL service, the major service providers (SBC, BellSouth, Verizon, and Earthlink) offer certified home networking products for use on their networks today, as well as support plans.

In addition, these providers either offer the enhanced broadband applications described above and/or make them available for an à la carte subscription. In all cases, DSL providers are subsidizing the cost of the equipment, providing a significantly lower cost than you would find in retail, because this is offset by the monthly charge for home networking support. Also, many of these providers ship residential gateway products (integrated modems and routers), which provide overall better performance than standard modems and off-the-shelf routers.

DSL providers (in most instances) can provide you with a "home network in a box" if you are interested. In other words, they can supply all of the equipment and pieces needed to get you up and running without your needing to go to the store and figure it out on your own. Because most providers don't provide details on their Web sites, call to get information about their offerings.

To learn more about their home networking products, visit 2Wire's Web site at www.2wire.com because all DSL providers currently offer the 2Wire HomePortal residential gateway.

Cable Service Providers

Cable providers also support home networking, albeit not as widely as DSL providers. The difference between the cable and DSL environments is that cable, for the most part, has not historically embraced router products. Instead, cable companies have insisted that each PC be assigned its own unique public IP address, which they assign to you. That means that cable providers will charge you a fee for each PC beyond your first that you want to connect to the Internet. Because the provider in this model generates a fee for each PC, there is no limit to the number of PCs that can be added to the network.

Some providers offer the associated networking equipment in conjunction with such service for an added cost. In many cases, they will direct you to retail. Note that in this context, given that each PC has its own IP address, a router isn't needed. For this reason, the equipment needs vary such that adapters are needed for each PC, then the PCs connect to the Internet through a simple hub or switch, rather than a router, which provides an interface to the broadband modem. It is worth noting that there is again no technical reason that a router can't work in this environment.

It is also worth noting that the cable industry is starting to welcome the router and residential gateway concepts. Accordingly, Cable Labs, the industry's nonprofit research and development consortium pursuing new cable telecommunications technologies, has been driving toward a more advanced model for service delivery into the home through its Cable Home initiative, developing the interface specifications necessary to extend high-quality, cable-based services to network devices within the home. One of the early adopters of router technology has been Time Warner Cable, which has conducted extensive trials with home networking products.

RETAIL AND ONLINE STORES

Most retailers and online stores these days offer home networking products. Although these can be popular destinations for some elements of your home network, such as adapter cards, hubs, switches, and even routers, you will always want to consider the potential offer from your service provider before making a decision to buy. Service providers are making tremendous offers that in most instances beat the discounts you would expect to find online. Do your homework in retail and online, then make an educated decision when talking to your service provider.

PLANNING AND INSTALLATION

Draw out a plan of your home. Note where the modem/residential gateway and PCs will be located; you will be on your way to deciding which technology to purchase. The following notes provide more background and suggestions for detailing your picture or technology blueprint.

Some Network Considerations

When mapping out your home network, consider the following questions as a starting point.

- Where will I locate my modem or residential gateway that connects to the Internet?

- How many PCs can I locate in the same room as that modem or residential gateway?

- How many PCs do I want to locate in other rooms?

- Are there any immobile objects to be dealt with?

- Is there a phone jack in that room?

- Will I want to move my notebook computers around the house?

- Are there a few locations, or many?

DVORAK'S NETWORKING RESOURCES

The following Web sites represent additional resources you can leverage in gathering more information on networking your home and/or office.

Practically Networked offers great reviews of the latest networking products:

www.practicallynetworked.com

Test your home network's security by visiting Gibson Research Corporation's security check site, where you can run the popular ShieldsUP! security test:

www.grc.com

Check your bandwidth to see what kind of performance you are getting by visiting 2Wire's Bandwidth Meter utility. Or, if you are looking for high-speed Internet, check 2Wire's DSL lookup service to find a provider in your area:

www.2wire.com

The first step in planning your network installation is getting an idea of the cost, scope, and size of the installation. Installing a network during a major remodel when the walls are open is a lot easier than retrofitting a network when the walls are closed up.

A star topology is the most cost-effective and easiest to build and configure. And I don't know of a house that's more than 100 yards long in any direction, so twisted-pair category 5 or 5e cabling will be the cable medium of choice. It offers easy installation at low cost, and CAT5e is capable of gigabit transfer rates.

With your professional/homemade blueprints, you need to locate a wiring closet location. A wiring closet should be out of the way from traffic (and isolated from tiny hands) and have an electrical outlet close by. If you are planning to connect the network to a cable, ISDN, or DSL line, then a phone jack or cable hookup is also going to be a requirement for the wiring closet.

After you have decided on where you're going to locate your hub and router, you should identify which rooms will receive network jacks or "cable drops." Each cable drop network segment will require a port on your hub or switch.

If you are retrofitting a network into an existing home and not during a remodel, you can get category 5/5e network cable that is designed to be run under carpets.

SUMMARY

Although networking may seem daunting to the newcomer, it's as important to using today's computers as knowing how to use a floppy disk was 20 years ago. There are plenty of people who will help you, too; just ask your friends. Everyone has an opinion on how to do things right. Above all, don't be afraid to experiment. Today's networking gear, despite its complexity, usually works better than anyone would have imagined even a decade ago.

19
HANDHELDS,
PHONES,
AND PDAs

Back in the late 1980s and the early 1990s, your choice of PC was limited to a desktop MS-DOS or Apple Mac. There were early *luggable* machines (weighing 10–12 lbs) that were called "portable" (a joke, in retrospect). As the size and weight of these machines decreased, they were called *laptops* and *notebook computers*.

Computing technology evolved. Computers became smaller and more portable. In 1988, Sharp introduced the Wizard, which featured a small LCD screen and a tiny keyboard. The Wizard was marketed as a replacement for paper-based appointment calendars and address books, and supplemented the PC.

Psion was the first manufacturer of a handheld computer, or personal digital assistant (PDA). There were many other, early handhelds. One was the Newton Message Pad, by Apple, released in 1993. In 1997, Apple released the eMate, but it was discontinued a year later before the handwriting recognition problems could be overcome.

Other entries to the market were by Hewlett-Packard, Motorola, Sharp, and Sony Electronics. These early devices required typing on a very small keyboard or some form of handwriting recognition system; neither were very effective. Although people were ready for the small devices, the technology hadn't quite arrived. These devices were too clunky and had the wrong feature set.

Arguably the most important PDA to date has been the Palm Pilot, which began life as something called the *Zoomer*. In 1995, Palm Computing was acquired by U.S. Robotics. The following year, a keyboardless PDA was introduced with a touch-sensitive screen coupled with the company's *Graffiti* handwriting system for data entry. (Graffiti is a simplified intuitive alphabet that is easily learned in about 20 minutes.) Using Personal Information Management (PIM), you could track appointments, addresses, notes, and to-do lists, and share this information with your PC or with others.

The Palm's keyboardless device segmented the market into PDAs with keyboards and those without. In the years since, the handhelds have been further reduced in size. Now there are palm-sized machines, on-the-go email machines, and PDA/telephone combination devices, among others. The evolution isn't over.

HANDHELD DEVICES TODAY

There are a number of PDA devices on the market today. An important difference between them is the operating system (OS). Three OSs struggle for dominance:

- Windows CE
- EPOC
- Palm OS

Windows CE

Windows CE, Microsoft's first purpose-built embedded OS, was released in 1996. The original CE supported monochrome devices. Support for color was introduced in CE 2.0, and support for RISC-based (Reduced Instruction Set Computer) processors was added in version 2.1. Although 40 manufactures were originally on board, the first CE devices were not well received by consumers. The main complaints were the limitations of the OS and a limited battery life, due to software that was too demanding for the environment. Another, more fundamental problem was that Microsoft had chosen to emulate the look and feel of the traditional Windows graphical user interface (GUI) on a much smaller form factor. The argument was that the OS was too complicated for a PDA device. Microsoft initially attempted to address this by splitting CE into two versions: Handheld PC Pro (H/PC Pro) for keyboard-based PDAs and the Palm PC (P/PC). Even with improvements, CE had a lot of ground to overcome to catch up with the other OSs on the market.

In 2000, Microsoft released a Pocket PC platform based on the CE foundation. It abandoned the idea of making a mini-desktop machine on a PDA and instead addressed functionality issues, simplified the user interface, and aimed at a more advanced handheld market. The focus would be on Intel's SA-1110 processor that was in Compaq's iPaq handheld, which was able to clock speeds of up to 206 MHz (compared with the 33 MHz on a typical low-end Palm with the Motorola Dragonball processor).

The shift in direction was significant. The move was toward the business market instead of the individual user. The latest version has support for Bluetooth, the Institute of Electrical and Electronics Engineers (IEEE) 802.11, and mobile phone technologies, such as CDPD (Cellular Digital Packet Data), CDMA (Code Division Multiple Access), and GSM (Global System for Mobil communications). Connectivity options range from VPN (Virtual Private Network), WAN (Wide Area Network), and LAN (Local Area Network) to PAN (Personal Area Network). Multimedia software Windows Media Player 8 is supported, which will allow digital music and movie clips to be played.

EPOC

This is an OS used by Psion PDAs since 1997. The name came from the company's belief that the world was entering into a *new epoch of personal convenience.* The original OS, Psion's Series 3 OS, ran only on RISC-based processors, using an ARM architecture (a proprietary microprocessor design). For the Series 5, EPOC became the name for the OS itself and evolved into a 32-bit open system. It was not until 1997 that Psion began to license its OS. Philips was the first manufacturer to license EPOC. In 1998, Psion joined with Ericsson, Nokia, and later Motorola, in a joint venture called *Symbian*. Symbian now licenses the EPOC32 OS and continues to develop it. The vision is a convergence of mobile computing wireless technology, Internet access, messaging, and information access with the aim of making EPOC the de facto OS for mobile wireless information devices.

Palm OS

The Palm OS was designed to fit into a palm-size device of a specific size and with a specific display size. (The other two OSs will work on a broader range of devices.) The OS uses task switching. In other words, a user can run only one task at a time. The space needed by the system for any application running is kept in dynamic, reusable RAM (random access memory). The application and databases are kept in what Palm calls *permanent storage*. In this case, the permanent storage is also RAM (which cannot be reused as the dynamic RAM can be). Palm OS does not use a hard disk. It divides an application into run code and data elements, such as user interface and icons. The data elements can be changed without rewriting code. The Palm OS has built-in applications such as date, address book, to-do lists, memo pad, and a calculator. Other applications can be easily added, and Palm has tried to encourage third-party development of these.

HANDHELD EQUIPMENT

In the future, wireless handheld devices will be a common way to access the online world. But you don't have to wait for some future world to realize the benefits of wireless handheld mobility. Wireless or wireless-enabled devices are available and useful right now. Their functionality and popularity are growing, and there are easy and cost-effective ways to get online with the 25 million handheld devices already purchased. Enter the world of wireless-enabled handhelds, data communicators, and smartphones.

The choices are unique in intent and purpose. They range from traditional PDA-style devices with integrated voice and data capabilities to mobile telephones with PDA features. Other makers are coming into the market with their own unique and innovative concepts. The industry is going in several directions at once. Palm and the Pocket PC-type devices are staying with the concept of a PDA focus, while Smart Phones and Blackberry have taken a different approach. All fall within the classification of *handhelds*.

Palm

Palm, Inc. makes it a point to emphasize that it builds *data-centric* devices. The concept is that people will use the device for its data capabilities and that voice is another added-on application. Palm's continued emphasis is on large displays and innovative input mechanisms. Their emphasis is on creating devices that look like a traditional PDA, rather than a telephone. (For comparison, consider that Handspring, Kyocera, and Samsung build phone- or voice-based devices, with data as a secondary consideration.) This path puts the Palm clearly in the business of competing with the big phone manufacturers—a daunting task at best. The design of these telephone-style devices does not yet suit the two basic requirements of a solid winner in this category—a great phone with a built-in PDA.

Pocket PC

Pocket PC is a generic term meaning any device that runs the Windows CE OS. They all share the same characteristics: lots of memory, big processors, poor battery life, and a complex user interface. If Pocket PC is anything like the OS model that spawned the IBM clones of the 1980s and 1990s, the devices, regardless of vendor, will all be compatible.

Smartphone

Historically, mobile phones were carry-about versions of their PSTN fixed-phone counterparts. (PSTN, Public Switched Telephone Network, is an international telephone system based on copper wires to carry analog voice data.) As telephone networks began to incorporate digital technology, their ability to transmit data improved and began to seek more data capability from mobile phones. The term *smartphone* means a wireless cell phone with other features not usually associated with telephones. These features might include some or all of the following features:

- Wireless email, Internet, Web browsing, and fax
- Intercom function
- PIM
- Online baking

- LAN connectivity
- Graffiti-style data entry
- Local data transfer between phone set and computers
- Remote control of computers
- Remote data transfer between phone set and computers
- Remote control of home or business electronic systems
- Interactivity with unified messaging

Blackberry

The original Blackberry device was a pager-sized handheld made by Research In Motion to deliver email and messages to roaming executives. Newer models have a keyboard and screen, more like a traditional PDA. In North America, the Blackberry uses four different wireless networks: GPRS (General Packet Radio Service), Datatrac, Mobitex, and the Nextel IDEN network. In Europe, Blackberry uses the global GPRS network.

Information packets are delivered over different backbones, including Microsoft Exchange Server and Lotus Notes Domino, as well as Internet-only email systems. The Blackberry architecture is designed to address security issues that pervade the wireless device world (eavesdropping, theft of equipment and information, viruses, denial of service [DoS] attack, spoofing, and hijacking).

SOME IDEAS

If what you want is an integrated, all-in-one voice and data device, you should consider one-piece solutions such as the Kyocera 6035, Samsung i300, Handspring Treo, or Palm Tungsten. These devices are ideal if you want to merge phone functionality into a PDA (or vice versa) and to access information wirelessly via your wireless service provider's data network. This solution is also ideal if you want to carry only one device. Although the units can be handy, they have their limitations, as well. One-piece solutions, in general, often wind up sacrificing key features or functionality of standalone devices because manufacturers need to hit certain price points. For example, the phone functionality in a one-piece is not likely to match all of the phone features that are in many of today's mid- to high-end mobile phones. Likewise, the screens may be smaller and have lower resolution, and the battery power may be less than that of a standalone PDA.

If you want to maximize the benefits of a separate mobile phone and a separate PDA, you should look at two-piece solutions. The two-piece approach, some-

---

times called a *best-of-breed approach*, allows you to select the best phone and the best PDA, then customize the solution for your own needs. Using this approach, the phone becomes a modem or gateway back to the network. By linking the PDA to the phone, either by a physical tether (cable) or by Bluetooth, the PDA can access the wireless network via the phone.

GO WIRELESS

So where are wireless browsers going? For the near term, think of a PC browser running on a 56K dialup connection. Blend that with the gamer's view of lots of input devices; keyboards; stylus; voice; mini joysticks; and authoring standards, such as XML/XHTML and Java; and give it a shot of vendor-specific special sauce, such as digital media players playing MP4 and proprietary content. The downside will be, of course, that lots of advertisers will know where you are at all times, so they can send you that fast food ad before you drive by. Nothing's perfect.

As with much of the digital community these days, a number of nontechnical matters, such as alliances, content types, and price points, will determine how fast you get a robust, PC-like experience on your wireless device. But in the meantime, there are services useful enough to justify investing in wireless Web browsing, such as finding a theater with the right movie playing and getting tickets while driving along—right after your significant other mentions that it's your anniversary.

Another reason to go wireless is that, although it's still not cheap, the cost of wireless connectivity is becoming more reasonable, even for average consumers. It is convenient to grab information on the fly. It's handy to be able to find the nearest services of a gas station, for instance, when you're in unfamiliar territory. Wireless can also give you the freedom to communicate with friends and family while you're out and about. Mobile professionals (sales and field service people) need access to corporate data when they're traveling. This group currently is the biggest target market for wireless handhelds.

However, today, wireless really refers to the ability of a device to communicate with another device or machine/infrastructure without using wires or a cable.

Sort of Wireless vs. Wireless

Many handheld vendors advertise their products as "wireless" or having wireless capabilities when what they mean is that it runs on an internal battery (therefore, needs no wires to connect to a power source). It is technically wireless, but not what we're talking about.

What makes a handheld wireless is that it can communicate with another device or remote infrastructure via one of the wireless technologies.

Until recently, wireless has been synonymous with networks based on WAN technologies. Most people associate wireless with roaming the countryside (to use the device in a car, in the middle of a field, or at the beach). Recently, however, connecting to a wireless infrastructure at a local coffee shop via 802.11 or using Bluetooth to turn a phone into a wireless modem while sitting in an airport have become more common.

WAN technologies are ideal for traveling executives and workers who depend on wireless coverage. (It's common for delivery, transport, shipping, and a multitude of other service-industry applications.) But 802.11 and, to a lesser extent, Bluetooth technologies are becoming far more prevalent today, and it is these technologies as they continue to evolve that will become the foundation of the true next generation of wireless communications around the globe.

Although you might select a handheld for the wireless technology it provides, there are other things to consider that will affect your purchase decision. Bear in mind that a handheld, as powerful as it might be, is really more like a watch than a PC, in that you will generally use it for lots of quick activities. For example, you might use it to look up a phone number or check your schedule to see when your next appointment is.

You probably will spend a significant percentage of your time doing activities such as keeping notes, looking up contact information, and managing your schedule. These are PIM activities. If PIM is actually at the top of your list, as it is for many handheld users, the Palm OS has the clear advantage. Tables 19.1, 19.2, and 19.3 give you a quick idea of handheld usage. Again, think of the watch metaphor.

CONSIDERATIONS BEYOND SOFTWARE

Choosing a wireless handheld wisely comes down to a couple of basic questions: What kind of wireless user am I, and what are my choices? When you choose any kind of handheld device, you need to think about what's going to work for you: how you intend to use the handheld and what you need wireless for. Core features to consider as you shop for your device include wearability and battery life, display, memory, and expandability. Battery life is a key aspect of wearability. For Palm Powered handhelds, battery life is measured in days and weeks, typically several times longer than that of Pocket PC devices. For you, it means being able to carry your handheld with you without constantly having to worry about recharging batteries. Battery life is an important consideration for laptops, but it is even more critical for handhelds. People tend to carry power cords along with their laptops, and it's fairly easy to find an electrical out-

---

let for supplemental power. With handhelds, it's inconvenient to lug around a carrying case and charger all the time. Doing so would, in fact, defeat the purpose of carrying a handheld. You have to be able to put it in your pocket or purse, or it simply isn't useful.

The screen should be large enough to read information easily and with the least amount of scrolling, especially if you have an email-intensive job. Resolution and screen technology specs can be confusing, and user experience is subjective. It's a good policy to compare devices in the same light, preferably both indoors and outdoors. Also, consider your need for color carefully. Although color may make reading easier, it also uses more battery power, and color devices generally cost more. Finally, you want to look at memory and expandability. RAM is important for storing applications, but expandability is also important. Check to see that the device has expansion slots and a way to connect other devices and accessories in the future.

Service Providers

Most of the larger wireless carriers in the United States now offer GPRS or CDMA 1X wireless data services. When selecting a carrier, you will need to take into consideration the network technology, coverage area—local vs. regional vs. national data coverage—cost of the service, and device selection. Like conventional mobile phones, integrated wireless PDAs are built to work on specific networks. For example, the Samsung i300 works only on Sprint's network in the United States, and it won't work on AT&T's network.

Wireless networks can be divided into the following categories:

- PAN
- Wireless LAN (W-LAN), such as 802.11a and b
- WAN, which encompasses networks based on Time Division Multiple Access (TDMA), CDMA, Mobitex, GPRS, and others

POCKET PC VS. PALM OS—THE USER EXPERIENCE

Microsoft Pocket PC OS provides an Internet experience that's closer to what you'd experience on a PC—if you were looking at a Web page on your PC through a keyhole. To find what you're looking for, you have to scroll up, down, left, and right. This can make navigating a Web site pretty tedious. Further, in some cases, the text is too small to read. Palm OS provides a generally faster Internet experience because the browsers are designed to strip out graphics and format the pages especially for the small screen. The data you see is specifically the information you requested, which can be nice when you're looking up movie times, for example.

TABLE 19.1 PDAs AND HANDHELDS

Smartphones

Manufacturer	Model	Palm OS	Memory	Battery	Input/Display
Handspring	Treo 300	3.5.2H	16 MB	Rechargeable	Built-in, backlit keyboard/Over 4,000 colors (12-bit color, backlit)
Handspring	Treo 270	3.5	16 MB	Rechargeable	Keypad/12-Bit (4,000 colors)
Handspring	Treo 180	3.5.2H	16 MB	Rechargeable	Built-in keyboard or Graffiti/Monochrome (16 shades of gray)
Kyocera	QCP-6035	3.5	8 MB	Rechargeable	Graffiti-handwriting/grayscale screen
Kyocera	7135	4.1	16 MB	Rechargeable and user Replaceable	Graffiti-handwriting/high-resolution screen with 65,000 colors
Samsung	SPH-I300	3.5.2	8 MB	Rechargeable	Graffiti-handwriting/160 by 240, STN screen displays 256 colors
Samsung	SPH-I330	3.5.3	16 MB	Rechargeable	Graffiti-handwriting/160x240, STN screen, displays 256 colors

TABLE 19.2 ADD-ON PHONE CAPABILITY

Manufacturer	Model	Battery	Web Browser
Handspring	Sprint PCS Digital Link	Rechargeable	Blazer 2.0
Handspring	Visorphone	Rechargeable	Blazer 2.0

Voice				
Browsers	**Network Tech**	**Mode**	**Talk Time/Standby (variable depending on a number of factors)**	**Carriers**
Blazer 2.0	CDMA 2000 (1xRTT) 1900 MHz	Dual mode	2.5 hours/150 hours	Sprint
Blazer 2.0	GSM; free GPRS upgrade	Dual mode	180 min/150 hours	Cingular or T-Mobile
Blazer 2.0	GSM; free GPRS upgrade	Dual mode	150 min/60 hours	Cingular or T-Mobile
HTML and WAP browsers	CDMA	Tri-mode	5 hours/180 hours	Verizon
HTML, Web Clipping and WAP	CDMA2000 1X	Tri-mode	3.2 hours/123 hours in digital mode	Carriers to be announced
Open-wave Mobile Browser 4.1, Web Clipping	CDMA	Dual mode	240 min/100 hours	Sprint
UP4.1-compliant, Web clipping	CDMA 2000 1X	Tri-band	4 hours/100 hours	Sprint

Network Tech	**Mode**	**Talk Time/Standby**	**Carriers**
CDMA	Dual mode	7 hours/300 hours	Sprint
GSM	Dual band	3 hours/3 days	Cingular or T-Mobile

TABLE 19.3 | DATA COMMUNICATORS (INTEGRATED WIRELESS RADIO)

			Data		
Manufacturer	**Model**	**Palm OS**	**Processor/ Memory**	**Battery**	**Input/Display**
Palm	i705	4.1	8 MB	Rechargeable	Palm mini or portable key-board (sold separately)/Transreflective Monochrome LCD with Backlight

Personal Area Network

PAN refers to wireless technologies (Bluetooth and infrared) that focus on short-distance wireless connections between devices. PAN is the interconnection of devices within the range of a person. It's a range of 15–35 feet. This means essentially that a person with a laptop, a PDA, a small printer, and a cell phone could connect them all together with some wireless technology. (The drawback to infrared is that it requires a direct, uninterrupted line of sight between the two devices.)

Hardware products that incorporate PAN technologies can be made smaller and cheaper than those built on other wireless technologies. PAN solutions, which reduce the speed at which data can be transmitted (up to 2 Mbps), are ideal for coordinating and managing communication with other devices.

WEAR YOUR COMPUTER?

The term *PAN* can also mean *wearable* computer devices that communicate with other computers, using the electrical conductivity of the human body as the data network, but to date, it's mostly theoretical *Buck Rogers* stuff. Wearables have been developed for the disabled, so this technology is probably not far off in the future.

The MIT Wearable Computing Web Page, MIThril, the next-generation research platform for context-aware wearable computing, describes wearable as:

> To date, personal computers have not lived up to their name. Most machines sit on the desk and interact with their owners for only a small fraction of the day. Smaller and faster notebook computers have made mobility less of an issue, but the said staid user paradigm persists. Wearable computing hopes to

| Wireless | Voice | | | | |
	Communications Software	Network Tech	Mode	Talk Time/ Standby	Carriers
Via Palm.Net service; Mobitex integrated wireless radio paging system transmitter-receiver	MultiMail Deluxe, AvantGo, and MyPalm Portal.	—	—	—	—

shatter this myth of how a computer should be used. A person's computer should be worn, much as eyeglasses or clothing are worn, and interact with a user based on the context of the situation. With heads-up displays, unobtrusive input devices, personal wireless local area networks, and a host of other context sensing and communication tools, the wearable computer can act as an intelligent assistant, whether it be through a Remembrance Agent, augmented reality, or intellectual collectives.

Thad Starner's concept, in development by Bradley Rhodes at the MIT Media Lab, is a computer to recognize and recall information about people in a room. Then it would whisper in your ear to remind you of their names and other mundane details of their lives or your last meeting with them. (It's not intended to be a spouse replacement, though.) Or it could be a "remembrance agent" and look for related documents while you were typing or take notes for you.

For more information, go to www.media.mit.edu/wearables/lizzy/.

Another term often used for this is *wireless personal area network* (WPAN). The technical difference would be that a PAN is centered around one person, and a WPAN is a connection without wires serving multiple users.

If you like a small, sleek, sexy cell phone and a small, sleek, sexy handheld, you might look at a PAN-based solution. Basically, you turn your phone into a communications module that never needs to leave your pocket or briefcase. And you turn your handheld into the brains of the system, dialing and answering calls using a Bluetooth headset establishing "high-speed" data connections using your phone as a wireless data modem. When you want to get away from email, you can leave your handheld at home and just carry that slim, sexy phone.

Bluetooth

Bluetooth is an evolving, short-range networking protocol to connect different devices. It is intended as a "global specification for wireless connectivity." This is a specification for a short-range (35-feet range) radio technology. Bluetooth allows short-distance wireless connections in a 360-degree circle to link network devices (mobile phones, laptop computers, and handheld organizers and/or cellular phones) or between network devices and the Internet without using Ethernet cables.

Bluetooth requires that a low-cost transceiver chip (utilizing the previously unused frequency band of 2.45 GHz) be installed in each device. They will then have a unique 48-bit (IEEE 802 standard) address. Data can be transferred at the rate of 1 MB per second. Encryption and verification are built in, and there is a frequency hop scheme to allow for communications during electromagnetic interference.

IEEE

The IEEE is a nonprofit, technical and professional association of more than 377,000 individual members in 150 countries. Through its members, the IEEE is a leading authority in technical areas ranging from computer engineering, biomedical technology, and telecommunications to electric power, aerospace, and consumer electronics, among others.

For more information, go to www.ieee.org/portal/index.jsp.

Wide Area Network

WAN, when it comes to cell phones, usually refers to wireless technologies (such as CDMA, TDMA, and GSM) that focus on longer-distance wireless connections between devices. The longer distance, accompanied by the fastest data speeds (300 Mbps and above), allows these solutions to give you the most flexibility. This technology is widely deployed around the world by wireless carriers, such as Sprint, Vodafone, and AT&T and historically has been used primarily to provide wireless voice communication services, but it is also in use by some data-only networks, such as CDPD and Mobitex. However, LAN solutions increasingly focus on providing faster combined wireless voice and data services to enterprise and retail consumers.

CDMA

CDMA is a digital cellular technology that uses spread spectrum. CDMA does not assign a specific frequency to each user but allows every channel to have access to the full available spectrum (multiplexing). This technology allows an optimization of the available bandwidth. It is an ultra-high-frequency (UHF) technology used in cellular telephone systems in the 800-Mhz and 1.9-GHz bands.

The technology was first used in World War II by the British to foil German attempts at jamming transmissions. The Allies decided to transmit over several frequencies instead of one, which made it difficult for a complete signal to be intercepted. Qualcomm, Inc. created communications circuits for CDMA, and once the information became public, claimed patents on the technology and was the first to commercialize it. Some of the cell phones in use in the United States use this technology (or TDMA), unlike in Europe, which uses the GSM standard.

If voice is a must-have and you need higher speed of data service, then a CDMA/1XRTT-based solution is the way to go, but not quite yet. For all the hype, coverage is simply not there yet, and rollout is far slower than the industry expected. The best bet right now is a GSM/GPRS solution, which is more readily available and provides worldwide roaming for both voice and data services. AT&T Wireless seems to be the carrier to watch. Its coverage is growing at unprecedented rates, and the service plans are reasonable.

TDMA

TDMA is a technology used in digital cellular phones. It allows a number of users to access a single radio frequency (RF). TDMA divides each cellular channel into three time slots. The current TDMA standard for cellular divides a single channel into six time slots, with each signal using two slots, providing a 3 to 1 gain in capacity over advanced mobile-phone service (AMPS).

The wireless industry needed to find a way to expand capacity in the early 1980s. One option was to convert the existing analog network to digital. In 1989, the Cellular Telecommunications Industry Association chose TDMA over Motorola's frequency division multiple access (FDMA). Suffice it to say that there is a very technical debate about the advantages and disadvantages of these various protocols. These debates will not be resolved but you can join in on any technical forum regarding cell phone technologies.

GSM

GSM telecommunication is a world standard for digital cellular communications using narrow-band TDMA, which allows for up to eight calls at one time on 800-MHz and 1,800-MHz frequencies. GSM assigns a specific frequency to each user. It was introduced in 1991 and is commonly used in Europe and Asia.

MOBITEX

If you frequent coffee shops, airports, or hotels and you just have to have super high-speed connectivity to the Internet, then an 802.11b solution is a good choice. Many people who are used to earlier-generation wireless connectivity (Mobitex, circuit switched, RD-LAP) are amazed at what their handhelds can do with 802.11. The device actually becomes a viable option for synchronizing wirelessly or downloading extensive emails.

W-LAN technologies have just started to evolve, with new variations being introduced regularly. Coverage is expanding, both with the emergence of aggregators, such as Boingo, and with private systems that are popping up all over major cities. In Seattle, for example, there is hardly a public place, from Starbucks to Marriott's, to a lodge in the middle of Woodlin's wine country, that doesn't provide 802.11 access. Right now, there are several W-LAN options for connecting handhelds, from sled attachments to integrated 802.11. This category of device should continue to get stronger and stronger, perhaps one day dominating the wireless handheld space.

If you can't live without voice and data combined in one device and you don't mind carrying something just a little larger than an average phone, then a combined voice/data integrated product might be right for you. The big question here is whether such a solution will meet your expectations for a great phone and a reasonable form factor. Although there are some great products on the market, manufacturers are still mastering the formula.

If you want data access without voice and don't need to wirelessly use the device internationally, then Mobitex is by far the best technology available today that suits these needs. There has been a lot of hype around next-generation networks, but the reality is that none exceeds Mobitex where coverage and reliability are concerned. If you want speed, however, hold off on Mobitex. With a gross throughput of 8 KB per second, it won't blow you away. However, Mobitex is ideal if you tend to send or receive short, bursty data, such as instant messages and text updates.

CONNECTING

The first thing you should know about getting online with a handheld is that it's not the same as connecting your PC or laptop. With PCs and laptops, you plug in a wireless modem PCMCIA card, configure it for an existing Internet-connected wireless network, and you're off and running. Well, it's not quite that easy, and of course, you have to boot up before you can do anything—which seems like overkill if all you want to do is check the weather.

Getting online with a handheld isn't hard; it's just different. What can be a little confusing, however, is that there seem to be so many ways to get online. Where do you start? To simplify matters, let's look again at the three types of wireless networks that will get you online: PAN, LAN, and WAN. These three wireless network types are different in the technology they use to provide a wireless connection and also in how they are used and in the solutions that are based on them.

In the United States, the following carriers offer GSM/GPRS services: AT&T Wireless, Cingular, and T-Mobile. On the CDMA front, Verizon and Sprint are the largest network operators. There are hundreds of other regional carriers, such as U.S. Cellular and AllTel, which offer similar wireless data services. Nextel operates its own proprietary network technology and offers wireless data services, as well.

Traditional Internet Service Providers (ISPs) also provide wireless service. Companies such as Earthlink and America Online (AOL) resell and/or aggregate a variety of networks. For example, if you bought service from Earthlink for wireless connectivity for a RIM 850, you would receive billing and customer support for the device and service from Earthlink. Even though Cingular may operate the actual network, your relationship would be with Earthlink, not Cingular.

802.11/WiFi AND FINDING A HOTSPOT

 For information on the business, technology, and the future of 802.11 networking, a good place to start is 80211-Planet.com (www.wi-fiplanet.com).

WiFi—which stands for wireless fidelity and is synonymous with 802.11b—is a term coined by the Wireless Ethernet Compatibility Alliance (WECA). WiFi products work with all access points and client hardware built to the WiFi standard.

To find an 802.11 access point anywhere in the world, check out www.hotspotslist.com. It lists thousands of locations and can be searched by city, state, or country. It claims that new sites are added every day.

Wireless Email Basics

To get wireless email, you'll need a wireless-enabled handheld. HandEra, HandSpring, Palm, and Sony all sell devices that can be made wireless with the addition of a modem or a module and a data-enabled mobile phone. Next, you'll need a wireless service plan and an email account. That could include ISP email, such as AOL, CompuServe, EarthLink, Juno, Mindspring, or Prodigy; Web mail, such as Yahoo! or Hotmail; corporate email; or Palm.Net Wireless Service. Finally, you'll need a wireless application that's compatible with your email service. If your handheld doesn't have integrated wireless or if you're not using a two-piece Bluetooth solution, you'll also need a way to get connected to the Internet.

Modem

Don't jump into buying a modem for handhelds without first checking with your wireless ISP. ISPs often require that you use their brand of modem. Some ISPs will waive standard wireless service activation fees, and some retailers may include a free modem with your PDA—although you may be required to sign up with a specific wireless ISP to qualify.

Novatel, WISP, and EarthLink offer CDPD modems for some Palm OS handhelds. Rebates are sometimes available, which reduces the up-front cost of the modem, but the real cost is in the service itself. Also, be sure to check CDPD coverage maps before you buy because service providers may offer plans that work only within the carrier's service area. Before you buy, make sure you find out if the CDPD service provider will also provide ISP services, Web browsing, and email; if not, you'll need to tack on the cost of an ISP, as well. Here are a couple of examples of wireless plans if you go the modem route.

Earthlink (formerly Omnisky) Wireless offers a variety of service plans. Regardless of the plan you choose, you get unlimited usage with no roaming charges. Monthly and annual service plans carry activation and early termination fees. The annual plans require a 12-month commitment; the monthly plans require a six-month commitment. As of the time of this writing, an annual plan for a Palm V handheld or a Handspring Visor Platinum, Prism, Edge, Neo, or Pro handheld includes a free modem and is available for a prepaid price of $432.00. On a monthly basis, the price is $39.95, and the modem is $49.95. The same service plans are available for the Palm m500 series, but the modem costs $269.95. Pocket PC plans are significantly more expensive. Prices and promotions are always subject to change, so be sure to check current service plan pricing.

GoAmerica (AT&T Wireless and Verizon Networks) has an activation fee of $29.95 for all of its service plans at the time of this writing. A Minstrel modem for a Palm III, Palm V, or Handspring Visor handheld is $99.00. The

Minstrel modem for the m500 is $369.00. For all devices, a Go.Unlimited plan is $44.95 per month, with other plans available.

Mobile Kits

You can also get wireless Internet access by using a compatible data-enabled mobile cellular phone and wireless Internet connection software. Once the software is installed, you complete the wireless Internet connection via a special cable, which you buy separately, or by lining up your handheld's integrated infrared (IR) port with the IR port of a compatible data-enabled mobile phone. Using a mobile phone/PDA combination for Internet access includes the cost of a monthly wireless ISP plan, plus telephone minutes.

THE PALM MOBILE INTERNET KIT

The Palm Mobile Internet Kit requires an IR-enabled mobile phone, a cable, which is sold separately, or a Palm-compatible modem. The kit, delivered on CD-ROM or via the Palm Web site, is easy to install and an affordable software solution for any Palm handheld supporting the Palm OS 3.5 platform. Upgrade software is included in the kit, which means that, if you have an upgradeable Palm handheld, you may be able to take advantage of new OS features. The kit allows you to access the Internet and Web content via hundreds of Web clipping applications available from the Palm.Net Web site.

Palm Handheld Requirements

- Palm m100, m105, III, IIIx, IIIxe, IIIc, or V series handheld
- Data-enabled mobile phone or a Palm OS compatible modem
- Palm OS v3.5 or later (3.5 upgrade included with kit)
- 660K memory required

System Requirements

- IBM-compatible 486 PC or higher
- Windows 95/98/2000/NT 4.0
- One available serial port
- CD-ROM

Other Requirements

- ISP
- Data services from mobile carrier

Data-enabled Phones

Data-enabled phones include many from Nokia, Kyocera/Qualcomm, Sagem, Samsung, Siemens, and Sanyo. You can find specific model numbers at the Palm Web site, www.palm.com.

You're Only as Good as Your Weakest Link

A fast PDA with a color screen is nice, but if you're on a 2G network, you might wait what seems like a lifetime for a color picture. Remember to set your expectations based on your PDA's resources (processor speed, memory, display), software capabilities (Wireless Application Protocol [WAP], HTML, digital media, etc.), and on your bandwidth (cellular 1/2/2/5/3G, 802.11, modem, etc.). Use it!

Although a lot of wireless devices and carriers tout wireless Web access, you really need to see it in action to understand whether it is right for you. Many third parties allow free downloads and trials that you can upload. The downside is that you can't get the content. Proxy or custom-content systems, such as AvantGo or Vindigo, offer a demo that you can download to your PC and sync to your PDA, which should give you a good idea of what they can do. However, because it is a demo and not an actual wireless connection, you will be browsing data faster than what you will experience with your wireless network.

WAP

WAP was a way for a coalition of wireless companies to get Internet data to their most minimal configuration devices (cell phones with minimal processing, limited RAM, and monochrome LCD displays) running over 2G networks. Essentially, this requires that data be in WAP Wireless Markup Language (WML) format (typically via a WAP gateway) before the WAP browser can view it. So you got what many users of PC-based browsers considered the worst of both worlds: basic black-and-white text with limited content access. Those in the industry generally agree that WAP in the United States was not the success they had expected. Although there is some useful content out there, even the WAP folks are gravitating to Extensible Markup Language (XML) as their future direction, so you probably should not expect a tremendous number of WAP-based services in the future.

CULTURAL VIEWS

If, like many in the United States, your Internet interface is a PC browser with broadband access, then wireless WAP at 2G speeds might make you dismiss wireless access before you experience any of its upside (like finding a movie time and theater in a new town while you're on vacation). Conversely, if you are from Japan, where iMode access was your main interface to the Internet, than using a browser that allows access to any Web page might be a refreshing change.

Proxy browsers, as their name suggests, use a proxy server. They are generally faster than proxyless browsers. What's more, they reformat information to make it look good on a handheld's small screen.

Proxyless browsers are generally slower than proxy browsers. They also force you to scroll horizontally, and that can take some getting used to because they show Web content exactly as it would appear on your PC. However, with a proxyless browser, your information does not reside on a server. Instead, the connection is made directly from the wireless device to the Internet, which makes it a more secure connection.

Palm OS devices offer both types of browsers.

PalmSource

PalmSource has a new Web site—www.palmsource.com—where you can find information, resources, and support for developing software or peripheral solutions for any handheld powered by the Palm OS. You can find information on the latest OS, programming support, simulators for testing and debugging, and more.

The PalmSource Web site also offers lots of developer documentation, some of which is free and some of which is available with a subscription service. A free trial membership is available for Palm OS Developer Program members, who receive a 15% discount on the yearly subscription fee.

PalmSource, Inc. 1240 Crossman Avenue Sunnyvale, CA 94089

Phone: (408) 400-3000

Fax: (408) 400-1500

Wireless Developers

Visual Basic and C/C++ developers can learn what they need to do to build, deploy, and troubleshoot custom enterprise applications that take advantage of available wireless coverage at http://palm.com/enterprise/products/wdbas/index.html. Palm WDBAS includes an easy-to-use, high-level data access API on handheld devices and a configurable server. This lets developers focus on applications, rather than on writing low-level networking and server-integration code.

SECURITY AND HANDHELD DEVICES

Handhelds are more easily lost or stolen than laptop or desktop computers, but the good news is that, with a few precautions, you can help protect your handheld data. Don't leave your handheld lying around. Be religious about synching. Use passwords.

Routinely synching your device with your PC will prevent you from losing your data if your device is stolen, lost, or broken. Beyond the software that comes with your device, there is an abundance of synchronization and backup software for Palm Powered handhelds.

Palm OS lets you assign a password to make your handheld inaccessible to others. You can also make selected records invisible to anyone but you. Antivirus software includes InoculateIT by Computer Associates and McAfee VirusScan and VirusScan Professional by Network Associates. Security applications for Palm Powered handhelds abound. The PalmSource Web site is a good starting point.

Palm OS 5, for future devices, will include a suite of best-in-class security services, which can be integrated into applications and corporate security policies when and how developers and enterprises want to incorporate them. These services were developed in cooperation with RSA Security and include 128-bit data encryption based on the RC4 algorithm and secure sockets layer (SSL) support for Internet email, Web browsing, and commercial transactions. SSL, encryption technology provided by RSA, is used in the new PalmSource Web browser. Encryption makes your message unreadable by anyone but the intended recipient. Encryption secures the transmission of private and sensitive information, such as your credit card number, password, and email messages. SSL protects both the messages you send and the messages you receive. When a wireless transaction is secured, you will see a little padlock icon on the title bar next to the name of the Web page.

SUMMARY

The future of wireless handhelds in all forms is secure. You'll either be carrying around a slim PDA that acts as a phone or a phone that acts as a PDA. The open question remains: How will these devices access and utilize the Internet and the Web? And what software will be needed to talk to these devices from the Internet? The trend that is emerging is not toward specialized browsers and device-specific coding to make sure that a Web page can be seen by any number of devices. Instead it is toward a universal system that can manage to take a normal Web page and adapt it to the device so that special coding is not needed. But that day is still a ways off, and if you want to communicate with the handheld world from the Internet, you're going to have to do some extra work—at least for now.

20
THE TEN-STEP
COMMUTE

You've heard of remote workers. They're the people sitting in their pajamas at the computer, working with their feet up, while you endure a 45-minute commute, only to be greeted by corporate politics and bad coffee. You know their enviable life has been made possible with *remote access*, but what exactly is it?

Remote access connects your computer to a network (or computer) at another location. With it, you can connect to your office computer and work from a home office, access a corporate network from an overseas subsidiary, or troubleshoot a distant network server from your office. It's in use in a variety of ways. Some examples would include teleworkers, traveling executives, help desk professionals, and meter readers.

The term *remote access* is actually a catchall term for a variety of products, each connecting to a network or computer in a slightly different way. True remote access makes a remote computer an actual part of a network, as with a virtual private network (VPN, discussed later in this chapter). This method is often used by businesses to provide remote network access to employees.

Another remote access method is *remote control*. The term might call to mind some long-distance mind control from a 1950s B-grade movie; it's actually a lot less sinister. Remote control is simply a way to connect to and control a computer from another computer. Because of its simplicity, individuals and small businesses often purchase remote control products for accessing one or a few computers remotely.

INFORMATION ANYWHERE: A BRIEF HISTORY OF REMOTE ACCESS

The ability to connect remotely to computers has been around as long as networks have been available. Decades ago, a computer operator could issue commands to a target computer through a remote console. But these commands were arcane, and the target computer was usually an expensive mainframe, so remote access was often restricted to professional computer types and the academic world.

Starting in the 1970s, companies began using leased lines (the telephone company dedicated this to one purpose, for a fee) and a protocol standard called X.25 to extend their private networks to wide area networks (WANs). These leased lines, although they kept information private and secure, were expensive to use and maintain. Faster technologies, such as frame relay (a telecommunications service designed to transmit traffic between local area networks [LANs] and WANs) later became the standard, opening the door to VPN technologies.

In the 1980s, remote access servers became popular with the improved speed and low cost of modems. Along with this form of network access, remote control

---

products began to make their mark. Initially called *remote takeover* products, remote control became more sophisticated as connection speeds and methods improved.

In the 1990s, remote access technologies started to become accepted with the computing masses. The market for VPNs got hot starting in the late 1990s after the protocols used to transmit and secure the data became more standardized and Internet connections became commonplace. With faster network and Internet connections and stronger security, remote control products became more sophisticated. The remote access market is getting bigger every year and is now a multibillion-dollar market.

WHO NEEDS REMOTE ACCESS?

Until recently, remote access was the domain of network administrators and a few brave telecommuters. With the combination of the Internet and easy-to-use products, however, remote access is now within everyone's reach, and there has been an explosion in its use by several groups:

- Full-time teleworkers and work extenders
- Remote offices and small office/home office (SOHO) workers
- Business travelers
- Systems administrators and support professionals

Teleworkers and Work Extenders

When you mention remote workers, most people think of the typical telecommuter, working full time from home five days a week. Although there are millions of telecommuters (or more accurately, *teleworkers*) in today's workforce, the modern remote worker now includes people who don't fit traditional definitions. Remote workers now include *work extenders*, a new class of worker who has unique remote access requirements. These employees require infrequent access to a corporate network from home after hours and during weekends.

Work Extenders: The New Teleworker

According to analysts, millions of work extenders now represent the largest segment of the remote user population. This is because work extenders come from all walks of life: They simply need access to their corporate network or office computer from home or while traveling. They typically put in extra hours at home in the morning or evenings, on weekends, or (believe it or not) while on vacation. For example, a work extender might want to catch up on email before driving into the office or check on the status of an important project while on vacation.

Work extenders, even though they represent a large portion of remote users, are nevertheless one of the most underserved groups when it comes to remote access. This is ironic because most employers would gladly provide work extenders with the remote access they need—it makes it easier for workers to put in additional time on the job, thereby making these employees more productive. Giving work extenders remote access makes sense for companies because these workers are immediately productive, thereby providing companies a fast return on their remote access investment.

Unfortunately, most remote access products are time-consuming to set up and difficult to configure for work extenders. What these workers typically want is remote access they can use from almost anywhere that doesn't take time to configure each time. Later in the chapter, we'll discuss hosted Web browser-based products, such as GoToMyPC (www.gotomypc.com), which might be appropriate for work extenders.

With highways becoming more congested, suburbs growing farther away from the urban core, a new sense of family, and the technology to support a remote workforce, workers have found they can increase their productivity, improve their job satisfaction, and add to their quality of life through telework.

Of course, the benefits are not all one-sided. Employers also get their fair share of rewards from a formal or informal program. The justification for implementing a program is not hard to come by. Employers with these programs have consistently reduced turnover, paid for fewer employee sick days, and obtained higher employee productivity.

For all these reasons, telework is growing quickly. There are over 30 million U.S. teleworkers currently. Analysts predict this trend will continue over the next few years. For more information and statistics, visit the International Telework Association & Council (ITAC) Web site at www.telecommute.org.

SELLING TELEWORK TO YOUR EMPLOYER

So, you're sold on the benefits of telework but don't think your employer will buy into it? Although many employers understand the benefits of telecommuting, they may have a few misconceptions about what it is. Therefore, you can do a little preparation to make sure they'll sign off on your proposal.

First, ask yourself whether you and your job are right for telework. Not everyone is suited for working away from the office. You'll need to be a self-starter who doesn't require a lot of direction from your boss. You'll also need good time-management skills so you won't be easily distracted at home. Of course, like any skill, these skills can be developed. In addition, if your job requires that you deal face to face with clients, it might not be a good fit for telework.

After you have thought about these factors, do your homework and prepare a proposal for your boss or management. Think in terms of what benefits your department or company will receive from your teleworking. Your manager probably won't approve your proposal out of generosity. You'll need to present specific answers to the following questions:

Why do you want to telecommute and why is your job right for telecommuting?

Where will you work, what equipment do you need, and is the space you will use right for working from home? Your manager or human resources department may want to know whether your office space and equipment is ergonomically correct.

How will your manager know you are working, and what quantitative measures will you use to show that you are productive?

How often will you telework? You might suggest that you start telecommuting only one or two days a week on a trial basis. After two or three months, you might plan to meet again to evaluate your success.

For assistance and information in deciding whether this is right for you, visit the U.S. government's Interagency Telework/Telecommuting Site at www.telework.gov.

Remote Offices and SOHO

Remote access technology can extend a company's network. Technologies such as leased lines were previously the domain of larger organizations, but newer technologies such as VPN make it cost-effective for smaller satellite offices to connect to main offices.

Remote access also makes it possible for employees or contract workers to provide services to a company whether they are 50 or 5,000 miles away. For example, an organization can use remote access software to connect customers to customer service employees sitting in distant remote locations, rather than in a central office. By doing so, the organization can reduce costs by hiring customer service employees in a lower-cost region.

SOHO (small office/home office)workers can also benefit from remote access. Because these workers are often self-employed, remote access and remote control products provide a cost-effective alternative to expensive hardware, software, and networking solutions intended for large enterprises.

Business Travelers

Today, many jobs in the business world require extensive travel. Although the traveling executive and the road-warrior salesman don't fit the mold of a typical remote worker, they are. These mobile professionals all need access to information, whether it is a sales report, an important presentation file, the company intranet, or email. Remote access solutions can give these workers the information they need.

Remote access companies are recognizing mobile professionals because they now make up about a third of all the remote and mobile workers. These on-the-go workers have little use for remote access software that requires significant configuration or that requires a fixed workstation. Instead, they rely on laptops, hotel business centers, and even Web terminals in Internet cafes for remote access.

Systems Administrators and Support Professionals

Our previous examples have been focused on telework and remote offices, but systems administrators and support people also use remote access solutions for troubleshooting computers and servers. For example, a system administrator might use a remote control program to troubleshoot a computer at 3 A.M. from home, rather than driving in to the office. Or a help desk professional might remotely run diagnostic software on an employee's computer, rather than walking down the hall to the employee's office.

YOUR REMOTE ACCESS CHOICES

Fortunately, the choices for remote access are as varied as the types of user. One popular method is to use remote control software to connect to a computer and operate that computer as though you were in front of it. A completely different method favored by businesses is to use a VPN to make a remote computer an actual part of the network. Still other solutions, such as application delivery servers, allow you to use your office applications without needing to install anything on a remote computer. In this section, we'll explain these different methods, describe why each might be appropriate for you, and provide a few examples of real products.

Remote Control Software

A popular way to give access to computers and a network is through remote control. This software relays the screen images and keyboard input between a host computer (such as an office computer) and a client computer (such as

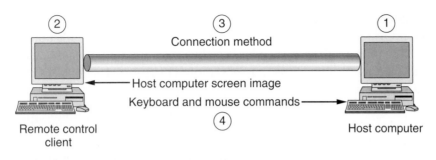

FIGURE 20.1 REMOTE CONTROL SOFTWARE.

your computer at home). Using remote control is like having your host computer in front of you wherever you are (Figure 20.1).

Remote control software is perfect for occasional teleworkers or mobile workers because they typically have a computer back at the office with a connection to the company network. This makes it easy to stop working on a file at the office, drive home, and resume working on the same file without any problems. Without a product like remote control, a mobile worker would need to get the file onto his computer at home by copying the file to a disk or sending the file to an email account at home, leaving the worker with duplicate files in different locations. Complicating issues even further, to read the file properly, the worker would need to have the same software programs at home as at work.

Remote control can be lumped into two general categories that we'll talk about later in this chapter. The first is traditional remote control software that you manually install on each computer. The second category, which is increasingly popular, is Web browser-based remote control. This method allows you to access your host computer from a Web browser without installing any software on the client computer. Remote control products come in a variety of flavors, and the product you choose depends on several factors, such as where you will access your computer, your operating system, your technical skill level, and your budget.

So what do you need to use remote control software? First, you'll need two computers with the right configuration to run the software. The exact configuration depends on the remote control software you choose, but you can usually find a product that fits your setup, whether it is a PC or Macintosh. Most products work on computers running Windows, but a few can accommodate other operating systems, such as Mac, Linux, UNIX, or Solaris. For example, Timbuktu Pro (www.netopia.com) provides a separate Mac version of its software.

Another necessary component is some sort of connection between computers. Many products, such as GoToMyPC (www.gotomypc.com), take advantage of Internet connections, whether they are initiated through dialup or broadband connections. This makes remote control of a computer possible, whether it's from your house down the street or from a computer overseas.

A few other products, such as pcAnywhere (www.symantec.com/pcanywhere), can utilize direct modem-to-modem dialup connections. A short list of products such as LapLink (www.laplink.com) allow direct serial, parallel, cable, or USB connections between computers sitting in the same room, enabling you to synchronize files quickly between, say, your laptop and desktop computer.

REMOTE CONTROL SET UP

Remote control gives teleworkers and mobile workers an efficient way to work, and setting up a remote control program is usually easy. With this in mind, if our remote worker wanted to set up and use a remote control product to access an office computer from home, they might perform the following steps:

First, install server software on the office computer. The computer you access remotely is often called the *host*.

Install client software on the home computer. The computer you use to access the host is often called the *client*.

Establish a connection between the computers. Depending on the product you're using, the connection can be a direct cable connection, modem-to-modem, LAN, or Internet connection. Some remote control products also secure the connection to protect your privacy.

Begin viewing the screen of the host computer and operating the computer remotely as though you were sitting in front of the host computer.

If you're familiar with remote access solutions such as a VPN, you can see the significant differences between them and remote control software: Remote access connects a remote computer directly to a network, and remote control connects the remote computer to another computer. With remote control, if that computer is connected to the network, you'll also have access to the network.

A typical remote control product has several features that make working on a remote computer easier. A few products have other features, but these are the essential elements:

- Interface to view the host computer. Most remote control software gives you a way to view and access the applications and data on your host computer. If your host computer is connected to a corporate network, you can usually view and access the network, as well.

- File transfer. You'll probably need a way to get a file from your office computer onto the computer where you are sitting. Most remote control software gives you a way to send and receive files from a distant computer; file transferring is a specialty with some software, such as LapLink Gold (www.laplink.com).

- Security features. You'll probably want to secure the data transmitted between computers, especially if you are using the Internet to establish the connection. This is particularly important if you are linked to a host computer that is connected to a corporate network. A few remote control products provide limited protection, and others provide robust security that can thwart eavesdroppers.

- Printing to your local computer's printer. If you are viewing a document on your host computer, you may need to print the document on the printer where you are currently. Many remote control products offer a way to print remote files on a local printer.

Earlier, we mentioned the two general categories of remote control products. The first is traditional remote control software installed manually on both client and host computers. The second and newer category is Web browser-based remote control, which is usually installed only on the host computer. Increasingly, these Web browser-based remote control products are offered as a service over the Internet. Let's talk more about each of these methods.

Installed Remote Control Software

Dozens of off-the-shelf software products are available for controlling computers remotely. These products usually require that you install the software from a CD or other method onto the computer you'll control remotely and on the computer from which you're working. A few big names have been around for years, such as Symantec pcAnywhere (www.symantec.com/pcanywhere) and Timbuktu Pro (www.netopia.com). A few products are available for download over the Internet, such as Virtual Network Computing (VNC), a free product from AT&T (www.uk.research.att.com/vnc/).

Still other choices are available free as a component of certain operating systems. For example, Microsoft Windows XP Professional (www.microsoft.com/windowsxp/pro/) includes a feature called Remote Desktop that allows you to view your Windows XP Professional computer from another computer running a 32-bit Windows operating system. Because the software is included in Windows, you don't need to pay anything to use it. However, with this software you're limited to accessing Windows XP Professional computers, so only a select group of people can utilize it. And, of course, you'll need to be technically savvy enough to configure the software.

Although remote control software is easy to use and makes telework possible for individuals or small businesses, there are a few disadvantages. For example, if you plan on installing remote control for more than one computer (for example, you're an administrator rolling out a telework program to several company employees), you'll need to consider software licensing and distribution issues. You'll need to purchase enough licenses to accommodate all your users, and you'll need to keep track of the software to make sure your users use the software according to the licensing agreement.

Another disadvantage to traditional remote control products is that they require that you install the software on both the client and server computers. This is inconvenient, especially for work extenders and mobile professionals, who would need to carry the software with them for installing on the client. In addition, these products require inbound Internet access to the host computer, often necessitating changes to the firewall security in place. These concerns are less of an issue with the next type of remote control software we'll discuss, Web browser-based remote control.

Web Browser-Based Remote Control

A recent innovation in remote access is the ability to connect to and view your host computer from a Web browser. This Web browser-based remote control offers a distinct advantage to traditional remote control software—you do not generally need to preinstall software on the client computer. This may sound trivial, but it's not. Because you don't need to lug software around for connecting to your host computer, you can utilize almost any computer connected to the Internet, such as from a customer's office, airport Internet kiosk, or business center. In addition, browser-based remote control can save you licensing fees, because many traditional remote control products charge you for each client computer you license. A few Web browser-based remote control solutions for teleworkers include GoToMyPC (www.gotomypc.com) and VNC.

With the growing popularity of application service providers (ASPs), many of the Web browser-based remote control products are becoming available as a service. These "hosted" products generally do not require that you purchase the software outright; rather, you pay a monthly fee for the privilege of using the software. Hosted Web-based remote control reduces the complexity of using remote control because the company takes care of much of the infra-

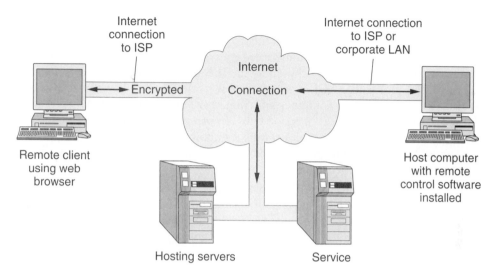

Internet
connection
to ISP

Internet connection
to ISP or
corporate LAN

Internet

Encrypted   Connection

Remote client
using web
browser

Host computer
with remote
control software
installed

Hosting servers   Service

FIGURE 20.2 **HOSTED WEB-BASED REMOTE CONTROL REQUIRES AN INTERNET CONNECTION THROUGH AN ISP.**

structure and software needed for remote access. A hosted Web browser-based service may wind up costing you more in the long run than a one-time software purchase, but the price is often offset by the added convenience.

As you can see in Figure 20.2, hosted Web browser-based remote control differs from the standard remote control configuration discussed earlier. One advantage of a hosted solution is that the hosting company maintains the servers used to make the connection between computers. Generally, the hosting companies take care of the encryption and other security settings, so you do not need to perform a complex setup or configuration.

REMOTE ACCESS SPOTLIGHT—GOTOMYPC

Although most remote control products are purchased off the shelf, a few are taking advantage of the efficiencies and convenience the Internet has to offer. One of those products, GoToMyPC (www.gotomypc.com), is unique among remote control products because it is easy to use and secure.

To get started, you register on the GoToMyPC Web site and install the remote software on the computer you intend to access. The software is easy for novices to install because no configuration is necessary. Once the software is installed, you can access your computer and network from most computers with Internet access and a Web browser.

GoToMyPC is a good choice for teleworkers because the security is preconfigured, making it acceptable for connecting to secure corporate networks. Each connection is secured by 128-bit advanced encryption standard (AES) encryption, a security standard (FIPS 197) chosen by the U.S. government as its encryption method. This means that hackers won't be able to view or decode your data as it travels between your host computer and Web browser. Because GoToMyPC is a hosted service, making the connection between computers is easy. You generally do not need to be concerned with firewalls or know the IP address of your host computer. You can learn more about remote access and GoToMyPC security at www.gotomypc.com/s/security.

Individuals can use GoToMyPC for remote access, and GoToMyPC also offers a product for larger telework implementations. GoToMyPC Corporate (www.gotomypc.com/corporate) is designed for companies with 10 or more teleworkers and provides administration tools to make managing a telework program easier.

Although most of the applications we've discussed so far use remote control in a teleworking situation, information technology professionals can also use remote control to maintain servers from a distance. For example, a network administrator might use remote control from home to restart a server that has crashed or to perform regular maintenance, such as backups. The list of products for network and server administration is extensive and includes NetOp Remote Control (www.netop.com) and Altiris Carbon Copy Solution (www.altiris.com). Many of the remote control products we've covered to this point also work perfectly well for server administration.

Remote control is also used extensively to support customers having problems with their computers and software products. Using a remote control product, a support engineer or help desk professional can view and control a customer's computer from a distance, significantly reducing support and travel costs. These products often take the form of Web browser-based remote control and include DesktopStreaming (www.desktopstreaming.com), Control-F1 (www.controlf1.com) and WebEx OnCall (www.webex.com).

Is Remote Control Right for You?

Although remote control is generally easy to set up and use, it may not be right for everyone. If your organization has a strict security policy, a remote control product may not meet its policy standards. For example, your organization may require that you use a firewall when accessing corporate resources. With remote control, the company is not able to monitor the security you are using from home. It also may not be able to maintain a formal record of the remote access taking place.

Another disadvantage of using remote control is that performance is limited by the connection speed. If you are working with a slow connection such as a modem, your view of the remote computer may occasionally lag behind your keyboard and mouse actions. If you're accessing a remote computer from home over the Internet, you'll probably want a faster connection, such as DSL or a cable modem.

Finally, for large enterprises with hundreds of users, it may not be cost-effective to purchase, distribute, and install remote control software. However, many remote control products are now providing distribution and administration tools that ease the headache of licensing and installing the software for large groups. Web browser-based remote control products ease an administrator's job further, because client software generally does not need to be distributed and installed, as with traditional packaged remote control software.

REMOTE ACCESS VPNs

Many businesses and organizations have turned to VPNs for connecting remote workers to a corporate network. Internet protocol (IP) VPNs are now a multibillion-dollar-a-year industry, and more providers are entering the arena every year. Because of their complexity, however, individuals do not generally install a VPN for remote access. VPNs can be found from smaller businesses all the way up to large, multinational enterprises with thousands of users. As a testament to the usual scale of a VPN, the larger the enterprise, the greater the chance that a VPN is in place for remote access.

Let's start by defining a VPN. In short, a VPN is a private network connection built within a public network such as the Internet. Because you're using a public network but transmitting your information using a secured tunnel within the network, using a VPN is often referred to as *tunneling*. Distant offices, remote workers, and business partners can all use this secure connection to access a corporate network.

If this concept isn't immediately clear, imagine that you need to cross the English Channel. You could cross the channel in a boat where everyone else in the channel could see you. However, if you were concerned about your security and privacy, you could travel through the Channel Tunnel instead. This way, people in the channel above cannot see you, and your privacy is protected. Similarly, you receive little privacy when transmitting your information on the public Internet—your data is fair game for anyone who wants it. By using a tunnel to transmit important information over the Internet, you're making sure that your information arrives securely and safely.

Although many companies use VPN technology to network distant offices or business partners securely, many are now using VPNs specifically for remote access. A remote access VPN makes a lot of sense for companies setting up telework programs, because they can use an existing Internet connection, rather than creating a separate, dedicated connection (such as a leased line).

In its most basic form, a remote access VPN connects a user's computer across the Internet to a corporate network. The user's computer is often called a *node*, because it essentially becomes a part of the main network, with access to network resources as though the user were in the office. This is an important distinction between a VPN and our previously discussed remote control products. Because a VPN connects a computer directly to a network, there is no need to have a second computer at the corporate end of the connection.

VPN configurations can range all over the map in terms of hardware and software; Figure 20.3 shows a typical remote access VPN. The employee (client) connects to the Internet using their standard Internet Service Provider (ISP) connection, whether it is a broadband or dialup connection. The VPN software on the client computer establishes a secure tunnel to a VPN gateway device at the edge of the corporate network; a user name and password ensure that only authorized users can access the network. Once the connection is made, all information sent between the client and gateway are secured using encryption, so data cannot be intercepted and read by eavesdroppers. Many configurations have additional components, such as corporate firewalls, routers, and other security devices.

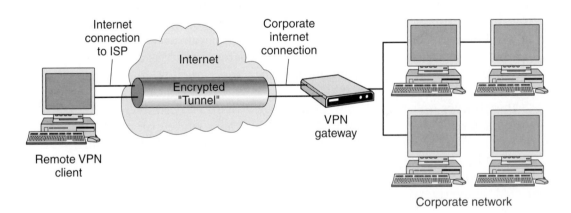

FIGURE 20.3 **TYPICAL REMOTE ACCESS VPN CONFIGURATION.**

Using this setup, you can see how a VPN might work for a teleworker performing work at home. In a typical remote work situation, the company provides client software to the worker, who installs it on a home computer. The worker can then gain access to the company network for accessing shared network files and resources. As long as the employee has the appropriate permission, any file or service that's available from the corporate network would be available at home. This might include email from a corporate email server, Web pages from the corporate intranet, or sales documents residing on a corporate file server.

One distinct disadvantage to VPNs is that if a teleworker has a computer back at the office, the files and resources located on the office computer are usually inaccessible (unless the employee has shared their computer and folders with the network). If you're a remote worker spending most of your time teleworking from home, this usually doesn't present much of a problem. But if you're an occasional teleworker spending a few days a month working from home, it can be a genuine hassle trying to coordinate your files between the office and home. Another disadvantage to VPNs is that you need to have the same application installed on your home computer as you have installed on your office computer to read files associated with that application. For example, you might not be able to view a presentation unless you have installed the same presentation software that is installed back at the office.

Setting up and running a VPN isn't a quick or easy proposition. To do it on your own, you'll need to dedicate quite a bit of time, expertise, and cash to get things running smoothly. Once a VPN is set up, it requires routine maintenance that may strain the budget of smaller enterprises. For these reasons, most businesses decide to outsource their VPNs to other parties. ISPs, network service providers (NSPs), and others vendors, such as AT&T (www.att.com) and Genuity (www.genuity.com), have all jumped onto the VPN bandwagon to provide VPN services. These so-called managed VPNs are simple to set up but usually require a hefty monthly fee in addition to an initial activation fee.

BUILDING A VPN FROM SCRATCH

You've decided that a VPN is right for your business. You've also concluded that you want to be in control of the VPN rather than farming it out to a vendor. What do you need to set one up? How do you, in industry terms, "roll your own?" What you need depends in part on your objectives, but here are the essential components:

Hardware

Depending on the scale of your VPN, you'll need several hardware components. For example, most VPNs use at least one VPN gateway device (also called a *VPN server*) on each network to control the connections to remote computers. Vendors such as Cisco Systems (www.cisco.com) and Lucent Technologies (www.lucent.com) manufacture VPN gateways. Larger implementations may require additional hardware, such as VPN routers or authentication servers.

Software and Protocols

Each remote computer usually has VPN client software installed to make the connection to the network. This client software is usually installed and configured by the network administrator. To get a VPN to communicate with the network, a protocol must be selected. Several protocols are available, although IPSec has become the leading industry standard.

Security

If you build your own VPN, you'll need to build security into your plan. Security encompasses many elements, such as firewalls, encryption methods, network address translation (NAT), and access control. We'll discuss security in detail later in the chapter.

VPN technology continues to evolve, so much so that the lines between a VPN and other technologies are blurring. An example is secure sockets layer (SSL). Some companies are adopting the SSL security standard for use as a remote access technology. Once SSL servers are configured on the company network, remote users can view the company network using only a Web browser—no client software installation is required. In another recent VPN variation, Multiprotocol Label Switching (MPLS) is combined with a VPN solution to improve the reliability of data transmission. Companies who need to meet high quality of service standards might use an MPLS VPN solution.

For businesses that want to set up a VPN quickly, there is yet another alternative. Remote access appliances, such as Instant Virtual Extranet (IVE) from Neoteris (www.neoteris.com), enable remote users to access corporate networks from a Web browser. These appliances, once configured on a network, allow users to access select network resources over the Internet without installing and configuring client software.

VPN: Not a Remote Access Cure-All

Although the VPN is surely a popular choice for corporate remote access, there are a few disadvantages to consider before committing to an implementation. The primary disadvantage is its complexity. To put a VPN into service requires an understanding of proper network deployment and security issues. Because users frequently connect to a corporate network from home, administrators often have a difficult time enforcing security policies. For example, the user might be connecting over an unsecured cable modem connection, allowing intruders to piggyback onto the connection.

Another issue with a VPN is its difficult administration requirements. Network administrators and help desk personnel need to deal with the complexities of supporting distant users who might have problems installing and using the client software. In addition, a significant amount of corporate resources must be dedicated to supporting an application that has limited usage, such as email. These disadvantages, when taken as a whole, may increase the overall cost of a VPN solution.

OTHER REMOTE ACCESS METHODS

A whole host of other products are available for remote access that don't fit into the typical remote control or VPN classifications. Most of these products have specific purposes, but they might be right for you.

Application Delivery Servers and Corporate Portals

Many companies implement application delivery servers and corporate portals for their remote access solution. Application delivery servers let companies install applications once on a server, rather than on every desktop throughout the company. Application delivery servers are useful if your company wants to keep close tabs on software licensing costs. Many application servers give users the ability to access applications remotely from wherever they are over the Web from a browser, such as Citrix MetaFrame (www. citrix.com) or GraphOn Go-Global (www.graphon.com).

To provide access to the applications, many companies create a corporate portal. The portal provides a way for users to access select content, services, applications, and data through a Web browser. Often, the corporate portal can publish information to users based on their identities. Together, these solutions work well if your users need to access information and data from Web-enabled "thin clients," such as wireless handheld devices.

If your company is running Microsoft Windows 2000 Server (www. microsoft.com) and you're technologically comfortable, you might consider running Windows Terminal Services, free software included with Windows 2000 Server. This software, when run in Application Server mode, lets administrators centrally deploy Windows-based applications to clients over different network connections, such as a LAN or dialup connection.

Dialup Remote Access Servers

You might think of remote access servers (RAS) as the precursor to today's VPN. However, rather than using the Internet or some other network to make the connection as a VPN does, RAS users dial in to a modem at the office and establish a dedicated network connection through a RAS server. Although this seems like a relatively straightforward solution, RAS is no longer used frequently because of its disadvantages and cost. Generally, RAS provides slower data transfer speeds than those available through a VPN. The hardware (usually a pool of modems) is expensive, and telecommunication costs can be high if users are dialing in long-distance or over a toll-free line.

However, many RAS solutions are still used by businesses for remote access. These businesses usually require banks of modems and client connection software for each client. Although the security threats aren't as severe as a network connection made over the Internet, you'll need to consider network security if you're using RAS on your corporate network.

Peer-to-Peer Products

With the advent (and eventual demise) of a few high-profile file-sharing products such as Napster, peer-to-peer products have received a substantial amount of press. The press is warranted, because peer-to-peer is a completely different and simpler method of connecting computers and users. In peer-to-peer architecture, each computer has equivalent capabilities, unlike the typical client/server relationship.

Although peer-to-peer connectivity has been used primarily for file swapping, the architecture can also be used for remote control. For example, the peer-to-peer remote control product from eBLVD (www.eblvd.com) displays your computer to all other registered users. This way, you can directly share a file or your entire computer to any user on the peer-to-peer network. Other products, such as those from Funk Software (www.funk.com), allow you to set up your own peer-to-peer remote control network. The primary apprehension with peer-to-peer products is that security is often compromised for convenience.

SHAREWARE PRODUCTS

If you are on a budget and want to experiment with remote control without a big commitment, consider shareware. Shareware is software usually distributed free of charge but for which you pay a small fee if you like the program. You can find remote access software at several shareware sites, such as Tucows (www.tucows.com) and CNET's shareware site (www.shareware.com).

Using FTP shareware, for example, you can transfer files back and forth between computers—especially useful if you are managing a Web site or need to transfer large files that can't be conveniently sent between email accounts. Shareware FTP

---

products, such as WS FTP Pro (www.ipswitch.com) or Serv-U (www.serv-u.com), allow you to set up an FTP server for transferring files to and from computers—a real timesaver if you're a teleworker who doesn't need the full features of a remote control product or the cost of a VPN.

File Transfer Products

One way to work remotely is to move files between computers and locations, such as when you want to work on a document at home over the weekend. Although the more traditional remote access products, such as VPN and remote control, have built-in file transfer, several specialized products are available to make the process easy. LapLink Gold (www.laplink.com) is one product that provides an advanced file transfer feature to synchronize files quickly between computers.

Telnet

Although the typical remote access user does not routinely use telnet, it does have its place. Telnet, or terminal emulation, is a protocol often used by network administrators to log on to and control servers from a distance. Using telnet software, the administrator enters commands that are executed as though they were entered directly on the server. Telnet is frequently used to administer UNIX-based Web servers remotely over the Internet. A variety of telnet clients are available, including the Telnet Client in the Microsoft Windows operating system.

MOBILE REMOTE ACCESS—HANDHELD DEVICES

As we've discussed, today's teleworker is no longer the typical home-based worker. Today, a mobile sales force and other on-the-go people now use devices that enable them to work, retrieve, and send data from virtually anywhere. Some of the more popular devices are simple email and text messaging tools, such as Blackberry (www.blackberry.net), which allow companies to integrate mobile email with their enterprise email systems.

Even the trusty personal digital assistant (PDA) is not immune to the mobile explosion. Using a PDA such as a Palm (www.palm.com) outfitted with a wireless card, you can obtain and send information to others back at the office. To take things further, several technologies are available to control a desktop computer back at the office remotely with a PDA, such as PalmVNC from Virtual Network Computing (www.uk.research.att.com/vnc/).

The concept of information anywhere has also expanded to the mobile phone. Products such as PCS Business Connection (www.pcsvision.com) enable mobile workers to get access to their office email and contacts from their Web-enabled phones.

For more information, go to Chapter 19.

PROTECT YOUR INFORMATION: REMOTE ACCESS SECURITY

If you use remote access, you need to concern yourself with security. Threats to your security can be sophisticated, such as an eavesdropper intercepting data over the Internet and reconstructing it to read email and other sensitive information. Or the threats can be something more ordinary, such as someone watching your computer screen in the office as you connect to it from home. For businesses, the threat can be even more insidious, with hackers gaining access to entire networks. The list of potential security threats to your information is lengthy, and an improperly implemented remote access solution can open the door to any or all of them.

One of the most common threats is losing confidential information to intruders. Corporate espionage and hacking, whether for fun or profit, is a very real threat in today's business world. Once hackers gain access to your network or computer, they can poke around, read private information, or delete files at will. The proliferation of newer technologies such as wireless networks makes the threats more widespread. You need to make sure any remote access solution you choose, whether it's a remote control product or a VPN, provides adequate security to block intruders from your network or computer.

You'll also want to make sure that once you access a computer or network from a public location, people using the computer after you cannot use your credentials to gain access to your information. For example, if you use a remote control product to access your office computer from an Internet café, make sure that you close the program, remove any memorized user information and password, and possibly uninstall the client software before walking away.

VPNs: SECURE OR NOT?

All remote access solutions and products have their security weaknesses, but there has been particular industry focus on the security drawbacks of the remote access VPN. Although data sent over a VPN is generally encrypted and therefore safe from the prying eyes of eavesdroppers, the connection is only as safe as its weakest link.

The weakest link of a VPN is often the user's connection. If your home computer and connection are not secure, it's only a matter of time before a hacker or other intruder tries to gain access. And once a hacker has penetrated a home system, it's possible to piggyback onto a corporate network through the VPN.

You might think of your Internet connection as secure, but it's generally not, especially if it's a shared connection, such as a cable modem. For this reason, make sure to set up a firewall on your client computer to protect your corporate network.

Security Choices

In general, the more computers that could be affected by a hacker or other intruder, the stronger your security requirements should be. You have a variety of security methods to choose from, so make sure that some or all of them are incorporated into your remote access purchase. For more information on security, refer to Chapter 11.

- **Encryption.** Many remote access methods use a technique called *encryption* to secure the information sent between computers or a computer and network. Data encryption scrambles the data in a way that only the receiving computer will be able to understand. In large part, the product you buy determines the encryption method. Some include industry-standard encryption methods, some use proprietary methods, and others use no encryption at all. If the product doesn't use encryption or requires significant configuration to obtain encryption, you might be better off choosing another product.

- **Authentication.** The product you choose should allow only you to access your remote computer or network. This process, called *authentication*, usually identifies you through a user name and password. Most remote access products provide a way to authenticate your identity, but not all methods are the same. The most secure methods encode your user name and password so snoopers cannot read this information on its way to your remote computer or network. A few less-secure products send your identifying information in clear text across the Internet, making it available for hackers to read.

- **Firewall.** Many remote access techniques connect you to a corporate network, and you should give the security of the network a high priority. One of the best ways to protect a network is through a firewall installed on your client computer. A firewall is hardware or software (or a combination of both) designed to prevent unauthorized access to a private network. Although a firewall is an effective technique for protecting networks, it may make the configuration of your remote access a little more challenging.

> Software-based firewalls such as Zone Labs ZoneAlarm (www.zonealarm.com) are inexpensive and easy to install. Hardware-based firewalls are more complex to install but allow you to secure several computers connected to the Internet.

GETTING STARTED WITH THE RIGHT REMOTE ACCESS

With all of the remote access options available, it may be daunting to choose just one. Before you make your purchase, you'll need to take into account several factors. You'll need to have a good grasp of how you'll use the technology, what hardware or additional software it requires, how much you can afford, and how much configuration you want to do. You'll want to avoid the trap of buying software or hardware you can't use because it's not right for your needs or too difficult to configure.

What Hardware and Software Do You Have?

The remote access technology you choose depends in large part on the hardware and software you currently have. If you need to connect to a Linux server, your choices are more limited than if you are connecting to your desktop computer running Windows 2000. If you are unsure what type of computer you'll be using to access your computer back at the office, you might select a Web browser-based remote control product, such as GoToMyPC (www.gotomypc.com). These products allow you to connect to your office computer from most Internet-connected Web browsers and are often not dependent on a particular operating system.

What Connection Do You Need?

The type of connection you'll need depends mainly on what type of technology you're using and where you're using it. If you are connecting through a VPN, you can utilize an existing Internet connection. If you're using a RAS solution, you'll probably use a modem to dial directly into the RAS server's modem. Still other solutions might be able to use a LAN or WAN solution if you're connecting across your organization's network.

If you intend to do any serious amount of telework, the faster the connection you have, the better. Not only will you be able to transfer data faster, your experience will be closer to what you might find on your office network or workstation. A faster connection usually means that you'll need to pay a little more each month to your ISP for a broadband Internet connection, rather than the more popular dialup modem connection.

For broadband connections, you generally choose between a digital subscriber line (DSL) or cable modem, although satellite connections may be available if you have access to neither. The extra cost is more than worth it for the improved productivity you'll find with an always-on Internet connection, and you might be able to have your employer subsidize all or a part of the cost.

REMOTE ACCESS AND BROADBAND

Using a remote access product to telework or provide support is one reason why broadband Internet access is becoming more popular. Before broadband, the typical home-based user had to rely on rusty dialup connections to the office, making work from home less productive. Now broadband gives users network speeds that, although they rarely approach the speed of an internal network, provide access as though you're there.

But even though four out of five U.S. households have access to broadband connections, only 10% take advantage of them. With the growth in remote access and telework, look for the statistics to change. Many analysts are claiming it will be one of the key drivers to broadband adoption. Broadband service providers recognize the advantageous combination of remote access and broadband; many providers, such as Earthlink (www.earthlink.com), are now promoting remote access products with their Internet service.

How Much Can You Afford?

Your number one consideration is probably your budget. You'll want to compare products on a per-computer basis and determine how long you intend to use the product. For example, if you're implementing a VPN, your initial start-up costs may be high, but over time and over 1,000 users, it may be more cost-effective than purchasing a packaged software product that you need to upgrade every two years.

On the other hand, if you're purchasing remote access for yourself or for a small office, a remote control product may suit your budget much more comfortably. If you intend to access your computer from multiple client computers, a Web browser-based product is probably more cost-effective for you.

If you are selling your remote access proposition to your manager, make sure to include the estimated savings you'll achieve in the way of productivity improvements. On the other hand, you'll also need to calculate the additional costs beyond the remote access solution itself. For example, if you're implementing a VPN, you'll need to consider costs for the additional application software you might need on client computers.

If you are considering remote access for your business or organization, the question of cost is only half the equation. The other, possibly more important, question is, How much will it save? This question falls into the category of return on investment analysis, but you don't need to perform complex calculations to determine whether remote access can save you money. You can generally show that remote access saves money in three ways:

- **Time savings.** For example, how much time would your company save if your network administrator didn't need to run to the office at 3 A.M. to reboot a critical server?

- **Productivity improvements.** As you've read, telework usually results in improved productivity. How much is it worth to improve productivity by 5% or 10% or more?

- **Overhead savings.** One of the main reasons companies implement a telecommuting program is to save costs such as the expense of office space. Quite often, companies start a telecommuting program because a municipality provides tax incentives for reducing parking or offering alternative work locations.

If you are considering a VPN, several calculators are available online that can help you determine if the numbers work for you or your company. Often, companies can justify the cost of a VPN by comparing the maintenance costs of an existing dialup RAS implementation. Keep in mind that these calculators are often developed by ISPs looking to sell you their managed VPN solution, so consider that as you review the results. You can find a good calculator made specifically for a managed remote access VPN by searching for "VPN calculator" at the Nortel Networks Web site (www.nortelnetworks.com).

How Much Security Do You Need?

When you're making your decision about which remote access product to use, make sure to take into account the security you (or your network administrator) require. The security you'll need depends on your business, company policies, and your own comfort level. For example, if the remote access is for a bank, consider that the transmitted information might contain sensitive financial data and, therefore, will need to be protected with the highest available security. On the other hand, if you're simply accessing your home computer while away on vacation, you might opt for a lower level of security.

Another consideration is whether there are any privacy regulations about protecting certain types of data. For example, if you are using remote access in a health care organization, the Health Insurance Portability and Accountability Act (HIPAA) dictates a certain level of security for protecting patient health privacy.

If you're a systems administrator, you know that the right remote access for your users involves trade-offs. On one hand, you want to give them a way to connect to the office that is easy to install and use, but on the other hand, the security of your network is paramount. To help ease the burden, choose a product with as many built-in security features as possible.

Ease of Use

Make sure to choose a product that fits your technical comfort level. If you don't have much experience with computers or don't want to spend time setting up the software, choose a product that requires little configuration. Remote access methods can vary widely in their reliability and ease of use. Unless you have a propeller-head friend nearby to help you troubleshoot your configuration at a moment's notice, an easy-to-use product such as GoToMyPC (www.gotomypc.com) might be right for you. However, if you don't mind customizing the software configuration to maximize your security, something like Symantec pcAnywhere (www.symantec/pcanywhere) or a VPN might be the right choice.

Purchasing a remote access product doesn't always entitle you to support. Many of the major commercial remote control products offer free, lifetime technical support. Some products provide free support for a limited duration, after which you'll need to cough up additional money for continued support. A few others offer no support at all. Unless you are inclined to spend hours troubleshooting, opt for a remote access product that provides lifetime support. Also useful is good online help and information.

Remote Access Administration

If you are responsible for administering remote access in an organization, the ease of administration is just as important as whiz-bang features and fast performance. After all, you'll need to spend time setting up users, managing their accounts, and reporting to management on the effectiveness of the new solution.

Understand the process for creating user accounts before you buy. Some products require several steps and many minutes for each user. If you are installing remote access for 100 users, this can amount to a serious chunk of your time. You'll also need to consider whether you need a full-time adminis-

TABLE 20.1 COMPARISON OF **VPN**, REMOTE ACCESS, AND WEB HOSTED REMOTE CONTROL.

	Remote Access VPN	Remote Control Product	Hosted Web Browser-based Remote Control
Required Hardware	VPN gateway device, client computer, possible additional hardware	Host computer and client computer	Host computer and client device (can be public)
Required Software	VPN server software; installed client software	Installed host software and installed client software	Installed host software; client access through Web browser
Required Connection	Usually Internet connection	Variety of connections including Internet	Internet connection
Cost	High startup costs, low recurring costs	One-time software purchase; occasional upgrades purchased	Usually recurring monthly service fee
Security	Included in protocol but must be configured; security only as strong as client connection; requires firewall adjustments	Must be configured; requires firewall adjustments	Usually included in service; firewall adjustments usually not necessary
Ease of Use and Implementation	Moderate difficulty to install; usually requires administrator to implement	Easy to moderate difficulty to install; configuration usually requires technical proficiency	Easy to install; configuration usually not required

trator or technical support person to monitor and troubleshoot the remote access. Often, the company's help desk is tapped to provide support to users.

To help you make your decision, Table 20.1 pulls together each of these questions and compares them across products. We've compared three of the more popular remote access products: remote access VPNs, traditional remote control software products, and hosted Web browser-based remote control.

SUMMARY

The growth of telework has spawned an entire industry around accessing computers remotely, so choose wisely. Before you sign on the dotted line or pull out that credit card for an online purchase, make sure you've thought about the issues we've discussed in this chapter. By doing so, you can be assured that you've made the right decision and will start realizing the freedom that remote access can give you.

RECOMMENDED READING

Books

Inside Network Perimeter Security: The Definitive Guide to Firewalls, Virtual Private Networks (VPNs), Routers and Intrusion Detection Systems. Karen Fredrick, Scott Winters, Lenny Zeltser, and Ronald W Ritchey. New Riders Publishing, 2002.

Complete Book of Remote Access: Connectivity and Security. Victor Kasacavage and Weikai Yan. Auerbach Publications, 2002.

Teleworking & Telecommuting. Jeffery D. Zbar. Made Ez Productions, 2002.

Telecommuting Success: A Practical Guide for Staying in the Loop While Working Away from the Office. Michael J. Dziak and Gil Gordon. Jist Works, 2001.

Web Sites

International Telework Association & Council (ITAC) at www.telecommute.org (an association promoting the economic, social and environmental benefits of telework).

Gil Gordon Associates at www.gilgordon.com (telework and alternative work Web site).

Interagency Telework/Telecommuting Site at www.telework.gov (the U.S. government General Services Administration/Office of Personnel Management Web site on telework/telecommuting).

Telework—the Future is Now at www.pueblo.gsa.gov/telework.htm (publication by the U.S. General Services Administration about telework information and statistics).

21
INTERNET
MARKETING

The Web Is Only Part of the Puzzle

Before you start down the path of promotions, ask yourself a few very important questions. How many sites do you have stored in your browser's Favorites or Bookmarks folder? Of those, how many do you visit on a regular basis? Do you have a general number in your head? Okay, now what's the first thing you do when you sit down to use the Internet? There is no right or wrong answer to any of these questions, but if you're like most people, you have dozens of *favorites* but visit only a handful on a regular basis, and you check your email before doing anything else online. Keep this in mind.

The power of email publishing can enhance your existing Web presence. Sure, it's great to have a Web site—but if nobody knows about it, what good is it to continue?

Aspirations will vary from publisher to publisher; some are in this industry for the thrill, some for the experience, some for the notoriety, and yes, some are in it for the money. There is no ultimate objective that every electronic publisher struggles to achieve. However, most of us have one thing in common: the need to be recognized. Simply publishing a marvelous e-zine (electronic magazine), then waiting for the world to read it ordinarily isn't good enough. You need name and product recognition; you need subscribers; you need a marketing strategy. Sometimes you have to turn right to go left; the immediate route isn't always the greatest or easiest way. This is the idea behind guerrilla promotions: achieving your goals by means of an indirect marketing campaign. Don't walk in the front door—use the back or side door.

Start Thinking

Before you can do anything, identify who you are and what you want to deliver to your readers. What do you find to be fun and/or interesting? That is to say, what topic or topics do you want your e-zine to cover? The world is your oyster, and if you want to publish a newsletter on oysters of the world, be my guest. If you have a fascination with paper airplanes, then why not write about them? Nobody's stopping you, and nobody should stop you. Here are a few things you should keep in mind when choosing your subject matter:

- Am I excited about my topic? If not, don't even start. Even those of us with passions find it frustrating to continue at times. When passion isn't there to begin with, those frustrations are only intensified.

- Do other resources cover my topic? How many? A quick search on Google will let you know about the competition. If the space is flooded, think about how you can make your resource different.

- Are those other resources doing a good job at covering my topic? Can I do better? Think about what's missing, then do your best to fill that void.

- How much information is out there (online) on my topic? Can I create new content? Unless you plan on being nothing more than a digital parrot, consider how you are going to present your information in a unique fashion.

- How many Web sites relate to my topic? Think about what you don't like about them, then create your own portal based on fixing those frustrations.

- How big an audience could I potentially attract with this topic? If you're tackling a niche, tackle it well. Think about percentages, not necessarily hard numbers.

- Is the information on my topic easily accessible?

- Do I know enough about my topic? If not, find others to complement your vision.

- How often do I want to publish? You can always change your mind down the road, but be realistic. If you don't have much time to devote to the project, that's fine—just make sure your audience knows how often you intend to publish new content.

- Who is my target audience? Are you aiming to appease novices or experts?

- What are my short-term goals for this e-publication? Long-term goals?

These questions should help you focus on what you really want to accomplish. I'm positive that working on the Internet is the "job of the future." I can think of no better way to start your career than with an electronic publication.

You Say Tomato

It's easy to call a sweater a sweater, but there are different kinds of sweaters (cardigan, pullover, and so on). In the same respect, there are many kinds of email broadcasts. The general umbrella term for an independently published document is *zine*. This word's concept predates computer distribution; people have been circulating various works using "unconventional" methods for decades. When the Internet started gaining popularity, e-zines (electronic zines) began to pop up. An e-zine can be delivered via email or simply put up on the Web (thus becoming a webzine). It's distributed in an electronic fashion, and that's all it needs to be in order to have that little e affixed to it. So, we've got this blanket term—now how many applications can we find for it? I'd like to believe the world will never run out of new ideas for electronic communications. However, for the sake of argument, let's look at the five major types of email publications around today: email newsletters, announcement lists, bulletins/action alerts, moderated discussion lists and unmoderated discussion lists.

NOTE

Some people choose to write the words *email*, *e-zine*, and *e-publication* without the hyphen. We've got a relatively new medium at our doorstep, so the rules haven't been completely written yet (which, for the most part, is a good thing for all). Whatever you decide, please be consistent. What's the correct pronunciation for e-zine? I believe *zine* should rhyme with *mean* or *teen*, but many people are rhyming it with *wine* or *mine*. My logic is this: Do you read magaZEENs or magaZYNEs? No matter what you choose to call your publication, you're correct. After all, it's yours. Isn't it nice to be yourself?

Bonus

Distribute your electronic mailings at Topica (www.topica.com). The free service is adequate (but somewhat limited). You'll have to put up with network advertisements if you don't pay for the service. It's a great place to start for people who just want to get up and running as soon as possible.

Email Newsletters

Pick a topic, any topic, and you can make an email newsletter for it. Just as a regular off-the-street newsletter isn't incredibly large, neither is one sent through email. Each one is content-driven; it is usually the publisher's job to come up with all the "stuff." For the most part, email newsletters tend to revolve around a particular topic. You might see an "eyeglass cleaner" newsletter here and a "dinosaur" newsletter there. Inside each issue, the reader might expect to see a new bit of information or insight regarding the given subject matter. An email newsletter may contain one article, a series of articles by the publisher and/or independent writers, links to other related Web sites or newsletters, and so forth. It's a simple venue that may be used for nearly anything the publisher desires. You're keeping people informed—that's the whole idea.

Email newsletters can be distributed in plain text, RTF (Rich Text Format), or HTML. HTML mail is essentially a Web page that is sent through email; not all HTML conventions are supported in every HTML-capable email client, but for the most part, you'll be able to use images, hyperlinks, tables, and colors. RTF mail is somewhere in between HTML mail and text, supporting formatting features such as underlining, italicizing, and bolding. A majority of today's e-publications are text-based, but you're probably going to see a major shift to HTML within the next five years. The content will hopefully remain of top quality, but users will have their text enhanced with pictures, sounds, colors, and so forth. As with anything, however, publishers will need to give their readers valid reasons to want an HTML newsletter over a text-based one.

Announcement Lists

Let's say that you already have an existing product or service, either online or offline. What better way to inform your installed user base about a price special or new development than through an announcement list? These lists aren't as long or as content-driven as email newsletters are, but they're just as valid. If you're trying to drive traffic back to your Web site, this is most likely the medium you're going to want to use.

This is not to say that you couldn't infuse a little content into your announcement list. Remember that your goal is not only to distribute the message, but also to have the end user read it. This has been a challenge for many electronic publishers.

At one point, someone got the bright idea that junk email would be an awesome idea. Well, it wound up hurting e-publications more than helping them. Junk email might disguise itself as a personal message or as some sort of announcement list. The idea is to trick the readers into believing that they subscribed to such a service. Of course, not everyone is that stupid. Most people don't want to read a message that looks like one big advertisement— do you? Nine times out of ten, the users delete the message without even looking at it. This could be a potential problem for you and/or your company's announcement list.

If your customer is accustomed to not seeing anything valuable in your e-publication, they will delete it without even thinking about it. You might have that customer listed in your subscriber database, but that doesn't mean anything. I could be sitting here with 400,000 subscribers. That's an impressive number, but if only 25% of them are reading what I'm sending out, I've got a major problem. For the most part, once you've lost a customer's interest, you've lost that customer for life.

If you're going to be pushing people back to your site for products, be sure you keep your content fresh; give them solid reasons to open your message every time they receive it.

Bulletins/Action Alerts

Bulletins and action alerts run along the same vein as announcement lists. However, they're typically geared more toward "this is what's new on my site this week" informative tidbits and less toward product announcements. The idea is to grab the reader's attention and get them to come back to your site. If you've created content on your Web site and want subscribers to visit, a small bulletin will keep subscribers "in the know." Give them a byte or two in the mailing, then point them to a URL for details.

Putting together a bulletin doesn't take much work, assuming that you already have content elsewhere on the Internet (Web site, newsgroups, and the like). If your advertising model is Web-based, a bulletin might be your best bet for e-publishing.

Push people back to your site to keep your advertisers and/or sponsors happy. If you have a Web site with original content, you should definitely send out something to your user base via email on a regular basis. Don't ever count on users to visit you more than once without prompting.

Moderated Discussion Lists

Imagine having a Usenet newsgroup come directly to your Inbox. That's pretty much what a discussion list (group) is. When you hear people talk about a LISTSERV, they're most likely referring to a discussion list. The two kinds of discussion lists are moderated and unmoderated.

Moderated means "supervised." Most Usenet newsgroups are unpoliced; anybody can post to them without fear of deletion (censorship). Some, however, are looked after by a designated individual (or individuals) who are authorized to remove unsuitable posts. Whether in newsgroups or on a list, moderation is great—in moderation. As the moderator, you have control over which posts your members view, but you don't want to take that control to the extreme.

The other key component is discussion. Because 99% of the list's content is going to be created and transmitted by members of the list, you need to keep them talking. If things are slowing down, give everybody a kick in the pants; don't be afraid to stir up controversy once in a while. For a list to be successful, you need participants who love to share their opinions.

Typically, discussion list messages can be mailed out to members either "as they are approved" or in a compiled digest format at regular intervals.

Many choose to receive the latter (which is easier on their Inboxes). It's the same stuff, no matter how you slice it; the different formats suit different users' needs.

If you get accused of being a fascist censor, press on. You are always going to find people who believe that they're right and you're dead wrong. You have the right to ban anyone from your discussion group—it's yours. My favorite thing to say to those who do nothing but complain about my publication is: "Make your own list." They seldom do.

Unmoderated Discussion Lists

An unmoderated list can be wildly unattractive to an electronic publisher; there is no censorship involved with regard to messages broadcast to the list. Imagine spilling a barrel full of candy bars into a room of preschoolers. The exact same thing could easily happen with an unmoderated discussion group (in one way or another). Your teeth won't rot, but you might not get anything accomplished; most people could be "bouncing off the walls."

Why would you want to start an unmoderated group? There are several reasons. Perhaps you want information to flow freely, and the members are people you know and trust. An unmoderated list works well when there is a small group of users that will continue to stay small and when the list's focus isn't too broad. It can also (obviously) save you a lot of time because you don't have to scrutinize and approve every message.

I would strongly advise against starting with an unmoderated list if you have never published through email before. Situations can get out of hand relatively quickly; without some form of control, you could be inviting disaster. Only if it is a small, closed group of individuals would I suggest operating an unmoderated list.

LOW COST, HIGH RETURN

Few e-publishers have either access to a sizable budget or the desire to work with venture capitalists and/or loan officers. There's nothing wrong with either of these two situations, but there's no point in wasting money. Too many Internet start-ups ultimately regretted funneling thousands of dollars into campaigns when they could have easily achieved the same results without spending a dime. Sure, sometimes you'll need to spend money, but when a cheaper road exists, you should consider taking it, especially if you're publishing independently and don't have much liquid capital on hand. That's the beauty of the Internet—there are few barriers to entry.

SUBSCRIBERS: YOUR GREATEST RESOURCE

Think outside the box for a moment. You've got capable list software, quality content, and a pretty darn good Web site. What's missing from this picture? What is the one element essential for your e-publication's success? Subscribers—without them, you're nothing.

These aren't simply email addresses in your database; they're real people. Your mission should be not only to keep users subscribed to your list, but also to turn them (eventually) into loyal readers. By offering users continual satisfaction, you're building a relationship that will not evaporate on a whim. Strive to maximize the time they spend reading every one of your mailings. Without a doubt, they're your greatest resource.

Subscribers should definitely be involved with certain significant decisions you make. At one time, I approached my subscribers with the idea of doing an audio show. Because I had no idea what its focus would be and how long it should last, I asked them for their candid opinions. The response was tremendous and very telling of what the average Lockergnome subscriber would like to hear. That informal poll will eventually help me focus on developing a show my readers want and avoid the features my readers do not want. I didn't hire a market analyst, as most companies might have done. You'll be able to craft your own publication to suit your readers' desires over time by simply asking them questions. This strategy will show them that you're willing to keep an open dialog. Do not allow their feedback to fall on deaf ears.

Peer Endorsements

You may not realize this, but you need a glimzorp. Even if you don't know exactly what one is, commercials keep telling you that life is incomplete without one. You've seen this product advertised dozens of times; it looks interesting, but you just can't see why or how it will do you any good. Suddenly, your good friend Byron stops by your home and shows off this amazing new tool. Wow, a good friend recommended it . . . Now are you a little more open to getting a glimzorp of your own?

Your list may be adding dozens of new subscribers per day, but how are those readers finding out about your publication? Did they discover you through the search engines? Was there a link on some random Web page they recently visited? Or did a friend take the time to recommend your site to them? By far, the most desirable new subscribers are the ones who received an endorsement from a close friend. These new members will be less likely to unsubscribe because they knew exactly what to expect from your publication before they joined. "I trust Byron. He says it's good, so it must be good." Compare this thought with: "Oh, a newsletter. I think I'll try it."

You can (and should) ask your readers to recommend your e-zine to friends, family members, and co-workers, but don't count on them doing it in droves. Some e-publishers will ask that subscribers forward an entire issue to someone else, which in theory is a good plan but doesn't usually translate into mass results. So how can you get people to start suggesting your work?

Free scripts and services available on the Internet will allow you to set up a recommendation form on your Web site. You can send traffic to the "recommend" page by providing a link to it in every issue, in the Welcome message, and in your email signature. You can find one of the better CGI scripts for this purpose at http://www.willmaster.com/. Or if you don't know much about programming, you might consider using a free service, such as http://www.recommend-it.com/. Most free services will append their own form of advertisements along with a user's "recommend" message, and they usually do not allow for tweaking (such as customizing fields, questions, and output format). The advantage of serving up your own script is that you can customize it to suit your needs and be able to track its usage in detail.

With Lockergnome's recommend script, users fill in their names and email addresses, the names and email addresses of friends, and possibly some personal comments. Then, upon completion, the script redirects to a page containing the same form, asking to recommend Lockergnome to another friend. Out of the blue, it asks users to suggest the site to another friend while their minds are still in "sharing" mode. And to top it off, names, email addresses, and personal comments have been carried over from the first recommend form. All the user has to do is think of some-one else, enter their email address, and press a button. Kablam! One solid recommendation just turned into two or more. It's potentially a never-ending loop.

Don't move forward without having some sort of recommend form set up on your Web site. Even if you don't "do" email publications, it is a valuable guerrilla promotion tool that shouldn't be overlooked.

The Precarious Post Boast

One excellent way to get your email publication known is by taking an active part in Internet discussions. The key word here is active. You're welcome to post whenever you have a question or an answer, but don't address the mem-bers of a group only when your interests are blatantly served. Advertising your services without some logical connection to the conversation is consid-ered rude—and some would go as far as to call it spamming. Your best bet is to sit back (lurk) and watch the regular users interact with one another. Then start answering questions confidently without mentioning your e-publication outright. After a while, you'll be seen as a "regular." Ask the moderator (if there happens to be one) if it would be okay for you to tell the members of the group about your resource. Who knows? You just may set up a strategic business partnership simply by asking!

You don't need to shove your subscription information down people's throats at any given opportunity, especially on mailing lists, Usenet news-groups, or Web forums. When you post to a group you're unfamiliar with, be very careful as to how you construct your message; every experienced nose has a built-in BS detector. If you're trying to get people to visit your site, don't come out and ask (or tell) them to go to it. Instead, contribute to a few con-versation threads and place your URL/subscription info in a four-line signa-ture of sorts (or underneath your real name if you don't have a "sig"). It's generally safe to speak when spoken to; you appear more legitimate when answering someone's question than you do by merely volunteering seemingly unrelated information. It's not your content that matters as much your tech-nique in presenting it.

You want group members to trust you as much as you need your sub-scribers to trust you. Unfortunately, this takes a lifetime to develop and only a moment to destroy. Still, the more familiar users are with you, the more they'll let you "get away with." Out of 100 posts over the course of a year, two messages may have been a little off topic. Compare this with posting three times over the course of one hour and having two messages be off topic. There is no comparison.

The Adventures of Links

A few years back, not very many "Windows" email newsletters were in existence (a primary reason for Lockergnome's inception). I contacted major shareware-related Web sites to inform them that I had started distributing a free Windows email newsletter on a regular basis. This announcement was intended to establish possible relationships with other content-oriented Internet resources. However, very few site managers paid attention to my blurb. I was the new kid on the block, desperately in search of the right stuff. To a certain degree, it is still difficult to get my foot in the door because I don't operate on a Web-centric model. I've seen subpar sites receive recognition and phenomenal email newsletters thrown to the wayside. This is a frustration that comes with the e-territory for the time being. Still, there are ways of getting your foot in the door with existing Web sites and/or email publications.

I began by offering reciprocal links to related Web sites. If they would place a link to Lockergnome on their site, I would do the same for them on mine. This worked for a while, until my list of links became unmanageable. Having a "reciprocal links" page is great for sharing resources with other site owners. By asking someone to swap links with you, you're effectively announcing your e-publication's arrival to the Internet. I strongly suggest working only with sites directly related to your subject matter; there's practically no advantage to having a kite newsletter link on a motorboat site (and vice versa). Yes, every link counts, but concentrating on strategies that will get you more recognition in your field is paramount.

It's also important to note that most FFA (Free-For-All) links pages do not work in the short or long run. At first, it may seem attractive to have your link on thousands of different pages, but recognize that your link will be lost amid hundreds of other links that are (more often than not) wholly dissimilar to your online resource. You stand a better chance of getting hit by a meteor than you do having someone discovering your link on an FFA page and actually clicking on it. If you really want to be listed in a directory, shoot for Yahoo!. You'll find that a listing in Yahoo! will bring you the most visitors by far. If you're smart enough to use the right keywords for your description, the chances of "user click-thru" will be even higher.

Design a Logo

Web surfers need to know who you are and what you do. If they see a link sitting on a Web page, it should be descriptive and/or intriguing enough for them to click on it. One way to help with name recognition on the Web is by designing a small logo. A standard graphic format for logos measures 88 pixels horizontally by 31 pixels vertically. This "button" can be animated or not. When Web sites approach you for a "button swap," they're most likely looking for this 88 × 31 image. Just about any graphics application will help you create a simple one; download an image-editing utility from your favorite shareware site (such as WebAttack.com; www.webattack.com) if you don't have one yet.

Web Ringmaster?

You may have heard of "web rings" before; as a rule, they're a waste of time and space. The idea is to link a handful of related sites together to form some sort of "virtual donut." If you stumbled upon a leather knapsack site that is a member of the leather knapsack web ring, you can see other leather knapsack sites with the click of a link (in theory). Here are the problems:

- Member sites might belong to more than one web ring.
- A member site might not display the web ring link in a highly visible area.
- Member links can change at a moment's notice, consequently disrupting the circle.
- There are usually no solid standards for member sites.
- It just doesn't look very professional.

You're better off working with a select group of sites if you want to create some sort of "network." You'll have more influence over implementation and be better acquainted with your affiliates. For example, if you have a "low carb" discussion list and know of someone who has a "low carb" email newsletter, you may consider working together. After users subscribe to your list, they can be automatically directed to sign up for that related newsletter. Of course, you'd expect to see a similar referral after a user signs up for the newsletter. It's a ring of sorts but in a more controlled environment. You'll all walk away as winners.

Sit Up and Give Notice

I knew that it would take a while for the world to recognize Lockergnome. So I decided that when I featured a resource in my newsletter, I would contact the authors to let them know that they had been formally recognized. I did this for a few different reasons: (1) it was courteous, (2) they probably wouldn't have known otherwise, and (3) I was hoping that they'd want to set up links on their sites pointing to Lockergnome's site. On the whole, authors have been very receptive to (and thankful for) these enlightening messages.

This is something that I've continued to do, and I advise that you do the same. You're consistently building qualified relationships that will (in turn) help build your publication.

Oranges and Oranges

Let's take the concept of reciprocal links a step further. If you have (or will have) an email publication, you're not alone. But your subscriber base is almost certainly unique, just as everybody else's is. Wouldn't it be fantastic if you could hook up with other e-publishers and exchange advertisements at a moment's notice? You can, and you should! This is a great way to legitimately gain access to a potentially fresh audience. And you don't necessarily need to have the same number of readers in order to swap with someone else. Here's the math: Newsletter A has 30,000 list members, and newsletter B has 55,000 list members. It's possible for newsletter A's host to approach newsletter B's and request a 2:1 advertisement swap (and vice versa). Even if newsletter A's subject matter is radically different from newsletter B's, both subscriber bases are used to receiving email publications and will consequently be more likely to subscribe to another one.

In fact, it's usually better if ad swaps are done with unrelated newsletters. This way, the subscriber bases are almost guaranteed to be completely unique. A graphic-design e-zine swapping with another graphic-design e-zine might not yield too many new subscribers, because there might be a high amount of duplication between the two lists. However, if a graphic-design e-zine were to ad swap with a newsletter that had the need for graphic design but wasn't necessarily focused on graphic design, the chances of each publisher walking away with more subscribers are higher. I've found that there's no better campaign for getting new subscribers than to work directly with other e-publishers. Forget about press releases, forget about prestigious awards, and forget about trying to do things on your own. By sharing resources with others in your industry, you're playing smart. It's okay to be independent, but don't let these opportunities pass you by.

On the flip side, seemingly worthwhile ad swaps might not be as fruitful as expected. Remember that subscriber count is not always representative of the number of regular readers. In an e-publication with over 100,000 email addresses in the database, only 70,000 might be verified as "good." And of those 70,000 working addresses, only 20,000 might actually read the publication on a regular basis. So don't let the numbers fool you. If someone approaches you with a phenomenal subscriber count, be very leery. Not every email publication is well read. Find out what kind of response their issues usually elicit (if possible). You, too, should be honest when approaching other email publishers; the chances for disappointment on either side will be far less.

I realize that approaching other electronic publishers can be daunting, especially if you're just starting your own email publication. Should you wish to initiate a relationship with another mailing-list manager, consider featuring their e-zine in your e-publication prior to contact. This way, when you finally do get in touch with that list owner, he may be more willing to work with you—especially if your mention had a noticeable impact. Understand, too, that often a well-written review from the list owner holds much more weight in a subscriber's eyes than does an advertisement. Method and presentation are important factors to bear in mind.

Get On, Stay On

When someone sees a URL while still online, they are more likely to visit it right then than when seeing the same URL offline. A user might be visiting a Web page, viewing a newsgroup post, or reading an email message, but the user is in "online mode." Suppose people see a flyer in the grocery store and become interested in your resource. At that point, they're far away from their computers and will probably forget your URL by the time they get online again. Now, what if they had seen the same URL while they were sitting in front of their terminals? Chances are, you'd have new subscribers.

Operating a business on the Internet can help keep your costs low, but you need to get out of the "traditional" mindset before you begin. Stop doing things offline; start doing things online. By focusing your efforts on Internet-related resources, you'll find the benefits far outweighing the drawbacks. Instead of posting flyers around town, it would be simpler, cheaper, more focused, and less time-consuming if you were to post a single message to a related newsgroup or mailing list. The Internet is global, and you need to use it to your advantage. Thinking small will produce small results. Though your focus may be strictly on people in your locale, expect that others from around the world will want to know more, as well.

Travel down those online avenues first! You shouldn't have business cards printed until you have a professional Web page up and running. And, don't think of getting T-shirts done until you have an interested subscriber base to buy them. Why have personalized pencils made if you never plan on handing them to people who would be interested in your e-publication? You can use other great promotional items to help create awareness of your online venture, but you should reserve them for use at trade shows, conventions, or speaking engagements. If you have money to burn, I suggest spending it on creating and fostering relationships with other email publishers first.

Whatever you decide to do, make sure you do it for a reason. If you don't have to spend money to get something, don't. I'm sure you'll discover on your own that online pursuits—targeted or not—will generate more results than anything done offline. Lockergnome has been featured in countless print publications with millions of regular subscribers, but email newsletters with fewer than 2,000 members have helped me more. You wouldn't expect that, but again, there's more than just one variable at play here. The largest variable is the environment in which the URL is seen—online, rather than offline.

> **TIP**
>
> When you do swap ads with other e-publications, be sure to include subscription information. A Web site and email address should suffice. Leaving either of these two things out completely nullifies the reason for doing an ad swap in the first place. Be descriptive, focused, and as upbeat as possible.

Offline Offensive

Don't get me wrong—it's okay to have items imprinted with your name and URL. But don't hand them out to unqualified strangers without a good reason. There are millions of people who have yet to jump online, and not all of them are going to be interested in what you have to offer once they get there. Still, I understand the thrill of seeing your logo or name on everyday objects. If you have a culinary e-zine, think about having customized placemats printed, then give them freely to restaurant managers. If you have a fitness email newsletter, what about customized duffel bags to be given away or sold at gyms? Dental discussion list moderators should have toothbrushes in hand. First-aid list owners would want bandages. You get the idea.

Business cards are important to sport at all times. When you need to explain your e-publication to someone but don't have a lot of time, give away a card. Let people visit your site and discover more on their own. Yes, it will probably be a few days, weeks, or months before they swing by, but if you personally give them a compelling argument as to why they can't live without your e-zine, they shouldn't quickly forget. The actual design of your card is completely up to you. However, keep in mind that you hand out these cards primarily to drive traffic to your Web site and/or email publication, not just to show people how to get in touch with you. Your URL should be the most noticeable object on your business card. Specific subscription instructions could be included, but remember that such instructions are prone to change over time.

Develop Writer's Cramp

Assumedly, you would like to have your email publication be as popular as dish soap. Although it probably won't be lemony fresh, you want people to know that you exist. When I started writing Lockergnome issues, my forte was "how to find cool stuff for my computer using the Internet." Virtually nobody knew who I was, and it was difficult to prove my worth to the world on my own. I would have had an easier time at building a name had I written articles in other electronic publications.

If you have a way with words, I strongly encourage you to do what I (and others) failed to. This bit of extra writing would have given me experience, visibility, and the opportunity (once again) to cultivate strategic relationships. Freelancing may not be your style, and the pay may not be exceptional, but you should do whatever you can to get your name and e-publication better known. Don't pull yourself in so many different directions that you neglect your regular administrative or editorial duties, but if a simple opportunity arises, you should take it. Not having enough time may be an issue. In that case, a simple syndication model might be worth pursuing with similar email publications.

The syndication idea is the concept that revolves around writing something one time and seeing it show up in several places. It's relatively easy to swap content with other e-zines; you wouldn't be writing any more, and you'd be getting more content for your own mailing list. The same benefits would be seen for the other e-publisher, if it is willing to work with you in this capacity.

Unrelated Relations

Having a Web page for your email publication is important for several reasons. You can use it for just about anything you'd like, including for "stuff" not exactly associated with your e-zine. Having a domain name works best for this tactic, because it is more recognizable for indirect association.

For example, suppose our friend Mr. Spatula registered http://www.mrspatula.com/ with the intent of publishing a free weekly email newsletter reviewing syrups of the world. The people who would most likely be interested in his offering would be pancake or waffle lovers, breakfast eaters, chefs, and so forth. But what about other people who might not be surfing specifically to uncover scrumptious syrups? They'll probably never visit http://www.mrspatula.com/.

Imagine that Mr. Spatula has another hobby—collecting bottle caps. He could easily make a separate section on his site using a subdirectory: http://www.mrspatula.com/bottlecaps/.

This would be designed, operated, and marketed much differently than his staple content (the syrup newsletter). Those interested in bottle caps would most likely visit his bottle caps page before they'd visit his main page.

It would be wise for Mr. Spatula to put a link, subscription form, or subscription instructions for his syrup newsletter on his bottle caps page. And did you know that Mr. Spatula also enjoys creating wallpaper images of baby seals? He might provide those for download at http://www.mrspatula. com/babyseals/. Are people who are interested in bottle caps or baby seals going to be interested in syrup? Quite possibly! The only drawback to this technique (as I see it) is in the outcome of your intentions. Visitors to the bottle caps page might believe that the subscription form is for a bottle caps newsletter, not a syrup newsletter; they'll probably wind up being disappointed. That notwithstanding, you would be attracting a different audience to your newsletter, simultaneously giving your URL more "airtime" in diverse venues.

Pressing Introductions

After you distribute your first email publication, you're a member of the electronic press. Your job is simple—to inform. The more people you inform, the more your publication will be worth in your industry. Now, how can you start getting companies to sit up and take notice of your online venture? Let them know two things: You're alive and you want to work with them in a mutually beneficial way. There is no better person to divulge this information to than a public relations (PR) professional or press contact. These people thrive on publicity. When you want to speak with someone, be sure you're barking up the right tree.

With luck, you're not the only person in the world interested in your chosen subject. You're going to have opportunities to cover topical events and/or review related products without having to spend a dime. For instance, let's say Katie has a recycled products discussion list, Recycle Receptacle. Company XYZ manufactures a mouse pad made from 100% recycled materials. Katie wants to give this accessory a whirl, so she uncovers a press contact and blasts off an email message to that individual.

Her message might have included more background information on the Recycle Receptacle mailing list, but saying very little is often as good as saying more than enough. Katie may never get a response from this company contact (or receive an evaluation unit), but at least she's introduced herself. If she decides to review the product, a link to the Recycle Receptacle might be placed on Company XYZ's Web site, potentially sending subscribers in Katie's direction. Understand, too, that the more expensive a product or service is, the less likely you will be to receive a "copy" of it.

Sweeping Idea

Some e-publishers have organized sweepstakes (of sorts) for their subscribers. Although not everybody has something of value to give away, it's possible to set up cross-promotional offers with other businesses. Recycling our example: Katie doesn't make products, but Company XYZ does. Once Katie has established a relationship with that company, she might offer to run a contest in conjunction with it. In essence, she would be pitching XYZ's products in her mailing list for free, in exchange for a few units for a few selected subscribers. Who wins? Katie gets coverage, the Recycling Receptacle subscribers get the chance to win, and Company XYZ gets to have its recycled products showcased in the mailing list. The most difficult part is finding a company willing to work with you.

For more details (and legalities) on running contests online, check out http://www.adlaw.com/RC/rf_sweeps.html.

You can promote your list in thousands of ways, and you'll discover more on your own. As long as you don't compromise your integrity, you should be in the clear. Respect yourself, respect your subscribers, and respect other list owners. In marketing your list, keep your ultimate goals in mind. Don't feel that you need to take advantage of every possible opportunity, either; some may not work particularly well for your list. It's great to have an email publication and to know how to promote it efficiently. Now how do you make it float? That is to say, how can you keep it running without running your wallet into the ground? It's time to answer the most important question: How can you make money with your mailing list?

Wipe those dollar signs from your eyes; email publishing is not a major cash cow at this time. Yes, you can make an adequate amount of money over time, but instant financial success is virtually impossible. Good money will come as a result of creating a powerhouse e-publication.

Although it's important not to lose money through electronic publishing, I don't suggest setting "wealth" as your ultimate goal. Your publication will almost certainly suffer. Subscribers are to publishers as students are to teachers; they can see right through you when you lie or mislead them. And remember: Without subscribers, you've got nothing.

I didn't start Lockergnome to make money; I started it to make waves. Any financial gains I do make from Lockergnome are merely icing on the cake. I'm a young college graduate with massive student loans who just got married and bought a house; I'm anything but well off. Despite those drawbacks, I've continued to publish a high-quality email newsletter and have driven my subscriber base higher than many of my competitors. Here's the kicker: I've been profitable! It hasn't been much, but at least I'm not in the red. Look around, and you'll find businesses losing money left and right on the Internet, but that's no reason why you should be in the same unsuccessful boat. Keep your costs extremely low by sharing and bartering resources, employing cost-effective, ground-level techniques, and listening to your subscribers. You'll be infinitely more satisfied—guaranteed.

CLICK HERE TO MAKE MONEY

"Yeah, but the Internet was made to make money!" No, it wasn't. It was created for the electronic distribution of information. Financial geniuses and marketing wizards decided that it was the next frontier for commerce. Consequently, too many underinformed and inexperienced users are logging on to line their pockets with "easy" money. We're in the middle of an electronic gold rush, and disenchantment hangs heavy in the air. I keep seeing circular arguments: Make money by clicking here to make money by telling people to click here to make money by clicking here . . . and so on. There's no content, there's no purpose, and there's no way you want to get involved in that game.

You may choose to found your publication on the principle that advertising will never be accepted. This is admirable but not always realistic. Can you foresee how popular your mailings are going to be? And who knows how much it will eventually cost you to distribute? By keeping your subscriber base small, you will avoid most financial annoyances. But not every e-publisher wants to restrict growth in that fashion. It's possible to start doing a separate, sponsor-supported email publication, provided that you have the time, energy, and resources for it.

THE FREE OR FEE DECISION

Face it: Revenue has to come from somewhere to keep your enterprise afloat. The obvious solution is to charge for subscriptions. But the average Internet user isn't ready to pay for online services or subscriptions yet. Some surfers are a bit more cavalier with their cash, but for the most part, users will pass you by if you start asking for their money up front. It's okay to offer your email publication for a fee, but you probably won't get an incredible number of subscribers in the beginning. It's wiser for you to offer a free newsletter alongside a "fee" one. The idea is to hook subscribers on something great, then offer them something even better for a little bit of money.

With a free subscription, you'll build subscriber numbers and brand recognition at a more rapid, steady pace. Under this system, you'll presumably fall into an advertising-based model for income.

How will the ads appear? It depends on your mode of publication. Although HTML email can accommodate either type of ad (text or graphic), text publishers are obviously stuck with text-only ads. Which style of ad is more effective? Well, advertisers are just starting to discover that text-based ads give them more bang for their advertising buck. You're going to be battling traditional banner-based models for a little while longer, though; not every businessperson is aware of the tremendous power of email quite yet.

Advertising and Email: A Great Match

When approaching potential sponsors for advertising support, you'll get asked how many "hits" your site receives. Kindly answer that your click-thru rates are not based on random hits but on a number of regular-reading, satisfied subscribers. You can then explain how newsletters are infinitely better than Web sites. But don't be surprised if they don't get it. Salespeople are currently of the mindset that "if it doesn't have a graphic, it isn't an ad." They're dead wrong and consequently missing out on remarkable opportunities with mailing lists. Is list advertising the way of the future? No, it's the way of today. Some email publishers want advertisers, and all advertisers want high click-thru rates. But most advertising businesses are turning to the wrong venue: the Web. Email publication readers digest more of the presented information than do Web page visitors viewing the same material. Trying to convince people of this phenomenon is difficult, but the logic is not that convoluted. You're in a different mindset when reading email (active), compared with surfing the Web (passive). Now, would you rather have 10,000 subscribers providing you with 1,000 click-thrus or 20,000 Web page visitors providing you with 50 click-throughs? By and large, a list will have a remarkably targeted, receptive, captive audience, whereas a Web page will generally attract random, unqualified, "mindless" visitors. I'm not asking you to believe me: See for yourself.

Sponsors would be considerably better off with mailing-list advertising. Whereas graphics take a while to download, need to be aesthetically pleasing, and generally can't get an idea across without trying to be cute, text-based advertisements are much more dynamic. Text ads can be written as the writer sees fit and customized for certain publications or campaigns, and they have the potential for being more descriptive than graphical banners.

The better a writer is, the stronger the advertisement's impact. However, just because you deal with salespeople doesn't mean you're dealing with powerful writers. You should always reserve the right to rewrite ad copy; who knows your audience better than you? If free stuff trips their trigger, make sure that gets mentioned toward the beginning of the ad (if possible). Keep it clean, honest, direct, and intriguing. You'll be happier with the wording, your subscribers will see the advantages of visiting, and your advertisers will be happier with the results.

When Can I Start and How Much Should I Charge?

People will pay more for Web advertising than they will for newsletter advertising. I realize this is messed up, but I can't directly control the way businesses think. So just how large should your subscriber base be before you can start accepting advertisements? Well, that "magic number" is entirely up to you! If you think 2,000 subscribers is enough, it's enough.

Some charge a fee per subscriber, and some operate on a flat fee. In a way, the amount depends on what kind of list you're publishing. Discussion group members are typically more active than newsletter readers. Advertising in a discussion group with 1,000 members could be considered more valuable than advertising in an email newsletter with 1,000 subscribers. An advertisement's value also hinges on how many businesses are trying to gain placement in the same ad spot.

How much should you charge per ad? That's entirely up to you. Start small, and as advertiser interest grows, increase your rates. It's better to undercharge than it is to overcharge. Your costs are low to begin with; it won't take much for you to turn a profit. A good rule of thumb is to charge well under a $1,000 per insertion when your mailing list has under 100,000 subscribers. The lowest rates I've seen have been $2 per thousand, and the highest have gone all the way up to $30 per thousand. Of course, if your list is smaller (under 1,000 subscribers) but extremely targeted, you may offer $50 or $100 per advertisement. Again, these numbers depend a lot on the demand of your list. For example, Lockergnome has 135,000 subscribers receiving the Text Weekly edition, and a "top" ad placement has run as high as $25,000 and as low as $10.

Do your best to have your ad spots filled in every issue; something is typically better than nothing. Try throwing together a few pricing packages for each potential advertiser. Everybody likes having options; give people a choice, and you'll wind up with greater success. It's much better to hear "no, no, yes, no" than simply "no."

You'll have some advertisers who are just looking to place one advertisement and move along. In those situations, don't be afraid to charge a higher rate. If the advertiser is not going to be around for long, you might as well get as much from the company as possible. However, with individuals and/or companies with whom you'd like a future relationship (advertising-centric or not), consider charging your normal rate.

Announcing that You're Open for Business

Advertisers can't read minds; tell them that you're receptive to sponsorship. Give them the opportunity to talk to you about advertising. Set up a separate Web page for ad-related information, and create a specific email alias for inquiries. Give out your phone number (if possible). If they don't know how to get a hold of you, how do you expect them to do it?

In a similar vein, why not tell your subscribers that advertising opportunities are available? You might even offer special ad discounts for your members—especially when ad sales are stagnant. Some people are just waiting for the right opportunity to come forth and express an interest in sponsorship.

Having a cool name and an awesome subscriber base often isn't enough to win over salespeople. You have to promise potential advertisers some value for their money. You don't want them to have to ask, "Why should I advertise in your email publication?" The answer should be obvious, and if it's not, you need to be able to educate them about your value. You'll need to be tactful, knowledgeable, and ready to wheel and deal. And don't feel that you have to accept every offer that comes across your desk; if you don't feel comfortable with a certain company, you don't have to work with that company!

Expanding Your Sales Operations

A few e-publishers have found that a few hundred-dollar ads in a single issue will cover all their costs (and then some). However, you may not be able to close those kinds of ad deals with ease, especially if you're not familiar with ad sales. As multiple companies begin to approach you to advertise, consider hiring a salesperson or outsourcing those responsibilities to a professional firm. Even if nobody is approaching you for ad placements, finding someone to represent you could prove advantageous.

Don't give away too much of the pie, though. Depending on the amount of work done, the percentage split might be anywhere from 20/80 to 40/60 (them/you). There is usually more involved in advertising sales than making contact with someone and negotiating a deal. Invoices have to be written, sent, and followed up; URLs may need to be tracked with special ID codes; performance reports and statistics should be released sometime after an advertisement's run. Delegating these tasks to other people is better if you don't function well in a high-pressure environment.

Associate with Affiliate Programs

Sponsored advertising isn't the only way to make money with your mailing list. You can actively seek advertisers, wait for them to come to you, or use that ad space for something other than traditional advertising. Associate- or affiliate-program popularity is skyrocketing at a phenomenal rate. The concept revolves around you getting paid to "associate" with other businesses. In exchange for traffic or purchases, you'll get a commission. Essentially, you become an independent sales representative. As an affiliate, instead of charging a fixed amount for an advertisement, you work on a percentage or predetermined fee. Your results will vary from placement to placement, program to program.

Finding an affiliate program is relatively simple. Most sites that offer products or services will have some kind of a commission-based plan already set up for content providers. Obviously, you'd like for your subscribers to act on any given advertisement. The closer you can match an affiliate program's offerings with your audience's interests, the more you will earn.

NOTE

Although minimum "impressions" aren't typically required to benefit from an associate program, some companies will not cut checks below a certain dollar amount. (An *impression* is the display of a banner or other type of advertisement on a Web page.)

You can start or stop working as an affiliate at any time, so you are free to advertise your participation sporadically or not at all. When you don't have a paying sponsor, you might as well use that space for something! It's important for you to do a little detective work before dealing with companies that offer associate programs. Some are legit, but others are not. What's the quickest way to determine the validity of a program's claims? Ask around; talk to other people you know and trust. Have they worked with this business before? What were their results? Did they see any "red flags?" Don't jump into something if it sounds too good to be true—there's almost always a catch.

BONUS

For a list of great affiliate programs, check out Commission Junction (www.cj.com). It will probably have campaigns targeted to your audience. If your Internet connection costs you $40 a month, and you make $50 a month through your resource, then wasn't it worth your time to look?

Sponsorship Foibles

I used to eat red licorice by the pound. As a result, I experienced the world's biggest stomachaches. Had I eaten only a few pieces at a time, my body wouldn't have minded, but I overdid it. Keep my tummy troubles in mind when you start placing advertisements in your email publication. I've seen far too many mailing lists alienate their users by engaging in "ad overkill." Nobody wins in these situations.

Would you be inclined to watch a television show that was 7 minutes long and had 23 minutes' worth of commercials? Probably not. Even if you enjoyed the show, there's no reason to sit through close to half an hour of sales pitches (unless, of course, you're an infomercial junkie). In time, if your email publication goes overboard with advertisements, your click-thru rates will suffer, as will your subscriber base. Most Internet marketing email publications miss the mark here; not only do they have a lot of duplicated content among them, but they're drowning their readers in ads. Subscribers are looking for substance. If you continue to pelt them with ads, they'll drop you. And where are you without subscribers?

It's also important for you to draw a clear line between advertising and editorial matter. A user should know when you are endorsing a product or service because you like it, as opposed to supporting everything that will bring in a buck. Should substance be indistinguishable from sponsorship, your integrity as an information provider will suffer. You may decide to accept only advertisements to which your readership will be attracted. In that case, the boundaries must be even more apparent. If you don't let subscribers know (visibly) where the content ends and the selling begins, you'll wind up with subscribers who feel used and misled.

Building to Sell

Your mailing list will be worth money from the start, should you decide to sell it. As to the exact amount, that's completely up to you. Some databases will be worth a penny per subscriber, and others will be worth $10 per subscriber. However, do you really want to sell your list of subscribers to the highest bidder? Yeah, you're making money, but you're doing so at other people's expense (indirectly). When I sign up for a belt buckle mailing list, I expect to receive messages regarding belt buckles. I don't want to have my address bought and sold to companies who just want to sell me stuff without asking me first.

You can do whatever it is you want to do, but remember that subscribers are people. They're (in all honesty) under your control and trust you enough to pass along their email addresses. When you sell lists, you're selling data, but in essence, you're also selling people. List brokers are profitable, but I've always questioned their motives. You should also ask yourself how long you plan to work with your e-zine. What do you want to gain from it in the long run? Do you have an exit strategy? What happens to your list when you're tired of running it? Is its success dependent on your involvement, or can it be easily handed to another company or individual? There's nothing wrong with wanting to sell your entire email publication to another party when the time comes. Just be sure to deal with honest, trustworthy people. You will have built a seemingly valuable resource, possibly around your own name. This list and everything it entails will become a large part of your life; don't throw everything away for a few bucks.

CAUTION

Be very careful when you're dealing with companies and Web sites that deal specifically with the generation of opt-in lists. By working with them, you're potentially misleading your readers in a dreadful way. Many believe they're signing up for newsletters also run by your organization when, in fact, those "other lists" are being operated by an outside source. It's a legitimate scheme, but too often, its presentation is deceptive.

SYNDICATION: WRITE ONCE, READ ANYWHERE

Some Net prophets claim that content will be king. I, for one, agree with them. For as many Web pages as there are on the Internet, very few worthwhile resources are available. Businesses are constantly struggling with ways to get visitors to return to their sites, but without good reason, most surfers won't come back. I've already covered how email publications take care of this problem, but how can you take this application to the next level? How can you acquire income without working any harder? It's not too good to be-true—it's syndication!

Pick up a newspaper. Chances are it's filled with syndicated features, editorials, and everybody's favorite—comics. These artists and writers don't spend their time writing the same things over and over again. Likewise, you don't have to compose the same content multiple times when you distribute via email. So why not give another content provider the right to run your stuff? Provided that you have style and substance worth reading on a regular basis, the benefits for other parties should be obvious: keeping their readers informed without having to hire a knowledgeable person to tackle the subject.

You're out nothing, getting name recognition, and possibly making a few dollars on the side. They're gaining content, keeping their readers happy, and increasing the value of their publications. The most difficult part of this strategy is finding companies willing to work with a syndication model. For that, you're pretty much on your own. Writing agents might be able to assist, but unless you know people on the "inside," this is a tough road to travel, especially for beginners.

THE CHALLENGE

I was minding my own business one afternoon when a Lockergnome subscriber emailed me from out of the blue. He felt that my publication was worth more than "free," so he offered to send me one American dollar. On top of this, he issued a "challenge" for all the other subscribers to do the same. I was extremely surprised with the results; although I didn't make a mint from his proposal, I am now the proud owner of a large box filled with envelopes from just about every country on the globe. Each piece of mail arrived with at least a dollar (some included up to $100). But the most impressive—and heartwarming—part of this situation was seeing the handwritten notes or letters thanking me for my services. When people try to tell me that the Internet is a cold, unprofitable place, I show them my challenge box. The Internet exists because people exist. Remember that.

If you publish without charging your subscribers, a voluntary donation drive might not be out of the question. I even set up a Web page for Lockergnome Challengers, to give them an incentive to help: http://www.lockergnome.com/challenge.html. They enjoy seeing their name "up in lights," and I enjoy reading their personal letters to me. They let me know that I'm truly making a difference. Good luck and fortune have nothing to do with it. You can't pay for or buy a contented subscriber.

> **BONUS**
>
> If you're looking for an easy way to accept donations for your site, check out Amazon.com (www.amazon.com). It has a free feature called the "Honor System." Sure, Amazon.com will take a small percentage from the overall gift, but you don't have to worry about anything on the back end (setting up a secure server, credit card processing, and so forth).

50 Ways to Make a Successful Online Publishing Business

1. **Be prepared to work.** Don't depend on someone else to do the job for you. Starting something successful on the Internet today is a tough job for anyone. You can't be in it for the short run; building a name and subscriber base will take time.

2. **Be sure you bite off only as much as you can chew.** Start small, and develop over time. In the beginning, you'll have tons of energy for your e-publication, but that enthusiasm will probably dissipate in less than six months.

3. **Do your technical homework.** Although you don't need to be a computer expert to manage an email publication, it would be wise if you had some practical experience on the Internet beforehand. Talk to other Internet-savvy friends; they might be willing to help and could offer suggestions.

4. **Target your audience.** If you like boating, why not make a boating e-publication? If you like pasta, why not make a pasta recipe e-publication? If you like antiques, why not . . . ? You get the point. Above all, be as specific as possible. The more precise the topic, the greater the chance of subscriber interest.

5. **Write about what you know and what you like.** If you don't know a thing about eighteenth-century homemade Amish swimwear, do yourself a favor and don't write about it.

6. **Keep your content relevant.** Even if the topic happens to be the latest craze, you'll find yourself in a daze within a few issues. If you stray from your primary objectives too often, your audience is likely to question their subscriptions.

7. **You can't be in it for the short run.** Email publications, although novel, aren't a quick moneymaker. You must build a subscriber base and work with other online entities to become a recognized name.

8. **Let your friends know.** Once you've decided you're going to create an email publication, contact your closest friends and let them know. Some of them couldn't care less, but others will support and applaud your efforts.

9. **Think of an original name.** "Bob's Cooking Tips" doesn't sound as catchy as "Pots & Pans." Steer clear of overused terms such as "Net," "Cyber," "Tech," or "Compu." Don't be afraid to have fun with the name.

10. **Try to do something new.** People are more apt to pay attention to something that hasn't been done before. Do it first, and people will remember you. Don't copy someone else's idea; you can take and build upon what you see, but if it doesn't scream "original," you might as well not even bother.

11. **Remember to have fun with your publication.** I realize that might not sound like much of a tip at this point, but hey, if your heart isn't into this, you're not going to give it all you've got, and your subscribers will pick that up immediately.

12. **Don't fear competition—welcome it.** You'll have a devout following of subscribers before long. It won't matter that similar e-zines are out there. If yours is good, your subscribers shouldn't leave you.

13. **Listen to your subscribers.** If 90% of them don't like something, knock it off. If a majority of them love something, think about doing more of it. If they're not reading what you're writing, try a new approach. You're not going to get anywhere without loyal and happy subscribers.

14. **Don't get discouraged.** The average start-up email publication reaches 2,000 people. Don't be depressed if you don't make it to this mark. You can't expect to have a million subscribers at the drop of a hat. Be proud of your accomplishments, and don't let anyone depress you with larger stats or larger subscriber numbers.

15. **Don't spam!** That is, don't cross-post to unrelated newsgroups, don't send unsolicited email messages to someone you don't know, don't purchase questionable email databases, and so on. Enough people out there are giving legitimate email publications a bad name.

16. **Don't purchase email databases from list brokers.** Purchasing lists sounds like the easy way out, but it is also an easy way to tarnish your reputation.

17. **Advertise your email publication in other email publications.** In my experience, it beats banner advertisement. You can be more descriptive with a text ad. Plus, people who subscribe to one email publication are likely to subscribe to another one. An email message is easier to read than a Web page; subscribers read an email publication at their leisure. Once it is in their Inboxes, they don't have to mess with being connected to the Internet anymore.

18. **Educate your advertisers.** When people ask how many impressions your Web site receives, tell them how many subscribers you have instead and why they would be more interested in advertising in your e-publication than on your Web site.

19. **Focus on your e-publication.** Although it is wise to accompany your email publication with some sort of Web page or site, you should use it only to advertise your e-publication's offerings. People often forget about the sites they visit, but once they're signed on to your e-pub, you've got a guaranteed audience (unless they unsubscribe).

20. **Keep your audience focused on your e-publication.** Make sure people know that your site advertises an emailed publication, not a webzine. Put the subscription form as close to the top on the front page as possible, and draw special attention to it.

21. **Contact people who have related resources on the Web.** If your email publication is about skateboarding, find all the skateboarding sites (big or small), and let them know about what you're doing. They could be helpful in spreading the word about your new publication.

22. **Advertise to defray costs.** In the beginning, you should be able to get by without advertising income, but if you get a domain name (whatever.com), you'll need to find a virtual host to carry your site, and that service costs money. Depending on your topic, you might be able to find some "small spenders" who will be willing

to plop down a couple of bucks to get the word out about their product or service.

23. **Make a graphical logo for your site.** A standard logo on a Web page is 88 pixels wide by 31 pixels high. A graphic catches Web surfers' eyes.

24. **Network with other sites.** When you mention a Web site in your email publication, contact someone from that site on the chance that he or she will want to announce that the site appeared in your email publication.

25. **Give yourself credibility.** It's a good idea to add a small description (annotation) or add a personal accolade to accompany *any* link. It gives you more credibility.

26. **If subscribers like what they see, they'll tell their friends.** There's no better advertisement than word of mouth. If you had to choose between 10 products and your friend recommended one of them, you'd probably go with that one.

27. **Count on your email publication reaching more people than those who are subscribed.** Many people print e-publications out and pass them around the office. That isn't a bad thing, either. At least you know that people are talking about what you're doing.

28. **Get links to your Web site and email publication on topically related Web sites.** If you had a car-related e-publication, you'd want your link on as many car-related pages as possible, for example. Links will drive more subscribers to your mailing list.

29. **If people see enough links to you, they'll eventually check you out.** Surfers become familiar with a certain name, and they begin to trust it. Some will come to you just because they keep seeing your button or link all over the place. They'll think, "Well, gee . . . If I keep seeing it everywhere, it must be good."

30. **Find out where people who subscribe are hearing about your publication.** If you're discovering subscriptions coming from a certain site or other email publication, see whether you can do something in conjunction with it.

31. **Choose your allies intelligently.** You don't want to get a bad name for yourself right out of the starting gate. If you feel that a site's content isn't as good as it could possibly be, you don't have to work with its owners. Everything will reflect back on your name and publication.

32. **Pursue joint promotions.** If you find a publication that complements yours, inquire about joint promotion opportunities.

33. **Be careful with banners.** Be careful about using banners on your site or in your HTML newsletter without researching them first. Some banner advertising schemes sound great, but unless you have a ton of traffic, chances are you're not going to gain any money by using them. And be sure not to place more than one banner in a row on your site if you want your visitors to see you as a "professional" site. Nothing looks worse than a page with five banners in a row. The page takes forever to load, and the banners don't improve the quality of your Web page or newsletter.

34. **Everywhere you go, talk about your publication.** Every subscriber counts.

35. **Encourage subscribers to refer others.** Don't be afraid to ask your subscribers to recommend your e-zine to their friends, family members, co-workers, supervisors, and so on. You don't want to beat them over the head with it, but a constant reminder is effective in getting more "quality" subscribers.

36. **Keep the line between advertising and editorial clearly drawn.** You'll lose your readers' trust if they can't tell the difference.

37. **Don't concentrate too much on promoting your online services offline.** You'll get more bang for your buck if you promote and advertise online.

38. **Keep costs low.** Don't employ more people than necessary. It's true that (for the most part) you need to spend money to make money, but you can keep your costs extremely low when e-publishing.

39. **Use a simple email program to distribute the e-publication in the beginning.** Try to find one that will suppress other subscribers' addresses (using a BCC feature). Broadcasting someone's email address to others is very bad manners.

40. **Avoid subscription fees if you can.** You can choose to charge a subscription fee, but I would strongly advise against it. The Internet's climate isn't ready for "pay" e-pubs yet. If you're going to charge for subscriptions, be sure you have a free version available, too. Remember how easy it is for an individual to pass along messages to an infinite number of others. It would be very difficult to keep control over that. If you really want to generate funds, try advertising.

41. **Start with a free Web page.** Plenty of services online host free Web pages. Or set up one with your current Internet account. Try GeoCities (http://geocities. yahoo.com) if you're looking for a service that will give you the right tools as you develop your online presence.

42. **Make sure you let your Internet Service Provider know that you're doing an email publication.** This way, if someone whines about you sending junk email, the service provider already knows.

43. **Use list services.** If your mailing list is small (5,000 subscribers or fewer), consider using a free mailing-list service. Once you get into the 10,000-subscriber range, consider going to a dedicated list service (which will most likely cost you a few pennies). You're entering the realm of "professional" at that point. Suits and ties are still optional.

44. **Treat your subscribers fairly, and don't be afraid to receive and implement feedback.** Yes, you'll get negative comments from time to time, but that's going to happen. Not everyone will be happy with your service. The subscribers aren't always right, but they do have valid points and ideas that can only help your readership grow. Give subscribers credit if they offer some content to your publication.

45. **Never share your list information (aside from total subscriber count) with anyone else.** If your subscribers start appearing on junk email lists after they sub-

scribe to your email publication, who do you think they're going to blame? Besides, there's little money to be made by selling name lists smaller than a million anymore.

46. **Give people an easy way to unsubscribe.** People's expectations might not match your email publication's content; they'll feel trapped and offended if you don't offer them an easy way out.

47. **Answer email personally and as soon as possible.** Answering every message takes time, but people enjoy knowing that you're not a computer. If you keep your replies personal, they'll feel a bond with you and be less apt to drop the subscription.

48. **Keep your subscription database clean.** When an address bounces, remove it. When a user needs to change their address, make sure it gets done. Certain list software packages work better than others with list management, so not everything needs to be done by hand.

49. **Maintain quality control.** People won't take you seriously unless you take yourself seriously first. If you want to run with the big boys, find a virtual host with a fast connection, purchase a Web domain, and hire a designer if you can't design your way out of a wet paper bag.

50. **Edit your stuff!** Go through each issue with a fine-tooth comb; check spelling, punctuation, grammar, and so on. If you're a good writer, people will love you. There's nothing better than an excellent writing style that keeps people entertained.

SUMMARY

The future of marketing is Internet marketing in one way or the other. Email marketing, Web-based marketing, or other forms of selling products using the power of the Internet will dominate all forms of selling in the future. This is largely because with the Internet it is easier to know who your customers are and how to cater to them. And, it should be noted, the speed of communications with the Internet rivals all other forms of communication. If you have a product to sell—use the Net.

22
WEBCAMS

Have you ever wanted to watch what's happening on the other side of the world? Wouldn't you like to see how much traffic there is on the highway before you leave for work in the morning? Or perhaps you'd just like to know whether the coffeepot in the next room is full without having to get up from your desk.

The idea of looking in on your pot of coffee from another room is actually not so far-fetched. In fact, there was a famous coffeepot. In 1991, some researchers in Cambridge, England had an idea. They worked on different floors of the same building and decided to save time during the day by pointing a video camera at the company coffeepot. The camera was connected to the company's internal network. The researchers would check to be sure that the coffeepot wasn't empty before leaving their desks to refill their cups.

Two years later, with the advent of the Internet, the coffeepot went from being an internal company convenience to a global destination on the World Wide Web. Although the coffeepot camera is no longer in operation, it is still known as the world's first webcam. It offered the first demonstration of Internet/webcam compatibility, which now delivers images from around the world (see Figures 22.1–22.3). The infamous coffeepot was sold (once the

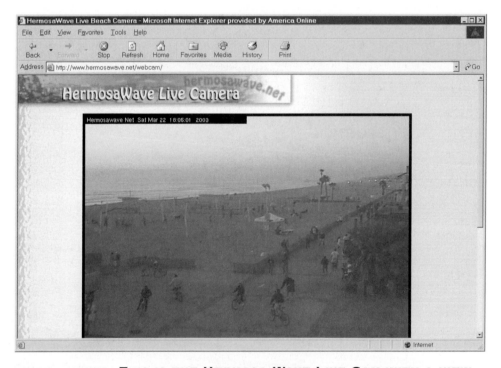

FIGURE 22.1 THIS IS THE HERMOSA WAVE LIVE CAM WITH A VIEW OF THE SOUTHERN CALIFORNIA BEACH.
WWW.HERMOSAWAVE.NET/WAVE/LIVECAM.ASP

FIGURE 22.2   NEW YORK TIMES SQUARE WEBCAM, ONE OF FIVE CHOICES OF VIEWS. WWW.EARTHCAM.COM/USA/ NEWYORK/TIMESSQUARE

FIGURE 22.3   FISH VOYEUR THE FISH SWIM. TOO BAD THE GUY DOESN'T HAVE A CAT. WWW.FISHVOYEUR.COM

webcam was turned off) for 3,350 English pounds (which is about US$5,606). Eventually, it will probably turn up on *Antiques Roadshow*.

A WEBCAM IS . . .

A webcam is a camera connected to the Internet. There are thousands upon thousands of webcam Web sites on the Web. Their content ranges from mild (a pet fish or lawn growing) to wild (porn). The uses are as wide as the imagination allows.

Technically, any camera can be a webcam. Some people have tethered a regular camera to the computer and used it as a webcam. In fact, a video camera can be used as a webcam. But there are many good choices for a camera that is designed to be a webcam on the market.

In the first days of webcams (way back in the early 1990s), a lot of the webcam Web sites were difficult to manage. Remote viewing users couldn't regularly refresh images. They were stuck looking at the same image for extended periods of time before their computer displayed a new image. This was due to slow technology and prohibitive costs.

All that has changed. The tools needed to set up a webcam and refresh images are affordable. Thousands of people are using their home PC and a webcam to stay in touch with relatives, entertain the masses, keep an eye on the house when they're away on vacation, or watch their business from home.

People can now share a moving image of themselves with others virtually anywhere in the world. It's not uncommon to find companies conducting business across the country and across the world with webcams.

In addition to the thousands of accessible personal webcams on the Internet, there are also thousands of webcams pointed at various places all across the globe. Your computer becomes a window on the world. From your desk you can sightsee New York's Times Square to California's Laguna Beach, from the Cats' Meow karaoke bar in New Orleans to Big Ben in London, and from the pubs in Dublin, Ireland to the streets of Mumbai, India. All of this may seem overwhelming at first, but don't worry, there are plenty of webcam directories to help you find the places you really want to see, as you'll see later in this chapter.

DRIVE ME INSANE

One very funny webcam site is www.drivemeinsane.com. It is a demonstration of home automation. Log on and you can control items in the home of Paul Mathis of Plano, Texas. You can turn on the lights, watch and manipulate cameras, tour his house, and drive a remote control car around. There is also chat so you can communicate with him, as well as a feature to let you listen in on his office.

According to his Web site, it all began in 1997. He decided to put his doorbell log on the Web after seeing something similar on another Web site. "I don't know why, but I just *had* to have *my* doorbell logs online for the world to see. I don't know why." Unfortunately, you can't ring it. He admits it's "perfectly useless in every way."

But this triggered something. He started to wonder what else he could put on the Internet. He came upon the idea of a lamp. The lamp would have a webcam trained on it, so not only could it be controlled by users hundreds or thousands of miles away, but they could see the lamp go on or off on their computers. One thing led to another, and now his Web site features ten controllable lights (not all are always in service) that you can flip on or off and attempt to drive him insane.

EARLY WEBCAMS

The coffeepot camera mentioned in the introduction to this chapter inspired other first-run webcams. Early webcams included the Netscape Fish Cam and the JenniCam.

Netscape claims that the Fish Cam is the second oldest live camera site on the Internet (created in 1995). The site uses two cameras to watch a fish tank. An Internet-viewable image is updated four times a minute.

JenniCam came onto the scene in 1996. Jennifer Ringley set up a webcam for her family to keep track of her at college. Jenni now has seven cameras in operation at her home. This shows the world details of her life 24 hours a day. The JenniCam site is well known across the globe. It was the inspiration for a series of voyeuristic sites that comprise a large portion of current webcam sites. Some webcam Web sites devote space to adult content. They are either for small advertisements or full-blown sites focused only on the adult entertainment industry.

WEBCAM PORTALS

Tommy's List Worldwide—www.rt66.com/~ozone/cam.htm
Webcam-Index.com—www.webcam-index.com
EarthCam—www.earthcam.com
Canon World Webcams—www.x-zone.canon.co.jp/WebView-E/sites.htm

U of Minnesota Crookston—www.crk.umn.edu/technology/webtech/cameras.htm

iCamMaster—www.icammaster.com/wlinks/wlinks.htm

Camscape—www.camscape.com

CURRENT USES

A growing trend is with state-installed traffic control webcams. Many state transportation departments now offer webcam views of mountain passes, bridges, traffic bottleneck points, busy commute streets, freeways, and so forth. This is a boon for the commuter or traveler. It's easy to decide whether a midwinter trip through a mountain pass is a good idea or not with a quick peek at the current weather conditions. It's one thing to hear that there are snow flurries, another to see that the webcam is in total whiteout. And the ability to check the traffic cams before a morning commute is valuable in locating alternate routes to avoid trouble spots.

But as mentioned, there are a great many other uses for webcams. Many cities have webcams set up in various locations. Zoos have webcams. Amusement parks, radio stations, sports arenas, and colleges have webcams. The following sidebar contains a list of webcam directories and other links.

BRIEF LISTING OF SOME WEBCAM SITES

Webcamworld.com is known as the first Internet portal devoted to web-cams. Webcamworld.com now offers users many resources for setting up webcams and for finding friends on the Internet.

Webcam.com separates out the adult content section from the other sections and allows you to type in search keywords for particular sites. There is also a list of the WebCam.com most-viewed webcam sites.

Camarades.com is a webcam community where you can find people online at all times of the day or night. The software is a little confusing in terms of the user interface, but it works. It's also hard to find people who share your interests. You may want to add your listing to the "People" section so that others can find you by browsing your section.

Webcamnow.com is a bit simpler than Camarades but is more limited. For example, if users want to see you at the highest possible speed, they have to pay WebcamNow a certain amount of money per month.

Eyeball.com's software is friendly, relatively easy to install and use, and is getting good reviews. Its directory of users and interests is good, but you have to copy and paste the person's username from the Web site into the chat. They've got categories for dating, politics, games, and more.

Camhoo.com This webcam search engine uses mostly text links to help you find your way around. The site prefaces all content with a warning that, although it is not an adult site, some searches will contain adult content, and it warns any users that they may be exposed to explicit content.

WEBCAM BASICS

You'll need a few things to set up a webcam: a computer, an Internet connection, a webcam, webcam software, and a Web server. Fortunately, webcam technology does not discriminate between PC users and Mac users—the required hardware and software are available for both operating systems. However, there are a few differences. Table 22.1 overviews the hardware, and Table 22.2 overviews the software.

Webcams

When selecting a webcam, pay attention to cost, quality, and ease of installation. You should expect to pay between $49 and $150 for a webcam, but the simplest webcams have dropped to below $100. However, as you would expect, higher-quality cameras cost more. Depending on how much use you'll get out of the camera, you should buy the highest-quality camera within your budget. The cheapest cameras will provide a poor to good quality image but won't be very versatile in image size, color, contrast, and editing features. Midpriced webcams have more features to adjust images and editing. They may still have a grainy image quality and may not allow much flexibility on how you structure your page. The higher-priced webcams have the best packages. They offer editing, adjustment, and flexibility. Another decision is between a webcam and a digital video camera. The difference is portability. A webcam is stationary. It will sit next to your computer with a six-foot cable, but a digital video camera can be taken with you to film events and the tape duped onto your computer when you return.

Snapshot or Streaming Webcam

A snapshot camera is for a series of still images on a Web page. The downside is that the image refreshes every few seconds. This means there is no continuous motion (like on television). However, the cameras use minimal resources and are usually easier to configure.

TABLE 22.1   WEBCAMS AVAILABLE

Product Name and Manufacturer	Cost	Platform	Description
AverMedia / Aver (http://www.aver.com/products/)	From $45 to $650	PC	Manufactures several video-capture devices, USB and Firewire.
Axis camera servers / Axis (http://www.axis.com/products/camera_servers/)	$1,200	PC/Mac	Network cameras that don't require a computer to work. Allow a modem to be attached.
Eggcam / Panasonic (http://www.panasonic.com/office/multimedia/multi.html)	$200	PC	Small but hi-quality webcam with video capture board connector for desktop usage only.
Ibot / Orangemicro (http://www.orangemicro.com/ibot.html)	$120	PC/Mac	First Firewire webcam of the market, nice design and functionality.
Icam / Perceptual Robotics (http://www.perceptualrobotics.com/misc/sitemap_error.shtml)	Up to $7,000	PC	Complete professional interactive webcam system (computer included) where you can pan, tilt, and zoom the webcam live.
PCA series / Phillips (http://www.quickcam.com/html/index.html)	From $55 to $180	PC	USB cams to fit all your needs. Logitech purchased the Quick-Cam series of webcams from Connectix. The first webcam ever released on the Web was a Connectix QuickCam B&W.

TABLE 22.2   AVAILABLE SOFTWARE

Software Name and Manufacturer	Cost	Display Type/ Platform	Description
Chillcam / Chillcam (http://www.chillcam.com/)	$25/ $50	Snapshot/ PC, Windows	Single/Multicamera webcam software with stunning user interface and many features that make it a good rival to other professional solutions.

EasySnap / Play Inc. (http://www.easysnap.com/)	$25	Snapshot/ PC, Windows	Software to use in conjunction with Snappy! hardware device which plugs into the parallel port.
ISpy / Surveyor Corporation (http://www.surveyor.com/ index.html)	$39.95	Snapshot/ PC, Windows	Single snapshot software. Past shots gallery, automatic Geocities support, and other interesting features.
IVista Suite/iNetCam software (http://www.inetcam.com/)	$49.95/ $99.95	Snapshot & Streaming/ PC, Windows	Single/Multicamera snapshot capable software. You can add modules (motion detection, screen capture . . .) to it too.
WebCam32/Surveyor Corporation (http://www.webcam32.com/ webcam32_software.html)	$39.95	Snapshot/ PC, Windows	This software is designed to be a one-way video product and is useful for people like Jennifer Ringley who want to share a part (or all) of their lives with the public. The Webcam32 software also comes with a simple chat application.
SiteCam / NuSpectra (http://www.nuspectra.com/ products/sitecam/index.htm)	$149/ $499	Streaming/ MacOS	Application for streaming live audio and video as well as time-lapse movies via the Internet with a Mac.
Coolcam / Evological (http://www.evological.com/ coolcam.html)	$20	Streaming/ MacOS	Fully featured webcam software for the Mac with a very WYSIWYG intuitive interface.
WebCam / NuSpectra (http://www.nuspectra.com/ sitecam/index.htm)	Free	Streaming/ PC, Windows	Free live video streaming software you can use in their online community. Professional solutions also provided.
WebcamNow/ WebcamNow.com Inc. (http://www.webcamnow.com/)	Free	Streaming/ PC, Mac	Exclusive software to broadcast live video through their on-line community.

A streaming camera allows a live video image, which, in theory, moves as it would on television. (At least, that's what streaming webcams are trying to do.) In reality, even with all the advances on the World Wide Web over the past few years, the Internet has trouble processing the large amount of data needed for a smooth, nonjerky image to be transmitted. Bandwidth is an important factor to send streaming video at a reasonable rate and quality. To stream live video consumes a system's resources at both ends of the connection.

SOME MAKERS OF WEBCAMS

Logitech—www.logitech.com

Axis Communications—www.axis.com

DLink—www.dlink.com/products/DigitalHome/DigitalVideo

VEO—www.veo.com

AIPTEK—www.aiptek.com/index2.php

Creative Labs—www.americas.creative.com/products

Winnov—www.winnov.com

TIP

Look for an image size of 640 × 480 pixels and the capability to do at least 15 frames per second (fps). Buy your camera from a reputable vendor that offers a return policy in case you run into problems.

Connection to the Computer

It is important to consider how you're going to connect the webcam to your computer to upload images onto the Internet. There are some choices.

If you're a PC user, you can use any of the following to connect your webcam to your computer:

- USB (Universal Serial Bus)
- FireWire/IEEE-1394
- Serial port
- Parallel port
- PCI card

A standard choice would be a USB connection. It is the best choice for most users because of its ease of use, cost, and availability. (Most of the newer webcam models use it.) Older webcams tend to use the serial and parallel ports. (These are rapidly becoming an obsolete option.) FireWire and PCI cards are popular with advanced webcam users. (These two connection methods heavily depend on which version of Windows is used. They also can have software conflicts that can be baffling.)

A Mac user has the following choices to connect a webcam:

- USB
- FireWire
- Video capture card

The easiest connection method of the three is USB. FireWire offers a high-quality video capture, but most webcam software cannot utilize the Mac's FireWire interface. This has changed with the release of iChat AV in Mac OS 10.3, especially when used in conjunction with the iSight FireWire camera (also available from Apple).

If your computer has a USB port, there is no need for a video capture card.

For the most part, video capture cards are for high-end applications, such as if you want to put streaming video or audio on the Web. (High-end streaming video and audio demand more bandwidth than the typical webcam offers.)

Other Connections and Cables

Cameras that don't use the USB connection have other connectors, such as composite cables, S-video connections, or FireWire connections.

Composite Video Cables

Composite video cables are the standard cables used for hooking a VHS player to a television. They're the simplest to use. If your camera comes with a composite cable, your video capture card will need to accept that cable type. The connector is a single male prong.

S-Video

S-video (supervideo) is a faster video and sound transfer. It provides a better quality of video and sound than does a composite. If your camera has S-video, you'll need a video card that has an S-video connection. Makers include Osprey Video Cards, Videum Cards, and Ads Tech.

FireWire

FireWire is a brand name of Apple Computer. It's generically known as IEEE 1394. The connectors are a compact rectangular/open box design. FireWire is the fastest choice to transfer video and sound from camera to computer. It is commonly used in professional video editing and DVD manufacturing. If you plan to make your digital videos or camcorder tapes into DVD, this would be the best choice. However, you would need a FireWire video capture card.

Software

Most cameras come with software but some of the software may be limited in functionality. But most likely, you also will need to purchase webcam software. Be sure the software you purchase meets all of the hardware requirements (operating system, memory, and so forth). Software varies in capability; for instance, some do not handle streaming video. So make a checklist of desirable features and requirements before shopping. PC users have a greater variety of software from which to choose. Macintosh users are offered a more limited number of selections.

Snapshot software is the cheapest and easiest way to add webcam images to your Web page. A dialup Internet connection will work to upload snapshot image files every few seconds. The streaming software is bandwidth-heavy and a resource pig. You'll still need extra hardware to manage the extra load, even if you're broadcasting only video or only audio. For a home user, you are probably better off with snapshots.

When it's all installed, the interchange is simple. The webcam software connects to the camera and periodically grabs a frame from it. The software turns the image into a normal JPEG file and uploads it to your Web server. The image can be placed on any Web page.

WEBCAM SOFTWARE INCLUDES:

Coffee Cup Cam—www.coffeecup.com/webcam
WebCam Ispy & Webcam32—www.webcam32.com
Beau Software WebCam Watcher—www.webcam-watcher.com
First Virtual Communications—www.fvc.com/eng/webconferencing/index.htm
iVisit—www.ivisit.info

The faster an Internet connection, the better a webcam viewing experience will be. This is particularly true with a streaming video webcam. The larger the webcam images are, the harder the viewer's Internet connections have to work to see them.

Consider carefully the image size. It doesn't matter whether you're using a streaming or snapshot webcam: Larger images will not refresh as frequently as smaller ones. For example, an image that is 640 pixels wide by 480 pixels high (640×480) might be a beautiful picture, but it will take a significant amount of time for someone with a slow Internet connection to view it. In fact, many would get frustrated at the wait and just go somewhere else on the Web. Internet surfers can be impatient. A reasonable user-accessible image size would be 320×240, particularly if you plan to refresh the image every 20–30 seconds.

The refresh rate is another important element when working with images. To refresh images more often, lower the image size to about 160×120. This will allow the image to refresh every 10 seconds. With video streams, try to keep the image to 160×120 so those with slow connections have the opportunity to see something.

Web Server

A Web server is what serves Web pages to a browser. When you type in a Web address (or URL) in your Web browser, it then uses a Web server to present the appropriate page and associated images. To upload images to a remote Web server, the most common method is with FTP (see Chapter 4). It is the most straightforward way to present webcam images. The disadvantage with FTP is that anyone viewing your image has to refresh the image manually by clicking the Refresh button on the Web browser. It is possible, however, to write scripts that automatically refresh the page for the viewers. We'll take a closer look at some of these scripts later in the chapter.

A **webcam server** is a specialized type of server. Unless you are terribly into hosting your own server, this isn't practical for most people. For more information on how to set up a webcam server and what hardware/software is needed, the following sites may be of help:

WebcamStat Server Software—www.surveyor.com/products/webcamstatserver.html

WebTermX with Secure Shell Security—www.powerlan-usa.com/webtermx.html

Windows Media Encoder—www.microsoft.com/windows/windowsmedia/wm7/encoder.aspx

WEBCAM VIDEO CHAT

Online video chatrooms are similar to text chatrooms, as described in Chapter 7. People collect in a virtual "room" to exchange small talk and debate about hobbies, and current events or, more often, look for love. Now there are places to meet for people with webcams. Yahoo!, for one, has separate rooms for this kind of connection. You also might find groups of people communicating over webcams in regular chatrooms.

It's technically called a *multiparty video* or *multiperson video*. Sites vary in the features offered. Some have multiparty video only, and others offer video, voice, text chat, and messaging, along with multiple simultaneous connections, call screening, and private meeting rooms. Security features may include things such as SSL encryption, password protection, unique user names, and scrambled images (to block users from viewing you).

SOME VIDEO CHAT WEB SITES

Yahoo Messenger—messenger.yahoo.com/messenger/webcams.html

PalTalk—www.paltalk.com

WebCamNow—www.webcamnow.com

iVisit—www.iVisit.com

ISPQ Videochat—www.ispq.com

SAFETY FIRST

The best advice is to be careful and don't be too quick to trust people. Be aware that not everyone is who or what they say they are. There are men posing as women and women posing as men. Also, many Web chat programs provide you with only a modest level of privacy. The city you live in can sometimes be traced through your computer's IP address. It is important to give out as little information as possible about yourself in order to protect yourself. (After all, you are talking with strangers.) There are software products you can purchase that can help to keep your identity under wraps.

ADULT ENTERTAINMENT INDUSTRY AND WEBCAMS

A review of the current state of webcams on the Internet would not be complete without spending some time discussing the adult entertainment industry's webcam use. During a standard Web search for webcams, you will be greeted on the results page by a warning that your "search has generated some sexually explicit results." While browsing the Web (and especially while perusing webcam directories and webcam-related Web sites), you're likely to see Internet Friends Network pop-ups advertising "personal intimate webcams." You can choose to "see or be seen" at many of these sites, and you can choose to see others from a wide variety of categories. Much of the spam you find in your email points you to sites where you can pay to watch men and women performing a variety of acts in front of their webcams.

You'll note that most of these sites require users to register and log in before displaying adult entertainment content. During the registration process, you'll be required to confirm that you're over the age of 18. Many times, you'll also be prompted for a credit card number. As mentioned above, if you choose to visit some of these sites, please exercise caution. Refer to the safety tips above before you give out personal information.

YOUR ONLINE WEBCAM

Okay, so you've bought your webcam, you've got all your hardware and software in place, and you know how you're going to send your images to the Web server. Now it's time to decide what you're going to do with your webcam. The best part about making this decision is that the options are limitless. You can point the camera out your window and add images to your own Web page, run your own video chatroom, use the camera to watch your room while you're away on vacation, or come up with something entirely different!

Once you've decided how you want to use the camera, you should also put some thought into how you want to present your images on the Internet. You might already have your own Web site where you'd like to display some webcam images or this may be your first opportunity to try your hand at HTML (Hypertext Markup Language). In either case, you should experiment with the type of page you'd like to use. If you're new to coding Web pages, you might try a standard HTML page featuring your webcam image as the main attraction. Or if you're more experienced, you should try to incorporate some additional features to make the page more usable and user-friendly.

Particularly if you're using a snapshot webcam and you don't want readers to have to push the Refresh button on their browsers to see the latest image, you have some options to get this done. To refresh the images automatically so that people don't have to reload your page, you should consider one of the following methods:

1. Add a *metatag* to the HTML of your Web page so that the server knows to refresh the page with a certain frequency. For example, you can add the following line of text to the HTML:

    <meta http-equiv="refresh" content="10">

    The number 10 represents the number of seconds between refreshes. This command reloads the entire page every 10 seconds, so you should try to keep the page short. Also, keep in mind that the larger the image is, the less frequently you should refresh it to make sure that users with slower Internet connections have the opportunity to view your images.

2. Add a *Java applet* (such as the one that comes bundled with the latest Webcam32 software package) to your site. An applet is a program that automatically grabs the image periodically. The main advantage here is that only the image refreshes, and the rest of the page does not.

3. Finally, you can use *JavaScript*, which will automatically refresh the page after a certain amount of time that you can specify in the code of your Web page.

Webcam Surveillance

Webcams are used to keep an eye on places and things that you want to protect. People are leaving their webcam live when they go on vacation so that they can periodically check their Web pages to make sure everything is okay at home or at work. The software is called both *surveillance* and *spy* software.

Video surveillance is in use in parking lots, stores, and playgrounds around the country. It's a good way to monitor and record suspicious events. By using a webcam as an inexpensive closed-circuit monitor, you can record video footage shot in your absence and route it to your computer. People have set them up to watch how the nanny treats the children and to see which pet dog is the one doing the damage while left alone. It's helpful to keep a watch on the side of a building frequented by vandals, to see who's visiting your elderly mother's house, or to keep track of what the kids are doing in the backyard (while you are busy working in your office). It could also be used to spy on a neighbor or capture somebody's keystrokes to gain access to their private password. In short, there are upsides and downsides to the technology.

There are a number of packages that offer just the software for surveillance. There are shareware and retail versions of software. There are also some software/hardware packages. Features include motion detection, scheduled recording and viewing, time stamps, saving files to compressed video clips, email alerts, broadcasting video images, or connecting to the Internet or a telephone line to let you watch from anywhere in the world. Some can let you access live remotes through your handheld PDA.

SURVEILLANCE SOFTWARE

 Surveyor Corporation—www.ispy.nl
Imagespro.com—www.imagespro.com
DigiWatcher—www.digi-watcher.com
Top Secret Software—www.topsecretsoftware.com
Sarbash Software—www.sarbash.com
Xcapturix Software—www.caturix.com/english/index.asp

SUMMARY

Webcams are great. They are the Dick Tracy and Jetsons future we've all been waiting for. You can sit down and talk—on your computer—face to face with friends and relatives. You can see your new grandbaby and visit with relatives on holidays. You can see the next blind date—which will take the terror out of that first meeting. It's easy to see the business applications, such as video conferencing and video mail. Right now there are many webcams monitoring the roads and passes. There is no reason that every restaurant, for example, can't have a webcam to show the activity and atmosphere of a restaurant or a bar so you can see if you want to go out before you go. ("How long is the line, honey?") Bus terminals, airports, parking lots, shopping malls, and other public facilities should all eventually be monitored by webcams.

With a video surveillance webcam, you can watch your house while on vacation or see what the neighbors are up to. You might even be able to record the license plate of the graffiti artist who scribbled all over your business. Red light runners can get tickets for the infraction, even if no one was around. Shopping center parking lots can watch for car thieves and maybe even do something to thwart it.

Web cameras are popping up everywhere. Someday everyone will probably have some sort of tethered cam on their computer, whether it's a traditional webcam or a high-priced digital still camera that can double as a webcam by using its USB port.

There is security in knowing that there will always be a watchful eye looking over our property and loved ones. The security and comfort of knowing that an area is under surveillance outweighs the fear of "Big Brother" for many.

However, a big issue in the coming years will be to enact rules and laws regarding the proper use and improper use of webcams. Privacy issues and modesty are going to become hot topics (do we really want the in-laws to see our dirty office and the beer cans on the desk?). It's unavoidable: In the near future, webcam issues will include regulations, restrictions, and laws regarding reasonable use.

But for now it's a novelty, and a fun one, at that.

23
CONTENT
MANAGEMENT

Content management is a general term. It is applied to many different practices and products in the computer industry. Content management was an issue for companies even before the Web. Questions arose about what to do with all the information printed on paper. The debate raged over filing schemes, microfiche, scanning technologies, storage, archiving, access, and the unfulfilled dream of the *paperless office.*

MANAGEMENT AREAS

The most important thing about content management is that it allows users or Web site owners to manage material (graphics, text, databases) in an automated fashion. The idea is that when you have a lot of data on a large Web site, you do not want to reorganize everything by hand each time a change is made. Content management software does it automatically.

The nebulous world of content management is comprised of many areas. Among them are: document management, digital asset management, knowledge management, and workflow management.

Document Management

Document management is best described as the process of creating, editing, reviewing, printing, and archiving documents (usually printed). It is about the control of the entire document life cycle. Document management systems often automate the tasks associated with digitizing printed documents, optical character recognition (OCR), indexing, and cataloging.

Digital Asset Management

This is an emerging field. It focuses on the arduous task of keeping track of the multitudes of pictures, graphics, documents, videos, audio files, and other content stored digitally. It has evolved from document management but distinguishes itself by focusing on the unique aspect of digital assets. Digital assets represent greater management challenges because of multiple formats and channels for both import and export. Another problem is in the management of the copyright and authorization issues associated with some corporate assets.

Knowledge and Experience Management

These are the two most valuable assets a company has. More often than not, a company's specific knowledge and experience are hidden and not readily accessible to anyone in the company who may need them. Companies usually focus on managing tangible assets, not the intangible collective expertise of the company. Knowledge is contained in a large variety of places, including databases, printed documents, filing cabinets, individual computers, and people's minds. It is often unorganized and unmanaged. Often, work is repeated, as are mistakes. Knowledge management systems attempt to seek out all these knowledge assets to record, catalog, and manage them.

Workflow Management

Here the focus is on the control and execution of business processes in an organization. This is how specific decisions are made in a company. Approval chains are automated and managed, as is the collateral associated with each process or decision.

In all, content management encompasses a wide range of topics that include content as well as process. The common element among content management solutions is the aim of simplifying management of content and the associated processes.

WHAT IS WEB CONTENT MANAGEMENT?

With the emergence of the Web and its millions of Web sites, managing the content contained on Web sites has become increasingly important. There is nothing worse than stale content on a Web site. Visitors don't want to see the Christmas graphics in July.

So how do companies keep their content under control? How do they change things in a timely and efficient manner? How do they allow actual content authors to update the content they create themselves? Three words: Web content management!

Web content management focuses on the specific tasks involved in managing the elements and objects that comprise a Web site. There may exist areas of overlap between Web content management and other areas of content management. For example, a company's document management system may be used for its user manuals that are also available on the Web site as PDF files. However, the primary goal of Web content management systems is to create a controlled environment that allows all groups involved in the creation, maintenance, and updating of a Web site to work together easily without significant overhead, duplicated work, or unnecessary delays.

CONTENT

After computers became commonplace but before the Web, content was managed within small groups. Products such as Lotus Notes and document management applications (dubbed *groupware*) were designed for teams of fewer than 20 people. These were used to fill in forms and create standalone documents, such as technical publications or applications for drug approvals, for example. Content was usually structured and homogeneous. Changes were infrequent. Business processes and the preparation of their associated documentation had defined life cycle.

The Internet explosion of the mid-1990s changed the way businesses store and access their information. These *digital assets* need to be referenced and connected to each other. The power of the Web is its ability to link knowledge and information in a variety of forms: text, images, graphics, and statistics. The Web allowed the information to be accessed (it could be "looked up"). For example, an HTML Web page could reference a Word document. The Word document could call up a PDF file, and all three elements could be combined by a Java JSP for dynamic content rendition addresses of content resources that could be "linked to" over the Web. URLs, or hyperlinking, completely transformed the way the world shares collective knowledge stores.

AN IMPERFECT ALLIANCE

This linking process wasn't seamless. It wasn't ideal. Marrying all kinds of content from HTML, Word files, PDFs, images, audio, and video all the way to executable code, the most complex form of content, was a potentially frustrating exercise. The sudden rush to combine sexy new content types into compelling Web sites slammed into cold reality. HTML pages didn't necessarily cooperate with PDF files.

There was room for improvement. Users had no concept of what was wrong. It was impossible to know what or where changes were needed. Tracking didn't exist. Content authors modified production Web servers directly or via FTP uploads. People were making changes with little concept of what they were doing. Accountability was questionable. It was a mess.

THE ORIGINS OF CONTENT MANAGEMENT

The need to organize the mess became apparent. In response, a new category of product was born—*content management*. A proliferation of start-up companies (nearly 200 at one point) claimed the territory. Few accomplished their mission.

Most of the solutions were limited in scope. They focused on one small aspect of the problem. They aimed low instead of addressing the bigger challenge—to create content in parallel.

This could be compared to the transition from horse and buggy to automobile. At the outset, manufacturers couldn't build enough automobiles quickly enough. Each car required the assembly of hundreds of parts. One person would craft the car, doing all the various assembly tasks from the beginning to the end. This production speed could not satisfy the demands of the customers. It was hampered by the problem of finding enough skilled workers to oversee and assemble the vehicle.

The solution, by Henry Ford, was to create a system to give each worker a specific task. An assembly line was created. Each person on the line became a specialist. Each specialist added a different part, in sequence. In this way, Ford could use lower-skilled workers to consistently create a quality product. A fleet of cars rapidly and efficiently rolled off the assembly line. Eventually, to further increase production, tasks were further specialized. There were tasks that needed human intervention and tasks that were automated.

This is the model for content management: a process to allow hundreds or even thousands of people to work together in the creation of content.

Although not exactly an assembly line, the best content management system (CMS) does automate many of the tasks associated with Web production and separates out the parts that need human intervention.

Separation of Content and Design

An essential part of content management is the separation of Web content from site design. Site design is the placement of elements (graphics, styles, fonts, colors, etc.) that affect how the page looks. The content is the text, pictures, links, and other items. An area of specialization has become *Web design.*

Web designers and developers work to make a Web site have a certain look. This look is created through layout, graphics, and fonts. The content has a secondary role in the look and feel of the site. This is especially true when most of the content is text. The separation of content from design keeps the appearance consistent across all pages, or versions, of the site. Updates don't cause the site to change how it looks or behaves.

Some CMSs separate the content from the design with templates to define consistent elements. For example, a template might define a common header and footer for all pages. When the page is published, content is inserted within the templates. Other CMSs use special tags to indicate the elements or areas of a page that are editable content. It can allow authorized content editors and authors to access specific areas but prevents changes in other areas.

In the creation of a Web site, the separation of content and design is the first step to allow content to change while keeping the look and feel consistent. The contents are handled independently of the site design.

File-Based Systems vs. Database Systems

CMSs fall into two distinct categories: *file-based systems* and *database systems*.

File-Based Systems

These directly manipulate the HTML files of the Web site. Content is designated with HTML tags. The pages can be broken up into different regions, with accessibility granted by a system access rights scheme. Because the content is specific to a page, it cannot be reused between pages (unless the designer explicitly designs the site to use small HTML files and includes them in multiple pages). (Web site content can be database-driven; however, with this scenario, the management tool itself is not.) To search for content, the system must look through all the Web site files. File-based systems have the advantage of rapid implementation. You don't need to extract existing content and rebuild your Web site from database-driven templates. It's also less complicated to manage, so it makes a good choice for small- to medium-size businesses with limited technical resources.

Database Systems

Database systems store chunks of Web content in a database. They use templates to reassemble the content into Web pages. Content is usually entered into the database with forms. This results in structured content that can be reused on different pages. The result is the system can take advantage of the features of a database for organizing, searching, and retrieving data. Database systems require more work in implementation to construct the page templates and content entry forms. Because the content is contained in the database and not in files, you must generate your Web site prior to publishing it.

STAGING AND PRODUCTION

A concept common to both Web development and content management is the practice of using a staging server and a production server (sometimes referred to as the *live server*). Directly editing a live Web site is a risky proposition. If mistakes are made, those accessing the site instantaneously see them. A better practice is to have a Web site "scratch pad" where changes are tested out before going live.

The staging server is a Web server (just like the live Web server) except that it is not accessible to the outside world. Many Web developers will make changes and test their Web sites on the staging server. Once the changes are ready for deployment, they are copied to the live server.

A Web CMS operates on the staging server. Features such as file locking, version control, workflow, and editing take place in a controlled environment. An administrator can publish the site once it is ready. In a file-based system, this involves the movement of the current files to the live server. In a database-driven system, the Web site is generated from the content stored in the database.

Staging servers are a useful tool to ensure that your live Web site is error free and reflects the content and changes desired.

No Reservations about Templates

With approximately 2,400 hotels scattered around the globe and "marquee properties" in most major cities, the Hilton Hotels brand is one of the best known worldwide. Following the acquisition of several new brands, the e-business team at Hilton Hotels wished to roll the new hotels' individual sites into the main Hilton platform. At the same time, the group felt the time was ripe for an upgrade to its overall IT infrastructure.

Previously, the chain had employed content entry "wizards," which allowed business owners to modify content as needed. But because these users updated content directly into production, there was no defined type of QA (quality assurance) or review process involved. And once content went onto the live site, if there were problems, it was difficult and time-consuming to identify their origin.

The Hilton IT team implemented a CMS that enabled the use of templates for content creation. These templates have made it simple for Hilton Hotels' subject-matter experts to create, review, and approve compelling online content, no matter what their technical skill level. Because the responsibility for content updates has been brought in house, Hilton is enjoying a significantly faster time-to-Web and a substantial return on its technology investment. The chain projected a $2 million reduction in its online publishing costs for 2002.

PARTS OF A CMS

What goes into a CMS? There are several things that a good system will include.

Work Areas

Also referred to as a *sandbox*, the work area looks and feels like a production Web site but is actually a virtual copy to let contributors add, remove, and modify assets. The use of multiple work areas encourages contributors to work on projects in parallel. This is a tremendous boost to productivity and shortens production schedules.

Staging Areas

Think of this as a "conference room" in which users can show and talk about what they've done in their individual work areas. The staging area contains a virtual view of the online property but also accepts changes to existing assets, captures a copy of any new assets, and keeps a record of who did what and when.

Editions

When the team has finished its production efforts, the new content can be published as an edition (like an edition of a magazine). These are read-only snapshots of the entire site, taken at various points in its development. Project managers can create hundreds of editions to see whether the work is production-ready or to see how an update might look on the live site. Editions are invaluable from an accountability perspective. An exact view of the site at any point in time from hours back to years back can be archived.

Virtualization

This gives contributors a virtual "view" of a site. Virtualization lets a user preview and test changes (code or content) to the live site without affecting other work. Contributors can test their work, knowing that their experimentation won't bring down the entire site.

Workflows

Coordinating the efforts of all contributors requires a defined system of checks and balances. Ideally, all contributors are assigned a title and a responsibility (such as author, editor, and so forth), with tasks spelled out to ensure content development and appropriate approval from an overseeing individual or group. Sequential workflow (the traditional model), parallel workflow, and distributed workflow are necessary for comprehensive workflow management.

Branching

Branches allow different development paths. They can be related to each other or completely different. Each will contain all the content for the site. A single branch contains all archived copies of the site (as editions), the staging area for content integration, and the individual work area. It can also contain subbranches, so teams can have alternate paths of development separate from each other. Branches facilitate distributed workflow because they allow separate teams to work independently on different projects.

Deployment

Deployment is performed when content has been developed, tested, approved, and is ready to be scheduled for release. The ideal deployment system will safely transport any changes to the content (as opposed to the entire content base), whether it originates in a database, a file-system, or as code from the development environment to the production server, with encryption features for secure distribution over the Internet.

CONTENT DEPLOYMENT: THE ULTIMATE CYA

In the financial world, timing *is* everything. More specifically, publishing one's financial information at the correct time can mean the difference between driving a luxury car to the country club and taking the bus to the unemployment office.

Case in point: A CIO was scheduled to post his Fortune 100 company's quarterly earnings release on the corporate site at 1 P.M. EST. Being a conscientious sort, the exec carefully prepared the summary several hours ahead of time, then archived the data in a temporary, "hidden" directory. Unbeknown to Mr. CIO, a search engine referenced and found his financials in the early morning hours . . . and *ka-boom*! The earnings went round the world, wreaking havoc inside the company and out. Needless to say, the exec in question immediately found himself jobless.

Of course, this faux pas was an unintentional, unfortunate mistake. But it was one that had dramatic repercussions. Without being able to schedule the exact time the earnings release should have been posted and lacking a "safe" haven for the file, the former CIO did what he thought was prudent. In hindsight, he's probably now aware that the proper content management and deployment system could easily have saved him (and his company) from such unnecessary grief.

CMS FEATURES

The large number of vendors in the content management space results in a dizzying array of features. A summary of common content management features includes the following:

- **User Management**—Some systems assign roles to specify the set of permissions and features a user can access by creating classes and groups of users.

- **Templates**—These are used in different ways. Page templates allow users a choice when creating new pages. Templates may define content objects in a system. Template editors specify content objects in a system or allow users to create and edit the templates to suit their purposes.

- **WYSIWYG Editor**—This allows a user to edit the content (or Web pages) with an editor that shows exactly what the final Web page will look like. It uses an old printing term, *WYSIWYG* (What You See Is What You Get). This is helpful when the design and formatting of a page is a critical element.

- **Version Control**—This feature keeps previous versions of a page to enable users to revert back to them if necessary. Systems may also highlight changes between file versions. Most systems will also ensure that only one user at a time can access a file.

- **Workflow**—This defines the way content is approved and published in a system. Systems that support complex workflow will have a workflow editor responsible for defining or changing the flow as necessary.

- **Scheduling**—This allows users to schedule when content will be published. Some systems allow scheduled content to expire and revert back to original content.

- **Reporting/Audits**—This tracks information on users, content, publishing, and a variety of other system activities.

- **Statistics**—Page hits, browsers used, and operating systems will be reported in a Web site activity log. These are accessible through the CMS.

- **Site Management**—These are the basic functions to maintain a Web site (cut, copy, delete, rename, upload, download, search, and replace content).

WORKFLOW

Content management is a tool to aid Web development. But even with the best tool, it's not a guarantee of content quality. That's where workflow comes in.

The workflow dictates how a new content should move down the "assembly line," finally arriving at the point prior to the final submission (usually the point where there is integrated testing and linking of images to text).

In companies with a simple *culture* (meaning the basic company structure is not complicated), the workflow will also be simple. One person creates content, another approves it, and out it goes. A large corporation, on the other hand, could labor through anywhere from 19 to 25 workflow steps before any kind of new product launch information could post to its corporate site.

These reviews and approvals must move through management systems built in vastly different eras, some stretching back to the 1950s. So even if a team member created a data sheet on the biggest, beefiest laptop available today, that content must still travel "back in time." It will start from the 1950s system, slowly make its way through the 25 approval steps, and get converted back and forth into different data types before it's finally published.

Clearly, structural collaboration is important. Workflow is important. But organizational efficiency and good practices are more important for a successful content management implementation.

EVALUATE THE COMPANY STYLE

It's crucial to understand the organizational culture of a company to ensure efficient content management.

- How do the teams actually work?
- Does the business employ internal or *outsourced* IT professionals?
- Does the company bring in third-party SI consultants?

Many naive companies say, "Just map our existing process." This may not be a viable option if the in-place system doesn't work well. Instead, organizations should take advantage of the implementation processes of content management. It's a good time to consider how to make the company, as a whole, more efficient.

Granted, the definition of the *system* is often highly contentious.

AVOID PROBLEMS

A CMS should support an *open*, standards-based architecture so that multiple data types work together. Ongoing development ideally should support dynamic HTML, XML, Java, .NET, and Web services, as well as other emerging technologies. A sound system should handle various content types to ensure compatibility with future technologies and protocols. (When a system supports only a specific content type, it is probable that at a later date, the retrofit of all existing content will be necessary.)

An open system goes beyond asset types and tools. There is also the issue of *legacy content repositories* (a fancy term for "old crap"). You never know when an old Web page, dusty data, or other archaic company information may be of value. With a flexible system in place, content discovery and reuse becomes possible at a global level, and the costs associated with the search for or duplication of content drops. Few content management solutions have this capability currently, although it can be a valuable tool.

MS Project
Visio
GIF, JPEG, MPEG1, MPEG2, MPEG3
ShockWave, Flash, MIDI, AVI, WinZip
tar file, RDB data
JavaScript, CGI, Java, JSP, ASP, JavaBeans
EJB, VB, VBScript, Visual Basic .NET
C, C++, C#, Perl, TCL, COBOL
ColdFusion
Games
CORBA
COM, DCOM, CRM applications
e-commerce applications, supply chain applications
home-grown applications, security applications, portlets, gears, channels
XML, DTD, SOAP, WSDL, Web services.

HOW TO CHOOSE A WEB CMS

The choice of a Web CMS can be a difficult process with so many products and features to consider.

Establish Goals

First, establish your needs. Specify practical goals. List the problems that have prompted a look at CMSs. Then list the problems that you hope a system will solve. If you have quantitative goals, specify them as well. For example, your goal may be the effective use of your technical personnel who are better trained to code than to edit copy for the marketing department.

Establish the Budget

How much money do you have to spend? The budget should cover the software licenses and implementation costs (typically the most expensive part). You may need to purchase other software, such as a database separate staging system or more hardware.

Review and Prioritize Features

A cursory review of products will introduce you to the available features. Select those that are important to your organization and prioritize them. This will help narrow the list of possible products. Products without a valued feature can be eliminated.

Evaluate Products

Compare the products with your budget and feature criteria. This should narrow the field even more. Ask the important question: Which product do I think my team would actually want to use?

Pay particular attention to client references and to case studies. Information from customers is important to determine whether a product is right for you. If a referenced company has characteristics similar to yours, ask to contact it directly. This will give you firsthand information about the product in actual use (that is, a review that is not buffed, polished, and spun by a sales and marketing team).

Request Personalized Demonstrations

It is important to understand how a product will work for you. A review of features lists and online demonstrations might help, but nothing beats a personalized demonstration. This makes the vendor learn about you and your company. You'll get a better feel for the company. Ask whether they can take some of your files to show you how the product would work. Their answer may be as revealing as the demo itself.

Evaluate the Vendors

Nothing is worse than going through the exercise of picking a product, only to learn that the vendor is going out of business. Market contraction and consolidation is a reality of the post-Internet-bubble world and of the content management market, as well. With so many vendors, some will undoubtedly not succeed. Consider whether the company has other sources of revenue. Look at its track record with other products and plans for the future for its content management offering. It is important to consider a company's history and future before investing in a product you hope to use for years to come.

Consider the Implementation

Implementation costs exceed software license costs. This will vary between products and in execution (in house, a consultant, or a combination of the two). An accurate estimate of the time, effort, and cost to implement the system is a variable in your buying decision.

When organizations began to realize they had repositories of corporate knowledge and information online, they started to realize that they had a problem: how to find any single piece of data. It was difficult, if not impossible. With this awareness came the concept of incorporating *content intelligence* into CMSs. In other words, "Let's make our content *smart*." The problem was not unlike the one that challenged libraries in the mid-1800s.

The answer then was the Dewey Decimal Classification (DDC) system. This system allowed a librarian to manage the books and readers to find what they were looking for. Each new book could be sorted by content—a locating criteria process—by the librarian. The DDC system was a boon to libraries. It made sense of the information explosion then. It's a solid system that still works. The Web needed something like it.

THE DEWEY DECIMAL CLASSIFICATION

Melvil Dewey was born Melville Louis Kossuth Dewey in 1851. He shortened his name to Melvil, dropped his middle names, and for a short time even spelled his last name as Dui.

In 1873, he devised the DDC system (as a 21-year-old student assistant in the library at Amherst College). It was first published in 1876. He had a long, illustrious career as a librarian. He is credited with helping to establish the ALA (American Library Association) and co-founded and edited the *Library Journal*. He promoted library standards and formed a company to sell library supplies, which eventually became the Library Bureau. He was a pioneer in library education.

His life wasn't all achievements. He was also a proponent of spelling reform. He founded the Spelling Reform Association. An example: "*Speling Skolars agree that we hav the most unsyentifik, unskolarli, illojikal & wastful speling ani languaj ever ataind.*" This concept was never embraced with any excitement in his lifetime or thereafter.

The DDC system has been largely replaced in large university and city libraries with the Library of Congress System. The DDC is still in use in schools and smaller libraries around the world. It is regularly updated and modernized. The system is built on the simple concept of being organized by general categories, such as:

000 Generalities

100 Philosophy & Psychology

---

200 Religion

300 Social Sciences

400 Language

500 Natural Sciences & Mathematics

600 Technology (Applied Sciences)

700 The Arts

800 Literature & Rhetoric

900 Geography & History

Then each main class is broken into 10 divisions, and each division into 10 sections (not all the numbers and sections have been used).

For more information, go to www.oclc.org/dewey.

The Web's classification system was to use a specific HTML tag to label the Web page. This was called a *metatag*. Metatags have many uses but, for the most part, site promoters focused on the keyword tag and description tags. For example, a porn site would have the description tag of PORN, and the keywords would be every dirty word ever used in the English language, plus some.

CHEATERS NEVER WIN

In the beginning, Web crawlers (aka spiders) and search engines would use meta information to help index a particular Web page. Over time, these tags were abused and often led to inaccurate listings and search results. As Google.com supplanted every other information portal on the planet, the reliance on these metatags decreased accordingly. Google uses a different system to rank the links in its database, relying more on direct user interaction and less on Webmaster savvy. Will you get more traffic if you submit your site to every search engine online? It's likely, but Google is the only one that counts right now. So metatags aren't what they used to be.

Some search engines would then look to the description tag as the first choice for a search engine listing, with alternate methods used if the tag was corrupted or missing. Some engines searched only the keyword tags. This method of Web searching has questionable effectiveness now, after many Web sites abused it. In fact, some of the misuse of tags included putting every possible keyword into the tag to increase the number of hits the Web site would receive. (This was back in the days of Web page banners paying big bucks based on hits.)

For content management, metatags are still used to track the Web page and locate it easily. Ideally, each piece of content will have good *metadata* assigned to it, a process that can be enforced for the content author through workflow. Thus, instead of the "librarian" standing by, the CMS will read an article that's just been written and will try to match it against metadata in a predefined *taxonomy* of products, markets, and geographies. Then through those individual terms, the CMS will classify the content.

TAXONOMY

A taxonomy is a structured dictionary or vocabulary created to exchange information in a logical, understandable manner. It is a way to organize relationships between items. It was originally used to refer to biological classification. Aristotle (384–332 B.C.) made the first recorded attempt to classify all the organisms around him. The next major attempt was by botanist Carolus von Linnaeus (1707–1778). Linnaeus classified organisms from broad to narrow groupings: kingdom, class, order, genus, and species, based on *significant figurative traits*. Taxonomy has become an important subfield of biology. The emphasis is on the classification of organisms based on their similarities and differences.

The concept of taxonomy in relation to Web pages is an attempt to sort them according to their presumed natural relationships. It's an ongoing process. Some of the major XML taxonomies are: MARC, LCSH, and MeSH. For a long list of the controlled vocabularies, thesauri, and classification systems available for the Web, go to www.lub.lu.se/metadata/subject-help.html.

Assigning content intelligence during the development process delivers two important benefits. The first: accurate, subject-based metadata. The metadata is created by the person who knows the content best—the author. The second is an enforcement of standards. It is unlikely that anyone would arbitrarily create metadata. It would not comply with the existing taxonomy. (The metadata should adhere to the corporate taxonomy.)

The *real* value of content intelligence is searchable and reusable content.

THREE WAYS TO BUILD TAXONOMIES

Use Someone Else's

This is a tried-and-true method used by corporations everywhere. There are thousands of industry taxonomies. An example is SNOMED. This medically related taxonomy contains over 250,000 (and counting) terminologies, including every single medical term, disease, and drug known to mankind. Plug SNOMED into your CMS when creating content for a health care portal, and you can be sure of the quick access to and integrity of all of your data.

> **Build One**
>
> The ideal content management solution will actually provide a user interface that will enable you to create your own taxonomy. It should be multidimensional, so you can construct different concepts, structures, and paths to get to the same base node or terminology. Keep in mind that two identical phrases can mean two very different things under different contexts. For example, "common cold" can be traced through *internal medicine*, *men's health*, *fitness and health*, *drugs*, and other categories. However, "apple" when searched under *fruit* and *computer* shows nothing in common!
>
> **Use Sample Documents**
>
> Your content management solution should be able to generate taxonomies automatically, based on existing collections of content. In this instance, you could "train" the CMS with a collection of corporate documents. The taxonomy generated with a training document set could be further refined.

CMS PRODUCT OVERVIEW

The content management industry has hundreds of vendors, from enterprise systems to small business solutions. The products being offered run the gamut in price and functionality. There are both highly specialized and mass appeal solutions available. To give you an overview of the market, six products are profiled below.

Enterprise Systems

Interwoven (www.interwoven.com/ecm/) is a company with a variety of content management products. From portals, external and internal Web sites to CRM, e-commerce, and knowledge management initiatives. Interwoven offers a full suite of content and business applications and integrates with a multitude of popular e-commerce applications.

Vignette (www.vignette.com) has content management and portal solutions. It offers a management framework to streamline the creation and management of electronic assets, no matter where they exist in the organization, by assigning an identity, meaning, and value to every asset. Manage the entire content life cycle, from collection and production to delivery and analysis.

Midrange Systems

RedDot Content Management Server Express (www.reddot.com/products/cms_express.htm) was adapted for companies with a limited budget, where only a few editors are needed to maintain the content. The product is designed for a single site with user accounts for one administrator, one template editor, and an unlimited number of content contributors (however, only five can concurrently log into the system). Express offers a straight-line workflow process so that all content is routed to the administrator in a WYSIWYG review to approve for release to a live site.

Microsoft Content Management Server 2002 (www.microsoft.com) is Microsoft's solution to content management. It may be a good choice for companies that rely heavily on Microsoft technology. Microsoft's push is that it is the enterprise Web CMS that enables companies quickly and efficiently to build, deploy, and maintain highly dynamic Internet, intranet, and extranet Web sites.

Small- to Medium-Size Business Solutions

GlobalSCAPE's pureCMS (www.cuteftp.com/purecms) is designed for the needs of small to mid-sized businesses. It's Web-based and Windows-like, so users will be familiar with how to use the product. Content changes are made in the staging area, never on a live site. It can define user groups and team leaders to manage approvals. Setup can happen in minutes, with no need to deconstruct your existing site and start from scratch.

Ektron CMS200 (www.ektron.com/cms200.cfm) is a full-featured Web authoring and publishing system enabling business users to author their own Web content while reducing cost, decreasing time to update, and automating Web content publishing workflow. It incorporates many of the functions necessary for more complex Web sites and intranets, using Microsoft ASP, ASP.NET, Macromedia ColdFusion, or PHP application server platforms in a Microsoft server environment.

MOLEHILLS OUT OF MOUNTAINS

The current industry buzz is all about Web services, but they're really just an extension of the "managing code and content together" concept. Web services break traditionally big programs into manageable, usable pieces. They help transfer the responsibility for their management from the developers to the users.

Let's look at both sides of the house for a moment. When engineering teams build programs, they usually build very *large* programs. These applications are difficult to reuse. The APIs are incompatible, and the components have heavy interdependencies. The concept of reusable code is more dream than reality. (Not to mention the bigger fantasy, where "business managers" could make changes.) In the competitive business environment where content and applications must be dynamic, fluid, and highly interactive, such a development model is hopelessly unrealistic and outdated.

For example, let's say that programmers are building an online product-ordering system for Costco. Initially, they might develop an application that requires customers to go through a five-step process each and every time they log on and purchase something. Changes are made. Two of the steps no longer apply. To make the process into a three-step operation, the business users would have to go back to the original programmers to re-engineer the entire program (to the tune of some $5 million or something equally outlandish). Obviously, depending on work schedules, this would take weeks or even months. In the meantime, the competition could eat into its market share.

Enter Web Services

Web services is a fancy way of saying "chop up this big, fat program into smaller pieces, and make it easy to be reused." It's sort of like the "Lego" concept. Blocks of programs can be snapped together, or snapped apart, to reconfigure the whole program.

Ideally, just the *product-ordering* part of the application could be changed. It would *not* require the services of the hardcore programmers to reconfigure an entire system. The job of Web services written in Java or .NET would simplify the process and allow for adaptability and flexibility.

XML: BRINGING ORDER TO CHAOS

When the Web was born, it was mostly comprised of unstructured content: miscellaneous forms, text, images, documents, and so forth. Given the Web design model we mentioned at the start of this chapter in which assets reference each other and the user moves freely from place to place, that was unimportant for several years.

But Web designers eventually found that unstructured content was "messy." The diverse code of the various unstructured assets made for some pretty hairy integration problems. Out of this need to bring order to the madness, XML was born.

XML (Extensible Markup Language) is a language for defining "markup languages" that, unlike HTML, provide for *structuring* content, rather than presenting it. Its flexibility is virtually unlimited, and it has changed the way content can be managed and communicated on the Web.

SUMMARY

Content management is here to stay. The most efficient development environment is one that encourages collaboration among content contributors. The newest document management applications do.

Because traditional, integrated document management (IDM) solutions were designed to "protect" documents and keep content locked up and available to only a privileged few, they have been of little value to organizations with hundreds of contributors who share and collaborate on content creation.

There is a need for collaborative document management (CDM). Without it, there are operational inefficiencies. People create documents on their desktops and email them to each other. Copies of files abound. There is confusion about which version is the "true" one, or where it may be. The situation is complicated when documents exist on file servers, as well as the desktop.

CDM is about bringing all of a business's documents together in a common sharing environment. With it, people can find the information they want with searchable content.

Next-generation CMSs will have granular collaboration. With a CMS that is truly collaborative, a cross-functional, multidimensional environment can go beyond pure content publishing alone. Add a few nodes, and suddenly you could create virtual teams to track the progress of an account and help team members see the activity. The future of the business resides in a collaborative environment.

REFERENCES

 Books

Content Management Bible. Boiko, Bob. Hungry Minds Inc., New York, NY. 2002.

Web Content Management, Nakano, Russell. Addison-Wesley, 2002.

Content Management Systems (Tools of the Trade). Dave Addey, et al. Glasshaus, 2002.

Web Sites

www.cmswatch.com

www.cms-list.org

24
THE BUSINESS
WEB SITE

After careful analysis of your business, you know it's time to create a *Web presence*. Unlike a personal Web site, this will be the portal for customers to find you on the Internet. It will provide information, services, and avenues to contact you. It will allow potential customers to find you, compare you with your competitors, and beat a path to your door.

A Web presence is a business Web site. It is often a collection of Web pages that are linked to a home page. Most individuals have a Web page that is a single Web address. Larger companies' *Web presence* may have multiple pages. For instance, one for each specialized division each brand name, or each geographic distinction (such as the different Disney properties—Disney World–Orlando, Disneyland, California Adventure–Anaheim, and so forth). The term *Web presence* has a more ethereal feel to it, as though it were not really tied to any one geographic location but instead "somewhere in the wild blue cyber." In reality, the terms *Web presence* and *Web site* are often used interchangeably, as they are in this chapter.

When you begin to define what your special needs will be from your Web presence, you need to take a broader perspective of the details of creating this Web entity. It's not unlike the business itself. These are questions that you probably ask yourself every day, anyway.

- What do you need to understand to make the right decisions for your business?
- How should you go about making them?
- How do you make sure the project succeeds?
- What can you expect from your Web presence over the long term?

CHOICES

There are options to consider: outsourcing, sharing resources, and customization are but a few. They are, however, important when it comes to how you will proceed. Would you rather not deal with it at all (outsource), share, or customize uniquely and specifically to you?

Outsourcing

This is an arrangement where one company provides services for another company. Most companies outsource at least some part of their Web sites. Even if all the servers live in your own building, the backbone won't. So you will outsource at least the connection to the Internet. In the past, the company usually would have done it all. But today, companies specialize.

Although companies can provide the services *in house*, they don't. It can be more cost-effective to outsource. Outsourcing allows a company to leave the details to the experts (instead of trying to become experts). It is common with information technology.

Outsourcing differs from subcontracting. With subcontracting, the company directs every phase of the process and supplies the materials. In outsourcing, the company does not own the raw material or manufacturing process. It only dictates the end-result specifications and the delivery method.

It is akin to a restaurant outsourcing bread from a bakery instead of baking loaves. The bakers prepare loaves of bread to produce the style and kind of loaf the restaurant desires. (They may or may not use the restaurant's proprietary recipe, depending on the agreement between them.) The bakery procures the flour, the eggs, and the yeast, and creates the end result—loaves of fresh bread. It is transparent to the restaurant's customers who made the bread. Outsourcing, in this case, frees up the restaurant ovens and personnel, and lets them focus on what they do best—prepare the meals.

Sharing Resources

When a resource is shared, the advantage is that the *cost is spread across multiple users*. On the other hand, in sharing a resource, there may be other considerations. There may be a security risk or sharing may impact the performance of other users. You are locked into the technology and operational selections of that resource. For example, your Web site is on a shared server. Another customer on the same server has a huge promotion, swamping the server. The result: poor response for *your* customers.

Customizing

The least expensive Web site is one already designed: You just plug in your information. This "cookie-cutter" approach is inexpensive. It is not a good idea. If the Web site is undistinguishable from your competitors, what have you gained? (Certainly not any strategic differentiation.)

Your business is different from others. Why shouldn't the Web site reflect those differences? Money invested to make the Web site reflect your company is a good investment. Choose the colors, font, and other features of the Web site with care. The Web site should reflect the quality of service you provide to your customers.

NEEDS

How much you decide to take off the shelf and how much you choose to customize will depend on your goals and the specific circumstances of your business. Variables include: host capacity, processing power, storage, bandwidth, availability, and security.

Capacity

How much Web traffic will the infrastructure have to handle? There are many ways to measure capacity. Some have to do with the amount of data you need to store (storage size), the size of the "pipe" carrying the data (bandwidth), and the speed with which your site handles user transactions (processing power).

For example, if your Web site will need to support document management in a large organization, capacity is a high priority. If, on the other hand, you want to stream music or a personal speech of the chairman over the Internet, bandwidth is more important. If the site will be a highly personalized, graphically demanding e-commerce site, processing power is more important.

Storage Needs

It is important to have an idea of the overall size and scope of Web presence. To calculate the amount of storage you will need in the next 6–12 months, take into account all of the following:

- number of pages on the site
- data requirements of any databases
- software size requirements
- log files for all the applications over the time period

A small or *regular* site will need less than 100 MB. Make sure the server space can handle that without a problem.

A medium or *mission-critical* site will need between 100 MB and 1 TB. Consider an entry-level storage management and backup solution.

A large or *lifeline* site will need over 1 TB of data storage. It will need an *enterprise-grade* storage management and backup solution.

Bandwidth

Bandwidth (also known as *throughput*) is, in general terms, the amount of information that can be carried over a wired or wireless communications connection in a second (or other measurement of time). One way to determine this would be to create a prototype implementation and measure the bandwidth consumption by a small sample of users, then extrapolate to the full system based on the amount of growth you can predict. This is a lot of work. Another way would be to use a bandwidth test program that sends a measured program of a certain file size over the network to a distant computer, then measures the download time to find this in a theoretical figure. However, bandwidth speeds can change from hour to hour, depending on a number of factors. During heightened Internet access times (or a catastrophic event somewhere in the world); excess geomagnetic, solar flare, or thunderstorm activity; or problems along any point of the Internet, connections speeds can slow to a crawl. Even telephone static can cause catastrophic problems. It is rare that there is any one, set number for bandwidth. It is usually a range. Test multiple times; take an average range.

CONSIDERATIONS

A small site will need less than 1 Mbps. It can share a T-1 circuit with other users or be housed in a small datacenter far away from the backbone.

A medium site will need between 1 and 10 Mbps. It should be housed in a datacenter with a small hop count to the backbone.

A large site will need over 10 Mbps. It will require multiple locations in first-class datacenters with top-notch connectivity as close to the backbone as possible.

A small site will need to handle less than 1 million *raw page hits* per day. Barring other considerations, you can get by with one or two reasonably powerful servers.

A medium site will need to handle between 1 and 10 million raw page hits per day. Consider a small farm of servers at each level of its architecture (such as the web layer, the application layer, and the database layer). Consider special-purpose servers for functions such as backup, traffic analysis, and back office integration.

A large site will need to handle more than 10 million raw page hits per day. This will require multiple load-balanced or clustered servers at each level of the architecture.

Critical Availability

Lets face it, the question is not whether technology breaks but how often and how long does it take to bring it back online? There are many ways to reduce the frequency and to shorten the recovery time. They all cost money. It depends on how much money you can afford, balanced with the amount of downtime you're willing to accept.

A regular site could be down for a day or two with recoverable losses. An informational site or archive site might have a bigger problem. A mission-critical site can be down only for an hour or two before the impact of the downtime is significant. (Good examples of these would be e-commerce sites or e-business sites that are major channels of communication with customers or partners.) Although you can engineer the site to have a few single points of failure, if they fail, you are taking an increased risk of significant downtime.

In any case, all components of the infrastructure should be backed up with spare parts handy on site and with reliable hardware support contracts. In addition, trained staff available to respond to outages is a given for a tight Service Level Agreement (SLA).

> SLAs are often described in terms of guaranteed response time. (*Response* generally means a human being is aware of the issue and has begun to troubleshoot and fix the problem.) Low-end SLAs would require the support team to respond within two hours of the problem occurring. A midgrade SLA would require a 60-minute response interval. A high-end SLA would require a 10-minute response. SLAs usually have credit provisions that the support team will give to the customer.

A *lifeline* site can be down for only a few minutes at a time before the impact becomes unbearable. (A stock trading site or online banking site are good examples.) Such a site will have multiple, fully redundant locations without any single points of failure and as few as possible double points of failure. Spare inventory must be available on site and backed up with reliable hardware support contracts. In addition, expert staff needs to be available on site to respond to outages for an extremely tight SLA.

Security

Security is an ever-present concern. From disgruntled employees to unscrupulous competitors, from foreign-based terrorists to teenaged "script kiddies," they represent a varied, constant, ever-escalating threat to your infrastructure. Make no mistake, you're at war with these threats the minute you connect your servers to the Internet. It is a never-ending war and one you can't win. You can only stave off defeat and recover as quickly as possible.

Few organizations have an infinite budget to ensure high levels of security. To balance the cost against the problem, it is important to define a level of tolerable risk.

Table 24.1 summarizes the dimensions of the different types of sites.

A regular site can get by with just enough protection to thwart a casual attack. It can be housed behind a shared firewall, as long as the servers themselves are *locked down* and known security vulnerabilities are addressed expeditiously.

A mission-critical site should provide a significant amount of protection to all layers of the architecture. Such a site would be engineered with several security layers to individually protect different data at appropriate levels. These layers should be separated by individually controlled, dedicated *choke points*, or firewalls.

A lifeline site must have the ultimate in protection. Such a site should add significant additional protection to the "mission-critical" facilities. Such technologies as intrusion detection, "honey pots," and people resources to conduct ongoing testing and monitoring of defenses are essential additions to the mix.

TABLE 24.1 **DIMENSIONS**

Dimension	Regular (Small)	Mission Critical (Medium)	Life-Line (Large)
Storage Capacity	<100 Megabytes	100Mb – 1 Tb	> 1 Tb
Bandwidth	<1 Mbits/sec	1 – 10 Mbits/sec	> 10 Mbits/sec
Processing Power	< 1 Million Raw Page Hits /day	1 – 10 M RPH/d	> 10 M RPH/d
Availability, or tolerance for downtime	1-2 days per outage	1-2 hours per outage	10-15 minutes per outage
Security, or tolerance for intrusion	Non-critical, Reactive	Critical, Dedicated, Reactive	Multi-layer, Dedicated, Actively Patrolled

How will you know whether your Web site is operating successfully? Set specific targets, then compare the data against those targets. Only by measuring these can you know whether you're operating at peak efficiency. And if not, identify trouble spots and address them.

Specifics to measure include:

Quality

This is the overall measure of the customer's satisfaction with the Web site and includes the other criteria on this list.

Time to Market

This is a measure of how quickly the Web site was constructed and brought into full operation. It can be measured in hours, days, weeks, or even months.

Availability and Reliability

How often is the Web site down? Is it wholly or partially unavailable to its intended users? This can be measured in total *unavailable* time per week, month, or year; the number of *defects*, the *total unavailable user minutes*, the *average downtime per incident*, or some combination of these. What percentage is downtime versus total available time?

Scalability

How quickly (and cost-effectively) can adjustments be made to increase capacity, and how much disruption will occur to accommodate the growth? This can be measured in time and resources necessary for growth.

Security

How resistant is your Web site to attack or other unauthorized use? How vigilant is your organization in dealing with them? Consider measuring the number of attacks detected and thwarted, the number of successful penetrations, and the time and other resources used to recover from them.

Operability, Maintainability, and Serviceability

How smoothly are normal, ongoing operational procedures performed? How easy is routine maintenance on the equipment performed? The time and other resources can be measured.

ORGANIZATION

The first decision you need to make is whether you will outsource all of your Web presence or keep it entirely or partially in-house. No matter the choice, you will still need some organization to support it. This is true, regardless of how large or small the Web site is, because the Internet runs 24 hours per day, 7 days per week, 365 days per year. Someone needs to be responsible.

No single human being can support this alone. There will always be a team, an organization. It may be completely within your company. It may be split between your company's staff and one or more external providers. Or it may be outsourced to an external organization, with someone in-house overseeing it.

Front-End Services

There should be a complete plan for acquisition, installation, configuration, testing, and launch of the Web site. This plan would include required tasks, the associated schedule, and budget. It should also define the lines of accountability for each task, including all outsourcing. To execute the plan successfully, the team needs to manage the acquisition process. This is as simple as making sure the right hardware arrives at the right location at the right time and that it is installed, configured, and checked. The Web site developers will need to bring up and test the site's content. (This should include function, integration, user experience, performance, stress, and security testing.)

ONGOING SYSTEMS MANAGEMENT SERVICES

Once the Web presence is up and running, there are many ongoing tasks. These include various management and administration functions.

- Application management assures that the applications operate correctly and at peak efficiency. It includes activities related to the applications, such as account administration, ongoing performance analysis, trend prediction, capacity planning, configuration management, upgrade management, and much more.

- Database administration is a specialized discipline to provide services similar to the above but for the specific database management systems that are part of the site. Modern database management systems are so complex that they require special expertise to support them. In addition to the activities listed above, this task includes overseeing data backups, data uploads, and data extracts. If the Web site includes a "high-availability" database configuration, such as a "cluster," this task will include data synchronization across multiple servers.

- System administration is the task of making sure the operating systems on the servers work at peak efficiency. It includes activities related to the system software, such as the ones described for application management.

Additionally, it oversees system backups, restores, and the writing of scripts to automate normal maintenance procedures.

- Security administration makes sure the Web site is not harmed by the security threats arrayed against it. Security also deals with any penetration, should it occur. It includes activities related to all security measures within the Web site, such as the firewalls, security features of the network equipment, servers, database management systems, application servers, and the applications themselves.

- Network administration is the task in charge of efficient network operations as they relate to the elements within the Web site (such as network routers and switches) and the network services provided to you by the companies that connect your Web site to the Internet.

- Alarm response activates and executes appropriate alarm response procedures based on information provided by monitoring systems. It includes an initial appraisal of the problem to determine whether it is real or an artifact of some other event within the system.

- Notification and escalation happen when it is determined there is a real problem. In that case, the necessary individuals are alerted that action is required. And if needed, an escalation plan is executed, with progressively higher-level staff notified.

- Problem resolution is the reaction to a problem, once detected. The right resources are moved to action, ideally without further help, or support contracts with hardware and software vendors may be triggered to address the problem.

- Regular maintenance is performed periodically to ensure correct and efficient operation of the Web presence. It includes regular data backups, sending storage media to secure, off-site locations, performing emergency procedure drills, and much more.

PROCESSES AND TOOLS

Any well-managed organization has clearly documented processes. Tools are used to support, document, and measure those processes.

> Many tools have been developed to support project planning and tracking. Some run on a desktop PC for use by a small team. Others run on a server for a Web-based user interface for a large group of participants. Some products offer proprietary technology, and others are developed and supported by open source developers around the world. The decision to use a planning tool is important to a project's success.

An operational Web site should be monitored for problems and to obtain measures for capacity planning. This is a thriving market for software companies. It is an area where the open source community has been active and has produced many excellent tools.

SOME COMPANIES THAT OFFER WEB SITE MONITORING

 Internet Seer Web site Monitoring—www.internetseer.com

Alertra—www.alertra.com

First Monitor—www.1stmonitor.com

WebSite Pulse—www.websitepulse.com

AtWatch—www.atwatch.com

AlertSite—www.alertsite.com

Net Mechanic—www.netmechanic.com/monitor.htm

Software QA Test—www.softwareqatest.com/qatweb1.html

TECHNOLOGY EXPERTISE

Another important aspect of supporting a Web site is technology expertise. If the support you've chosen does not have the experience needed to architect, deploy, and support the right technologies or products, you may be stuck with a suboptimal infrastructure that is too expensive, not capable enough, not stable enough, or in some other way inferior. Of course, over time, these skills will be learned. Although this may be acceptable for an internal organization, it is a poor decision for an outsourced project.

 Depending on the complexity of your infrastructure, the support organization may have to be expert in all aspects of current technology. These include:

Major server platforms: Intel, Sun, HP, IBM

Operating systems: MS Windows, Linux, Solaris, AIX

Database management systems: Oracle, MS SQL Server, MySQL, PostgressSQL

Application Servers: BEA WebLogic, IBM WebSphere, Tomcat, JBoss

Middleware servers: BEA Tuxedo, WebSphere MQ, MSMQ

Load Balancers: F5 Networks, Cisco/Alteon, Array

Firewalls: Checkpoint, Netscreen, Sonic, Watchguard, Cisco

Network elements: Cisco, Juniper, Netgear, Linksys

Outsourcing to a Datacenter

Data centers are facilities essential to the operation of a Web site. These are physical locations with servers, equipment, and people. There are some key buzzwords that you should know when looking for this kind of outsourcing solution.

Real Estate is the whole physical structure but specifically means the servers themselves, usually housed in individual cabinets, wire-fence cages, or cooled server rooms.

Bandwidth and Peering Arrangements are common in datacenters, although a growing number of external datacenter providers don't actually deliver these themselves but invite major network providers to locate access points within the datacenter and sell their circuits directly to the colocated customers. In either case, the bandwidth can be delivered via an Ethernet handoff or a telephone circuit, such as a DS-1 or a DS-3. You need to know what the arrangements are and adjust the architecture accordingly. For example, if the chosen facility hands bandwidth via an Ethernet connection, you will need a network switch to connect to it. If the hand-off is to a DS-3 circuit, you will need a router and a CSU/DSU to connect to it. Both are acceptable, but you need to know which one to buy.

Make sure the hand-off has sufficient redundancy to support availability requirements. You should look deep into the internal network of the bandwidth provider to make sure that the connectivity from the datacenter to the rest of the Internet has adequate redundancy to support your availability requirements, as well as wide peering arrangements to define performance requirements.

Clean, Redundant Power is a critical service in a datacenter. It is essential that the datacenter provide uninterruptible, well-conditioned power to the infrastructure and to the network elements that provide the connection to the Internet. Service should be delivered with at least N+1 redundancy across at least two modes of delivery. N+1 redundancy means that if you need two generators to run the facility at full load, you will actually have three at your disposal, and if you need 10, you will actually have 11, and so on. A good Data Center will have both backup battery power and backup generators (diesel or turbine). Furthermore, there should be at least one spare generator over and above the generator capacity necessary to run the entire datacenter at full electrical load, including climate control. N+2 redundancy is better, and some datacenters may even have 2N redundancy in some systems (that is twice as many components as needed).

Stable Climate Conditions are another critical service in a datacenter. It is usually provided by a redundant system of air conditioners and relies on carefully designed airflow to carry the heated air from the servers out of the facility and pump the cold air to the servers. N+1 redundancy is required in this service.

Physical Site Security for the site may include human guards, video surveillance systems, access card systems, and biometric systems, such as fingerprint, iris, or hand geometry scanners.

A Web site is more than bandwidth, scripts, and pages to view. There is a business side to it, as well. The issues that are key to a Web presence include risk management, relationships with the various participants, expectations, and other elements needed for a sound business decision that are discussed in this section.

Risk Management

There is a fashionable concept that all risk within a business can be managed across the enterprise. This includes classical financial risks (such as currency fluctuations that affect profits on exported goods) and operational risks (such as a failure of critical information systems). To effectively manage risk, you need to plan how the Web site and its supporting organization will continue to deliver value in the face of partial failure. This *business continuity planning* is the flip side of disaster recovery in the event of total failure.

Business continuity focuses on the delivery of value while recovering from failure. In disaster recovery, the focus is on the speediest possible fix of the outage. Although related, they have different priorities. For example, you could choose to install an extra server in the infrastructure to provide business continuity if the primary server fails by malfunction. However, the spare server will do you no good if the primary datacenter is on fire. The disaster recovery plan would outline procedures to install a spare server in another datacenter, transfer the Web presence (network connectivity, firewalls, servers, storage, and so forth), and be up and running before the firemen have finished their job.

Relationships: Provider vs. Partner

The go-go days of the Internet bubble gave rise to a strange situation where the customers cared more about being the *first to market* than about quality. Corners were cut in the name of expediency, especially where it came to building long-term relationships with trusted technology partners. Providers were overwhelmed by work beyond anything they believed possible. But worst of all, a number of organizations were created out of the culture of short-term profits at the expense of client success. This resulted in spectacular project failures.

Those days are over. Now a sound business plan requires all parties working toward meeting expectations, communicating openly, delivering on promises, and building mutual confidence and trust.

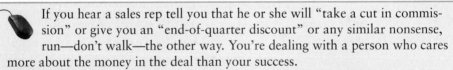

A contract might contain:

Introduction, to describe the parties and their relationship

Scope of work, usually as an addendum

Duration of contract

Intellectual property issues, such as nondisclosure, as well as specifics of ownership of any custom developments

Warranties provided, Service Level Agreements (SLAs) and what happens if the SLA is not fulfilled

Dispute resolution procedures

Dissolution, or what happens if things don't work out

It is vitally important to make sure that your attorney approve any contracts before you sign them. You can expect that the larger the project, the more you should negotiate the contract.

Pricing and Packaging

There is a great deal of price pressure in this market. Most providers have fixed price schedules. Contract negotiation and price negotiations lack much "wheeling and dealing." In fact, if a stereotypical slick salesman shows up who'll "cut you a special deal," check it out thoroughly. (Buyer beware!)

If you hear a sales rep tell you that he or she will "take a cut in commission" or give you an "end-of-quarter discount" or any similar nonsense, run—don't walk—the other way. You're dealing with a person who cares more about the money in the deal than your success.

A good sales rep understands the precarious balance between charging more than the market expects and what it really costs to deliver the service. They can't overprice the service for fear of losing the deal, and they can't underprice it because Wall Street is no longer patient with companies that don't earn a profit.

A good sales rep will work with you to make sure that you get the maximum value within your budget and schedule. This improves the chances that the project will succeed, and you will do business with that company again in the future.

Although it would be nice if most vendors had the incentive to treat their customers well, unfortunately, many of them don't. The ones that do will significantly contribute to the success and satisfaction of your project. The best source of honest assessment will be the vendor's current and past customers.

Challenge, compare, and validate the proposal, but tell the sales rep what the real priorities and decision criteria are. If they don't know how you will make the decision or what the real budget is, they have to guess. (This means that most of the proposals will miss!) In this case, nobody wins. Don't start out a potential long-term relationship with mutual distrust and dissatisfaction.

Infrastructure

All of these models are based on the same fundamental number—the hourly cost of the staff needed to perform the support tasks. Hourly rates vary greatly in the industry and depend on the location and skill level of the staff. They could be as low as $20/hour for technical staff located offshore in Asia, Eastern Europe, or the Caribbean. Alternately, rates could be as high as $300/hour for an Oracle DB with 15 years of production experience in the Wall Street environment and a sterling reputation within that very tight community.

To get more insight into how you can evaluate proposals, let's look at how some of the providers package and price their offerings.

Real Estate

This can be as small as a little space in a rack or a cabinet or as large as thousands of square feet in a separate room in the datacenter.

On the smaller end of the scale, real estate is measured in rack units, or just "U." Each U is 1.75" of vertical space in a rack or a cabinet. The racks are usually 19" wide, to fit most standard rack-mount hardware. Some providers have wider cabinets that provide more space for hardware.

Because all hardware generates heat, it is important to have extra space in an enclosed cabinet to allow the air to move around the hardware and take away the generated heat. In this respect, enclosed cabinets with built-in electrical fans provide more consistent cooling than do open racks or cabinets without fans. Pricing could be as low as $200/month for 1 U in an open rack or up to $1,200/month for a fully wired, enclosed, individually secured cabinet.

On the larger end of the scale, real estate is usually priced on a per-square-foot per-month basis. Prices range from $25 per ft²/mo for basic raised floor to $40 per ft²/mo for world-class facilities. The latter may include sophisticated security system (biometrics, video, armed guards), highly redundant power sources (2N redundancy), and high-end management tools to support operations. The more real estate you purchase, the less it will cost per square foot.

Power

Depending on how much real estate you purchase and in what form, all the necessary power may be included in the price. However, if the infrastructure is unusually power-hungry hardware, such as larger mainframe or storage devices, you may need to make custom arrangements for power. Pricing for custom power varies widely between providers.

Bandwidth

Most providers price bandwidth in monthly precommitted packages. For example, a provider can offer you a package with 2 Mbps of Committed Information Rate (CIR) at $1,500/month with overage priced at $800/month per sustained 1 Mbps.

This means that the Web site can generate up to 2 Mbps on a continuous basis and even burst over that limit for some period of time each month. But if the traffic bursts over that limit more than 10%, the provider will bill you an additional $800 for that month for each additional 1 Mbps of sustained traffic.

A different model, usually appropriate for smaller sites, measures the total amount of data transferred to and from the Web site. For example, a provider can offer you a package of 20 GB per month for $200/month and each additional 1 GB for $12. If your site generates more traffic than that, the provider will bill you for the overage amount at the higher rate.

Shared Hardware

There is some controversy about the appropriate use of shared hardware in a Web presence. The trade-off between shared and dedicated hardware is the lower budget of the former and the more predictable performance and security of the latter.

An additional element to consider is the "barrier to exit" that shared hardware represents. What happens if you decide to leave the provider? If you included a significant amount of shared hardware in the architecture, you will need to duplicate this hardware either by purchasing your own or by selecting a new provider with the same shared hardware. Neither one is a particularly palatable alternative, especially if it is outside the budgetary constraints of your organization.

So shared hardware becomes a major factor in staying with a provider that you are not happy with, which is not a good situation for you or the provider.

However, if you're on a tight budget, you may have to go with shared hardware if you cannot afford dedicated hardware. Also, consider sharing peripheral hardware. For example, many projects succeed with shared storage and backup solutions. Other alternatives include shared load balancing and security elements (such as firewalls). These solutions, although not ideal, are a way to fit a tight budget.

> The price of shared elements varies so much between providers that it is nearly impossible to define the boundaries of a good deal.

Rent vs. Own

Another long-standing controversy within the industry is the question of owning the hardware versus renting it. There are pluses and minuses to each.

When you rent the hardware, you don't have a large capital expense at the start of the project. On the other hand, the provider that is renting the hardware to you needs to finance the hardware and make a profit on it, so you end up paying much more over time.

When you own the hardware, you can pick it up and move it to another provider at any time. On the other hand, you may need to arrange financing or convince your management to increase the initial capital budget.

> Most providers price services in one of four ways:
>
> **Fixed Cost**
> You pay a fixed fee based on the scope of a project. This usually applies to a project with fixed scope and duration, such as deployment and launch of a Web site.
>
> **Incident Package**
> You pay a fixed fee for a certain number of support incidents, however long each takes and however long it takes to consume the number of incidents you paid for.
>
> **Retainer**
> You pay a fixed fee per month for a specific quantity of services each month, whether you use them or not.
>
> **Time and Materials**
> You pay hourly rates for support.
>
> Risk differentiates these pricing models. In the fixed-cost model, the risk is entirely with the provider. In the time and materials model, the risk is entirely with the customer. The other two models offer a gradual spectrum of trust and risk sharing. Most providers can offer more than one pricing model and will work with you to fit the risk and the budget to your specific requirements.

Monitoring

The prices for these services vary widely, from almost free to several hundred dollars per monitored host per month. The difference seems to be in the type of software system used for monitoring, the depth and frequency of monitoring, and the type and speed of notification. The tighter the response SLA, the more expensive the service.

- Most providers base the price of monitoring on the complexity of your infrastructure, the type of hardware in it, and the depth to which you wish to monitor it.

- There may be additional charges for customization of either the centralized monitoring systems or the monitoring agents that are deployed on the hardware.

- Finally, there may be additional charges for designing and implementing custom notification and escalation procedures, if the provider supports this at all.

With some planning, and some good choices, you'll end up with a Web home for your company's Web presence.

SUMMARY

It's time to check the calendar if you don't have a business Web site. You are overdue. Even a token Web site is better than nothing. What we've discussed in this chapter should get you started in the right direction. You'll thank yourself for doing it, and your customers will thank you even more. If you already have a businbess Web site, use this information to improve it.

25

ENTERPRISE INSTANT MESSAGING

Not since Alexander Graham Bell invented the telephone in 1876 has there been a communications revolution as significant as instant messaging. It is a technology that facilitates real-time, one-to-one communication. Instant messaging (or *IM*, as it is now commonly referred to) initially allowed the exchange of simple text messages over a network. IM has grown to encompass different instant communications applications and devices, including voice over IP (VoIP), voice conferencing, pagers, personal digital assistants (PDAs), and cellular phones. What began as a consumer fad morphed into an online phenomenon as IM established a pervasive presence among consumers and businesses alike.

According to Jeff Tyson (www.howstuffworks.com), IM became ubiquitous in the late 1990s. The technology originated as early as the mid-1980s as a real-time communication feature in online bulletin boards and IRC chatrooms. As common interest groups, chatrooms, and bulletin boards became virtual online communities of people who wanted to chat directly and immediately about their passions, IM began to foster a sense of immediacy.

IM got a boost when online services, such as America Online (AOL), included IM in their dialup client software. They expanded the technology through the addition of *buddylists* and rudimentary presence detection (the ability to determine who is online and available to talk with). The growing popularity of the Internet transformed IM from a technology into a phenomenon. In 1996, Mirabilis, an Israeli company, was founded by Yair Goldfinger, Arik Vardi, Sefi Vigiser, and Amnon Amir. These four launched ICQ (short for "I Seek You"), which expanded IM beyond closed-end online services, such as AOL, Prodigy, and CompuServe. IM was released to the burgeoning Internet. Mirabilis created what became the foundation of today's IM platform.

CONSUMER IM TAKES OFF

What developed in the late 1990s was a surge in IM proliferation. This allowed instant and direct connection of people across the entire Internet. Consumers (many of whom were kids and teenagers) who began to use the technology to chat with friends drove the initial wave. As IM became more popular, it began to feed on itself, driving "viral marketing," essentially a phenomenon where the people who have it create more of a need for it (word-of-mouth marketing).

AOL acquired Mirabilis for approximately $287 million in 1998, when the service had expanded to more than 10 million users. Soon thereafter, AOL introduced its own IM platform, AOL Instant Messenger (AIM).

Adding to the ranks of ICQ and AIM, Microsoft and Yahoo! developed their own IM products. As each of these competing services grew, they did so in virtual isolation. AIM and ICQ would not allow access to their networks from competing services (in fact, to this day, AIM and ICQ—essentially the same service from the same company—are not configured for interoperability). With more than 100 million users of IM worldwide, the Gartner Group predicts that by 2006, IM will be used more often than email as the preferred method of interpersonal messaging.

Lacking a single standard—and owned by three fierce competitors—in 1999, IM became a metaphoric though very real battleground for AOL and Microsoft. At the heart of the issue was interoperability (the ability to connect users of one service to users of another). Microsoft devoted substantial resources to tapping into AOL's network. AOL resisted the push through technology, as well as in the legal system. AOL was determined to quash interoperability with threats of legal action against Microsoft for unauthorized use of its network.

AOL has remained intent on keeping its IM network closed. It sees the user base as a strong marketing platform for its fee and subscription-based offerings (magazines, movies, paid AOL dialup service, etc.). Microsoft decided to back down and acquiesce after a series of attempts at "hacking" a bridge to AOL's service failed. For now, anyway, AOL is maintaining a closed network.

According to CNET, ICQ achieved its 200 millionth download on May 20, 2002. Microsoft, Yahoo!, and AOL's AIM all have had a similar trajectory. There are literally hundreds of millions of downloads and tens of millions of users. The numbers are rather staggering and only serve to underscore the immense popularity of IM as a dominant conduit for today's communications.

THE RISKS OF CONSUMER IM SYSTEMS

The convenience of IM carries risks. Traditional IM systems lack the security features needed to protect a company's assets. Message sessions on consumer platforms are susceptible to electronic eavesdropping, and hackers have the capability not only to get into a user's computer but also into the enterprise network and the intellectual property that resides there. Many consumer IM systems offer direct, peer-to-peer file-sharing capabilities. These lack security and leave corporations more vulnerable to hackers. Viruses have the ability to spread quickly throughout insecure IM systems—paralyzing a corporate network in no time. Many companies that offer free IM services, such as AOL,

MSN, and Yahoo!, have been infected with viruses: Aplore was spread through AIM, and MSN messenger was infected by Choke and CoolNow.

Corporations without a secure enterprise IM (EIM) system find that their employees rely on publicly available IM technology. Those publicly available solutions do not offer management mechanisms. The decentralized structure prohibits IT department control over who within the organization uses IM and how. This said, Gartner Group found that 60% of all enterprises have some form of IM behind their firewalls. And very few CIOs and CTOs have developed a strategy to manage, or extend their IM infrastructures.

BUSINESS IM

A trend surfaced in the late 1990s. The phone companies saw that their data service line usage begin to eclipse voice usage. (Most of the data was comprised of email and Internet traffic.) Just as email obviated the need for faxes and snail mail, IM was impacting telephone usage (and in-person conversation). Telephone tag, frequent conversations, and face-to-face meetings could be replaced by short messages. An immediate response could be received without the need to stop working.

Soon, many in business discovered the advantages of IM in the workplace. Buddylists became a vital reference point because people could now get a sense of who was available and who was out to lunch. IM began to offer tangible advantages, such as presence detection, immediate response, and back-and-forth dialog. Questions could be asked and answered not only in real time but in less time than face-to-face communication, telephone calls, or email. The efficiency grew as the network expanded.

ENTERPRISE IM

Businesses adopted these systems "unofficially" as employees loaded the client software on their computers and found ways to overcome firewalls and other hurdles presented. Companies were concerned with the proliferation of these consumer communications platforms within their companies.

Unlike email, where people using Outlook can send and receive mail from AOL, Hotmail, and Yahoo!, IM remained proprietary. Some consumer users found that the best solution to this problem was to keep two or three IM applications running simultaneously. As a business tool, the situation was becoming more problematic. IT administrators fretted about unauthorized open ports on the corporate networks. Other IM issues were discovered.

In mid- to late 2001, there were several publicized cases of IM traffic intercepted and posted to public Web sites. These exposed the companies to additional liability and compromise of trade secrets. In one particularly famous example, the CEO of the Internet start-up eFront had his ICQ logs hacked and posted to dozens of Web-based message boards. The incident wreaked havoc on eFront's business and accelerated the decline of the company.

Electronic viruses spread through email systems. This brought awareness of the threat that an insecure, widely deployed network such as IM posed, could be susceptible to an electronic virus. There were dozens of high-profile articles warning of additional risks associated with AIM and MSN messenger. The basic theme was how a hacker could gain access to a user's computer hard drive through the consumer IM clients. With the risks beginning to surface, several smaller IM firms sprang up to offer alternatives.

It began as a simple tool for text messaging. Today's IM has become a much more robust offering. It has integrated chat, VoIP, voice conferencing, and mobile devices. Several firms have augmented these features to establish a business tool based on real-time communication technology. IM products now include the addition of security measures (such as applying encryption technology) to secure communication and greater centralized controls to cut down the risks of a distributed, pervasive communications network.

Wall Street embraced IM. It found a welcome home in many trading and brokerage firms. Then the issues of security and control became even more important. Stock trades have a specific requirement governing the logging and auditing of messages sent to and from the company, as mandated by the Securities and Exchange Commission (SEC). The need was even more demanding than that of investment banks and brokerage houses. In fact, the SEC regulations stipulate that all electronic communications be recorded and kept in a secure, nonchangeable format for up to three years.

Characteristics of the Enterprise Market IM

The only large player in the EIM space is IBM's Lotus unit. With Notes and Sametime, Lotus has long offered a strong suite of applications for corporate collaboration. While Notes developed as an earlier email system and evolved to become a sophisticated and powerful corporate communications platform, Sametime debuted as a simpler, more streamlined version for users who needed some of the collaborative features of Notes but not all of them. The result has been a solid application for business use that has become a de facto player in the EIM space.

Not surprisingly (even given the current market environment), smaller firms have emerged to stake a claim in EIM. Security features, centralized controls, message encryption, and a host of integrated features and customization are their strong sales points. Firms such as FaceTime, Communicator, Omnipod, and Bantu are competing to offer cost-effective, secure, and scalable alternatives

Each of the EIM players has approached the market differently. The following is a brief description of the seven primary characteristics of EIM systems.

Interoperability

A frustrating aspect of consumer IM is that each of the big systems is mutually exclusive of the others. Users on AIM cannot connect to or converse with users of MSN Messenger. Interoperability, a concept originated by a few smaller consumer IM applications (such as Cerulean Studios' Trillian and Odigo), can allow users of one service to add buddies and IM with users of a different system. Interoperability is a key feature for enterprise users to keep in touch with colleagues on another system.

Security

After the events of September 11, 2001, virtually every company became even more sensitive to the security of their intellectual property, as well as of their employees. IT administrators previously could turn a blind eye to the risks associated with employees on AIM or Yahoo!. The course of events created a heightened sense of insecurity. IM came to represent a hole in the corporate armor. Most EIM firms now offer some form of encrypted messaging, such as secure sockets layer (SSL) or triple encryption using DES (Data Encryption Standard), and some enterprise products restrict the ability to execute text through the IM window to reduce the threat of viruses spreading through IM sessions.

Scalability and Robustness

The major consumer IM systems support millions of people. They were not built with important features to scale throughout a company efficiently. EIM, on the other hand, has focused on the specific needs of a particular corporation. The corporate network system must be able to handle millions of IM users, as well as adequately support the user base. Most of the successful EIM providers are based on client/server architecture. (The consumer IM is essentially a distributed network of peered clients.) The IT department is able to maintain control by routing all messages through a centralized server, providing an added level of administration and security.

Integration

There are many options—too many. In fact, corporate employees are becoming overwhelmed with too many options and choices, especially on their computer screens. Successful enterprise applications now focus on integration with existing platforms and infrastructure to streamline both the introduction and use of new systems (especially ones with similar purposes). Just as CRM (customer relationship management) and sales automation applications are a natural fit, many of the EIM platforms have focused on integrating with existing intranets, contact lists, and file servers (among others) as a means of improving efficiency of use and reducing application clutter on the desktop.

Extensibility

In addition to "out-of-the-box" solutions, many EIM providers offer extensible solutions that can be customized specifically to address a corporate need. In particular, several IM providers now offer customizable user interface designs that incorporate a firm's logo and corporate identity.

Logging and Tracking

Electronic records are required for firms in the securities business. It is important for companies concerned about liability and security to keep logs of IM sessions. Providing an intuitive way to view and search the logs is a valuable tool. Several EIM firms have addressed this issue though the development of administrative controls that include features such as logging toggle; keyword search; and search by date, user, system, etc.

Standards-Based

Session Initiation Protocol (SIP, RFC 3261) is a basic request-response signaling protocol used to establish a connection in an Internet Protocol (IP) network. By extension, SIP for IM and Presence Leveraging Extensions (SIMPLE) is a standard being developed and advocated by the Internet Engineering Task Force (IETF) to enable basic text messaging and presence information to be passed from one IM system to another. The development of standards such as SIMPLE will allow IM systems to route messages using various devices, systems, and protocols, including cell phones, pagers, PDAs, Wireless Application Protocol (WAP) applications, SIP applications, Short Messaging System (SMS) messages, email, and IM.

EIM and Instant Security

Security problems can be serious, but they are not insurmountable. EIM must securely facilitate communication both within and between organizations. Some popular EIM offerings now provide secure messaging and file transfer with other sophisticated administrative features. Valuable features include the ability to mimic existing corporate hierarchical structures and interoperability with other IM networks.

EIM systems must be less susceptible to most common computer viruses that infect IM systems. One common EIM virus-prevention tactic is to make sure that the text within EIM sessions is not executable. With centralized administrative controls, it is easier to provide message logging, auditing, and strict hierarchical domain structures to dictate access control levels for internal and external users. EIM services should offer a state-of-the-art firewall, sophisticated security software, and scalability to accommodate hundreds of thousands of users.

Platform for Interaction and Information Sharing

Instant electronic communication is now available in several different forms and iterations, from straight IM and chat to file sharing and identity management. These features have traditionally been found only in separate and competing applications. The future will be integration.

The survivors over the next period of consolidation will manage to differentiate themselves, either through a leading market position or through their ability to develop a more holistic offering. IM as a standalone product holds less promise than systems that can build on IM with other applications and features, such as file sharing, content delivery, and identity management.

Centralized Storage and File Sharing

IM and information-sharing systems with centralized storage can eliminate the need for synchronization of files and enable users to access stored information from any Internet-enabled PC. Centralized storage allows for advanced security features and usage monitoring, offloading the overhead of data storage and management for users and IT departments. In the case of file sharing, centralized storage eliminates the proliferation of various file versions and ensures that the most recent iteration is always available for a collaborative work group. Documents and folders of any size or type can be shared, transferred, stored, and backed up in a secure environment with log-based audit trails and clearly defined access control levels. With file-sharing transactions occurring within a centralized server, zero bandwidth is required to share a file, whether it is 2 KB or 50 MB.

Managed IM

IM can quickly lose its appeal with unmanaged free access. The right EIM solution should establish a system of rules to communicate and collaborate securely.

From a central administrative level, EIM systems can be overlaid by rules-based protocols that determine who can chat with whom via IM. For example, a CEO may want to have the ability to send messages to anyone in the company but may prefer to receive incoming messages only from direct reports and select individuals both within and outside the company, including key customer contacts. The purchasing department may wish to communicate with select individuals in each department of the company and with all of the company's suppliers but may not want to allow identification of or communication among its suppliers. Stipulating who can see and correspond with whom on the EIM network should be easy for an administrator to set and change frequently.

Ease of Use, Flexibility, Productivity, and Security Equal Effective IM

Businesses will get the most mileage out of a system that enables rapid deployment and requires no additional investment in hardware or software. The easier it is to deploy, manage, and maintain, the more companies can enjoy the benefits of IM and file sharing without compromising network security, proprietary integrity, and intellectual property. Retrofitting an existing IM system to provide this level of security and structure is a difficult task, and most companies will look for an EIM platform with an architecture built to manage and control IM and information-sharing activities within their organizations or collaborative groups.

Architecture

As more and more computers have come online in recent years, the desire to expand the network and exchange information has grown exponentially. Consumer IM systems have hundreds of millions of users worldwide. File-sharing services (such as Napster and Gnutella) have tens of millions of devotees. Conversing and sharing files have given the Internet an entirely new dimension of interactivity and utility.

Peer-to-Peer vs. Client/Server

Basic architectures for IM and file-sharing networks essentially fall into two camps: peer-to-peer and client/server. Most of the consumer applications that spread so rapidly and (in)famously a couple of years ago relied on peer-to-peer architectures to track presence information and user location, as well as to share information from one user to another throughout the network.

For companies such as Napster and Limewire, these decentralized peer-to-peer systems were part of the appeal. In fact, Napster famously claimed early on that, due to its system structure, it had no control over who sent what through its network (claiming that, thus, the company was not responsible for illegal music swapping). Similarly, consumer IM systems such as AOL, Microsoft, and Yahoo! all rely on a decentralized peer-to-peer network to scale exponentially, quickly, and cost-effectively. However, most peer-to-peer file-sharing and consumer IM systems rely on some central server functions, such as tracking presence and handing off requests. The central servers act as directories, while the exchange is handled directly from client to client.

The primary advantage of peer-to-peer is that resources are distributed, so conversations and file transfers between users can use local bandwidth, storage, and CPU resources. The Napster usage model was successful for this reason: The amount of bandwidth and storage needed was large but did not need to be provided by the service.

Client/server systems were less promoted during the peer-to-peer craze. They are now seen as a more stable and long-term solution to online communication networks. With messages and information routed through central servers, client/server overcomes many of the problems with peer-to-peer. It benefits from being more firewall-friendly, as well as more conducive to administrative oversight. The traditional drawback of client/server is that it requires significantly greater resources (at least centrally) to operate. Although the cost of centralized networks made this choice less viable, compared with the advantages of distributed networks, as the costs of bandwidth, storage, and servers has fallen dramatically in recent years, the resource constraints have become less important over time.

Ironically, Internet Relay Chat (IRC), the first iteration of online chat and predecessor to IM, employs a client/server architecture. Originally developed in Finland by Jarkko Oikarinen in 1988, IRC was designed as a multiuser chat system where people convene on "channels" to talk either privately or in groups. The system works by linking various users' clients to a central IRC server that routes the messages.

Platforms

One of the strengths of IM and presence services is the real-time communication they allow. The power of these systems is evidenced in the great lengths that cellular companies and two-way pager manufacturers have gone to supply various forms of text messaging on their respective mobile devices. With "wireless anywhere" becoming a mantra of both the cellular providers and the PDA and equipment makers, these devices are becoming more sophisticated and powerful. PDAs and phones now have options such as color screens, long battery life, expanded memory capacity, and more and more options for connectivity. WiFi and GPRS promise higher speed connections, and wireless providers are busy rolling out these offerings in major markets nationwide. With SMS technologies so prevalent throughout Europe and Asia, and Palm and Blackberry offering IM and presence detection, users can now "take their conversations with them," literally.

As bandwidth prices have fallen and sound quality has improved, IP telephony is emerging as a more viable technology. Because IP phones already can be controlled through a computer, using standard network links instead of hard-wired phone lines, several IM providers have begun developing tools that interface with the telephone. Soon, IM users will be able to interface directly with their phones to place and manage calls, conduct conferences, and share files and documents directly.

Plain old Web browsers have become an outlet for IM. Slower and less robust than a true client, HTML browsers are the standard interface for most Web-based operations. Several IM providers, including AIM and IMLogic, provide browser-based IM. Most browser IM uses Java to provide a more real-time experience. The primary advantage of browser/Java solutions is that they are cross-platform. They work on Mac and Linux, as well as on Windows and UNIX.

The consumer IM platforms all offer cross-platform client options that work on Windows, Mac, and UNIX, but the corporate market has largely ignored Mac and UNIX. Because Windows is the de facto corporate standard, most EIM clients have tended to focus their development resources almost exclusively on this operating system. Unless Apple begins to make a substantial comeback in the corporate world or Linux suddenly dethrones Windows as the operating system of choice, expect more and more cross-platform offerings to focus on browser/Java clients.

The Competitive Landscape and Outlook

The competition between enterprise-class IM and collaboration solution providers will intensify. The long-term market leaders will offer organizations a secure, easy-to-use, rapidly deployable, and cost-effective integrated communications platform. Companies must continue to refine the means by which employees, business partners, and customers electronically communicate and collaborate with each other. Those able to provide a solution to address the myriad needs will be in the best position to survive and capitalize on a substantial market opportunity. The product will need to address such diverse requirements as administrative capabilities, advanced presence detection, IM, chat, email, file sharing and file collaboration, application sharing, threaded discussions (e.g., bulletin boards), and shared resources (e.g., team calendars, shared contacts).

The widespread adoption of consumer-based IM solutions among end users has prompted all three major providers (AOL, Yahoo!, and Microsoft) individually to begin development on an enterprise-class IM and collaboration solution. There are numerous individual users actively using each network.

It is unlikely that corporate IT departments will purchase solutions from organizations whose roots are embedded in media and advertising. At last count, the emerging enterprise-level IM and collaboration market had more than 30 participants, ranging from solutions offered by large, multinational corporations, such as Microsoft and IBM (Lotus), to smaller, more focused players, such as Omnipod and Jabber.

Those that ultimately succeed will likely share the following characteristics.

- **Broadly defined communications platform.** Successful EIM and collaboration software vendors must offer more than just IM and chat or file sharing and workflow automation functionality. The most successful companies will be able to integrate disparate applications and technologies elegantly while offering sophisticated administrative capabilities.

- **Robust administrative capabilities.** Successful enterprise communications solution providers must offer an easy-to-use yet very robust administrative solution. IT professionals must be able not only to manage end-user permissions granularly but also to import user definitions from existing corporate resources. The ability to mirror an existing corporate organizational hierarchy—whether based on geographic location or functional group—in a communications platform, then to assign localized administration capabilities to each subsegment grouping is critical. In addition to being able to monitor, log, and audit end-user activities, such as IM and file-sharing activities, administrators must be able to assign permission-based controls on a user-by-user basis. Finally, enterprise communications solution providers must provide extensibility to other applications and vendor platforms.

- **Rapidly deployable and intuitive interface.** To ensure widespread adoption of EIM and collaboration platforms, successful vendors must be able rapidly and cost-effectively to deploy solutions that require minimal end-user training. With the substantial proliferation of consumer IM clients, the transition from consumer-based offerings to EIM and collaboration solutions by end users will be most seamless with those solutions that best resemble the consumer IM interfaces.

- **Platform extensible outside of organization.** As with current email solutions, EIM and collaboration providers must provide solutions that enable end users to communicate with individuals beyond the enterprise. The overall effectiveness of any communications solution is amplified by the pervasive characteristics of the network.

THE INTEROPERABILITY WARS

AOL got a jumpstart on the IM phenomenon with its purchase of Mirabilis in the summer of 1998. Microsoft had to delay its own entry into the space because the company was determined to have its MSN Messenger tightly integrated with Hotmail, its free email service. In late July 1999, MSN Messenger debuted with features similar to those offered by AOL Instant Messenger and ICQ; however, it had one new key feature—the ability to interoperate with AIM. MSN, hoping to tap into AOL's network of some 35 million IM users, had added a bridge to AOL's network, allowing users of MSN to search out and communicate with users on AIM.

AOL immediately responded by changing its protocols, effectively cutting off MSN's efforts to connect to its network. MSN retaliated with yet another patch that circumvented AOL's means of blocking access to its network. Microsoft and Yahoo! were vociferously supporting open standards for IM through the IETF, a volunteer organization that seeks to develop new Internet standards specifications. AOL fought hard to keep "unauthorized hackers" off its proprietary network. The game of cat and mouse continued between Microsoft and AOL for much of the rest of 1999, until Microsoft finally threw in the towel in November, claiming that its efforts to interoperate with AOL IM posed a potential security risk for MSN users.

Ironically, while Microsoft and Yahoo! sought to tap into AOL's network and goaded AOL to join the IETF and support a common standard for IM, users of MSN and Yahoo! Messenger were unable to IM each other. And although AOL owns and operates both AIM and ICQ, the two systems, each with tens of millions of users, are mutually exclusive and unable to communicate with each other. One condition of AOL's merger with Time Warner was to effect an interoperable platform for its messaging system. The company issued a statement in August 2002, claiming that interoperability was proving much more difficult than was originally envisioned.

The few consumer-oriented products that have emerged with a focus on interoperability have met with the same resistance from AOL. Both Odigo and Trillian offered interoperable IM, the latter releasing a client that allowed users to conduct IM sessions with AIM, Yahoo!, and MSN from a single Trillian interface. Although Trillian has experienced approximately 4.5 million downloads and counts more than a million users, it has had little commercial appeal and shows limited promise as an enterprise solution.

SUMMARY

As IM has grown in popularity among business users, the issue of interoperability has come to the forefront. With no system of standards in place, users on AIM at company X have no way to communicate with those on MSN within the same organization (much less with users of another network outside the company). In early September 2002, the IM Standards Board (IMSB), a newly created consortium that includes the Wall Street firms Lehman Brothers, J.P. Morgan Chase, Merrill Lynch, Morgan Stanley Dean Witter, UBS, and Deutsche Bank, met with AOL, Microsoft, IBM, and Yahoo! to encourage the development of common standards within the IM industry.

At issue is the substantial surge in IM popularity and the problems caused by lack of standardization. The IMSB seeks to prod the industry to work together on developing interoperability.

The IMSB appears promising. It is still subject to the whims of companies (such as AOL). In fact, AOL had similar efforts, such as the IETF advocacy of the SIMPLE standard, as well as a Federal Communication Commission (FCC) order to open its network to others. By abandoning the IETF and dismissing the FCC's order as being "too difficult," AOL effectively halted those efforts at interoperability.

26
PEER-TO-PEER
COMMUNICATION

One of the buzzwords in the computer business is *peer-to-peer,* or P2P. It is communication between two (or more) computers directly. It could be called *one-to-one* because they are essentially the same. This is unlike other communications models, such as *master/slave* or *client/server.* It denotes a level of operating inequality between the two (generally, one is more centrally located). In some cases, the P2P exchange might give each computer client/server capabilities. This exchange can be either public or private.

This chapter is about file sharing—hooking two computers together. It allows for an efficient way to exchange data without servers. It's a hot topic. The nuances between a P2P and a client/server connection are slight, but there are differences. The easiest way to explain this is to start by defining the terms and their associated parts.

THE CLIENT/SERVER MODEL

The term *client/server* was originally used to distinguish networked computing from the monolithic centralized mainframe model of computing. (In reality, this distinction is a moot point, because today's mainframe applications are heavily client/server and networked.) A client/server communication relationship is never equal. The computers communicate through the server program that establishes a hierarchy.

The program running on a computer can ask for and receive only a very particular and specialized type of data. The other computer will send only the data requested. Neither computer can vary from the limitations of the specific client/server program. This is a common network setup and a convenient way to interconnect computers at different locations to share common data in a very controlled way. These transactions are very common. For instance, if you check your account balance at a bank from your home computer, it initiates a client/server program. The client program in your computer forwards a request to the bank's server computer. That request will be forwarded on to other programs in the system, ultimately sending the request to the database server to retrieve your account balance. It's given back up the line of command to the bank's server, then passed to your client program and displayed for you.

The client/server model is a foundation of network computing. Most business applications use it. The basic Internet communication protocol, TCP/IP, supports the client/server model. One server, commonly called a *daemon*, is activated and awaits a client request. Many people can access the same server program at the same time. On the Internet, your Web browser program is a client program and can request services from a dedicated Web server. These services can include the sending of Web pages or files. This is called Hypertext Transport Protocol (HTTP). Your computer's TCP/IP allows you to make client requests from File Transfer Protocol (FTP) servers in other computers on the Internet.

Client

Clients communicate only with servers for information. Clients cannot request information from other clients. Clients and servers can be both software and/or hardware in their design. Web browsers are a good example of client software. The Web browser on your computer requests a Web page from a Web browser located on a remote online computer, where a server program fulfills the request and sends a *response* back to the browser. The browser then renders and displays the information it receives back from a server.

A browser is an application program that provides a way to look at and interact with information on the Internet. The browser is a client program that uses HTTP to make requests to other computers. Some browsers in common use are: Mosaic, Microsoft Internet Explorer, Netscape, Lynx (a text-only browser for UNIX shell and VMS users), and Opera.

Server

A server is a program running on a computer waiting to process a request that originates from a client. The server then provides the results to the client. Servers are the workhorses of the Internet.

In Greek mythology, a *daemon* was an attendant power or spirit. In a similar fashion, this is an ever-ready program. It exists only to handle periodic service requests that a computer system may receive. It's a little like the coat check clerk whose sole employment purpose is to wait for someone to check or fetch a coat. The daemon program forwards the request to other programs, as needed. Each server of pages on the Web has an HTTP daemon (HTTPD) that continuously waits for requests to come in from Web clients. This is not to be confused with a *demon*, which is a program or part of a larger program. The program will lay dormant until something wakes it to action, such as a help system or the annoying little animated paper clip in Microsoft Office Help.

Distributed Computing

Distributed computing is the idea that resources on other computers in other locations can contain information that your computer can access (as though it were on your computer). Distributed computing has various computers working with each other to increase computing power. Distributed comput-

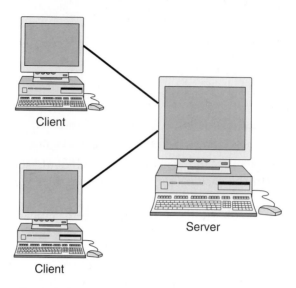

FIGURE 26.1 **CLIENT/SERVER CONNECTIVITY.**

ing can have a central location that routes the communications (host/master, or client/server; see Figure 26.1) or can exchange data without a central point (P2P; see Figure 26.2) or can have a hybrid of the two.

THE P2P MODEL

P2P has come to describe a way for people to use the Internet to exchange files with each other directly or through a mediating server. To put this simply, a group of users decide they want to make files on their computers avail-

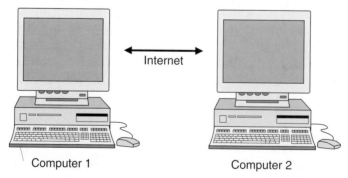

FIGURE 26.2 **P2P COMPUTERS AND CLIENTS ALSO ACT AS SERVERS.**

able to other users who might want them; a central computer is set up to index these files; and all the users use the same software and formatting to make everything work. You decide you want a specific file. You go search on the central computer for an index for the file you want. Three are located. Sammy, Betty, and Joe each have a file you want. (You don't know any of these people, but they've got the same software you do, and the files have been designated as accessible.) You've accessed from Joe's computer before, and his files are good quality. So you go directly to Joe's computer and download the file. This is very similar to how the MP3 file-sharing software on Napster worked. (In the case of Napster, however, files went through a centralized server.)

Ironically, this is very similar to early online practices when one person with a modem would contact another person with a modem to exchange files. In those days, the contact might be made because of a listing on an old bulletin board system. Let's say that someone was looking for a specific computer program, and the listing said that Bob had it and gave information on how to contact Bob.

Now it's a transient network. A group of users with the same networking program can find each other without going to a bulletin board, listing server, or other third party. The person with files to offer will list them, and people who are looking can browse. The two will connect with each other directly to access files from one another's hard drives. To facilitate the process, there are software-based listing programs to serve as intermediaries. The program will list the people who have the file you're looking for. Because there is no central location, these listings are always in flux. You may not see a file source twice, depending on how many people are connected.

Most of today's P2P networking software programs are freeware or shareware. These are distributed in a variety of ways (Figure 26.3). You can go to a Web site and download a copy, usually at the recommendation of a friend, or a friend can give you a copy of it. To date, the most popular clients have been Kazaa Media Desktop (kazaa.com), BadBlue (badblue.com), and BearShare (bearshare.com). Napster, Gnutella, and IRC are examples of software designed for of P2P interaction.

BENEFITS OF P2P

- Simple way to share files with friends
- Quick access to other shared files online

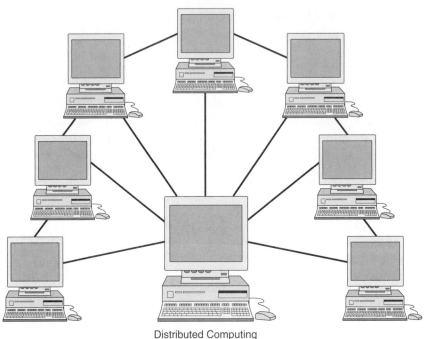

Distributed Computing

FIGURE 26.3 **DISTRIBUTED COMPUTING.**

DRAWBACKS OF P2P

- Your P2P client may come bundled with spyware. For more information on spyware, please refer to Chapter 11.

- You need to open a "port" on your network, giving people access to certain files on your hard drive.

- You may very well inadvertently download and install a virus or Trojan. More information on these malicious programs can be found in Chapter 12.

Napster

This was a P2P program that worked as an intermediary. It was a central server that looked at your computer/song list. When someone logged on and searched for a specific song, Napster would look through the index and locate a list of the available versions of that song on various computers. You'd then contact an individual who had the song on their list. (Napster sold to Roxio for $5.3 million in 2002.)

Gnutella (not to be confused with Nutella, the hazelnut/chocolate spread)

This program was developed by NullSoft (creators of WinAMP). It was never publicly released. (Nullsoft's parent corporation was AOL. AOL declared the work an "unauthorized publication.") However, the beta version became an open source program. The offspring of the beta version were free from AOL control.

This system was similar to Napster. Individuals could exchange files over the Internet directly. Also like Napster (and similar Web sites), Gnutella is a way to download and share music files (which is why it has been of concern for the music publishing industry). Unlike Napster, Gnutella is not a central Web server. Instead, it's a sort of daisy-chain. Gnutella users directly see the files of a small number of other users, who in turn can see the files of others. Napster was limited to MP3 music files. Gnutella allows downloads of any file type.

With the Gnutella software the user's computer becomes a node. It's both a client and a server in the network. It shares designated files with other Gnutella users. Individuals exchange information with each other without supervision or restriction of an intermediary or third-party server.

IRC

Internet Relay Chat (IRC) is a system to converse with other people via text on your computer. It is similar to AOL's Instant Messenger (AIM) and ICQ ("I Seek You"). It involves software you install on your computer that is P2P in nature. For more information, see Chapter 7 and Chapter 25.

Current and Future Uses

During the last 10 years, there have been many changes in P2P applications in different scenarios and environments. The advancement of telecommunication technologies, such as cable, satellite, wireless, and broadband, form the foundation of digital communications. Increased demands for communication and file sharing will increase the demand for P2P software.

DVORAK'S LEGALITIES TIP

P2P software can be used in both an authorized and an unauthorized capacity. Illegal uses include the sharing or transferring of illegal information, intellectual property, and so forth. As more laws come into place to protect these things, the likelihood of legal retribution will increase. The user will need to stay informed and aware of what constitutes *legal* and *illegal*.

Private

Private P2P networks are a way for clubs and groups to communicate and exchange information. Most people online today are using email to communicate and exchange files. P2P software would make the communication more dynamic and personal. For instance, private clubs such as the Boy Scouts, the Sierra Club, the Girl Scouts, and church groups could use P2P networking to provide private and secure information to their members.

Private computer clubs and user groups have also found many uses for P2P software. In fact, in the last five years, it has become more commonplace for people to participate in discussions and attend meetings online than in person.

Personal Use

A personal P2P can keep family members in touch. It is an efficient way to discuss personal topics with friends and associates. It's also a way to keep track of personal appointments, to coordinate events, to share information, and to stay in touch.

Public P2P

Most public P2P systems were created to solve problems inherent in email, such as latency, junk mail, spam, and restrictions (such as attachment size). Email has been a basic way for the public to stay in touch and exchange files, pictures, and programs. The new generation of P2P software programs perform these functions more efficiently. They are expected to be embraced by the online community.

THE PROBLEMS WITH EMAIL

Email's biggest problems concern time and space. Email is very slow and requires storage on four systems. You have to wait for it to be sent, processed, stored, then read. Email works like this:

The sender creates a message on his/her local machine.

They then "sends" or uploads the message to the POP server at their Internet Service Provider (ISP).

This POP server then transfers the message to the POP server at the receiver's ISP.

The message is then finally downloaded to the receiver's machine to be read.

> P2P systems bypass the slower email protocols and enable users to send and receive messages with fewer servers in the loop. Even better, they allow for instant messages, real-time communications, and the exchanging and sharing of files with fewer steps involved.

The Security of P2P

Programmers who developed today's public P2P systems were motivated by personal reasons. Privacy and security were not high on their priority lists. Today's systems normally connect through a Web port (80) and route all communications through central servers, where it is easier for snoopers and hackers to monitor them.

Small companies have recently introduced add-on software in an attempt to plug these security holes. One such program is IMPasse, a $20 program that sits on a machine alongside AIM, MSN Messenger, and Yahoo! Messenger and encrypts whole or parts of conversations. Akonix released a similar security application earlier in 2002. Though these are admirable attempts to plug security holes "after the fact," new P2P systems are designed at the protocol level to be secure, giving users a more complete security solution.

CORPORATE/ENTERPRISE SYSTEMS

It is not surprising that corporations have become interested in P2P technologies to enhance efficiency in their daily operations. It could facilitate employee communications with things such as instant messaging and data management programs.

Finance, administration, marketing, and sales are particularly well suited for P2P programs because of the real-time communication and collaboration capabilities. There are now several corporate versions of P2P programs that can be customized in numerous ways. IBM/Lotus's new P2P software, Sametime AnyPlace, and HBN's new Enterprise Guide with Business Messaging are just a few of the new P2P systems that can provide quality, secure solutions to the corporate world.

The main reason for the growth of corporate P2P software is because the public versions of P2P software (such as ICQ, AIM, and Yahoo! Messenger) have deficiencies that need to be addressed in the competitive markets of today. Deficiencies in *privacy* and *security* are high on the list. Corporate versions of P2P programs developed to overcome such deficiencies are costlier to implement and maintain.

EDUCATION

Education-based P2P technologies are beginning to be used by major institutions, such as colleges, universities, and private schools. It may be a natural fit for P2P software to become part of the education process because the majority of the people currently using P2P software are students and teenagers. Of the over 100 million users of current public P2P chat and file-sharing programs, approximately 60 million are between the ages of 13 and 24.

Specialized educational P2P software will need to connect student users with the faculty in a more efficient and manageable way than current Web-based intranets. Remote learning programs will benefit the most by using P2P software because of their reliance on the Internet and on successful communication and collaboration.

The biggest challenge for the schools that choose to implement P2P technologies will not be what content to share or information to distribute; it will be providing a P2P system that will address *privacy* and *security* for both the administration and the students.

ENTERTAINMENT

The big question in the entertainment industry is, "How do we make money from P2P software?"

There are many legal issues surrounding the use of P2P technologies and the entertainment industry. Most issues are centered on the illegal copying and sharing of copyrighted materials. There is a legal push to secure copyrighted materials on behalf of the music industry, in particular. This will directly affect all other areas of entertainment.

The "Holy P2P Grail" that the entertainment industry is seeking will likely be a combination of a TV/cable guide and an entertainment network-based search engine. This network guide will have to include pay-for-view and pay-to-play capabilities, as well as the basic P2P functions, such as chat, instant messaging, and file sharing.

Once IPv6 (the new broadband IP addressing protocol for the Internet) becomes widely deployed, expect more movies, music, TV, and other basic analog-based broadcast technologies to migrate to the community. However, the entertainment industry will probably be the last place that legal P2P technologies are deployed successfully.

Government

The government is one of the biggest users of P2P technologies. P2P technologies are specifically suited for government work because of their dynamic ability to communicate and transfer information in both the wired and wireless environments. When used as a complementary system to VPNs (Virtual Private Networks), today's secure P2P technologies are providing the kinds of collaboration and networking tools needed for real-time communication systems in both peacetime and wartime.

During the late 1990s, the government was involved in the review and implementation of different types of P2P technologies rapidly becoming available in the public sector. The Department of Defense authorized various types of P2P software for use in the campaign against terrorism in the Middle East. (Some of the 9/11 terrorists used P2P technologies to collaborate prior to the attack on America.) By using applied cryptography, burst technologies, frequency skipping, and other high-tech techniques, P2P technologies can become more secure.

A Basic Overview of P2P Legal Issues

This section lays out some of the laws related to P2P networking. There are a few things to remember when trying to decide whether certain P2P software is illegal to use or whether certain uses of it are considered illegal. Understanding how these laws can affect you and which actions may cause you some legal discomfort may help you avoid such situations.

This overview is not to be considered as legal advice but more as a source for understanding the possible legal issues that may arise from the use of various P2P software programs. Check with qualified legal counsel before using any P2P software that the United States judicial system has deemed illegal. If you are using a P2P network for your business, you may also want to check into any security and privacy compliance issues.

The best safeguard against legal action when using P2P software is to follow some simple, common-sense rules. Ask yourself the following questions.

- Am I doing something I know is wrong?
- Am I doing something I know (or should know) is illegal?
- Am I willing to pay the price if caught?

Once you have made it past those three questions, ask yourself the next three questions.

- Is the software legal to use in the manner I wish to use it?

- Was the software designed to be used in the manner I wish to use it?

- Have the software and/or its designers been involved in any current or past legal actions?

The Laws

There are some major laws now on the books that could affect P2P technologies. Most of these laws work in unison with other laws against fraud, theft, and harassment. The scope of this isn't to discuss all legal ramifications but just to provide a short overview.

17 USC 00 101-810 United States Copyright Act

The copyright laws of the United States of America are meant to protect the creators of art, music, movies, and literature from loss due to unauthorized use of their works.

Current copyright law originates from the copyright clause of the United States Constitution.

The Copyright Act of 1976 states that any work submitted to be copyrighted must be original and independently created, and must possess a measure of creativity.

It is interesting to note that actual registration is not required for copyright protection. Original works are now considered protected upon their creation. The only good reason to actually register an original work is that it provides the creator with additional legal protection if an infringement suit arises.

COPPA 1998 Children's Online Privacy Protection Act

COPPA protects the privacy of children using the Internet. It puts parents in control over the information collected from their children online and is flexible enough to accommodate the many business practices and technological changes occurring on the Internet.

The statutes and rules apply to commercial Web sites and online services that are directed to or that knowingly collect information from children under 13. To inform parents of their information practices, these sites will be required to provide notice on the site and to parents about their policies with respect to the collection, use, and disclosure of children's personal information.

With certain statutory exceptions, sites will also have to obtain "verifiable parental consent" before collecting, using, or disclosing personal information from children. The rule became effective on April 21, 2000, giving Web sites six months to come into compliance with the COPPA regulations and requirements.

CALEA 1994 Communications Assistance for Law Enforcement Act

CALEA was passed in 1994 in response to rapid advances in telecommunications technology, such as the implementation of digital technology and wireless services that have threatened the ability of law enforcement officials to conduct authorized electronic surveillance.

CALEA requires telecommunications carriers to ensure that their equipment, facilities, and services are able to comply with authorized electronic surveillance. These assistance capabilities were originally due to be available by October 25, 1998, but the Commission deferred the deadline until June 30, 2000.

Carriers that were unable to provide the required capabilities could petition the Commission for an extension of the deadline or for a determination that compliance is not reasonably achievable.

TCA 1996 Telecommunications Act

On February 1, 1996, the 104th Congress of the United States passed the United States Telecommunications Act. This act promotes competition and reduces regulation in order to secure lower prices and higher quality of services for American telecommunications consumers, as well as to encourage the rapid deployment of new telecommunication technologies. The Telecommunications Act recognizes the telecommunications network as a network of interconnected networks.

DMCA 1998 Digital Millennium Copyright Act

The U.S. Congress passed the Digital Millennium Copyright Act on October 12, 1998. President Clinton signed the act into law on October 28th of the same year.

The DMCA was originally supported by both the entertainment and computer software industries. It is interesting that scientists, librarians, and educational groups were opposed to the DMCA, citing that it could possibly constrict technological development. The reason the DMCA was implemented was to include various laws that were ratified by the World Intellectual Property Organization (WIPO) at its conference in Geneva in December 1996.

The DMCA makes it illegal to circumvent antipiracy measures built into most commercial software and outlaws the manufacture, sale, or distribution of code-cracking devices used to copy software illegally. Even though the DMCA does not permit the cracking of copyright protection devices, it does allow developers to conduct encryption research, assess product interoperability, and test computer security systems. The DMCA also provides exemptions from anticircumvention provisions for such areas of commerce as nonprofit libraries, archives, and educational institutions under certain circumstances.

One of the more positive sides of the DMCA is that it protects ISPs from copyright infringement liability for transmitting information over the Internet. Service providers, however, are expected to remove material from users' Web sites that appears to constitute copyright infringement.

The DMCA also requires "webcasters" who broadcast streaming video or audio content on the Internet to pay licensing fees to the creators of the streamed media, such as record companies. This act alone led to the shutdown of most online radio stations and streaming media sites during 2000 and 2001.

USAPA 2001 United States of America Patriot Act

The USAPA was passed "to deter and punish terrorist acts in the United States and around the world, to enhance law enforcement investigatory tools, and for other purposes." The law also creates a new relationship between domestic criminal investigations and investigations related to foreign intelligence. Most of the new surveillance powers granted will expire after four years, pursuant to the statute's sunset provisions.

The USAPA provides federal agencies with more surveillance options and less judicial supervision. The court order permitting surveillance, like the statute, will require investigators to submit to various forms of limitations and judicial supervision, but because the point is to gather intelligence rather than evidence, challenges to the legality of surveillance aren't likely. The USAPA allows surveillance and monitoring of U.S. citizens, who may never even know they have been under surveillance.

Three Common Legal Defenses in P2P Suits

Defendants in P2P copyright infringement suits usually assert one of three defenses. There will undoubtedly be more to come in the continued legal wrangling between the developers and marketers of P2P software and the entertainment giants who wish to control the marketplace.

- **No Direct Infringer** ("all users are innocent fair users"): The main difficulty with this defense is it can be difficult to ensure that every end user is indeed engaged in fair use. The future of P2P file sharing is entwined, for better or worse, with copyright law.

- **The Sony Betamax Defense** ("capable of substantial noninfringing uses"): Until the recent Napster decision, this was perhaps the most promising defense. In light of the Ninth Circuit's interpretation of this defense, it may be of limited value once anyone receives a "cease and desist" letter from a copyright owner.

- **The DMCA Section 512** ("safe harbors"): These may provide a defense for certain systems (search engines, instant messengers, P2P software, and ISPs) that satisfy the stringent statutory prerequisites applying to the safe harbors. Because basic architecture decisions may influence a system's eligibility for these defenses, an IM/P2P developer would be well advised to consider the limits of each possible defense in order to evaluate the legal risks posed by any particular system design.

A Legal Look at Napster

Three major technologies brought P2P technologies to the forefront of the legal scene: MP3s, CDR/RWs, and chatrooms/file exchange programs, such as ICQ. Napster's Shawn Fanning was the one person to pull them all together to provide a free "music-sharing" network. Without the legal rulings that caused Napster's demise, P2P systems might be regarded as just another basic networking utility. Unfortunately for Shawn and Napster, the original reason for creating Napster (documented in Napster's business plan) was illegal.

NAPSTER TIMELINE

The following timeline will highlight the very up-and-down saga of Napster, Shawn Fanning, and the music industry's legal fight to shut down the music-sharing service. It is meant to give you a history of the legal battles and an idea of the money that becomes involved when technologies such as P2P take on giants such as the music industry.

6/1999—Napster, Inc. launched from simple core of about 30 users.

12/1999—The RIAA (Recording Industry Association of America) brings a 20 billion dollar lawsuit against Napster in federal court for copyright infringement.

4/2000—Metallica sues Napster for copyright infringement and racketeering. Shawn Fanning gets "bummed out" about the suit.

4/2000—Dr. Dre files suit against Napster, and Napster starts to get some major press play on the three lawsuits (RIAA, Metallica, and Dr. Dre). Napster's user base increases almost tenfold.

5/2000—Metallica produces a list of over 335,000 people the band says illegally shared their songs through Napster.

5/2000—"Napster is not entitled to 'safe harbor' protection under the Digital Millennium Copyright Act," states U.S. District Judge Marilyn Hall Patel.

7/2000—Judge Patel grants RIAA's request for a preliminary injunction. Napster is ordered to shut down but vows to appeal the decision.

7/2000—"Substantial questions are raised about Patel's injunction," states the Ninth U.S. Circuit Court of Appeals, which stays the lower court injunction.

10/2000—U.S. Court of Appeals hears oral arguments by Napster and RIAA attorneys.

10/2000—Shawn Fanning is on the cover of *Time Magazine*.

10/2000—Bertelsmann AG announces a partnership with Napster to develop a membership-based distribution system to guarantee payments to artists. Bertelsmann AG (a former plaintiff against Napster) agrees to drop its lawsuit and allow Napster users access to its music catalog. Bertelsmann retains the right to buy a larger stake in the service.

10/2000—Napster announces it will develop a "legalized" file-sharing system. Napster looks into additional investments, such as a medical marijuana import service, "authorized" celebrity pornography, and offshore gambling.

2/2001—Napster has a court order to shut down due. Napster experiences first big loss of its users to other P2P programs, such as Morpheus and Kazaa.

2/2001—The Ninth Circuit Court of Appeals rules Napster must prevent its subscribers from gaining access to content on its search index. RIAA wins its first battle against the music-swapping service.

2/2001—The recording industry laughs at Napster's offer to give $1 billion to the record companies if they agree to drop their suit.

2/2001—The Ninth Circuit Court of Appeals orders Napster to cease facilitating the swapping of copyrighted songs. The U.S. District Court for Northern California is ordered to rewrite its injunction before closing Napster.

3/2001—Napster lawyers offer to provide a service to install software over the weekend to help satisfy the order to stop swapping copyrighted songs with Napster. Napster claims the software would block the swapping of approximately a million songs that had been singled out by the record labels and recording artists. New software does not work, and copyrighted songs are still traded.

3/2002—Shawn Fanning decides to sue Napster and its two directors.

4/2002—Napster claims, "A reduced need for foosball playing is the reason for recent employee layoffs."

5/2002—Bertelsmann AG acquires Napster for $8 million. Total invested in Napster by Bertelsmann AG, including the $8 million acquisition, now exceeds $85 million. Shawn slips into the background.

6/2002—Napster announced it would file for Chapter 11 bankruptcy protection. After accepting an $8 million buyout offer from Bertelsmann in May 2002, which is as of this writing still pending approval by the bankruptcy court, Napster would be controlled entirely by Bertelsmann.

7/2002—Despite the possible buyout by Bertelsmann, the various songwriters, recording artists, and music companies still seek damages owed from the exchanging of music on Napster. Alleged damages by the plaintiffs are estimated to be in the billions of dollars.

8/2002—The new executives at Bertelsmann suggest they might shut Napster down.

9/2002—Napster's chief executive says the company is headed for liquidation, and he is letting his staff go. He resigns.

SUMMARY

At the end of the day, P2P networks work. Sometimes all too well. Although friends may encourage you to hop aboard the "free music gravy train," remember what you're jumping into. Beyond legal issues surrounding this dynamic type of data exchange, you may have to contend with software headaches that would not have plagued you, had you not opened your computer to these various file-exchange systems. If you want to "try before you buy," you'll find that many "official" sites allow you to sample tracks or demo software.

It's what all the cool kids are doing.

27
INTERNET LAW

The chances are slim that anything you do on or with the Internet will get you into legal trouble. But it is possible. Downloading music, libeling, offering *warez* software, trying to auction stolen items, running a kiddie porn site—there are a lot of possibilities. Although we don't think the readers of this book are likely to get into such trouble, it's often good to know what the limits are regarding the law and the Internet.

With that said, the next 20 or so pages will not disclose a thousand ways to use the Net fraudulently and get away with it. This chapter is about the Internet and the law—from a social, historical, and most important, practical perspective.

But if your actions won't be subject to legal scrutiny, why read any further?

Who really cares about the Internet and the law, especially if you're neither a lawyer nor an Internet professional? Although there are probably dozens of answers to this question, here are three good ones:

- To know what actions break the law and what the consequences are

- To protect yourself from others who break the law and may infringe on your freedoms—speech, privacy, ownership of property, and unhindered access to technology

- To get the inside story on those who break the law and get caught— because such stories generally pique interest

DISCLAIMER

The writers, publishers, and editors of this book (collectively, the publishers), including but not limited to its assignees, licensees, subsidiaries, and partners, assume no liability for the actions of you, the reader, regardless whether they are the direct or indirect consequence of the materials discussed in this forum. The writings set forth in this chapter are the sole views of the authors and make no claims to the content's accuracy. The work should not be construed as legal advice or an unbiased recount of factual proceedings. By reading further, you acknowledge that you have read and agree to the aforementioned statements made in this disclaimer and indemnify the publishers against any act committed by you, the reader. If you do not agree to the terms set forth or if any portions of such terms are unclear, do not continue to read this chapter.

HOW INTERNET LAW DIFFERS

All laws are subject to change. This in itself is not unique. In 1776, slavery was legal. In 1876, segregation was legal. And in 1976, neither was legal. But unlike more traditional areas of law, the Internet has novel elements that cause legal uncertainty and volatility, as discussed in the following sections.

AGE OF THE INTERNET

The Internet is so young that only a fraction of its legal implications have been addressed. Passing laws and adjudicating cases involving them takes time.

GLOBAL REACH

A country's border defines the reach of its laws. Every country in the world has its particular version of *the law*. An act illegal in one country may not be in another. Laws between countries have always been agreements, treaties, and other diplomatic arrangements. For the most part, the law is enforceable only in that country. The Internet muddies this because communication over the Internet is oblivious to territorial borders. It may be impossible to adhere to all the laws in all the areas the Internet touches. It may be impractical. The question becomes one of whether any country can impose laws on users outside its jurisdiction.

CONSTANT EVOLUTION

Internet technology changes so rapidly that it is difficult to produce a set of rules specific enough to regulate it effectively yet general enough to remain current and complete.

Historians claim that history repeats itself; the cause and effects of yesterday can be used to predict or at least explain today and tomorrow. The Internet is a frontier of sorts. It is a place where the sheriff is in charge so long as someone with more strength or wit doesn't come along. On this frontier, the view rapidly changes as gold seekers settle unexplored territory and in the process introduce unforeseen side effects, making the traditional rules governing our way of life inadequate for or inapplicable to all cases.

Similar to other areas of communication law, Internet law is primarily concerned with protecting citizens' rights with regard to four areas—ownership of property, privacy and security, and freedom of speech.

Ownership of Property

Copyright, patent, and trademark law (the law of *intellectual property*) protects rights of ownership to published work, invention or innovative method, and business mark of identity. The ironic supposition is that the government needs to be involved at all in *your* ownership of *your* own work.

From the U.S. government's standpoint, its role is not to limit natural and rightful ownership of property (intellectual or otherwise). It is to uphold an uncontested right over it. It's not to say that you don't own something until the government says you do. It's when a problem arises. When someone else says they also own *your* something. That is when the need arises for unquestionable verification for proof of ownership (if the need so arises). It's at that point the government may step in.

There has been an alarming rise in copyright infringement by individuals. It is trivial now for the average person to duplicate and distribute published information. This is due largely to the increased personal use of computers and the Internet. Faster computers, high-speed Internet connections, CD and DVD burners, and new media formats offer better quality of sound and smaller video files. Most notably, the popularity of peer-to-peer (P2P) file-sharing programs (such as Napster) have allowed millions of Americans to trade pirated copies of music and other media files online—an act that is socially acceptable in the eyes of many Internet users yet illegal in the eyes of the law.

From a technical standpoint, P2P file sharing (covered in Chapter 26) involves a publicly accessible private network to share content efficiently among multiple computers. Although this network is accessible to the public, it is private in the sense that it uses a specialized communication protocol. In other words, special software is needed to connect to and communicate over the network. This network is made up of a collection of personal computers that act both as servers (providers of content) and as clients (requesters of information). P2P file sharing operates around a central indexing server that keeps track of the computers on the network and what content they have to share.

As an example, if someone is looking for a file (e.g., an MP3 copy of Elvis Presley's *Jailhouse Rock*), the computer will query the indexing server for the names and locations of the computers on the network having files that contain the word *jailhouse* and/or *rock*. The indexing server returns its findings. Then the seeking computer can directly contact one of the computers listed and download the file.

Nothing is inherently illegal or immoral with file-sharing technology. In fact, it has revolutionized the relationship between servers and clients. It is an important technology in many ways. What is illegal is 50 million people sharing copyrighted media files without the permission of their respective owners.

NAPSTER

The practice of sharing copyrighted files was unregulated for almost two years. A highly publicized copyright lawsuit turned the tables. The Recording Industry Association of America (RIAA) accused Napster of violating the Digital Millennium Copyright Act (DMCA) by allowing copyrighted material to be illegally distributed through the Napster network. Napster facilitated two parties in finding each other in order to break the law—knowingly and repeatedly.

Napster's defense was that it was an Internet Service Provider (ISP). Therefore, it was not Napster's responsibility to monitor user activity, and Napster was protected under a "safe harbor" clause of the DMCA. The law protects an ISP by not holding it accountable for a crime committed when one of its users transcribes copyrighted text and transmits it through email.

Napster's claim was that it should not be held liable for individuals' copyright violations. The question was, Did the users have the right to trade music under a *fair use* policy?

This is a provision that allows copyrighted materials to be exchanged, published, or copied without the permission of the owner in certain specific (and limited) instances. It's why people are allowed to make audiotaped copies of records and use videotapes to record a program for viewing later or to give to a friend.

In July 2000, federal judge Marilyn Patel issued a preliminary injunction against Napster. It mandated a halt to the distribution of copyrighted material. In her ruling, she found that the exchange of copyrighted material was not "fair use" and made up the vast majority of Napster usage. The users of the service were able to take advantage of a product they'd normally have to pay for. The economic benefit was at the expense of the recording companies (not fair use).

NAPSTER'S ATTEMPT TO SURVIVE

From the ruling came a challenge to try to allow the continued legal use of the service while preventing the transfer of copyrighted materials. It could be feasible to block specific files with specific file names or specific keywords from being transferred. These two methods of filtering were not accurate enough to stop Napster's illegal use. As quickly as measures were put into place, enthusiastic music fans devised creative ways to circumvent Napster's efforts.

Most notably, a program called *Aimster Pig Encoder* scrambled file names and searches in a pig-Latin-like fashion. Aimster's encoding scheme was simple. It would take a file name, such as *Another One Bites the Dust,* and rename it to *notherA neO itesB het ustD.* As a counter-measure, one would expect Napster to employ a simple decoding method to block searches and file transfers with the Pig Encoder in use. But there's a catch: The DMCA (the same copyright act that put the nail in Napster's coffin) also made it illegal to reverse-engineer encryption designed to *protect* copyrighted works.

COPYRIGHT

To obtain a registered copyright, you must submit a copy of the work (as well as a fee and application form) to the Unites States Copyright Office. It in turn files it in its archives and supplies you with a certification document. For more information on the benefits of and how to obtain a registered copyright, visit the United States Copyright Office Web site at www.copyright.gov or talk to an intellectual property attorney.

Other Protection Methods

If you don't feel the need to register your work officially but do want to protect it and notify others that you are the rightful owner, you simply assert copyright. Although this is not a registration, it is for practical purposes sufficient to protect your rights as the author (or owner) of a work.

Asserting copyright asserts your ownership of a work of authorship. If you need to assert such ownership in a United States court, however, you may be required to have registered a copy of your work. Luckily, you can retroactively register a work if you can prove the work was created at a certain time.

 To assert a copyright over your work, whether or not you've registered it, all that is needed is a copyright notice. Generally, such a declaration consists of:

The copyright symbol (©) or the word *copyright*

The year of creation

The phrase "all rights reserved"

Thus, a copyright notice looks like:

© 2003 Prentice Hall, or Copyright 2003 Prentice Hall

DOMAIN NAMES

If you've gotten rights to a domain name, particularly within one of the more common top-level domains (.com, .net, .org), you know how hard it can be to find one. What makes it even more frustrating is that many desirable ones have been registered but are not in use. This is called *squatting*.

This commonplace scenario is frustrating, especially when a domain name is desired for a specific use, such as corporate branding. Domain squatting is quite common. Recent legal precedents have set tight restrictions on it, especially when trademark infringement is at issue.

> The clash of domain names and trademark law is a broad, changing subject. *The Domain Name Handbook: High Stakes and Strategies in Cyberspace* by Ellen Rony and Peter Rony, R&D Books: Lawrence Kansas, 1998 (www.domainhandbook.com/dd.html) is a good choice if you want more information on this slippery subject. The book provides a practical history of the policies, controversies, and initiatives associated with the domain name system.

THE ODD COUPLE: INTERNET AND TRADEMARK LAW

Loosely defined, a trademark is a symbol, picture, phrase, or other representation (a "mark") used to identify a company. The *golden arches* are a widely recognized symbol (and trademark) of McDonalds. They give it a particular persona to identify the business.

A trademark is generally protected within the geographic locale of a business and within a specific business sector. As an example: You are in Omaha, Nebraska and want to start a pen and stationery business called *Ink, Inc.* A New York company has the same (or similar) name. This will not prevent you from doing business unless the New York company already has a store in Omaha, Nebraska. What's more, you can start a heating and cooling business called *AA Hot* even if there's already a hot dog company by the same name.

The catch is, the Internet knows no such boundaries. To operate an online bookstore on the Internet is to operate it in Hartford, Connecticut; Dallas, Texas; Jacksonville, Florida; and every other city and town in the United States (and sometimes the world). Traditional *brick-and-mortar* trademarked companies have established an online presence. The problem arises when those with similar names (or even identical trademarks) that once were in isolation are now in competition.

Delta Airlines, for example, has trademarked its name and has registered the domain name *delta.com*. Delta Faucets, on the other hand, has also trademarked its name and probably would jump at the chance to acquire the domain name currently being used by Delta Airlines. Cases such as this are treated on a first-come, first-serve basis. When two companies both have unquestionable legal uses for or rights to a domain name, the first one to register it obtains indefinite control.

As long as the domain name holder has an unquestionable right to the name, this practice causes little concern. It is the squatter who obtains an attractive domain name with the intent to sell it for an excessive profit or registers a name that is similar to that of another site (with the intent of benefiting from the confusion) who is infringing on others' rights. However, some companies have gone after a domain even though the holder of it had no intention of selling it.

VERONICA, POKEY, AND STRICK

In 1999, a trademark-driven domain battle was well publicized in the media. It involved veronica.org. The Web site was set up by David Sams to honor his then two-year old daughter, Veronica. The site featured photos of the toddler. Archie Comics wanted the name and claimed that it held a trademark on the name Veronica, the brunette character in its classic series. After a media focus, bad publicity and all, the company backed down. This never reached court.

A similar fight ensued between the Prema Toy Company and 12-year-old Web designer Chris Van Allen's pokey.org. The toy company wanted to shut down the child's site, due to trademark infringement. (Prema Toy owns Gumby and his horse, Pokey.) The toy company backed down when the creator of Pokey, Art Clokey, stepped in and said the boy should have his site. It still belongs to Chris Van Allen.

In the case of *James B. Strickland v. Strick Corporation*, the company sought the rights to the domain *strick.com*. Mr. Strickland was a computer consultant and software developer. In 1995, he tried to get his last name, found it was taken, then registered his nickname (strick) as strick.com. The corporation wanted the name and claimed unfair competition and trademark dilution.

Judge Bruce W. Kaufman of the U.S. District Court, Eastern District of Pennsylvania, found in Mr. Strickland's favor. "It is clear that nothing in trademark law requires that title to domain names that incorporate trademarks or portions of trademarks be provided to trademark holders. To hold otherwise would create an immediate and indefinite monopoly to all famous mark holders on the Internet, by which they could lay claim to all .com domain names. . . . Trademark law does not support such a monopoly."

This was a key ruling. Prior to this decision, courts generally ruled that individual domain name registrants were required to release domain names that contained trademarks to the trademark holders. This ruling, as well as others, reversed the trend. A decision such as this shows that the courts seek a balance between the rights of individual domain name holders and the need to apply trademark law to the Internet.

Internet Corporation for Assigned Names and Numbers

Network Solutions, Inc. (NSI) was the original grantor of domain names. It assigned names on a first-come, first-serve basis. NSI was quickly sued for helping infringement by granting registrations that were similar or the same as valid trademarks. It avoided liability by citing the absence of knowledge of wrongdoing and setting up a domain dispute policy that allowed owners of federally registered trademarks to complain against holders of identical domain names. If the holder had no federal trademark registration, the ownership of the domain was forfeited.

The policy was flawed. It did not recognize that trademark rights do not apply to noncommercial users. It did not protect state and common law trademark holders. *Reverse domain hijacking* began, where a trademark owner would use NSI to leverage its rights where the law would not have permitted it. This is how Archie Comics tried to grab veronica.org, as discussed earlier.

The NSI policy was flawed in other ways, as well. For instance, it could be used against only domain names that were exactly the same as the federal trademark. Misspellings and obvious typos, among other things, were not covered. (Errors on a Web address could take a person from a legitimate site to a porn site that floods the screen with unrelenting multiple windows, the only recourse for which would be to turn off the computer.)

THE ORIGINS OF THE INTERNET CORPORATION FOR ASSIGNED NAMES AND NUMBERS

In 1993, NSI was given a contract with the U.S. National Science Foundation (NSF). It was called the *cooperative agreement* to administer the domain name system (DNS). The terms of the agreement covered only second-level domain (SLD) names, such as *dvorak* in *dvorak.org* (within the top-level domains *.com, .net,* and *.org),* which were to be given free, on demand, on a first-come, first-serve basis). No one anticipated back then that it would be anything more than a low-demand, simple administrative job. No one else wanted to do it.

InterNIC (Internet Network Information Center) and NSI were the subject of a great deal of criticism by 1995, when the cooperative agreement was amended to allow a fee for the service ($100 for two years; only $30 went to the NSF). In 1996, the critics became louder. NSI was accused of slow service and an ineffective resolution policy. The detractors mounted a campaign to challenge NSI's hold on the service. There was a great deal of infighting and debate.

The Internet Corporation for Assigned Names and Numbers (ICANN), a nonprofit global organization, was formed as part of a new U.S. Government Statement of Policy in October of 1998. A compromise was reached. NSI, ICANN, and the Department of Commerce agreed to let NSI provide several million dollars of funding support for ICANN in exchange for the right to maintain exclusivity over the registry function for four to possibly eight years, depending on certain conditions and provisions. Then the service would be open to competition, as it is today.

In late 1999, the ICANN, the central authority in the United States for the administration of domain names, adopted the Uniform Domain Name Dispute Resolution Policy. In it, ICANN states the exact circumstances in which a domain name license can be disputed or revoked. Explicitly, it states that your rights to a domain name can be retracted if:

- The domain name is identical or confusingly similar to a trademark or service mark in which the complainant has rights.

- You have no rights or legitimate interests with respect to the domain name.

- It is used in bad faith.

Bad faith exists when the individual has registered the domain in order to sell or rent it, prevent a trademark owner from possessing rights over it, disrupt the business of a competitor, or attract traffic from the confusion of the domain with another domain or trademark.

KODAK THEATER

In the summer of 2001, the Eastman Kodak Corporation brought a complaint against a California resident who purchased a set of eight domain names (including kodaktheatre.com and kodaktheatre.org) after Kodak announced a business venture using the name Kodak Theatre. It wasn't until Kodak was approached and given the opportunity to buy the domains for $100,000 apiece that Kodak noticed the infringement. The company brought the dispute to the National Arbitration Forum. Former judge Carolyn Marks Johnson ordered that the domains be transferred to Kodak, concluding that they had been registered in bad faith and were similar to a trademark held by Kodak.

Domain Disputes

If you feel your rights to a domain name have been challenged, you have recourse. You can hire an attorney. Or you can file an ICANN dispute. A complaint can be made to one of several dispute resolution service providers (your choice) listed on ICANN's Web site. In addition to the list of providers, you'll find sample complaint forms, additional rules and limitations on filing a complaint, and a copy of the dispute resolution policy.

PRIVACY AND SECURITY

With the advancement of technology comes greater efficiency. But it comes at a price—privacy and security. In the days before computerized commerce, trade was less efficient. Centralized inventory systems did not exist. Statistical analysis of buying trends was more primitive. Goods in transit could not be tracked with the precision that we have today. Even supermarket checkout was manual.

There was a time when everyone would cut coupons from the newspaper and bring them to the store. Groceries were individually priced. The checker would enter the price of each item individually. Today, the cashier scans items with a barcode reader. The register, in turn, notes the price of the product. In place of coupons, a discount card is scanned in a card reader. Items can be purchased in an all non-cash transaction (ATM or credit cards). All this information is tied together in one or more databases. The information about your buying habits is mined and used for market research purposes, direct marketing, or whatever other uses various companies can think of. For example, a person buying disposable diapers on a Friday may also buy beer, or peanut butter purchases might also often include bread and sandwich baggies.

In our everyday shopping expeditions, there are at least half a dozen places where privacy could be compromised, especially if the security of the system that holds the information was itself compromised. Fortunately for consumers, there are some laws that protect our privacy. In many states, if we wish to be taken off mailing lists or have phone solicitors stop calling us, there are easily accessible means to such ends. But the Internet is a frontier where the laws of yesterday were not necessarily written (or appropriate) for the Internet. Consequently, many rights such as privacy will be compromised until legislation exists to protect us.

In January 2000, one of the Web's largest advertising networks, Double-Click, came under fire when it openly admitted to using Internet cookies to track surfing habits, online purchases, and other private personal data. It had announced plans to combine online consumer information with personally identifiable consumer data from its newly merged subsidiary, Abacus Direct. The point would be to compile a dossier to improve target advertisements to consumers based on their Web surfing habits. This triggered a tidal wave of protests from consumer groups and consumers alike.

The New York Attorney General's office began a 30-month investigation into the company. In August 2002, DoubleClick vowed to give consumers more information about how it collected data online. The agreement between DoubleClick and 10 states requires the company to explain on Web sites how it tracks and profiles Web surfers' usage data. In the agreement, it didn't admit wrongdoing but paid $450,000 to the states to cover the costs of the investigations and for consumer education. The states joining New York in the settlement were Arizona, California, Connecticut, Massachusetts, Michigan, New Jersey, New Mexico, Vermont, and Washington.

In May of that same year, DoubleClick paid $1.8 million and enacted new disclosure rules to settle an action brought by the Federal Trade Commission (FTC). Although neither the suits nor the investigation found DoubleClick in violation of any state or federal law, its practices served as a red alert for consumers.

DoubleClick's focus changed to building anonymous profiling products that take advantage of Abacus's wealth of data-mining capabilities without triggering further privacy problems. The company went ahead with plans for PredictiveMail, a combined email and direct mail marketing service. It's called an *intelligent targeted advertising service* that taps into the database of some 100 million anonymous online profiles.

Cookies

An Internet cookie is a small text file that a Web server places on your computer to store and retrieve information temporarily or permanently (or until you manually delete it from your computer). There are hundreds of legitimate uses for cookies. For example, go to your favorite Web site and sign in; there is usually a checkbox that asks whether you want the site to remember your user name and password in future visits. If you check the box, your information will most likely be stored in a text file (hopefully encrypted) on your machine—a cookie. Likewise, if you visit Amazon.com and search for a book on the Beatles, the chances are great that later in your session or even on a different day, you'll see a promotion for Beatles merchandise. This customization is made possible in part by the use of cookies.

The information stored in a cookie by a particular site is accessible only to that site when you visit. But you don't have to be viewing a site in its entirety or even voluntarily for a cookie to be written to your machine. HTML allows content from multiple sites to be shown within one Web page. (A page's advertising is often hosted by a third party that can write and read cookies.)

An advertiser such as DoubleClick is in a very unique position. It serves ads across multiple sites and can write and read cookies specific to the ad and the Web site on which the ad was viewed. If a user visits a financial site, a weather site, and a casino site that all use DoubleClick to serve ads, they use cookies to track the user path from one site to another to form a comprehensive profile of the user over time. Plainly, cookies do store information about you that you may not want other people to have access to.

Spam

Spam is a serious problem. It is annoying and intrusive, especially when the content of the solicitation is objectionable. Spam also puts an unwarranted burden on the corporate and commercial email servers whose job it is to deliver email communications.

There are no federal regulations to put specific limits on marketing communication via email. Although congressmen, FTC officials, and consumer advocacy groups have all drafted proposals that they feel are adequate solutions to the problem, none are likely to see the light of day anytime soon. Many states have introduced and ratified antispam laws. In Kansas, it is illegal for commercial email messages to have misleading or false subject lines. In California, unsolicited commercial email messages are required to have contact information and opt-out policies (which must be honored) stated within the email. In Wisconsin, unsolicited commercial email messages with obscene or sexually explicit material must include the words *adult advertisement* in the subject line. The biggest problem is enforcing these laws.

The Internet is international. Unfortunately, the scammers of foreign countries have devised clever ways to spam people in this country with plots, schemes, and ploys to rid us of our excess money. On a regular basis, some foreign national will email you with a plea for help (in exchange for a reward), or there will be an urgent request to call an 809 area code (this is the area code for the Dominican Republic).

The reasons you are encouraged to call are varied (examples: to avoid litigation, to get information about a relative or friend, or you won a prize). Calls placed to the 809 area code seem just like any other long-distance call. No international codes are necessary. The basic rate for a call to the Dominican Republic is $3 a minute, but some 809 numbers have a pay-per-call service that permits the levy of additional fees. You won't know what the call costs until you get the bill. Because the numbers are located offshore, they aren't subject to U.S. laws; there are no legal requirements that consumers be informed in advance. The FCC has a warning on its Web page about this, and they advise people to file an informal FCC complaint. (It's unknown what, if anything, happens to such FTC complaints.) The long-distance companies are forced to collect because you did place the call (although it seems as though they could add a country code or something to protect you).

More such area codes are starting to show up (011, 268, 664). The best advice is to check all unfamiliar area codes with a quick glance at the front of your telephone book, a call to the telephone operator, or through your computer's search engine. A Web site that keeps track of questionable Internet practices is www.scambusters.org, or go to the www.dvorak.org/home.htm Web page—its *phone links* has a huge amount of information about everything under the sun, including scams and area code searches.

FREEDOM OF SPEECH

Americans hold freedom of speech as important as taking a breath. Speech is scrutinized from every angle. The Internet is unique. It's probably the first communication tool involving freedom of speech without needing freedom of assembly.

One-on-one communication (talking on the telephone or writing letters) has traditionally been a universal way for citizens to communicate. Until now, communication from one to many has been reserved for public gatherings or for publishers, news bureaus, television stations, and other mass media. Although these may claim to speak on behalf of the people, they do not assure that all voices or opinions are heard.

This is a wonderful breakthrough for free speech in the world. It places a high value on Internet communication. As well, we've come to expect a certain entitlement to its access through this conduit. But the Internet is complex and has a lot of issues to understand. There are still a lot of decisions to be made. Along the way, there will be a lot of misjudgments, confusion, and mistakes in the process of drafting relevant legislation.

E-Rate

In December 2000, the United States government enacted a spending bill with a significant amendment attached. This amendment stipulated that to receive technology "e-rate" funding, a library or school must install filtering software on any and all computers that allow children access to the Internet. These filters were to censor Web sites that contain questionable (inappropriate for children) content. The intent was to prevent kids from using library and school computers to look at porn.

The drawback: Due to the way it is configured, most filtering software on the market also prevents women from learning about breast cancer or grandmothers from finding recipes to prepare chicken breasts. (There is nothing in the Constitution that guarantees the right to tender chicken.) Civil liberties groups argue that the law violates First Amendment rights.

Filtering

Content filtering is a tricky business. Computer filters always filter too much and too little at the same time. There is no accurate way to filter unwanted information while including wanted content (aside from simply not using the Internet at all).

There are two approaches to content filtering. The first is list-based filtering. Sites are indexed for content and reviewed. A decision is made (by someone) regarding the appropriateness of the site for the group intended to view it. Keyword-based filtering relies on a list of *taboo* keywords or phrases. Most filtering software uses a combination of these methods.

These two methods are fine for home use. But as filtering solutions, they are inherently flawed when it comes to public use. The methods rely on human opinion to classify hundreds of thousands of Web pages for content. These decisions are made out of context. Some information, especially for health and medical sites, can be denied because words that relate to the human body are also used on some porn sites. (A breast cancer survivor site might be barred because of the word *breast*.) Additionally, content keyword filtering generally cannot decipher words connected to screen pictures.

Shortly after Congress passed the filtering law, free speech advocates filed a flurry of motions. The underlying argument was that mandatory content filtering violates citizens' First Amendment rights:

- Filtering discriminates against people who use public libraries as their sole conduit to access content on the Net.

- It is unconstitutional to force all citizens, especially adults, to browse the Net through a content filter.

The result? A few months after this law was put into effect, the issue of mandatory content filtering was put to rest on the federal level (and the state level, in many states) by being held unconstitutional.

WHERE THE HARM LIES

Most citizens in the United States are law-abiding people. Although not all of them are voters, regular churchgoers, or even nice people. The vast majority do not murder, steal, loot, or even lie on a regular basis. But in one sense or another, all are lawbreakers. We all break a minor law once in a while. (It's almost impossible not to, given the sheer numbers of laws on the books, including the arcane ones.) We don't consider our actions criminal or question our moral integrity. One reason is that laws usually fall into one of two categories—those that prohibit or punish harmful actions to citizens (such as murder) and those that proscribe actions that cause little harm. Internet law generally falls into this latter category.

To kill a man unjustifiably by dropping a computer on him is harmful, illegal, and unacceptable by society's standards. To kill his reputation by publishing defamatory accusations on the Web is still illegal yet construed as less harmful.

LAW

The Internet is unique. Its roots are anchored in American soil, but its branches and leaves cover the globe. The simple act of sending an email to your next-door neighbor might have the document pass through servers around the world.

The imposition of laws and limitations on the Internet cannot be entirely in America's jurisdiction. The U.S. government claims regulatory power. So can every other country. Unlike traditional industries (where international law is well defined), the Net is a new, rapidly growing, ever-changing industry. The governing bodies of the world have not had enough time jointly or appropriately to understand the real issues, let alone take wise action. Consequently, users may unknowingly become subject to laws they may have never even heard of from countries they don't even know exists.

MONOPOLIST, THE GAME?

The Internet has created a world of muddy international law. It reveals the semantic differences between language and the law. As an example, if an American writer published an online article calling Microsoft a *monopolist*, this would raise eyebrows in Canada. In America, it's not illegal to say that a corporation is a monopolist. In Canada, it is just not done. (It is analogous to calling someone a rapist.) The irony is that even if a company had been tried and found to be a monopoly in America, it still would not be called a monopolist in a Canadian publication. It's just how things are.

The difference is in the libel and slander laws. The United States does have defamation (libel and slander) laws. Accusing someone in print of an illegal action can be construed as libel if, in fact, the claim is totally unfounded, malicious in nature, and damages reputation. (This principle is why tabloid newspapers sometimes can and other times cannot get away with the half-truths that they often print.) American law in this area is broad, complex, and convoluted. It is a gray area. It weighs the degree of defamatory effect and malicious interest. There are other requirements, such as the offense must be about someone who can be identified and must be "published" to someone other than the offended party. (Telling someone to their face that they are stupid and ugly is not slander; it's an opinion. Writing a letter to the person to that effect is also an opinion, not libel. Publishing it in a full-page ad in a newspaper or posting it on every bulletin board and telephone post in town is a different issue.) The law is obviously open to interpretation.

In Canada, the judicial system is fragmented, with each territory and province having its own interpretation of defamation laws. A defamatory statement exists if the publication tends to lower the plaintiff's reputation in the estimation of those who are commonly referred to as *right-thinking* members of society. An individual or corporation may sue for any defamatory statement that affects its property, goodwill, financial position, or reputation. In Canada, the liability of a defamatory statement extends to all those who participate in its dissemination. If it were a newspaper, then the editor, the section head, the newspaper owner, and even the person who distributes the newspaper would all be held liable.

Needless to say, Canadian libel law is difficult to grasp. There are different criteria than the American conditions for libel. And to find common ground between the two is akin to making comparisons between European football

> (soccer) and American football—two different games with two different sets of rules.
>
> The confusion arises in the blurred borders of the Internet and what International law applies. If an American writes an online column (read in Canada) and calls a Canadian corporation a monopolist, could the writer be sued in Canada? Probably. And therein lies the confusion.

Where the Chips May Fall

Historically, the country of its creation governs new technology. To expedite enactment of regulations concerning the technology, lawmakers consult with experts in that field to explain how the technology works and what impact it will or may have. Lawmakers write, ratify, and impose laws to address concerns of the technology. Sometimes this works, although often laws are too general, unfocused, or unworkable. The law is then revised and interpreted via court actions and decisions. It is a process and an art.

International law is no different.

In mid-2002, Greece enacted a law that was absolutely absurd in the eyes of most people. In Greece, illegally operated electronic gaming machines were becoming a problem. They were allowing citizens to lose large sums of money without having any legal protection. Consequently, the issue was brought to the high court, where lawmakers entertained a ban on all public gaming. One official noted the obvious. Banning computer gaming systems from public places would just send the systems underground. As a solution, the country decided to ban all computer gaming, both public and private. Greek police made a bust on an Internet cafe where patrons played computer games (chess and Doom). When this case reached the high court, the law was overturned.

CYBERLIBEL

Email is more like conversation than anything else. It is often hasty, ungrammatical, rash, and tends toward emotional outbursts. It can lead people to saying things they would probably not say in person or normally write, especially for publication.

But there is liability for defamatory statements over email. Libel based on email has won in court in Australia, England, Canada, and the United States.

In the case of *Rindos v. Hardwick* (March 25, 1994, Supreme Court of West Australia), the court held that the academic competence of Rindos was defamed by a fellow anthropologist in a message posted on the DIALx science anthropology computer bulletin board. Several posts to the board were outright gossip, questioning both the character and qualifications of Rindos. The posts were published for all to see in a very specific online community. The publisher of the message was held liable for damages in the amount of $40,000 at 8% per annum. The court did not judge it appropriate to treat the Internet context as different from other means of communication.

In Geneva, Switzerland, Dr. Laurence Godfrey of CERN was awarded a cash settlement for libel on a Usenet located in England. An action by an American businessman against a defendant journalist was settled in the case of *Suarez v. Meeks*.

In Canada's Ontario Province Court of Justice, the case of *Egerton v. Finuncan* (May 25, 1995) involved a college professor's supervisor sending out a broadcast email to the entire faculty instead of only its intended recipient. The message listed concerns over Egerton's performance and reasons for his termination. Mr. Egerton initiated a wrongful termination suit against Finuncan. The interlocutory decision cited "the manner in which the allegations against Mr. Egerton were published to other persons rather than being communicated to Mr. Egerton on a confidential basis." The claim of defamation was allowed to go to trial as separate action.

The moral: Beware when posting comments, writing email, or forwarding things that could be considered libelous. In the eyes of the law, it can be viewed as no different than taking out a full-page ad in the *Wall Street Journal*.

SUMMARY

The Internet seems to offer participants anonymity. The illusion of invisibility leads people to believe that their actions are not subject to the scrutiny of others. What people do in private and what they do in public are often vastly different. Appearances and the perceptions and judgments of one's peers keep many people more moral than they would like to admit. Behind the Internet veil of anonymity, actions are less hindered by the threat of consequences.

The reality of the extent of this anonymity is up for debate. You can usually be tracked down somehow. Thus, some attention must be paid to the law and what you are allowed to do on the Net legally. And because the international aspect of all this has yet to be resolved, with contradictory laws in various countries, the best approach is the most conservative. In other words, don't do anything on the Internet that you wouldn't do in the 3D world in which you live.

Internet law has a long way to go before it is clear and well understood. It is larger than one country or one set of opinions. Some of the law will be international law. Other parts of the law will be country- and state-specific. The important thing to do is to be informed and aware of how the laws might affect you.

28
VOICE OVER INTERNET PROTOCOL

Voice over Internet Protocol (VoIP) is a technology to use the Internet Protocol instead of phone-switching technology for voice, facsimile, and message services. The typical consumer probably hasn't heard of VoIP yet. However, the technology is already commonly in use. The main example would be the dominance of inexpensive prepaid telephone cards on the market. VoIP is the technology in use for almost all the prepaid telephone long-distance cards. It's how their per-minute charges are so competitive, compared with traditional long-distance service.

Until just a few years ago, every telephone call utilized the traditional Public Switched Telephone Network (PSTN). With PSTN, a long-distance call first goes through a local telephone company, then to the long-distance provider (for a connection fee) in an all-analog voice signal. Large telephone switches are in place to make the transfer. With VoIP prepaid telephone cards, you pick up your phone and dial a special number, then the long-distance number. The route that the call takes differs from that of traditional PSTN. VoIP simplifies the system with an advanced combination of hardware and software. The analog call is converted to digital. The digitized call is compressed and translated into IP packets for transmission over a private IP network or the Internet. The call bypasses the traditional route through the expensive telephone switch at a telephone company's central office. At the other end of the wire, the process is reversed: The digital signal is converted back to an analog signal, and it's again routed through regular telephone equipment.

Like many nascent technologies, VoIP was originally considered a cute novelty. But it's gaining momentum as a viable technology. VoIP holds several solid advantages, both in the home and in business, over traditional PSTN networks. A few include:

- Cost Reduction—VoIP eliminates traditional circuit-switched networks and reduces the associated per-minute long-distance fees. VoIP reduces the amount of hardware needed (infrastructure overhead) by converging voice and data networks. Network efficiency improves with shared equipment. Excess bandwidth, rarely exploited, can be fully utilized. In short, it's a bargain.

- Simplicity—A single piece of equipment supports both voice and data communications. Less hardware means less cost.

- Advanced Applications—Like PSTN, basic telephony and facsimile are the core elements of VoIP. However, because VoIP uses a compressed, packetized digital format, the possibility for advanced multimedia (and multiservice) applications is limitless. A few possible applications include: Web-enabled call centers, collaborative white boarding, remote telecommuting, and personal productivity applications.

The History of VoIP

VoIP had been talked about long before Vocaltec, Inc. released Internet Phone Software in 1995. This software was designed to run on a home PC (486/33 MHz) with sound cards, speakers, microphone, and modem. The software compressed the voice signal, translated it into voice packets, and shipped it out over the Internet. The technology worked as long as both the caller and the receiver had the same equipment and software. Although the sound quality was nowhere near that of conventional equipment at the time, this effort represented the first IP phone. By converting analog voice into compressed digital IP packets, the software enabled PC-to-PC Internet telephony.

It's tempting to view the advent of VoIP as a singular technological event. In reality, however, VoIP is an evolutionary extension of decades-long communications and network technology progress. The highly reliable telephone network has been in a state of constant evolution for more than 100 years.

Today, billions of calls traverse the world's phone systems every day with little human intervention. This hasn't always been the case. In the early 1900s, each call was switched manually by a live telephone company switchboard operator and again with private board operators hired by each company. An important development for the telephone company network was the automation of the call switching function. With the invention of the Private Branch Exchange (PBX), companies were able to cut their payrolls from many in-house operators to just a handful of receptionists.

The next big step forward for the telephone network was in the early 1960s, with the introduction of pulse code modulation (PCM) technology. PCM addressed the inherent signal problems of transmitting voice in the analog world by converting the analog signal to binary 0s and 1s. This reduced the distance and interference noise on the line. (In fact, on transatlantic calls, one could hear the waves as transient noise moving over the cable.) The binary voice signal became as clear at the receiving end of the line as at the sending end. In the 1980s, Time Division Multiplexing (TDM) became a popular way to deliver analog voice over digital networks. With TDM, many analog channels were digitized and allocated a specific time slot. The technology allowed different speeds for each channel and supported traffic aggregation. TDM transformed analog voice to digital over switched networks, laying very important groundwork for VoIP, because voice could now be viewed as data.

TDM provided the major advantage of putting more voice channels onto a single line. For example, two pair of copper wires could now support a T1 line, or 24 channels. The downside of TDM was that allocated channel bandwidth couldn't be dynamically reassigned when not in use. It was for this reason that a different way was sought to transmit voice and data over a single network—a significant challenge because of their differing natures.

Data is sporadic. It comes in bursts. Voice is time-sensitive. If a large data file takes up system bandwidth, voice packets can drop out or be delayed, a condition considered unacceptable for voice transmissions. It would be very difficult to follow a conversation in which large chunks of a sentence are missing.

The Asynchronous Transfer Mode (ATM) technology solved this problem in the early 1990s. ATM is a high-bandwidth, low-delay, packetlike switching technique. It has the quality of service (QoS) built in to integrate voice and data. Although many of today's international backbones utilize ATM, it has proven to be too costly for most corporate environments.

At the same time, however, many companies had started to integrate different types of data on their networks with low-cost frame relay, wide area networks (WANs). IT managers added intelligence to their networks to support different applications and protocols to utilize the same pipe. This became a universal method to transport a variety of applications. IP spread rapidly. Data and telecommunications managers could see the promise of IP as a universal transport mechanism.

Voice is the latest core function making its way into the IP world. It's only logical because to an IP network, voice is just another application. The PBX can be a highly reliable application server. It seems natural to converge traditional voice with existing data networks.

In the years since VoIP was introduced, a growing list of technology providers have begun to offer PC telephony software. There is a spate of gateway manufacturers entering the market. Until recently, VoIP provided PC-to-PC telephony primarily over intranets typically found in a business environment. With the introduction of gateway infrastructure outfitted with VoIP technology, users can now look forward to the widespread proliferation of Internet telephony. VoIP infrastructure is the real on-ramp to the Internet itself.

HOW DOES VoIP WORK?

It's simple: Voice becomes another data application running over the IP network. The PBX becomes a large server.

Technically, a VoIP call takes place in the following way:

A user picks up the handset, which signals an off-hook condition to the signaling application portion of the VoIP in the network. Then the session application portion of VoIP issues a dialtone and waits for the remote client to dial the number. When a number is dialed, the numbers are stored by the session application. After a sufficient number of digits are accumulated, the number is mapped to an IP host through the dial plan mapper. The IP host has a direct connection to either the destination telephone number or a PBX to complete the call.

Next, the H.323 session protocol (a standard discussed a little later in this chapter) establishes a transmit and receive channel over the IP network. If a PBX is handling the call, it will forward the call to the destination telephone. The VoIP system then starts a coder-decoder compression scheme for both ends of the connection. The remote client's communication is with Real-Time Transport Protocol/User Datagram Protocol/Internet Protocol (RTP/UDP/IP) as the protocol stack (also discussed further later in this chapter).

Call progress indications cut through the voice path as soon as an end-to-end audio channel is established. Additionally, any signaling that the voice port detects, such as inband dual-tone multifrequency (DTMF), is captured by the session application at both ends of the connection and carried over the IP network in Real-Time Control Protocol (RTCP), using the RTCP application-defined (APP) extension mechanism.

Finally, when either remote user hangs up, Resource Reservation Protocol (RSVP) reservations are undone if they are used, and the session ends. Each remote terminal is now idle and waits for the next off-hook state to trigger another call setup.

THE SPECIAL REQUIREMENTS OF VOICE

Though voice is just another data application in an IP system, it nevertheless has some distinct requirements. Some unique characteristics set voice apart. These include all of the following:

- Voice is a real-time application. This means data packets must be processed as they happen in the real world. They do not have the same tolerance for delay and packet loss as other data applications.

- Data traffic sometimes happens at unpredictable intervals, or "bursts." Voice, on the other hand, follows a consistent flow and is more predictable.

- Data transmissions are generally "asymmetrical" because file transfers are typically much larger on the download side than they are on the upload side. Conversely, voice transmissions are typically "symmetrical" because the rate of transfer is almost the same in both directions.

- An industry concern is the reliability in a migration from traditional PSTN-based voice to packetized voice. It is a critical application (and one people have come to expect rock-solid reliability from). Any voice network, traditional or digital, must provide nearly 100% reliability of uninterrupted service. Voice service must be accessible and predictable to provide the continuity human conversation depends on. In a digital voice network, this continuity requires that digital voice packets arrive in the same order in which they were transmitted and be assembled in proper order. Otherwise, it would not be an accurate representation of the source analog input.

How IP Gateways Packetize Voice

The first step in transforming voice into an IP application is to collect raw analog voice data. To simplify design and efficiently utilize bandwidth, most packet systems transmit a constant number of samples (these typically span several milliseconds for each data packet). This series of samples is usually referred to as a *frame*. The size of the frame is often determined by the voice compression algorithm in use. In fact, most popular voice compression algorithms require a predetermined size of the input frame. Likewise, they produce a predetermined output frame. The time the system uses to create voice packets from raw analog voice creates latency. Latency is defined as the average time for a packet to work its way across the network. A typical voice system will gather at least 8 milliseconds of voice data before transmitting the packet. That 8 millisecond latency is introduced into the real-world conversation between two people.

In the world of VoIP, echo cancellation is the next step after raw voice samples have been collected and packetized. The echo cancel function removes the echo (inherent to the analog equipment used in the phone network). In addition, echo cancellation removes the perception of an echo created by the latency introduced when raw analog voice is digitized and broken into packets.

When the echo cancellation procedure is finished, the frame is compressed. This process typically falls within the special domain of a digital signal processor (DSP), which is a specialized processor optimized to handle real-time signals in the digital domain. The DSP may compress the frame in ratios ranging from 1:1 to as much as 10:1, depending on the protocol being used. In addition to compression, the DSP minimizes additional latency caused by the time used to compress the packet.

The VoIP system collects several frames of data before sending a voice packet. This is due to the series of protocol headers added to every packet. When the system has collected enough data for a packet, the DSP adds the headers at the beginning of the data to indicate the destination and the type of packet. It is then put in line for transmission.

How long do all these steps take? The whole process from raw analog voice to a packetized, transmission-ready compressed voice takes no more than 20 milliseconds. VoIP is virtually transparent.

GOALS FOR VoIP IMPLEMENTATION

The goal of the implementation of a VoIP system is quite simple. It is to add telephone-calling capabilities to IP-based networks. Then it interconnects them to the public telephone network and to private voice networks to maintain voice quality standards and preserve the features users expect from their telephones.

A VoIP system should have specific characteristics:

- Voice quality should be comparable to what is available using the PSTN, even over networks with variable levels of QoS.

- The underlying IP network must meet strict performance criteria, including minimal call refusals, network latency, packet loss, and disconnects. This goal should be met even during congested periods or when multiple users must share network resources.

- Call control must make the telephone process transparent so that callers are unaware of the technology they are using.

- PSTN/VoIP service interworking should involve gateways between the voice and data network environments.

- System management, security, addressing, and accounting should be provided, preferably consolidated with the PSTN operation support systems (OSSs).

The Challenge of VoIP

Speech quality should be at least equal to the PSTN (usually referred to as "toll-quality" voice). Some experts argue that a *cost-versus-function-versus-quality* trade-off should be applied.

QoS usually refers to the fidelity of the transmitted voice and facsimile documents. QoS can also be applied to network availability (i.e., call capacity or level of call blocking), telephone feature availability (conferencing, calling number display, etc.), and scalability (any-to-any, universal, expandable).

The quality of sound reproduction over a telephone network is fundamentally subjective, although standardized quality measurements have been developed by the International Telecommunications Union (ITU). These measures represent special challenges in implementing VoIP and can profoundly impact QoS. Challenges include:

- Delay—Two problems result from high end-to-end delay in a voice network. These are echo and talker overlap. Echo becomes a problem when the round-trip delay is more than 50 milliseconds. Because echo is a significant quality problem, VoIP systems must address the need for cancellation. Talker overlap (the problem of one caller stepping on another talker's speech) becomes significant if the one-way delay becomes greater than 250 milliseconds. The end-to-end delay budget is therefore the major constraint and driving requirement for reducing delay through a packet network.

- Jitter (delay variability)—Jitter is the variation in interpacket arrival time as introduced by the variable transmission delay over the network. Removing jitter requires collecting packets and holding them long enough to allow the slowest packets to arrive in time to be played in the correct sequence, which causes additional delay.

- Packet Loss—IP networks cannot guarantee that packets will arrive at all, much less in the right order. Packets will be dropped under peak loads and during periods of congestion (caused, for example, by link failures or inadequate capacity). However, because of the time sensitivity of voice transmission, normal TCP-based retransmission schemes are not suitable. Approaches used to compensate for packet loss include interpolation of speech by replaying the last packet and sending of redundant information. Packet losses greater than 10% are generally intolerable.

All of these technical conditions do present challenges. However, the major benefits of VoIP are fueling the industry to work through standards and technology advancement to make them nonfactors for the user.

Standards

VoIP represents a potential for users to enjoy advanced services such as unified messaging, Web-based call centers, *follow me anywhere* services, and other forward-looking applications. The key to any technology is standards. VoIP currently has a glut of standards.

Traditional voice service has a strong set of international standards to specify and clarify design principles, communication processes, test procedures, and environmental conditions. Since H.323, the first VoIP standard, was ratified in 1996 by the ITU, a host of standards and variations of those standards have emerged from the ITU, as well as from other standards bodies. In addition, there are many more VoIP standards in the works. The following is an overview of the major standards governing the way in which traditional circuit-switched networks and packet-switched networks interact.

H.323

This standard was originally created for established multimedia applications. H.323 is part of a broad family of standards developed by ITU. It describes how audio, video, and data communications take place among terminals, network equipment, and services on IP networks. By 1997, H.323 was accepted as the prevailing VoIP network standard, a position it still enjoys today. H.323 allowed designers to get products to market by giving them a platform for packet network communications and interoperability among early vendor equipment. Because it was originally developed for multimedia applications, H.323 does burden VoIP systems with unnecessary overhead. Nevertheless, its wide use makes it the de facto choice for interoperability among VoIP equipment. The standard describes four major functions of networked communications:

1. Terminals—These are LAN client terminals that enable two-way communication.
2. Gateways—Gateways are designed for real-time, two-way communication between H.323 terminals on a network and other ITU terminals residing on a switched-based network or on another H.323 gateway.
3. Gatekeepers—Within a given zone, gatekeepers are the nexus for calls, providing services to endpoints.
4. Multipoint control units (MCUs)—MCUs function as endpoints for three or more terminals and gateways, enabling multipoint conference communication.

Session Internet Protocol

Session Internet Protocol (SIP) is relatively new on the VoIP standards scene. SIP is an application-layer control protocol that makes up for many of H.323's inherent faults. The standard, developed by the Internet Engineering Task Force (IETF), addresses the call setup and teardown, error handling, and interprocess signaling that are functions of every point-to-point connection. It also changes and terminates multimedia sessions, including conferences, Internet telephony, distance learning, and other applications. SIP enables VoIP gateways, client endpoints, PBXs, and other systems to communicate over packet networks from an equipment perspective.

Compared with H.323, SIP is a simpler protocol with less overhead. The minimum number of message exchanges to set up a call between two endpoints is three. SIP locates the recipient of a call, ensures that the equipment is congruent with the caller's equipment, then allows other protocols to take care of other functions, such as data transfer and security. In addition, SIP differentiates itself from H.323. SIP distributes much of the call management and routing among different areas of the network. Like H.323, SIP has morphed into several related protocols. Furthermore, SIP is a text-based and largely free-formatted protocol, making it easy to debug protocol implementations and to add new features to the protocol to meet new industrial demands.

Media Gateway Control Protocol

Also created by the IETF, Media Gateway Control Protocol (MGCP) is a proposed standard to convert audio signals on the PSTN to data packets that traverse the Internet. The protocol is based on an architecture to move call-control intelligence away from the gateway for processing by external call-control or call agents. MGCP allows media gateways to communicate.

Megaco/H.248

Megaco/H.248 is a new protocol born of a joint effort between the ITU (ITU-T Study Group 16) and the IETF (Megaco is work group of the IETF). Functionally, the proposed standard enables a control of media gateways. Megaco/H.248 is designed to succeed MGCP, adding peer-to-peer interoperability and ensuring a way to control IP telephone devices operating in a master/slave manner. The standard breaks the H.323 gateway function into separate subcomponents. It also determines the protocols employed by each communication component.

So Why All the Standards?

With all of the established VoIP standards and a veritable plethora of others in the works, the obvious questions arise: Why all the standards? Are they all necessary? Probably. First and foremost, standards deliver on the promise of interoperability. This is the ability for myriad VoIP-enabled products to communicate successfully. Interoperability, in turn, delivers an open platform for which many different solutions providers can create innovative products. Perhaps most important, standards and interoperability together give consumers a greater choice in products and technology. They lower the cost of ownership through free-market competition.

Overall, standards are good. Yet this still leaves the question of why there are so many standards, each seemingly with its own unique merits and faults. As discussed earlier, H.323 was originally established for multimedia applications. It was utilized for VoIP because of its maturity and the lack of a perfected standard for voice over packet communications. Nevertheless, despite shortcomings for voice, it enabled designers to get to market quickly with early VoIP products. It provided a vehicle for packet network communications and interoperability among early VoIP vendor equipment. By 1997, H.323 had achieved preeminence as the prevailing standard, a position it still maintains today.

H.323 served communication efforts among early VoIP equipment well. However, early equipment interfaced primarily with other packet-based VoIP equipment within an intranetworking environment, but VoIP systems must interface with legacy POTS (plain old telephone system) phones—the PSTN—and their accompanying standards were not well served by H.323. VoIP requires voice detecting and transmission via the packet network. It also requires tones, which are part of a body of incumbent switched-network standards initiated at the transmitting device.

Today, most VoIP systems don't employ IP from one end to the other. Accordingly, it is necessary to have a standard way of transmitting DTMF tones, as well as to provide a communication mechanism for other named telephony signal events to be transmitted in RTP packets. Request for Comment (RFC) 2833, created by the IETF and formally named *RTP Payload for DTMF Digits, Telephony Tones and Telephony Signals*, is part of the standards track of the Networking Working Group at the IETF. It describes how to carry and format tones and events in an RTP packet. With separate payloads, RFC 2833 ensures a common way to avoid voice encoder payloads and insure redundancy for accurate reception.

Many VoIP applications will use RFC 2833. In Internet phones, it can emulate DTMF functionality. This alleviates the need to create legacy tones. In the receiving phone, it eliminates tone detection. As mentioned previously, VoIP gateways utilize DTMF relay support from RFC 2833.

In RTP, the packet network serves in place of the circuit-switched network. There is another possible application to benefit from the derivative standard. Here, RFC 2833 offers a way to perform transparent communication of telephony signals and events between Class 5 switches and IP networks or endpoints. One real-world example would be to allow MSOs (multisystem operators, such as a cable provider which also offers VoIP) to deploy services more quickly and cost-effectively than through use of the standard in IP telephony. Legacy equipment provides an interface between the Packet Cable network and the Class 5 switch through an IP terminal communicating the necessary GR303 signaling.

Further Standard Evolution—Vocoders

Today, most VoIP applications use voice codecs (also called *vocoders*), which were created for existing digital telephony applications. Like H.323, they are robust and proven. They allow designers to get interoperable products to market quickly. The downside, however, is that they are limited to the telephony signal band of 200–300 MHz with 8-kHz sampling. This worked fine when VoIP quality goals were to achieve the same levels as existing switched networks. However, this level of quality is far below real-world, face-to-face communication. It requires a much wider bandwidth of 50–7,000 Hz.

Just as the industry addressed previous limitations with VoIP service, it is now developing new wideband codec standards designed to push the technology to higher levels of service. The ITU G.722.1 vocoder delivers 24-Kbps and 32-Kbps data rates, and it enables wideband performance with a 16-kHz sampling rate. It is currently being used in some IP applications. Meanwhile, another wideband standard, the Adaptive Multi-Rate Wideband (AMR-WB) in the 50- to 7000-Hz bandwidth, has been jointly developed by the ITU-T and the Third-Generation Partnership Project (3GPP)/ETSI. Recently approved by the ITU and referred to as G.722.2, the standard further improves voice quality over G.722.1, and it enables seamless interface between VoIP systems and wireless base stations.

Ongoing Standards Development

Some may see the ongoing development of new VoIP standards as an alphabet soup and a cumbersome way to negotiate the development of a new technology. In reality, however, the process of continually creating new and more evolved standards is the single most influential force in the promotion and proliferation of a new technology. Standards allow manufacturers to get to market quickly with open systems; they create across-the-board interoperability; and they reduce the consumer's cost of ownership.

VoIP in the Enterprise

Within an enterprise or business communication environment, there are some distinct advantages of combining voice, fax, data, and multimedia traffic onto a single multipurpose network. Lower recurring transmission charges, reduced long-term network ownership costs, and the ability to implement a host of new and powerful voice-enabled applications all are compelling arguments. They have sparked interest in the business world for VoIP technology. At the same time, however, IT leaders have several reasons to move cautiously into the largely uncharted world of converged networks and packetized voice. Quality of voice calls on the data network, stability of VoIP solutions, and the consequences of being prematurely locked into a given architecture are areas of concern within the enterprise. This section will first look at the advantages of VoIP in the enterprise, then it will give some consideration of the risks.

There may be much discussion of the hows and whens of converging voice with other data services in the enterprise. However, the benefits of doing so are very convincing and an idea already being proven by early adopters in the enterprise.

Lower Transmission Charges

Reduced monthly phone charges are one clear advantage of converging voice calls with the corporate data network. For some companies, this reason may be the most compelling of all, depending on several factors, including the volume of calls within the company and the distance between company offices. Companies with offices overseas stand to reap the biggest rewards by eliminating international long-distance charges, especially to countries with monopolistic long-distance markets. In addition to intracompany calls, savings can also be realized for extracompany calls. First the call is routed to a destination outside of the company over the corporate network to the nearest remote office. It then interfaces with the PSTN. As an example, a company with offices in Los Angeles and Tokyo could route calls to and from each office over the corporate network, then hand the call off to a local carrier for another destination outside of Tokyo but still within the country of Japan. In this case, not all but a significant portion of long-distance charges have been avoided.

Economically speaking, it is attractive to use data networks for voice for a couple of reasons. First, data networks nearly always offer spare capacity; second, voice typically requires little bandwidth when compared with other data transactions. Compression of voice data typically makes it possible to integrate the new service into the existing network without additional capacity investments.

Reduced Cost of Ownership

The lower cost associated with VoIP systems is not just relegated to lower monthly bills. Converged data networks also reduce the recurring cost of owning two separate networks, one for voice and one for data. With any network, there are both human and equipment costs associated with purchase, implementation, maintenance, software licensing, and traffic monitoring. Personnel costs have always been a major concern for businesses, and now more than ever it is cost-intensive to attract and retain qualified IT personnel. Convergence of voice service with other data services gives companies an effective way to streamline their networks and make the most of their IT manpower. This in turn gives VoIP adopters a distinct advantage in the marketplace.

Powerful New Converged Applications

Saving money is an important way for companies to promote the interests of their employees and shareholders. Beyond this, companies exist to be profitable, win in their markets, and better serve their customers. By providing a host of new converged voice and data applications, such as Web-enabled call centers, unified messaging, and real-time collaboration, VoIP allows companies to serve their customers better, giving them additional advantages in their markets.

As an example, Web-enabled call centers present a way to overcome the communication problems inherent in turning site visitors from browsers into buyers. Historically, Web-based interaction between buyer and seller has been problematic at best. However, Web-based call centers, allow a customer with a question simply to click on a hyperlink to initiate a conversation with a live customer service agent who can answer questions and move the customer to a purchase decision more quickly.

Real-time multimedia/audio conferencing, distance learning, and embedding voice links into electronic documents are other coming applications. And these are just the beginning. There are many VoIP-enabled applications yet to be thought of.

Voice Quality

Most companies view any degradation in the voice quality provided by current switched networks as a significant concern. Within a data network, packets move around in a somewhat nonlinear fashion, and sometimes they are even lost or dropped. This is especially true in Ethernet networks that make up the most common enterprise computing environments. With most data applications, this doesn't present much of a problem, because Ethernet or IP error correction readily compensates for these events. Voice data, where there must be an efficient, real-time packet flow throughout the network, is much more sensitive to these problems.

Reliability

Anyone who has worked with computers and network data applications understands the frustrations of having the system or the network down. At the same time, most take for granted that when they pick up their telephone receivers, there will always be dialtone, along with reliable, uninterrupted service. VoIP must achieve close to this same level of reliability before it as seen as a wholesale replacement for switched networks.

Technology Adoption Issues

As businesses move to adopt converged voice and data networks, there is the concern that they will prematurely buy into the wrong technology. First, there is the concern over "buyer's remorse," the idea that a superior solution will become available just as the company has invested significant dollars in another solution. Second, the more far-reaching concern is that buy-in to a particular solution will result in a long-term commitment to a particular (possibly inferior) architecture that may limit the ability to choose services and management tools.

The continuing evolution of VoIP standards, as discussed earlier in this chapter, will in many ways alleviate this concern over time.

Risk vs. Reward

The reality with VoIP and converged networks is simply put: They *are* coming, and the companies that implement them in an effective way will be the ones to benefit first from the new services and cost savings they enable. The companies that integrate VoIP technology will enjoy significant competitive advantages.

THE ELEMENTS OF A VOIP SYSTEM

Every VoIP system is made up of four essential functions: hard and soft clients, communication servers, client and trunk media gateways, and application servers. Together, these building blocks are spread over a telephony or business-grade IP network, providing the necessary levels of reliability, voice quality, and traffic management.

Client Side

For end users in the enterprise, the VoIP client is their personal way of interfacing with the network. Traditional switched networks offer one primary interface, which is typically the phone sitting on the user's desk. VoIP client equipment, however, may take several forms, including a dedicated IP telephone (which may look very similar to an ordinary phone), a wireless LAN telephone, or a PC running client software. In general, fixed-function devices, such as the IP phone, are much more reliable, while PC-based systems offer more flexibility.

The number and types of client equipment, which will grow with market demand, roughly fall into two categories: thin clients and thick clients. As their name implies, thin clients feature less inherent intelligence, relying primarily on network intelligence provided by the communication server to initiate communications and manage feature operation. Likewise, thick clients are more highly integrated and use built-in intelligence to serve the user.

Communication Servers

The heart of every VoIP system in the enterprise is the communication server. It provides the control that allows call establishment across the network. How much intelligence a particular call server integrates depends on whether thick clients, such as PCs, or thin clients, such as IP phones, are being used as endpoints. The functional purpose of a communication server is to coordinate address translation and handle call signal processing, call setup, management, resource management, and admission control in an IP network. The state of active calls and accompanying logs are maintained by communications servers, and with thin clients, H.323 clients, and some SIP clients, they also record state tracking. Signaling is also typically the domain of communication servers because a network may support multiple protocol stacks.

With integrated application programming interfaces, communication servers can integrate application servers into a VoIP system, and they are easily replicated for high availability and networked for scalability. The two most common types of communication servers are server-based and purpose-built.

Server-Based Communication Servers

Software is the underlying technology for server-based communication servers. The software components reside on industry-standard computing platforms, such as Windows or UNIX servers, delivering call processing and resource management functions for both media gateways (the next VoIP functional element) and VoIP clients. Advantages of server-based implementations include easy integration of third-party software; disadvantages include susceptibility to outside hackers.

Purpose-Built Communication Servers

In the enterprise, purpose-built communication servers are typically integrated into a multifunctional PBX running an embedded operating system in a closed environment. The advantages of purpose-built servers are that they are scalable and secure, and through integration in existing equipment, they allow maximum return on equipment investment.

Media Gateways

Media gateways come in two varieties: client-side and trunk-side. They serve as liaisons between VoIP packet data and analog or digital T1 voice trunks and analog or digital telephone set interfaces. A media gateway's purpose is to provide media mapping and/or transcoding functions between the IP network and circuit-based networks. Specific functions include compression, silence suppression, and echo cancellation. In addition, media gateways are responsible for H.323 or SIP on the VoIP side and other signaling required on the client or trunk side.

The three common implementations of client- and trunk-side media gateways are:

1. Standalone—Used in networks that utilize purpose-built communication servers, standalone media gateways provide client- and/or trunk-side media gateway functionality. They can be implemented anywhere, and they can expand without regard to underlying network architecture.
2. Network-based—These media gateways are consolidated with other network devices, such as routers and access devices. The clear benefit of a network-based media gateway is that there are fewer systems to support, and its functions can be coupled with routing, bandwidth, and traffic management aspects of the network. Reliability is an issue, however, due to the fact that they require the same software fixes and upgrades as other network functions.

3. Integrated media gateways—Typically, integrated media gateways are found in association with a PBX. Their feature set is closely coupled with the PBX and includes: call routing, trunk selection, and telephony class-of-service capabilities. As an advantage, they maintain the reliability and scalability of the PBX, but their disadvantage is also tied to the PBX, in that they may not be as modular as a standalone or network-based gateway.

Application Servers

Application servers act as a bridge between the VoIP and legacy worlds. They support a host of services and applications, such as unified messaging, conferencing, and collaborative multimedia services, regardless of whether the client uses VoIP or legacy voice systems. They can reside anywhere on the network to maintain application performance balance and optimal network conditions.

THE FUTURE OF VoIP

As with any new technology, widespread adoption depends on a complex mix of market needs and market resources set against the new application's potential to transform the user experience. Customers must see the clear advantages of the new technology over their present systems; they must have financial incentive to adopt the new technology; and they must feel confident that it will make them more productive, save money, or fulfill other pressing business or personal requirements. More and more every day, VoIP is living up to these tough criteria. Still, as illustrated earlier, there are important issues that the industry must continue to address. The continual evolution of complementary standards and robust product offerings are just a few.

So where is the VoIP market today, and where is headed? Currently, the enterprise, in the form of corporate intranets and commercial extranets, holds the most immediate promise. VoIP is particularly attractive in these environments because IP-based infrastructures allow operators to decide who can and cannot use the network.

The VoIP gateway is another factor propelling the proliferation of packet voice technology. Gateway functionality, which once resided on a PC-based platform, has now migrated to robust embedded systems, each able to process hundreds of simultaneous calls. For corporations, the economies of scale from this integration will allow them cost-effectively to deploy large numbers of VoIP connections that merge data, voice, and video into integrated networks. In fact, the reduced expenses and competitive cost advantages associated with integrated IP networks will be the most compelling factor for many companies.

Outside of the corporate intranet setting, commercial extranets are also pushing VoIP acceptance. These carefully engineered IP networks are already delivering voice and fax over the Internet to customers. As an example, many of the calling cards available at the local convenience store checkout stand are really private IP extranets that earn a profit on the margins that data networks enjoy over traditional switched networks.

VoIP on the Internet

Realistically, it will be a few years before VoIP is a widespread phenomenon in the home. VoIP products that use the Internet will, for the time being, be niche markets that can deal with the varying performance levels. In the next three to five years, however, VoIP on the Internet will make significant strides in the wake of two important developments:

- Backbone bandwidth and access speeds will increase by several orders of magnitude, made possible by the deployment of IP/ATM/synchronous optical network (SONET), cable modems, and digital subscriber lines (DSL).
- The Internet will become tiered, requiring users to pay for the particular services they need or want.

Fax over IP (FoIP) products and services over the public Internet will proliferate more quickly than voice and video, mainly because it is more cost-effective and less technologically challenging. In fact, it is believed that most corporations over the next couple of years will take their fax traffic off the PSTN and move it to the Internet and corporate intranet.

Summary

VoIP's adoption in the industry and the home is happening incrementally, yet inexorably. By the end of the decade, videoconferencing with data collaboration will be the standard way to communicate in the workplace. Video cameras in the workplace are now paving the way for inexpensive equipment in the home, a development that should propel packet video and accompanying packet voice into the mainstream. When this happens, VoIP will become interwoven in the fabric of daily life.

INDEX

timeline, 653–655
P2P model, 642–647
security of, 647
Peer-to-peer connectivity, 524–525
Peer-to-peer gaming sites, 201
Peer-to-peer (P2P), 121
Peer-to-peer vs. client/server, 634–635
Pegasus Mail, 238
Pentium Celeron chip, 25–26
Pentium chip, 25–26
Perceptual audio coding, 116
Perl, 232, 364
Personal area network (PAN), 496–497
Personal firewalls, 454
Phase shift keying (PSK), 430
PhatNoise Phatbox, 119–120
Phone line networking, 466–468
Phonograms, 166
Photolog Tutorial, 376
Photologs, 376
Photoshop (Adobe), 350
PHP, 364, 383
Physical memory, 31
PING, 220
Pirillo, Chris, 12
pirillo.com, 12
Plasma display panel, 52
Plug-ins, 224–225
pMachine, 383
Pocket PC, 489
  Palm OS vs., 493
PocketPC, 3
PocoMail, 238
Pogo, 196–197
Political blogs, 373
Polymorphic viruses, 304
Polyphony, 46
POP3 (Post Office Protocol 3), 240–241, 289
PopCap, 197–199
Popdex, 388–389
Pop-up ads, 106–108, 208–209
  pop-up killers, 108
  Realistic Internet Simulator, 106–107
Popup Manager, 108
Portable CD MP3 Player, 119
Portable MP3 hardware:
  for automobiles, 119–120
  compatability, 118
  features, 118–119
  manufacturers, 119
  memory, 117–118
  reviews, 119
Positional audio, 47–50
  A3D (Aureal), 48
  EAX (Creative Technology), 48–49
POST, 17
Powerline networking, 475–476
Priority arrangement, peering, 61
Privacy Net, 236
Privacy policies, 293–294
Private peering, 60
Processor speeds, 25–27
Prodigy, 502
Programming languages, 596–597
Programming tutorials, 363
Programs, 16, 21
Project Gutenberg, 8, 102

PROM, 33
Protocols, 74, 219, 404–405
Proxy browsers vs. proxyless browsers, 505
Proxy Connection, 236
Psychoacoustics, 115
Public domain software, 226
Public Switched Telephone Network (PSTN), 678
Pulse Code Modulation (PCM), 430–431
pureCMS (GlobalSCAPE), 603
Purpose-built communication servers, 693
Python, 364

Quadrature Phase Shift Keying (QPSK), 430
Quality of service, and Home PNA technology, 468
QuickTime, 224, 406–407, 419

Rabbit program, 308
RAM (random access memory), 31
Rant blogs, 375
RAT (Remote-Access Trojan), 269–270
RDRAM, 32
Read-only memory, See ROM (read-only memory):
RealAudio, 342
Reality simulations, 194
RealNetworks, 225, 406, 418, 419
RealPlayer (RealNetworks), 225
Real-Time Transport Protocol/User Datagram Protocol/Internet Protocol (RTP/UDP/IP), 681
Real-Time Control Protocol (RTCP), 681
Reciprocal links, 545, 547
Recording Industry Association of America (RIAA), 124–126
Red Hat, 22
RedDot Content Management Server Express, 602–603
Refill-FAQ, 10
Regional dating, 184
Regular site, 613
Remote access, 507–533
  administration, 531–533
  application delivery servers and corporate portals, 523
  brief history of, 508–509
  comparison of VPN/remote access/Web hosted remote control, 532
  connection, 528
  cost of, 529
  dialup remote access servers, 523–524
  file transfer products, 525–526
  hardware/software, 528
  peer-to-peer connectivity, 524–525
  remote control software, 512–515
    installed, 515–516
  security, 526–528, 530–531
    authentication, 527
    encryption, 527
    firewalls, 527–528
  teleworkers/work extenders, 509–512

VPNs (virtual private networks), 519–523, 526–527, 532
Web browser-based remote control, 516–518
Remote control products, 524–525
Remote Desktop, 288
Remote-access software, 269–270
rentmychest.com, 12
Replacements, Ltd., 13
Replicator technology, 102
Reserve auction, 144
Residential gateway, 462–463
Resource Index, 353
Resource Reservation Protocol (RSVP), 681
RIMM (Rambus inline memory modules), 37
Rindos v. Hardwick, 674–675
RJ-11 and RJ-45 connectors, 465
RM356 (Netgear), 477
Robot crawlers, 75
Role playing games, 193
Rolling Stone Web site, 5–6
ROM, 16–17
ROM (read-only memory), 16–17, 32–33
Routers, 461–462
RPM, 41
RPM/seek time, 41
RTOS (real-time OS), 17

Safe harbors, 653
Samsung, 119
Sandbox, 591
SandNet, 179
Sarbash Software, 583
Sargent patent, 70
Satellite Internet access, 452–453
Satellite modems, 217–218
Scanners, 317–318, 324
Script kiddies, 165, 262
Script sources, 352–353
Scrolling/flooding, 168
SCSI (Small Computer System Interface), 40–41
SCSI-2, 40
Scumware, 108
SDRAM, 32
Search engines, 75, 79–104
  algorithms, 80–81
  AltaVista, 94–95
  Beaucoup, 98–99
  Boolean operators, 83–84
  Dogpile, 98
  FAST/AlltheWeb, 95–97
  FindArticles, 99–100
  fuzzy search, 82
  Google, 85–92
  KartOO, 93–94
  keyword frequency/placement/prominence, 81–82
  keywords, 83
  optimization, 81
  pay for placement, 83
  ranking/relevance/recall, 82
  site popularity, 82
  stemming/spelling, 82
  Yahoo!, 92–93
SearchAbility site, 96–97
Secondary memory (storage), 31
Second-level domain names, 77

Topical blogs, 373
Top-level domain names, 76–77
Torvalds, Linus, 21
Traceroute, 220
Trademarks, 663–664
Transmission Control Protocol
     (TCP), 219
Travelocity, 7
Treadmill gaming, 193
Trend Micro, 330
Trillian, 172
Trojan horses, 263, 266, 304
Truste, 293–294
tutorial.lockergnome.com, 12
Twisted-pair cables, 464
Twitch games, 194
2-pass encoding, 411
2Wire.com, 480–481

Ultra SCSI, 41
Ultra2 SCSI, 41
Ultra160 (LVD), 41
Undernet, 181–182
Unified memory architecture, 45
United Nations Web site, 6
United States Copyright Act (17 USC
     00 101–810), 650
United States of America Patriot Act
     (USAPA), 652
University of Minnesota Crookston
     webcam, 572
UNIX, 121, 271
Uploading, defined, 214
Upper memory area (UMA), 45
URI (Uniform Resource Identifier),
     75
URLs (Uniform Resource Locators),
     75–76, 292
URN (Uniform Resource Name), 75
US Government Whois, 237
US Military Whois, 237
USA Today Web site, 6
USB, 440, 466
Usenet, 4–5, 108–111
     newsgroups, 109–110
User management, 594
UVA (University of Virginia),
     102–103

V.42 protocol, 435
V.42bis protocol, 436
V.44 protocol, 436
V.90 modems, 215
V.92, 443–444
Valhall.net, 179
Variable bit rate (VBR) encoding,
     411
VBScript, 360
VCM, 33
VEO, 576
Version control, 594
Video card, 44–45
Video chat, 580
Video memory (frame buffer), 45
Vienna virus, 313
Vigilantism, and hackers, 296
Virtual memory, 31
Virtualization, 592
Virus protection, 221
Viruses, 241, 264–266, 303–334
     avoiding, 324–327
     categories of, 304

future, 330–334
glossary of terms, 304
history of, 305–308
infections/epidemics, 309–311
and Linux, 332–333
and mobile phones, 331–332
top historic, 313–316
Visual Basic (VB), 365
Visual Net, 9
Vocoders, 688
Voice over Internet Protocol (VoIP),
     629, 677–695
     advantages of, 678
     client side, 692
     communication servers, 692–693
     in the enterprise, 689–691
     future of, 694–695
     history of, 679–680
     how it works, 680–681
     implementation goals, 683–688
     on the Internet, 695
     media gateways, 693–694
     standards, 684–688
          ongoing development, 688
     system elements, 691–694
     voice, special requirements of,
          681–683
Voiceband, 442
Volatile memory, 31
von Neuman, John, 307
VPNs (virtual private networks),
     508, 519–523, 526–527, 532
VRAM, 38

Wall Street City, 7
WAP, 504
War dialing, 272
Warez, 180, 222–223
Warped, 179
WAV format, 121
WaveTracing, 48
Wayback Machine, 101–102
Wearable computer devices,
     496–497
Weather.com, 7
Web design, dos/don'ts, 336–337
Web graphics, 348–351
     compatibility, 349
     creating, 350
     libraries, 351
Web mail, 239–241
Web programming languages,
     357–365
     client-side languages, 358–362
     server-side languages, 362–366
     W3Schools, 358
Web services, 602–603
Web sites, 335–356, *See also* Business
     Web site
     domain name registration,
          342–344
     domain names, 338
     hosting, 337–342
          options, 339–340
          Windows vs. UNIX/Linux,
               340–341
     HTML editors, 344–349
     Hypertext Markup Language
          (HTML), 336–337
     Web design dos/don'ts, 336–337
     Web tools, 351–353
Webcamnow.com, 572

Webcams, 567–584
     and adult entertainment industry,
          581
     basics of, 573–578
     cables, 577
     connecting to the computer,
          576–577
     defined, 570–571
     FireWire, 578
     history of, 571
     Internet connection, 579–580
     makers of, 574–576
     portals, 571–572
     safety factors, 580–581
     setting up, 581–582
     snapshot/streaming, 573–574
     software, 578
     surveillance, 582–583
     video chat, 580
     webcam servers, 579–580
Webcamworld.com, 572
WebExpress (MicroVision
     Development), 346
Webrings, 389, 546
Web site hoaxes, 281–282
White hats/blackhats, 296–297
Wide area networks (WANs),
     498–500
Wide SCSI, 41
Wide Ultra2 SCSI, 41
WiFi, 501
Wi-Fi (wireless fidelity), 58–59
Win95.CIH virus, 315
Windows operating system, 16,
     18–20
     complaints about, 18–19
     instability of, 18
     timeline, 19–20
     upgrades, 19
     Windows 1.0, 19
     Windows 3.0, 19
     Windows 95, 19
     Windows 98, 19
     Windows 2000 Professional, 20
     Windows CE, 487
     Windows for Workgroups 3.11,
          19
     Windows Media, 406
     Windows Millennium Edition
          (Windows ME), 20
     Windows XP, 20
WinMX, 123
Winnov, 576
Win.Tentacle virus, 314
WinWhatWhere Corporation, 269
WinZip, 122
Wireless, 471–473, 491–498
Wireless access point, 462
Wireless bridge, 462
Wireless email, 502
Wireless Markup Language (WML),
     359
Wireless personal area network
     (WPAN), 497
Wireless phones with Web services, 3
WISP, 502
WOL (Wake on LAN) technology,
     43–44
WordPad, 319
Work areas, 591
Workflow management, 587
Workflows, 592, 594–595